INTERNATIONAL MIGRATION STATISTICS

INTERNATIONAL MIGRATION STATISTICS

GUIDELINES FOR IMPROVING DATA COLLECTION SYSTEMS

*R.E. Bilsborrow, Graeme Hugo,
A.S. Oberai and Hania Zlotnik*

A study published with the financial support
of the UNITED NATIONS POPULATION FUND
(UNFPA)

INTERNATIONAL LABOUR OFFICE · GENEVA

Copyright © International Labour Organization 1997
First published 1997

Publications of the International Labour Office enjoy copyright under Protocol 2 of the Universal Copyright Convention. Nevertheless, short excerpts from them may be reproduced without authorization, on condition that the source is indicated. For rights of reproduction or translation, application should be made to the Publications Bureau (Rights and Permissions), International Labour Office, CH-1211 Geneva 22, Switzerland. The International Labour Office welcomes such applications.

Libraries, institutions and other users registered in the United Kingdom with the Copyright Licensing Agency, 90 Tottenham Court Road, London W1P 9HE (Fax: +44 171 436 3986), in the United States with the Copyright Clearance Center, 222 Rosewood Drive, Danvers, MA 01923 (Fax: +1 508 750 4470), or in other countries with associated Reproduction Rights Organizations, may make photocopies in accordance with the licences issued to them for this purpose.

R. E. Bilsborrow, Graeme Hugo, A.S. Oberai and Hania Zlotnik
International migration statistics: Guidelines for improving data collection systems
Geneva, International Labour Office, 1997

/Guide/, /international migration/, /migrant/, /data collecting/, /measurement/, /methodology/, /developed country/, /developing country/. 14.09.2
ISBN 92-2-109517-7

ILO Cataloguing in Publication Data

The designations employed in ILO publications, which are in conformity with United Nations practice, and the presentation of material therein do not imply the expression of any opinion whatsoever on the part of the International Labour Office concerning the legal status of any country, area or territory or of its authorities, or concerning the delimitation of its frontiers.

The responsibility for opinions expressed in signed articles, studies and other contributions rests solely with their authors, and publication does not constitute an endorsement by the International Labour Office of the opinions expressed in them.

Reference to names of firms and commercial products and processes does not imply their endorsement by the International Labour Office, and any failure to mention a particular firm, commercial product or process is not a sign of disapproval.

ILO publications can be obtained through major booksellers or ILO local offices in many countries, or direct from ILO Publications, International Labour Office, CH-1211 Geneva 22, Switzerland. Catalogues or lists of new publications are available free of charge from the above address.

Printed in Singapore

PREFACE

The sweeping economic and political reforms taking place in the world today have not only created the prospect of dramatic changes in labour migration patterns, but have also affected the whole approach to migration policies. Policy-makers are now showing much greater interest in migration issues, together with a greater willingness to bring these issues to the core of policy dialogue and international cooperation.

While concerns about international population movements have increased in recent years, adequate and reliable data for understanding the processes shaping such movements and for developing an appropriate policy response are still lacking.

Recent concerns about international migration stem from two major factors. First, increasing globalization of economic networks, rapid population growth in the South, and growing poverty have led to increased pressures towards emigration. More than 70 million people, mostly from developing countries, are now working (legally or illegally) in other countries. Second, increasing unemployment, mounting nationalism and xenophobic sentiments have led to social tensions in the migrant-receiving countries in the North and have encouraged many governments to adopt more restrictive immigration policies.

Some of these perceptions about the causes and consequences of international migration are not necessarily based on sound analysis. Rather, they often reflect a broader social unease stemming from poverty and growing social and economic imbalances. They sometimes develop in reaction to migration episodes that, even if of limited dimensions, have been quite visible and striking in the eyes of the public and of the media.

There is thus a growing interest among governments and scholars, in both North and South, in quantifying the volume of international migration flows and in assessing their economic and social implications. The carving up of the world into distinct regional blocs, the liberalization of trade, and the relocation of production units in labour supply countries are also likely to have important implications for intra-regional and inter-regional migration flows, and for types of labour movement. It will be necessary, therefore, to study the impact of these changes on future migration trends.

International migration statistics

Unfortunately, the limited availability of migration statistics poses a severe constraint on conducting any systematic analysis of the social (e.g. migrants' adjustment, cultural assimilation, role and status of women), demographic (e.g. population growth, age and sex structure of the population) or economic (e.g. labour market, technological change, savings and investment, balance of payments, income distribution) impacts of migration in either the sending or receiving countries. In the absence of such an analysis, the discussion on migration is often at a speculative level and its consequences are analysed more in terms of impressions than in terms of impact. Policy formulation therefore rests, unfortunately but unavoidably, on a shaky basis.

The major objective of this volume is therefore to strengthen national capacities for generating the relevant and more meaningful data (on migration flows, return migration, remittances, etc.) required for migration policy analysis. Within this framework, it has three immediate objectives: first, to provide a critical review of the adequacy of current sources of data on international migration; second, to discuss the conceptual and analytical issues related to the measurement of stocks and flows of international migrants, and the problems related to the international comparability of migration data; third, to suggest improved methods of data collection (through administrative records, population censuses, sample surveys, etc.) and ways of enhancing the international comparability of migration statistics.

The volume has been prepared with the financial support of the United Nations Population Fund (UNFPA) as part of the activities of the ILO's Interdepartmental Project on Migrant Workers implemented in 22 selected countries during the biennium 1994-95.[1] One component of this project was concerned with increasing the capacity of sending and receiving countries to collect and process reliable statistics on movements of migrant workers. Another was to develop, in the Office, basic statistics on international migration for the purposes of analysis and dissemination.

Besides collecting core data on migration flows/stocks and related socio-economic information, the Office collected methodological information on sources, concepts and definitions.[2] This information was used to assess current sources and methods of data collection and to identify gaps and shortcomings (special consideration being given to data on socio-economic and demographic characteristics, skills, wages, remittances, gender, and regional breakdown of migrant workers).

Based on a critical review of existing sources of data in the 22 countries covered by the Interdepartmental Project, as well as on experience of data collection in many other countries, the present guidelines were prepared in order to pave the way for an improved data collection system on international migration.

Many people have contributed to this volume. It is difficult to single out individuals, but a large number of officials working in national statistical agencies and government departments dealing with emigration/immigration have provided useful information on problems of migration statistics and on their experience of handling data collection issues. Particular thanks go to

Preface

Ms. Linda Gordon of the United States Immigration and Naturalization Service.

Significant inputs and materials were provided by colleagues working on similar issues in regional and other international organizations such as the Organisation for Economic Co-operation and Development (Mr. Georges Lemaitre), the Statistical Office of the European Community (Ms. Thana Chrissanthaki and Mr. Curt Grundström), the Economic Commission for Europe (Mr. John Kelly), the International Monetary Fund (Mr. Jack Bame and Mr. Mohinder Gill), the United Nations Statistics Division (Mr. K. Gnanasekaran, Ms. Cristina Hannig, Mr. Jan van Tongeren and Mr. Viet Vu) and the Economic and Social Commission for Asia and the Pacific (Mr. Jagdish Kumar). We are indebted to all of them.

A special word of acknowledgement is reserved for Mr. Bela Hovy, Statistician, Office of the United Nations High Commissioner for Refugees (UNHCR), who contributed an earlier version of Chapter V on "Data collection systems providing information on asylum-seekers and refugees".

Several colleagues at the ILO have contributed to the evolution of this volume through their support, comments and observations. Thanks are particularly due to Mr. J. Lönnroth, Mr. W. R. Böhning, Mr. F. Mehran, Mr. M. Abella, Mr. R. Paratian and Mr. A. Khan.

Special thanks go to Mr. Eivind Hoffmann and Ms. Sophia Lawrence of the ILO's Bureau of Statistics, who generously provided intellectual inputs and helpful suggestions throughout the period of this study.

The work of preparing the manuscript for publication was handled by Ms. Joan Robb, Ms. Julie Locascio and Ms. Valerie Boobier. We gratefully acknowledge their assistance.

Finally, we wish to express our thanks to the UNFPA for its support of this work.

Needless to say, the views and opinions expressed in this volume reflect our own positions, and not necessarily those of the organizations to which we belong. The responsibility for any errors or shortcomings must, therefore, rest solely with us as authors.

R. Bilsborrow, G. Hugo, A. S. Oberai and H. Zlotnik

January 1997

Notes

[1] These include: Argentina, Belarus, Côte d'Ivoire, the Dominican Republic, Gabon, Indonesia, Jamaica, Japan, the Republic of Korea, Kuwait, Lebanon, Morocco, Pakistan, Poland, Portugal, the Russian Federation, Senegal, South Africa, Sri Lanka, Switzerland, Thailand and the United States.

[2] Data were gathered from secondary sources through a structured questionnaire. No specifically designed surveys were envisaged as part of this work.

CONTENTS

Preface V

Chapter 1. The need to improve international migration statistics 1

A. Purpose and scope of this book 8
B. Major findings and limitations of this book 10

Chapter 2. Concepts underlying international migration statistics 15

A. Citizenship 16
B. Residence 18
C. Time 21
D. Purpose of stay 24
E. Place of birth 26
F. Considerations in the assessment of international migration statistics . 29
G. Framework for the identification and classification of international migrants 32
H. International migration and economic activity 48

Chapter 3. Data collection systems concerning all international migrants 51

A. Population censuses 52
B. Population registers 75
C. Registers of foreigners 102
D. Administrative sources 114
E. Border statistics 136

Chapter 4. Data collection systems concerning labour migration 161

A. Work permit statistics 161
B. Reports by employers 179
C. Statistics derived from the control of contract labour migration by countries of origin 182
D. Statistics derived from regularization drives 197

Contents

Chapter 5. Data collection systems providing information on asylum-seekers and refugees 213

A. Dynamics of change of the refugee population 216
B. Statistics derived from the provision of assistance 221
C. UNHCR practices regarding the gathering of statistics on refugees . . 226
D. Statistics on asylum-seekers 229

Chapter 6. Design of surveys to investigate the determinants and consequences of international migration 237

A. Use and limitations of existing sample surveys 238
B. Design of surveys for the analysis of the determinants and consequences of international migration 245
C. Sample design 267
D. Other data collection approaches relevant for international migration . 288
E. Content of questionnaires in surveys to analyse the determinants and consequences of international migration 293
F. Questionnaire for surveys in countries of destination and origin . . . 305

Chapter 7. Measurement of remittances 321

A. Definition of remittances in the system of national accounts and in the balance of payments 321
B. Problems involved in measuring migrants' remittances and other international transactions relative to international migration 332
C. Financial flows at the micro-level: Remittance data from household surveys 339
D. Concluding remarks 360

Annex 1. Model questionnaires for country of destination 363

A. Household questionnaire 363
B. Individual questionnaire 368
C. Community-level questionnaire 398

Annex 2. Model questionnaires for country of origin 403

A. Household questionnaire 403
B. Individual questionnaire 404

Bibliography 411

Index 427

List of tables, boxes and figure

Tables

2.1.	Framework for the characterization of different categories of international migration	33
2.2.	Framework for the classification of migrants for family reunification	35
3.1.	Distribution of countries according to national practices regarding the inclusion or exclusion of particular population groups	54
3.2.	Countries conducting population censuses during a given period by whether data on place of birth was published	57
3.3.	Countries conducting population censuses during 1975-84 according to whether they published data on place of birth or on citizenship	58
3.4.	Countries conducting population censuses during a given period by whether data on citizenship was published	59
3.5.	Characterization of immigrating and emigrating citizens according to the mode of operation of the population registers of different countries	84
3.6.	Characterization of immigrating and emigrating foreigners subject to free-movement provisions, according to the mode of operation of the population registers of different countries	85
3.7.	Characterization of immigrating and emigrating foreigners, excluding those subject to free movement, according to the mode of operation of the population registers of different countries	86
3.8.	Data on international migrants gathered by countries maintaining population registers	93
3.9.	Visa categories allowing the holder to work in Australia and number admitted under each category, 1990/91	122
3.10.	Schematic classification of arrivals and departures by duration of absence from and presence in a given country	139
3.11.	Countries reporting only overall number of arrivals and departures for selected periods	144
3.12.	Countries reporting long-term immigrants and emigrants for selected periods	146
3.13.	Categories of citizens and foreigners used in the tabulation of arrival and departure statistics of Mexico	150
3.14.	Arrivals and departures in 1973 and 1980 according to the border statistics of Mexico and the United Nations *Demographic yearbook*	152
4.1.	Relevant characteristics of systems to control contract labour migration in Asian countries of origin	183
5.1.	Sources of change of the refugee population	216
5.2.	Recommended tabulation on the results of the process to consider applications for asylum	232
5.3.	Recommended tabulation on the mode of reaching positive decision on asylum applications	232

Contents

5.4. Recommended tabulation indicating number of asylum applications by status of persons filing them, and decision taken by status of applicant . 233
5.5. Recommended tabulation on the reasons for rejecting applications for asylum or for denying asylum 233
6.1. Focal groups for data collection at origin and destination to study the determinants of international migration 250
6.2. Focal groups for data collection at origin and destination to study the consequences of international migration 256
6.3. Factors relevant for the analysis of the determinants and consequences of international migration at the micro-level 295
7.1. Migrant remittances in selected countries 322
7.2. Gross inflows of private unrequited transfers (including remittances) of selected countries, 1993 (in million US$) 333
7.3. Remittances sent through informal channels as a percentage of total remittances 337

Boxes

2.1. Characterizing different types of migrants 36
3.1. Population subgroups according to special treatment in population censuses 54
6.1. Steps involved in conducting a specialized survey on international migration 264
7.1. Balance of payments: Standard components 323
7.2. The concept of residence in the 1993 system of national accounts . . . 326
7.3. Pakistan: National reporting system 335
7.4. Thailand 335
7.5. Republic of Korea: Recording of remittances 336
7.6. Sri Lanka: Private transfers 337

Figure

6.1. Illustration of multi-level model of determinants of international migration 305

THE NEED TO IMPROVE INTERNATIONAL MIGRATION STATISTICS

The twentieth century has witnessed unprecedented increases in population mobility made possible by revolutionary advances in transportation and communication systems. The world has become smaller and more densely populated. At the same time, it has become more compartmentalized, as the modern system of nation States has crystallized into a finer partition of the inhabitable surface of the planet. As the number of States has increased so has the potential for population mobility to become international in character. Despite the barriers imposed by nation States to control international movements of people in accordance with the principle of State sovereignty, the number of international travellers has risen steeply. Only a few of those international travellers, however, can be considered to be international migrants. At the world level, it is estimated that the total number of international migrants reached 120 million by 1990 (United Nations, 1995a). Yet, there is no single characterization of what constitutes an international migrant. The question of how to distinguish international migrants from the generality of international travellers has long been recognized as crucial in trying to assess the magnitude and characteristics of international migration.

The quest for an appropriate characterization of international migration to serve as the basis for the collection of statistics on the subject dates back at least to the first quarter of the twentieth century. In 1922, the International Labour Conference, at its fourth session, recommended that agreements be reached on a uniform definition of the term "emigrant" and on a uniform method to record information regarding emigration and immigration (United Nations, 1949). In 1932, the International Labour Organization sponsored an International Conference of Migration Statisticians which adopted the first set of international recommendations for the improvement of migration statistics (United Nations, 1949). According to the 1932 Conference, "in principle, every act of removal from one country to another for a certain length of time should be included in the statistics of migration, with the exception of tourist traffic" (United Nations, 1949, p. 3). In an attempt to distinguish between permanent and temporary migration, the Conference suggested that "when the removal is for one year or more the migration should be regarded as permanent migration" and "when the removal is for less than a year the migration should be regarded as temporary, frontier traffic being excluded" (United Nations, 1949, p. 3).

In 1949, when the United Nations Population Division assessed the recommendations made by the 1932 Conference, it noted that "tourist traffic" was not defined and that no criteria to distinguish "tourist traffic" from "temporary migration" had been proposed. It expressed doubts about the possibility of distinguishing one from the other solely on the basis of duration of stay, since seasonal migrant workers could remain in the country of immigration for shorter periods than certain tourists or business visitors. It concluded, therefore, that both the purpose of the movement and its duration had to be taken into account. It thus suggested that "temporary migrants" be defined as persons who enter a country for the purpose of finding temporary employment (or to exercise temporarily an occupation on their own account) together with their dependants (United Nations, 1949).

Such suggestions were partially reflected in the set of recommendations for the improvement of international migration statistics that the United Nations adopted in 1953 (United Nations, 1953). Those recommendations maintained the distinction between "permanent" and "temporary" migrants on the basis of duration of stay (over a year versus at most a year), and established that "temporary" migrants should be distinguished from "visitors" on the basis of purpose of stay. Thus, "temporary immigrants" were defined as non-residents intending to exercise for a period of one year or less an occupation remunerated from within the country of arrival. Their dependants were to be classified as "visitors".

The text accompanying the 1953 recommendations itself noted that "differences between countries in the length and geographic nature of frontiers, volume of migration, national legislation regarding the control of migration, and other factors, do not make it possible to lay down a set of even minimum standards which all countries can forthwith implement fully" (United Nations, 1953, p. 15, para. 2). In the event, the 1953 recommendations were not successful in achieving a significant improvement in the comparability of international migration statistics. In the 1970s, concerned about the lack of improvement and recognizing the inadequacies of the 1953 recommendations, the United Nations undertook their revision and a new set of recommendations was adopted in 1976. The report on the new set noted that "an important complicating factor in developing a satisfactory definition of a migrant for statistical purposes is the close relationship between this term and the concept of residence in a country. For example, an immigrant must not currently be a resident of the country he or she has entered and an emigrant must have been a resident of the country from which he or she is departing. The concept of residence, however, is a legal concept on which there is as yet no consensus among countries even in regard to the minimum period of presence in a country needed to determine residence.... The possibility of securing internationally comparable migration statistics based on any definition of migrant expressed in terms of residents and non-residents appears, therefore, to be remote at best" (United Nations, 1980a, p. 4, para. 21).

In order to avoid a lack of comparability resulting from the use of criteria based on residence, the 1976 recommendations defined migrants in terms of actual and intended periods of presence in, or absence from, a country. Thus, "long-term immigrants" were characterized as "persons who enter the country with the intention of remaining for more than one year and who must never have been in the country continuously for more than one year or, having been in the country continuously for more than one year, must have been away continuously for more than one year since the last stay of more than one year" (United Nations, 1980a, p. 7). "Long-term emigrants" were defined in equivalent terms from the perspective of departure. In addition, echoing the 1953 recommendations, four categories of "short-term" migrants were identified on the basis of both length and purpose of stay. A "short-term immigrant", for instance, was characterized as a person who enters the country with the intention of remaining for one year or less for the purpose of working in an occupation remunerated from within the country and who must never have been in the country continuously for more than one year or, having been in the country continuously for more than one year, must have been away continuously for more than one year since the last stay of more than one year (United Nations, 1980a).

The 1976 recommendations present the most coherent and logical framework available to date for the identification and classification of "long-term" immigrants and emigrants, as well as for the special categories of "short-term" migrants that they distinguish. Nevertheless, as in the case of their predecessors, the 1976 recommendations have not been implemented widely. The United Nations is currently engaged in revising again its recommendations on international migration statistics. It is therefore particularly timely to consider how existing systems of data collection characterize international migrants and to assess whether the approach followed so far to ensure greater comparability is likely to produce the data needed to address the questions being posed daily around the world regarding the nature, magnitude, characteristics, causes and impact of international migration.

Even with all their deficiencies, the available statistics on international migration validate the view that, at the world level, the number of persons who can be considered international migrants has increased more rapidly in recent years, the growth rate of the international migrant stock being 2.5 per cent annually during 1985–90 in comparison to 2.1 per cent during 1975–85 (United Nations, 1995a). Flow statistics for key countries of destination further corroborate an increasing trend. The persistence of economic disparities between developed and developing countries, the political transformation taking place in the former communist countries, and the instability or even conflict that has plagued certain countries or regions have all contributed to spur the international movement of people. Faced with the prospect of rising inflows, countries of destination have recently been closing their doors and host societies have been reacting negatively to the international migrants already in their midst. In such a context, international migrants are not necessarily equated with persons changing their country of residence and even less with persons satisfying the strict definitional criteria set out in United Nations recommendations. Both the public at large and policy-makers in host countries tend to characterize international migrants as foreigners, that is, non-citizens. In a world organized into mutually exclusive States whose borders are deemed to coincide with the social boundaries of the people under their jurisdiction, international migration becomes a process whereby individuals are transferred from the jurisdiction of one State to that of another, thus becoming *de facto* members of the host society (Zolberg, 1981). In order to maximize the collective welfare of society while maintaining the identity and exclusiveness of that society, the State has the right to restrict the entry of foreigners. This universally recognized attribute of State sovereignty both conditions and curtails international migration, and lends it relevance as an object of policy-making. Consequently, to be relevant, any approach to the measurement of international migration must take into account the crucial role that the State plays in controlling and shaping the international migration of non-citizens.

In exercising control over the inflow of foreigners, States usually make distinctions among various categories of international movers. Such distinctions are normally stipulated in pertinent national laws or regulations and, on occasion, may be established by international treaties or agreements. Despite the many inter-country variations in the national laws and regulations establishing the conditions under which foreigners may enter and stay in a State's territory, certain common practices and approaches can be identified. Countries usually make clear distinctions between the admission of foreign tourists, refugees, migrant workers, permanent settlers, and migrants for family reunification. Since there is general agreement that persons admitted as tourists should be excluded from international migration statistics, foreigners belonging to the other categories listed can be considered international migrants. In fact, in most receiving countries, the types of questions relevant for policy formulation demand that statistical information be available on the different categories of non-tourist foreigners admitted under existing laws and regulations. Thus, although knowing the annual number of "long-term immigrants" as defined by the United Nations would be useful, even the best statistics in that regard would not allow an assessment of the degree to which family reunification has been fuelling migration inflows. Nor would information on "long-term immigration" necessarily reflect well the number of persons admitted for the sole purpose of exercising an economic activity in the country of destination.

Given that the identification of international migrants in several statistical systems is closely related to laws and regulations establishing who qualifies as an international migrant or, equivalently, who can establish residence in a country's territory, even if for a limited period, it is unlikely that a universal definition of international migrant that by-passes any consideration of such laws and regulations could ever be fully adopted and implemented by most countries. Furthermore, it is also questionable whether a single definition of international

The need to improve international migration statistics

migrant can adequately satisfy the data needs of researchers and policy-makers interested in identifying specific types of migrants that are the object of particular policy initiatives. The various sets of United Nations recommendations have attempted to cope with the most pressing needs in that regard by making special provisions for the reporting of certain types of international movers. They all include, for instance, special categories for the reporting of refugees, arguing that "population transfers and refugee movements are different in character from the normal movement to which migration statistics have previously related almost exclusively" (United Nations, 1953, p. 15). Today, similar arguments can be made regarding other types of movements, some of which may fall within the traditional concept of international migration. To cite but a few examples, consider persons subject to free movement provisions within the European Union; persons who, because of their descent, have the right to settle or to obtain the citizenship of countries such as Germany, Israel or Japan; or foreigners admitted for the specific purpose of providing services under international treaties such as the General Agreement on Trade in Services (GATS). The growing relevance of particular categories of international movers implies that, to the extent possible, international migration statistics must also reflect those categories even if the persons involved do not move from one country to another for an interval longer than a year.

A crucial aspect of the characterization of international migrants is their citizenship. From the policy perspective, citizenship is a key factor in determining the rights of individuals to enter, reside or exercise an economic activity in a country. Often, there is not only a sharp difference between the rights of citizens and those of foreigners but, in addition, not all foreigners are treated equally. Thus, through a variety of international agreements, governments often grant preferential treatment to the citizens of certain countries. Usually such differential treatment is reflected in the statistics gathered, be it because those subject to preferential treatment are officially excluded from statistical accounting or because they are more likely to be included since they need to fulfil only minimal requirements to obtain the necessary permits. Citizenship is therefore a key variable for the analysis of international migration and should be given prominence in both data collection and tabulations of the information obtained. Especially in the case of data collection systems producing information on migration flows, the separate identification of citizens and foreigners for each of the flows recorded is essential since governments are interested in knowing not only whether their populations have grown or decreased because of international migration but also whether there is a net gain or loss of foreigners.

An aspect of international migration that has long attracted attention is its impact on the labour markets of countries of destination. Most data sources producing information on economically active international migrants equate them with foreigners. That is the case, for instance, of labour force surveys that produce information on the labour force participation and other economic characteristics of foreigners; of population censuses in certain countries; of registers of foreigners; and of statistics derived from residence permits, work permits and reports by employers. There are also significant differences in the populations covered by each source. Thus, whereas censuses and population registers cover, in principle, all foreigners irrespective of the reason for their admission, statistics on work permits refer only to migrant workers, meaning only those foreigners admitted specifically for the purpose of exercising an economic activity. Although the impact of migrant workers on the labour forces of receiving countries is recognized as relevant for policy formulation, that of all foreigners, irrespective of the reason for their admission, is also important and should not be neglected.

There are also a number of crucial questions regarding the relevance of the economic processes that are considered to be at the root of most international migration. For example, it has been argued that successful development will, over the long run, reduce the migration pressures in developing countries. It is also recognized, however, that over the short and medium term, the process of development itself sets in motion forces that may actually increase international migration (United States Commission for the Study of International Migration and Cooperative Economic Development, 1990). Yet, given the serious deficiencies in international migration statistics and the complexity of the issues involved, the empirical bases for such assertions remain weak. Other issues relevant for effective policy formulation also cannot be settled without recourse to better and more comprehensive data on international migration. They include: the extent to which foreign direct investment or foreign aid can be a substitute for international migration; the effects of increased economic linkages through trade or capital flows on international migration; the kind of trade most likely to reduce (or enhance) the potential for emigration from developing countries; and the effects of remittances on development. The analysis of any of these issues requires detailed information not only on flows of international migrants over time but also on related social and economic variables, including migrant remittances, which are weakly covered by existing statistical systems.

In addition, since individuals and families are the international migrants, it is crucial to obtain adequate data for the analysis of the determinants and consequences of international migration at the micro-level. Such data can best be gathered through specialized, intensive surveys of international migrants and non-migrants. Only through such surveys can sufficiently detailed information be obtained to permit the comprehensive assessment of the factors that can affect the decisions of people regarding international migration and the outcomes of a move. The need for a comprehensive quantitative approach must also be underscored in this regard, since all potentially relevant factors have to be analysed simultaneously in order to determine which ones are the most important in a particular country context. The analysis of the consequences of international migration requires the systematic consideration of the various dimensions on which migration has an impact, be they social, demographic, economic or political. In addition, because international migration depends on the linkages between sending and receiving countries and is itself a means of interaction between the two, determinants and consequences cannot be looked at from a single country perspective. Linkages between the societies of origin and destination must be brought to bear both in the manner in which data are collected and in the ensuing analysis.

Given that the genesis of international migration flows between countries can often be traced to governmental or institutional actions – such as the recruitment of workers in a given country by agents working for employers or for the government of another country – the collection of information relative to the determinants of international migration cannot focus exclusively on the individual or household level. Processes operating at a higher level, be it the community or the country of origin, may be equally or more relevant in triggering migration, so it is necessary to design appropriate data collection instruments to capture such processes. In addition, it is well known that, once established, international migration flows tend to develop their own momentum through the operation of migrant networks (Kritz and Zlotnik, 1992). Migrant networks link communities of origin and destination, serving as channels for information and resources. While economic and political processes operating at the macro level may explain why certain international migration flows emerge, the operation of networks helps explain why they continue and why certain people migrate while the vast majority do not. The systematic analysis of migrant networks requires the development of specific data-collection instruments at the micro level and their use in a variety of settings.

As the twentieth century draws to a close, many countries find themselves hosting sizeable migrant populations and having to deal with the long-term consequences of growing stocks of international migrants. Among many host countries, the perception that international migrants are more of a liability than an asset is growing. The lack of adequate statistics on the numbers and characteristics of international migrants in major receiving countries and the scarcity of careful studies on the consequences of international migration continue to provide fertile ground for the proliferation of misinformation and its exploitation for tendentious purposes. Claims are often made about international migrants that underscore common stereotypes and prejudices. Thus, although most existing studies indicate that international migrants are positively selected from the better-off members of the societies of origin, the view persists that they are poor and uneducated. Industrialized countries with generous welfare systems tend to view migrants from developing countries as intent on taking advantage of those systems and other public services. The deficiencies of existing statistics and the lack of appropriate survey data severely constrain an objective assessment of the impact of international migration on the receiving country's economy and society.

This book attempts to respond to the urgent need for improvement in the quality and availability of data on international migration, its determinants and consequences. By documenting the strengths and weaknesses of available statistics on international migration, providing suggestions on how to improve the operation of existing systems of data collection and dissemination, and proposing new approaches to measuring the factors leading to international migration and its consequences, this book attempts to provide a solid basis for systematic efforts to improve data on international migration. In addressing the measurement of factors leading to international migration and the consequences of international migration, attention will be paid not only to the migrants themselves and their families, but also to their communities and countries of origin and destination. Information at both the individual or micro-level and at the community or intermediate level is crucial for a comprehensive assessment of the costs and benefits of international migration that may provide a better basis for policy formulation.

A. PURPOSE AND SCOPE OF THIS BOOK

Since its creation in 1919, the International Labour Organization has devoted attention to international migration issues, including the availability and quality of international migration statistics. The present book continues that tradition. Its purpose is to set forth the basis for strengthening national capacities to generate the data required for policy analysis in the area of international migration.

To fulfil its purpose, this book discusses the conceptual and analytical issues related to the measurement of international migration and their implications for the international comparability of international migration statistics. It then provides a critical review of the adequacy of current sources of data on international migration and suggests ways of improving such data so as to enhance their usefulness and international comparability. A similar review has not been undertaken since at least 1949 when the United Nations issued the report entitled *Problems of migration statistics* (United Nations, 1949).

Attention is also paid to the use of specially designed surveys to gather information for the analysis of the determinants and consequences of international migration. A better understanding of the processes giving rise to international migration flows and their consequences, for both the migrants themselves and their communities of origin and destination, is crucial for developing realistic and effective policies.

This book is divided into seven chapters, the first of which is this introduction. In addition, it contains annexes presenting model questionnaires for use in surveys carried out in countries of destination and countries of origin, respectively. To guide the reader in the use of this book, a brief description of the content of each chapter and annex follows.

Chapter 1 discusses the need to improve international migration statistics so as to permit both a more accurate measurement of flows and stocks of international migrants and a clearer analysis of the determinants and consequences of international migration.

The need to improve international migration statistics

Chapter 2 addresses the conceptual basis for the identification of international migrants in existing statistical systems. It discusses the meaning and limitations of the different concepts used to identify international migrants and reviews their use according to country practices. A comprehensive framework for the classification of international migrants into different categories, together with definitions of the categories, is presented. Since that framework is used as reference for the discussion of international migration statistics throughout the book, it is recommended that Chapter 2 be read by all users of this book. The framework presented reflects the concepts most commonly used by researchers and policy-makers, and thus embodies a user's perspective in terms of data needs.

Chapter 3 provides a detailed description of the various data collection systems used to gather information about international migrants in general, as distinguished from those which provide information only about migrant workers. The data collection systems examined include population censuses, continuous population registers, registers of foreigners, administrative statistics and border statistics. The type and quality of data gathered on international migrant stocks and flows through those sources are assessed to identify gaps and shortcomings, and to suggest ways of improving the performance of each system.

Chapter 4 reviews data collection systems used to gather information specifically on migrant workers, including work permit systems, reports on foreign workers by employers, data on contract workers collected by countries of origin and statistics from regularization drives. The coverage of each system and the quality of data it yields are assessed critically to identify ways of improving available statistics.

Chapter 5 is devoted to the measurement of forced migration, including the movement of refugees and asylum-seekers. It examines the conceptual problems involved in identifying and measuring such population movements and assesses the performance of existing data collection systems. Examples derived from current country practices are used to pinpoint the strengths and limitations of various systems and to suggest ways of improving the statistics they yield.

Chapter 6 discusses the use of sample surveys to provide data for the analysis of the determinants and consequences of international migration. It discusses the type of data collection approach needed to study the determinants or the consequences of international migration in different contexts and the selection of appropriate comparison groups; it provides an overview of the type of information that is most relevant for the analysis of the factors leading to migration and of its likely consequences; and it discusses specialized methods of survey and sample design appropriate for collecting data on international migration.

Chapter 7 focuses on the conceptual and methodological problems related to the measurement of remittances, a crucial aspect of the consequences of international migration. The chapter discusses both aggregate statistics and statistics at the household level. Difficulties in gathering the appropriate information

International migration statistics

and inconsistencies across countries with respect to the definitions used are documented. Since it is unlikely that the deficiencies characterizing the information on remittances produced through balance of payments and national accounts will disappear soon, a case is made for the collection of data at the household level using surveys. Detailed questionnaire modules are presented for incorporation into the questionnaires presented in the annexes.

Annex 1 presents model questionnaires for specialized migration surveys in countries of destination, including a community-level questionnaire for the study of the determinants and consequences of international migration.

Annex 2 presents model questionnaires for specialized migration surveys in countries of origin.

B. MAJOR FINDINGS AND LIMITATIONS OF THIS BOOK

Given that the authors of this book have spent their careers mostly as users of international migration statistics, the approach used in describing and analysing existing data collection systems and the statistics that they produce tends to reflect the perspective of users rather than that of producers. As the book stresses throughout, however, users cannot hope to employ available statistics correctly unless they are well informed about the salient features of the systems that produce them. Providing that information to users as well as making producers aware of possible ways in which their efforts can lead to better statistics are the dual purposes of this work. The task has not been straightforward, largely because there is scant information about the systems producing international migration statistics in most countries of the world. Statistics relative to developing countries and countries with economies in transition, in particular, are scarce and even more so is information about their meaning and scope. Consequently, the material contained in this book has often been drawn from a handful of secondary sources reflecting the results of efforts made in recent years to document better the state of statistical systems producing immigration statistics in particular world regions. The availability of such sources has made a more comprehensive treatment of the subject possible, but biases in coverage remain, with the experience of developing countries being considerably less well documented than that of developed countries.

Incomplete documentation regarding existing sources has also prevented a systematic assessment of the precise changes necessary to improve the usefulness of the statistics produced. For example, it is often not possible to establish from available documentation which information is actually collected, which is processed, and which is eventually published. Without such knowledge, it is impossible to establish whether the production of improved statistics requires the modification of data collection instruments, changes in the processing of the information collected, or just the preparation of a different set of tabulations.

Whenever that distinction was possible, it was made. In all other instances, the relevant information was lacking.

Despite the incompleteness of the information available, a major finding of the book is that most data collection systems fail to exploit the richness of the data already gathered. Indeed, as shown in Chapters 3 to 5, most of the information recorded about persons identified as international migrants is not used to produce tabulations. The tabulations published or otherwise disseminated tend to be very few in number and consist at most of cross-tabulations of two variables at a time. All too often, only overall numbers are released, thus preventing an analysis of even the most basic characteristics of international migrants. Given the increasing complexity of international migration movements and the diversification of flows, detailed tabulations crossing several variables are necessary to improve our understanding of the process. Key attributes allowing the identification and classification of international migrants must be consistently used in cross-tabulations; these attributes include sex, country of citizenship and reason for admission. A thorough analysis of the data gathered according to the various characteristics recorded would go a long way in allowing a better characterization of international migrants and of the likely consequences of their movement.

The data collection systems assessed in Chapters 3 to 5 are concerned primarily with the identification and measurement of international migration. While they occasionally provide information describing some of the basic characteristics of international migrants, they do not provide sufficient data to study either the determinants or consequences of international migration. As this book explains, household surveys are flexible data collection instruments well suited for the in-depth analysis of various aspects of the migration process and are therefore the best potential source of information for the analysis of both the determinants and consequences of international migration. But to collect the necessary data, surveys of international migration should meet certain conditions. First, they should cover both the international migrants of interest and the relevant comparison group of non-migrants, which will require surveys in both the countries of origin and destination. Second, the questionnaires used should solicit detailed information on the wide range of factors potentially affecting international migration and its consequences for the migrants. This will require retrospective information on the situation prior to migration as well as at the time of interview. Third, specialized sampling methods are necessary to deal with the relative rarity of international migrants in most sending and receiving countries. Given the growing interest in understanding better the causes of international migration and its consequences, the importance of designing appropriate data collection instruments for their analysis cannot be overstressed. The discussion in Chapter 6 should therefore be useful to both users and producers of international migration statistics.

With respect to the overall measurement of international migration, the review presented in this book shows that there is considerable variation in the way that the statistical systems of different countries characterize international migrants. As is well known, such variation reduces the comparability of measures of international migration across countries. However, the book also documents that there is considerable compatibility in the data produced by similar data collection systems. Therefore, as long as perfect comparability continues to be elusive, it is important not to lose sight of the fact that much can be done to improve the relevance and facilitate the use of existing statistics, especially by promoting the dissemination of the statistics already available and by publishing data that are more disaggregated in terms of key characteristics. It is also essential to ensure that the statistics available are well understood by their potential users. To that end, a description of their meaning and scope in terms of concepts, definitions, relevant regulations and groups of persons excluded from the statistics should systematically accompany their publication.

As the United Nations noted in 1953, "migration movements are so closely related one to another that it is desirable for a given country to be informed not only of the volume, direction and composition of the immigration and emigration affecting that country, but also of the movements affecting other emigration and immigration countries" (United Nations, 1953, p. 6). Given the difficulties faced by countries of origin in collecting data on persons departing, it was suggested that countries of origin rely on the statistics gathered by countries of destination to estimate their levels of emigration. Today, even countries that gather some information on emigration have an interest in checking the accuracy of their statistics by comparing them with those obtained by the major countries of destination. Consequently, efforts to promote the exchange of information between countries of origin and those of destination should be fostered.

To conclude, it should be noted that certain administrative records which are potential sources of data on the labour force participation of foreigners have not been covered in this book. They include comprehensive government-run social security systems and national health insurance schemes which cover foreigners who are economically active. Such sources are not discussed here because, to our knowledge, they have generally not been used to yield information on working foreigners and are potential sources of such information only in a few developed countries. Developing countries mostly lack social security or health insurance systems covering the total economically active population. Consequently, such systems are unlikely to be adequate sources of information on foreigners, particularly when a large proportion of the latter work in the informal sector.

In sum, although the review of data collection systems on international migration in this volume is more comprehensive than anything produced during the past fifty years, it cannot claim to be complete or unbiased. Nevertheless, this review reflects the state of such systems today; by documenting the operation of these systems in a wide range of countries, it shows that much potentially useful data are already collected and only need to be made available through wider dissemination. Although the harmonization of concepts underlying the international migration statistics gathered by existing data collection systems is desirable, much can be achieved with existing data even in the absence of perfect comparability in the definitions used. Implementation of the detailed recommendations made with respect to each data collection system in Chapters 3 to 5 would, nevertheless, substantially improve the state of international migration statistics in the world. But as reiterated throughout this volume, the information needed to understand the complex process of international migration involves much more than mere counts of international migrants. Therefore, while improving the dissemination and exploitation of existing data is crucial, planning and implementing specialized household surveys in countries of origin and destination is also essential. To increase the resources devoted to data collection, governments themselves must be convinced of its usefulness. Data producers have therefore a strong interest in ensuring that the data they collect are used more widely and that their policy value is well understood.

CONCEPTS UNDERLYING INTERNATIONAL MIGRATION STATISTICS
2

This chapter presents a framework for the characterization of international migrants that provides a basis for the assessment of the statistics yielded by the various data sources available in different countries. Although such an assessment is carried out in greater detail in Chapters 3 to 5, it is desirable to present here an overview of how international migrants are currently characterized in statistical systems. A major problem faced in trying to analyse the concepts underlying the data collection systems of different countries is the lack of information on the concepts actually used. Data on international migrants are considerably more accessible than documentation regarding the definitions underlying those data. Perhaps the most comprehensive source of information on the definitions underlying data on flows of international migrants is the list compiled during the 1970s by the Statistical Office of the United Nations, which was published in the *Demographic yearbook 1977* (United Nations, 1978). That source is used throughout this chapter to analyse the conceptualization of international migration in data collection systems. It is therefore important to describe its limitations. First, the list is not universal in coverage: information on the concepts underlying immigration statistics is available for 116 countries or areas while that for emigration statistics is available for only 96 countries or areas. Second, the definitions presented are those underlying a variety of data collection systems, spanning the spectrum from arrival/departure statistics to data derived from continuous population registers. Third, the definitions are provided in concise form and are therefore unable to convey the complex nature of the characterization of migrants in the different statistical systems (Zlotnik, 1987). Lastly, all definitions refer to practices during the 1970s, some of which may have changed since then.

In addition to the information contained in the *Demographic yearbook 1977*, use is made, as appropriate, of the information gathered by the ILO from the 22 countries selected for in-depth study under the Interdepartmental Project on Migrant Workers implemented during 1994–95. Special questionnaires were sent to the institutions responsible for gathering or publishing international migration statistics in each of the countries selected so as to ascertain the coverage, scope and meaning of the statistics available. Detailed information on the concepts underlying the different sources of international migration statistics in those countries was thus obtained.

Five basic concepts are normally used, alone or in combination, to characterize international migrants, namely, citizenship, residence, time or duration of stay, purpose of stay and place of birth. They constitute the building blocks that allow the construction of more complex structures. By focusing on them, the discussion below sheds light on how apparently similar structures may be, in practice, essentially different. Understanding how such differences arise is a necessary first step to make proper use of international migration statistics and to devise ways of improving their quality and comparability.

A. CITIZENSHIP

A key attribute of international migration that sets it apart from other types of population mobility is that it links two distinct sovereign States and that persons moving from one State to another are not all treated equally. Citizenship is a decisive factor determining a person's rights in a country and has traditionally been used to determine who is subject to control when crossing international boundaries. Differentiation between citizens and foreigners at the time of border control is justified on the basis of international law as, according to the Universal Declaration of Human Rights, every person has the right to leave any country, including his or her own, and every person has the right to return to his or her own country. Such provisions validate the tendency of governments not to exercise anything but minimal control over two groups of persons: all those leaving a country's territory, and all citizens entering their own country's territory. That is, control is most likely to be exercised over persons entering a country other than their own (foreigners) and, to the extent that migration statistics are derived from the administrative procedures associated with such control, they often reflect only the inflow of foreigners. Canada and the United States, two of the major countries of immigration in the world, provide typical examples of countries where the statistics available on flows of international migrants refer only to the admission of foreigners.

Citizenship is also relevant in considering the consequences of international migration for the migrants themselves since persons who are allowed to stay in a country other than their own on a conditional basis may be subject to discriminatory practices in terms of employment, access to services or freedom of movement. Furthermore, all international instruments relating to the protection of the rights of migrant workers, such as the ILO Migration for Employment Convention (Revised), 1949 (No. 97), and the ILO Migrant Workers (Supplementary Provisions) Convention, 1975 (No. 143), or the United Nations Convention on the Rights of All Migrant Workers and Members of Their Families (opened for ratification in 1990), focus mostly on the situation of persons living in countries other than their own.

Concepts underlying international migration statistics

Given the relevance of citizenship for the assessment of policy implications, it is important to consider the extent to which countries use citizenship to characterize international migrants. According to the set of definitions compiled in 1977 by the United Nations, out of the 90 countries that identify international migrants from the generality of international travellers, 45 use citizenship as the identifying factor (Zlotnik, 1987). In addition, among the countries whose censuses for the period 1965-85 gathered data on either the foreign or the foreign-born population, those publishing detailed tabulations by legal nationality were: 34 out of 40 in Africa, 10 out of 33 in the Americas, and 16 out of 23 in Asia. (The totals correspond to countries with data available). It thus appears that, at least in Africa and Asia, legal nationality is used as a key criterion for the identification of international migrants (United Nations, 1993a). The same observation holds for European market-economy countries that gather data on international migrants through population registration systems or administrative procedures. Furthermore, among the countries that responded to the ILO questionnaire, the large majority (16 out of 17) reported having at least one source of international migration statistics where citizenship was a key factor in identifying international migrants.

One of the advantages of citizenship to identify or classify international migrants is its potential objectivity since, if data are gathered at the point of entry into or departure from a country, it is almost certain that proof of citizenship will be required to complete the admission or departure formalities. Thus, unlike other possible identifiers, citizenship is established on the basis of tangible evidence (usually a passport). Cases of double or multiple nationality, however, add some confusion to the data and may be the source of noticeable inconsistencies if the number of persons switching from using one passport to using another during travel is significant.

Even when data are gathered through other procedures, such as through the issuance of work or residence permits, population registers, or regularization drives, identity papers providing proof of legal nationality usually need to be presented. The accurate determination of citizenship can therefore be ensured. In contrast, censuses, surveys and other data collection systems that depend solely on self-reporting may not be equally successful in eliciting accurate information on citizenship, particularly if migrants have some vested interest in hiding their true legal nationality. Lack of proof of citizenship has also been a problem in the case of asylum-seekers, many of whom lack the necessary documents to prove their identity (some asylum-seekers believe that, by destroying their passports, they will be less likely to be returned to their countries of origin). However, lack of data on the number of asylum-seekers who are believed to or can be proved to have misreported their citizenship prevents an assessment of the potential magnitude of reporting errors.

B. RESIDENCE

Perhaps the most widely used and yet the least well defined concept to identify international migrants is that of residence, implemented either in terms of a change of residence or in terms of a change of resident status. Among the set of definitions compiled in 1977 by the United Nations, out of the 90 that distinguish international migrants from other international travellers, 73 use residence as a criterion to effect the distinction (Zlotnik, 1987). However, residence is seldom defined in terms of measurable elements.

Countries tend to identify immigrants as non-residents who enter the country with a view to establishing residence (that is, of becoming residents) and emigrants as residents who intend to give up residence (that is, to become non-residents). Although such definitions appear to be clear and straightforward, serious difficulties arise in their implementation because the term "residence" is not well defined, especially for mobile individuals. The meaning of residence can be interpreted from a legal (*de jure*) perspective or from a *de facto* perspective. According to the former, a person establishes residence in a country if he or she fulfills all the requirements to become a legal resident of that country. Being a resident on a *de jure* basis usually implies having a place of abode in the country concerned as well as acquiring certain benefits and obligations, such as the right for children to attend local public schools or the duty to pay local and national taxes. From a *de facto* perspective, establishing residence implies actually living in or being present in a given place for more than a minimum length of time. In countries that adopt the second approach, the minimum length of time needed to establish residence usually varies between three months and a year.

Because the *de jure* interpretation of residence derives its meaning from the laws and regulations of the countries concerned, it can and does vary from one country to another. Furthermore, the conditions for establishing residence in a given country are also likely to differ according to whether the person concerned is or is not a citizen of the country in question; in most countries, there may be no explicit criteria to judge whether a citizen is or is not a resident. Indeed, given the principles set by international law, there is a strong presumption that all citizens of a country have the right of abode in it and consequently their mere presence in the country may qualify them as residents. It may thus happen that a person may be considered simultaneously a *de jure* resident of two countries: his or her own country of citizenship, where the person may be present only temporarily, and the country where the same person, as a foreigner, has his or her usual abode.

Another consequence of the fact that citizens are presumed to be legal residents of their own country-irrespective of the time that they have actually spent in it – is that they would not qualify as "immigrants" according to the definition that equates immigrants with non-residents entering a country to establish residence in that country. Hence, if citizens are not to be eliminated from international migration statistics altogether, a specific category to accommodate them needs to be created. That seems to have been the solution chosen by 52 of the 115 countries whose consolidated statistics on international arrivals were published in the *Demographic yearbook 1985* (United Nations, 1987): those 52 countries listed "returning residents" under a separate category. Although it is likely that the definition of returning resident varies from country to country, its mere use indicates that the need to make explicit allowance for the return of persons who already "belong" to the receiving country is real.

The use of a *de facto* definition of residence to identify international migrants would avoid some of the problems associated with the *de jure* approach if all countries would adopt the same cut-off point regarding the minimum length of stay required to establish residence. This strategy, however, is not entirely devoid of problems, especially in cases where the minimum length of stay necessary for a person to be considered a resident is long. The longer that period, the more likely that the person concerned may travel abroad and thus break a continuous length of stay. To illustrate the drawbacks of using actual length of stay as the sole criterion to identify migrants, consider a country that defines international migrants as foreign persons who stay in the country for more than a year after initial admission. Then, strict application of that definition would imply that a foreigner who settles in the country for a period of years but spends at least one month of every year abroad would never qualify as a resident and thus never be counted as an international migrant. Thus, defining migration strictly on the basis of time actually spent in a country, though appealing in theory, is less than ideal in practice, not only because of the difficulties involved in determining actual length of stay, but mainly because, ultimately, it is not the uninterrupted presence of a person in a country that is important. The purpose of a person's stay, at least as interpreted through existing regulatory mechanisms, may be more relevant.

To illustrate how a *de facto* approach to the determination of residence is used in gathering international migration statistics, consider the case of the Netherlands, where data on migration are derived from a population registration system. In principle, all persons having residence in the Netherlands are inscribed in the population register. The card of a resident person is removed from the register if the person leaves with the intention of staying abroad for at least a year. Dutch citizens who have been abroad are inscribed in the register of the locality in which they intend to live if they expect to stay in the Netherlands for at least one month, but foreigners are inscribed only if they intend to stay in the Netherlands for at least six months (Verhoef, 1986). This example illustrates how the concepts of residence, legal nationality and duration of presence in or absence from the country concerned can be intertwined to identify international migrants. Note that the undefined term "residence" is used to specify the universe (total population) being considered. Only by making explicit the rules governing the entry and removal of personal cards from the population register does it become clear what residence really means. For Dutch citizens, it implies having been present in the Netherlands for at least one month at some time and, since then, having been present at least one day of every year. By following this strategy, a Dutch citizen would be initially inscribed in the register and, because no subsequent period of absence would be at least a year in duration, his or her personal card would not be removed from the register. For foreigners, the initial period of presence should be of at least six months followed by a yearly return of at least one day. Clearly, such extreme situations are not those typically evoked by the term "residence", nor are they likely to occur often in practice. However, they point to weaknesses in the definitions adopted and underscore the fact that residence, even if apparently defined in terms of length of stay, does not necessarily imply presence.

The case of Australia is also illustrative of the pitfalls surrounding the use of the concept of residence. According to Australian sources (Australian Bureau of Statistics, 1984), the definitions underlying the data on migration flows gathered through border control are the following:

Permanent immigrants are persons arriving with the intention of settling permanently in Australia (settlers).

Permanent emigrants are Australian residents (including former settlers) departing with the intention of residing permanently abroad.

Long-term movements include: (a) overseas arrivals and departures of *visitors* with the intended or actual length of stay in Australia of 12 months or more; (b) departures and arrivals of *Australian residents* with intended or actual length of stay abroad of 12 months or more.

Once more, the term "resident" is not explicitly defined. However, the definition of permanent emigrants implies that Australian residents include both Australian citizens and persons who, at some earlier date, were admitted as settlers, that is, were granted the right to reside in Australia. Thus, in spite of the appearance to the contrary, the term "resident" is used from a *de jure* perspective, rather than as an indicator of presence or absence. This conclusion is corroborated by the fact that the definition of long-term movements includes those of Australian residents, suggesting that once persons are granted the right of abode in Australia they do not lose it even if they subsequently leave to spend several years abroad. Clearly, such an interpretation of residence, if not made explicit, can be very misleading, especially if one does not have access to the laws and regulations establishing who is a resident and under what conditions residence may be acquired or lost. In this case, the essence of the concept of residence is similar to that of citizenship or legal nationality, both being attributes that do not depend on a person's actual presence in or absence from a State. However, while the limitations of citizenship in this respect are always clear, the variability in the concept of residence and its connotations regarding presence constitute a fertile ground for confusion.

Since residence is not equivalent to presence and, as a legal attribute, is subject to far greater variations of interpretation than citizenship, is it wise to use it at all? Although a negative answer to this question would be appropriate from purely theoretical considerations, the widespread use of the concept of residence is too closely linked to the basic tenet of international migration, namely, the State's prerogative to grant residence privileges to foreigners, for it to be totally discarded. Even the most recent efforts by the United Nations Statistical Division to produce a new set of recommendations regarding international migration statistics give prominence to the concept of residence in identifying international migrants (United Nations Statistical Division and European Communities Statistical Office, 1995). Residence is therefore very likely to remain a basic element in the definition of international migration; consequently, strategies to render it less misleading and easier to capture statistically should be devised.

Several suggestions can be advanced in this respect. The first involves a campaign to make explicit the meaning of residence whenever it appears in the definition of migrant categories used by a statistical system. Such definitions should accompany every published set of data relating to those categories so as to promote awareness about the many nuances of the terms resident, non-resident and residence. Especially when residence is used as a legal attribute, the explicit presentation of the laws and regulations determining resident and non-resident status should be standard practice. Personnel charged with the collection of information need to be instructed about the meaning of residence and about how to establish the resident status of travellers. Countries of origin and destination linked by migration flows should be encouraged to exchange information about their respective regulatory and administrative practices to establish resident status with a view to devising data collection strategies that depend, as far as possible, on objective evidence (for example, a citizen's declaration of intention to depart permanently from his or her country of nationality might be validated by possession of the appropriate entry or residence permits issued by the country of destination).

Ensuring that the meaning of residence is well understood by those gathering information on international migrants is crucial to elicit more accurate responses from the persons involved. It is also essential to ensure that the instruments used for data collection (forms, instructions on how to fill them in, etc.) are well designed and convey the appropriate concepts to the respondent. In several statistical systems yielding information on international migration, recording the country of previous residence or the country of intended residence of those persons identified as international migrants is standard practice. However, unless respondents have a clear understanding of what "residence" refers to, the data obtained will be less than ideal. This matter is further discussed in Chapters 3 and 4 in dealing with specific data collection systems.

C. TIME

As illustrated above in discussing residence, time is a criterion often used to determine international migrant status. Time can be used in different ways.

International migration statistics

Compare, for instance, the definition of immigrants adopted by the United States: "aliens lawfully accorded the privilege of residing permanently in the United States" (United States Immigration and Naturalization Service, 1993), with that used by the United Kingdom: "persons intending to reside in the country for a year or more after having resided outside the country for a year or more", or that of the Netherlands: "nationals intending to stay in the Netherlands for more than 30 days and aliens intending to stay for more than 180 days". Although time is an element of all these definitions, it clearly has different levels of concreteness in each. In the cases of the Netherlands and the United Kingdom, durations are not only expressed in terms of definite numbers, but they are also meant to represent actual durations of stay or absence since there is the expectation that intended durations will become actual ones. In contrast, in the case of the United States, the term "permanently" cannot be interpreted, even ideally, as an actual duration of stay. Time, in this instance, refers to the length of validity of the privilege granted by the United States. It is a potential time accorded to the immigrant, who may or may not realize that potential. The term "legal time" has been suggested to denote a time criterion that is expressed in terms of the limitations (or lack of them) set by the receiving State on the potential period of stay of an international migrant as opposed to "actual time" which refers to the intended or actual duration of stay of the migrant concerned (Zlotnik, 1987).

Legal time is closely associated with the concept of legal residence. It represents the time constraints (or lack of them) set by laws or regulations on the right to legal residence granted by the receiving State to a foreigner. Legal time differs from the actual time criterion in that the latter tries to reflect actual outcomes by representing either actual or intended lengths of stay. In contrast, legal time is regulatory in nature and is related but is not equivalent to actual time outcomes. Consequently, an international migrant's actual stay in the receiving country may differ considerably from that specified by the legal time criterion. The case of temporary migrant workers is typical: through permit renewals they may stay in the receiving country for lengthy periods even though, at any given time, their permission to stay is restricted to a year or less. Thus, although at any given stage of the process the expected *de jure* length of stay is limited, the potential for *de facto* permanence exists. However, since it is not possible to know *a priori* what the actual length of stay will end up being, statistics are likely to reflect only the limited, *de jure* period of stay granted to temporary migrant workers at any given time.

Although few statistical systems make explicit the fact that their definitions of migrant categories are based on the concept of legal time, it often underlies them. One may even posit that legal time influences the declaration of intended length of stay made by international migrants subject to border control. Indeed, when a foreigner entering a country is asked by immigration authorities to state his or her expected length of stay, it is unlikely that the person would report a length that contravenes the one allowed by law or by the specific visa or entry permit that he or she holds.

Concepts underlying international migration statistics

The use of specific time limits to determine migration status is not all that widespread. Only 29 out of the 90 countries or areas providing some characterization of international migration to the United Nations in 1977 made explicit use of specific durations (that is, durations other than "permanent"). Lack of consistent information about whether those durations refer to the actual or intended presence or absence or to statutory lengths of stay does not permit an accurate assessment of the relative importance of the use of legal versus actual time. It is likely, however, that the use of legal time predominates (Zlotnik, 1987).

Among the countries for which information on definitions of international migration were collected by the ILO, several indicate that legal time is the concept used in classifying migrants. Japan, for instance, reports that in gathering data on persons entering or leaving the country, the type of work or residence permit of incoming foreigners is recorded together with its period of validity. Japan's alien registration system is also geared towards maintaining records on foreigners by type and duration of residence permit. In Poland, migrant workers are classified into two main categories according to the length of validity of their work permits. Short-term migrant workers are granted permits of up to three months whereas long-term migrant workers are granted permits with a validity of 3 to 12 months. Since permits can be renewed a number of times, Polish statisticians recognize that the current duration of a work permit does not reflect the actual length of stay of an international migrant worker in the country. Portugal reports that in gathering immigration statistics, a "permanent immigrant" is a foreigner who, irrespective of his or her time of arrival in Portugal, requests for the first time from the competent authorities a residence permit valid for a period of one year. In Sri Lanka, the Department of Immigration and Emigration gathers data on the number of residence visas issued to foreigners. Residence visas have a validity not exceeding two years and are renewable. Lastly, Switzerland maintains information on the foreign population according to type of residence permit. The categories of migrants identified separately in Swiss statistics include persons holding "establishment permits" (which allow permanent residence in Switzerland), those granted "annual permits" (whose length of validity varies between 9 and 12 months, and which are renewable), and persons granted "seasonal permits" (which allow a stay in Switzerland of up to 9 months in any given year).

In contrast, only Portugal reports the use of a concept of time that is not *de jure* in nature. Thus, Portugal defines temporary emigrants as persons leaving the country with the intention of working in gainful employment and staying abroad for at most a year. Permanent emigrants from Portugal are defined as persons leaving the country with the intention of residing abroad more than a year.

It is noteworthy that, as the definitions cited above reveal, terms that have a certain connotation or meaning are often used to mean something quite different. The definitions reported by Portugal provide a good example: the term "permanent" is used to describe persons who, as immigrants, obtain permits valid for only one year and, as emigrants, intend to stay abroad more than a year but not necessarily forever. In both cases, the label "permanent" is misleading. In Switzerland, an "annual permit" may be valid for only 9 months, whereas in Poland a "long-term permit" needs to be valid for only slightly more than three months. It is such misuse of terminology together with confusion about the true meaning of the time concepts used in determining migration status that leads to common misunderstandings about the international migration process. Thus, it is often claimed that the distinction between temporary and permanent migration is breaking down. In reality, that distinction has never been clear-cut when actual lengths of stay abroad are considered: there have always been cases of foreigners granted permanent residence in a country who nevertheless decide to leave it after only a short stay, and of persons admitted temporarily who end up staying for long periods. The relevant difference is that between being granted the right to reside permanently in a country and being granted instead a temporary right of residence, even if the latter is renewable. Such a difference is further accentuated by the fact that restrictions on the right to residence are usually accompanied by statutory limitations affecting other spheres of life as well, including choice of employment, freedom of movement within the receiving State, and the possibility of family reunification. The problem, therefore, is not that the distinction between the permanent and the temporary status of international migrants is disappearing but rather that it persists even when, in fact, many migrants with a temporary status actually remain in the receiving State for periods comparable to those of migrants who, because of their "permanent" status, are granted a more comprehensive set of rights.

Just as in the case of citizenship and residence, understanding that issues of time and duration of stay cannot be divorced from the State's role in controlling international migration helps to explain why attempts to measure international migration based on actual outcomes have had little success. That is not to say that actual outcomes matter little, but that they are usually not the ones being reflected in available statistics. The challenge is to devise data gathering procedures that provide information on both: statutory limitations on duration of stay and actual time spent by international migrants in the receiving country.

D. PURPOSE OF STAY

Purpose of stay is particularly important in determining international migrant status when it is related to the exercise of an economic activity. Thus, 21 out of the 90 countries or areas that provided specific definitions of immigrants and emigrants to the United Nations in 1977 considered the exercise of an economic activity in a country other than their own as a characteristic distinguishing international migrants from other travellers (Zlotnik, 1987). Yet, working abroad is not the only purpose of stay relevant for the characterization of international migrants. Studying abroad, being trained in another country, moving to join family members living abroad, and fleeing persecution or seeking a safe haven from conflict in one's own country have all been recognized by States as purposes of stay that warrant special treatment.

As in the case of the residence and time criteria, there are two ways of interpreting purpose of stay: as a reflection of the subjective intentions of an international migrant or as the reason for admission validated by the receiving State. Although there is probably a high correlation between the two, it is important not to assume that the purpose of stay validated by the State is an accurate reflection of the intention of the migrant. Furthermore, because a person's intentions are complex and changeable, statistical accounting should not be based upon them. The State's view, in contrast, is relevant not only from a policy perspective but also because it determines the conditions under which a person can be legally admitted into its territory. Note, however, that where a State's own returning citizens are concerned, the power of the State to impose conditions on admission is limited.

Given that the State's control over the international migration of foreigners usually starts in the country of origin through the issuance of visas or other permits allowing entry, stay or the exercise of economic activity in the State's territory, the type of visa granted can be used to establish purpose of stay. Thus, there are visas allowing the admission of foreigners for the purpose of pursuing specific programmes of study; visas allowing foreigners to engage in a particular type of economic activity, often only during a specific period of stay; visas granting permission to reside permanently in the State's territory; visas permitting admission strictly for tourism and restricting considerably the length of stay; and visas allowing the short-term sojourn of foreigners to engage in business activities. Generally, the restrictions imposed by visas refer not only to the type of activities that a foreign person can legally engage in but also to the duration of stay. Thus, the duration and purpose of stay allowed are often closely linked criteria from the regulatory perspective and, together with citizenship, they provide the most useful elements in determining the migrant category appropriate for classifying someone entering a country.

The purpose of stay abroad is also an important criterion used by some countries of origin to identify relevant emigrant groups among their citizens. Thus, among the 22 countries providing information to the ILO in 1994-95, those known to be important sources of migrant workers often cited the purpose of stay abroad as a key criterion to identify international migrant workers. Belarus, for instance, reported collecting information on citizens who registered their intention to take up short- or long-term employment abroad as well as on persons who already had labour contracts that would allow them to work abroad. In Pakistan, an emigrant was defined as a person departing for the purpose or with the intention of working abroad for hire or engaging in any trade, profession or calling. In Poland, the Central Labour Office gathers information on Polish citizens going abroad to work under the framework of bilateral agreements (the vast majority perform seasonal work abroad lasting no more than 90 days). In Sri Lanka, the Bureau of Foreign Employment gathers information on Sri Lankan citizens engaging in contractual employment abroad; and in Thailand, the Overseas Employment Administration Office gathers information on Thai citizens who depart to work abroad, whether they obtained job offers individually or through contract agencies.

The variety of these characterizations of international emigrants suggests that, although purpose of stay is indeed a relevant criterion to identify international migrants, it is also a frequent cause of the lack of international comparability in the statistics available. Thus, in some of the definitions provided by governments there is confusion between the purpose of stay intended by the migrant departing and the purpose of stay established by the receiving State. In Belarus, for instance, both citizens registering their intention to work abroad and persons already in possession of labour contracts seem to be treated equally for statistical purposes. One cannot but wonder if those "registering their intention" have any tangible reason for believing that they would ever find work abroad. In Pakistan as well, emigrants were characterized as persons departing with the *purpose or the intention* of working abroad. Again, it is not clear whether purpose and intention are being treated as distinct, what their meaning is, and which has greater weight.

As in the case of legal time, the use of purpose of stay in identifying and categorizing international migrants needs to be given more attention, especially in order to understand how purpose of stay is used during the data collection process and to devise ways of improving its relevance as an indicator of actual rather than intended outcomes. Furthermore, just as in the case of residence, personnel charged with the collection of information on international migrants need to be instructed about the meaning of purpose of stay and about how to establish it in the case of particular travellers. To that effect, it is important to promote the exchange of information between countries of origin and destination linked by migration flows, so that knowledge of the receiving countries' practices to regulate purpose of stay could be used to devise objective means to establish that of emigrating citizens.

E. PLACE OF BIRTH

Place of birth is relevant because it is the criterion most often used to identify international migrants in population censuses and is also commonly used in other demographic data sources, such as household surveys. Information on place of birth has the advantage of allowing the identification of not only international but also internal migrants using a single question. Given that census questionnaires must be kept short to keep costs low and ensure data quality, the multiple uses of information derived from a question on place of birth make it attractive for inclusion. Furthermore, because persons born in a place different from that in which they are enumerated must have moved from the place of birth to the place of enumeration at some time during their lifetimes, it is appropriate to equate them with migrants (sometimes called *lifetime* migrants). In contrast, there is no guarantee that foreign citizens enumerated in a given country would necessarily have migrated to that country since there are countries in which citizenship is not automatically granted to persons born in the country's territory. Consequently, the children of foreigners, even if born in the country, remain foreigners.

Place of birth is preferable to citizenship as a classifying variable because it does not change over the life of an individual, whereas citizenship can and does change, particularly among internationally mobile persons. However, place of birth is generally not a basic attribute used in characterizing international migrants in continuous recording systems, although information on place of birth is often gathered by those systems and may be used as a classifying variable in producing tabulations about migration flows.

Although it is common practice to equate the number of foreign-born persons enumerated in a census with the stock of international migrants in a country, other data sources may identify international migrants on the basis of different criteria. In Canada, for instance, immigrants are foreigners granted the permission to reside permanently in the country. Canadian statistics use the term "landed immigrant" to distinguish persons granted such a right from other foreigners admitted on a temporary basis. Because it is common for landed immigrants to become Canadian citizens, current citizenship (that is, citizenship at the time of the census) would not be an adequate criterion to use for identifying the stock of all persons who had been admitted as international migrants. Instead, the 1991 census of Canada, though still including a question on place of birth, identified the stock of immigrants on the basis of whether or not persons enumerated had ever held the status of landed immigrants (Canada, 1992). Thus, the 1991 census tabulations present separately the number of persons who are non-immigrants (22,427,745), 84,430 of whom were born outside Canada, and the number of persons who had been landed immigrants (4,342,890), 4,335,185 of whom were foreign-born. Although the total number of foreign-born (4,419,615) would be only 1.8 per cent greater than the actual number of immigrants in the population, the Canadian data indicate clearly that the foreign-born population, being the group of *de facto* international migrants, is not necessarily equivalent to the number of persons who, having been granted immigrant status, remain in the population (the *de jure* group).

In the United States, where the naturalization of immigrants is also common, population censuses have traditionally gathered several items of information to establish the immigrant stock. According to United States Bureau of the Census definitions, natives are persons born in the United States, the Commonwealth of Puerto Rico, or a possession of the United States. Natives also include the small number of persons who, although born in a country other than the United States or at sea, have at least one parent who is both born in the United States and is a citizen of that country. The foreign-born are then defined as all persons not classified as native (Shryock and Siegel, 1975). That is, the foreign-born exclude persons born outside United States territory who have the right to United States citizenship because at least one of their parents was a United States citizen born in the United States. Consequently, the foreign-born population normally used as an indicator of the international migrant stock includes only those foreign-born persons who, at the time of their birth, had parents neither of whom were citizens of the United States born in the United States. The number of those persons conforms better than all foreign-born persons to the concept of international migrant used in other statistical sources (a foreign person granted permission to stay in the United States).

In France, international migrants are normally equated with foreigners. The Ministry of the Interior, for instance, compiles statistics on the number of foreign persons having valid residence permits. Furthermore, although France usually grants citizenship to persons born in its territory, qualifying foreigners need not make a petition for French citizenship until they are 18 years of age. Consequently, persons under age 18 may remain foreigners even if born and having lived continuously in France. Therefore, the total number of foreigners residing in France at any given time will include a mixture of both persons born in France and persons born abroad. Similarly, the number of foreign-born persons will include both foreigners and French citizens born abroad. In the case of France, the difference between the number of foreigners and the number of foreign born is large. Thus, according to the 1990 census, there were 3.6 million foreigners and 5.9 million foreign-born persons in metropolitan France (excluding French overseas territories). Clearly, if only the number of foreigners were available, one would have a quite different view of the impact of international migration in France than one has knowing both the number of foreigners and the number of foreign-born.

France's practice of gathering information in its censuses on both place of birth and current citizenship is to be commended. Other countries experiencing sizeable inflows of international migrants should give serious consideration to doing the same. It is also crucial to stress that, if data on both place of birth and citizenship are collected, tabulations of the total population classified simultaneously by place of birth, citizenship and other relevant variables should be published. All the enumerated population should be included in such tabulations, as opposed to only the foreign-born or only those with foreign nationality, since it is important to identify all the possible groups of relevance, namely, citizens born abroad, foreigners born abroad, foreigners born in the country of enumeration (sometimes called "second generation migrants"), and citizens born in their own country.

Concepts underlying international migration statistics

F. CONSIDERATIONS IN THE ASSESSMENT OF INTERNATIONAL MIGRATION STATISTICS

The preceding review of concepts shows the major influence that legal and regulatory considerations exert, whether explicitly or implicitly, on the characterization of international migrants in statistical systems. One of the main problems faced in understanding how international migration is viewed and measured by national statistical systems is to clarify and interpret the legal or quasi-legal nature of the concepts underlying their operation. Although there have been several attempts to expurgate international migration statistics from their legal dimensions, they have not been successful largely because international migration is so inherently linked to a State's basic prerogatives that the depuration sought tends to reduce the policy relevance of the statistics obtained. For that reason, a more expedient approach is to take explicit account of the views and practices of governments in trying to set up a usable framework for the categorization and analysis of international migration statistics. That is the approach followed below in which we propose a framework for the discussion and evaluation of the statistical systems presented in the rest of this book.

Before proceeding with that task, let us consider first the basic question: "Who is an international migrant?" Unfortunately, there is no single or simple answer to this question, and part of the reason that statistics on international migration are deficient is that the group of people identified as international migrants varies not only across countries, but also between different data sources within a country and even on occasion within the same data source over time. Furthermore, there are at least two possible and not always compatible approaches to ascertain who is an international migrant. The first, which may be described as the outsider's approach, is to construct from basic principles the set of criteria that a person should meet to be considered an international migrant. The second, which may be characterized as the insider's approach, consists of taking the identification procedures that are already used by countries and trying to organize them into workable concepts and definitions.

The approach followed here is a combination of the two described above, though it favours the outsider's approach in the sense that the concepts and definitions proposed will not necessarily reflect the practices of any particular State. In selecting those definitions, however, account will be taken of actual State practices so that the latter can be accommodated by the proposed framework. The usefulness of following an outsider's approach lies mostly in recognizing that its output is normative, that is, it establishes models with which to compare actual practices, although it may not influence those practices in any significant way. Thus, deciding that international migrants are persons who have moved at least once in their lives from one country to another does not alter the fact that the stock of "international migrants" in Germany or Japan is usually obtained from registers that include only foreigners, many of whom have never moved. The existence of the model makes us aware that existing statistics do not fit it and that adjustments may be necessary to get a better measure of the normative concept; it does not change the nature of the statistics themselves.

The first step in deriving a normative framework is to establish the concepts to be given priority. Let us consider again the issue of citizenship. Given that today's world is partitioned into sovereign States, each of which has the right to determine who enters its territory and under what conditions, one of the distinctive features of international travel is that it is only possible if one country allows the admission of the citizens of another. Although countries generally allow the entry and short-term stay of foreigners, their long-term stay or the exercise of particular activities, such as an economic activity, may be permitted only under certain circumstances. It is clearly this prerogative of governments to control the length of stay and type of activity of foreigners in their territories that sets international migration apart from other types of international or internal movement. Citizenship, therefore, matters a great deal in understanding the dynamics of international migration and the circumstances of international migrants. Yet because the laws and regulations governing citizenship allow for the existence of persons who, despite having always been present in a country, have the citizenship of another country, citizenship cannot be the only identifier of international migrants. It must, however, play a key role in their characterization.

Citizenship also matters because, once migration has taken place, persons who spend lengthy periods in a country other than their own cannot always count on the government of the host country to protect their interests or to uphold their rights. Depending on the conditions for their admission and stay, foreigners may be subject to discriminatory practices in terms of employment, access to services or freedom of movement. Aware of such problems, the international community has adopted several international instruments dealing with the protection of the rights of specific groups of persons moving to countries other than their own. Thus, the ILO has adopted the Migration for Employment Convention (Revised), 1949 (No. 97), and the Migrant Workers (Supplementary Provisions) Convention, 1975 (No. 143); the United Nations has opened for signature and ratification the Convention on the Rights of All Migrant Workers and Members of Their Families (1990); and about two-thirds of the countries in the world have ratified the 1954 Convention Relating to the Status of Refugees or its 1967 Protocol. All these conventions deal with the rights of foreigners who, depending on the conditions of their admission, fall into either the category of migrant workers (and members of their families) or that of refugees. Having information on those types of international migrants is therefore highly relevant for policy assessment.

The essence of migration is movement; therefore, international migration should involve a move from one country to another. But to be relevant, international migration must be distinct from international travel and consequently more than movement must be involved. Either a minimum length of stay in the country of destination or a particular purpose for moving to that country or for leaving the country of origin must be factors distinguishing international migration from international travel. Purpose of stay, as validated by the receiving State, will therefore be used as one of the key identifiers of international migrants in the framework proposed. The emphasis on State validation is justified for two reasons. The first is that it is the only way of ensuring that objective rather than subjective criteria are used. Thus, a person moving from one country to another may have several purposes for doing so or may have a purpose that is not sanctioned by the receiving State, which would therefore be unlikely to be reported. Detailed surveys might try to probe into those aspects of migration, but it would be unwise to use them as the basis for the identification or classification of international migrants. The second reason is that State actions matter the most for policy assessment. That is, from a policy perspective, the admission of a foreign male of working age as a worker is not equivalent to the admission of the same man as the spouse of a citizen. In the first case, the State has maximum discretion regarding the admission of the person involved, whereas in the second the State's actions are constrained by the rights of citizens. For the purposes of policy analysis and of understanding the immediate determinants of international migration, distinguishing the two is extremely relevant.

To sum up, citizenship, purpose of stay as defined by the receiving State, and the fact that a person has actually moved from one country to another will be the three key factors allowing the identification and characterization of international migrants. The use of citizenship, however, should not be interpreted to mean that only foreigners matter. There are many reasons for ensuring that international migrants are not restricted to being only persons moving to countries other than their own. From a demographic perspective, the addition of a person to a population through international migration has the same effect whether the person is a foreigner or not. From an economic perspective as well, an additional worker represents one more economically active person irrespective of his or her legal nationality. Consequently, persons returning to their countries of origin or persons moving to countries where they have a right to citizenship should not be excluded from international migration statistics, since their economic, social and demographic impact in the countries receiving them is likely to be relevant.

Lastly, although there is much in the framework presented that can be justified in terms of the needs of policy-makers and researchers wishing to obtain a better measurement and understanding of the different aspects of international migration, it cannot be claimed that the framework satisfies all possible user needs or that it was derived having only the needs of users in mind. As stated above, the framework proposed is a normative construct that adopts elements of what already exists and organizes them within a coherent structure so as to permit a better understanding of the phenomenon at hand. Furthermore, because of its normative character, the framework is maximal in nature and it is not expected that every country will admit all the categories of international migrants identified. The expectation is, however, that any specific categories already in use by countries may find their equivalent within the framework.

G. FRAMEWORK FOR THE IDENTIFICATION AND CLASSIFICATION OF INTERNATIONAL MIGRANTS

Tables 2.1 and 2.2 present in schematic form the framework for the identification and classification of international migrants that guides the discussion of existing statistical systems in the rest of this book and provides a model for their assessment. In addition, box 2.1 presents succinct definitions of the different categories of international migrants included in the framework. Note that, because of its maximal character, the framework incorporates some types of international movements of people who are not generally considered international migrants. Those groups are included in the interest of comprehensiveness and to make the point that certain short-term international movements are also relevant for the study of migration although they do not necessarily involve the exercise of an economic activity. The distinction below makes explicit the extent to which the framework proposed is based on existing country practices regarding the identification of international migrants in statistical systems and points out the cases in which the equivalence between particular types of migrants identified by existing systems and the categories included in the framework is not straightforward.

Before embarking on a discussion of the elements constituting the framework proposed, a number of points must be highlighted. First, all categories refer to persons who have moved from one country to another. In discussing the meaning of most categories, it is assumed that migrants are identified and characterized at the time they enter the country. However, the definitions presented can generally be applied either to migrants admitted during a given period (flows of migrants) or to migrants present in the country of destination at a given time (stocks of migrants). The framework itself does not make a distinction between the two.

A second and most important point is that, in defining different categories of migrants, the framework accords primacy to the *conditions set by the receiving State* for the admission of an international migrant. Only rarely are the intentions, desires or wishes of a person crossing international borders used to determine migrant status. Such exceptions arise mostly in the case of the admission or readmission of citizens, which according to international law should not be subject to restrictions.

The third point is that the categories presented are meant to be used in counting international migrants and not international migration (that is, number of moves) and that a person is expected to belong to one and only one category at a time. Decisions about the allocation of cases that could potentially

Concepts underlying international migration statistics

Table 2.1. Framework for the characterization of different categories of international migration

Citizenship	Legal basis for admission	Category	Sub-category	Admission of family members	Period of stay
Citizens	Right of entry and abode	Return migrants	Returning students or trainees	Allowed	Unrestricted
			Returning emigrants	Allowed	Unrestricted
			Returning migrant workers	Allowed	Unrestricted
			Repatriating foreign-born citizens	Allowed	Unrestricted
			Repatriated refugees	Allowed	Unrestricted
			Returning asylum-seekers	Allowed	Unrestricted
			Returning irregular migrants	Allowed	Unrestricted
Foreigners	Right to citizenship	Returning ethnics		Allowed	Unrestricted
	Right to free movement	Free-movement migrants		Allowed	Unrestricted
	Provisions for short-term admission of foreigners	Non-migrant categories	Consular personnel	Allowed	Open ended
			Military personnel	Allowed	Open ended
			Tourists	Not applicable	Restricted
		Possible migrant categories	Students	Sometimes allowed	Restricted
			Trainees	Sometimes allowed	Restricted
			Retirees	Allowed conditionally	Open ended
	Immigration laws	Immigrants	Settlers	Allowed	Unrestricted
	Labour migration laws	Migrant workers	Frontier workers	Not allowed	Restricted
Foreigners			Seasonal migrant workers	Not allowed	Restricted
			Project-tied migrant workers	Not allowed	Restricted
			Contract migrant workers	Rarely allowed	Restricted
			Temporary migrant workers	Sometimes allowed	Restricted

International migration statistics

Table 2.1. (*continued*)

Citizenship	Legal basis for admission	Category	Sub-category	Admission of family members	Period of stay
Foreigners (cont.)			Established migrant workers	Allowed conditionally	Open ended
			Highly skilled migrant workers	Allowed	Restricted
	Economic migration laws	Business travellers		Not applicable	Restricted
		Immigrating investors		Allowed	Unrestricted
	Laws on asylum	Asylum migration	Convention refugees	Sometimes allowed	Open ended
			Humanitarian admissions (refugees type B)	Sometimes allowed	Open ended
			Asylum-seekers	Not allowed	Uncertain
			Temporary protected status	Not allowed	Uncertain
			Stay of deportation	Not allowed	Open ended
	Unauthorized	Irregular migration	Unauthorized entry	Not applicable	Not applicable

belong to two different categories at the same time should always be made explicitly. An important feature of the framework is that it should not be used as a static model. Given the number of categories included, the task of presenting all possible transitions between categories is far from straightforward and will not be attempted. It is, however, important to bear in mind that persons belonging to one category at a specific point in time may move to another category as time elapses and their status changes. Such transitions are particularly important when they involve a move from a non-migrant category, such as that of a tourist, to a migrant category. That type of transition may mean that a person is counted as an international migrant only some time after the actual move has taken place. Other key transitions of interest are noted below in the discussion of the categories included in the framework.

Another related issue is that the different categories, though relevant for both the country of origin and that of destination, are presented here from the perspective of the country of destination. To the extent that a majority of arriving migrants eventually depart, the most likely transition is from a certain category of arriving migrants to its counterpart as departing migrants. For instance, most arriving migrant workers will become departing migrant workers from the perspective of the country of destination and become return migrant workers for the country of origin. Separate consideration of migrants by citizenship (distinguishing citizens and aliens) allows, to a certain extent, the perspectives of countries of origin and destination to be incorporated simultaneously within the same framework.

Concepts underlying international migration statistics

Table 2.2. Framework for the classification of migrants for family reunification

Citizenship of sponsor	Migration status of sponsor	Type of reunification	Foreign relatives allowed to join the sponsor				
			Spouse	Dependent children	Other children	Parents	Siblings
Citizens	Non-migrant	To join	Yes	Yes	Often	Often	Sometimes
	Return migrant	To accompany	Yes	Yes	Often	Often	Sometimes
		To join	Yes	Yes	Often	Often	Sometimes
Foreigners	Returning ethnic	To accompany	Yes	Yes	Sometimes	Sometimes	No
		To join	Yes	Yes	Sometimes	Sometimes	No
	Free-movement migrant	To accompany	Yes	Yes	Sometimes	Sometimes	No
		To join	Yes	Yes	Sometimes	Sometimes	No
	Foreign student	To accompany	Sometimes	Sometimes	No	No	No
		To join	Sometimes	Sometimes	No	No	No
	Foreign trainee	To accompany	Sometimes	Sometimes	No	No	No
		To join	Sometimes	Sometimes	No	No	No
	Retiree	To accompany	Yes	Yes	No	No	No
	Settler	To accompany	Yes	Yes	Sometimes	No	No
		To join	Yes	Yes	Sometimes	Sometimes	Sometimes
	Frontier-worker	Not applicable	No	No	No	No	No
	Seasonal migrant worker	Not applicable	No	No	No	No	No
	Project-tied migrant worker	Not applicable	No	No	No	No	No
	Contract migrant worker	To accompany	No	No	No	No	No
		To join	Rarely	Rarely	No	No	No
	Temporary migrant worker	To accompany	Sometimes	Sometimes	No	No	No
		To join	Sometimes	Sometimes	No	No	No
	Established migrant worker	To join	Yes	Yes	Sometimes	Sometimes	No
	Highly-skilled migrant worker	To accompany	Yes	Yes	No	No	No
		To join	Yes	Yes	Rarely	Rarely	No
	Business traveller	Not applicable	No	No	No	No	No
	Immigrating investor	To accompany	Yes	Yes	No	No	No
		To join	Yes	Yes	Sometimes	Sometimes	Rarely
	Humanitarian admission	To accompany	Yes	Yes	No	No	No
		To join	Yes	Yes	Rarely	Rarely	Rarely
	Asylum-seeker	To accompany	Yes	Yes	No	No	No
	Temporary protected status	To accompany	Yes	Yes	No	No	No
	Unauthorized entry	Not applicable	No	No	No	No	No

International migration statistics

As shown in table 2.1, the framework makes a major distinction between the admission of migrant citizens and that of foreigners. Among the latter, a further distinction is made between foreigners whose admission is sanctioned by the receiving State and those whose admission is not authorized. The latter are part of the category of *irregular migrants*. Among foreigners admitted legally, those granted only very short periods of stay for the purpose of tourism or business travel are generally not considered international migrants, but other categories are. Table 2.1 makes a detailed inventory of the latter. The main reason for including tourists and business travellers in the framework is that they can become irregular migrants if they stay beyond the time allowed by law or if they violate the terms of their admission by, for instance, engaging in an economic activity not sanctioned by the receiving State. The last two columns of table 2.1 reflect important attributes of the categories identified with respect to the possibility of being accompanied or joined by immediate family members and relative to the period of stay allowed by the receiving State (legal time). The term "unrestricted" for the period of stay indicates that the receiving State imposes no restriction on the duration of stay of the persons concerned. The term "restricted" implies that the State imposes strict limits on the duration of stay, whereas the term "open ended" implies that the limits established (if established at all), are generally more flexible.

Migrants for family reunification constitute a major group of the international migrants alluded to in table 2.1 but one that requires a more explicit treatment. That group is not included as a separate category in table 2.1 because the admission of migrants for family reunification can be linked to the admission or presence of several other categories of international migrants. Under such circumstances, adding a single category for family reunification would not be satisfactory. Instead, table 2.2 indicates that, ideally, international migration statistics should distinguish migrants admitted for family reunification according to both the timing of their admission (whether they migrate with the primo-migrant or not) and the type of sponsor making their admission possible (that is, according to the status of the primo-migrant at the time of family reunification). The last five columns of table 2.2 serve to characterize further the persons who may qualify for family reunification in each case and, though attempting to reflect the general thrust of government practices, should be interpreted as merely indicative and not as definitive. This and other questions regarding the meaning of each of the migrant categories included in the framework are discussed in more detail below.

Box 2.1. Characterizing different types of migrants

Citizens

1. *Returning migrants* are persons who have been abroad as migrants in a country other than their own and who return to their own

Concepts underlying international migration statistics

country to settle in it. Among persons entering their own country, returning migrants should be distinguished on the basis of the time that they have spent abroad and the time that they intend to spend in their country of citizenship. A year is a reasonable cut-off point in both cases, so that returning migrants are citizens who have been abroad for at least a year and who intend to remain in their own country for more than a year.

Foreigners

2. *Returning ethnics* are persons who are admitted by a country other than their own because of their historical, ethnic or other ties with that country and who are immediately granted the right of permanent abode in that country or who, having the right to citizenship in that country, become citizens within a short period after admission.

3. *Migrants with the right to free movement* are persons who have the right to enter, stay and work within the territory of a State other than their own by virtue of an agreement or treaty concluded between their State of citizenship and the State in which they reside.

4. *Foreigners admitted for special purposes:*

(a) *Foreign students* are persons admitted by a country other than their own for the specific purpose of following a particular programme of study. In some countries, foreign students are allowed to work under certain conditions.

(b) *Foreign trainees* are persons admitted by a country other than their own to acquire particular skills through on-the-job training. Foreign trainees are therefore allowed to work only in the specific institution providing the training and are allowed to stay for a limited period.

(c) *Foreign retirees* are persons beyond retirement age who are allowed to stay in the territory of a State other than their own provided that they do not become a charge to that State. They are generally allowed to be accompanied by their spouses.

5. *Settlers* are persons who are granted the right to stay indefinitely in the territory of a country other than their own and to enjoy the same social and economic rights as the citizens of that country. Settlers are usually accorded the opportunity to become naturalized citizens of the receiving State once minimum requirements have been met. The terms *permanent migrants* or *immigrants* are often used to refer to settlers.

6. *Migrant workers* are persons admitted by a country other than their own for the explicit purpose of exercising an economic activity.

(a) *Seasonal migrant workers* are persons employed in a State other than their own for only part of a year because the work they perform depends on seasonal conditions.

(b) *Project-tied migrant workers* are migrant workers admitted to the State of employment for a defined period to work solely on a specific project carried out in that State by the migrant workers' employer. The employer is responsible for providing the inputs needed to complete the project, including labour. The employer or an agent who may have acted as an intermediary must ensure that project-tied migrant workers leave the country of employment once the work is completed.

International migration statistics

(c) *Contract migrant workers* are persons working in a country other than their own under contractual arrangements that set limits on the period of employment and on the specific job held by the migrant. Once admitted, contract migrant workers are not allowed to change jobs and are expected to leave the country of employment upon completion of their contract, irrespective of whether the work they do continues or not. Although contract renewals are sometimes possible, departure from the country of employment may be mandatory before the contract can be renewed.

(d) *Temporary migrant workers* are persons admitted by a country other than their own to work for a limited period in a particular occupation or a specific job. Temporary migrant workers may change employers and have their work permits renewed without having to leave the country of employment.

(e) *Established migrant workers* are migrant workers who, after staying some years in the country of employment, have been granted the permission to reside indefinitely and to work without major limitations in that country. Established migrant workers need not leave the country of employment when unemployed and are usually granted the right of being joined by their immediate family members, provided certain conditions regarding employment and housing are met.

(f) *Highly skilled migrant workers* are migrant workers who, because of their skill, are subject to preferential treatment regarding admission to a country other than their own and are therefore subject to fewer restrictions regarding length of stay, change of employment and family reunification.

7. *Economic migration* covers persons who move internationally in connection with the exercise of an economic activity that is either not remunerated from within the country of destination or demands a certain investment from the migrant concerned.

(a) *Business travellers* are foreigners admitted temporarily for the purpose of exercising an economic activity remunerated from outside the country of destination.

(b) *Immigrating investors* are foreigners granted the right to long-term residence on the condition that they invest a minimum amount in the country of destination or start a business employing a minimum number of persons in the country of destination.

8. *Asylum migration* covers the whole spectrum of international movements caused by persecution and conflict. Specific types of migrants that are part of asylum migration are listed below.

(a) *Refugees* are persons who, owing to a well-founded fear of being persecuted for reasons of race, religion, nationality, membership of a particular social group or political opinion, are outside of their country of nationality and are unable or, owing to such fear, are unwilling to avail themselves of the protection of that country. Persons recognized as refugees under this definition are sometimes called *Convention refugees* and are usually granted an open-ended permission to stay in the country of asylum. When they are admitted by another country for resettlement, they are called *resettled refugees*.

(b) *Persons admitted for humanitarian reasons* are persons who, being outside of their country of nationality, are in refugee-like situations because they cannot avail themselves of the protection of their own country and therefore require the protection of the State in which they find themselves. Sometimes such persons are characterized as *refugees type B* because they do not fully meet the criteria stipulated in the 1951 Convention. They usually receive treatment equal to that of Convention refugees.

(c) *Asylum-seekers* are persons who file an application for asylum in a country other than their own. They remain in the status of asylum-seeker until their application is considered and adjudicated.

(d) *Persons granted temporary protected status* are persons who are outside of their country of nationality and cannot return to that country without putting their lives in danger. The temporary protected status granted to them by the country in which they find themselves allows them to stay for a limited though often open-ended period (as long as return to their country is considered detrimental to their security).

(e) *Persons granted stay of deportation* are persons who have been found not to qualify for refugee status or to be in an irregular situation and who are under deportation orders but who have been granted a temporary reprieve from being deported because their lives would be in danger if they returned immediately to their country of nationality.

9. *Irregular migrants* are persons in a State other than their own who have not fully satisfied the conditions and requirements set by that State to enter, stay or exercise an economic activity in that State's territory.

10. *Migrants for family reunification* are persons admitted by a country other than their own for the purpose of accompanying or joining close relatives migrating to that country or already living in that country. Because most migrants for family reunification are relatives of other migrants, they should be considered as a distinct sub-category of that to which the primo-migrant belongs. A scheme for classifying migrants for family reunification is presented in table 2.2.

1. Citizens

As is shown in table 2.1, in considering international migration, the first important distinction to be made is that between *citizens* and *foreigners*. If international migrants are identified when they enter the country of destination, persons entering a country of which they are already citizens can be considered *return migrants* if they have been absent from their country of citizenship for more than t months and plan to stay in that country for more than t months. The category of *return migrants* may also include persons born outside their country of citizenship who enter it for the first time with the intention of staying for at least t months (repatriating foreign-born citizens). Return migrants often move in family groups but, if each family member is a citizen of the country of

International migration statistics

destination, family ties can be considered incidental and each person can be considered a return migrant in his or her own right. However, if some of the immediate relatives of return migrants are *not* citizens of the country of destination, they would have to be admitted under family reunification provisions, as suggested in tables 2.1 and 2.2.

Return migrants can be further classified according to the status they had while abroad. Thus, distinctions could be made between returning students or trainees, returning emigrants, returning migrant workers, repatriating foreign-born citizens, repatriating refugees, returning asylum-seekers, and returning undocumented migrants (some of whom may have been deported back to their country of origin). The category of repatriating foreign-born citizens would include the children of former emigrating citizens who themselves may have settled abroad for lengthy periods but whose offspring maintain the right to citizenship of the country of origin and eventually return to it. Foreign family members accompanying or joining later a return migrant should be attached, as appropriate, to the relevant category of the return migrant concerned. Note that, although in principle return migrants must be distinguished from other arriving citizens only on the basis of their length of stay abroad and their intended (or actual) stay in their own country, the length of time t used above may have to vary from sub-category to sub-category. Thus, migrant workers may return to remain in their country after only a few months of work abroad. Refugees and asylum-seekers, as well, may be out of their country only for a short period before they return voluntarily or are forced to return. Undocumented migrants may also return after short periods abroad, especially if caught and deported. Thus, time abroad may not be the only relevant criterion in ascertaining whether an arriving citizen is a return migrant or not. The reason for the return as well as that for departure may be equally important.

2. Returning ethnics and free movement

Although it is an attribute of sovereignty that every State can decide which foreign persons can enter its territory and under what conditions, certain countries have either adopted laws or concluded agreements with other countries that in effect limit their right to restrict the entry or stay of certain foreigners. Thus, some countries have provisions that grant an almost automatic right to citizenship to persons of certain ethnic or religious backgrounds. The term *returning ethnics* has been selected to refer to those groups of persons who, because of historical, ethnic or other ties with a country, have a right to its citizenship and who, once admitted, become legally indistinguishable from other citizens (see table 2.1). Ethnic Germans admitted by Germany, Jews admitted by Israel and Pontian Greeks admitted by Greece all belong to this category of migrants. As in the case of return migrants, returning ethnics may be accompanied by immediate family members. If those family members do not qualify on their own for admission as returning ethnics, a separate but related category of admissions due to family reunification would be added.

Another case in which the sovereign right of States to control the entry and stay of foreigners is diluted arises when zones of *free movement* are set up through international agreements or treaties (table 2.1). Under those conditions, the citizens of the States that are parties to such agreements or treaties are subject to minimal control when they enter the territory of other State parties. Although freedom of movement need not be accompanied by freedom of establishment, when the two apply, citizens of member States can move to and stay in the territory of other member States without obtaining prior permission. Usually their length of stay is not subject to restrictions and is subject to few controls. An example of a fairly comprehensive regime of free movement is that currently existing among the member States of the European Union.

3. Irregular migration

Irregular migration occurs when a person does not fully satisfy the conditions and requirements set by a State other than his or her own to enter, stay or exercise an economic activity in that State's territory. Thus, among foreigners entering a country, a distinction needs to be made between those whose admission is sanctioned by the receiving State and those whose entry is unauthorized (see table 2.1). Unauthorized migrants are *ipso facto* in an irregular situation. In contrast, foreigners admitted legally may move into an irregular situation if they violate any of the provisions governing their stay or exercise of economic activity in the receiving State. Thus, persons entering as tourists who remain in the receiving country longer than their visas allow or who work for wages become irregular migrants. Foreign students who drop out of school to work full time and do not change their visa status generally become irregular migrants. Asylum-seekers whose applications for asylum are rejected but who nevertheless stay without authorization in the country concerned also join the ranks of the irregular migrants. In fact, almost any type of legal migrant can become an irregular migrant by violating the terms of his or her admission to the receiving country. Furthermore, a migrant in an irregular situation need not have that status forever. A transition in the other direction, from irregular status to a regularized status, is also possible, and not only through explicit regularization or legalization. Thus, a foreign student whose terms of admission prohibit him or her from working and who nevertheless works but only for a month or two may be in an irregular situation only for that period. Transitions of that sort add to the difficulty of measuring irregular migration, even if the illegality involved did not present another major obstacle to its proper quantification.

4. Foreign persons admitted on a short-term basis

With regard to the generality of foreigners admitted legally, a number of categories can be identified. The list presented in table 2.1 is unlikely to be definitive, although it covers most of the groups identified as relevant for the study of international population mobility. In the interest of comprehensiveness, some of the categories refer to people who move from one country to another but who are generally not considered to be international migrants, either because of the purpose of their trip or because the time they spend in a country other than their own is too short. Thus, *consular personnel* are usually excluded from international migration statistics. So are the armed forces of a country stationed in the territory of another, even though the *military personnel* involved may be accompanied by family members and may remain in the host country for years. *Tourists* are also normally excluded from the group constituting international migrants. In contrast, foreigners admitted to study (*students*) or to be trained (*trainees*), being likely to spend longer periods in the receiving country, are often considered migrants. Foreign *retirees* also tend to be considered as migrants, especially in countries wishing to attract them as residents because of the foreign currency that they receive as pension income.

5. Settlers

The other categories of legally admitted foreigners in table 2.1 constitute the core of what is normally considered international migration. Three major groups can be distinguished: settlers, migrant workers and refugees. *Settlers*, also known as immigrants or permanent immigrants, are persons granted the right to stay indefinitely in the territory of a country other than their own. The receiving country usually allows or even encourages the naturalization of settlers. Thus, many become citizens of the receiving country and, at least legally, cannot be distinguished from natives thereafter. Furthermore, even without naturalization, settlers usually enjoy equal economic and social rights to those of citizens. Settlers need not stay permanently in the receiving country, and significant numbers return to resettle in their country of origin. Others may leave the receiving country for lengthy periods (a few years) but return later. Countries admitting settlers usually do not deprive them of the right to stay indefinitely when they spend only a year or two years abroad. It is the right to remain indefinitely that characterizes settlers and not their actual presence in or absence from the receiving country.

6. Migrant workers

Migrant workers are persons admitted by a country other than their own for the explicit purpose of exercising an economic activity. Migrant workers are

Concepts underlying international migration statistics

usually admitted only for a limited period at a time, though the permission to stay and exercise an economic activity may be renewed or extended as time elapses. There are many modalities for the admission and control of the movement of persons considered to be migrant workers. The most commonly used lead to special categories of migrants, such as those listed in table 2.1. In fact, some of the categories listed in table 2.1 are, strictly speaking, usually not considered part of international migration. Thus, frontier workers and seasonal workers are often excluded from statistics on labour migration. Frontier workers have also been explicitly excluded from the provisions of key international instruments relating to migrant workers, such as the ILO Migration for Employment Convention (Revised), 1949 (No. 97), and the ILO Migrant Workers (Supplementary Provisions) Convention, 1975 (No. 143). However, the 1990 Convention on the Rights of All Migrant Workers and Members of Their Families includes explicit provisions regarding frontier workers and provides a definition of persons belonging to that category. Essentially, *frontier workers* are persons who work in a State other than their own but whose habitual residence is located in a neighbouring State to which they return every day or at least once a week. The 1990 Convention also makes reference to *seasonal migrant workers* and to *project-tied migrant workers*. The former are characterized as persons who are employed in a State other than their own for only part of a year because the work that they perform depends on seasonal conditions. *Project-tied migrant workers* are migrant workers admitted to the State of employment for a defined period to work solely on a specific project being carried out in that State by the migrant workers' employer. The employer concerned is usually another foreign person or a foreign company operating in the country where the project is being executed. In project-tied migration, the enterprise hired to carry out a project usually makes arrangements to provide all the necessary inputs, including labour.

Although international instruments do not mention explicitly the other types of migrant workers listed in table 2.1, the categories presented are often used by governments and researchers to characterize migration for employment. Thus, *contract migrant workers* are persons working in a country other than their own under contractual arrangements that set limits on the period of employment and on the specific job held by the migrant. Once admitted, contract migrant workers are not allowed to change jobs and are expected to leave the country of employment upon completion of their contract. They differ from project-tied migrant workers in that the jobs they hold are expected to exist over a long period, although each migrant worker may hold a given job only for a limited time. Depending on the circumstances, renewal of contracts may be possible, but migrants may have to return to their countries of origin before such a renewal takes place, thus ensuring that long and uninterrupted stays in the country of employment do not materialize.

Temporary migrant workers are foreigners admitted for a limited period to work in a particular occupation or in a specific job. In contrast with contract migrant workers, temporary migrant workers have flexibility in changing employers and can have work permits renewed without having to leave the country of employment for a significant time. Consequently, temporary migrant workers can accumulate relatively lengthy and largely uninterrupted periods of stay in the country of employment. A number of countries of employment allow temporary migrant workers to be accompanied or joined by their immediate family members. Some countries also permit a change of status for temporary migrant workers: once their length of stay surpasses a certain threshold they can become *established migrant workers*, that is, persons having the permission to reside indefinitely in the country of employment and to work without major limitations. Established migrant workers need not leave the country of employment when unemployed and are usually granted the right of being joined by their immediate family members provided certain conditions regarding employment and housing are met.

Although it has not been explicitly stated as yet, the migrant workers covered by each of the migrant-worker categories mentioned above are, in their vast majority, unskilled or semi-skilled workers. Because some countries already distinguish highly skilled migrant workers from the rest, use of a separate category is recommended. Many countries that tend not to admit migrant workers make exceptions for the highly skilled. In others, only highly skilled migrant workers can become settlers. Thus, persons belonging to the category of *highly skilled migrant workers* can be distinguished from other migrant workers not only because of their level of skill but also because they receive preferential treatment regarding admission, length of stay, type and conditions of employment, and the possibility of being accompanied by family members. Thus, countries wishing to attract and retain highly skilled migrants usually have distinct admission categories in which to accommodate them.

7. Economic migration

Many countries have provisions allowing the admission of foreigners to exercise an economic activity that is not necessarily remunerated from within the country of admission. The term *economic migration* is used here to cover that category of migrants, most of whom are admitted on a temporary basis but some of whom may be granted long-term residence rights provided that they invest a minimum amount of money in the receiving country or that they establish a business employing at least a certain number of workers in the receiving country. The term *business travellers* is used to denote the temporary component of economic migration and it encompasses persons such as journalists, performing artists, members of the clergy and traders or investors on short-term assignments. The term *immigrating investors* is used to denote the category of foreign employers establishing businesses in the country of destination or of foreign persons making other types of major investments in that country in exchange for the right to long-term residence.

Concepts underlying international migration statistics

8. Refugees

Refugees constitute one of the major categories of international migrants. Given that the international instruments relating to refugees are widely recognized (as of June 1995, both the 1951 Convention Relating to the Status of Refugees and its 1967 Protocol had been ratified by 120 countries and a further 8 had ratified one or the other), it is standard practice to define a refugee in terms consistent with the definition established by those instruments. Thus, *refugees* are persons who, owing to a well-founded fear of being persecuted for reasons of race, religion, nationality, membership of a particular social group or political opinion, are outside of their country of nationality and are unable or, owing to such fear, are unwilling to avail themselves of the protection of that country. Although certain regional instruments, such as the Convention Regarding the Special Aspects of Refugee Problems in Africa adopted by the Organization of African Unity (OAU) in 1969 and the 1984 Cartagena Declaration of the Organization of American States (OAS), include definitions that expand the accepted reasons giving rise to refugee outflows, their definitions are only accepted at the regional level. Furthermore, largely because of the consequences of recent geo-political changes, matters related to asylum are currently being re-evaluated by a number of countries and country practices regarding the granting of asylum have been changing. In particular, increases in the number of persons seeking asylum in industrialized market-economy countries and the reluctance of those countries to grant refugee status to persons fleeing war or internal conflict in their countries of origin have led to the creation of various categories of foreigners whose status is tentative at best. That is the case, for instance, of persons granted *temporary protected status* who are allowed to stay in the receiving country for as long as return to their country of origin would put their lives in danger, but who are nevertheless subject to a number of restrictions aimed at precluding their long-term settlement. Another such category consists of persons whose applications for asylum are rejected but who are not deported immediately: they are allowed to stay under a *stay of deportation* decision. Deportation, however, is only postponed, not annulled. Since it is not always clear whether persons in such groups will end up departing soon or staying for a lengthy period, it is not easy to determine if they should be considered fully fledged international migrants or not in the meantime.

Although persons recognized as refugees frequently face equally uncertain situations regarding eventual return to their country of origin, refugees differ from other categories of forced migrants in that they are usually granted a more open-ended if not indefinite permission to stay. In fact, countries of immigration tend to grant legal immigrant or settler status to persons recognized as refugees, particularly when those persons are admitted under resettlement programmes. Some countries also grant an open-ended permission to stay to foreigners considered to be in need of protection for *humanitarian* reasons. Although those persons are generally not granted formal refugee status (sometimes they are considered to be *refugees type B*), they are treated in a manner similar to Convention refugees (i.e. persons meeting the criteria set out by the 1951 Convention and its 1967 Protocol). Chapter 5 discusses further the statistics available on these categories of migrants.

9. Migrants admitted for family reunification

As table 2.1 indicates, the receiving State may admit certain categories of international migrants together with their immediate relatives or allow migrants to be joined later by their immediate relatives once certain conditions have been met. Whether accompanying the migrant at the time of migration or joining the migrant at a later time, immediate relatives can be considered to constitute a sub-category of their own, albeit a sub-category inextricably linked to the category of the migrant they are related to. In most receiving countries, immediate relatives are restricted by law to include only the spouse and dependent children of the migrant concerned. Thus, the 1990 Convention on the Rights of All Migrant Workers and Members of Their Families stipulates that, in the case of migrant workers who are in a regular situation, "State Parties shall take measures that they deem appropriate and that fall within their competence to facilitate the reunification of migrant workers with their spouses or persons who have with the migrant worker a relationship that, according to applicable law, produces effects equivalent to marriage, as well as with their minor dependent unmarried children" (Article 44, para. 2). In fact, as table 2.1 shows, migrant workers whose stay in the country of employment is subject to stringent restrictions are unlikely to be granted permission to be accompanied or joined later by their immediate relatives. A common exception is the case of highly skilled workers who, being subject to less stringent conditions of stay and work, can usually be accompanied by immediate family members.

Family reunification is most commonly allowed in the case of settlers, that is, migrants who are granted not only the right to stay indefinitely in the receiving country but who enjoy, in addition, social and economic rights equal to those of citizens. In fact, countries of immigration have generally allowed not only the admission of the immediate relatives of settlers (spouse and dependent children) but also that of other relatives, including married children, parents and siblings. In addition, since countries of immigration have provisions that facilitate the naturalization of settlers, once they become naturalized citizens, their rights regarding family reunification improve. Migration for family reunification has thus constituted a very sizable proportion of immigration to Australia, Canada, the United Kingdom and the United States over recent decades (United Nations, 1992).

One component of family reunification that is not reflected explicitly in table 2.1 but that appears as the first entry in table 2.2 is the migration of foreigners to join a citizen of the receiving State who is not a migrant. Since most countries have nationality laws that favour the naturalization of the foreign spouses of citizens and either facilitate the naturalization of the minor children of citizens or directly grant citizenship to those children, the admission of foreign spouses and foreign minor children of citizens is generally allowed under conditions similar to those of settlers: they usually obtain unrestricted permission to stay in the receiving country with the expectation that naturalization will take place within a short period. It is important that, in organizing international migration statistics, a special category be created for those family members so that it is clear that their admission is determined by their relationship to a citizen.

A special case worth mentioning is that of foreign persons admitted not strictly as immediate relatives but rather as fiancés or fiancées of citizens. Women are especially likely to be in that category of migrants. Fiancés or fiancées of citizens are usually admitted for a limited period beyond which, if marriage has not taken place, they must depart. Once marriage takes place, another period of conditional stay may be allowed to ensure that the marriage is genuine. If the marriage survives, the migrant is granted open-ended permission to stay and the possibility of opting for naturalization. That is, the migrant either takes on the attributes of settler or has to leave the receiving country. It is desirable that countries admitting a significant number of persons as fiancés or fiancées of citizens present data on those admissions separately.

As table 2.2 suggests, in gathering and tabulating statistics on migrants admitted on family reunification grounds, it is crucial to classify them simultaneously according to at least three criteria: (a) the type of sponsor of their migration, that is, the migration status or category of the immediate relative whose presence in the country of destination has made their admission possible; (b) the timing of their migration in relation to that of the sponsor, that is, whether family members are accompanying the primo-migrant or joining someone already present in the country of destination; and (c) the type of relationship that migrants for family reunification have with the sponsor, that is, whether they are spouses, dependent children, other children, parents, siblings or yet other relatives of the sponsor. The availability of such a multidimensional classification of statistics on family reunification would help clarify how chain migration operates. Since migration for family reunification is highly restricted in most countries, implementation of the classification scheme proposed would be fairly straightforward in most of them because the cells most likely to be filled would be those referring to spouses and dependent children. The use of this scheme would be somewhat more complicated in countries where other relatives may be admitted on family reunification grounds, since those relatives may themselves be accompanied or joined later by their immediate family members. Married children and siblings, in particular, are likely to be accompanied by their own spouses and dependent children at the time of admission. If so, special categories for the accompanying family members of married children and of siblings would need to be created.

10. Changes of status

Although the framework presented in tables 2.1 and 2.2 appears static, in reality international migrants often move from one category to another. Some examples of relevant changes of status have already been mentioned, including tourists who become irregular migrants or temporary migrant workers who become established migrant workers. The rules and regulations governing international migration usually establish which changes of status are possible in a country. Since changes of status have important implications for the management of international migration, it is important for statistical systems to reflect them appropriately. Yet most statistical systems fail precisely in providing adequate measures of changes of status among international migrants. Even the fairly straightforward transition from asylum-seeker to refugee is poorly measured (see Chapter 5). Therefore, in analysing the performance of different statistical systems, special attention should be paid to their ability to track the most relevant changes of status.

H. INTERNATIONAL MIGRATION AND ECONOMIC ACTIVITY

The above description of the main categories of international migrants that are relevant for the study of international migration suggests that, although migrant workers constitute a major component of all migration for employment, they are by no means the only type of migrants engaging in economic activity while abroad. Foreign trainees, for example, are a special category of economically active migrants who are generally not considered to be among migrant workers because the main purpose of their work abroad is to acquire new skills rather than to perform a needed task for the country of employment. Yet one may question whether the work they perform is really only of marginal value, especially when the persons involved are already highly skilled. The United States, for instance, has long had a programme allowing persons with advanced degrees to work in research institutions as trainees to enhance their knowledge and skills. In recent years, the Government of Germany has set up a sizeable scheme to improve the skills of trainees from Central and Eastern European countries, and Japan and the Republic of Korea have done the same for trainees originating in neighbouring Asian countries (Kuptsch and Oishi, 1994). Training programmes are thus being used by employers to obtain needed workers without having explicit recourse to migrant worker programmes.

Foreign students constitute another group of international migrants who may work under certain circumstances. The numbers involved are far from trivial. It is estimated that in 1991, about 1.5 million students were enrolled in tertiary level programmes in countries other than their own, about a million in Organization for Economic Cooperation and Development (OECD) countries (OECD, 1994). Although foreign students are admitted only for the time it takes them to complete their programme of study and are generally expected to return to their countries of origin thereafter, the ties they develop in receiving countries often lead to international migration later. Student migration can thus be a first step in a process of brain drain, although it also contributes to the transfer of technology and the expansion of networks linking highly skilled personnel at the global level.

The number of foreign students or trainees pales in comparison to those of persons admitted as settlers or returning ethnics who are entitled to full economic rights, including the right to work, and to the sizeable numbers of refugees and other foreigners in need of protection admitted by countries that grant them working rights. The realization that settlers and refugees can be economic actors whose rights as migrants for employment need to be recognized is not new. As early as 1949, the ILO adopted the Migration for Employment Recommendation (Revised), 1949 (No. 86), which included as an annex a model agreement on temporary and permanent migration for employment, including the migration of refugees and displaced persons. Indeed, although the negative connotations associated with the term "economic refugee" seem to suggest that any economic motivation among persons fleeing persecution is suspect, in reality, every international migrant is a potential worker and is more likely to become one if pushed by necessity. Refugees and asylum-seekers are no different from other migrants in that respect: if the international community or the country in which they find themselves cannot provide for their subsistence needs, they will have to work, whether legally or clandestinely. Thus, although asylum migration is not motivated primarily by economic considerations, it cannot be ignored if the economic consequences of international migration are to be assessed.

A clearer case for inclusion can be made with respect to irregular migration, especially when the main reason for irregularity is the exercise of an economic activity. It is generally assumed that persons who enter a country other than their own without authorization do so in order to work. Similarly, most persons who enter a country as tourists and stay beyond the time allowed by their visas are presumed to be working. Equally relevant are persons who have permission to reside in a country other than their own but who lack permission to work and nevertheless do so. Women are especially likely to be in such a situation, since they are more likely than men to be admitted as dependants and thus to lack the right to work (United Nations, 1995b). Yet, whatever the mechanism that first leads to the irregularity of someone's status, working without permission is the factor that most worries receiving countries since irregular migrants who work are more likely to be exploited and, by being paid lower wages, to distort the labour market dynamics of their place of destination.

These observations suggest that, in assessing the determinants or impact of international migration on the labour market of countries of destination, attention should be focused on all persons who may be considered international migrants and are likely to work, whether as salaried workers or on their own

International migration statistics

account. International migrants officially classified as migrant workers are important, but they are not the only group that matters. Thus the labour market experience of settlers, trainees, refugees, other migrants seeking protection from persecution, irregular migrants, and all accompanying family members is also relevant. Therefore, in discussing data sources in subsequent chapters of this book, the availability of and need for information on the economic activity of all types of international migrants is given attention.

DATA COLLECTION SYSTEMS CONCERNING ALL INTERNATIONAL MIGRANTS   3

This chapter reviews the operation of data collection systems producing information on the generality of international migrants, including population censuses, population registers, registers of foreigners, statistics from administrative sources border statistics. The systems considered are assessed in terms of the types of data that they yield and the extent to which those data reflect or have the potential to reflect the different categories of international migrants identified in Chapter 2. Recommendations on how to improve the data gathered by each system are made systematically. Because of the heterogeneity of the systems in operation in different countries and the lack of information on how they operate, comprehensiveness is not the objective of this chapter. Instead, examples are drawn, as appropriate, from the experiences of various countries to illustrate the strengths and weaknesses of the different systems considered. Discussion is organized according to the mode of operation of each system, rather than on the basis of the type of information a system yields. In fact, a given system is usually capable of producing various types of data depending on the basic information recorded and the use made of it in the preparation of complex cross-tabulations.

The measures of international migration most commonly used are of two types: measures of stocks of international migrants and measures of flows. The migrant stock is defined as the total number of international migrants present in a given country at a particular point in time. It is a static measure and it represents a count, that is, the number of persons that can be identified as international migrants at a given time. Migration flows also tend to be measured in terms of counts, with the inflow of migrants being the number of international migrants arriving in a given country over the course of a specific period, usually a calendar year, and the outflow being the number of international migrants departing from a given country over the course of the year. Because flow measures reflect the dynamics of the process, they are considerably less tractable than stock measures. Thus, although the definitions of migrant inflows and outflows seem straightforward, they do not make allowance for the possibility that a migrant might arrive in and depart from the same country several times during a year. Is that migrant to be counted several times or only once? There is no definitive answer: it depends on how the statistics reflecting flows are gathered and used. That is, even seemingly straightforward measures of international migration may not be easily obtained in practice. For that reason, alternative measures are constantly being used, although it is rarely explained how they differ from the ideal. The discussion that follows will try to make such differences clear.

A. POPULATION CENSUSES

Population censuses are perhaps the most comprehensive source of internationally comparable information on international migration in the world. Their strength stems from their universal coverage (all persons living in a country are counted) and their reliance on short questionnaires with limited flexibility, applied repeatedly at long intervals, usually of ten years. Those characteristics, unfortunately, are also associated with major limitations. On the positive side, because censuses can accommodate only a small number of questions eliciting straightforward answers, they cannot introduce much variability in the range of questions or concepts used. Consequently, there is greater uniformity in the type of data they produce across countries than for any other data collection system. Censuses also have the advantage of covering the complete population of a country. Since international migrants usually constitute only a small proportion of the population of most countries, censuses are often the only data collection instruments that can assure an adequate coverage of the international migrant population.

Another advantage of censuses is that they have the potential for permitting the characterization of international migrants in terms of certain basic demographic and socio-economic characteristics recorded in the census questionnaire. They often are the only source of information on the distribution by age and sex of international migrants, their distribution by place of residence in the receiving State, or their distribution by educational attainment, marital status, participation in the labour force, occupation and level of income. Thus, censuses have been particularly useful in providing evidence regarding the high levels of female participation in international migration (data derived from censuses have shown that women are almost as numerous as men among persons identified as international migrants) and in providing the data used to assess the economic impact of international migrants or their degree of integration (United Nations, 1995b; Borjas, 1990).

However, censuses have a number of limitations. First, because in most countries censuses are carried out only once every ten years, they cannot capture or reflect rapid changes in international migration on a timely basis. Second, because censuses can accommodate only a limited number of questions, they cannot provide the detailed information needed for a meaningful analysis of either the determinants or the consequences of international migration. Third,

Data collection systems concerning all international migrants

most censuses fail to achieve a complete and accurate count of the population of a country, and it is quite possible that the degree of accuracy with which they cover international migrants is even lower, especially if international migrants have a vested interest in avoiding being counted or in misreporting their migrant status. Fourth, given that census takers receive minimal training, they are unlikely to spot reporting errors and because the respondent to a census questionnaire is not always the person most knowledgeable about the characteristics of other members of the household, errors in reporting migrant status may ensue. Lastly, in processing and tabulating the data gathered by censuses, low priority is often accorded to international migration, with the result that the data gathered often take several years to become available and only a very limited number of relevant cross-tabulations are published.

Another possible drawback of the statistics produced by censuses is that countries use different approaches to define the population enumerated. Censuses may aim at enumerating the *de facto* population and thus include all persons physically present in the country at the census reference date, or they may cover only the *de jure* population, covering only the usual residents of the country in question, some of whom may not be physically present in the country at the reference date. Straightforward as these concepts seem, strict conformity to either is rare. In particular, there are groups of potential international migrants that may be included or excluded from census counts on arbitrary grounds. Thus, some censuses claiming to cover the *de facto* population may nevertheless exclude foreign military and naval personnel or diplomatic personnel and their accompanying family members and servants present in the country, while at the same time including merchant seaman or fishermen outside the country at the time of enumeration. Censuses based on a *de jure* approach may also include groups of aliens who may not strictly qualify as residents, such as short-term foreign workers (United Nations Statistical Division, 1994).

The United Nations (1980b) has identified fourteen distinct population groups that are often subject to special treatment in censuses (see box 3.1). Several of the sub-groups, particularly those of civilian aliens, (j) to (m), are relevant for the study of international migration. Although there is no comprehensive set of information indicating to what extent those groups are excluded from censuses, data compiled by the United Nations Statistics Division for selected countries carrying out censuses during the 1970 and 1980 rounds suggest that, in most instances, subgroup (l), consisting of civilian aliens working in the country, is included in censuses, whether the latter are carried out on a *de facto* or a *de jure* basis (United Nations Statistical Division, 1994). Civilian aliens who are not working and are only temporarily in the country tend to be included when a *de facto* approach is followed and may or may not be included if the census is carried out on a *de jure* basis (see table 3.1). Military, naval or diplomatic personnel stationed outside the country are likely to be excluded except in some *de jure* censuses. It is therefore possible that some groups may end up being excluded from the censuses of both countries of origin and

International migration statistics

> Box 3.1. Population subgroups according to special treatment in population censuses
>
> (a) Nomads.
> (b) Persons living in areas to which access is difficult.
> (c) Military, naval and diplomatic personnel and their families located outside the country.
> (d) Merchant seamen and fishermen resident in the country but at sea at the time of the census (including those who have no place of residence other than their quarters aboard ship).
> (e) Civilian residents temporarily in another country as seasonal workers.
> (f) Civilian residents who cross a frontier daily to work in another country.
> (g) Civilian residents other than those in (c), (e) and (f) who are working in another country.
> (h) Civilian residents other than those in (c) to (g) who are temporarily absent from the country.
> (i) Civilian aliens temporarily in the country as seasonal workers.
> (j) Civilian aliens temporarily in another country as seasonal workers.
> (k) Civilian aliens who cross a frontier daily to work in the country.
> (l) Civilian aliens other than those in (i), (j) and (k) who are working in the country.
> (m) Civilian aliens other than those in (i) to (l) who are temporarily absent from the country.
> (n) Transients on ships in harbour at the time of the census.
>
> Source: United Nations (1980a), p. 67.

Table 3.1. Distribution of countries according to national practices regarding the inclusion or exclusion of particular population groups

Type of group	Group identifier	Number of countries	De facto census Included	De facto census Excluded	De jure census Included	De jure census Excluded
Nomads	(a)	14	2	4	7	1
Military, naval and diplomatic personnel	(c)	23	0	9	8	6
Seafarers	(d)	16	7	3	5	1
Seasonal workers abroad	(e)	26	1	6	13	6
Foreign military and diplomatic personnel	(i)	33	10	9	8	6
Foreign migrant workers	(l)	42	13	0	29	0
Aliens temporarily present	(m)	34	12	1	10	11
Transients	(n)	25	10	1	14	0

Source: United Nations (1994).

destination. The information presented in table 3.1, however, covers only a small number of countries. Clearly, more comprehensive information on national practices is needed to assess the performance of censuses regarding the coverage of particular groups of international migrants.

There is a tendency to assume that censuses gather information only on persons who are legally present in a country. That is not the aim of any census. Even censuses carried out on a *de jure* basis tend to adopt definitions of "resident" that have nothing to do with legal status. The case of Burundi's 1979 census provides a typical example. According to census documentation, the enumerated population consisted of residents present, residents absent and visitors (Burundi, Département de la Population, 1982). The definitions of each category are as follows:

"Residents present" are persons who have lived usually in the household for more than six months and who were present in the household during census night (the reference date). Also included are persons who were present during census night and who have lived in the household for less than six months but who intend to stay.

"Residents absent" are persons who usually live in the household but who were absent on census night and who have been absent for less than six months.

"Visitors" are persons who are not usual residents of the household but who were present during census night and have been present for less than six months.

Aside from the fact that these definitions can lead to double counting (a person may be a resident absent from a household and at the same time qualify as a resident present in another household), they indicate that even persons whose presence is temporary (visitors) are to be included in the census count. Furthermore, there is no mention of the legal status of the persons considered. Actual presence and absence are the criteria used to establish the category to which different persons belong. There is no reason to expect, therefore, that migrants in an irregular situation would be purposely excluded from the census count. The practice of using a six-month period of presence to determine residence status is common. The censuses of Burkina Faso, Cameroon, Côte d'Ivoire, Rwanda and Senegal, among others, use definitions similar to those of Burundi to determine who is a resident.

Perhaps the best example of a case in which a census has covered a substantial number of migrants in an irregular situation is that provided by the 1980 census of the United States. At the time the census was being planned, the United States Congress was considering the possibility of allowing the regularization of undocumented migrants present in the country. Pro-immigrant groups, especially those in the Hispanic community, conducted campaigns to ensure that persons of Hispanic origin were well covered by the census, arguing that, by being counted, migrants in an irregular situation could later prove that they had been present in the United States. The 1980 census enumerated the population on a *de facto* basis and a comparison of the foreign-born population that it yielded with estimates of the number of foreign-born expected to be legally present in the country showed that between 2 and 3 million undocumented migrants had been included in the census count (Warren and Passel, 1987). The

International migration statistics

census thus proved to be a useful instrument for the measurement of irregular migration. Recently, similar assessments of the 1990 census results have shown that it too covered a substantial number of migrants in an irregular situation, even though it was not preceded by campaigns promoting their inclusion. It is important, therefore, not to underestimate the capacity of censuses to yield information on all international migrants present in a country, irrespective of their legal status.

1. Use of place of birth and citizenship

Censuses can use a number of criteria to identify international migrants. The two most commonly used are place of birth and current citizenship or legal nationality. Place of birth is one of the most frequently included items in population censuses. The usual question in census questionnaires is: "Where was this person born?", with the answer recorded in different ways depending on whether the person was born within the country of enumeration or outside it. For those born abroad (the foreign-born), the country of birth should be recorded. To enhance international comparability, the United Nations recommends that information on country of birth be recorded according to the national boundaries existing at the time of enumeration (United Nations, 1980b). It is, however, recognized that in the case of countries that have been created from the partition of larger units, the correct identification of country of birth may entail recording the major territorial division or even the specific locality in which a person was born. Since censuses cannot go into such detail, few adjustments are made in practice. Generally, the tendency is to rely on the respondent to decide which adjustment, if any, is appropriate in answering the question posed.

It is not easy to assess whether the use of a question on place of birth in censuses has become more common over time, partly because the number of countries or areas conducting censuses has increased so markedly. Out of the 131 countries or areas that conducted a population census between 1955 and 1964, 95 (73 per cent) had gathered and published some information on the population classified by place of birth, whereas among the 198 countries or areas that conducted censuses between 1975 and 1984, only 120 (61 per cent) published such information. Table 3.2 shows the distribution of the two sets of countries by region. Only in the Americas, a region where the number of countries carrying out censuses did not change between the 1960 and the 1980 rounds of censuses, did the proportion publishing data on place of birth increase. By the 1980 round of censuses, 44 out of the 47 countries in the Americas that conducted population censuses had gathered and published information on place of birth. In other regions, particularly in Africa and Oceania, there was actually a decline in the proportion of countries that published data classified by place of birth. By the 1980 round, the lowest relative

Data collection systems concerning all international migrants

Table 3.2. Countries conducting population censuses during a given period by whether data on place of birth was published

Region	Census in 1955-64			Census in 1975-84		
	Conducted census	Published data on place of birth	Percentage publishing	Conducted census	Published data on place of birth	Percentage publishing
Africa	25	16	64	50	18	36
Americas	47	33	70	47	44	94
Asia	21	16	76	36	19	53
Europe	24	16	67	35	19	54
Oceania	14	14	100	30	20	67
Total	131	95	73	198	120	61

Source: United Nations (1993a).

availability of information on place of birth was found in Africa, though the number of countries producing the required information had not changed markedly since the 1960s. Although the number of African countries carrying out censuses doubled between the 1960 and the 1980 rounds of censuses, the number that did not publish the data of interest also rose.

The better than average performance of the Americas is likely to be related to two factors: the well established tradition of conducting population censuses in most countries of the region, combined with a special initiative by the Latin American Demographic Center (CELADE) of the United Nations Economic Commission for Latin America and the Caribbean (ECLAC) to promote the use of data on place of birth for the analysis of international migration. During the 1970s, CELADE launched the IMILA project (so called because it dealt with international migration in Latin America), one of its objectives being to promote the gathering and tabulation of information classified by country of birth (Arretx, 1987). As part of the project, CELADE (in Santiago, Chile) became the depository of census tapes containing the records of either the whole foreign-born population in a country or of a representative sample. Such tapes were produced by most of the major Latin American countries. In addition, the United States Bureau of the Census and Statistics Canada collaborated in the project by producing more detailed tabulations of the foreign-born population enumerated in their 1980 and 1981 censuses, respectively, than ever before. Using the tapes collected, CELADE then prepared a series of comparable tabulations on the foreign-born population classified by a number of variables. Those tabulations were published and widely distributed (CELADE, 1986 and 1989). The IMILA project was thus instrumental in facilitating access to comparable information on international migrants living in Latin American countries and in promoting the exchange of information between countries. Although the IMILA project is still operational, budget-imposed reductions in the data processing capabilities of CELADE are hindering its further expansion.

International migration statistics

Table 3.3. Countries conducting population censuses during 1975-84 according to whether they published data on place of birth or on citizenship

Region	Countries conducting censuses	Countries with data on place of birth	Countries with data on place of birth and citizenship	Countries with data on citizenship	Percentage publishing both
Africa	50	9	9	15	27
Americas	47	33	11	0	25
Asia	36	11	8	6	32
Europe	35	8	11	8	41
Oceania	30	13	7	2	32
Total	198	74	46	31	30

Source: United Nations (1993a).

No other developing region has benefited from an initiative similar to the IMILA project of Latin America. Censuses in Africa and Asia are less likely to publish information on the population classified by place of birth and more likely to gather information on citizenship as an identifier of international migrant status. Out of the 33 countries in Africa publishing some information on either place of birth or citizenship, 24 published data on citizenship. In Asia, the corresponding numbers were 25 and 14. In Europe, countries publishing information on place of birth or citizenship were about equally divided, whereas in Oceania as well as the Americas, place of birth was preferred (table 3.3).

As discussed in Chapter 2, using country of birth as the criterion to identify international migrants ensures that the persons considered have actually moved from one country to another at some time before enumeration, whereas the use of citizenship as the identifying criterion does not. For purposes of assessing migrant integration or the effects of differential rights because of foreign status, however, citizenship is the criterion that matters. Consequently, the best strategy is for censuses to gather information on both current citizenship and place of birth, and to publish tabulations crossing both variables with other relevant characteristics. As shown in table 3.3, only 30 per cent of the countries conducting a census during the 1980 round and publishing information on place of birth or citizenship did so for both, but cross-tabulations were not necessarily produced. The percentage of countries gathering and publishing information on both variables was highest in Europe and lowest in the Americas, but the range of variation was rather narrow (from 25 to 41 per cent). Thus, much remains to be done to improve the availability and use of data on citizenship and place of birth gathered through censuses.

To gauge whether there has been a tendency for countries to increase their reliance on citizenship as an indicator of international migration, we consider the distribution shown in table 3.4 of countries publishing data on citizenship among those that conducted censuses during the 1960 and 1980 rounds. Just as in the case of place of birth, there has been a general decline in the percentage of

Data collection systems concerning all international migrants

Table 3.4. Countries conducting population censuses during a given period by whether data on citizenship was published

Region	Census in 1955-64			Census in 1975-84		
	Conducted census	Published data on citizenship	Percentage publishing data	Conducted census	Published data on citizenship	Percentage publishing data
Africa	25	11	44	50	24	48
Americas	47	15	32	47	11	23
Asia	21	15	71	36	14	39
Europe.	24	17	71	35	19	54
Oceania	14	7	50	30	9	30
Total.	131	65	50	198	77	39

Source: United Nations (1993a).

countries publishing data on citizenship. Among the 131 countries conducting censuses during 1955–64, nearly half published the relevant data, whereas among the 198 conducting censuses during 1975–84, only 39 per cent did so. Furthermore, declines in the percentage of countries publishing data on citizenship were noticeable in all regions except Africa. Given that the number of African countries conducting censuses doubled during the period, the increase in the percentage publishing data on citizenship is noteworthy. Africa is the only region where citizenship has gained ground as an indicator of international migration status.

2. **Quality of data on place of birth**

In most cases, data on the place (country) of birth will be among the most straightforward pieces of information collected in a census, since most people know in which country they were born. However, when the borders of a country change over time, the question arises as to whether the respondent should be expected to provide the name of the country that existed at the time of birth or that of the current country. Indeed, in some situations, someone who has never moved in his or her lifetime may appear as an international migrant by virtue of a change in international boundaries that convert part of a country into part of another. The United Nations recommends that reports on country of birth be made in terms of the national boundaries in existence at the time of enumeration. However, even when that recommendation is followed, errors may arise when neither the respondent nor the enumerator has a sufficiently precise knowledge of boundary changes to ensure that the information recorded is accurate. Furthermore, even if the names of localities within the original country of birth are recorded, the appropriate allocation may not be made at the editing stage because of the difficulties involved in identifying accurately the localities reported by respondents.

To avoid such problems, some countries have sought to record country of birth in terms of the national boundaries in existence at the time of the respondent's birth. In addition, the inclusion or exclusion of certain countries in the list used for tabulation purposes may depend on whether they are recognized or not recognized by the country conducting the census. Thus, the United States continued to recognize the Baltic States – Estonia, Latvia and Lithuania – as separate entities long after they had become *de facto* parts of the Soviet Union. Other countries failed to distinguish between the Federal Republic of Germany and the German Democratic Republic. Although the boundary changes that have taken place since 1990 have, in a way, validated these particular practices, other problems have arisen with the further disintegration of nation States. It may be instructive to recall that after the break-up of the Austro-Hungarian empire, for example, United States census takers had problems allocating persons born in it to its various successor States, including Austria, the former Czechoslovakia, Hungary and Yugoslavia. In 1950, allocation was based on the surname of the person enumerated. In 1960 information on mother tongue (a new question added to the 1960 census schedule) was used as a basis for allocation. Although the change probably led to more accurate results, it also reduced the comparability of statistics between the two censuses (Shryock and Siegel, 1975). It is still too early to tell how the reconfiguration of States that has taken place in that region since 1990 will be handled by future censuses.

In addition to biases arising from the respondent's ignorance about the country in which his or her birthplace is located at the time of enumeration, other biases may arise because of deliberate misreporting. Some of the foreign-born who have long lived in the country of enumeration may claim that they are natives. The type of information requested, the wording of the question used and the instructions given to enumerators may influence the extent of this bias. Thus, it is less likely for a foreign-born person to claim that he or she is a native if the information sought is the exact province within the country of enumeration or the country of birth for those born abroad than if it is only the dyad, native versus foreign-born. The use of specific instructions for enumerators regarding distinctions of particular relevance, such as noting the difference between Ireland and Northern Ireland, or between the Federal Republic of Germany and the German Democratic Republic have also proven to elicit information of better quality.

In some countries, the level of non-response to the question on place of birth is large, particularly in comparison to the number of persons who declare they are foreign-born. In Kenya, for instance, the number of persons who did not declare a place of birth in 1969 was 78,756, whereas the number declaring that they were born abroad amounted to only 158,692. In the Central African Republic in 1975, the number of persons with place of birth unknown (36,995) was almost as large as the number of foreign-born (44,583). In both cases, the tabulations lacked explanations about whether persons with place of birth unknown were, in fact, born in the country of enumeration but did not know their province of birth or were persons born abroad who did not know their country of birth or included both types.

One way of handling the cases of non-response is to prorate them according to the distribution of those who do provide information. Another is to assume that they are all natives. In the United States, for example, during the processing of the 1960 census all those with place of birth not stated were assumed to be natives unless their census report contained some information suggesting otherwise (for example, if the person reported the use of a language other than English at home).

3. Quality of the data on citizenship

According to the United Nations recommendations for population censuses (United Nations, 1980b), citizenship is the legal nationality of a person. A citizen is a legal national of the country in which a census is conducted, and an alien is a non-national of that country. The United Nations recommends that, in countries where aliens are numerous, the country of citizenship of aliens be recorded and that countries having substantial numbers of naturalized citizens gather information distinguishing citizens by birth from citizens by naturalization. Additional questions on previous legal nationality and mode of naturalization may be included. Enumerators should be instructed about how to deal with the cases of stateless persons, persons with dual or multiple nationality, and persons in the process of becoming naturalized citizens. It is recognized that persons whose citizenship has changed recently because of the emergence of newly independent States or because of territorial changes may have difficulty providing adequate information on their current citizenship.

One possible source of confusion in gathering data on citizenship is the ambiguity characterizing the unqualified term "nationality" which, in certain countries, is used to mean ethnic group rather than legal nationality or citizenship. To avoid such ambiguity, the term used should be "country of citizenship". Also to be avoided is the practice of obtaining information on citizenship in adjectival form (e.g. Austrian, British, Chinese, German, Indian), since some of the adjectives involved would seem to describe an ethnic group rather than legal nationality. Although censuses cannot be expected to reflect the complexity of national laws regarding citizenship and legal nationality, there may be cases that need to be accorded special treatment. British citizens originating in Hong Kong, for instance, mostly lack the right of abode in the United Kingdom and should be distinguished from persons who have fully fledged rights as nationals of that country. It is also important to distinguish Chinese citizens originating in Taiwan, China, from those originating in the mainland.

As in the case of place of birth, long-term foreign residents of a country often tend to declare themselves as citizens, but there is little quantitative

International migration statistics

evidence indicating the extent of such a bias. In fact, some counter-examples exist. In France, for instance, an estimated 220,000 persons of Algerian origin enumerated by the 1982 census had the right to French citizenship by virtue of having been born in Algeria at a time when that country was part of France. However, they declared themselves as Algerian citizens, artificially inflating the number of foreigners in France (Magescas and Charbit, 1985).

The number of foreigners enumerated in a country may vary noticeably according to whether or not the census covers certain categories of aliens identified in box 3.1. Although censuses carried out on a *de facto* basis would be expected to enumerate more foreigners than censuses covering the *de jure* population, this depends on the treatment accorded particular groups of aliens. It is crucial, therefore, that censuses provide adequate information both about the population actually covered and about aliens explicitly excluded from census counts.

4. Other relevant questions often included in censuses

In a recent addendum to the recommendations for population and housing censuses, the United Nations suggests that the immigrant stock of a country be defined as all foreign-born persons present in the country for more than a year (United Nations, 1990). To ascertain which foreign-born persons qualify, information on time of arrival in the country of enumeration should be gathered. Both calendar year and month of arrival must be recorded for all foreign-born persons. Although it is not stated explicitly, time of arrival probably should refer to the first time a foreign-born person entered the country and stayed for a lengthy period. For persons who travel often, the most recent time of arrival would probably not be useful. Clearly, it is important to provide an explicit definition of the time of arrival that should be recorded to avoid confusion and misinterpretation by enumerators, respondents and data users.

Note that if time of arrival is defined in terms of first arrival for a lengthy period, the availability of information on month and year of arrival allows the identification of foreign-born persons who entered the country for the first time during a specific period preceding enumeration and who are still present (or resident, if the census is conducted on a *de jure* basis) in the country at the time of the census. If the period selected spans the time from a year and a half to half a year before enumeration, the number of foreign-born persons arriving for the first time during that year and being in the country at the time of the census would represent people who, on average, have spent a year in the country and could be equated with the inflow of new migrants during the year in question. Such data would therefore provide a measure of migration flows, even though not all the movements that flow statistics usually reflect would be covered. In particular, censuses cannot yield reliable information on persons who have left the country and are therefore no longer present at the time of enumeration.

Data collection systems concerning all international migrants

Another item of information often gathered by censuses is the place of residence at some pre-specified time in the past (five years prior to enumeration, for instance). Such information is often obtained primarily for the purpose of studying internal migration, and consequently place of residence is recorded in terms of territorial divisions within the country of enumeration. In the case of persons living abroad at the time specified, country of residence has generally not been recorded, though census procedures could easily be modified to record it. Many countries include questions on place of residence at a particular time in the past in their censuses: among the 166 countries or areas conducting censuses during 1965-1973, 61 used such questions (Courgeau, 1988). Since the question on place of residence at a pre-specified time is normally posed to the whole population (or a representative sample), it may provide information useful for measuring return migration. To identify return migrants, persons living abroad at the pre-specified time should be cross-classified by both place of birth and current citizenship. A first approximation of the number of return migrants is the number of citizens who lived abroad at the pre-specified time. However, in countries where naturalization is common, return migrants may best be identified as natives (that is, persons born in the country of enumeration) who lived abroad at the pre-specified time. Use of information on place of residence at some time in the past is especially important for countries experiencing important inflows of returning ethnics or for those where the temporary migration of citizens to other countries is sizeable.

Some countries alternatively obtain information on place of previous residence and on time of arrival in the current place of residence. Although such information is again mainly used for the measurement of internal migration, it allows the identification of persons whose previous place of residence was outside the country of enumeration. Knowing that a person has moved from abroad to the country where the census is conducted is not, however, enough to derive useful migration measures: the timing of the move is also crucial. Hence, if a question on previous place of residence is included in a census, the timing of the change of residence (or the length of residence in the current place of abode) should also be included (Courgeau, 1988). Among the 166 countries or areas which conducted censuses between 1965 and 1973, 43 included both questions. As in the case of the question on place of residence at a pre-specified time, the country of previous residence is generally not recorded for those living abroad. Nor are special tabulations made of those whose previous place of residence was outside the country of enumeration. Thus, valuable information remains unexploited. Tabulations of persons whose previous place of residence was outside the country of enumeration by place of birth, citizenship and length of time in current residence would be useful in understanding the dynamics of international migration.

The questions discussed here are recommended by the United Nations (1980b) for inclusion in census questionnaires. As explained above, they are useful in measuring various aspects of migration into the country of enumeration. In many countries, major information gaps also exist regarding emigration. It is not surprising, therefore, that some have tried to use censuses to obtain information on emigrants, as discussed below.

5. Questions used to measure emigration

Attempts to use censuses to count the number of persons who, though still belonging in some way to the population being enumerated, have been abroad for some time, date back to at least the beginning of the twentieth century. In Swaziland, for instance, the census carried out in 1921 tried to count the number of "employed absentees" among the African population (Jones, 1968). The practice of counting that population subgroup was also adopted by later censuses, and in 1966 an attempt was made to attain a more general coverage of the absentee population by dropping the requirement that absentees be employed. Enumerators were instructed to identify "people who normally live in Swaziland but who are temporarily absent from the country in South Africa, overseas or elsewhere either studying, at work, on holiday or for some other reason. For the purpose of the census only those occupants of the homestead who have been away for three years and less and whom a responsible occupant of the homestead expects to return to Swaziland should be enumerated. The only details which are required are the name, sex, age, and ethnic group of such persons. Because they may have been away for some time, you should obtain these particulars only from a responsible person such as the absentee's father, mother or wife" (Jones, 1968, p. 16).

Although apparently straightforward, the identification of "absentees" on the basis of such instructions is problematic. The characterization provided suggests that absentees are men (a wife is mentioned as a possible provider of information on the absentees but not a husband) and that they are only "temporarily" absent. However, the instructions also indicate that the persons in question "may have been away for some time" and a time limit of three years or less is set (too long for absentees to be really "temporary", one might argue). Ultimately, it is left to a "responsible occupant of the homestead" to decide whether the person is expected to return or not. Only if a return is considered likely will the enumerator record the "absentee" on the census form. Consequently, true "emigrants" (persons who have left for good) would not be recorded.

This example is typical of the approach followed by many countries in trying to count the population living abroad. Usually, the respondent providing information for members of a household is asked whether a person who used to be a member of the household is abroad. Once such a person is identified, the person's name and characteristics are recorded if certain other criteria are met, such as that the person has been abroad or is intending to be abroad for more than a certain minimum period (six months, for instance) or that the person is currently employed or studying abroad. Often the suggestion is made that the only persons that matter are those who are "temporarily" absent. The 1981 census of Botswana explains that questions on members of the household absent from Botswana refer "only to citizens of Botswana who are absent from the country. All those persons who are absent but who would live in the household if they were in Botswana should be included (for example, citizens working or temporarily living with relatives in South Africa or studying abroad)" (Botswana, n.d., p. A.33).

This approach to the estimation of temporary emigrants has important drawbacks. As the examples quoted above show, the instructions provided to enumerators are vague and open to a variety of interpretations. It is therefore unlikely that all the nuances and complexities can be transmitted easily or consistently to respondents in the context of a census operation, so errors of many types are likely to ensue. In addition, there is no claim to comprehensiveness because the information sought refers only to a subset of all possible emigrants. To be reported, the persons must be considered as still "belonging" in some ill-defined way to the household enumerated and as being abroad for only a limited period. Furthermore, they must have left someone behind to report on them. Those who have left for good, those who have been away for too long, and those whose former household has disintegrated or who lack former household members to report their absence (because the whole family moved abroad) will not be reflected in the statistics. Consequently, the reported number of absentees will almost certainly underestimate even the temporary component of international emigration and certainly will not reflect the true extent of total emigration. This conclusion has been reached by most of those considering the results obtained by countries that have tried such an approach, including the cases of Egypt, Nepal and Singapore (Oberai, 1993).

There is a better approach to the estimation of emigration from a country. It is based on demographic principles and consists of using information on the current place of residence of persons related in specific ways to the people enumerated. The approach was first proposed by the Working Group on International Migration of the International Union for the Scientific Study of Population (IUSSP) (see Somoza, 1977 and 1981a) and has been used for the estimation of the emigrant stock from Paraguay in 1982 (Zlotnik, 1988), Colombia in 1985 (Ordoñez-Gómez et al., 1988), Uruguay in 1985 (Jaspers-Faijer, 1993) and Bolivia in 1992 (Jaspers-Faijer, 1993). The censuses of those countries have incorporated the relevant questions.

Two methods for the estimation of the stock of emigrants were proposed by the IUSSP Working Group. They are based on different types of information on persons living abroad. The first relies on data on the place of residence of the siblings of all persons enumerated. Thus, for every enumerated person one needs to record the number of brothers and sisters (reported separately) who live in the country of enumeration and the number of brothers and sisters who live abroad (again reported separately). The brothers and sisters of interest are those who have the same mother as the enumerated person. Ideally, reports on numbers of siblings should not include the person enumerated. To facilitate data collection, however, enumerators may be instructed to include the person enumerated as a sibling living in the country. Such practice ensures that the reports corresponding to different siblings living in the same household are the same in terms of numbers of brothers and sisters and their distribution by country of residence.

Once the data are gathered, a distribution of number of persons enumerated according to their own age, the number of same sex siblings present in the country, and the number of same sex siblings abroad can be derived. On the basis of such data and using demographic models, it is possible to estimate not only the total number of emigrants from the country but also their distribution by age and sex (Hill, 1981; Zaba, 1986 and 1987). Although the estimation method available has been proved to be fairly robust to deviations from the basic assumptions underlying it, it has not been recommended for use in censuses because of the complications involved in gathering the data that it relies upon. Indeed, experience regarding the gathering of information on residence of siblings in demographic surveys has shown that, unless enumerators are well trained, it is not always easy to ensure adherence to rules regarding the inclusion of the respondent in (or the exclusion from) the sibling count. Consequently, serious biases often affect the basic data. Furthermore, the information on residence of siblings has no other use for demographic estimation, so the added cost of gathering it in censuses cannot be fully justified.

In contrast, the second method of estimation proposed by the IUSSP Working Group relies on information that is already gathered by many censuses and which only needs to be refined further (Somoza, 1981b). To estimate mortality in childhood, censuses have been recording for every woman of reproductive age the number of children she has ever borne alive and the number of children surviving. The estimation of emigration requires that similar data be gathered using three categories of children: children dead, children surviving and living in the country of enumeration, and children surviving and living abroad. In addition, each category of children needs to be classified by sex, and the questions on children dead and surviving need to be posed to all women aged 15 years and over and not just to those of reproductive age (15 to 49 years). Then, on the basis of the number of children living abroad, classified by sex, and age of mother, it is possible to estimate the total number of persons living abroad by estimating two categories of other emigrants: persons who are abroad but whose mother is dead and cannot therefore report their absence from the country, and persons who do not have a mother to report on them because the mother herself is an emigrant (Somoza, 1981b; United Nations, 1986; Zaba, 1986 and 1987; Zlotnik, 1989). Estimation is most straightforward if data on the incidence of maternal orphanhood are also available. This requires that the census have a question recording, for each person enumerated, the survival status of his or her mother. Availability of data on maternal orphanhood is useful not only for the estimation of emigration but also for the estimation of adult female mortality. Thus, although the estimation of the emigrant stock based on information on the residence of children also demands several items of information, which in turn require the inclusion of several additional questions in the census, those questions yield data that are also useful for other purposes and amply justifies their inclusion in census questionnaires.

Up to now, only countries in Latin America and the Caribbean have gathered the data needed to estimate the emigrant stock on the basis of information on the residence of children. Such data have been gathered through both censuses and household surveys. Countries including the necessary questions in their censuses include Bolivia (1992), Colombia (1985), the Dominican Republic (1981), Haiti (1982), Paraguay (1982) and Uruguay (1985), but only the data for Bolivia, Colombia, Paraguay and Uruguay have been analysed (see citations above). The other countries have not produced the necessary tabulations. An assessment of the results in the cases analysed indicates that application of the estimation method needs to be tailored to the particular circumstances of each country and that the results obtained need to be validated by comparison with additional evidence (Jaspers-Faijer, 1993). Nevertheless, although the estimates obtained may not be perfectly accurate, they have been useful in providing upper bounds for the number of irregular migrants in receiving countries. In the case of Colombia, for instance, data on the residence of children obtained through a national household survey in 1980 included information on whether children abroad lived in Venezuela or elsewhere. It was therefore possible to estimate the total number of Colombian migrants living in Venezuela and compare that number with data gathered in Venezuela itself on the number of Colombians legally resident in the country. The difference provided an estimate of the considerable number of Colombian migrants who lived in Venezuela in an irregular situation in the early 1980s (United Nations, 1986).[1]

One of the major advantages of the approach based on the residence of children is that it relies on data that reflect demographic ties between individuals rather socio-economic ties (such as "household membership"). The estimation methods used can therefore be based on demographic models that are amenable to testing (see Zaba, 1987). Consequently, although the approach proposed still needs to be tried in a wider variety of contexts, it represents a clear advance over the other approaches described above, which are marred by poorly defined concepts unlikely to yield accurate measures of any component of the emigrant stock.

6. Census information relevant for the characterization of international migration

One of the advantages of censuses is that they produce a comprehensive, albeit limited, profile of the population in a country. Clearly, information about the socio-economic characteristics of the population in general is also relevant for the characterization of international migrants. It is useful to know the distribution by age, sex, marital status, educational attainment, labour force participation, occupation, etc., of that subgroup of the population identified as international migrants. In addition, there are some items of information that are often particularly relevant for the study of international migration, such as language ability, ethnicity and religion.

There are three types of information on language that can be gathered by censuses: mother tongue, defined as the language usually spoken in the individual's home in his or her childhood; usual language, defined as the language currently spoken, or most often spoken by the individual in his or her present home; and ability to speak one or more designated languages (such as those considered the official languages of the country concerned). Since each of these types of information serves a distinct analytical purpose, each country should decide which is most appropriate for its needs. Information on language should be collected for all persons (and the criterion for determining the language of children not yet able to speak should be clearly indicated). In countries having significant numbers of international migrants, recording both their usual language and their ability to speak the country's official language or languages is desirable to indicate the degree of integration of international migrants into the host society.

In recording mother tongue or usual language, one of the problems encountered is the variety of languages possible. Listings in census reports often group languages by linguistic affinity. That practice is not recommended when mother tongue or usual language are to be used as indicators of origin or religion. Thus, it would not be useful to have speakers of Yiddish (or Creole) grouped together with speakers of German (or French), no matter how close the languages are in linguistic origin (Shryock and Siegel, 1975).

National circumstances generally dictate the type of information on ethnicity that is relevant. Some of the bases on which ethnic groups are identified include: ethnic nationality, which refers sometimes to ancestry and other times to country or area of origin and should not be confused with citizenship or legal nationality; tribe; race; colour; and usual language. Because most of these terms lack clear definitions, international comparability cannot be ensured. Given the various connotations that terms such as "tribe", "race", "origin" or "colour" may have, countries using them should specify explicitly the criteria used to classify individuals and ensure that appropriate explanatory notes accompany any tabulations produced. In general, countries gathering information on ethnicity have not related that information specifically to international migrants. There may, however, be cases where the identification of the ethnicity of international migrants is relevant.

Religion is another attribute that allows for the classification of the population into particular groups. For census purposes, religion may be defined as: religious or spiritual belief or preference, regardless of whether or not this belief is represented by an organized group; or affiliation with an organized group having specific religious or spiritual tenets. Countries including a question on religion in their censuses can use whichever definition is most suitable,

Data collection systems concerning all international migrants

but they should make it explicit in census guidelines. The degree of detail with which information is gathered will depend on the country's circumstances. In some countries it may be important to record not only the main religious affiliation but also the particular sect to which a person belongs. With respect to international migrants, religious affiliations that differ from those of the majority of the host society can be a factor in retarding integration and are therefore sometimes of interest with respect to studies of the consequences of migration.

Some censuses include questions on reasons for migration, usually accompanied by pre-coded answers directed mostly to the study of internal migration. The two main categories of reasons are economic – to find a job, to change jobs, to earn more – and personal or family reasons – to join family members, to accompany family members, or to get married. The information obtained from such questions is of limited use because a small set of pre-coded reasons cannot capture the complexity of migrants' motivations. Furthermore, since the migrants themselves are not always the ones answering census questionnaires, reporting biases due to proxy respondent error are common. Consequently, questions on the reasons for migration are not recommended for inclusion in census questionnaires, though they may be useful components of more intensive household survey questionnaires.

Lastly, censuses may be used to gather information on the migration status of international migrants. For example, it has been suggested that censuses include a question to ascertain if a foreign-born person has ever been or is currently a refugee. The inclusion of such a question would be especially useful in determining the extent to which censuses cover refugees in developing countries, where other types of registration systems are extremely weak. Sudan has included such a question in its most recent census. It is not clear, however, whether this question will be successful in eliciting accurate information from respondents, especially where refugees fear being singled out. Since questions designed to ascertain migrant status are also likely to result in misreporting by persons whose status is irregular, their use is not recommended in situations where irregular migrants are common. Burdening census schedules with questions that may lead to poorer overall coverage of the population or to higher levels of misreporting about other more important items is never a wise course of action. Careful pre-testing of any questions on international migrant status should therefore be done before they are included in census questionnaires.

7. Use of sampling in censuses

As censuses grow in scale and complexity, it is increasingly common for them to cover a number of items only at the level of a sample of the whole population being enumerated. According to the recommendations on population censuses issued by the United Nations (1980b), sampling may usefully be employed in collecting information on any topics which need not be tabulated for small areas. That is, a sample of the population is selected to receive a longer questionnaire than the basic census schedule. Sampling should usually be avoided, however, when the aim is to cover population groups that are small in relation to the country's population. International migrants usually constitute one such group. Nevertheless, in major receiving countries where international migrants constitute a sizeable proportion of the total population (over 5 per cent) and where census samples are also large (covering 10 or 20 per cent of the total population), information on the international migrant stock obtained from a census sample may be adequate to characterize international migrants. It is important nevertheless to recognize that the full population has not been covered and that sample results are subject to some degree of random variation.

8. Tabulations

According to United Nations recommendations, there are three main sets of tabulations of potential interest for the analysis of international migration. The first is constituted by the five tabulations in the *Principles and recommendations for population and housing censuses* (United Nations, 1980b) which incorporate place of birth, citizenship, and place of previous residence as classifying variables. They are:

1.1 Foreign-born population by country of birth, age and sex;
1.2 Population x years of age and over by place of usual residence, place of residence at a specified time in the past, age and sex (foreign country as a single category);
1.3 Population by place of usual residence, duration of residence, place of previous residence, and sex (foreign country as a single category of place of previous residence);
1.4 Population by country of citizenship, age and sex.

An addendum to the United Nations recommendations, issued in 1990, suggests that the following tabulations be added (United Nations, 1990):

2.1 Immigrant stock by period of arrival, country of birth, age and sex;
2.2 Immigrant stock by marital status, age and sex (cross-classification by country of birth also useful);
2.3 Immigrant stock x years of age and over by usual (or current) activity status, age and sex;
2.4 Economically active immigrant stock x years of age and over by period of arrival, occupation and sex (cross-classification by country of birth also useful);
2.5 Immigrant stock x years of age and over by educational attainment, age and sex.

Compliance with these recommendations has been poor. With respect to the first set of tabulations recommended, the most useful are those presenting data classified by country of birth or country of citizenship simultaneously with a breakdown by age and sex. Yet the number of countries publishing such information is small. Perhaps the best compliance is that found in the Americas, where out of the 47 censuses conducted between 1975 and 1984, a table on the foreign-born population classified by age, sex and country of birth is available for 35. For many countries in the region, however, the table available was that produced by CELADE through the IMILA project, rather than by the countries themselves. Thus the availability of the recommended tabulation would have been considerably more restricted without the IMILA tabulations. In Africa, out of 50 countries with censuses conducted between 1975 and 1984 only 13 published a tabulation on the foreign-born by age, sex and country of birth, although 22 (not all different from the previous 13) published the equivalent table for foreigners (non-citizens). In Asia, out of 36 countries with a census in the 1980 round, only 13 published a tabulation of the foreign-born population classified by age, sex and country of birth, and only 5 the equivalent tabulation for foreigners. In Oceania as well, a tabulation regarding the foreign-born was available in more countries than that on the foreign population: out of 30 countries or areas conducting censuses between 1975 and 1984, 11 published a tabulation of the foreign-born by age, sex and country of birth whereas only three produced the equivalent tabulation for the foreign population.

In other words, although the potential for using the data gathered by censuses for the measurement and characterization of international migration is high, this potential has largely failed to be realized because the data on the foreign-born are seldom tabulated in sufficient detail. Even the most basic tabulation on the foreign-born population classified by sex, age group and country of birth is not usually available in printed form. It is important, therefore, to devise mechanisms for a more thorough exploitation of census information on international migration.

With respect to economic activity, the United Nations recommendations suggest that the following tabulations be prepared and published:

3.1 Population x years of age and over by activity status, marital status, age and sex;
3.2 Economically active population by occupation, age and sex;
3.3 Economically active population by industry, age and sex;
3.4 Economically active population by status in employment, age and sex;
3.5 Economically active population by status in employment, industry and sex;
3.6 Economically active population by status in employment, occupation and sex;
3.7 Economically active population by industry, occupation and sex;
3.8 Economically active population by occupation, educational attainment, age and sex;
3.9 Economically active population by industry, educational attainment, age and sex;
3.10 Economically active population by occupation, place of usual residence, duration of residence, age and sex;
3.11 Economically active population by educational attainment, place of usual residence, duration of residence, age and sex;
3.12 Economically active female population by occupation, marital status and age;
3.13 Economically active female population by status in employment, marital status and age;

International migration statistics

3.14 Population not economically active, by functional categories, age and sex;
3.15 Employed population by hours worked during the week, age and sex;
3.16 Economically active population, by months worked during the year, age and sex;
3.17 Employed population or total economically active population by time worked, occupation and sex;
3.18 Employed population or total economically active population, by time worked, industry and sex;
3.19 Economically active population by monthly income, occupation and sex;
3.20 Households and population in households by annual income and size of household.

The recommendations go on to suggest that status in employment include the categories of employer, own-account worker, employee, unpaid family worker, member of producers' cooperative, and not classifiable. Occupation is to be recorded according to or convertible to the latest revision of the *International standard classification of occupations* (ILO, 1990), at least down to the minor groups (two-digit level). Lastly, industry should be recorded in conformity with or be convertible to the latest revision of the *International standard industrial classification of all economic activities*, at least to the major (three-digit) groups.

Among the tabulations recommended in the three lists cited above, only two provide some information on the economic characteristics of international migrants (2.3 and 2.4) but they are mostly not produced in practice. Only through the IMILA project have census data been used to produce, in a systematic way, information on the labour force participation, sector of economic activity and occupation of the foreign-born population. Even the IMILA project has not gone far enough in exploiting the richness of census information, since it provides only three tabulations on economically active migrants:

4.1 Economically active foreign-born population aged x years and over by country of birth, sex and age group;
4.2 Economically active foreign-born population aged x years and over by country of birth, sex and branch of activity;
4.3 Economically active foreign-born population aged x years and over by country of birth and occupation.

Several strategies can be suggested to improve the use of census data for the analysis of international migration in relation to economic activity. The first and most direct is for census takers to make provisions for the preparation and dissemination of tabulations such as those listed under 3.1 to 3.20 above for international migrants (the foreign-born population, for instance). The second is to promote the production and dissemination in machine-readable form of census samples or, for certain purposes, subsets of census information referring only to international migrants. In the United States, for instance, the widespread availability of census samples has made possible the use of census data for a variety of analytical studies related to the adaptation of international migrants and to the economic impact of international migration.

9. Census data in relation to the framework characterizing international migrants

Given that censuses can include only a few questions relating to international migration, they cannot be expected to provide information on each of the various types of international migrants characterized in the framework presented in Chapter 2. If a census records information on country of birth, on current citizenship, and on the means of acquisition of current citizenship, it is, however, possible to distinguish the following: foreign-born persons who are citizens by birth and who must have been return migrants at some point in their lives; foreign-born persons who are naturalized citizens, a group that, depending on the country considered, may be equated with "settlers"; persons who, by being born in particular countries, are likely to belong to the group of those who have the right to citizenship by virtue of their ancestry and that can therefore be equated with returning ethnics; and foreigners who are economically active and who would mostly qualify as migrant workers except in countries where the admission of settlers is common.

If a census includes, in addition, a question on place of residence at some reference date prior to the time of enumeration, return migrants may be identified as persons born in the country who were living abroad at the reference date or, to make the identification more precise, as persons born in the country of enumeration who are citizens by birth and who were living abroad at the reference date. Although the group thus identified would not include all return migrants (it would exclude native persons who had both emigrated and returned since the reference date), it would nevertheless represent an important part of return migration which is often not covered well by other data sources.

10. Recommendations for the improvement of international migration statistics derived from censuses

- Census schedules should include questions on both place of birth and country of citizenship.
- The question on place of birth should record the country of birth for all persons born abroad and allow for the identification of those whose place of birth is within the country of enumeration but is not exactly known. Thus the question should have the form:

In which province of this country or in which foreign country was this person born?

Province: _____

Province unknown (check):
Other country, specify: _____

Country unknown (check):

International migration statistics

- The question on citizenship or legal nationality should record both country of current citizenship and mode of acquisition of citizenship. Thus:

  What is the current citizenship of this person?
  △ Citizen of this country (of enumeration) by birth
  △ Citizen of this country (of enumeration) by naturalization
  △ Citizen of another country, specify _____

- If a question on place of residence at a certain reference date prior to the census is included, it should allow for the recording of country of residence in some detail. Thus:

  Where did this person live on [reference date]?
  In this country, province: _____
  In another country, specify: _____

- If a question on the previous place of residence is included, it should be accompanied by a question on the length of stay in the current residence. Responses to the question on place of previous residence should also allow for the recording of different countries. However, inclusion of these questions should usually be accorded lower priority than those regarding place of birth and citizenship.

- If the measurement of emigration is considered important, questions on the place of residence of children should be included in the census (see section 3.A.5 above). Questions on the place of residence of absentee household members should not be included.

- The publication of tabulations of the enumerated population classified by age, sex and country of birth, and of the enumerated population by age, sex and country of citizenship should be given priority.

- If information on the place of residence at a certain reference date before the census is recorded, a tabulation of the population residing abroad by age, sex and country of residence at that time should be produced.

- All tabulations referring to the migrant population should be classified by sex.

- The census tabulation plan should include tabulations relative to the economic activity, sector of economic activity and occupation of the migrant population by sex. Preparation of tabulations 3.2 to 3.9, presented in section 3.A.8 above, for the migrant population (the foreign-born) are highly desirable.

- High priority should be given to the preparation and dissemination of census samples in machine-readable form to permit in-depth comparisons of international migrants to non-migrants.

Data collection systems concerning all international migrants

- The dissemination of a machine-readable public-use file containing information only on the international migrant population (that is, only on households having members who can be considered to be international migrants, either because they are foreign-born or because they are foreigners) is also recommended to facilitate further study of international migration.

B. POPULATION REGISTERS

A population register is a data system providing for the continuous recording of selected information pertaining to each member of the resident population of a country. Both the organization and the operation of a population register must have a legal basis (United Nations, 1969). While the main purpose of population registration is administrative, a population register can be used for the compilation of up-to-date statistical information on the size, characteristics and location of a country's population.

Population registers are built up from a base consisting of an inventory of the inhabitants of an area, modified continuously by current information on births, deaths, adoptions, legitimations, marriages, divorces, changes of name, and changes of residence, including those brought about by international migration (United Nations, 1969). For purposes of measuring international migration, the registration of changes of residence is the main focus of attention. Since population registers cover only the *de jure* population that – having the right to legal residence in a country – the rules establishing who is a resident determine who gets inscribed in and who should be deregistered from the register. The term "deregistered" is used instead of the terms "removed" or "deleted" because, in some countries, the records of persons who have left the population are maintained in the population registers with appropriate notations to ensure that those records are disregarded when estimating stock measures.

Population registers have a long history. The earliest known registers operated in China (over 2,000 years ago) and Japan. The parish registers of Finland and Sweden, established in the seventeenth century were among the earliest population registers in Europe. At the beginning of the twentieth century, population registration was in operation in 15 countries (United Nations, 1969). During the 1960s, 65 countries reported to the United Nations that they maintained population registers, though only 35 used them to produce statistical data. Among the latter, only 13 derived statistics on international migration from population registers (United Nations, 1969). They were: Cuba and Suriname in Latin America; Israel, the Republic of Korea and Taiwan, China, in Asia; and Belgium, Bulgaria, Denmark, the Faeroe Islands, the Federal Republic of Germany, Hungary, the Netherlands and Sweden in Europe.

International migration statistics

Today, population registers are still more common in Europe than in any other region. Austria, Belgium, Denmark, Finland, Germany, Iceland, Italy, Liechtenstein, Luxembourg, the Netherlands, Norway, Spain, Sweden and Switzerland all maintain current population registers that produce some data on international migration. In addition, several countries of Eastern and Central Europe have population registers, but they are not being used to derive international migration statistics. In Asia, population registration is still operational in Japan and the Republic of Korea, but it is not a source of international migration statistics in either. The existence and use of population registers for statistical purposes in other world regions has not been documented recently.

In Europe, a recent effort to document the role of population registers in producing international migration statistics has been undertaken under the aegis of Eurostat as part of a project to improve the comparability of international migration statistics within the European Union and the European Economic Area, thus encompassing Iceland, Liechtenstein and Norway in addition to the 15 member States of the European Union. Consequently, most of the information available on the operation of population registers for the production of international migration statistics refers to member States of the European Union or of the European Free Trade Association.

1. Structure and operation of population registers

To be an effective tool for the generation of statistics, a population register must have nationwide coverage and its operation must be authorized by a legal instrument (that is, a law, a regulation, a royal decree, etc.) that makes the provision of information by each person resident in the country compulsory. The more the administrative uses of the register are judged essential by both a country's authorities and its people, the more effective the operation of the register. Thus, when proof of inclusion in the register is required to have access to the public health system, to education, employment or housing, a person will have an interest in registering and remaining in the register. Indeed, a problem often encountered in the operation of population registers is that persons who are registered are reluctant to deregister when they leave the country.

Although all the registers which produce statistics on international migration have nationwide coverage, not all are organized at the national level. In a number of countries, registers operate at the local level – that is, at the level of the commune, the municipality or the province – often under local legislation that may vary from unit to unit. Compliance with certain minimum standards is established at the national level through federal or national legislation, thus setting the basis for the exploitation of the local registers for statistical purposes at the national level. Germany, the Netherlands, Spain and Switzerland provide

Data collection systems concerning all international migrants

examples of countries whose population registers still operate mainly at the local level, meaning that the agencies in charge of compiling statistics at the national level cannot generally have access to the detailed information contained in local registers. In Austria and Italy, local registers are also still dominant, but a strategy to institute centralization is being implemented.

The case of Switzerland illustrates the operation of a highly decentralized type of population register, where the issuance of detailed regulations regarding the residence of Swiss citizens falls within the competence of the 26 cantons constituting the country. Only with respect to foreigners does the confederation have the power to establish the legal conditions for stay and residence in Switzerland. Consequently, the administration of the local population registers is mainly the concern of the cantons and the 2,912 communes into which the cantons are subdivided (Gisser, 1992). The production of statistics at the national level has to cope, therefore, with the existence of substantial heterogeneity at the local level. In particular, individual data on the migration movements of Swiss citizens cannot be produced by the majority of the communes. Instead, communes report aggregate data to the Federal Statistical Office. Thus, every year since 1980, the communes have been under the obligation of producing tabulations based on their population registers on the migration of Swiss citizens into and out of each commune. The tabulation form that the communes have to fill is prepared by the Federal Statistical Office and requests very basic information: number of Swiss in-migrants to a commune according to sex, place of previous residence (in a country other than Switzerland, in another Swiss canton, or in another part of the same canton) and month of registration; and similarly for Swiss out-migrants. The tabulations are sent to the Federal Statistical Office every January and constitute the basis for the publication of information on the migration of Swiss citizens at the national level. In recent years, some communes have been fulfilling their reporting obligations by transmitting to the Federal Statistical Office individual records on electronic media. As of 1992, individual records were received from communes accounting for 44 per cent of the population of Swiss origin (Gisser, 1992).

In Germany, the most recent rules on maintaining and adjusting the local population registers are laid down by the Federal Registration Law of 1980 and the Registration Laws of the Länder, which came into effect during the period 1982–86. Although the Registration Laws of the Länder differ slightly from one to another, they are similar in all essential parts (Bretz, n.d.). They establish that, with some exceptions, every person who moves into a dwelling or another type of accommodation has to register at the local registry office and every person who leaves a dwelling or other type of accommodation has to report to the local registry office to be deregistered. Special forms are filled out at the local registry office when a new registration or deregistration takes place and, according to the Law on Population Statistics, a copy is sent to the statistical offices of the Länder for processing. The processed information is then transmitted to the Federal Statistical Office which is in charge of compiling and publishing data for the country as a whole.

International migration statistics

In the Netherlands, the population register is described as decentralized, but there is considerable uniformity in its operation at the municipal level. Municipalities are required to report monthly to the Netherlands Central Bureau of Statistics (NCBS) the occurrence of births, deaths, marriages and migration. Special forms are used to effect such reporting. Every person in the register has a "person card" on which events in that person's life are recorded. In the event of emigration, the person card of the person is forwarded to the Central Government Inspectorate in The Hague where the card is filed. The card is accompanied by a special form (notification form A) which records data relative to the emigrant. After administrative use, this form is transmitted to the NCBS for statistical processing. Similarly, when an immigrating person is to be registered, his or her person card is retrieved from those kept in the Central Government Inspectorate or, if the person has never been a resident of the Netherlands before, a new person card is issued. Notification form B is filled out for every immigrating person and sent to the NCBS for statistical processing (van der Erf et al.).

In Spain the operation of the municipal registers is coordinated by the National Institute of Statistics (NIS) which on 30 December 1986 issued technical instructions to the mayors of municipalities on the operation of the local population registers and their annual verification. When a person changes residence from one municipality to another or from abroad to a Spanish municipality, he or she must apply for registration in the local register. A standard registration form is filled out, copies of which are transmitted to the NIS on a monthly basis for processing. They serve as a basis for the production of statistics on international inflows (Escribano-Morales, n.d.). Data on outflows do not seem to be collected.

As these examples indicate, there is considerable variation in the functioning of decentralized population registers and, although decentralization cannot be equated with heterogeneity of operation at the local level, there is certainly a greater possibility for such heterogeneity to arise. In recent years, to promote uniformity and to enhance the use of the data from population registers, the tendency has been to increase their centralization. Often, centralization has involved the creation of a parallel central population register that operates simultaneously with those at the local level. The Nordic countries are among those having the most developed centralized population registers. In Sweden, for instance, Statistics Sweden has been charged since 1991 to maintain a total population register that is computerized. This register includes most of the information kept in local registers and is constantly updated. Every week, an average of 40,000 changes are reported to Statistics Sweden through electronic media. It is estimated that the delay between the occurrence of a migration and its entry into the central register is only about four weeks (Poulain, 1992).

In Denmark, population registers at the municipal level have been in operation since 1924, but in 1968 a computerized central population register was established. Both the local registers and the central population register are updated as part of a coordinated administrative process administered by the

Secretariat for Personal Registration of the Ministry of the Interior. The responsibility of producing statistics derived from the central population register rests with Danmarks Statistik (Lange, n.d.).

In Finland, population registers are also maintained both locally and centrally. The central population register was created by law in 1969 and its coordination with the local registers is carried out by the population register centre of the Ministry of the Interior. As of 1 April 1990, any change of residence must be reported to the postal service which, aside from noting the change of address of the person concerned, reports it to the local population register using special forms. The latter then transmits the information to the central population register. The Central Bureau of Statistics of Finland has access to the data contained in the central population register (Poulain, 1992).

In Norway, local population registers have been in existence for over two centuries but a central population register was created only in 1964. Until 1991, the Office of the National Registrar responsible for the operation of the central population register operated within Statistics Norway but it has since been put under the Directorate of Taxes and a new centralized register has been constructed. All of Norway's municipalities are currently electronically linked with the new central population register.

Among other European countries, those having centralized population registers include Belgium, Liechtenstein and Luxembourg. In Belgium, for example, the communes have traditionally maintained a number of population registers for administrative purposes. In 1967, to facilitate data exchanges between the different registers, the Belgian Council of Ministers authorized the setting up of a computerized and centralized population register, named the national population register. Since 1969 until its official recognition by the law of 8 August 1983, the national population register functioned as an extra-legal framework through the voluntary affiliation of communes. According to the law of 1 August 1985, the National Institute of Statistics (NIS) can use the data in the national population register for statistical purposes and study. As one of its tasks, the NIS annually produces tabulations on international migration using the data from the national population register (Poulain et al.).

In Liechtenstein, the 11 communes of the country maintain local population registers. At the national level, a central population register (*Wohnbevölkerungsstatistik*) is maintained by the Office for the National Economy. Although until 1992 there was no link between the local and the central registers, there were plans to give the communes and other national offices access to the central population register. All registers are computerized but the updating of the central population register is carried out on the basis of inscription and deregistration forms sent by the communes to the Office for the National Economy (Gisser, 1992).

In Luxembourg, population registers at the level of the commune coexist with a central register known as the general register of natural persons which is managed by the state computing centre within the Ministry of Communications. At the local level, only the larger communes have computerized their registers and every two weeks they transmit information on changes to the general register. Other communes transmit information regularly to the state computer centre so that the necessary changes can be made in the general register. Until 1986, the communes transmitted annually to the National Statistical Office (Statec) a list of the persons whose names were entered or deregistered from the local registers because of changes of residence and Statec processed the data to produce migration statistics. Since 1987, the state computer centre has been in charge of transmitting the relevant information to Statec (Langers and Ensch, n.d.).

Lastly, in Iceland there is only a centralized population register operating under the national registry office established in 1953 within the Statistical Bureau of Iceland. Persons changing residence must report that change to the local municipal administrations which transmit the information to the national registry. In the capital, registration may be carried out at police posts or directly at the office of the national registry (Poulain, 1992).

The existence of a centralized register facilitates timely processing of information regarding population change, especially when the national statistical office has direct access to the data in the central population register, as in the case of Belgium, Iceland, Norway and Sweden. In some countries, concerns about the possible misuse of a centralized population register in ways that may infringe the right to privacy of individuals has either prevented centralization altogether or curtailed the possible use of the central register for statistical purposes. Furthermore, the simultaneous operation of registers at the local and central levels requires that both systems be checked periodically to ensure their compatibility and consistency in terms of coverage. In Liechtenstein, for instance, the contents of the central population register are compared with those of the local registers at the end of every year and adjustments are made after mutual consultation. In Belgium and Luxembourg, the coherence between the local registers and the computerized central register is also checked at periodic intervals. In Luxembourg, those checks have tended to yield relatively important inconsistencies, particularly regarding the coverage of the foreign population resident in the country (Langers and Ensch, n.d.).

In some countries, population registers, whether centralized or not, are checked and adjusted at the time of every population census. This has been the practice in Belgium, Germany and Spain. In addition, Spain conducts a special population count (*Padrón Municipal de Habitantes*) at the mid-point of every intercensal period to check and update its municipal population registers (Escribano-Morales, n.d.). In contrast, in a few other countries censuses have been completely replaced by population counts based on population registers. The Netherlands, for instance, has not conducted a population census since 1971 and derives its population statistics exclusively from the population registers (van den Brekel, 1977).

In some countries, concerns about the confidentiality of statistical information have prevented the comparison of different data sources to check the accuracy of population registers. For example, in Sweden the 1990 census could not be used to assess the coverage of population registration. In such cases, other forms of assessment must be used. In Sweden, the use of the registers for taxation and insurance purposes implies that the authorities communicate periodically with most of the adult population in the country and such communication provides a means of controlling the accuracy of the registers (changes of address are detected when mail is returned, for instance). Swedish statisticians are confident that the degree of coverage of the total population register is very high. In other countries, the police collaborate with municipal authorities in checking dwellings that have become empty or are occupied by new tenants to ensure that the proper deregistration or registration has taken place.

Of particular concern in all countries is the tendency of persons who leave with the intention of settling abroad to avoid reporting their out-migration to the authorities in charge of maintaining population registers. Thus, emigration is often underestimated, especially in the case of foreigners. Although periodic checks allow for the identification of those who have left and result in their eventual deregistration, in some countries such adjustments result in a change of the *de jure* population but are not incorporated in international migration statistics. In the Netherlands, for instance, administrative corrections to the local population registers change the population stock but are not used to adjust the international migration statistics published by the Netherlands Central Bureau of Statistics (van den Erf et al.).

2. Definition of international migrants in population registers

Given the mode of operation of population registers, the identification of international migrants depends on the rules in place to determine who should be inscribed in or deregistered from a population register. The task of determining what those rules mean in practice is far from straightforward, partly because the statistical officers in charge of compiling and publishing international migration statistics derived from population registers are often not fully apprised of the legal requirements to be met for registration, especially in the case of foreigners. It is common for those in charge of statistical accounting to provide definitions of immigrants and emigrants that appear to be based only on the desires or intentions of the persons involved when, in fact, registration involves providing proof that certain requirements have been met to stay legally in the country concerned.

In the European countries that use population registers to derive international migration statistics, the rules for inscription in and deregistration from the population registers vary according to whether the person concerned is a citizen of the country or a foreigner. In addition, among countries that have entered into international agreements allowing the free movement of citizens, a further distinction is made between foreigners in general and foreigners subject to free movement. In Europe there are two sets of countries among which free

International migration statistics

movement has been established: the European Union and the Common Nordic Labour Market. The current member States of the European Union are Austria, Belgium, Denmark, France, Finland, Germany, Greece, Ireland, Italy, Luxembourg, the Netherlands, Portugal, Spain, Sweden and the United Kingdom. The Common Nordic Labour Market was established in 1954 by Denmark, Finland, Iceland, Norway and Sweden. Among each group of States, citizens of member States generally have the right to enter and establish residence in any member State other than their own provided certain minimal conditions are met. Within the European Union, the free movement of workers was established in the founding documents of the European Communities and took effect in 1968. Then, as other countries acceded to the Communities, transitional periods were established in some cases before free movement of workers took effect for the citizens of new members. In addition, as part of the process leading to the emergence of the European Union, freedom of movement was extended to persons other than salaried or self-employed workers and their dependants. Today, freedom of movement operates not only among the 15 member States of the European Union but also in relation to the European Economic Area that also encompasses Iceland, Liechtenstein and Norway. In the Common Nordic Labour Market free movement was established in 1954 when the group was constituted (Plender, 1987) and the right of citizens of Nordic countries to settle in a Nordic country other than their own was guaranteed by an agreement signed in 1982 that came into force on 1 August 1983. In both groups of countries, free movement implies that citizens of member States can enter member States other than their own without a visa and establish residence without having requested permission to do so before arrival. Free movement does not mean, however, that citizens of member States are entirely free from control when they change residence from one member State to another. Particularly with respect to registration, foreigners having free movement rights have the obligation to register and to satisfy several conditions that limit their right to settlement (within the European Union, having appropriate health insurance and otherwise not being a burden on the receiving State, for instance). Thus, in Denmark, nationals and citizens of other Nordic countries can stay and register without requesting a residence permit, but citizens of other member States of the European Union must obtain a residence permit before they are allowed to register (Lange, n.d.).

All other foreigners – those not having the right to free movement – must obtain a visa, residence permit or work permit before entering any of the European countries listed above to settle. Holding the appropriate permit is generally a necessary precondition for inscription in the population registers of the receiving State. However, this is frequently not made explicit in defining who must register. In addition, some foreigners may be admitted without having a visa or may enter with a tourist visa and then try to stay after the visa expires. Asylum-seekers, for instance, need not have the necessary visas or permits to enter the country where they seek asylum and may remain in that country for lengthy periods before their status is determined. Whether they are inscribed or not in population registers often depends on the type of accommodation they occupy: those settling in normal housing may be registered while those staying in government hostels or in detention centres may not be. In most countries, however, asylum-seekers will register when they are granted refugee status. Since in most countries, asylum-seeker cases take several months or even years to be adjudicated, delays in registration bias the resulting international migration statistics. Unfortunately, the definitions of international migrants provided by countries deriving statistics from population registers usually lack the necessary detail to indicate the extent to which the registration process covers either asylum-seekers or foreigners whose status is irregular.

Tables 3.5 to 3.7 characterize international migrants according to the population registers of various European countries. Table 3.5 refers to the international migration of citizens and the conditions under which citizens must be inscribed in or deregistered from the population register in cases where international mobility is involved. Note that even among the small number of countries considered (14), there is considerable variation in the criteria used to characterize returning and emigrating citizens. With respect to returning citizens, eight countries use a time criterion to determine if inscription should take place, but the expected length of stay varies from 30 days in the Netherlands to over a year in Finland, Iceland, Liechtenstein and Sweden. In two countries, Austria and Germany, the fact of occupying a dwelling is the main criterion used in determining if inscription should take place; in the remaining four countries – Belgium, Italy, Luxembourg and Spain – citizens are registered if they intend to "establish residence" in their own country. Whether the establishment of residence must be proved by any concrete act (renting or buying a dwelling; returning to an established dwelling etc.) is not indicated. There is also considerable vagueness about what "having been resident abroad" means. In no case is it indicated that a citizen must have been abroad for a certain minimum period before being considered "resident abroad". In Italy, Italian citizens can be registered as return migrants after having spent abroad periods shorter than three months. One practical way of interpreting the meaning of "having been an emigrant" or "having been resident abroad" is to consider the characterization of emigrants in terms of the conditions for deregistration. Six countries – Denmark, Finland, Iceland, the Netherlands, Norway and Sweden – quantify the identification of emigrating citizens by establishing minimum periods of stay abroad beyond which emigration is assumed to take place. In most other cases, "establishing residence abroad" tends to be the criterion used to determine if citizens should deregister. In Germany, the fact of "giving up a dwelling" and in Denmark departure without retaining a "residence" in the country (probably meaning a dwelling) are reasons for deletion from the register. In fact, Danish citizens need not deregister if they leave the country for at most six months while still retaining a dwelling in Denmark.

With respect to foreigners subject to free-movement regimes, the conditions for registering and deregistering are presented in table 3.6. Among member States of the European Union, the tendency is to require that citizens of member

International migration statistics

Table 3.5. Characterization of immigrating and emigrating citizens according to the mode of operation of the population registers of different countries

Country	Requirements to register	Requirements to deregister
Austria	Moving into a dwelling after having been resident abroad	Not available
Belgium	Establishing residence after a period of residence abroad	Departing with the intention of residing abroad
Denmark	Returning after emigrating abroad with the intention of residing in Denmark for at least three months	1. Departing with the intention of staying abroad for more than six months, or 2. Departing without retaining a residence in Denmark
Finland	Returning after residing abroad with the intention of staying more than a year	Departing with the intention of staying abroad for more than a year
Germany	Returning after emigration and intending to reside in Germany in an owner-occupied home, as a tenant or a sub-tenant	Departing and giving up the dwelling occupied in Germany
Iceland	Returning after residing abroad with the intention of staying more than a year	Departing with the intention of staying abroad for more than a year
Italy	Returning after a period of residence abroad	Departing with the intention of residing abroad
Liechtenstein	Returning from abroad with the intention of staying more than a year	Departing with the intention of establishing residence abroad
Luxembourg	Returning from abroad to establish residence	Departing with the intention of establishing residence abroad
Netherlands	Returning from residence abroad and intending to stay in the Netherlands for more than 30 days	Departing with the intention of staying abroad more than 360 days
Norway	Returning after residing abroad with the intention of staying more than six months	Departing with the intention of staying abroad for more than six months
Spain	Returning after emigrating and intending to establish residence	Not covered
Sweden	Returning after residing abroad with the intention of staying more than a year	Departing with the intention of staying abroad for more than a year
Switzerland	Returning after residing abroad to establish residence (intending to stay for more than three months)	Departing with the intention of establishing residence abroad

Source: Adapted from Poulain (1992) and Poulain et al. (n.d.).

States register if they intend to stay more than three months, as in Belgium, Denmark, Italy, Luxembourg and Spain. Among member States of the Common Nordic Labour Market, registration in Finland, Iceland, and Sweden takes place only if a Nordic citizen intends to stay more than one year, whereas in Norway citizens of Nordic countries are inscribed in the register if their intended period of stay is more than six months. Denmark, which until 1993 was the only

Data collection systems concerning all international migrants

Table 3.6. Characterization of immigrating and emigrating foreigners subject to free-movement provisions, according to the mode of operation of the population registers of different countries

Country	Requirements to register	Requirements to deregister
Belgium	Entering Belgium with the intention of staying more than three months	Departing with the intention of establishing residence abroad
Denmark	Entering Denmark with the intention of staying for more than three months	Departing with the intention of residing abroad
Finland	Entering Finland with the intention of staying for more than a year	Departing with the intention of staying abroad for more than a year
Germany	Entering Germany with the intention of residing in an owner-occupied home, as a tenant or sub-tenant	Departing and giving up the dwelling occupied in Germany
Iceland	Entering Iceland with the intention of staying for more than a year	Departing with the intention of staying abroad for more than a year
Italy	Entering Italy with the intention of residing for more than three months	Departing with the intention of residing abroad
Luxembourg	Entering Luxembourg with the intention of residing for more than three months	Departing with the intention of residing abroad
Netherlands	Entering the Netherlands with the intention of staying for more than 180 days	Departing with the intention of staying abroad more than 360 days
Norway	Entering Norway with the intention of staying for more than six months	Departing with the intention of staying abroad for more than six months
Spain	Entering Spain with the intention of staying for more than three months	Not covered
Sweden	Entering Sweden with the intention of staying for more than a year	Departing with the intention of staying abroad for more than a year

Source: Adapted from Poulain (1992) and Poulain et al. (n.d.).

country that was simultaneously a member of the Common Nordic Labour Market and of the European Union, uses a three-month cut off point instead. With respect to the deregistration of foreigners having the right to free movement, Finland, Iceland and Sweden do so when the expected period of absence exceeds a year. Norway uses six months of absence and Denmark bases deregistration on the intention to reside abroad. Among other member States of the European Union, Belgium, Italy and Luxembourg also make use of the intention of residing abroad, whereas Germany stipulates further that deregistration is needed only if the dwelling occupied by the foreigner in German territory is given up. Lastly, both with respect to registration and deregistration, the Netherlands applies to foreigners subject to free movement the same criteria as to all other foreigners.

Table 3.7 summarizes the criteria for the registration and deregistration of all other foreigners. Note that the criteria are similar to those applied to foreigners having the right to free movement except that other foreigners must

International migration statistics

Table 3.7. Characterization of immigrating and emigrating foreigners, excluding those subject to free movement, according to the mode of operation of the population registers of different countries

Country	Requirements to register	Requirements to deregister
Austria	1. Staying in a hotel for more than two months after admission, or 2. Occupying a dwelling after admission	Not available
Belgium	Entering with the necessary permit to establish residence	Departing with the intention of establishing residence abroad
Denmark	Entering with the necessary residence permit and intending to stay for more than three months	Departing with the intention of residing abroad
Finland	Entering with the intention of staying for more than a year and having the necessary permit to do so	Departing with the intention of staying abroad for more than a year
Germany	1. Intending to reside in Germany in an owner-occupied home, as a tenant or sub-tenant, or 2. Intending to stay in a hotel for more than two months	Departing and giving up the dwelling occupied in Germany
Iceland	Entering with the intention of staying for more than a year and having the necessary permit to do so	Departing with the intention of staying abroad for more than a year
Italy	Entering with the intention of residing in Italy for more than three months and having the necessary residence permit to do so	Departing with the intention of residing abroad
Liechtenstein	Entering with the required residence permit	Departing with the intention of establishing residence abroad
Luxembourg	Entering with the intention of residing in Luxembourg for more than three months and having the necessary residence permit to do so	Departing with the intention of residing abroad
Netherlands	Entering with the intention of staying for more than 180 days	Departing with the intention of staying abroad more than 360 days
Norway	Entering with the intention of staying for more than six months and having the necessary permit to do so	Departing with the intention of staying abroad for more than six months
Spain	Entering with the required residence permit	Not covered
Sweden	Entering with the intention of staying for more than a year and having the necessary permit to do so	Departing with the intention of staying abroad for more than a year
Switzerland	Entering with a residence permit allowing a stay of more than a year	Departing with the intention of establishing residence abroad

Source: Adapted from Poulain (1992) and Poulain et al. (n.d.).

possess the necessary permits to stay for the period required or to establish residence. Some countries, namely Austria, Germany and the Netherlands, do not explicitly mention the possession of permits. In Austria, where occupying a dwelling is a key criterion for registration, landlords and homeowners are charged with reporting the presence of new tenants or lodgers in their property; and managers of hotels have similar obligations regarding foreigners staying in their establishments. Since those reports are made to the police, internal control of foreigners is thus effected and cases of foreigners who fail to register can be detected (Gisser, 1992). In the Netherlands, registration does not seem not involve a compulsory check of the legitimacy of stay of the foreigners in the country, and therefore some migrants in an irregular situation are probably inscribed in the register (van den Erf et al.).

Since the conditions for the registration or deregistration of persons from a population register determine who is counted as an immigrant and as an emigrant, respectively, tables 3.5 to 3.7 can be considered to present the definitions underlying the data on flows of international migrants produced by the countries considered. In comparing those definitions, a problem that is immediately evident is that there are a number of cases where persons moving between country A and country B may be considered emigrants according to A but not immigrants according to B and vice versa. Thus, a Dutch citizen moving to Norway for 8 months would not be considered an emigrant according to the population register of the Netherlands but would be considered an immigrant according to that of Norway. Similarly, a Danish citizen moving to Sweden for 10 months would be considered an emigrant according to the population register of Denmark but not an immigrant according to that of Sweden.

The possibility of such inconsistencies is clear from the definitions in tables 3.5 to 3.7, and their existence and magnitude have been the object of analysis of the Conference of European Statisticians, which reports to the Economic Commission for Europe (ECE) and which has been trying since 1971 to improve the comparability of international migration statistics among European countries (Kelly, 1987). As part of that effort, a systematic comparison has been made between the number of emigrants recorded by country A with country of destination B and the number of immigrants recorded by country B with country of previous residence A. The discrepancies between the two figures have often been significant. In order to reduce them, some countries have modified their procedures to gather or to tabulate information on international migrants. The member States of the Common Nordic Labour Market, for instance, have opted for greater integration of their population registers in relation to the migration of Nordic citizens. Thus, when a citizen of country A moves to country B and registers there, the population registry of country B sends a copy of the registration form to the registry of country A so that the citizen in question can be deregistered in country A and counted as an emigrant. That is, among the Nordic countries, the definition of an emigrating citizen varies according to the country of destination but has the advantage of being consistent with that of immigrant when the country of destination is another Nordic country.

Another strategy to improve the consistency of international migration statistics between countries consists in using different definitions of immigrant and emigrant in preparing tabulations from those officially used for registering and deregistering persons. Such a possibility arises, for instance, when countries register persons who intend to stay more than x months, where x is less than 12. Then, once a year has elapsed since registration, it is possible to use the information contained in population registers to ascertain how many of the persons admitted for at least x months have actually stayed more than a year. Tabulations on persons who have stayed more than a year are more directly comparable with those of countries where a year is the cut-off point to define emigrants. The Netherlands is one of the countries producing special tabulations for comparative purposes. The data normally published by the Netherlands Central Bureau of Statistics, however, are still those reflecting the official definitions presented in Tables 3.5 to 3.7.

3. Meaning of "establishing residence" in the case of foreigners

Since the characterization of foreigners as international migrants through the operation of population registers depends on the process that must be followed by a foreigner to "establish residence" in the receiving country, it is useful to provide further details about this procedure. The case of Belgium will be used as an example (Poulain, 1987).

In Belgium, the rules governing the registration of aliens are set by the law of 15 December 1980. To enter Belgian territory an alien must be in possession of the documents required under bilateral agreement between Belgium and the country of citizenship of the alien concerned. In the absence of reciprocal agreements, the alien must be in possession of a visa stamped on his or her passport obtained from one of the Belgian consular or diplomatic offices abroad. To obtain a visa, an alien must prove that he or she has sufficient means to stay in Belgium without being considered in need of assistance. Upon arrival at the border, the alien's passport will be stamped (irrespective of whether a visa is required or not). Then, if the alien stays in a hotel or inn, a form will be filled in to comply with the procedure for the control of travellers; but if the alien intends to stay at least eight working days in the country and is not staying in a hotel or inn, he or she must apply for a permit in the commune where he or she is staying. The alien will be issued with a declaration of arrival, valid for a maximum of three months from the date of arrival and subject to the length of validity of his or her visa. The administration of the commune will complete the declaration of arrival in triplicate, the original will be given to the person concerned, the second will be forwarded to the Aliens Department (*Office des Étrangers*), and the third will be kept at the commune.

An alien cannot remain more than three months in Belgium unless he or she is allowed to settle or obtains special permission to remain. Several successive stays cumulating over 90 days within a six-month period are considered equivalent to staying more than three months. Persons admitted temporarily are informed that they are forbidden to earn a living in Belgium, either as employed or self-employed workers, without permission from the Ministry of Labour. The administration of the commune is required, after the date of expiration of the declaration of arrival, to check by police inquiry whether the alien stayed or has left the country. The result is made known to the Aliens Department, which makes a decision regarding future handling of the person concerned.

To stay more than three months in Belgium, an alien must apply for permission from the Minister of Justice or the Aliens Department while outside Belgium. If the application is successful, the alien will receive a permit for temporary stay. Before 1974, such a permit could be obtained only after a work permit had been issued to the potential migrant by the Ministry of Employment in response to an application made by a potential employer.

Within eight working days of arrival in Belgium, an alien holding a permit for temporary stay must register in the register of aliens of the commune where he or she will reside. The administration of the commune will enrol the person in the register of aliens (part of the local population register) and issue a certificate of enrolment valid for a year and renewable.

To settle in Belgium, an alien must apply for permission from the Ministry of Justice and the Aliens Department. Subject to having satisfied the conditions of entry and stay, an alien is granted permission to settle if he or she fulfils one of the following conditions: (a) has stayed legally in Belgium for five continuous years; (b) complies with the legal conditions, other than those of residence, for the acquisition of Belgian nationality; (c) is a woman who was Belgian by birth but has lost that nationality by marriage or following the acquisition by her husband of another nationality; (d) is the spouse or foreign child of an alien authorized to settle in Belgium and will live with the latter. If permission to settle is granted, the alien will receive an identity card which implies that his or her record has been transferred from the register of aliens to the population register of the commune in which he or she resides.

Absence from Belgium and the right to return is granted to aliens holding a valid certificate of enrolment or an identity card indicating settlement. If the alien intends to leave Belgium for more than three months, he or she must report his or her departure to the administration of the commune in which he or she resides and indicate his or her intention to return. If the intended absence is longer than a year, the alien must also prove that the centre of his or her interests remains Belgium, in which case his or her record remains in the register during his or her absence. Upon his or her return, he or she must report to the commune of residence and must be in possession of a valid certificate of enrolment or identity card to ensure that his or her records are not deregistered.

If the alien leaves without the intention of returning, he or she is required to make a declaration to that effect to the administration of his or her commune of residence and to return his or her certificate of enrolment or identity card. The records will then be removed from the register of aliens (if he or she had a certificate of enrolment) or from the population register (if he or she had settled and had an identity card). Given that foreigners departing may be reluctant to give up the possibility of returning to Belgium, it is common for them to leave without making the necessary declaration to the commune of residence. To detect such departures, the local police carry out inquiries and, if these lead to the conclusion that the alien has left for good, his or her records will be deregistered three months after the discovery of his or her departure. Such deregistration has to be approved by the local mayor and alderman. All deregistrations, whether by declaration or through administrative adjustments, are reported to the National Institute of Statistics.

This example illustrates how the processes of alien control and data collection are closely intertwined. Thus, full understanding of the scope and meaning of the data cannot be attained without understanding the administrative procedures through which alien control is carried out. Unfortunately, only rarely are both described in sufficient detail so as to make the necessary connections between them.

4. Groups subject to special treatment regarding registration

As in the case of censuses, there are certain groups of persons who, by law, are given special treatment regarding their inscription in the population registers or their deregistration from them. In Belgium, for instance, Belgians whose names are kept in the register even if they actually reside abroad include: (a) Belgian members of the armed forces; (b) members of the diplomatic corps, administrative and technical staff in Belgian diplomatic missions, Belgian officials and employees in the consular service and their families; and (c) Belgian workers in cooperative services abroad. The latter, however, may request to be removed from the population register (Poulain, 1987). In the Netherlands, certain groups of Dutch nationals living abroad are not deregistered from the municipal registers, including: (a) Dutch nationals entitled to diplomatic immunity and those in the diplomatic service; (b) Dutch nationals in the armed forces stationed abroad and their families; (c) Dutch civilian staff employed by the armed forces abroad and their families (van den Erf et al.).

In addition, there are certain categories of foreigners who are not inscribed in the population registers of some countries even when they live there for lengthy periods. In Belgium, those categories include: (a) members of the foreign diplomatic corps and their families; (b) officials of international organizations established in Belgium and members of their families if they hold a special permit marked "exempted from registration in the register of aliens"; (c) foreign consular officials and their families; and (d) foreign military personnel in bases in Belgium (Poulain, 1987; Poulain et al.). In the Netherlands, aliens exempt from registration include: (a) aliens entitled to diplomatic immunity and aliens in the diplomatic service together with their families; (b) alien armed forces stationed in the Netherlands; and (c) alien civilian staff employed by the foreign armed forces

Data collection systems concerning all international migrants

stationed in the Netherlands and their families (van den Erf et al.). In Denmark, NATO personnel and other foreign armed forces stationed in the country need not register (Lange, n.d.). Similar exceptions with respect to both deregistration of citizens or registration of aliens are likely to exist in other countries, but are not well documented in general.

Asylum-seekers constitute another group of foreigners often treated in exceptional ways in terms of registration. In Austria, for instance, asylum-seekers are excluded from local registers if they are housed by territorial authorities (Gisser, 1992). In some of the German Länder, asylum-seekers and even refugees are excluded from population registers if they live in provisional accommodation or camps for less than two months (Bretz, n.d.). In Switzerland, asylum-seekers are registered only after they have spent a year in the country (Gisser, 1992).

A review of state practices regarding the inclusion of asylum-seekers in international migration statistics among EU and EFTA countries concluded that in almost all cases some asylum-seekers were included in international migration statistics and generally could not be identified separately from other international migrants (Eurostat, 1994a and 1994b). Among countries whose international migration statistics were derived from population registers, Belgium, Denmark, Germany, Luxembourg, the Netherlands, Norway and Sweden reported that some asylum-seekers were included in the international migration statistics because there were grounds for including them in the population registers while their cases were being adjudicated. However, the exact grounds on which registration takes place were usually not explained. In Belgium, for instance, it was reported that only asylum-seekers whose cases were being processed through the regular adjudication procedure and who were registered in the local register of aliens were included in international migration statistics. In Denmark, only persons admitted as immigrants on grounds other than the search for asylum and who subsequently filed an application for asylum were included in the population register and therefore in international migration statistics. In Germany, Luxembourg and the Netherlands, it was recognized that some asylum-seekers may be included in the population registers, though it was not explained why they were included. In Norway, the usual practice before January 1994 was to inscribe asylum-seekers in the population registers without identifying them as asylum-seekers; only those whose cases were rejected within a week or two after arrival were excluded. Since January 1994, persons who apply for asylum in Norway have been included in the central population register with a marker indicating that they are not residents of Norway. In Sweden, only those asylum-seekers who have obtained a residence permit are included in the population registration system and therefore in international migration statistics. It is not clear, however, whether asylum-seekers whose cases have not yet been adjudicated may obtain residence permits.

In most countries, asylum-seekers whose cases have been adjudicated and who are granted either refugee status according to the 1951 Convention or the permission to stay on humanitarian grounds receive residence permits that

International migration statistics

allow them to register in the population registers of the municipality in which they plan to reside. Although there may be some delay between a favourable adjudication and the registration of the person in the population register, such registration usually takes place at some point. Once this has occurred, the person can no longer be considered an asylum-seeker, since his or her status has been established as either a Convention refugee or a refugee admitted on humanitarian grounds. In particular, Iceland, Italy and Spain report that only asylum-seekers formally granted permission to stay as refugees or for humanitarian reasons are included in the population register. Otherwise, as long as people remain asylum-seekers, they are not included in the international migration statistics generated by population registers.

Clearly the treatment of persons seeking asylum while they are waiting for a decision on their cases is problematic both from the regulatory and from the statistical perspective. The fact that no clear rules seem to exist regarding when and under what conditions their inscription in the population registers can take place is conducive to confusion and misinterpretation of the international migration statistics derived from those registers. It is important, therefore, that such rules be spelled out clearly and that efforts be made to identify asylum-seekers and refugees explicitly in the population registers.

5. Data on international migrants gathered by population registers

The forms used to inscribe persons or family groups in the population registers or to deregister them record a limited amount of information regarding the persons involved. Typically, a single form has to be filled in for each family group, since it is common for all persons in a family to move together. A separate line or column is allocated to record the characteristics of each member of the family, and only the most basic data items are recorded. Among the European countries using population registers to produce data on international migration, the characteristics most commonly recorded are sex, date of birth, place of birth, citizenship or legal nationality, and marital status (see table 3.8). In addition, the place of previous residence and the place of intended residence are usually recorded for the family as a whole, often in the form of a previous address in another country and a new address in the country of registration for incoming migrants, and as a future address abroad and a previous address in the country of departure in the case of departing migrants.

In a few countries, the date of migration is recorded explicitly (that is, it is not assumed to coincide with the date of registration or deregistration), while in others, specific questions are posed regarding accompanying family members, such as their number or their relationship to the head of the family. Such questions are not posed on an individual basis, but are directed to the head of the family. Some countries also include a question on religion, usually addressed to the family as a whole. Questions on occupation and economic activity are

Table 3.8. Data on international migrants gathered by countries maintaining population registers

Type of information	Austria	Belgium	Denmark	Finland	Germany	Iceland	Italy	Liechtenstein	Luxembourg	Netherlands	Norway	Spain	Sweden
Sex	✓	✓	✓	✓	✓	✓	✓	—	✓	✓	✓	✓	✓
Date of birth	✓	✓	✓	✓	✓	✓	✓	✓	✓	✓	✓	✓	✓
Place of birth	✓	✓	✓	✓	—	✓	✓	✓	✓	✓	✓	✓	✓
Citizenship	✓	✓	✓	✓	✓	✓	✓	✓	✓	✓	✓	✓	✓
Marital status	✓	✓	—	✓	✓	✓	—	✓	—	✓	—	—	—
Religion	—	—	—	✓	—	—	—	—	—	—	—	—	✓
Previous residence	✓	✓	✓	✓	✓	✓	✓	✓	✓	✓	✓	✓	✓
Intended residence	✓	✓	✓	✓	✓	✓	—	✓	—	—	✓	—	✓
Date of migration	—	—	✓	✓	—	✓	—	✓	—	—	—	—	—
Date of entry into country	—	—	—	—	—	—	—	—	✓	—	—	—	—
Expected length of stay	—	—	—	—	✓	—	—	✓	✓	✓	—	—	—
Occupation or economic activity	—	✓	—	✓	—	—	—	—	✓	—	✓	✓	✓
Accompanying family members	—	—	—	✓	—	—	—	—	✓	✓	✓	—	✓

Source: Kuijsten (n.d.), Poulain (1992) and Poulain et al. (n.d.).

used by a number of countries and are also usually directed only to the head of the family. They vary considerably in content. Some record the profession, others the occupation, and yet others simply whether the person involved has an economic activity. Austria and Spain record "academic degree", an item that can indicate both educational attainment and profession. Clearly, the types of questions posed regarding economic activity and occupation could be improved in terms of both scope and comparability between countries.

Some countries pose, in addition, a number of questions regarding the international migration process. Date of entry into the country of registration and intended length of stay are examples of questions asked by Luxembourg and the Netherlands. Luxembourg also records the type of documents presented to certify that a migrant has permission to reside in the country (passport, visa, residence permit, etc.) and the necessary means of subsistence. The Netherlands uses a number of questions to ascertain whether an incoming migrant has been previously present in the country. Thus, for those who have immigrated after 1940, the date of inscription in the population register is recorded, together with the name of the Dutch municipality in which the person was last inscribed in the population register, and the date of removal of the person's card from that register. If the person has earlier been an emigrant from the Netherlands, the country of destination is recorded, together with the country of last residence.

With respect to key variables for the characterization of international migrants, it is worth noting that there are still some countries that do not gather the relevant information. For example, Liechtenstein fails to record the sex of international migrants, and Germany does not gather information on place of birth.

There is, therefore, considerable room for concerted action to improve the comparability of the data gathered on international migrants and, perhaps more importantly, to ensure that certain key characteristics of international migrants are recorded systematically by population registration systems in all countries with these systems.

6. Tabulations of data from population registers

Although some countries having population registers publish international migration statistics in some detail, they do not exploit well the potential richness of the data gathered through population registration systems. Since population registers maintain up-to-date demographic and socio-economic information on every person resident in a country, many types of tabulations useful in the study of the characteristics of international migrants and their impact on the host society are possible. Yet in practice, even some of the most basic two-way tables are not published. This is the case, for example, regarding tables giving the distributions of international migrants by country of origin and sex, and by country of origin and age group. Many countries do not include these tabulations in the statistical yearbooks they publish.

Data collection systems concerning all international migrants

Furthermore, in some countries, the data on international migration yielded by population registers are far from comprehensive. In Austria, for instance, the population register does not yield data on international migration for the country as a whole. In Liechtenstein, the population register produces no information on the international migration of citizens, whereas in Switzerland only the migration of Swiss citizens is monitored through the general population registers, with available tabulations showing Swiss citizens immigrating and emigrating by canton of origin and destination, respectively; Swiss immigrants and emigrants by marital status; net migration of Swiss citizens by sex; and net migration of Swiss citizens by age group (Switzerland, Office Fédéral de la Statistique, 1994a).

In Italy, the general population registers produce information only on immigrating foreigners. Three tabulations are published annually, all showing the number of foreign international migrants registering in the year by region of registration and the following variables: age; country of previous residence; and country of citizenship. No information on the distribution by sex of foreign international migrants is published, nor are data available on any socio-economic characteristics.

In Spain, the population registers produce data only on immigrants, covering both citizens and foreigners. Two sets of tabulations are published annually. In the first, immigrants are classified by province of destination and citizenship (Spanish versus foreign) and then by the following characteristics: sex and place of birth (Spain and abroad); age group; educational attainment; and region of birth (Spain, European Union, other Europe, Africa, the Americas, Asia and Oceania). In the second set, immigrants are classified by country of previous residence and citizenship (Spanish versus foreign) and then also by each of the following variables: province of destination; size and type of municipality of destination; sex; age group; educational attainment; and region of birth. Additional tabulations show the total number of immigrants by country of previous residence and country of citizenship; by province of destination and region of citizenship; and by province of destination and region of previous residence (Spain, Institut Nacional de Estadística, 1994).

A 1989 review of the types of tabulations published by countries deriving statistics on both immigrants and emigrants from population registers indicates that they vary considerably from country to country, and that most countries produce only a small number of tabulations (Kuijsten, n.d.). Belgium, for instance, publishes only four relevant tabulations each year from its population register, which indicate the numbers of immigrants and emigrants by citizenship and sex. In two of the four tabulations, only the crude categories "citizen" and "foreigner" are used to indicate citizenship. In a third tabulation, country of citizenship is presented in some detail, except that most developing countries are grouped together by geographic region. The fourth tabulation uses country of origin and country of destination to classify immigrants and emigrants, respectively. No tabulation presents information on international migrants by age.

International migration statistics

Denmark produces tabulations of immigrants and emigrants by sex and age; sex, age and marital status; and sex, age and destination within Denmark or region of origin, respectively. Two other tabulations indicate the citizenship of international migrants. One presents immigrants and emigrants by citizenship (citizens vs. foreigners), sex, age and country of origin or destination. The other presents immigrants and emigrants by sex and country of citizenship.

Luxembourg publishes only two tabulations on international migrants and does not distinguish them by citizenship. One tabulation shows immigrants and emigrants by sex and age, and the other shows immigrants and emigrants by sex and country of origin or destination, respectively.

The Federal Republic of Germany publishes a fairly comprehensive set of tabulations on immigrants and emigrants. In a set of tabulations where immigrants and emigrants are always classified as German or foreigner, other variables used include: age and marital status; country of origin or destination; region of residence in Germany and country of origin or destination; sex, age and country of origin or destination; sex, economic activity and country of origin or destination; sex, economic activity, region of residence in Germany, and country of origin or destination. A second set where immigrants and emigrants are always classified according to country of legal nationality, includes as additional variables: sex and age; economic activity; and type of residence permit.

The Netherlands also produces a number of useful tabulations on immigrants and emigrants based on the population registers. As in Germany, in tabulations where immigrants and emigrants are classified according to whether they are Dutch citizens or aliens, the additional variables used are: country of origin or destination; sex and country of birth; year of (previous) entry to the Netherlands and country of destination in the case of emigrants; year of previous departure from the Netherlands and country of origin for immigrants; region of residence in the Netherlands; and sex, age and marital status. In other tabulations where immigrants and emigrants are always classified by country of citizenship and sex, the additional variables used are: age; age, marital status and family status; and country of origin or destination. In addition, immigrants and emigrants are tabulated by sex, region of residence in the Netherlands and family status.

In all of the above cases, the tabulations refer to the numbers of immigrants or emigrants registered over the course of a year and therefore represent international migration flows. In fact, most countries with population registers fail to derive from them data on the stock of international migrants. The Nordic countries are among the few that obtain both flow and stock data from their population registers. Thus, Denmark, Finland, Iceland, Norway and Sweden all publish annual data on the population classified by place of birth or citizenship, using therefore the same criteria as in their censuses to identify international migrants. The tabulations most commonly available present the data classified by sex. Distributions of the population classified simultaneously by age group, sex and place of birth or citizenship are unfortunately not as common.

Furthermore, no country produces a tabulation of the population cross-classified by both place of birth and citizenship, and no attempt is made to identify international migrants using other criteria (such as persons who have ever migrated internationally or who have migrated during a certain period, for instance).

In addition to producing tabulations that allow some measurement of the stock of international migrants, all Nordic countries publish tabulations on the numbers of immigrants and emigrants moving during a given year. Thus, Finland presents the number of immigrants and emigrants by age group (Finland, Tilastokeskus, 1994); Iceland tabulates the number of immigrants and emigrants by country of citizenship and country of birth (indicating if the two coincide), and by country of previous residence and country of citizenship (Iceland, Statistical Bureau, 1994); and Norway shows the number of immigrants by sex and country of previous residence, and the number of emigrants by sex and country of destination (Norway, Statistisk Sentralyrå, 1994). Sweden publishes annual data on the flow of immigrants and emigrants by age and sex; age, sex and citizenship; and age, sex and marital status. Also published are tabulations on immigrants by age, sex and country of previous residence; emigrants by age, sex and country of destination; immigrants by country of citizenship and country of previous residence; and emigrants by country of citizenship and country of destination (Sweden, Statistiska Centralbyrån, 1995).

Clearly, ensuring a more thorough exploitation of the data gathered by population registers would go a long way towards improving the characterization of international migration in Europe. Working towards the preparation of comparable tabulations by the countries having population registers would be a desirable first step towards improving the usefulness of the data. As section 3.B.5 above suggests, most countries do gather similar information on international migrants. There is thus considerable potential for improving international comparability by ensuring that, at the processing stage, similar tabulations of the data are produced.

7. Potential for deriving international migration statistics from population registers in countries of Central and Eastern Europe

Population registration is not restricted to the market economies of Europe. Several of the European countries with economies in transition have also had population registers for a long time. However, during the communist era, such registers were used as an instrument of internal control rather than as administrative or statistical tools. During that time, restrictions on travel and on emigration virtually closed Central and Eastern European countries to international migration by preventing the exit of citizens and restricting the admission of foreigners. Population registration was also often a means of reducing and controlling internal mobility through the issuance of "internal passports" used to regulate the movement of people from one place to another. With the process of liberalization currently under way in Central and Eastern European countries, the regulatory mechanisms to control international mobility are changing. Thus it is increasingly evident that adjustments have to be made in the statistical systems if international migration is to be measured adequately. The use of population registers for this purpose ought to be given serious consideration. To judge the potential usefulness of existing population registers, a brief review of several of those in existence is presented next, in alphabetical order.

Bulgaria maintains a centralized population register that covers only Bulgarian citizens. The register, which is computerized at both the regional and national levels, is used to issue identity cards to citizens. Persons are inscribed in their place of residence but are allowed to have both a permanent place of residence and a temporary one. Because of restrictions concerning the establishment of residence in certain towns or cities, persons who effectively live in those cities declare them as the site of a temporary residence. Changes of permanent residence are to be reported to the local authorities and are still subject to control. It is not clear whether citizens who emigrate are required to report their departure to the authorities in charge of registration.

The former Czechoslovakia also had a central computerized population register that is now divided between the Czech Republic and Slovakia. As in Bulgaria, citizens of each country can declare both a permanent and a temporary place of residence, and changes of permanent residence must be reported to local authorities and are entered in the register. Only citizens are inscribed in the register. Apparently, no provision exists as yet for the deregistration of emigrating citizens.

The situation in Hungary is similar. The population register covers all persons who officially reside in Hungary. Individuals are registered in the place of their permanent residence but have the option of declaring also a temporary residence. All persons changing their permanent residence must report such change to the municipality of arrival. Many changes of residence are said to go unrecorded, however, because there are advantages associated with maintaining a residence in certain places.

In Poland, the population registers operating at the level of communes were centralized and computerized in the early 1980s. They cover all persons residing permanently in Poland, including foreigners. Persons registered can declare a permanent and a temporary residence. Changes in the permanent place of residence must be reported to the communes of origin and destination. Although persons leaving the country for more than two months should inform the authorities so that a change is recorded in the register, few do so. International migration statistics for Poland are not normally derived from population registration data.

In Romania, population registers still operate at the local level only, though they are in the process of being computerized and centralized. The local police are in charge of maintaining the registers. Changes of permanent residence must be reported. A temporary residence can also be declared. It is not clear whether the register includes only Romanian citizens or not. The population register has not been a source of international migration statistics.

In the Russian Federation and in all the successor States of the former Soviet Union, each individual is registered in one and only one residence, a fact that is certified by a residence permit delivered by the Ministry of the Interior. The permit, called *propiska*, is used as an identity card. All changes of residence are subject to prior authorization and involve deregistration from the place of origin and registration in that of destination. However, the number of registrations at destination often surpasses the number of deregistrations in places of origin by as much as 50 per cent. The system does not seem to have been used to measure international migration in the former Soviet Union, and it is not clear whether movements between the successor States of the former Soviet Union and the Russian Federation are still being recorded using such a system.

In Slovenia, a central computerized population register has been in operation since 1971. It is maintained by the Statistical Office of Slovenia. As in other countries with economies in transition, Slovenian legislation recognizes the right of individuals to have a permanent and a temporary place of residence. Changes of permanent residence must be reported but no mention is made of changes of residence brought about by international migration.

From these brief descriptions of the operation of population registers in countries with economies in transition, it is clear that they have the potential for generating international migration statistics, provided citizens become convinced that there are no penalties for leaving the country. Extending the coverage of population registers to include foreign persons residing legally in the countries involved would also permit the measurement of the full spectrum of international migration movements.

8. Types of international migrants identified by population registers

In terms of the types of international migrants characterized in Chapter 2, population registers generally produce information on the international migration of citizens and, whenever they also cover resident foreigners, they are capable of yielding data on a number of the migrant categories defined earlier. Population registers are often the best means of obtaining statistics on the emigration and return migration of citizens. Furthermore, because a person's citizenship usually determines the types of procedures that must be followed to be inscribed in the register or deregistered, citizenship is an important classifying factor. Consequently, it is common for data derived from population registers to be presented separately for citizens and foreigners, and thus to permit the direct identification of emigrant citizens and return migrants as defined in Chapter 2.

International migration statistics

With respect to foreigners, population registers have the potential for identifying several categories of international migrants although currently they do not fulfil such potential because they either fail to publish the appropriate tabulations or do not record certain information about international migration. The categories that can potentially be identified include: returning ethnics; migrants with the right to free movement; settlers; migrant workers; refugees; asylum-seekers; and the dependants of each of those categories. Depending on the detail in the register on the type of residence permit that a foreigner holds, the identification of other categories may also be possible. Note, however, that the identification of even the limited set of categories listed requires that the register record some information on the reason for admission. Perhaps the only exception is migrants subject to the right of free movement, which can usually be identified in terms of citizenship alone. Returning ethnics may also be identifiable on the basis of citizenship, provided they do not become naturalized citizens before they are inscribed in the register.

A concerted effort is needed on the part of those deriving statistics from population registers to obtain information on each of the migrant categories listed above and to produce relevant cross-tabulations regarding the demographic and socio-economic characteristics of the international migrants belonging to each category. Given the relevance that those categories have for policy discourse and for the evaluation of policy outcomes, such efforts should be accorded high priority.

9. Recommendations for the improvement of international migration statistics derived from population registers

- An effort should be made to ensure that countries maintaining population registers record in a similar fashion a core set of information on all persons inscribed in the register or deregistered because of a change of residence. Such a core set should include: date of birth; sex; date of registration or deregistration; date of change of residence; place of birth; citizenship; place of previous residence; place of intended residence; marital status; highest educational level completed (primary, secondary or tertiary); current occupation; number of accompanying family members; relationship to head of family; and type of document or documents presented to claim residence rights (passport, visa, residence permit, work permit etc.). In addition, for foreigners, the register should record: allowed duration of stay; reason for granting the person permission to stay; and whether the person has or does not have permission to exercise an economic activity. This information should be recorded for each foreign person in a family group.
- Concerted action should be taken among interested countries (particularly those belonging to the European Union) to ensure that a set of core tabulations based on the information maintained in population

Data collection systems concerning all international migrants

registers is prepared annually. The set might include:
(a) Immigrating citizens by age group, sex and country of previous residence;
(b) Emigrating citizens by age group, sex and country of intended residence;
(c) Immigrating foreigners by age group, sex and country of previous residence;
(d) Emigrating foreigners by age group, sex and country of intended residence;
(e) Immigrating foreigners by age group, sex and country citizenship;
(f) Emigrating foreigners by age group, sex and country citizenship;
(g) Immigrating foreigners allowed to work by age group, sex, country of citizenship and occupation;
(h) Immigrating foreigners allowed to work by age group, sex, country of citizenship and educational attainment;
(i) Immigrating foreigners allowed to work by age group, sex, country of citizenship and type of residence permit;
(j) Foreigners admitted as dependants by age group, sex, country of citizenship and relationship to the primo migrant;
(k) Immigrating foreigners by age group, sex, country of citizenship and reason for admission (i.e. type of residence permit);
(l) Emigrating foreigners who were allowed to work while in the country by age group, sex, country of citizenship and occupation;
(m) Emigrating foreigners who were admitted as dependants by age group, sex, country of citizenship and relationship to the primo migrant;
(n) Stock of foreigners present in the country at a given time by age group, sex, country of citizenship and type of residence permit;
(o) Stock of foreigners present in the country at a given time and allowed to work by age group, sex, country of citizenship and occupation;
(p) Stock of foreigners present in the country at a given time and admitted for family reunification by age group, sex, country of citizenship and relationship to the primo migrant; and
(q) Stock of citizens who returned from abroad over the five years preceding a set date by age group, sex, country of previous residence and occupation.

- All published tabulations on international migrants based on population registers should present the data classified by sex.
- To facilitate the wide dissemination of complex tabulations, the possibility of using electronic media such as compact discs, diskettes, or electronic mail networks should be explored.

- In countries that maintain population registers which exclude resident foreigners, an effort should be made to expand the coverage to include the latter.
- Published tabulations derived from population registers should indicate succinct definitions of all international migrant categories used. In cases where the conditions for inscription or deletion of a person from the register depend on the citizenship of the person, such distinctions should be spelled out.
- The administrative unit in charge of maintaining a population register should prepare and update as necessary a guide to the operation of the register that, among other things, spells out the conditions under which citizens and foreigners are inscribed in the register or deregistered.
- Measures should be taken to assess periodically the degree of coverage and the quality of data yielded by population registers. Information about the performance of a population register with regard to the coverage of international migration flows and stocks should be disseminated through specialized publications.
- The authorities in charge of maintaining a population register should ensure that sufficient information to identify the major types of international migrants is included in the register and that tabulations are made on the numbers of persons in each migrant category. Of particular interest is the identification of refugees, asylum-seekers, foreigners granted permission to exercise an economic activity, and foreigners admitted for family reunification or as accompanying dependants of other migrants.

C. REGISTERS OF FOREIGNERS

A register of foreigners can be characterized as a variant of a population register that includes only persons who are not citizens of the country in which they reside. Like a population register, a register of foreigners is modified continuously as it records current information on changes in marital status, citizenship and address, as well as deaths of and births to foreign residents. More importantly, a register of foreigners generally records changes in the migration or residence status of aliens.

Austria, Germany, Japan, Liechtenstein, Spain and Switzerland are among the countries that have or are in the process of setting up registers of foreigners. In Austria, the creation of a national register of aliens (*Fremdendatei*) was announced in 1992. The national register was to centralize data obtained from local registers, which had been providing information to the authorities responsible for dealing with matters concerning aliens (Gisser, 1992). Until 1992 most of the local registers of aliens were kept manually but their computerization is planned. Aside from recording the basic demographic characteristics of foreigners, the national register would record information on date of arrival in Austria, expected duration of stay, purpose of travel, source of livelihood, occupation and employer.

In Germany, the Central Register of Foreigners is maintained by the Federal Office of Administration (*Bundesverwaltungsamt*) mostly for administrative purposes, which include keeping track of the residence status of foreigners living in Germany. Local offices for foreigners (*Ausländerbehörden*) are in charge of maintaining a form for each resident foreigner indicating date of birth; sex; marital status; citizenship; date of first arrival; date of departure/date of new arrival (when a foreigner returns, the date of departure is deleted and replaced by the date of most recent arrival); economic activity; whether the foreigner is an asylum-seeker; whether the foreigner is a quota refugee; and the type of residence permit that the foreigner holds (Bretz, n.d.). In 1991 a law regulating the operation of the Central Register of Foreigners was being considered. It provided for the recording and maintenance of all departure and arrival dates for each foreigner so that the actual length of stay could be ascertained.

In Japan, the Alien Registration Law of 1952 establishes that any alien residing in Japan must apply for registration to the mayor or headman of the city, town or village in which the foreigner plans to reside, submitting a request for registration within 90 days of having entered Japan for the purpose of establishing residence (Japan, Immigration Bureau, n.d.). Foreign children born in Japan who stay for more than 60 days also have to be registered. The mayor of a city or the headman of a town or village keeps an alien registration card for each foreigner and issues a registration certificate which the foreigner must carry at all times. The information recorded on the alien registration card includes date of registration, date of birth, sex, citizenship, domicile in the country of citizenship, place of birth, occupation, port of entry, residence status, period of stay as provided for in the Immigration Control Act, address in Japan, name of employer, and place of employment (address). Diplomatic and consular personnel as well as foreign armed forces stationed in Japan are not included in the register.

Registered foreigners who change their place of residence within Japan must report that change to the local authorities maintaining the register of aliens so that the change can be recorded. Foreigners must also report any change of name, citizenship, occupation, employer or place of employment. In addition, every five years, the registration certificate must be renewed. In case of death, the registration certificate must be returned to the registration authorities. When resident foreigners leave Japan, their registration certificates are retained by immigration authorities at the port of departure unless the foreigners are in possession of re-entry permits. The mayors or headmen in charge of alien registration must report any registration card alterations, the issuance of new registration certificates, and their return or withdrawal to the Ministry of Justice, which compiles statistics on resident aliens at the national level.

In Spain, the General Directorate of the Police, which operates under the Ministry of the Interior, is in charge of controlling the entry, departure and stay

International migration statistics

of foreigners in the country. The Directorate issues residence permits according to the guidelines established by the Organic Law 7/1985 of 1 July, the Royal Decree 1119/1986 of 26 May relative to the admission of the generality of foreigners, and the Royal Decree 1099/1986 of 26 May relative to the admission of citizens of other member States of the European Union. On the basis of the different types of residence permits granted to foreigners, the General Directorate of the Police has been maintaining since 1985 a Central Register of Resident Foreigners which is continuously updated (Escribano-Morales, n.d.). The data recorded for each foreign head of household include: date of birth, place of birth, sex, marital status, occupation, address, type of economic activity, employer, number and type of dependants accompanying the foreigner (spouse, children, parents and other relatives), and type of permit (Izquierdo-Escribano, n.d.).

In Switzerland, the central register of foreigners was established in 1972 by an ordinance of the Federal Government. The Federal Office for Alien Affairs is in charge of maintaining the register which serves three main purposes: as a tool to control the stay and establishment of foreigners in Switzerland; to maintain up-to-date statistics on foreigners residing in the country; and to contribute to the efficiency of the aliens police (Gisser, 1992). The central register of foreigners is centralized and computerized, and since 1988 there has been full automation of all changes and additions. The communes report arrivals and departures of foreigners; changes and amendments of personal data (particularly name, date of birth, sex, marital status and citizenship); deaths; adoptions; and children born in Switzerland of foreign parents. The cantons report the issuance of first permits; renewals of seasonal, annual or border permits; conversions of seasonal to annual permits; changes of occupation or employers within a canton; newly issued establishment permits; prolongation of permits; and ordinary naturalizations. Federal agencies report facilitated naturalizations and repatriations; applications for and recognitions of asylum; orders of internment; and the old-age insurance number for each foreigner. For registration purposes, the place of residence of a foreigner is the commune in which the permit of stay or establishment was issued. Generally, all changes relative to a foreigner remain stored in the central register. Even information on foreigners who once lived in Switzerland but have left the country is maintained in the register. The aliens police and the employment authorities of the Confederation and the cantons have access to the information kept in the central register.

There is also in Switzerland an automated register of asylum-seekers, known as AUPER, which is maintained by the Federal Office for Refugees (Gisser, 1992). The AUPER covers all persons who have applied for asylum in Switzerland, including those who have been recognized as refugees according to the 1951 Convention Relating to the Status of the Refugees. Personal data on the applicants, collected at the federal reception posts or by the cantons, are entered in a file that is linked with the relevant information on the asylum procedure. The AUPER database is used for administrative decisions, case follow-up and documentation, as well as for the production of statistics on asylum-seekers and refugees. Data on recognized refugees and asylum-seekers

Data collection systems concerning all international migrants

holding permits of stay are provided to the authorities in charge of maintaining the central register of foreigners, but the link between the two had not been computerized as of 1992. It was expected that sometime in 1993 or 1994, the central register of foreigners and the register of asylum-seekers would be merged to create a single register.

Liechtenstein maintains a central register of foreigners that operates in a way similar to that of Switzerland since, according to an agreement with that country, the aliens police (Fremdenpolizei) of Liechtenstein generally follows the relevant Swiss regulations. There is cooperation between the police authorities of the two countries and data are exchanged between their respective central registers of foreigners. The data on foreigners recorded in Liechtenstein's register include: previous address; current address; date of entry into Liechtenstein; date of birth; marital status; citizenship; occupation; employer; reason for stay if not working; type of residence permit; and number of persons in the foreigner's household. The data recorded are gathered by the aliens police from the foreigner himself or herself, from the authorities of the commune of residence, and from the foreigner's employer. The central register of foreigners is used both for administrative purposes and to obtain up-to-date statistics on resident foreigners.

1. Characterization of international migrants according to registers of foreigners

Just as in the case of general population registers, the conditions under which foreigners are inscribed in registers of foreigners or deregistered from them provide a characterization of persons who are considered to be international migrants. Furthermore, given their administrative nature, registers of foreigners usually accord priority to the recording of migration status and thus have the potential to provide a more detailed characterization of international migrants than other statistical systems. The following cases illustrate the extent to which such potential is realized in practice.

In Germany, foreigners who are not citizens of member States of the European Union may not enter the country with a view to remaining in it for more than three months unless they are in possession of a residence permit. Decisions on the issuance of residence permits are based on the interests of Germany. According to the administrative provisions of the Law on Foreigners, a residence permit is granted initially for a limited period of one year, after which two extensions, each for a two-year period, are possible. After five years of uninterrupted lawful residence, a foreigner may obtain a residence permit of unlimited duration (Plender, 1987). Holders of all such permits nevertheless require work permits to exercise an economic activity within Germany. Work permits, in turn, are of two types: *general work permits* which are valid for at most two years and only for the district in which they are issued; and *special work permits* which do not confine the migrant to working in a specific establishment, occupation or location (Mammey et al., 1989). Foreigners holding special work permits can, after eight years of lawful residence in Germany, obtain a permanent residence permit provided they can prove they have adequate housing and a sufficient knowledge of German. A permanent residence permit is not subject to any temporal or spatial limitations and cannot be withdrawn solely because a foreigner becomes unemployed or receives public assistance.

Citizens of member States of the European Union do not require a residence permit to enter Germany and search for work (Esser and Korte, 1985). However, they must apply for a residence permit if they intend to reside in Germany. Under minimal conditions, they are entitled to receive an unrestricted residence permit for themselves and for accompanying family members (spouses, children under the age of 21 years and certain other dependants).

The issuance of residence permits for family members of other resident foreigners is left to the discretion of the authorities in charge of foreigners affairs. Generally, foreigners who have resided in Germany for at least three years (one year in the case of foreigners coming from countries with which Germany had labour recruitment agreements)[2] and having adequate housing and sufficient means to support their immediate relatives are allowed to be joined by their spouses and minor children. The upper age limit determining minority has changed over the years, passing from age 21 years to age 18 years in 1975 and then to age 16 years in 1981 (Mammey et al., 1989). In addition, the admission of spouses of second-generation foreigners (i.e. persons whose parents are foreigners) who have lived in Germany for less than eight years, who are themselves under 18 years of age and whose marriage has not yet lasted a year is generally not allowed.

Foreigners married to German nationals are normally granted a first residence permit valid for three years and then one of unlimited duration (Mammey et al., 1989). Foreigners wishing to study in Germany must obtain admission to a German university prior to entering Germany and must also secure a residence permit while still abroad. Foreign students are not entitled to be accompanied by their spouses or minor children (Mammey et al., 1989).

Persons granted refugee status, either because they enter the country as quota refugees or because they are recognized as refugees as a result of an asylum adjudication procedure, are entitled to receive a residence permit with no time limitation and a work permit, irrespective of the labour market situation of the country (Mammey et al., 1989).

The data contained in the central register of foreigners, by reflecting the type of residence permit that each foreigner has at a given point in time, have the potential of allowing an analysis of the composition of the foreign stock by type of permit. However, very few tabulations based on those data are published and disseminated widely. The information derived from the central register of foreigners published in the *Statistisches Jahrbuch* varies from year to year, but normally includes only the total number of resident foreigners present at the end

Data collection systems concerning all international migrants

of the year classified by country of citizenship, combined with each of the following: age group, sex, duration of residence, and province of residence (Germany, 1982 and 1994). Tabulations of annual inflows and outflows of foreigners from the central register of foreigners do not, however, seem to be available, thus precluding an assessment of the grounds on which new foreign migrants are granted residence permits and of the selectivity of emigration in relation to the type of residence permit. Thus the data contained in the central register of foreigners remain underexploited.

In Japan, the entry, residence and departure of foreigners are controlled through different residence categories established by the Immigration Control and Refugee Recognition Act of 1951, which was amended in December 1989. As a result of that amendment, the number of residence categories was expanded from 18 to 28. The different categories are divided into four groups according to the rights accorded to each with respect to the exercise of an economic activity or potential length of residence (Japan Immigration Association, 1994). The first group includes the categories of foreigners who are allowed to work in Japan but whose salary is generally paid by a foreign source. They include professors, artists, persons engaged in religious activities, and journalists. The second group, which includes categories of foreigners allowed to work in Japan for a limited period only, comprises: investors and business managers; persons engaged in legal or accounting services; persons providing medical services; researchers; instructors; engineers; specialists in the humanities or in international services; intracompany transferees; entertainers; and skilled workers. Categories of foreigners admitted for limited periods who are not allowed to work in Japan include: temporary visitors and tourists; college students; pre-college students; trainees; persons engaged in cultural activities; and dependants of other foreigners who are themselves admitted for a limited period. Lastly, categories of foreigners granted long-term residence rights and allowed to work include: spouses and children of Japanese nationals; persons granted a special right to permanent residence as a result of the provisions of the Special Law on the Immigration of, *inter alia*, Persons Who Have Lost Japanese Nationality on the Basis of the Treaty of Peace with Japan, most of whom are Korean; persons granted permanent residence on the basis of an agreement with the Republic of Korea; spouses and children of permanent residents; and persons granted long-term residence, usually because they are the descendants of ethnic Japanese.

The Ministry of Justice derives statistics from the register of foreigners on the number of foreign residents by citizenship and type of residence permit, thus reflecting each of the categories enumerated above (Japan Immigration Association, 1994). The data are published by the Ministry itself. The number of tabulations derived from the register of foreigners remains small, however, and information on the number of resident foreigners by citizenship, sex and age group, for instance, is not readily available. In addition, only information on the stock of foreign residents is obtained from the register. Information on annual inflows or outflows, which the register can generate, is not available. As in other countries, therefore, much remains to be done in exploiting the register's richness.

In Spain, foreigners can be granted different types of residence permits according to their status (Escribano-Morales, n.d.). Citizens of member States of the European Union can obtain three types of residence cards:

Temporary residence card: Valid for a period ranging from three months to a year, it is granted to citizens of member States of the European Union wishing to work in Spain and is limited to the duration of economic activity, whether as own-account or salaried workers.

Provisional residence card: Valid for at most six months, it allows citizens of member States of the European Union wishing to work on their own account to apply for a residence card.

Residence card: Valid for five years and renewable, it allows citizens of member States to settle anywhere in Spanish territory and exercise any type of economic activity.

Citizens of all other countries must obtain a residence permit if they plan to stay in Spanish territory for more than three months. The types of residence permits are:

Initial residence permit: Valid for a period ranging from three months to two years, it is granted to foreigners who have not resided legally in Spain for two years or more and who, being legally present in the country, wish to establish residence.

Ordinary residence permit: Valid for up to five years, it is granted to foreigners wishing to establish residence in Spain and who have already lived in the country legally for at least two years.

Special residence permit: Valid for up to ten years, it can be granted to foreigners who have resided continuously in Spanish territory for at least two years and who belong, in addition, to one of the following categories: are retired persons receiving a pension from abroad; were born in Spain; are the descendants or the parents of Spanish citizens; are citizens of Latin American countries, Equatorial Guinea, Portugal, the Philippines or Andorra; are Sephardic; or satisfy one of the conditions established in the Royal Decree 1119/1986 of 26 May.

The data recorded in the register of resident foreigners include the type of permit held by each foreign person inscribed in the register. For statistical purposes, the number of foreigners residing in Spain as of 31 December of each year is published annually by the National Institute of Statistics in the publication entitled *Migraciones*. The tabulations published present the number of resident foreigners classified by citizenship and by either province of residence within Spain or major community of residence. No information is provided on type of residence permit or on demographic or other characteristics (Spain, Instituto Nacional de Estadística, 1994). Clearly, exploitation of the information contained in the register is still in its infancy.

In Switzerland, foreigners wishing to work or stay in the country must apply for permission while abroad (Gisser, 1992). Foreigners who do not require a visa to enter Switzerland must obtain assurance abroad that a residence permit will be granted to them when they reach Swiss territory. Normally, their prospective employer applies for a permit and, if the application is approved, the aliens police sends the required assurance to the foreigner. Those foreigners who

Data collection systems concerning all international migrants

require a visa to enter Switzerland must obtain an authorization for residence from a Swiss diplomatic mission abroad. These include workers, students and family members of persons who already hold Swiss residence permits.

Upon arrival, foreigners who intend to reside or work in Switzerland must register with the aliens police within eight days or before starting to work. They must present proof of having an assurance that a residence permit will be issued and evidence of having appropriate accommodation. All foreigners staying or working in Switzerland must have a permit. There are various types of permits: seasonal; annual; establishment; short-stay; and border permits granted to foreigners who work in Switzerland but who return daily to their home outside Switzerland (Gisser, 1992). The issuance of most permits is subject to the approval of the Federal Office for Alien Affairs. However, cantons can issue permits of stay with a validity of up to two years to persons who are not economically active; to students for the duration of their studies; to in-patients until their discharge; to domestic and agricultural workers for up to five years; and to seasonal workers for up to nine months, though the latter are subject to certain ceilings by occupation as established by the Federal Office for Industry, Trade and Labour. In case of urgent demand for foreign workers, the cantons can issue provisional permits of stay.

Newly admitted foreigners are usually granted residence permits allowing only a limited period of stay. Seasonal work permits are the most common and can be valid for a period of at most nine months. Seasonal workers are considered to have a residence abroad and cannot be joined in Switzerland by their immediate relatives. A foreigner who has held a seasonal work permit and worked for at least 36 months over four consecutive years has the right to obtain an annual permit. After three years of holding annual residence permits, foreigners have the right to have them renewed automatically (OECD, 1986). Establishment permits are granted at the discretion of the pertinent authorities, after a stay of five to ten years in Switzerland, depending on the citizenship of the foreigner (Hoffman-Nowotny, 1985). Five years are required for citizens of Belgium, Denmark, Finland, France, Iceland, Ireland, Italy, Liechtenstein, Luxembourg, the Netherlands, Norway, Sweden and the United Kingdom; ten years are required for all other foreigners (OECD, 1987). An establishment permit grants the holder the right to remain in Switzerland for an unlimited period and can be revoked only under special circumstances. The spouse and minor children of a foreigner holding an establishment permit are also entitled to be included in that permit and hence to enjoy the same residence rights as that foreigner. Seasonal, annual or short-stay permits are terminated when they expire or upon the deregistration or actual departure of the migrant. Establishment permits are terminated with deregistration or with an actual stay abroad of more than six months by the migrant (the period of absence may be prolonged to two years by special request). Resident foreigners who leave Switzerland with the intention of establishing residence abroad must notify the aliens police and deregister from the central register of foreigners. Foreigners who do not deregister do not receive their documents back. In addition, the landlords and employers of foreigners who leave the country have to notify the authorities of that departure within eight days of its occurrence.

The Swiss central register of foreigners is used to produce about 200 tabulations annually, but they are kept in microfiche and only a small subset is published. Three reports are issued every year: one presenting the stock of foreigners in Switzerland at three points in time over a year; a second one showing the number and types of changes in the register; and a third analysing the changes taking place. The tabulations published include the annual inflow and outflow of foreigners holding annual and establishment permits by participation in the labour force; by branch of industry; by citizenship; and by age group. In addition, the Federal Statistical Office publishes in the *Annuaire statistique de la Suisse* the number of foreign residents (that is, foreigners holding annual or establishment permits) classified by citizenship; by type of permit; by marital status, sex and labour force participation; and by age group, sex and type of permit.

2. Problems affecting the data derived from registers of foreigners

As with general population registers, registers of foreigners tend to underestimate the level of emigration of resident foreigners since reporting a long-term departure to the authorities in charge of the register often results in the revocation of the residence permit that the foreigner holds. Consequently, to avoid overcounting the foreign resident population, other special means of keeping track of the presence or absence of foreigners in a country must be devised. Making employers or landlords of foreigners responsible for reporting the discontinuation of their employment or of their rental contracts, as in Austria, Liechtenstein or Switzerland, is one way of ensuring that the departure or change of address of foreigners is detected on a timely basis. Japan, being a country of islands, is in a better position to control the departure of foreigners and ensure that resident foreigners leaving without a re-entry permit have their residence permit withdrawn before departure.

In some countries, the comparison of different data sources has been a means of checking the accuracy and degree of coverage of the register of foreigners. In Germany, for instance, the central register of foreigners was compared with the results of the 1987 census. This comparison showed that there were fewer discrepancies between the central register of foreigners and the census than between the local population registers and the census. Nevertheless, the central register of foreigners was found to overcount the foreign population by 389,000 persons, or 9.4 per cent of the total number of foreigners residing in Germany at the time, a sizeable difference. With respect to the inflows and outflows of foreign residents, it was found that the central register of foreigners yielded better estimates than the local population registers (Bretz, n.d.). However, flow statistics are less commonly available from the central register of foreigners than from the local population registers.

In most countries maintaining registers of foreigners, the potential for comparing the data obtained from such registers with those yielded by other sources is high but remains largely underutilized. One factor that is likely to hinder periodic assessments of the coverage and quality of the data gathered by registers of foreigners is the fact that they are usually maintained by authorities in charge of controlling international migration rather than by statistical offices. Because an aliens register is a tool for control, access to its contents may raise issues of confidentiality and the right to privacy that can derail attempts to check its contents or produce statistics. Furthermore, because errors in the data yielded by the register may be interpreted as a failure of existing control mechanisms, the authorities may be reluctant to acknowledge them. Much can be gained, however, by identifying and quantifying the possible deficiencies of registers of foreigners, since they are one of the potentially richest sources of policy-relevant information on international migration.

3. Types of international migrants identified by registers of foreigners

Although registers of foreigners can only reflect the international migration of aliens, they have the advantage of recording fairly detailed information on the specific type of permit under which foreigners are admitted and reside in a country, and are thus better suited than other sources of information on international migration to produce data relative to the types of international migrants identified in Chapter 2.

The description of national practices in section 3.C.1 above suggests that registers of foreigners are capable of producing information on migrants having the right to free movement (as in the cases of Germany and Spain); seasonal migrant workers (Switzerland); temporary migrant workers (Germany, Japan and Switzerland); established migrant workers (Germany and Switzerland); refugees (Germany, Japan and Switzerland); settlers (Japan); foreign students and trainees (Japan); and returning ethnics (Japan and Spain). Although the definitions of certain categories of migrants implicit in the way registers of foreigners operate sometimes do not coincide perfectly with the general definitions presented in Chapter 2, the latter provide a useful framework to carry out international comparisons. To realize the full potential of such comparisons, however, tabulations by type of residence permit must be available for all countries having registers of foreigners. Yet, as documented above, very few countries publish the detailed tabulations necessary to facilitate comparative international analysis and policy evaluation. Thus, as in the case of the general population registers, much remains to be done to realize the potential that specialized registers of foreigners have for producing policy-relevant information on the international migration of foreigners.

International migration statistics

4. Recommendations for the improvement of international migration statistics derived from registers of foreigners

- Countries maintaining registers of foreigners should be encouraged to gather in a similar fashion a core set of information on foreigners inscribed in the register or deregistered. Such a core set should include: date of birth; sex; date of registration or deregistration; date of change of residence; place of birth; citizenship; place of previous residence; place of intended residence; marital status; highest educational level completed (primary, secondary or tertiary); current occupation; number of accompanying family members; relationship to head of family; type of document presented to claim residence rights (passport, visa, residence permit etc.); length of validity of residence permit; reason for granting the foreigner a residence permit; whether the foreigner has an authorization to work; length of validity of work authorization; and place of employment.
- All published tabulations derived from a register of foreigners should present data classified by sex.
- The institutions in charge of maintaining registers of foreigners should be encouraged to produce annually a variety of tabulations on the characteristics of the foreign stock and its changes during the year. A basic set of tabulations might include:

    (a) The stock of resident foreigners by age group, sex, country of citizenship and type of residence permit;

    (b) The stock of resident foreigners by age group, sex, country of citizenship and duration of residence;

    (c) The stock of resident foreigners allowed to work by age group, sex, country of citizenship, education, and occupation;

    (d) The stock of resident foreigners admitted for family reunification by age group, sex, country of citizenship and relationship to primo migrant;

    (e) Immigrating foreigners by age group, sex, education, and country of previous residence;

    (f) Emigrating foreigners by age group, sex, education, and country of intended residence;

    (g) Immigrating foreigners by age group, sex and country citizenship;

    (h) Emigrating foreigners by age group, sex and country citizenship;

    (i) Immigrating foreigners allowed to work by age group, sex, country of citizenship and occupation;

    (j) Immigrating foreigners allowed to work by age group, sex, country of citizenship and educational attainment;

    (k) Immigrating foreigners allowed to work by age group, sex, country of citizenship and type of residence permit;

Data collection systems concerning all international migrants

    (l) Foreigners admitted as dependants by age group, sex, country of citizenship and relationship to primo migrant;

    (m) Immigrating foreigners by age group, sex, country of citizenship and reason for admission (i.e. type of residence permit);

    (n) Emigrating foreigners allowed to work while in the country by age group, sex, country of citizenship and occupation;

    (o) Emigrating foreigners admitted as dependants by age group, sex, country of citizenship and relationship to primo migrant;

    (p) Deaths of foreigners by age group, sex and country of citizenship;

    (q) Naturalizations of foreigners by age group, sex and previous citizenship;

    (r) Births of foreign children by age group and citizenship of mother.

- To facilitate the dissemination of complex tabulations, the possibility of using electronic media, such as compact discs, diskettes, or electronic networks, should be explored.

- Published tabulations derived from registers of foreigners should include succinct definitions of the migrant categories used. In cases where the inscription or deletion of a person from the register depends on the citizenship of the person, such distinctions should be spelled out.

- The administrative unit in charge of maintaining the register of foreigners should prepare and update a guide to the operation of the register that would describe the conditions under which foreigners are granted a permission to reside or to work in the country.

- Measures should be taken to assess periodically the degree of coverage and the quality of the data yielded by registers of foreigners. Information about the performance of the register with regard to the coverage of stocks of resident foreigners and flows of different types of foreign migrants should be disseminated through statistical publications.

- The authorities in charge of maintaining a register of foreigners should ensure that sufficient information to identify the major types of international migrants is recorded in the register and that tabulations are made on the number of persons in each migrant category. Of particular interest is the separate identification of refugees, asylum-seekers, foreigners granted the permission to exercise an economic activity, and foreigners admitted for family reunification.

- Efforts should be made to use the information recorded in the register of foreigners to analyse the dynamics of migration and status changes among resident foreigners. Of special interest for policy assessment and formulation are the transitions from one permit to another among migrants and the impact of those transitions on length of stay. It is also important to understand better the dynamics of family reunification in terms of timing, characteristics of the relatives admitted, and impact on the educational system, the health care system, and the labour market.

D. ADMINISTRATIVE SOURCES

In many countries, continuous statistics on international migration can be derived from the administrative procedures involved in controlling the admission and stay of foreigners. Because such procedures vary greatly from country to country, the statistics themselves take several forms, reflecting sometimes the number of residence visas granted, at other times the number of residence permits of different types, and at yet other times the number of foreigners undergoing a medical examination in order to be admitted as residents. Although it may be argued that the data yielded by population registers and special registers of foreigners also reflect the administrative procedures involved in obtaining permission to reside in a country, the difference between those sources and the ones considered in this section stems from the fact that the latter usually produce statistics on documents and not on persons. Consequently, although there is usually a good one-to-one correspondence between a person and a document, the possibility of double counting cannot be ruled out, especially when a person can change migrant status during a given year. In contrast, in population registers and registers of foreigners, the person is the unit of statistical interest, and changes in his or her status are recorded in ways intended specifically to avoid double counting.

Although most administrative sources produce statistics relative to the admission of foreigners, there are also some that reflect the emigration of citizens. The internationally recognized right of every person to leave any country including his or her own does not imply that certain controls on persons leaving a country cannot be exercised. Citizens, in particular, generally require passports to travel abroad. In countries where a passport is issued almost automatically to any citizen who requests one, the number of passports issued is not indicative of international migration, but in countries where the issuance of passports is restricted, passport statistics may be useful indicators of international migration. Countries that impose barriers to emigration, often in contravention to the right of free movement of their own citizens, are also likely to have administrative data sources relative to the number of exceptional cases in which emigration is allowed. Information on the nature, scope and functioning of such sources, however, is often not readily available.

This section documents the variety of data sources producing international migration statistics as a by-product of administrative procedures. To the extent possible, examples from all regions of the world are presented, though detailed information on the operation of the data sources of developed countries is more readily available than for developing countries. In fact, one of the major deficiencies of administrative sources is that, in many countries, they are not considered useful sources of statistical information and are therefore underutilized. Another factor hindering the use and dissemination of statistics from administrative sources is their political sensitivity in contexts where the admission of foreigners is controversial. The close links between the operation of administrative sources and the implementation of policy is in some cases not conducive to full disclosure.

1. Residence permits

The statistics derived from the issuance of residence permits or visas allowing residence for different purposes and durations of stay sometimes provides a useful basis for the measurement of the inflow of international migrants. Under certain circumstances, they can also provide information on the total number of legally resident foreigners. When the administrative procedures to issue residence permits or visas ensure that the permits issued to newly arrived foreigners are identifiable, their number can be used as an indicator of migrant inflows. Problems in the use and interpretation of data on residence permits arise when those permits are granted not only to newly arriving foreigners but also to those who have already been present in the country for some time. When the procedures used in gathering statistics on residence permits make no distinction between permits issued for the first time, permit renewals and changes of status within the country (from non-resident to resident), their use as indicators of migrant inflows is problematic.

The following review outlines the experience of countries where residence permits, visas or other types of documents regulating the length of stay of foreigners are used to derive statistics on those foreigners who may be considered international migrants. Usually, countries issue various types of residence permits to regulate the stay and economic activity of different categories of foreigners. To the extent possible, these types of permits are described in detail since they provide the basis for the identification of some of the migrant categories distinguished in Chapter 2. Unfortunately, for a number of countries there is virtually no information on the conditions under which residence permits are granted or on the types of permits that may be issued. Clearly, much remains to be done to ensure that statistics derived from residence permits or equivalent documents are accompanied by adequate documentation regarding their meaning and scope.

Europe

Portugal provides an example of a member State of the European Union where the issuance of residence permits differs according to whether the applicant is or is not a citizen of the European Union. Foreigners who are not citizens of the Union and who wish to establish residence in Portugal must obtain a resident visa abroad and exchange it for a residence permit once in Portugal. Citizens of the European Union do not require a visa to enter Portugal but most obtain a residence permit if they intend to stay. Both groups of foreigners must apply for a residence permit during the first three months of their stay in Portugal. Diplomats, their dependants and domestic workers, and political refugees do not require residence permits (Peixoto, n.d.). Since 1980, the Service of Foreigners and Borders (*Serviço de Estrangeiros e Fronteiras-SEF*) of the Ministry of the Interior has been in charge of issuing residence permits. A permit may take a year or more to be issued once the application is received.

Citizens of the European Union may qualify for one of three types of residence permits: a normal residence permit, valid initially for five years and renewable, granted to those who gain the right to stay indefinitely; a European Union residence permit, valid for five years and granted to persons having an employment contract for a year or more or planning to work on their own account; and a temporary residence permit, granted to persons with employment contracts of 3 to 12 months duration and valid for the duration of the contract.

All other foreigners are granted initially a residence permit valid for a year and renewable. After five years of continuous and legal residence, the foreigner can apply for a five-year residence permit; and after 20 years of continuous residence, a residence permit of indefinite validity may be obtained. Children under the age of 14 years are included in the residence permit of their father (or mother), but at age 14 years they must obtain a residence permit in their own right. Before 1986, statistics derived from residence permit information did not make allowance for the children included in the permits of adults (Peixoto, n.d.).

By law, any change of residence by a holder of a residence permit must be reported to the SEF, but it is known that foreigners who leave the country tend not to report their departure. Furthermore, since the data on residence permits only began to be computerized in 1992, keeping the files up to date before that was far from straightforward. The SEF publishes data on the stock of foreigners residing in Portugal based on the residence permits it compiles. The numbers published are likely to be affected by a number of biases, including the omission of citizens of the European Union who do not apply for residence permits but nevertheless reside in Portugal; the double counting of persons when permit renewals are processed as if they were new issues of permits; and the inclusion of persons whose permits are valid but who have left the country. The SEF publishes an annual statistical report containing data on the stock of foreigners with valid residence permits classified by age group and sex; by citizenship; and by occupation. In addition, since 1986 the National Statistical Institute publishes similar tabulations annually (Peixoto, n.d.).

In France, every foreigner aged 18 years and over (16 years before passage of the Law of 2 August 1989) and wishing to reside in France for more than three months has to obtain a residence permit from the Ministry of the Interior. Different procedures exist for citizens of other member States of the European Union, other foreigners, quota refugees and asylum-seekers (Tribalat, n.d.). When citizens of the European Union apply for a residence permit, they first obtain a temporary document valid for three months that is exchanged for another permit valid for five years. Upon expiration, the latter can be exchanged for a permit valid for up to ten years. Other foreigners must obtain a visa before entering France and then apply for a residence permit. When they do, they are given a temporary document valid for three months that is renewable for as long as it takes for their cases to be considered. If their application for a residence permit is approved, they obtain either a temporary residence permit valid for a year or a residence permit if they belong to categories of migrants having such a right (Algerians obtain a residence certificate). Holders of temporary residence permits can renew them and, after three years of continuous residence in France, can apply for a residence permit. Residence permits are normally valid for three years.

Persons admitted to France as quota refugees (that is, resettled refugees) are granted upon arrival a temporary document valid for six months. When their status as refugees is granted by the *Office Français de Protection des Réfugiés et Apatrides* (OFPRA) they receive a residence permit valid for ten years and marked "refugee". Asylum-seekers obtain initially a provisional authorization to reside in France valid for a month and renewable. During that month they must present an application for asylum to the OFPRA where they receive a document indicating that the application is being considered. With such a document, asylum-seekers can obtain temporary permission to reside, work and obtain assistance in France during the time it takes for their case to be decided. Those being granted refugee status by OFPRA can then obtain a refugee residence permit.

On the basis of the issuance of residence permits, the Ministry of the Interior produces some statistics relevant to the evaluation of migration policy but, since its mandate does not include the dissemination or processing of data, the tabulations produced are mostly for internal use and have several limitations. Information obtained from persons applying for residence permits or their renewal is processed manually at the level of the prefecture and summary tables are assembled at the Ministry. Reports on the flows (new permits issued, renewals, cancellations and the expiration of permits) are transmitted every six months to the Ministry, and reports on stocks (the number of valid permits existing at the end of each year) are transmitted annually. The stock at the end of a year is obtained by adding the net flow to the stock estimated at the end of the previous year. The measure of flows, however, is incomplete: foreigners leaving the country are generally not counted unless they receive aid from French authorities to return to their countries of origin. Deaths of foreigners and naturalizations are, in principle, taken into account but probably not completely (Tribalat, n.d.). Few statistics are released for public use and do not include those on flows. Data on the number of residence permits valid at the end of each year were published annually until 1985. Compared to census results, they overestimate the foreign population residing in France. Although residence permit statistics have the potential for providing useful information on certain components of change of the foreign population by tracking the issuance of new residence permits by type of migrant and the renewal of residence permits, such potential is largely not realized by the mechanisms now in place at the Ministry of the Interior.

International migration statistics

There is, however, another source of information on certain international migrant flows to France. The *Office pour les Migrations Internationales* (OMI) is in charge of admitting foreign workers and foreigners joining family members already resident in France. Information on the migrants involved is gathered when they undergo a medical examination in France, so foreigners exempt from the examination, such as citizens of other member States of the European Union, are not included in the statistics produced by OMI. Other groups excluded are foreigners whose entry and stay is governed by international agreements, as in the case of citizens of the Central African Republic, Gabon and Togo, and of Algerians until 1985 when a revision of the Franco-Algerian Agreement of 1968 established that Algerian workers would also undergo a medical examination. Over the years, the statistics released by OMI have varied considerably in their coverage. Before the active recruitment of foreign workers was stopped in 1974, the number of foreigners who entered France as tourists and later regularized their status as migrant workers was added, with some delay, to OMI's statistics. However, since 1974, when regularization programmes became exceptional, the number of persons regularized has not always been properly integrated into OMI statistics. Then, in 1987, certain groups of migrants (such as foreign students) who had not been subject to medical examinations were also required to undergo such examinations and began appearing in OMI statistics. However, the 1987 regulations also allowed medical examinations to be carried out at OMI missions abroad and, because the operation of those missions was not consistent, the statistics gathered were deficient. In 1989, a new circular established that medical examinations of foreigners other than salaried workers and family members had to be carried out in France. Hence, it has only been since 1990 that the statistics of OMI have had the possibility of covering completely the groups of foreigners that they are meant to represent.

The statistics gathered by OMI have been published annually since 1967. From 1967 to 1976 the data published referred mostly to foreign workers and migrants admitted for family reunification by country of citizenship. The number of migrant workers by occupation and the number of seasonal workers were also presented. In 1977, 1980 and especially since 1985, the part devoted to statistics on family reunification was expanded to include information on the year of birth of spouses, children, parents and "collaterals", as well as other information on family groups. Since 1985, data on the number of temporary work permits for students and trainees have also been published, and a new annual publication on the numbers of foreigners returning to their countries of origin with assistance from the French Government has been issued. Finally, since 1987 a volume devoted to foreigners other than workers, and family members who are subject to a medical examination, has been released annually. Yet, despite the large number of tabulations published, the data available have several limitations, particularly with regard to family reunification. Information on the status of the sponsor of family members (worker, family member, refugee, person born in France etc.), sex of the family members admitted, year of

Data collection systems concerning all international migrants

reunification, and year of marriage is all necessary to study the dynamics of the process and is not currently available (Tribalat, n.d.).

In Greece, the Office for National Security of the Ministry of the Interior and Public Order is in charge of issuing residence permits to foreigners. Any foreigner wishing to reside in Greece for more than three months must be in possession of a residence permit. Statistics on the number of residence permits issued and on their renewal are prepared by the Ministry of the Interior but are not published (Koszamanis, n.d.).

In Italy, the Ministry of the Interior is in charge of issuing residence permits to foreigners legally present in the country. In doing so, statistics on the number of residence permits are collected and published annually. Foreigners planning to stay for more than one month require a residence permit. Citizens of member States of the European Union are not exempt from such a requirement. The data produced by the Ministry of the Interior show the number of valid permits at the end of each year, the number of permits issued during a year (including renewals), and the number of permits cancelled or expiring during a year, all classified by country of citizenship of the holder, thus allowing an approximation to both the stock of foreigners in the country and the annual flows (CENSIS, 1993). However, because the residence permits issued during a year include the renewals of those expiring, they are not the same as migrant inflows. Nor can the number of those cancelled or expiring be equated with migrant outflows. The net increase or decrease of residence permits is used to update the number of valid residence permits existing for foreigners from one year to the next. No allowance seems to be made, however, for the naturalization or death of foreigners, and it is not clear to what extent the emigration of foreigners is covered.

The Ministry of the Interior also issues data on the number of residence permits valid at the end of each year classified by reason for residence of the foreign holder of each permit. The reasons listed include: employment, self-employment, studies, family reunion, choice of residence, religious motives, tourism, asylum, health reasons, training, and adoption. Also available are data on the number of valid residence permits at the end of the year classified by both reason for residence and citizenship of holder; by sex and age group of holder; by marital status and country of citizenship of holder; by region of residence within Italy and region (but not country) of origin; by sex and current region of residence; by marital status and region of residence; and by age group and region of residence (CENSIS, 1993).

In Ireland, citizens of the European Union must obtain a residence permit if they plan to stay in the country for more than three months. Other foreigners must obtain a work permit first and then are required to apply for a residence permit within their first seven days in Ireland. Initial residence permits are valid for a year and are renewable. The Ministry of Justice is in charge of issuing residence permits. The data gathered only began to be computerized in 1992, but manual tabulations had been made showing the number of valid residence permits as of 31 December of each year, classified by citizenship of holder. That number does not include foreigners under 16 years of age who do not require residence permits but it does include students. It is also likely to include foreigners whose permits are still valid but who have left the country (Poulain, et al., n.d.).

In the United Kingdom, the Home Office is in charge of responding to requests from foreigners for permission to settle or extend the time limits of their permits. Citizens of the European Union can stay in the United Kingdom for up to six months without requiring permission to settle. If they then apply for settlement, they are included in the statistics of acceptances for settlement. Other foreigners are usually admitted initially for a limited period, and information on their citizenship, date of birth, sex, date of settlement grant and settlement category is computerized. Publication of the number of acceptances for settlement by citizenship, sex and settlement category occurs annually in the series entitled *Control of immigration statistics* (Salt, n.d.).

In the Czech Republic, the Ministry of the Interior maintains information on residence permits issued to foreigners and produces estimates of the number of foreigners residing in the country. Before 1990, permanent residence permits were granted to refugees and to persons wishing to join close family members in the Czech Republic. Since October 1991, foreigners must apply for residence permits while abroad. Long-term residence permits are usually valid for a year and are renewable according to the length of the employment contract of the foreigner or the programme of studies followed by the foreigner (Economic Commission for Europe, n.d.).

In Hungary, the Service of the Police of Foreigners of the Ministry of the Interior issues residence permits and, since the 1980s, maintains a database on the number of valid permits. Permits can be temporary or permanent. The data recorded include sex, citizenship, profession and type of permit (Economic Commission for Europe, n.d.).

Traditional countries of immigration

Among the countries of immigration – Australia, Canada, New Zealand and the United States – Canada and the United States gather statistics on immigrants using a hybrid system that combines the issuance of residence visas or permits at their embassies and consulates abroad with border control procedures to verify entry into the country. However, in the United States a large number of persons granted permanent resident status obtain it by changing their status within the country, mostly after having been present there under other types of permits. Thus, in 1989, 63 per cent of the immigrants recorded by United States authorities were already residing in the country. In Canada, changes of status from temporary to permanent residence are normally not possible, but persons granted refugee status after applying for asylum while in the country are in effect changing their status without leaving Canadian territory and are included in the immigration statistics published annually. Yet Canada gathers statistics on settlers mostly at the border, when foreigners with immigrant visas arrive to take up residence in the country. Canada and the

Data collection systems concerning all international migrants

United States also collect information on incoming foreigners admitted as "non-immigrants", some of whom are granted permission to stay for temporary, albeit lengthy, periods to work or study. However, both Canada and the United States lack statistics on either the inflows and outflows of their own citizens or on the outflows of foreigners. Consequently, they cannot be said to gather comprehensive border statistics.

In contrast, Australia and New Zealand gather border statistics that reflect the full range of possible movements, including those of citizens and former settlers, and those of foreigners admitted on a temporary basis.[3] Their statistical systems, therefore, include comprehensive border statistics. Australia allows the foreigners to change their residence permits from temporary to permanent while living in the country. Statistics on those changes, derived from administrative sources, are published (Australia, Bureau of Immigration, Multicultural and Population Research, 1995). Furthermore, Australia issues visas under 24 separate temporary residence categories, some of which allow the exercise of an economic activity (Sloan and Kennedy, 1992). Table 3.9 shows the main temporary visa types that allow the holder to work. Most are used for the admission of highly skilled or specialized personnel. Although data on those categories of temporary migrants are not published, the Australian Department of Immigration and Ethnic Affairs maintains a database on temporary migrants and can produce requested tabulations on the information available (Hugo, 1994).

In Canada, the Immigration Statistics Division of Immigration and Citizenship Canada is in charge of processing and disseminating statistical information on both settler migration and the admission of foreigners on a temporary basis. An annual publication entitled *Immigration statistics* contains data on the number of "landed immigrants" admitted annually and on foreigners admitted on a temporary basis, including documented visitors, foreign students and temporary foreign workers. Landed immigrants are foreigners who have received lawful permission to enter Canada and establish permanent residence. They are counted when they "land" in Canada, that is, when they enter the country for the first time after having received the required visa abroad. The statistics therefore are a better reflection of the number of immigrant visas issued than of the full inflow of foreigners into Canada and are thus more akin to administrative statistics than ideal border statistics. Published tabulations on landed immigrants show: the number admitted annually classified by country of birth, age group and sex; age group, sex and marital status; country of last permanent residence, age group and sex; country of citizenship and province of intended destination; occupational group, age group and sex; and selected intended occupations and province of intended destination (Employment and Immigration Canada, 1988).

In the United States, migration is regulated through the issue of different kinds of visas that allow the holder to enter the country and, under certain conditions, to work and reside in it. Statistics on persons granted permission to reside permanently are gathered either at the time the person arrives in the

Table 3.9. Visa categories allowing the holder to work in Australia and number admitted under each category, 1990/91

Visa class	Description	Length of stay	Whether extension of stay possible	Visas issued 1990/91
Executive	Allows entry of senior management personnel to join established businesses in Australia or to establish branches of overseas companies in Australia	Up to 4 years	Yes	2 236
Specialist	Allows entry of highly skilled workers from overseas where employers in Australia have been unable to meet their needs from the Australian labour market or through their own training efforts	Up to a maximum of 2 years	Yes, up to a maximum of 2 years provided total stay in Australia does not exceed 4 years	21 050
Educational	Allows entry of staff for Australian educational institutions and research organizations	For senior academic and post-doctoral research, up to 4 years For other staff, up to 2 years	Yes, extensions of 4 years on a continuing basis provided they stay at the same institution Yes, up to 2 years provided total stay does not exceed 4 years	1 467
Working holiday	Allows young people to enter Australia to experience its culture and by doing this improve international understanding by holidaying and travelling in Australia with the opportunity to work to supplement their funds	Twelve months unless date of departure is expected to be within 4 weeks of visa issue. This may be 13 months, giving applicant up to one month's travel time to Australia	No	41 753
Visiting academic	Allows entry of people as visiting academics at Australian educational institutions and research organizations	Up to 12 months	Yes, assessed on a case-by-case basis	2 028
Entertainment	Allows entry of entertainers, models and mannequins and their associated personnel for specific engagements or events in Australia, and of actors and support staff engaged in the production of films, documentaries or commercials in Australia which may involve local workers or which are being produced for the local market	Consistent with time sufficient to enable specific project to be completed	Yes	5 410

Sport	Allows entry of sports people, including officials, and their support staff, to take part in specific events in Australia, and of sports people joining Australian sports clubs or organizations	Consistent with that sought in the sponsorship up to 12 months. Special arrangements for basketball and soccer players	Yes, in certain circumstances	13 088
Media and film staff	Allows the entry of foreign correspondents to represent overseas news media organizations in Australia, overseas journalists, reporters, camera operators, television teams and photographers, including actors and support staff, involved in the production of films, documentaries or commercials in Australia which will not involve local workers and are not being produced for the Australian market	Consistent with sponsorship	Yes	4 007
Religious worker	Allows the entry of religious and evangelical workers to serve the religious objectives of religious organizations in Australia	Consistent with length of sponsorship	Yes, if permitted entry for 6 months or less, cannot be granted an extension beyond 6 months. Otherwise, extension possible on a case-by-case basis	1 234

International migration statistics

United States with a valid immigrant visa issued by the United States Department of State abroad or when an alien already present in the United States is granted immigrant status by the Immigration and Naturalization Service. The source of information on new arrivals is the immigrant visa, and the source of information on status adjustments is the form granting legal permanent residence. After the immigrant is admitted, the immigrant visa and adjustment forms are forwarded to the Immigrant Data Capture Facility of the United States Immigration and Naturalization Service for processing. Information gathered on immigrants admitted includes: age; sex; marital status; port of admission; type or class of admission; country of birth; country of previous residence; country of citizenship; occupation; original year of entry and class of entry for those adjusting from temporary to permanent residence; and the state of intended or current residence. The number of immigrants admitted for legal permanent residence in a year is not at all equivalent to the number entering the United States that year because many immigrants adjust their status after residing in the United States for some time, and they are included in the annual "admission" statistics at the time of their adjustment in status, rather than when they originally entered the United States. In addition, other international migrants, such as some asylum-seekers, parolees and refugees, may reside permanently in the United States but never be counted as legal permanent residents because they are not required to adjust their status.

In addition to admitting immigrants for permanent residence, the United States admits several "non-immigrant" categories of foreigners who are allowed to reside in the country on a temporary but often lengthy basis. The group of non-immigrants also includes tourists and persons travelling to the United States on short business trips. Statistics on non-immigrants are gathered through the Non-immigrant Information System (NIIS) which was established in 1981 and is designed to provide a record of legal admission and departure for each person admitted as a non-immigrant. The NIIS is based on recording the arrivals and departures of non-immigrants, each as a separate record. The NIIS includes data on parolees and refugees. It records information on the age, country of citizenship, class of admission, visa-issuing post, port of entry and destination in the United States of non-immigrants arriving. A separate automated system, the Student/School System (STSC), is used to keep track of foreign students and allows the derivation of detailed statistics on foreign-student arrivals and departures, as well as the stock of foreign students present in the United States.

Upon arrival in the United States, a non-immigrant presents the entry visa together with a special form that is numbered and has two parts. One part is kept by the immigration officer and sent for statistical processing. The other must be handed back by the non-immigrant upon departure from the United States. The latter is then sent for processing and eventual electronic matching with the part collected upon arrival (United States Commission for the Study of International Migration and Cooperative Economic Development, 1990). The NILS does not include data on permanent resident aliens returning after short

Data collection systems concerning all international migrants

visits abroad or on the millions of citizens of Canada and Mexico who cross the border for brief periods of stay in the United States. Most aliens entering the United States from Canada or Mexico do not require the documentation recorded by the NIIS. Canadians may enter the United States for purposes of business or pleasure and remain for up to six months without any travel restrictions. Mexicans who cross the border frequently may apply for border crossing cards which allow them to visit the United States for business or pleasure provided they leave within 72 hours and remain within 25 miles of the border.

The data on persons granted permanent residence status and on non-immigrants by class of admission gathered through the different systems are published in some detail in the annual *Statistical Yearbook of the Immigration and Naturalization Service*. With respect to immigrants, the tabulations published show: immigrants admitted over a given year classified by age group and sex; country of birth, age group and sex; marital status, age group and sex; type of admission, region and selected country of birth; selected class of admission, region and selected country of birth; and calendar year of entry, type of admission, region and selected country of birth. In addition, the number of immigrants admitted whose status was adjusted to permanent resident is tabulated by selected status at entry, region and selected country of birth (United States, Commission for the Study of International Migration and Cooperative Economic Development, 1990). It is unfortunate that no tabulations are produced on the education of immigrants. For non-immigrants, the tables published include the number admitted in a year by selected class of admission, region and selected country of citizenship; by age group and selected country of citizenship; and by class of admission. Other tables provide the numbers admitted as temporary workers, exchange visitors and intracompany transferees classified by country of citizenship.

Africa

In Côte d'Ivoire all foreigners, except citizens of member States of the Economic Community of West African States (ECOWAS), are required to obtain visas before entering the country. Since 1990, foreigners wishing to work in Côte d'Ivoire must also obtain residence permits before becoming employed. Permits granted are initially valid for one year. There are, however, no statistics derived from the issuance of residence permits.

In South Africa, the Home Office is in charge of issuing residence permits for persons intending to reside or settle in the country. Information on the number of persons admitted annually for settlement by country of citizenship is published in the *Statistical Yearbook of South Africa*.

Asia

In Asia, Israel is a major country of immigration, admitting two types of settlers – immigrants and potential immigrants. Immigrants are persons who enter to take up permanent residence under the Law of Return or the Law of Entrance. Potential immigrants are persons entitled to an immigrant visa or an immigrant certificate under the Law of Return who enter Israel with the intention of staying for more than three months. Israeli statistics further distinguish the category of immigrating citizens, constituted by the children born abroad of Israeli parents. Data on the number of immigrants and potential immigrants entering Israel have been gathered since 1988 by the Ministry of Immigrant Absorption at points of entry and by the Ministry of the Interior at the district offices of the Population Administration. Immigrants have to fill in an immigrant registration questionnaire which records the following: country of birth; country of previous residence; citizenship; date of birth; sex; marital status; occupation while abroad; number of persons accompanying the head of the family; years of schooling; and first address in Israel. The data thus gathered are processed by the Ministry of the Interior and a file on immigrants and potential immigrants is used by the Central Bureau of Statistics to produce an annual set of tabulations published under the title *Immigration to Israel* (Israel, 1992).

In Sri Lanka, the Department of Immigration and Emigration is responsible for processing requests for residence visas which allow foreigners to reside for up to two years. Since residence visas are not issued by Sri Lankan Missions abroad, a foreigner qualifying for a residence visa must first enter the country under a visitor visa and then apply for a residence visa immediately upon arrival. Foreigners who enter under a visitor visa and do not apply immediately for a residence visa cannot change their status later. Holders of residence visas can travel to and from Sri Lanka as often as they wish during the period of validity of the visa, so that they do not need to stay in the country for the entire period. Residence visas issued to registrants under the special residence guest scheme approved by the Board of Investment can be issued for a maximum of five years. All residence visas are renewable. Foreigners residing in Sri Lanka who are exempt from the requirement of holding a residence visa include: members of Her Majesty's Naval, Military or Air Force stationed in Sri Lanka and their immediate family members; diplomats, members of their families and their household staff; experts, advisers or technicians working for the United Nations or its agencies and present in Sri Lanka at the request of the Government as well as their family members; trainees and immediate family members sent to Sri Lanka by the United Nations or its agencies; and any foreigners admitted to render services to the Government of Sri Lanka and their immediate family members (Sri Lanka Department of Immigration and Emigration, 1993). For each foreigner granted a residence permit, the Department of Immigration and Emigration gathers the following information: sex; age; date of birth; country of birth; marital status; citizenship; educational attainment; current employment status; occupation; sector of economic activity; date of first entry into the country or of admission as a resident; reason for migrating; type of residence permit; duration of permit; length of contract; type of employer (public sector versus private sector); and number of accompanying immediate relatives. Data on the number of valid residence permits at a particular point in time are published in the *Annual administration report* and in the *Bulletin on immigration and emigration statistics*, which was published in 1990 and 1993. The information gathered is not computerized.

In Kuwait, the number of residence permits by year of issue and citizenship of holder has been presented since 1965 in various statistical publications (Kuwait, 1974 and 1979). More recent issues contain information on the number of residence permits issued annually by country of citizenship and type of permit: study, dependant, servant, commercial activity, private business, and government business (Kuwait, 1979).

In Oman, the offices of the Immigration Department located in different regions gather information on the number of residence permits issued or renewed each year. Data classified by type of permit are published in the *Statistical Year Book of the Sultanate of Oman*. Residence permits can be granted to persons working in the public or in the private sector. Newly issued permits are valid for two years and are renewable for further two-year periods. The statistics show whether the permits are newly issued, renewals or cancellations (Oman, 1986).

In Saudi Arabia, the Department of Passports and Nationality is in charge of issuing residence permits to foreigners. Data on the number of residence permits granted every year have been published continuously since at least 1965 but the tabulations printed vary from year to year. In 1965 and 1966 residence permits were classified by type: new permit, renewal, gratis and temporary (Saudi Arabia, 1965), but between 1967 and 1974, only temporary versus permanent residence permits were identified. In 1975, permits were classified by citizenship of holder for the first time (Saudi Arabia, 1975) and in 1978 the information was also classified by sex (Saudi Arabia, 1978). More recently, the number of persons accompanying the foreigners granted residence permits has also been published (Saudi Arabia, 1993).

The United Arab Emirates publishes data on residence permits issued in a given year by citizenship of holder (United Arab Emirates, 1977). The number of visas issued in embassies abroad by type of visa, which includes residence visas, is also presented.

In Yemen, the Social Welfare Department used to produce statistics on the number of residence permits granted to foreigners, classified as Arab and other foreigners, by year of issue (Yemen Arab Republic, 1972). In 1976 it was indicated that residence permit statistics were compiled by the Department of Passports (Yemen Arab Republic, 1976) and in 1978 statistics on residence permits were no longer published (Yemen Arab Republic, 1978).

Latin America

In Argentina, the National Directorate for Migration (*Dirección Nacional de Migraciones*) produces statistics on the number of foreigners granted establishment permits. The so-called "register of resident foreigners" was established in 1977 and includes all the "*radicaciones*" of foreigners (that is, information on foreigners who obtain establishment permits). The issuance of permanent and temporary residence permits is also recorded. Establishment permits are issued by the National Directorate for Migration whereas permanent and temporary admission permits are issued by Argentine embassies and consulates abroad (Giusti, 1993). The data maintained in the register of resident foreigners also include information on persons who have regularized their status. When applying for a permanent or temporary establishment permit, foreigners are requested to declare: name, address in Argentina, type and number of travel document, sex, date of birth, citizenship, country of birth, country of origin, educational attainment, marital status, occupation, religion, date of most recent entry, place of entry, and whether the migrant has Argentine relatives or relatives who already hold establishment permits in Argentina. When applying for a permit for admission, the migrant is requested to declare: name, citizenship, age, marital status, educational attainment, relationship (if accompanied by relatives), occupation, place of residence, and place of destination.

In Venezuela, the *Dirección General Sectorial de Identificación y Control de Extranjeros* (DIEX) issues identity cards to foreigners who are legally present under the status of sojourners (*transeúntes*) or residents. The data on the stock of foreigners thus gathered are usually tabulated annually by citizenship and type of identity card (sojourner or resident), but those tabulations are not published (Torrealba, 1987).

2. Assessment of the scope and limitations of the residence permit data available

As the preceding review of country practices shows, there is considerable heterogeneity in the statistics derived from residence permits, visas or other equivalent documents. Given that heterogeneity, it is crucial for the user of such statistics to obtain accurate information on their meaning and scope. Because residence permit statistics are administrative in nature, they are closely related to the application of laws and regulations relative to the admission and stay of foreigners and reflect the idiosyncrasies of such regulations. A full understanding of the statistics available usually demands some knowledge of how those laws and regulations operate. It is essential, therefore, that the agencies in charge of producing or publishing statistics derived from residence permits provide explanations of the procedures they use and definitions of the populations covered, in conjunction with the data themselves.

Statistics derived from the issuance of residence permits can be used to provide two types of measures: those relative to stocks, which usually reflect the number of valid residence permits at a given point in time, and those relative to the different flows that bring about changes in the stock. Ideally, the number of valid residence permits at a given time can be equated with the number of foreigners residing legally in the country at that time. In practice, however, problems in capturing the changes in status of foreigners over time prevent residence permit statistics from reflecting accurately the size of the legally resident foreign population in a country. The major limitation of resident permit statistics is that the procedures that give rise to them are not equivalent to those involved in maintaining a register of foreigners (as discussed above). Thus, agencies in charge of issuing residence permits usually are not mandated to maintain a continuous follow-up of the status of each foreigner. In terms of data collection *per se*, the issuance of multiple residence permits to the same foreigner as time elapses is not necessarily statistically linked. More importantly, there are few, if any, procedures to ascertain whether persons with valid residence permits are still resident in the country later; even when foreigners are required to return their residence permits to the issuing agency upon departure to reside abroad, the implementation of such a requirement is lax. Consequently, the total number of valid residence permits often overestimates by wide margins the actual number of legally resident foreigners in a country. Possibly for that reason, few countries use residence permit statistics to estimate stocks of foreigners. Among the countries whose experiences are reviewed above, only seven produced statistics on stocks, with five of the seven being in Europe (namely, the Czech Republic, France, Ireland, Italy and Portugal).

In order to produce meaningful measures of stocks, changes over time must be accurately measured. With respect to the number of valid residence permits, the type of changes possible include: (a) the issuance of new permits to newly arriving foreigners and to those changing status; (b) the renewal of existing permits upon expiration; (c) the expiration of existing permits; and (d) the cancellation of existing permits before they expire. Cancellations may occur for a variety of reasons, including the change of status of the foreign holder, and his or her death, naturalization or definite departure. In the last three cases, the permit of the holder should be entirely withdrawn from the stock of valid residence permits; but when a change of status is involved, the cancelled permit should be exchanged for a new permit. If the stock of valid residence permits at the end of a year is to be calculated as the stock at the end of the previous year plus all permits counted under (a) and (b) during a year, minus those under (c) and (d), it is necessary for all expiring permits to be counted under (c) irrespective of whether they are renewed or not: otherwise foreigners whose permits are renewed would be counted twice. If such procedures are used and the statistics published display the sum of (a) and (b) as "inflows" and the sum of (c) and (d) as "outflows", those quantities cannot be interpreted as reflecting the actual inflows and outflows of foreigners. Only one component of (a), the new permits issued to newly arriving foreigners, and the components of (c) and (d) that represent the number of expiring permits that are not renewed and the number of permits cancelled because the foreign holder is departing, are indicative of actual flows. Yet, as the review of country practices suggests, no country publishes statistics allowing the identification of all these components. Furthermore, in several cases information to calculate (d) is lacking, since data on the deaths, naturalizations and particularly the departures of foreign residents are not readily available.

International migration statistics

Partly because of the problems involved in calculating stocks accurately when information on the emigration of foreigners is deficient or even nonexistent, residence permit statistics are more commonly reported in terms of flows than in terms of stocks. When that happens, flows are usually restricted to the presentation of "inflows", that is, to the number of new residence permits issued over a year, the number of permits renewed, or a combination of both. Only rarely is information on the number of permits cancelled or expiring produced. Furthermore, in countries granting permanent residence permits, such as Canada, Israel and the United States, the possibility of expiration does not exist and cancellations are extremely rare and are not reported.

Out of the countries whose experiences were reviewed above, 14 produce some statistics on the number of permits issued per year and France produces information on new arrivals through admission procedures. Among those issuing temporary residence permits with various lengths of validity, only Oman and Saudi Arabia have published statistics differentiating newly issued permits from those renewed, but such differentiation has not been made consistently over the years. Among the countries granting permanent residence permits, Canada makes no distinction between foreigners who adjust their status from within the country (who are generally few) and newly arriving foreigners, whereas in the United States such a distinction has been made consistently over the years. With respect to data on foreigners granted temporary residence permits that allow the holder to work or study in the country, Canada publishes information on the number of employment and student authorizations issued every year but does not make clear whether the data include renewals or only permits issued for the first time. The equivalent data for the United States represent the number of entries recorded by the Non-immigrant Information System by type of permit presented and thus count a single permit holder several times if the person involved travels abroad more than once during a year.

In general, countries publishing statistics on the number of residence permits issued during a year also fail to provide sufficient information on the exact meaning of the data or on the types of permits. For those that do, the interpretation of the data available is generally far from straightforward since they do not represent actual flows of people but, rather, changes of status of permit holders. Residence permit statistics are, however, useful indicators of policy implementation because they tend to reflect the conditions under which foreigners are admitted and thus allow the identification of several of the main categories of international migrants characterized in Chapter 2, including settlers, migrant workers, temporary migrant workers, highly skilled workers, foreign students, foreign trainees, persons admitted for family reunification, refugees and persons admitted for humanitarian reasons. While the relevant categories of migrants vary from country to country, they can usually be identified if the residence permit data are classified in detail. Flexibility is needed in both the use and the interpretation of residence permit statistics because their administrative character limits their international comparability and is a poor basis for the homogenization of either concepts or data collection procedures.

Data collection systems concerning all international migrants

Yet information derived from residence permits or other documents regulating the admission and stay of foreigners is often the main source of statistics on international migration in major receiving countries and cannot be dismissed. Understanding its nature is the best avenue to ensure its proper use and the exploitation of its strengths.

3. Recommendations for the improvement of residence permit statistics

- Agencies in charge of publishing data derived from the processing of residence permits, visas or other documents regulating the admission and stay of foreigners should ensure that the statistics published are accompanied by a sufficiently detailed description of how the data are collected, what the data represent and which migrants are covered. Categories of foreigners who do not require residence permits should be listed.

- In the process of issuing residence permits, a core set of information should be recorded for each permit holder, including the following items:

  Socio-demographic information:
  Name;
  Date of birth;
  Sex;
  Country of citizenship;
  Country of birth;
  Country of previous residence;
  Marital status;
  Educational attainment:
   Highest level of education attended;
   Number of years of schooling completed;
  Occupation;
  Sector of economic activity;
  Number of dependants;
   Spouse;
   Number of children under 18 years of age.

  Administrative information:
  Date of application;
  Date of issue of the residence permit or visa;
  Date on which the permit or visa takes effect;
  Length of validity of the residence permit or visa;
  Type of residence permit or visa;
  Whether the residence permit is:
   Issued for the first time to the holder;
   A renewal of an existing permit;
   A permit implying a change of the migrant status of the holder;

International migration statistics

If appropriate, occupation for which the residence permit is valid:
Type of work: salaried or own-account;
Occupation group;
Sector of economic activity;
Whether the holder is accompanied by any dependants:
Spouse;
Number of dependent children.

Migration history:
Whether the holder has just arrived in the country of destination;
Whether the holder has already been living in the country of destination. If the holder has already lived in the country for some time:
Date of arrival;
Initial admission status.

The availability of the information listed above makes possible the classification of residence permits issued according to whether they are first-time permits, renewals or changes of status. Such administrative information in combination with knowledge of whether the foreign holder has already been living in the country of destination for some time allows a distinction to be made between residence permits issued for the first time to newly arriving foreigners and those granted to foreigners who were already present in the country. For purposes of understanding migration dynamics, separate identification of those categories is essential. It is strongly recommended, therefore, that countries that do not yet gather the necessary information, do so.

- The following core tabulations should be produced:

  (a) Number of residence permits issued in a year according to issuance category (first-time, renewal and change of status), sex and citizenship of holder.

  (b) Number of first-time residence permits issued per year by sex, age group, citizenship and presence of holder in the country (newly arrived versus already living in the country).

  (c) Number of first-time permits issued per year according to presence in the country (newly arrived versus already living in the country), sex and occupation of holder.

  (d) Number of first-time permits issued per year according to presence in the country (newly arrived versus already living in the country), sex and sector of economic activity of holder.

  (e) Number of first-time permits issued per year according to presence in the country (newly arrived versus already living in the country), sex, citizenship and occupation of holder.

  (f) Number of first-time permits issued per year according to presence in the country (newly arrived versus already living in the country), sex, citizenship and educational attainment of holder.

Data collection systems concerning all international migrants

- (g) Number of spouses and dependent children accompanying holders of first-time permits issued per year by sex, citizenship, and presence in the country of the holder.
- (h) Number of spouses and dependent children accompanying holders of permits renewed or modified (change of status) per year by sex and citizenship of holder.
- (i) Number of renewed permits and number of changes of status processed per year by sex, age group and citizenship of holder.
- (j) Number of renewed permits and number of changes of status processed per year by sex, citizenship and occupation of holder.
- (k) Number of renewed permits and number of changes of status processed per year by sex, citizenship and sector of economic activity of holder.
- (l) Number of renewed permits and number of changes of status processed per year by sex, citizenship and educational attainment of holder.

- Countries producing data on the number of valid residence permits at a particular date should consider preparing the following tabulations:

  Number of valid residence permits by type of permit, sex and citizenship of holder.

  Number of valid residence permits by sex, age group and citizenship of holder.

  Number of valid residence permits by sex, citizenship and occupation of holder.

  Number of valid residence permits by sex, citizenship and sector of economic activity of holder.

  Number of valid residence permits by sex, citizenship and educational attainment of holder.

- Countries having the relevant information on the cancellation of residence permits or their expiration should prepare the following tabulations:

  Number of residence permits expiring over a year by type of permit, sex and citizenship of holder.

  Number of cancelled residence permits by sex, citizenship of holder, and reason for cancellation (death, naturalization, departure, other).

- All tabulations produced, whether in the lists of recommended tabulations presented here or not, should show data classified by sex of the permit holder.
- An effort should be made to publish regularly the tabulations derived from residence permit or visa statistics, preferably through specialized

publications. In addition, at minimum, tabulations (a) to (c) above should be included in more general publications, such as statistical yearbooks of the country. To the extent possible, tabulations (f) to (j) should also be included in widely available statistical sources.

- Agencies in charge of processing statistics derived from residence permits should consider the possibility of developing a computerized database on residence permits issued to facilitate in-depth analysis. The possibility of electronically linking the permit history of each foreigner residing legally in the country should also be explored.

- Countries that derive stock statistics from residence permit data should explore ways of assessing their level of coverage of stock data by, among other things, comparing them with census results or other independent sources of information on the foreign stock.

4. Exit permits

This section reviews the cases of countries that have used administrative sources to produce information on the emigration of their citizens. Such an approach is feasible when emigration is restricted and government approval is necessary to leave the country, be it for short-term travel abroad or for a long-term change of residence. Such practices were common among the former communist countries of Central and Eastern Europe before 1990. Since then, the regulations governing international travel have been relaxed and most restrictions have been eliminated, thus weakening the basis for the control of emigration and for the production of statistics on citizen outflows. In any case, the statistics gathered during the period of restricted emigration have not been widely disseminated and have only recently begun to be released. Both restrictions on the dissemination of the statistics gathered and the lack of information about the exact procedures used to control the international mobility of citizens result in considerable uncertainty about the meaning and scope of such limited data as do exist. The overview presented here is therefore limited and largely based on information gathered by the Economic Commission for Europe (n.d.) in 1992-93. Similar information could not be found for countries in other regions known to restrict the international mobility of their citizens. In all such cases, the withholding of information is common and statistics are rarely released. Hence, if any recommendations are to be made, they relate first and foremost to the need for disseminating whatever information is available accompanied by appropriate explanatory notes. Given the status of the information discussed below, further recommendations will not be made in this case.

Until the late 1980s, the international migration of residents of the Baltic States was regulated by the laws of the former Union of Soviet Socialist Republics (USSR). In Lithuania, however, the processing of emigration visas was somewhat more liberal that elsewhere in the former USSR and therefore some people, albeit living elsewhere in the USSR, particularly those of German or Polish origin, tried to obtain Lithuanian residence in order to have easier access to an emigration visa. The first step toward developing a more independent migration policy in the Baltics took place in 1988 when the Council of Ministers of the Estonian Soviet Socialist Republic and the Council of Trade Unions of the Estonian Republic adopted Decree No. 36 on measures reinforcing the control of population registration in the Estonian SSR. That decree served as a model for the formulation of more liberal emigration policy in Latvia and Lithuania prior to their independence. By the early 1990s, therefore, the Baltic States had liberalized their international migration policies, imposing only minor limitations on emigration. In Estonia and Latvia, the right of every person to leave was enshrined in the new constitutions adopted, whereas in Lithuania it was established by the new Emigration Law. However, emigration is still possible only for those persons who possess exit visas. Those persons can obtain a passport allowing international travel only if they can produce an invitation from the prospective country of destination. Persons emigrating to other successor States of the former USSR do not require an exit visa and are therefore not reflected in exit visa statistics.

In the former Czechoslovakia, persons wishing to emigrate prior to 1989 needed to obtain an official authorization to leave. If the authorization was granted, a special passport allowing emigration was issued and a form providing information about the emigrant was filled out for statistical purposes. It was, however, also possible to obtain a tourist visa and to leave without declaring one's intention to emigrate. Persons who followed that route were often discovered through checks by the local police and their absence was recorded. Statistics on such "illegal emigration" have been released recently. Since 1991, special passports allowing emigration are no longer issued and the obligation of citizens to report their intention to emigrate has been eliminated. This source of statistics is, therefore, no longer viable.

In Hungary, exit visas were required until January 1990 for persons wishing to travel to non-socialist countries and the former Yugoslavia. Exit visas were abolished as of that date. Those leaving before 1990 had to declare their country of destination and present proof that they could be admitted there. They also had to declare which family members stayed in Hungary.

In Romania, prior to 1990, the main sources of statistics on international migration were the General Directorate for Passports and the Border Police. Romanian citizens wishing to leave permanently had to obtain permission from the General Directorate before being issued with a passport. Those travelling abroad for fixed periods were issued with passports that had to be returned to the General Directorate upon return to the country. The Directorate could therefore keep statistics on both the emigration and the return of citizens. In 1990, Decree No. 10 of 8 January established that every Romanian citizen had the right to obtain a passport that would enable the individual to travel and

International migration statistics

remain abroad if desired. Entry and exit visas for Romanian citizens were discontinued. Romanian citizens holding passports may now leave the country at any time without further formalities from the Romanian authorities, and may remain abroad for the entire period of validity of the passport. Romanian citizens wishing to settle abroad may request a passport showing their expected address abroad. Romanian citizens who maintain a domicile in Romania are under no obligation to inform the authorities of their departure. Such legislative changes imply that the issuance of passports and exit or entry visas for Romanian citizens can no longer be used to measure international emigration or return migration.

Prior to 1 January 1993, citizens of the Russian Federation and of the former Soviet Union before 1992 needed exit visas to leave the country. Until the disintegration of the Soviet Union, citizens wishing to leave the country temporarily needed to obtain the permission of the Ministry of Foreign Affairs. Some statistics on the number of Soviet citizens allowed to emigrate from the former USSR are beginning to be made available.

This overview indicates that by issuing special passports allowing international travel to non-communist countries and requiring exit visas to leave the country, the countries of Central and Eastern Europe had the administrative machinery in place to gather fairly reliable statistics on the small number of persons allowed to emigrate and on those who, even without official permission to emigrate, nevertheless managed to travel abroad and remain there for lengthy periods (the so-called "illegal emigrants"). Because exit visas are now no longer required in most countries and passports allowing travel to any destination are more easily accessible, those sources of statistics on emigrating citizens are no longer adequate. Procedures being followed now, and the resulting shortcomings with respect to the measurement of international migration, are now becoming closer to those of the market economy countries of Western Europe. It is of historical and research interest, however, to secure the release of the data gathered before travel restrictions were lifted, preferably in time series form. The publication of special issues presenting a full set of the statistics available for the period 1950-90 together with an analysis of their meaning and the trends that they indicate would be most valuable.

E. BORDER STATISTICS

Border statistics have traditionally been considered a major source of information on international migration flows. Border statistics are derived from the collection of information at points of entry into a country and at points of departure, regardless of whether they are actually located at the border (they include airports and other sites at which persons formally enter or leave a national territory). Border statistics have the advantage of reflecting actual moves with a high degree of accuracy in terms of timing, mode of transport and

Data collection systems concerning all international migrants

place. The task of gathering information from all persons arriving and departing from a national territory is, however, usually well beyond the means at the disposal of many countries. As early as 1949, when the United Nations published its first study on the adequacy of international migration statistics, doubts were expressed about the capability of border statistics to capture all the relevant movements across borders (United Nations, 1949). At the time, a distinction was made between port statistics, based on the lists of passengers that shipping companies or ships' masters had to submit to maritime authorities, and land frontier control statistics collected at land borders. The latter were considered especially difficult to collect with accuracy since traffic was higher across land borders and control operations therefore had to be rapid. The example of movement between Mexico and the United States was cited. During 1920-25, Mexican statistics showed that 489,748 nationals had returned from the United States, whereas United States statistics indicated that the number of Mexicans returning to their home country was only 38,740 (United Nations, 1949). The equivalent data are not available today, since the United States no longer collects any information on persons leaving the country. However, the magnitude of border flows may have increased by up to a thousandfold since then. In 1989 alone, the total estimated number of arrivals of aliens and citizens in the United States amounted to 429 million. Clearly, gathering information on all those moves to identify the million or so persons admitted as permanent residents that year, or the further 1.1 million granted special permits to work or study in the United States, would be wasteful. Instead, as explained in section 3.D, the United States uses administrative procedures combined with border controls at certain ports of entry to gather the relevant information.

Another approach to the problem of handling large numbers of moves is to obtain information on only a selected sample. The United Kingdom, for instance, gathers information on international migration through the International Passenger Survey (IPS) which covers the principal air and sea routes between the United Kingdom and countries outside the British Isles. However, the routes between the United Kingdom and Ireland and those between the Channel Islands or the Isle of Man and the rest of the world are excluded, as is the movement of all diplomats and armed forces personnel. The IPS samples between 0.1 and 5 per cent of passengers depending on the route and time of year. Migrants are distinguished from other travellers on the basis of their intentions to reside in the United Kingdom or abroad for more than a year. More specifically, a migrant into the United Kingdom is a person who has resided abroad for a year or more, and who states on arrival the intention to stay in the United Kingdom for a year or more. A migrant from the United Kingdom is a person who has resided in the United Kingdom for a year or more, and who states on departure the intention to reside abroad for a year or more (United Kingdom Office of Population Censuses and Surveys, 1995). The IPS questionnaire collects nearly 100 items of information on each passenger interviewed and uses five questions to establish whether the person is or is not a resident of the United Kingdom, that is, whether the person has (or has not) lived at least

International migration statistics

12 months in the United Kingdom or abroad before departing (or arriving). Citizenship is established by checking the passenger's passport but no mention is made of checking that a person has the necessary visas or permits to validate declared intentions of staying in the country for a year or more.

The United Kingdom's practice illustrates yet another drawback of border statistics, namely, that declared intentions are often used to distinguish international migrants from other travellers, but those intentions may not match actual outcomes. Yet intentions need not be the only basis for such a distinction. Passports indicating citizenship and the requirement for holding special types of visas or permits are another way of identifying migrants, particularly among foreigners. Citizens returning after living abroad for a time may be more difficult to identify, though the use of exit/entry forms or of stamps in passports indicating the time of previous departure may make the task less dependent on subjective reporting. In the case of citizens, however, there is no substitute for declared intentions when it comes to ascertaining whether they plan to remain in their own country for a lengthy period.

In many countries, border statistics are derived from information collected through special forms filled in by arriving and departing passengers. Commonly, duplicate forms are filled in by all non-residents arriving in the country, one copy of which is kept by immigration authorities at the time of arrival, while the other must be submitted at the time of departure. Residents of the country in question also fill in duplicate forms at the time of departure, submitting one to immigration authorities as they leave the country and handing in the second one when they return. The matching of forms can then allow an accurate assessment of the length of stay or absence of the persons involved. Even without matching, if complete coverage of inflows and outflows of people could be ensured, such a system would yield an estimate of net migration over a year by subtracting the total number of departures from the total number of arrivals, which might be done for resident and non-resident categories of travellers separately. In practice, however, such a procedure usually yields poor estimates of net migration because of the great volume of movements involved: small errors in the coverage of either arrivals or departures may lead to very large errors in the difference between the two, which is usually several orders of magnitude smaller. For that reason, if border control is to be used to gather international migration statistics, an effort needs to be made to distinguish international migrants from other travellers at the time of data collection so that the gathering of information can be targeted more effectively and the resources available can be spent on recording data of better quality.

1. Problem of identifying migrants at the border

At its most abstract, the problem of measuring flows of international migrants can be described in the following terms: the set of persons present in

Data collection systems concerning all international migrants

Table 3.10. Schematic classification of arrivals and departures by duration of absence from and presence in a given country

Arrivals

Future presence	Past absence	
	$\leq t$	$> t$
$\leq t$	Commuters	Outsiders arriving
$> t$	Insiders returning	**Outsiders settling**

Departures

Past presence	Future absence	
	$\leq t$	$> t$
$\leq t$	Commuters	Outsiders departing
$> t$	Insiders departing	**Insiders emigrating**

a country at any given time can be divided into two subsets, those belonging and those not belonging to the country, a set of "insiders" and a set of "outsiders". Migration is the process by which insiders become outsiders and vice versa. The difficulty lies in the fact that outsiders can enter the country and remain outsiders, and insiders can leave the country and remain insiders even while abroad. This is the case of the huge volume of tourists, for example. Therefore, criteria must be adopted to establish when the transformation of outsiders into insiders and that of insiders into outsiders takes place.

The most general criteria are based on actual or intended durations of stay in or absence from a country, as suggested by the Statistical Commission of the United Nations in its *Recommendations on statistics of international migration* issued in 1980 (United Nations, 1980a). Table 3.10 presents in a schematic and generalized form the basic approach underlying such recommendations. For a fixed length of time t months, four mutually exclusive sets of travellers can be distinguished among each group of arriving and departing persons. With respect to arrivals, the four sets consist of: commuters, or a type of short-term movers, that is, persons who have been absent from the country for at most t months and who return with the intention of staying at most t months; insiders returning, that is, persons who have been absent from the country for at most t months and who return with the intention of staying in the country for more than t months; outsiders arriving, that is, persons who have been absent from the country for more than t months and who enter the country with the intention of staying at most t months; and outsiders settling, that is, persons who have been absent for more than t months and who enter the country with the intention of staying for more than t months. The Statistical Commission recommends that the last category be included in international migration statistics under the label "long-term immigrants".

International migration statistics

With respect to departures, the equivalent categories are: commuters, that is, persons who have been in the country for at most t months and who plan to remain abroad for at most t months; insiders departing, that is, persons who have lived in the country for more than t months and plan to be absent for at most t months; outsiders departing, that is, persons who have been in the country for at most t months and plan to remain abroad for more than t months; and insiders emigrating, that is, persons who have been in the country for more than t months and who plan to remain abroad for more than t months. Once more, the Statistical Commission recommends that the number of persons in the last category be included in international migration statistics under the label "long-term emigrants".

The recommendations of the Statistical Commission are consistent with the following conceptualization: insiders are persons who have been present in the country for more than t months. All others are outsiders. Therefore, outsiders who, on arrival, declare their intention to remain in the country for more than t months can be considered as having the potential to become insiders and should be counted as international migrants. Similarly, insiders who upon departure declare their intention of remaining abroad for more than t months have the potential of becoming outsiders and should be considered also as international migrants. All other categories identified in table 3.10 would not change their character as insiders or outsiders and should therefore not be counted as international migrants.

The terms "insider" and "outsider" have been used here purposely to stress the point that it is the duration of presence in a country that qualifies a person as either an insider or an outsider. Although these terms are not devoid of connotations, they are more neutral than the ones used in presenting the United Nations recommendations and thus help to highlight their crucial conceptual underpinnings.

According to the United Nations recommendations, time t should be set at 12 months, but some countries use other time limits. The essential point is that the same time limit be used for the identification of migrants in both arrival and departure statistics and, perhaps more importantly, with respect to both presence and absence. As table 3.10 illustrates, when t is the same in all cases, there is a natural correspondence between the arrival and departure cells in the table. Thus, the category of "insiders returning" is the natural counterpart of "insiders departing". So is that of "outsiders arriving" to "outsiders departing". When this type of consistency is lacking, the data can be misleading. In the Netherlands Antilles, for instance, immigrants are defined as "persons who intend to take up residence in the country for at least a year" and emigrants as "persons intending to reside abroad for at least a year" (United Nations, 1978). According to table 3.10, immigrants thus defined are the sum of "insiders returning" and "outsiders settling", whereas emigrants are the sum of "outsiders departing" and "insiders emigrating". Since the category of "insiders returning" does not represent the arrivals of persons included in "outsiders departing", there is a fundamental inconsistency in the immigrant and emigrant categories defined by the Netherlands Antilles.

Data collection systems concerning all international migrants

This example illustrates the crucial importance of taking into account the identification of "insiders" and "outsiders" before migration is defined in a country. Thus, the definitions used by the Netherlands Antilles would be correct if they were modified slightly to read: immigrants are outsiders who intend to take up residence in the country for at least a year and emigrants are insiders who intend to reside abroad for at least one year. In fact, formulations such as those of the Netherlands Antilles are considerably more common than those recommended above for "insiders emigrating" and "outsiders settling", but they take a slightly different form: the term "insiders" is substituted by "residents" and the term "outsiders" by "non-residents", so that the definition of long-term immigrants becomes "non-residents who intend to stay in the country for more than t months" and that of long-term emigrants is "residents who intend to stay abroad for more than t months". Use of the terms "resident" and "non-resident", though appropriate at first sight, has the drawback of incorporating the legal connotations that the term residence has (see Chapter 2) and thus introducing ill-defined concepts in the identification of international migrants. Yet their use is so widespread that even the United Nations recommendations could not avoid them entirely (United Nations, 1980a).

It is useful therefore to compare two approaches to the identification of international migrants among all arriving travellers. According to the one summarized in Table 3.10, a long-term immigrant is a person who has not been present in the country during at least the previous t months and who enters the country with the intention of staying for more than t months. According to a residence criterion, a long-term immigrant is a non-resident who enters the country with the intention of establishing residence. Both coincide if being resident is interpreted to mean being present in a country for more than t months. However, that is rarely the case. A "resident" may be interpreted to mean being a citizen, having a valid residence permit, having a domicile in the country, paying taxes in the country, or simply declaring oneself a resident if no documents are checked. Non-residents are likely to be equated with foreigners, except when the latter have residence permits. Citizens are unlikely to be considered non-residents, especially if lengths of stay abroad are not recorded or otherwise subject to control. Consequently, when countries define immigrants or emigrants in terms of residence criteria, unless those criteria are spelled out in practical terms, it may be impossible to ascertain the meaning of the statistics produced.

2. Influence of United Nations recommendations

The full set of United Nations recommendations on international migration statistics is considerably more complex than suggested above. For the purposes of this section, however, only the most salient features will be described. Although the core of the recommendations is the definition of long-term

International migration statistics

immigrants and emigrants as presented above, allowance is also made for the relevance of certain short-term movements that can be considered to be international migration. Thus, persons who arrive in a country having been absent from it for more than a year and who intend to stay for at most a year for the purpose of taking up employment remunerated from within the country are considered short-term immigrants. Their accompanying dependants and employees are automatically put into the same category. Upon departure, they are considered short-term immigrants departing. In addition, persons who have lived in a country for more than a year and who depart with the intention of working abroad for at most a year are considered short-term emigrants. Once more, their accompanying dependants and employees are put in the same category. Upon return, that is, when they arrive back in the country after having been working abroad for at most a year and having the intention of staying for a year or more in their "home" country, they are considered short-term emigrants returning.

Although the United Nations recommendations issued in 1980 have not been fully implemented by any country, many countries have adopted certain elements of the recommendations and have either modified their own procedures to implement them or have tried to fit existing categories into the moulds recommended by the United Nations. Unfortunately, the fit is not always exact and many sources of inconsistency remain. Some can be inferred from the arrival and departure statistics published by the United Nations Statistics Division through its *Demographic yearbooks*. The tabulations published try, to the extent possible, to present arrival and departure statistics according to the main categories suggested by the United Nations recommendations including long-term immigrants and emigrants, and short-term immigrants and emigrants. Additional categories include: visitors of various kinds; persons in transit; and returning residents, a category that usually covers residents who are returning from short trips abroad, mostly for tourism.

Since 1975, two issues of the *Demographic yearbook* (1977 and 1989) have presented detailed statistics on international migration flows. Because the *Demographic yearbook 1977* (United Nations, 1978) reflects the situation just before the United Nations recommendations on international migration statistics had been disseminated, and the *Demographic yearbook 1989* (United Nations, 1991) reflects those at a time when the recommendations had time to be adopted and implemented, their contents will be compared here. Regarding flow statistics, the two *Demographic yearbooks* have five tabulations in common, showing: departures to another country or area, by major categories; arrivals from another country or area, by major categories; long-term emigrants and immigrants by country or area of last or intended permanent residence for selected years; long-term emigrants by age and sex; and long-term immigrants by age and sex. For purposes of examining the performance of border statistics, the first two tabulations are the most relevant, since they focus on the type of data generally gathered at the border. Furthermore, the data are presented in categories that, as noted above, attempt to approximate those recommended by the United Nations. A cursory examination of the data in the *Demographic yearbooks* indicates, however, that certain countries have reported information that is not obtained through border control. Thus, the data for several European countries are derived from population registers and those for the United States are obtained from the administrative sources described in section 3.D. Unfortunately, the *yearbooks* do not provide thorough and consistent information about the exact source of the statistics presented. It is known, however, that most European countries do not gather migration statistics through border control procedures. In fact, border controls between certain member States of the European Union are being dismantled. In Canada and the United States, as well, generalized border control is not the source of most international migration statistics. In contrast, in many developing countries, border control is often the only source of information on international migration flows. Consequently, the following analysis will focus mostly on developing countries but will also include a few developed countries such as Australia, Japan and New Zealand where border control is used to derive information on international migration flows.

Two aspects of the arrival and departure statistics contained in the *Demographic yearbooks* will be analysed in some detail. The first relates to the countries that report only overall numbers of both arrivals and departures without making any differentiation between migrants and other travellers. A list of these countries is presented in table 3.11. The periods for which data are available are also indicated for each country. The *Demographic yearbook 1977* covers the period from 1967 to 1976 whereas the 1989 issue covers the period from 1979 to 1988. The second aspect relates to the availability of data that allow the identification of long-term immigrants and emigrants. Table 3.12 shows the countries that reported such data for specific periods. Trends in data availability may be assessed on the basis of both sets of information. Notice that some countries appear in both tables 3.11 and 3.12, meaning that at some point they only had overall numbers of arrivals and departures, while at another they reported different categories of persons arriving and departing, including those corresponding to long-term migrants. Changes are observed in both directions. For Ethiopia, Peru, Singapore, Sri Lanka, Thailand, Turkey and Niue, the data published in the *Demographic yearbook 1977* show long-term migrants as a separate category, whereas those published in the *Demographic yearbook 1989* provide no breakdown by category. In contrast, for the Falkland Islands, the Republic of Korea, Macau, Fiji, New Caledonia and Norfolk Island, more recent data are published by category (including that of long-term migrants) whereas older data did not make any differentiation between migrants and other travellers. Overall, therefore, there seems to have been little progress toward a more consistent reporting of data on long-term migration.

At the regional level, tables 3.11 and 3.12 indicate that there has been a noticeable deterioration in the availability of data for African countries or areas. Those providing overall numbers of arrivals and departures without identifying migrants declined from 11 to 5 between the 1977 and the 1989 issues

International migration statistics

Table 3.11. Countries reporting only overall number of arrivals and departures for selected periods

Region, country or area	Demographic yearbook 1977		Demographic yearbook 1989	
Africa				
Angola	1967-72	–	–	–
Botswana	–	–	1979-83	1986-87
Cape Verde	1967-73	–	1981	–
Comoros	1972-73	–	–	–
Ethiopia	–	–	1979	–
Gambia	–	–	1980-81	–
Guinea-Bissau	1967-70	–	–	–
Libyan Arab Jamahiriya	1967-68	–	–	–
Madagascar	1967-68	–	–	–
Mauritania	1969-71	–	–	–
Mozambique	1967-71	–	–	–
Sao Tome and Principe	1967-71	–	1981-86	–
Tunisia	1967-73	–	–	–
Western Sahara	1974	–	–	–
Latin America and the Caribbean				
Antigua	1974	–	1982-83	–
Bermuda	–	–	1982-84	1987-88
Costa Rica	1967-71	–	–	–
Grenada	1975	–	1979	–
Guadeloupe	–	–	1979-80	–
Guatemala	1967-69	–	–	–
Honduras	–	–	1985	–
Martinique	–	–	1983-84	1987-88
Montserrat	1967-76	–	–	–
Puerto Rico	–	–	1979-88	–
St. Pierre and Miquelon	1967-69	–	–	–
St. Vincent	1972-73	–	–	–
Bolivia	1967-72	–	–	–
Falkland Islands	1967-69	–	1980-81	–
French Guiana	–	–	1983-86	–
Peru	–	–	1979-86	–
Asia				
Bahrain	1967-68	–	1985	–
India	–	–	1985-88	–
Iraq	1972-73	–	–	–
Jordan	1967-69	1972-76	1979-88	–
Korea, Republic of	1974-76	–	–	–
Kuwait	1967-73	–	1979-85	–
Macau	1967-70	1972-74	–	–
Qatar	–	–	1982	1986-87

Data collection systems concerning all international migrants

Table 3.11. (*continued*)

Region, country or area	Demographic yearbook 1977		Demographic yearbook 1989	
Singapore	–	–	1979-88	–
Sri Lanka	–	–	1979-84	1986-88
Thailand	–	–	1979-81	–
Turkey	–	–	1980	1983-85
Oceania				
American Samoa	–	–	1979-84	1987-88
Fiji	1967-76	–	–	–
New Caledonia	1967-68	1973-76	–	–
Niue	–	–	1981	1986-87
Norfolk Island	1974-76	–	–	–
USSR	–	–	1987-88	–

Source: United Nations (1978; 1991).

of the *Demographic yearbook*. The number of those producing some data on long-term migration dropped from 18 to 7 between the two issues. In recent years, only a handful of African countries seem to have been producing time series data on international migration flows, mainly small islands such as Mauritius, Saint Helena and the Seychelles, plus South Africa and Zimbabwe. For the last two, it is not clear whether the data available cover all international migration flows. In Zimbabwe, the data available before 1980 refer only to the movements of the "European, Asian and the coloured population" (excluding blacks) (United Nations, 1991, p. 531).

In Latin America and the Caribbean, most island countries or areas have gathered some information on international arrivals and departures, but only about half of those having data distinguish long-term migrants from the generality of travellers. For the region as a whole, the number of countries or areas reporting only overall numbers of arrivals and departures increased from 9 to 10 between the 1977 and the 1989 issues of the *Demographic yearbook*, while the number reporting data on long-term migrants declined from 19 to 14. Furthermore, only 10 countries or areas reported information on long-term migrants in both 1977 and 1989, suggesting that the data collection efforts were continuous in those ten countries. Yet, as table 3.12 shows, only Panama and Trinidad and Tobago had virtually uninterrupted series on long-term immigrants as covered by the respective *Demographic yearbooks*, and only Trinidad and Tobago also had such a series for long-term emigrants. On the whole, therefore, the situation regarding the availability of flow statistics in Latin America and the Caribbean does not seem to have improved between the late 1970s and the late 1980s.

In Asia, although the number of countries or areas reporting statistics on either long-term immigrants or long-term emigrants remained virtually

International migration statistics

Table 3.12. Countries reporting long-term immigrants and emigrants for selected periods

	Long-term immigrants		Long-term emigrants	
	Demographic yearbook 1977	*Demographic yearbook 1989*	*Demographic yearbook 1977*	*Demographic yearbook 1989*
Africa				
Egypt	1972-73	—	1968-73	—
Ethiopia	1967-69	—	1967-69	—
Ghana	1967-70	—	1967-70	—
Kenya	1967-76	1985	1967-76	—
Liberia	1970	—	1970	—
Mauritius	1967-76	1979-88	1967-76	1979-88
Morocco	1967-73	—	1968-73	—
Nigeria	1967-73	—	1967-70	1972-73
Rwanda	1967-68	—	1967-68	—
St. Helena	1967-69	1979-86	—	1979-86
Seychelles	1967-74	1979-87	1967-74	1979-87
Somalia	1971	—	1971	—
South Africa	1967-74	1984-88	1967-74	1984-88
Swaziland	—	1983-84	—	—
Uganda	1967-74	—	1967-74	—
Tanzania, United Rep. of	1967-68	—	1967-68	—
Zaire	1970	—	—	—
Zambia	1967-71	1974	—	—
Zimbabwe	1967-76	1979-88	1967-76	1979-88
Central America and the Caribbean				
Barbados	1967-68	—	—	—
Belize	1967-69	1972-73	1967-69	1972-73
British Virgin Islands	1967-70	1973-75	1967-71	1973-75
Cayman Islands	—	1981-82	1975-76	1981-82
Cuba	—	1983	—	1983
Dominica	1967	—	1967	—

146

Data collection systems concerning all international migrants

Dominican Republic	1967-70	1972-73	1985-86	—	1967-70	1972-73	1985-86
Haiti	1968-73	—	—	—	1968-75	—	—
Mexico	1967-73	—	1979-82	—	1967-73	—	1979-85
Panama	1967-76	—	1979-88	—	—	—	—
St. Kitts and Nevis	1967-71	—	—	—	1967-71	—	—
Trinidad and Tobago	1967-76	—	1979-87	—	1967-76	—	1979-87

South America

Argentina	1967-68	1971-73	—	—	—	—	—
Brazil	1967-75	—	1983-84	1986	—	—	—
Chile	1967-71	1974-75	1979-80	—	1967-72	1974-75	—
Colombia	1967-69	—	1980-81	—	1967-69	—	—
Ecuador	—	—	1979-82	1986-88	—	—	1979-88
Falkland Islands	—	—	1988	—	—	—	—
Guyana	1969-70	1972-75	—	—	1969-70	1972-75	—
Peru	1967-68	—	—	—	—	—	—
Suriname	—	—	1981-82	1985-86	—	—	1981-82	1985-87
Uruguay	1967	1970-72	1980-81	1983-84	—	—	1979-82	1985-88
Venezuela	1967-71	1974	1979-82	1985-88	1967-71	1974	1979-82

Asia

Afghanistan	—	—	1979-81	—	—	—	1979-81
Brunei	1971-73	—	1980-85	1987	—	—	—
Cyprus	1967-68	1972	1981-88	—	1967-75	—	1979-88
Hong Kong	1967-76	—	1979-88	—	—	—	—
Indonesia	—	—	1983	—	—	—	1983
Israel	1967-75	—	1979-88	—	1967-72	—	1984-86
Japan	1967-76	—	1979-88	—	1967-76	—	1979-88
Korea, Republic of	—	—	1982-86	1988	—	—	1983-88
Macau	—	—	1981-82	—	—	—	1981
Myanmar	1968	1971-73	1988	—	1968	1971-75	1980-83	1987-88
Philippines	1967-68	—	—	—	1967-68	1972-73	1981-84	1986-88

147

International migration statistics

Table 3.12. (continued)

	Long-term immigrants			Long-term emigrants		
	Demographic yearbook 1977	Demographic yearbook 1989		Demographic yearbook 1977	Demographic yearbook 1989	
Singapore	1967-76	—		—	—	
Sri Lanka	1967-71	—		1967-71	—	
Syrian Arab Republic	—	—		—	1980-81	
Thailand	1967-70	—		—	—	
Turkey	1967-74	—		1967-75	—	
Yemen, Democratic	1968-70	—		1968-70	—	
Oceania						
Australia	1967-74	1979-84	1986-87	1967-74	1979-87	—
Christmas Island	1967-68	—		1967-68	—	
Cook Island	1973-74	—		—	—	
Fiji	—	—		1973-76	1979	1981
Nauru	—	—		1967	—	
New Caledonia	—	1979-88		—	1987-88	
New Zealand	1967-76	1979-88		1967-76	1979-88	
Niue	1967	1969-71		1967-71	—	
Norfolk Island	—	—		—	1980	
Papua New Guinea	1974-75	1980-81	1983-88	1967-75	1980-81	1983-88
Samoa	1975-76	—		—	—	
Solomon Islands	1972	—		—	—	
Wallis and Futuna	1969	—		1969	—	

Source: United Nations (1978; 1991).

Data collection systems concerning all international migrants

unchanged between the 1977 and the 1989 issues of the *Demographic yearbook*, there was a tendency for countries that had such data in 1977 to present only overall totals in 1989, thus precluding the identification of migrants. Yet, in the cases of Afghanistan, Macau and the Republic of Korea, new or more detailed information was available in the late 1980s compared to the late 1970s. In addition, fairly complete time series of statistics on long-term immigrants were available for Hong Kong, Israel and Japan, but data on long-term emigrants were more sparse. On the whole, most countries or areas reporting data on long-term migration in Asia only did so in a few years.

Lastly, in Oceania, Australia and New Zealand have consistent and complete series of statistics on international migration flows that conform well to the definitions of long-term migration suggested by the United Nations. For other countries or areas in the region, the availability of flow statistics is less consistent and has shown some tendency to decline over time, especially for long-term migration. Thus, whereas nine countries or areas reported some data on long-term immigrants in 1977, only four did so in 1989.

This overview suggests that even in terms of mere data availability, the situation in developing countries has not improved between the late 1970s and the late 1980s, and in certain regions there are clear signs of deterioration. In addition, it is not certain that the data published by the United Nations actually conform to the definitions suggested. The trend in the number of countries or areas reporting short-term migration separately suggests that there is little consistency in the data reported over time. Quick fixes are likely to have been adopted by countries to make their data appear to conform to new United Nations definitions without really changing their nature. In Africa, for instance, eight countries or areas reported separately data on short-term immigrants and emigrants in the late 1970s, but only four did so in the 1980s, only two of which were also in the earlier group (Saint Helena and the Seychelles). In Latin America and the Caribbean, 10 countries reported data on short-term immigrants and emigrants in the 1970s, and nine did so in the 1980s, but the two groups differed almost entirely. Only Chile was present in both, providing data on short-term immigrants in the 1970s and on short-term emigrants in the 1980s. In Asia there was somewhat more consistency, with countries or areas such as Cyprus, Hong Kong, Japan and Myanmar reporting short-term migrants in both periods. In addition, three other countries did so in the 1970s and four different ones in the 1980s. In Oceania, six countries or areas provided reports on short-term migrants during each period but only two, Pacific Islands and Papua New Guinea, had the relevant data for both periods. In a few countries – Kenya, South Africa and the Cayman Islands, according to the *Demographic yearbook 1989* – the data on long-term migrants include short-term migrants. It appears that for several of the countries listing short-term immigrants, the condition that they be admitted explicitly to work for less than a year is not always met.

The task of clarifying the exact meaning of the statistics published is far from straightforward. To cite but one example, consider the case of Mexico

International migration statistics

whose arrival and departure statistics have been published with some consistency since the 1960s. Mexican law recognizes the existence of different categories of migrants, and the border statistics gathered reflect those categories. Table 3.13 presents a description of the different categories used and Table 3.14 shows the numbers reported for 1973 and 1980. Those numbers served as the basis for

Table 3.13. Categories of citizens and foreigners used in the tabulation of arrival and departure statistics of Mexico

Category	Definition
Citizen	
Arrivals	
Turistas residentes en México (tourists residing in Mexico)	Mexican citizens who reside in Mexico and return from a short visit abroad
Turistas residentes en el extranjero (tourists residing abroad)	Mexican citizens who reside abroad and enter Mexico for a short visit
Diplomáticos (diplomats)	Mexican officials returning from a posting abroad
Repatriados (repatriating citizens)	Former Mexican emigrants who return to the country after having resided at least two years abroad
Deportados (expellees)	Mexican citizens expelled from a foreign country filing form FM II
Departures	
Turistas residentes en México (tourists residing in Mexico)	Mexican citizens who reside in Mexico and leave for a short visit abroad
Turistas residentes en el extranjero (tourists residing abroad)	Mexican citizens who reside abroad and leave Mexico after a short visit
Diplomáticos (diplomats)	Mexican officials departing (presumably to be posted abroad)
Emigrantes (emigrants)	Persons leaving the country with the purpose of "establishing residence" abroad (Art. 77). According to the law, an emigrant should be able to show the documents allowing him/her to resettle in another country (Art. 78)
Foreigners	
Immigrants	
Inmigrantes (provisional immigrants)	Persons entering the country with the purpose of residing in it (Art. 44). Immigrants are granted five-year residence permits that must be validated annually (Art. 45). Statistics on arrivals present data on *inmigrantes por primera vez* (first-time immigrants) and *inmigrantes de regreso* (returning immigrants). Departures show different categories for immigrants leaving temporarily and leaving permanently
Inmigrados (permanent immigrants)	Persons who acquire the right of permanent residence in Mexico. Temporary immigrants may apply for permanent residence after five years of stay in Mexico (Art. 53). Arrival data show *inmigrados de regreso* (returning permanent immigrants), while those on departures distinguish permanent immigrants who leave temporarily from those who leave for good

Data collection systems concerning all international migrants

Table 3.13. (*continued*)

Category	Definition
Non-Immigrants	
Tourists	Foreigners admitted for up to six months for recreational purposes (Art. 42.I). They are not permitted to work for a salary. This category is recorded in both arrivals and departures
Transmigrantes (transit migrants)	Persons in transit to another country. They may remain in Mexico for up to 30 days (Art. 42.II)
Visitantes (visitors)	Persons who will exercise some activity, whether lucrative or not, for up to six months, with a possible extension of another six, or in some cases, another year (Art.42. III). Arrival data distinguish between visitors arriving for the first time and returning visitors. Departures show separately visitors departing permanently and visitors departing temporarily
Visitantes provisionales (provisional visitors)	Persons whose entry is allowed for a stay not exceeding 30 days when their papers are not in perfect order (Art. 42.IX). Arrivals and departures of this type of travellers are presented separately
Consejeros (advisers)	Persons granted a permit valid for six months and good for multiple entries provided no stay is longer than 30 days (Art. 42.IV). Arrival statistics distinguish advisers entering for the first time from those returning after a trip abroad. Permanent and temporary departures are also distinguished
Asilados políticos (asylum-seekers)	Persons allowed to stay for a limited time so as to protect their liberty and life from political persecution in their country of origin (Art. 42.V). Arrival data distinguish between first-time asylum-seekers and returning asylum-seekers. Departure data present separately asylum-seekers leaving temporarily and those departing permanently
Students	Persons allowed to study in Mexico under annual permits (Art. 42. VI). Arrivals distinguish students entering for the first time from those returning. Departures indicate whether students are leaving permanently or temporarily
Diplomáticos (diplomats)	Foreign government personnel whose arrivals and departures are recorded
Deportados (expellees)	Foreigners expelled by Mexican authorities
Other	A few other categories of aliens admitted for short periods under special conditions (which exclude the permission to work)

Sources: *Ley General de Población, 1974* (specific articles are shown in parenthesis within the table), and interviews with personnel of the "Dirección General de Servicios Migratorios" as reported by García y Griego (1987), pp. 1247-1248.

the derivation of the statistics published by the United Nations under different categories. The 1973 data were published in the *Demographic yearbook 1977* and the 1980 data in the 1989 issue. Table 3.14 uses code numbers to indicate which of the categories of migrants or travellers that are used to classify the border statistics of Mexico were combined to yield the categories presented in the

International migration statistics

Table 3.14. Arrivals and departures in 1973 and 1980 according to the border statistics of Mexico and the United Nations *Demographic yearbook*

Code	Category	Number	Code	Category	Number
	Total arrivals 1973	**3 986 574**		**Total arrivals 1980**	**5 521 878**
	Citizens	938 974		Citizens	1 691 065
7	Tourists residing in Mexico	340 985	7	Tourists residing in Mexico	1 027 368
2	Tourists residing abroad	337 571	2	Tourists residing abroad	527 699
1	Repatriates	15 407	1	Repatriates	9 267
1	Deportees	239 120	1	Deportees	120 683
1	Diplomats	5 891	1	Diplomats	6 048
	Foreigners	3 047 600		Foreigners	3 830 813
	Provisional immigrants:			Provisional immigrants:	
1	First time	2 135	1	First time	1 389
7	Returning	17 865	7	Returning	22 616
	Permanent immigrants:			Permanent immigrants:	
7	Returning	36 532	7	Returning	49 255
	Non-immigrants:			Non-immigrants:	
2	Tourists	2 901 183	2	Tourists	3 613 044
6	Transit migrants	32 514	6	Transit migrants	48 116
3	Students, first time	3 888	3	Students, first time	4 253
3	Students returning	10 208	3	Students returning	16 190
5	Asylum-seekers, first time	309	1	Asylum-seekers, first time	403
5	Asylum-seekers returning	14	7	Asylum-seekers returning	60
1	Diplomats	21 175	1	Diplomats	26 544
5	Special permits	4 544	0	Special permits	2 535
4	Visitors, first time	17 233	0	Visitors, first time	30 035
			0	Visitors returning	16 181
			0	Provisional visitors	6
			0	Advisers first time	153
			0	Advisers returning	33
	Data according to *Demographic yearbook 1977*			Data according to *Demographic yearbook 1989*	
	–		0	Short-term immigrants	48 943
1	Long-term immigrants	283 728	1	Long-term immigrants	164 334
	Visitors:			Visitors:	
2	Holiday	3 238 754	2	Holiday	4 140 743
3	Education	14 096	3	Education	20 443
4	Business	17 233		–	
5	Other	4 867		–	
6	Transit visitors	32 514	6	Transit visitors	48 116
7	Residents returning	395 382	7	Residents returning	1 099 299
	Total departures 1973	**3 118 598**		**Total departures 1980**	**4 482 382**
	Citizens	601 521		Citizens	1 310 261
7	Tourists residing in Mexico	375 408	7	Tourists residing in Mexico	981 020
2	Tourists residing abroad	210 015	2	Tourists residing abroad	320 227
1	Temporary emigrants	10 226	1	Emigrants	2 444

Data collection systems concerning all international migrants

Table 3.14. (*continued*)

Code	Category	Number	Code	Category	Number
1	Diplomats	5 872	1	Diplomats	6 570
	Foreigners	2 517 077		Foreigners	3 172 121
	Temporary emigrants:			Temporary emigrants:	
7	Provisional immigrants	19 464	7	Provisional immigrants	23 279
1	Permanent immigrants	37 573	7	Permanent immigrants	49 234
	Permanent emigrants:			Permanent emigrants:	
1	Provisional immigrants	1 291	1	Provisional immigrants	521
1	Permanent immigrants	65	1	Permanent immigrants	86
	Non-immigrants:			Non-immigrants:	
2	Tourists	2 380 929	2	Tourists	2 961 822
6	Transit migrants	27 737	6	Transit migrants	39 008
3	Temporary students	11 605	3	Temporary students	19 556
3	Permanent students	1 018	3	Permanent students	1 013
5	Temporary asylum-seekers	21	7	Temporary asylum-seekers	17
5	Permanent asylum-seekers	77	0	Permanent asylum-seekers	39
1	Deportees	2 026	1	Deportees	12 947
1	Diplomats	20 721	1	Diplomats	25 326
5	Special permits	4 557	1	Special permits	2 740
4	Visitors	9 993	0	Temporary visitors	23 130
			1	Permanent visitors	13 340
			1	Provisional visitors	0
			1	Temporary advisers	41
			1	Permanent advisers	22
	Data according to *Demographic yearbook 1977*			**Data according to *Demographic yearbook 1989***	
			0	Short-term emigrants	23 169
1	Long-term emigrants	77 774	1	Long-term emigrants	64 037
	Visitors			Visitors	
2	Holiday	2 590 944	2	Holiday	3 282 049
3	Education	12 623	3	Education	20 569
4	Business	9 993		–	
5	Other	4 655		–	
6	Transit visitors	27 737	6	Transit visitors	39 008
7	Residents departing	394 872	7	Residents departing	1 053 550

Sources: Mexico (n.d. and 1981) and United Nations (1978 and 1991).

Demographic yearbooks. Several problems can readily be detected. First, the definitions underlying the statistics gathered by Mexico do not conform to those suggested by the United Nations. For example, there is the category of "transit visitors" which, according to the United Nations, includes persons who do not spend even one night in the receiving country and who remain in special holding lounges in airports or ships because they do not undergo formal passport control (United Nations, 1987 and 1991). But the category of *transmigrantes*, as

International migration statistics

used by Mexico, includes persons who, albeit in transit, may spend up to 30 days in Mexican territory.

A more serious problem stems from the fact that Mexican statistics do not differentiate travellers from migrants according to expected length of stay or absence, at least not in the sense of using one year as the cutoff point for differentiation as recommended by the United Nations. Consequently, in deciding which categories of arriving and departing persons are considered long-term immigrants and emigrants, subjective considerations (of the Mexican government clerks and officials) based on citizenship, purpose of travel or stay, and place of residence are made. Furthermore, the decisions made by the authorities are not consistent over time so that the groups considered to be long-term migrants in 1973 were not the same as those used for 1980. In terms of arrivals, in the 1970s long-term immigrants were equated to the sum of repatriating Mexicans, Mexicans deported by United States authorities, Mexican diplomats returning from postings abroad, foreigners admitted as "provisional immigrants" for the first time, and foreign diplomats. In the 1980s the category of asylum-seekers admitted for the first time was added as well. Greater differences between one period and the next can be observed with respect to the identification of long-term emigrants, which in the 1970s included: emigrating Mexicans (temporary emigrants); departing Mexican diplomats; foreigners holding permanent residence permits and leaving the country temporarily; foreigners holding temporary or permanent residence permits and leaving the country definitely; foreigners deported by Mexican authorities; and foreign diplomats departing. By the 1980s, several categories were added to that list, namely: foreigners on special permits departing; foreign visitors holding permanent or provisional permits departing; and foreign advisers holding temporary or permanent permits departing. In addition, the category of foreigners holding permanent residence permits who left the country temporarily was taken out of the long-term emigrants category and put in that of returning residents. Although one can debate whether the groupings used in the 1970s are more or less appropriate than those used in the 1980s, the main point is clear: they were different. Because this is not made explicit in the data published by the United Nations, use of the data can lead to considerable confusion and misrepresentation of trends.

In 1989, the data published for Mexico included the categories of short-term immigrants and emigrants. The latter, short-term emigrants, was equated with the sum of permanent asylum-seekers departing and temporary foreign visitors departing. According to United Nations recommendations, short-term emigrants are persons who have been in the country of reference (departure) for more than a year and who leave to work abroad for at most a year. In contrast, according to Mexican definitions, temporary foreign visitors (*visitantes*) are those who are considered unlikely to remain in Mexico for more than a year, even though they may work while in Mexico. But when these persons leave Mexico, it is not known that they will be leaving to work abroad for less than a year, since they may be returning to their permanent jobs and residences.

Data collection systems concerning all international migrants

Thus, the numbers reported by Mexico under "short-term emigrants" better represent the United Nations category of "short-term immigrants departing" (United Nations, 1980a), namely, persons admitted as short-term immigrants who depart within a year of arrival. The confusion between the two categories stems from the traditional interpretation of emigrants as the counterpart of immigrants, and suggests that the producers of statistics in Mexico have not yet become familiar with (or accepted) the less-than-straightforward concepts being proposed by the United Nations.

In conclusion, problems encountered in determining the exact meaning of the flow statistics published in the *Demographic yearbook* are likely to be similar for many other countries and thereby compromise the usefulness of the data derived from border statistics. Thus, in the absence of any guarantee that the statistics published truly conform to the definitions suggested by the United Nations, they may be quite misleading. Furthermore, in several respects, even if the statistics on long-term and short-term migrants were perfectly consistent and complete over time, problems related to their interpretation would still arise, partly because they fail to distinguish key components of international migration, mainly the participation of foreigners and citizens in the various types of flows.

3. Relevance of border statistics

Although border statistics are ideally suited to reflect international migration flows as they occur, problems related to the consistent and comparable identification of international migrants between countries and within the same country over time continue to plague them, as noted above. Furthermore, countries gathering border statistics do not always publish them at regular intervals or publish only overall numbers of arrivals and departures that are virtually useless for the measurement of international migration flows. Lack of easily accessible time series statistics from border control prevents their use for either the measurement of international migration or their evaluation. By their very nature, border statistics are unlikely to provide a complete coverage of international migrants, but an assessment of their completeness cannot be carried out on the basis of gross numbers of arriving and departing persons.

Countries publishing the statistics derived from border control in some detail often provide information not only on gross levels of inflows and outflows of international migrants but also on some of the categories of migrants characterized in Chapter 2. It is, however, often difficult to infer from the published data exactly what different types of migrants are. In the case of Mexico, for instance, without access to the text of the law, it would not have been likely to infer that the category of "visitors" encompasses foreigners admitted for short periods with the possibility of exercising an economic activity. The need to produce not only detailed tabulations of the data gathered but also adequate documentation explaining the meaning and scope of the data cannot be stressed enough.

It is important to emphasize that border statistics can provide useful information even when they do not conform to international standards. The quest for international comparability should not be pursued at the expense of rendering existing statistics meaningless by imposing moulds that country practices cannot fit into. The availability of comparable and consistent statistics on long-term migration as defined by the United Nations can yield adequate estimates of net migration that are a necessary ingredient for the preparation of population projections. Yet, even their general availability would not satisfy all data needs in regard to international migration. Information on long-term migration, *per se*, does not address most questions posed about the migration of labour, immigration for permanent settlement or return migration. It is important, therefore, to increase the flexibility of statistics derived from border control by gathering information on both the type of migration involved according to national laws or regulations and according to the expected duration of presence or absence of persons in a country's territory. By thus enriching the data available, statistics may be derived to satisfy a variety of needs.

Because the use of border control as a source of statistics on international migration is more common in developing than in developed countries, any broad effort to improve the quality and availability of border statistics needs to focus on developing countries. Better information is needed on actual country practices to ascertain which changes in data collection procedures are likely to be most effective. Personnel will need to be trained and a sustained effort made to ensure that any changes introduced actually result in better statistics. All this can only be done with the commitment of the relevant authorities. Countries experiencing important changes in levels of international migration are prime candidates for improvements in border statistics. The recommendations below are intended to guide their efforts.

4. Recommendations to improve border statistics

- Countries deriving statistics from border control should publish them at regular intervals in conjunction with information describing their meaning and scope. This information should include definitions of each of the categories of arrivals and departures identified in the statistics as well as a list of categories of travellers not covered by the statistics. The procedures used in gathering the statistics published should also be described.
- The information gathered on persons subject to border control should include the following:

Data collection systems concerning all international migrants

Socio-demographic information:
  Name;
  Date of birth;
  Sex;
  Country of citizenship;
  Country of birth;
  Marital status;
  Educational attainment:
    Highest level of education attended;
    Number of years of schooling completed;
  Occupation;
  Sector of economic activity.

Mobility history for persons arriving:
  Date of arrival;
  Country from which the person arrives (country of origin);
  Whether the person has ever lived in the country of arrival;
  If the person has been in the country of arrival:
    Date of most recent departure from country of arrival;
    Purpose of stay abroad;
  Intended length of stay in the country of arrival;
  Purpose of stay in the country of arrival.

Mobility history for persons departing:
  Date of departure;
  Country of destination;
  Whether the person has ever been abroad;
  If the person has been abroad:
    Date of most recent arrival in the country of departure;
    Purpose of stay while in the country of departure;
  Intended length of stay abroad;
  Purpose of stay abroad.

Administrative information:
  For foreigners:
    Type of visa, entry or residence permit;
  For citizens:
    Type of passport:
      Tourist;
      Diplomatic;
      Worker's passport;
      Other.

The information on mobility is needed to implement the United Nations recommendations on the identification of long-term immigrants and emigrants as well as that of short-term migrants. Modifications to the questions are possible if different sets are posed to citizens and foreigners. It is also possible to

International migration statistics

try to establish a difference between "insiders" and "outsiders" by recording the country in which the person lives. Thus, the information recorded on a person's mobility history can be modified in the following way:

Mobility history for persons arriving:
  Date of arrival;
  Country from which the person arrives;
  Country in which the person lives;
  If the person lives in the country of arrival:
    Date of most recent departure from country of arrival;
    Purpose of stay abroad;
  Intended length of stay in the country of arrival;
  Purpose of stay in the country of arrival.

Mobility history for persons departing:
  Date of departure;
  Country of destination;
  Country in which the person lives;
  If the person lives abroad:
    Date of most recent arrival in the country of departure;
    Purpose of stay while in the country of departure;
  Intended length of stay abroad;
  Purpose of stay abroad.

- The following tabulations should be published:
  (a) Number of persons arriving classified by migrant and non-migrant categories, sex and citizenship (citizens versus foreigners);
  (b) Number of persons departing classified by migrant and non-migrant categories, sex and citizenship (citizens versus foreigners);
  (c) Number of migrants arriving by category, sex, age group and country of citizenship;
  (d) Number of migrants departing by category, sex, age group and country of citizenship;
  (e) Number of migrants arriving by category, sex, age group, citizenship (citizens versus foreigners) and country of origin;
  (f) Number of migrants departing by category, sex, age group citizenship (citizens versus foreigners) and country of destination;
  (g) Number of migrants arriving by category, sex, age group and country of birth;
  (h) Number of migrants departing by category, sex, age group and country of birth;
  (i) Number of long-term immigrants by sex, age group and country of origin;
  (j) Number of long-term emigrants by sex, age group and country of destination;

Data collection systems concerning all international migrants

- (k) Number of short-term immigrants and short-term immigrants departing by sex, age group, citizenship (citizens versus foreigners) and country of origin/destination;
- (l) Number of short-term emigrants and short-term emigrants returning by sex, age group, citizenship (citizens versus foreigners) and country of destination/origin;
- (m) Number of migrants arriving by sex, citizenship (citizens versus foreigners) and occupation;
- (n) Number of migrants departing by sex, citizenship (citizens versus foreigners) and occupation;
- (o) Number of migrants arriving by sex, citizenship (citizens versus foreigners) and educational attainment;
- (p) Number of migrants departing by sex, citizenship (citizens versus foreigners) and educational attainment;
- (q) Number of migrants arriving by sex, citizenship (citizens versus foreigners) and marital status;
- (r) Number of migrants departing by sex, citizenship (citizens versus foreigners) and marital status.

- All tabulations produced should show data classified by sex.
- An effort should be made to publish regularly the tabulations derived from border statistics, preferably through specialized publications. Those publications should provide time series relative to specific tabulations, including (a) and (b) above. Tabulations (i) to (l) above should only be made if the data to identify long-term migrants and short-term migrants are gathered in accordance with United Nations recommendations. Otherwise, it is preferable to present the migrant categories used by each country according to its own rules and definitions, which may at least allow internal comparability over time. In all cases, the preparation of tabulations (a) to (e), (g) and (h) should be given priority.
- Countries that derive statistics from border control should explore ways of assessing their level of coverage by, among other things, comparing them with intercensal changes in the migrant stock or with other relevant sources of information.

Notes

[1] It was estimated that the number of Colombian migrants illegally present in Venezuela around 1980–81 was 100,000 (Zlotnik, 1989).

[2] Germany concluded recruitment agreements with Greece, Italy, Morocco, Spain, Tunisia, Turkey and Yugoslavia (Plender, 1987).

[3] The gathering of comprehensive border statistics is facilitated by their status as island (or continent) countries, with no land borders with other countries.

DATA COLLECTION SYSTEMS CONCERNING LABOUR MIGRATION

4

This chapter reviews the operation of data collection systems that are mainly geared to gathering data on international migrant workers, that is, persons admitted by a country other than their own for the explicit purpose of exercising an economic activity. During the past 50 years, a number of countries have adopted policies favouring the admission of international migrant workers to satisfy their labour needs. Often, the implementation of those policies has been accompanied by the development of complex administrative machinery to control the movement and activities of migrant workers after they arrive. In a parallel development, countries of origin have adopted policies favouring the emigration of workers and placing them in the international labour market. Regulatory mechanisms have therefore been developed to control the outflow of workers and ensure the protection of their rights. As a by-product, data on the migrants have been gathered by both countries of origin and countries of destination. The most common types of statistical systems emanating from such operations will be discussed here. They include: work permit statistics; statistics derived from reports by employers; and statistics derived from the control of contract labour migration by countries of origin. In addition, this chapter will discuss the data obtained through regularization drives since a precondition for regularizing a migrant's status is usually that the migrant be gainfully employed. Thus, it seems valid to assume that regularized migrants would have been international migrant workers had they not found themselves in an irregular situation.

A. WORK PERMIT STATISTICS

In most countries, foreigners wishing to exercise an economic activity must obtain official permission to do so before they enter the territory of the country in question. Usually the prospective employer of a foreigner is required to apply to the authorities for a work permit before the migrant is given permission to enter the country. Hence the number of new work permits granted

International migration statistics

during a given period is closely correlated with the number of new migrant workers admitted. For that reason, statistics on the number of new work permits issued are useful indicators of the size of the inflow of migrant workers.

Countries using work permits as a means of controlling the length of stay of migrant workers usually limit the duration of their validity while at the same time allowing their renewal when certain conditions are met. Since the administrative processes for renewing a permit are often similar to those involved in the issuance of a new work permit, it is common for the agency in charge of issuing work permits to make no distinction between renewals and new permits in its statistics on the number of permits processed over a given period. In those cases, the number of permits reported is a poor indicator of the actual flow of migrant workers. Furthermore, because the number of renewals depends on both the policies being pursued (allowing a longer or shorter stay for migrant workers, for instance) and the distribution of the existing stock of migrant workers by length of validity of their work permits, data that do not make a distinction between permits being renewed and those being issued for the first time do not have a straightforward interpretation. It is therefore crucial that data on the number of work permits be compiled and published by type (first-time permit versus renewal) as well as by duration of permit.

Another complicating factor is that in countries where migrant workers are allowed to be accompanied by family members, those family members may, under certain circumstances, be allowed to apply for and obtain work permits. Therefore, they will be given first-time work permits even though they may have already been present in the country for some time. Similarly, in some countries, foreigners admitted for purposes other than that of exercising an economic activity may be allowed, under certain circumstances, to apply for a work permit while already being present in the country. That was the case, for instance, of numerous migrant workers in France during the 1960s who did not follow the official procedure requiring that work permits first be obtained abroad. Instead, they entered France as tourists, found jobs, and then applied for regularization of their status. Another example is provided by persons admitted as students who in some countries are allowed to work for a limited period once their training is completed. Clearly, when there are numerous exceptions to the rule that first-time work permits be obtained abroad or immediately upon admission, the number of first-time work permits issued will not be a good indicator of the flow of migrant workers. In such cases, gathering information on whether or not the holder of a work permit has already been a resident of the country granting the permit would allow the identification of new arrivals and their differentiation from persons already there merely changing status. From a policy perspective, however, knowing how many foreigners have been allowed to enter the labour market for the first time is useful, irrespective of whether they are new arrivals in the country.

Another important statistic for policy-makers is the number of foreigners who are legally exercising an economic activity at a given point in time. Assuming that all foreigners having valid work permits are actually employed, the number of valid work permits would be equivalent to that statistic. Unfortunately, most agencies in charge of issuing work permits lack statistical systems capable of producing that number from available information. That is, record keepers tend to focus almost exclusively on the ongoing process of issuing or renewing work permits and do not keep track of the work permit history of individual migrants over time. Developing databases that allow the identification of the number of migrants having valid work permits at any given point in time would be useful. The technology exists; the question is whether the agencies in charge of issuing work permits have the will and resources to implement such innovations. Another crucial factor is the extent to which governments want to keep up-to-date, easily accessible records on international migrant workers and wish to disseminate the statistics derived from those records. In countries where international migrant workers constitute high proportions of the labour force, governments are often reluctant to release the relevant statistics.

The statistics derived from the issuance of work permits have several potential advantages. The first is that they refer only to migrant workers as defined in Chapter 2, and thus reflect the methods used by governments to control a foreigner's exercise of an economic activity. Consequently, they are more likely than other sources of information to permit the identification of different types of migrant workers, especially those belonging to the categories proposed in Chapter 2. In addition, because the issuance of a work permit usually depends on the existence of a job that a migrant worker will occupy and requires the existence of a contract, information obtained on the occupation, sector of economic activity, salary and other occupational characteristics of a migrant is likely to be more accurate than that obtained from self-reporting. Lastly, because the statistics on work permits reflect the actual performance of policy, they provide the necessary basis for policy evaluation. In this respect, gathering and publishing data on the numbers of requests for first-time permits and for renewals over a given period and on the numbers granted and refused would be most useful. Information on the length of time that it takes for a request to be processed would also provide a means for assessing the efficiency of policy implementation.

Among the drawbacks of work permit statistics, perhaps the most salient is that they reflect the economic activity only of those foreigners subject to control. In countries where common market arrangements exist, citizens of States that are members of the common labour market are likely to be exempt from the need to secure a work permit to work in a State other than their own. In some countries, citizens of former colonies may also be exempt from work permit requirements. In other countries, foreign corporations or foreign contractors may be granted collective work permits allowing them to bring in several foreign workers for a given period: their numbers are not likely to be adequately recorded if they are admitted on a collective basis.

Work permit statistics also have the drawback of not covering those foreigners who work illegally, that is, who do not obtain the necessary work permit to engage in an economic activity. However, some types of irregular

International migration statistics

migrant workers are reflected by work permit statistics, including persons who keep on working when their permit has expired or those who change employers in contravention of regulations.

Almost all countries of the world have some provisions for the admission of foreigners intending to exercise an economic activity. Those provisions often stipulate that such foreigners must obtain a work permit. Hence, work permit statistics are available or potentially available from many countries. However, there has not yet been a concerted effort to obtain worldwide information on such statistics. The overview provided below will therefore be less than comprehensive. Selected country experiences will be used to illustrate the various modes of operation of work permit systems.

1. Europe

As a result of their experience as labour importers, several market-economy countries of Europe have developed elaborate systems of work permits to control the admission and exercise of an economic activity by foreigners. Although most European countries have ceased being importers of migrant workers in recent years, the work permit systems used at the height of labour migration remain largely in place and are being used to regulate the entry into the labour force of family members (children and spouses) of the original migrant workers. In addition, all countries still allow the admission of highly skilled international migrants who are also subject to work permit requirements, and some countries are developing new labour importing schemes for seasonal and project-tied migrant workers.

In Belgium, the Ministry of Labour is in charge of issuing work permits to foreigners whose employers have the permission to hire them. In principle, such permissions ceased to be issued when the decision to restrict labour migration was issued on 8 August 1974. Some foreign workers are, however, still being admitted: for example, in 1989, 3,697 work permits were granted to new immigrants (Poulain et al., n.d.). Work permit statistics in Belgium do not reflect several groups of foreigners who are exempt from the requirement of holding a work permit. Thus, citizens of the European Union, having the right of free movement within the Union, do not need work permits to work in Belgium. In addition, certain categories of foreigners settled permanently in Belgium, including some citizens of Burundi, Rwanda and Zaire, are exempt, as are aliens registered as seamen in the Belgian merchant marine, ministers of religion, and some journalists.

There are two general categories of work permits in Belgium: temporary work permits denominated B and C; and permanent work permits, denominated A (OECD, 1986). Temporary permits are valid for a year and are renewable. Holders are restricted to work in a particular branch of industry, are required to sign labour contracts, and must possess a medical certificate validating their physical fitness. On the other hand, a permanent work permit can be obtained only after a foreigner has lived and worked continuously in Belgium for a certain period (or has specific family ties with a migrant worker), and allows the holder to work in any type of employment.

The Ministry of Labour compiles and tabulates the statistics on work permits. Three types of tables are available, showing: the number of temporary and permanent work permits issued by sex and country of citizenship, and by whether the work permit was issued to a new immigrant or to a foreigner already present in Belgium; the number of temporary and permanent work permits issued by industrial sector and by whether the permit was issued to a new immigrant or to a foreigner already residing in Belgium; and the numbers of persons receiving work permits over a year by age group, sex and country of citizenship (26 countries are identified separately). Some of the statistics in these tables are published in the statistical yearbook of the National Institute of Statistics (Poulain et al., n.d.).

In Belgium, foreigners wishing to become own-account workers do not require work permits but must be in possession of either a professional card or a hawker's card (for those exercising an ambulatory activity), both of which are issued by the Ministry of the Middle Classes. Professional cards are valid for five years, and hawker's cards can be valid for up to six years and are renewable. The National Institute of Statistics publishes data on the number of hawkers by citizenship (but only by Belgian versus foreign), sex and place of residence. The Ministry of Economic Affairs, in collaboration with the National Institute of Statistics, publishes annual data on professional cards in a publication entitled *Statistics on internal trade and transport* (Poulain et al., n.d.). The tables published include number of professional cards by citizenship, age group and marital status; number of professional cards by citizenship and place of residence; professional cards by citizenship and region; and cards by type of economic activity and region of origin of holder.

In Greece, foreigners wishing to exercise an economic activity must be in possession of a work permit issued by the Bureau of Employment and Labour. Citizens of the European Union cannot be denied a work permit but are required to have it. Other foreigners must file an application to the competent office in each prefecture which transmits such application to both the Ministry of the Interior and Public Order and the Bureau of Employment and Labour. Data relative to the number of work permits issued annually are transmitted to the National Institute of Statistics which is in charge of their publication (Koszamanis, n.d.).

In Ireland, the Department of Labour issues work permits to employers who can prove that there are no qualified workers either in Ireland or in other countries of the European Union available to perform a certain job. Statistics on work permits issued differentiate those granted for the first time from renewals (Poulain et al., n.d.).

In the Netherlands, foreigners usually require work permits to secure employment. Application must be made jointly by the foreign worker and the prospective employer (OECD, 1986). Categories of foreigners exempted from holding a work permit include: citizens of the European Union; foreigners granted permanent residence in the Netherlands; foreigners holding a residence permit of unlimited duration by virtue of being dependants of other migrants; refugees; and foreign nationals covered by special treaties (van der Erf et al., n.d.). Work permits are issued by the Ministry of Social Affairs and Labour. Normally, a foreigner is first granted a temporary work permit which is generally valid for three years after which the foreigner can apply for a permanent work permit. Dependent family members of holders of permanent work permits may apply directly for the permanent work permit without having to obtain first a temporary permit. It must be noted that if a foreign person has several employers at the same time, he or she may be covered by more than one work permit simultaneously. The Ministry of Social Affairs and Labour registers all the temporary and permanent work permits issued in the Netherlands. The information gathered on each permit holder includes: name, date of birth, sex, citizenship, type of permit, length of validity, and date on which the permit takes effect. The Ministry produces tabulations on the data gathered and publishes some of them in its annual report, with more detailed tables for internal use only (van der Erf et al., n.d.). The latter include information on the number of temporary and permanent permits granted and refused by citizenship of applicant.

In Spain, foreigners wishing to work either on their own account or as salaried workers must obtain a permit which is issued jointly by the Ministry of Labour and the Ministry of the Interior. Citizens of the European Union and their dependants need a work permit only if they are to be salaried workers. Other foreigners can obtain one of five types of permit according to their length of stay and type of economic activity (Escribano-Morales, n.d.). Holders of type A permits can undertake seasonal or occasional employment. Type A permits can be renewed only either twelve months after their issuance or three months after their expiration date. Holders of type B permits are constrained to work in a particular occupation and a particular region of the country. Type B permits may be renewed but only for the duration of another contract. Holders of type C permits are not subject to any restrictions with respect to employment type or location. Type C permits may be granted to foreigners who have worked legally in Spain for five continuous years. The period of continuous work is reduced to two years in the case of citizens of Andorra, Equatorial Guinea, Latin American countries, the Philippines or Portugal. Persons of Sephardic origin, those from Gibraltar, Ceuta and Melilla, and descendants of former Spanish citizens residing in Spain can also obtain type C permits after two years of continuous employment. Type C permits may also be granted to persons who have resided legally in Spain for eight years and who have worked continuously during the 12 months preceding the application for a type C permit. Lastly, foreigners wishing to work on their own account must obtain a type D permit which can restrict their activity to a certain location. Upon expiration, type D permits may be exchanged for type E permits, which do not subject the holder to any limitation in the exercise of an economic activity as an own-account worker.

Data collection systems concerning labour migration

Data gathered by the Ministry of Labour on the number of work permits issued per year are published in the *Anuario de Estadísticas Laborales*. The tabulations published include the number of permits granted by: type of permit and country of citizenship; type of permit, sex and age group of holder; type of permit and sector of economic activity; type of permit and occupation; type of permit and location of employment; country of citizenship, age group and sex; location of employment, age group and sex; country of citizenship, type of work and sector of economic activity; sex, age group and type of holder (European Union citizen, other foreigner, family member of resident foreigner); and country of citizenship and type of holder (Escribano-Morales, n.d.). The number of applications for work permits granted and rejected classified by the body responsible for the decision is also presented.

Spanish sources tend to qualify type A permits as "temporary" because their renewal is subject to waiting periods after the permit expires. Other types of permits are considered "permanent" because their renewal without leaving Spain is possible. Yet because all permits have a time limit, those terms are misleading and should be avoided. Given that certain permits may be renewed twice over a given year, statistics on work permits issued are distorted by a certain degree of double-counting. Furthermore, since no differentiation is made in the statistics published between new work permits and renewals of existing permits, those statistics cannot be used to ascertain the number of foreign workers that are actually new additions to the labour force during a given period.

In the United Kingdom, the Overseas Labour Section of the Department of Employment grants work permits to employers wishing to hire foreigners to perform specific jobs. Ordinary work permits are granted to employers planning to hire foreigners living outside the United Kingdom. Permits known as "first permissions" are granted to employers wishing to hire aliens already residing in the United Kingdom. To grant such permissions, the Home Office must ascertain whether the foreigner in question has a residence status allowing the exercise of an economic activity and, if not, must take steps to change that status if possible. Once ordinary work permits or first permissions expire, an employer may apply for an extension. If the foreign worker wishes to change employment, the prospective new employer must request that the work permit be modified. Employers may also apply for permits allowing them to engage foreigners as trainees or as persons gaining work experience (Salt, n.d.).

Categories of foreigners not requiring a work permit before engaging in an economic activity in the United Kingdom include: citizens of the European Union; dependants of work-permit holders; and Commonwealth citizens aged 17 to 27 who work in Britain only during the holidays. Work permits may be granted for both short-term work (less than 12 months) and for long-term work (one year or more). Until 1982, data on the numbers of short-term and long-term work permits issued were published annually in the Department of Employment *Gazette*. The data were classified by occupation, industry and main country of origin. The data are no longer published by the Department, but the tabulations are available and have been included in the United Kingdom SOPEMI (OECD Continuous Reporting System on Migration – *Système d'Observation Permanente sur les Migrations*) reports since 1985 (Salt, n.d.). In addition, in *Control of immigration statistics*, the Home Office publishes the total number of work permits issued annually and the number of dependents admitted, with holders of work permits classified by major area of origin (Old Commonwealth, New Commonwealth and Pakistan, and other countries).

Although the use of work permits to control access to a country's labour market by foreigners is more common in market-economy countries, some countries with economies in transition also use them. In Hungary, for instance, foreigners who wish to work must obtain a work permit from the Ministry of Employment. Information recorded about each foreigner obtaining a work permit includes: citizenship; sector of economic activity; type of occupation (manual versus non-manual); and educational attainment. There is no information about whether the data are processed or published. In Poland, the 1989 Act on Employment and Counteracting Unemployment establishes that local Labour Offices can grant short-term and long-term work permits to employers seeking to hire foreigners. Short-term work permits are valid for up to three months and long-term for up to 12 months. Renewals are possible and employers must return expired work permits to the Labour Office if they are not renewed. Information gathered about the persons covered by work permits includes: sex; date of birth; citizenship; previous country of residence; current occupation; sector of employment (public, private or mixed); and duration of permit. Tabulations of the number of work permits issued by selected characteristics of foreign workers are made manually and are presented in the *Quarterly information on structure of legal employment of foreigners*, prepared by the National Labour Office.

2. Latin America and the Caribbean

In Latin America and the Caribbean there are few countries that have had explicit policies favouring the admission of migrant workers and, consequently, statistics on such migrants appear to be rare. It is likely, however, that more countries than those identified below use work permits to control labour migration, but they either do not publish any statistics or do not disseminate widely the publications in which pertinent statistics appear. Indeed, one of the major obstacles faced in studying labour migration in Latin America and the Caribbean is that statistics on migrant workers are not easily available. In many instances, it is not clear whether any statistics are gathered at all. More information on the practices of countries in the region is certainly necessary.

Information on the use of work permits is available for only three countries: the Dominican Republic, Guatemala and Venezuela. Of the three, Guatemala is not a major receiver of migrant labour. The Dominican Republic

Data collection systems concerning labour migration

has traditionally admitted Haitians to work in sugar harvesting and processing, and Venezuela is a major destination of workers from neighbouring countries, especially Colombia. Yet as the descriptions below indicate, the data sources available in all three countries remain underexploited.

In the Dominican Republic, the General Directorate for Labour (*Dirección General del Trabajo*) of the Ministry of Labour is in charge of authorizing the hiring of foreigners and thus permitting the issuance of residence visas allowing the exercise of an economic activity. The Directorate checks that foreigners working in the country have adequate contracts and that the proportion of foreign workers in each national enterprise remains below a certain level. Information gathered on each migrant worker includes age, sex, citizenship, marital status, educational attainment, occupation, duration of contract, employer, post to be occupied, and wage. Data on the number of applications received, classified according to whether approved or not, are published by the *Dirección Técnica Laboral*, though it is not clear with what periodicity. Cross tabulations of the information do not appear to be available.

In Guatemala, foreigners wishing to work must obtain a work permit from the Ministry of Labour (*Ministerio del Trabajo y Previsión Social*). Data on the number of new work permits granted every year, classified by citizenship of worker, are published by the Ministry. Only a few hundred work permits are issued annually, the majority to citizens of El Salvador, Nicaragua and the United States (Pellecer-Palacios, 1993).

In Venezuela there are two sources of statistics on migrant workers. One covers border workers from Colombia and the other produces information on skilled workers hired by national enterprises. In accordance with the Andean Instrument on Labour Migration concluded under the 1977 Cartagena Agreement and ratified by Colombia and Venezuela, a Department of Labour Migration associated with the *Dirección General Sectorial de Identificación y Control de Extranjeros* (DIEX) was established. The Department is in charge of controlling the hiring of Colombians to work in the western states of Zulia and Táchira, and the municipality of Paez in the state of Apure. A border identity card (*carnet fronterizo*) is issued to those workers. It is initially valid for 6 months and may be extended for up to five months thereafter. Enterprises wishing to recruit migrant workers must register with the Department of Labour Migration and must apply for the certification of prospective migrant workers. For each enterprise registered, DIEX maintains a single card listing all the persons working for that enterprise. However, neither the data on those registration cards nor those on the issuance of border identity cards are used as sources of statistics on international migration (Carvallo-Hernández, 1993). Nevertheless, the total number of enterprises registered and the total of border identity cards issued during a year is sometimes presented in the annual report of the Ministry of the Interior as indicators of the work load of DIEX.

As part of the admission and control of foreigners, the Office for Selective Immigration (*Oficina de Inmigración Selectiva*) of the Ministry of Labour evaluates and decides on the issuance of labour permits requested by national

International migration statistics

enterprises for the admission of foreign skilled workers to Venezuela. The Office maintains a register of applications and labour permits by citizenship, sex, occupation and type of enterprise making the application. The data gathered are published annually in the *Memoria y Cuenta* of the Ministry of Labour (Torrealba, 1987).

3. Asia

As major destinations of migrant workers, the countries of Western Asia have used work permits as a means of controlling labour migration. Even among countries best characterized as sources of international migrant workers, the use of work permits to control the access of foreigners to their labour markets has been common. Statistics derived from the issuance of work permits, however, remain underdeveloped in both groups of countries. Furthermore, information on the conditions under which work permits are granted and on the types of foreigners that require a work permit to become employed is hard to find. In some cases, the statistics published suggest that work permits are granted only to a subset of all foreigners allowed to work, but confirmatory evidence is not available. Consequently, published statistics remain difficult to interpret and are often misleading.

In Western Asia, Jordan, Lebanon and Yemen provide examples of countries that, having been major sources of migrant workers, have instituted the requirement of obtaining a work permit before foreigners can work within their territories. In Jordan, data on the number of work permits issued annually by the Ministry of Labour are presented by citizenship of holder and sex; by occupational group and sex; and by whether the permits are being issued for the first time, renewed or issued for a change in place of work (Jordan, 1989 and 1992). In Lebanon, the Manpower Department of the Ministry of Labour issues and maintains a register of work permits granted to foreign workers. In Yemen, until 1978 the Social Welfare Department gathered information on the number of foreign workers granted work permits and produced at least one tabulation on the number of foreigners granted permission to work by country of citizenship and occupation, which was published in the *Statistical year book* (Yemen Arab Republic, 1972 and 1975). In 1978, published data indicated that the data source had switched to the Ministry of Labour (Yemen Arab Republic, 1978), and by 1986 it was the Ministry of Labour and Social Affairs and Youth (Yemen Arab Republic, 1987). Since unification with the Yemen Democratic Republic, work permits have been issued by the Ministry of Labour and Vocational Training (Yemen, 1992). Data for 1986 and 1992 show the numbers of work permits issued to Arabs and non-Arabs by occupation and citizenship.

Among the oil-producing countries of Western Asia, Bahrain has tended to publish regularly information on the number of work permits issued annually to Bahrainis and non-Bahrainis. The data are produced by the Ministry of

Labour and Social Affairs (Bahrain, 1973). No explanation is given as to who requires a work permit, but it is clear that work permits are not simply a means of controlling the employment of foreigners, since Bahraini nationals are also expected to have them. Published tabulations on work permits granted vary somewhat from year to year, showing sometimes a distribution by country of citizenship, or by occupation, or by both occupation and citizenship (Bahrain, 1973 and 1976).

During the 1960s, Iraq published tabulations on the number of work permits granted yearly to foreigners according to country of nationality (Iraq, 1968). Those data included both permits issued for the first time and renewals. In 1970, the number of foreigners renewing work permits by country of citizenship was published (Iraq, 1970). The numbers involved were small. During the 1970s, publication of such data ceased (Iraq, 1976).

In Kuwait, work permits are issued by the Ministry of Social Affairs and Labour to persons seeking employment in the private sector. Labour offices in the main cities issue the permits. The Ministry compiles information on all work permits issued annually and provides it to the Central Statistical Office for publication. In the 1970s, a tabulation on the number of work permits classified by country of citizenship of holder was published with some regularity in the *Statistical yearbook* (Kuwait, 1974 and 1978). More recently, the number of work permits issued annually by type (renewals, first time permits, permits for the self-employed, for those entering for work purposes, and for unskilled workers), as well as the number of cancellations or transference of sponsors, have been published regularly (Kuwait, 1994).

Oman publishes the number of work permits issued by the Directorate General of Labour Affairs to foreigners working in the private sector, classified by major economic activity and year of issue; by occupational group and year of issue; by occupational group and country of citizenship; and by country of citizenship and year of issue (Oman, 1986 and 1992). The first two tables have also included at times the number of active work permit holders who left Oman by year of departure (Oman, 1986).

In Saudi Arabia, both Saudi nationals and foreigners require work permits to work in certain occupations. The Department of Municipalities is in charge of issuing such permits. The number of such work permits granted to Saudis and non-Saudis by year of issuance is published regularly (Saudi Arabia, 1965, 1975 and 1990), but the number of workers involved clearly excludes most of the foreigners working legally in the country in other occupations or sectors.

During the 1970s, the United Arab Emirates issued work permits on both an individual and a collective basis. Collective permits were issued to employers who wished to hire a group of migrant workers to carry out a task. Data were published on the number of individual and collective work permits granted in a given year by Emirate of issuance, by country of origin, and by citizenship (United Arab Emirates, 1977). More recent statistics reflect the number of work visas issued annually by the Ministry of Labour and Social Affairs. The tables published show the number of work visas by year of issue and Emirate; by year of issue and citizenship of holder; and by citizenship of holder and Emirate (United Arab Emirates, 1991). In addition, information is published on changes in the work permit sponsor approved by the Ministry of Labour and Social Affairs in a year, classified by citizenship of worker (United Arab Emirates, 1977 and 1991).

Outside of Western Asia, less information is available on the use of work permits to regulate the labour force participation of foreigners. In Malaysia, for instance, employers wishing to recruit foreign workers must apply to the Department of Foreign Labour of the Ministry of Home Affairs for the necessary work permits, providing documentary evidence that no Malaysian workers are available to perform the work required. Employers must present a signed contract of employment, bear the costs of recruitment and repatriation, and deposit a security bond with the Immigration Department. Employers who hire migrants in an irregular situation are liable to heavy fines or imprisonment. A Special Task Force on Foreign Workers must approve the request to hire foreign workers, and such approval must be supported by the Immigration Department. Once all required authorizations are granted, migrant workers can obtain the required visas from Malaysian embassies abroad and enter the country. Upon arrival, a foreign worker obtains a one-year work permit that is renewable and allows employment with a specified employer. The Immigration Department publishes statistics on the number of requests received, the number of approvals, and the number of foreign workers issued identity cards (Awad, 1995).

In Thailand, the Alien Working Act of 1978 stipulates that any person wishing to employ a foreigner has to submit an application on behalf of the foreigner to the Alien Occupational Control Division of the Department of Employment, Ministry of Labour and Social Welfare and to secure a work permit before the foreigner is recruited. Currently, foreigners are banned from working in 39 occupational categories, which include manual workers and traditional craft skills. There are two types of work permits: temporary and permanent. Temporary work permits may be renewed and, after three years with such permits, a foreigner can apply for a permanent one. Information recorded on each foreigner requesting a work permit includes: sex; date of birth; age; country of birth; citizenship; marital status; length of contract; sector of employment (public or private); educational attainment; date of first entry into the country; type of work permit; duration of permit; and current occupation. However, the information is not computerized. Special tabulations of the number of work permits issued during a certain period, classified by selected variables such as country of citizenship and occupation can be obtained from the Department of Employment. The information gathered also allows some estimation of the number of foreigners working in Thailand at a given time, since temporary permits which are not renewed are removed from the Department's files. There is, however, no mechanism to ensure that foreigners who leave before their work permit expires report that fact to the Department of Employment.

4. Scope and limitations of the work permit data available

The preceding review of the practices of 22 countries indicates that there is considerable heterogeneity in work permit statistics. Given that heterogeneity, perhaps the main obstacle in using and correctly interpreting work permit statistics produced by labour-importing countries is that adequate information on their meaning and scope is lacking. Because of their administrative character, work permit statistics reflect the application of laws and regulations relative to the formal sector of the labour market. As such, they are often a better reflection of how those regulations operate than of the labour market itself. As the review of country practices reveals, countries such as Bahrain and Saudi Arabia require that their own citizens obtain permits in order to work in certain sectors of the economy. In those cases, data on work permits may be an indicator of the extent to which those sectors are dependent on foreign labour, but they cannot be used as measures of migrant worker flows.

Although the majority of countries issuing work permits to foreign workers gather considerable information on the characteristics and working conditions of the workers, most information is neither processed nor tabulated. When tabulations are made, they are often not published. Such tabulations as exist in publications show little more than the overall numbers of work permits issued classified by a few variables, usually one at a time. Published data also often fail to indicate whether the numbers presented refer to the number of work permits issued during a given time period (usually a year) or simply the stock of valid permits in existence at a particular point in time. The user must thus be careful to ascertain which variant is being used. Generally, it has been assumed in the preceding overview that data which are poorly labelled refer to the number of work permits issued in a year, but there is ample room for misinterpretation. To cite one example, consider the case of professional cards issued in Belgium. Tabulations are described only as showing "the total number of professional cards", a phrase that can mean either the total number of cards in circulation at a given point in time or all cards issued during a specific period. More information is needed to establish which interpretation is correct.

Among the 22 countries considered, only Thailand makes clear its use of work permit statistics to derive the number of migrant workers having valid permits at a given time (a measure of the stock of such workers). However, because the system in place has no way of eliminating from its statistics migrant workers who have left the country while their work permits are still valid, the number of valid work permits at a given time overrepresents the actual number of foreign workers employed in the country at that time.

The data produced by 17 of the 22 countries considered have been interpreted as representing the number of work permits issued in a year, a flow measure. For the rest of the countries, there is no information about any tabulations regarding work permits. Among the 17 countries producing tabulations, only four – Belgium, Ireland, Jordan and Kuwait – distinguish between newly issued permits and renewals. Given that permit renewal is generally possible, in countries where certain types of permits have an initial validity of only a few months, the likelihood of counting a single migrant worker several times during a given year is high. Poland, Spain and the United Kingdom are among the countries where that potential exists, and none produces tabulations distinguishing newly issued permits from renewals. The case of the Netherlands offers yet a different example of a situation leading to double-counting: a foreign worker having two employers simultaneously requires two different work permits and would be counted twice. In contrast, in countries such as the United Arab Emirates, where collective work permits are used, the total number of work permits issued will provide a significant underestimate of the number of migrant workers involved unless explicit allowance is made for the fact that a single collective permit represents a specific number of workers. In the data published by the United Arab Emirates, it is unclear whether such allowance has been made.

Another source of diversity in the data gathered by different countries is that not all migrant workers are required to have work permits. In Europe, Belgium, the Netherlands and the United Kingdom do not require citizens of other member States of the European Union to obtain a work permit to work in their territories, and Spain also exempts self-employed citizens of member States from the need to obtain work permits. Foreigners who have become settled also tend to be exempted from work permit requirements, as in Belgium and the Netherlands. Consequently, a potentially large number of economically active foreigners are not reflected in work permit statistics. In developing countries, the group excluded is sometimes several times larger than that included. In Venezuela, for instance, work permits are required only for highly skilled workers and thus fail to reflect the larger number of less skilled foreigners working legally in the country. In Kuwait, only private sector workers require work permits, while in Saudi Arabia only those in certain occupations require them, thus excluding most international migrant workers.

Such varied practices as reported here evidently compromise the international comparability of work permit statistics and make them generally poor indicators of the migration of labour. But to judge their adequacy, it is useful to set a standard with which they may be compared. It is common simply to seek to measure the economically active foreign population in a country, either in terms of its stock (the number of economically active foreigners present in a country at a given time) or in terms of flow (net number of foreigners added annually to the economically active population in a country). The latter requires both inflows and outflows from the economically active foreign population, with inflows including foreigners already present in a country who become economically active during a given year plus newly admitted foreigners who become economically active soon after arrival. Similarly, outflows consist of economically active foreigners who stop working during a given year but do not necessarily leave the country plus economically active foreigners who do leave the country. Work permit statistics usually reflect only part of the inflows to the economically active foreign population, but this does not necessarily mean that they underestimate their target population. Indeed, let us recall the definition of migrant worker provided in Chapter 2: "Migrant workers are persons admitted by a country other than their own for the explicit purpose of exercising an economic activity".

It must be stressed that work permit statistics refer to migrant workers characterized by this definition. Consequently, they ought to reflect only those foreigners admitted explicitly for the purpose of exercising an economic activity and for no other reason. Foreigners admitted as settlers and who then become economically active; persons granted refugee status who are also allowed to work; foreigners admitted as tourists or students who work illegally are all groups of migrants that are not meant to be covered by work permit statistics. Consequently, little is gained in assessing the adequacy of work permit statistics by cavilling about their "missing" such groups of migrants. The real issue is whether work permit statistics cover all foreigners admitted for the explicit purpose of working. In the cases of Kuwait, Saudi Arabia and Venezuela, they clearly do not. In the cases of Guatemala, Malaysia and Thailand, they do. Other cases are less clear, either because information on the actual coverage of the statistics available is lacking or because the situation is more complex.

In the case of the Netherlands, for instance, the categories of economically active foreigners exempted from holding a work permit include: (a) refugees; (b) foreigners holding a residence permit of unlimited duration by virtue of being dependants of other migrants; (c) foreigners granted permanent residence in the Netherlands; (d) foreign nationals covered by special treaties; and (e) citizens of the European Union. As already noted, refugees are properly excluded from work permit statistics, as are persons admitted by virtue of being dependants of other migrants. It is also appropriate to exclude foreigners granted permanent residence, except that some may have been originally admitted as migrant workers. With respect to (d), it is not clear which special treaties are referred to, but they are unlikely to be related to labour migration, so its exclusion is probably justifiable. Lastly, citizens of the European Union belong to the category of migrants subject to free movement and, according to the framework proposed in Chapter 2, are distinct from migrant workers. Consequently, they are rightly excluded from work permit statistics. On the whole, therefore, the Netherlands system excludes categories of migrants that ought to be excluded so that its work permit statistics cannot be faulted on that account.

One may argue, however, that until the end of 1992 citizens of the European Union had the right to free movement mostly in relation to the search for employment, so that their admission was not entirely divorced from labour market considerations on the part of the receiving State. Accordingly, inclusion of economically active citizens of the European Union in work permit statistics could be justified prior to 1992. Although such an approach is not fully consistent with the framework proposed in Chapter 2, it has some merit and reflects the practice of countries such as Greece and Spain. To allow for international comparability, it is important that States that include migrants subject to free movement in their work permit statistics present that group separately in the data published.

Work permit statistics can therefore refer exclusively to migrant workers as defined in Chapter 2 or may also include migrants subject to free movement when such prerogative is granted precisely because they are workers. With respect to migrant workers, according to the country practices reviewed above, the statistics on work permits may reflect contract migrant workers (as in many Western Asian countries); temporary migrant workers (as in most European countries); workers who have already acquired some establishment rights (such as those obtaining permanent work permits in Thailand); and seasonal migrant workers (as in Spain). However, for most countries, information about the conditions of admission of migrant workers requiring work permits that would allow the identification of the major migrant worker categories identified in Chapter 2 is not readily available. Hence, it is not possible to assess, except in very general terms, the extent to which those categories are consistent with actual country practices.

Further information on the practices of most countries is necessary to assess whether work permit statistics cover all migrant workers and only migrant workers. In some countries, foreigners who would not qualify strictly as migrant workers according to the definition presented in Chapter 2 may be included in the statistics. That may be the case, for instance, of foreigners admitted as dependants of other migrants who are granted permits to work after their admission. However, as the practice of the United Kingdom illustrates, a case could be made for the validity of such inclusion in terms of a change of status. Indeed, the United Kingdom work permit system allows for the possibility of granting work permits to aliens who are already residing in the country provided their status allows them to work or, if not, that their status can be changed. The authorities thus assert their prerogative to change the status of a migrant into that of "migrant worker" by admitting him or her explicitly to the labour market. Such a change of status is equivalent to "being admitted for the purpose of exercising an economic activity" and not only validates but makes mandatory the inclusion of such migrants in the work permit statistics if the latter are to cover properly all migrant workers. A change of status also validates the inclusion of irregular migrants working illegally whose situation becomes regularized by the granting of a work permit. Thus, if a regularization drive causes a sudden increase in the number of work permits issued, it cannot be claimed that the coverage of the latter improves. The increase reflects rather a true increase in the migrant worker population strictly brought about by changes of status. The distinction is subtle but pertinent, and must be made when judging the adequacy of work permit statistics.

To conclude, it bears stressing that work permit statistics are not meant to cover all inflows of economically active foreigners into a country. They reflect, at best, that part of the foreign labour force that is subject to controls in terms of its admission and exercise of an economic activity. Given their administrative nature, work permit statistics often represent documents, not persons, and they are therefore often better reflections of changes in the rules or regulations governing the work of foreigners than of true changes in their economic activity. Nevertheless, as indicators of the effects of policy, they are useful, provided the data are processed, disseminated and described in a much more thorough manner than has been the case in most countries to date.

5. Recommendations for the improvement of work permit statistics

- Agencies in charge of publishing data derived from the processing of work permits should ensure that the data are accompanied by a precise description of how the data are collected, what they represent and which migrants are covered. Categories of economically active foreigners who do not require work permits should be listed.
- In the process of issuing work permits, a core set of information should be recorded for each work-permit holder, including the following items:

Socio-demographic information:
  Name;
  Date of birth;
  Sex;
  Country of citizenship;
  Country of birth;
  Country of previous residence;
  Marital status;
  Educational attainment:
    Highest level of education attended;
    Number of years of schooling completed;
  Identification and number of any dependants:
    Spouse;
    Number of children under 18 years of age.

Administrative information:
  Date of application;
  Date of issue of work permit;
  Date when permit takes effect;
  Type of work permit;
  Length of validity of work permit;
  Whether work permit is:
    Issued for the first time to the holder;
    A renewal of an existing permit;
    A permit validating a change of employer;
  Occupation for which the work permit is valid:
    Occupation group;

International migration statistics

Sector of economic activity;
Employer which the work permit assigns the holder to, if any:
  Type of employer (private, public, mixed);
  Location of employment;
Wage;
Whether the holder is accompanied by any dependants:
  Spouse;
  Number of dependent children.

Migration history
Whether the holder has just arrived at the country of employment;
Whether the holder has already been living in the country of employment;
If already living there:
  Date of arrival;
  Initial migrant status;
Whether holder has ever worked in the country before;
If so:
  Beginning and ending dates of most recent previous employment;
  Type of permit held during that period.

The availability of the information listed above would make possible the classification of work permits issued according to whether they are first-time permits, renewals or changes of employer. Such administrative information, in combination with knowledge of whether the holder has already been living in the country of employment for some time, allow the identification of work permits issued for the first time to newly arrived foreigners and those granted for the first time to resident foreigners. For the purposes of understanding entry into the labour force in relation to migration dynamics, separate identification of all those categories is essential. It is strongly recommended, therefore, that countries that do not yet gather the information above do so.

- The following core tabulations should be produced:
    (a) Number of work permits issued over a year according to issuance category (first-time, renewal and change of employer), sex and citizenship of holder;
    (b) Number of first-time permits issued in a year by sex, age group, citizenship and presence in the country of holder (newly arrived versus already living in the country);
    (c) Number of first-time permits issued in a year by presence in the country, sex, and occupation of holder;
    (d) Number of first-time permits issued in a year by presence in the country, sex, and sector of economic activity;
    (e) Number of first-time permits issued in a year by presence in the country, sex, citizenship, and occupation;

(f) Number of first-time permits issued in a year by presence in the country, sex, citizenship, and educational attainment of holder;

(g) Number of spouses and dependent children accompanying holders of first-time permits issued in a year by sex, citizenship, and presence in the country of the holder;

(h) Number of spouses and dependent children accompanying holders of permits renewed or modified in a year by sex and citizenship of holder;

(i) Number of renewed or modified permits by sex, age group, and citizenship of holder;

(j) Number of renewed or modified permits by sex, citizenship, and occupation of holder;

(k) Number of renewed or modified permits by sex, citizenship, and sector of economic activity of holder;

(l) Number of renewed or modified permits by sex, citizenship, and educational attainment of holder.

- All tabulations, whether in the recommended list or not, should present data classified by sex of the work permit holder.

- An effort should be made to publish regularly the tabulations derived from work permit statistics, preferably through specialized publications devoted to international migration statistics. In addition, as a minimum, tabulations (a) to (c) above should be included in general country publications, such as statistical yearbooks or yearbooks of labour statistics. To the extent possible, tabulations (g) to (j) should also be included in widely available statistical sources.

- Agencies in charge of processing statistics derived from work permits should consider the possibility of developing a computerized database that, in addition to facilitating the cross-tabulation of several variables at a time, permits the identification of the number of work permits valid at a specific point in time and is thus able to produce indicators of stocks. To enhance the performance of work permit statistics as potential indicators of stocks, the possibility of making employers responsible for returning to the appropriate authorities the work permits of foreigners who leave their employment before the permit has expired should be explored.

B. REPORTS BY EMPLOYERS

In some countries, information on the stock of employed foreigners is obtained from reports of employers or enterprises. Such reports may be mandated by law or may be obtained through censuses or surveys of enterprises. In certain countries, the public sector reports annually the number of employees by citizenship. In most cases, data derived from reports by employers fail to cover the entire spectrum of legally employed foreign workers since not all employers are covered by the reporting procedures used. However, for those sectors covered, the information obtained is valuable, since it indicates the current role of foreign employment in the sectors concerned. Unfortunately, the information available on the coverage, scope and legal basis for the reports is sketchy at best. It is not possible, therefore, to make an accurate assessment of the strengths and weaknesses of the information gathered. To illustrate the variety of situations, the experience of a number of countries in gathering information from employers is reviewed below.

In Venezuela, the Labour Law stipulates that all enterprises registered with the Ministry of Labour must submit, at regular intervals (currently set at six months), information on the number and characteristics of their employees, including citizenship. The Ministry of Labour processes the information from 20 per cent of the forms submitted and tabulates such information twice a year. However, those tabulations are not published (Torrealba, 1987; Carvallo-Hernández, 1993).

In South Africa, the Chamber of Mines, the main employer of foreign workers in the country, annually publishes data on the average number of contract foreign workers employed by the gold and coal mines that are members of the Chamber, classified by country of origin of the worker (South Africa, Chamber of Mines, 1987).

In Japan the Ministry of Labour introduced in June 1993 a system whereby employers must report the number of foreigners working for them. By early 1995 a first set of reports had been received, but the level of non-response was high (about half of all employers had failed to file a report). Improvements in the performance of the system are expected as it becomes established.

In Kuwait, the Central Statistical Office has carried out three censuses of employment by the public sector, in 1966, 1972 and 1978 (Kuwait, 1978). The data gathered in 1972 and 1976 were published in some detail, showing the number of Kuwaiti and non-Kuwaiti civil servants classified by various variables (Kuwait, 1974 and 1978).

Other Western Asian countries that publish information on the number of employees in the public and mixed sectors of the economy by citizenship (nationals versus foreigners) include Iraq, Oman, Qatar and the United Arab Emirates. However, none documents well the source of the information published. For Iraq, tabulations showing the number of foreign workers in the public and mixed sectors of the economy ceased to be published around 1975 (Iraq, 1976). Data on the number of foreign workers in industrial enterprises, which were also published before 1975, indicated that the enterprises covered were those "liable to the Labour Law" (Iraq, 1968). In the case of Oman, the data published refer to the number of workers in the civil service and those employed by public corporations, classified as Omani and non-Omani (Oman, 1986 and 1992). Qatar reported the number of workers in each government ministry at the end of the year by sex and citizenship (Qatari, Arab national and foreigner), as well as the number of workers in the mixed sector of the economy

Data collection systems concerning labour migration

(Qatar, 1981). Lastly, the United Arab Emirates published information on the number of workers by sex and citizenship (citizens and foreigners) in establishments, government ministries, and the oil industry (United Arab Emirates, 1977).

Clearly, the use of employer reports to derive statistics on the number of foreigners employed at a given time is less well developed than other sources of information discussed in this chapter. However, since several of the countries known to be important destinations of labour migration already have such employer reports, it is appropriate to suggest ways in which their use could be improved. Before doing so, it bears stressing that the types of existing reports by employers can be representative only of foreigners employed in the formal sector and, in many cases, only for a particular sector of economic activity. Furthermore, although employers may not be asked to provide proof that the foreigners that they report are both legally resident and legally employed, there is a strong likelihood that foreigners who find themselves in an irregular situation with respect to employment or to residence may not be reported. Understanding the extent of an employer's liability in the case of hiring an irregular migrant is therefore an important factor in assessing the quality of the reports made.

Recommendations for the improvement of statistics on employed foreigners derived from reports by employers

- Agencies in charge of collecting or publishing data derived from reports by employers should ensure that the data are accompanied by a careful description of how they are collected and what they represent. It is particularly important to describe which types of employers must submit reports (those belonging to a particular sector, those employing more than a certain number of workers, those having official licences, etc.), the date to which the reports refer, and whether all employees must be reported (even those working part-time or hired temporarily).

- To the extent possible, the following information should be recorded for each employed worker:

    Name;
    Sex;
    Country of citizenship;
    Occupation;
    Number of years employed by the person or enterprise reporting;
    Current wage.

- The following tabulations should be produced:
    (a) Total number of employees reported by sex and country of citizenship;

(b) Total number of employees by sex, country of citizenship and occupation;

(c) Total number of employees by sex, country of citizenship and length of employment (for example, less than one year, 1–4 years, 5–9 years and more than 10 years);

(d) Total number of employees by sex, country of citizenship and wage level;

(e) Total number of employees by sex, citizenship (national versus foreign), occupation and wage level.

- All tabulations produced, whether in the list of recommended tabulations or not, should present data classified by sex of employees.
- An effort should be made to publish the tabulations derived from reports of employers. Of particular importance are tables (b), (d) and (e), since they allow an assessment of the role of foreign workers in the formal sector of the labour market and a comparison with citizens. These tables should be included in widely available publications such as statistical yearbooks or yearbooks of labour statistics. The other tabulations, if not published, should be made available upon request to interested agencies and researchers.

C. STATISTICS DERIVED FROM THE CONTROL OF CONTRACT LABOUR MIGRATION BY COUNTRIES OF ORIGIN

The data sources discussed thus far in this chapter relate to international migrant workers in the country of destination. Countries of origin also have statistical sources producing information exclusively on international migrant workers, generally as a by-product of procedures established to provide emigration clearance for workers. Especially in the labour-exporting countries of southern and south-eastern Asia, governments have instituted complex procedures to regulate the outflow of labour, ostensibly to ensure that migrant workers are protected against abuse or exploitation in the country of destination. In order to facilitate and control the outflow of labour, countries of origin have set up agencies within their government structures. As Athukorala (1993a) argues, it is essential to understand the salient features of their administrative mechanisms to assess the meaning, scope and possible deficiencies of the data they yield. One problem faced in this is that both the structures and mechanisms have been changing as the migration process evolves and are usually not well documented.

In the early 1970s, labour migration became significant from countries such as Bangladesh, India, Pakistan, the Philippines, the Republic of Korea and Thailand, to the oil-producing countries of western Asia. At that time,

Data collection systems concerning labour migration

Table 4.1. Relevant characteristics of systems to control contract labour migration in Asian countries of origin

Country	Year of new emigration legislation	Agency and year established	Percentage of recruitment by government	Coverage of emigration clearance by government agency	Restrictions on labour outflow
Bangladesh	1976	BMET (1986)	1985: 1.6 1991: 0.1	All workers	Female domestic workers not allowed unless accompanied by husbands
India	1983	PGE and FPEs (1983)	1989: 0.6	Designated categories only (mostly blue-collar workers)	Female domestic workers under age 30 are not allowed in western Asia and northern Africa
Indonesia	1978	*Pusat AKAN* (1978)	–	All workers[1]	Female domestic workers under age 22 not allowed
Pakistan	1979	BEOE (1971)	1980: 8.8 1985: 6.9 1991: 4.0	All workers	Female domestic workers under age 40 (previously 45) not allowed unless accompanied by husbands. Nurses not allowed
Philippines	1974[2]	BES (1974) POEA (1982)	1982: 1.6 1991: 1.3	All workers	Ban on all female domestic workers until 1987 when it was lifted for those who obtain approval from Filipino embassies in country of employment
Sri Lanka	1980	FEU (1976) SLBFE (1985)	1975: 10.5 1991: 1.6	None	None
Thailand	1985	OEAO (1985)	1990: 0.2	All workers	Ban on all female workers except to certain countries

Key: BMET: Bureau of Manpower, Employment and Training; PGE: Protector General of Emigrants; FPEs: Field Protectors of Emigrants; BEOE: Bureau of Emigration and Overseas Employment; BES: Bureau of Employment Services; POEA: Philippine Overseas Employment Administration; FEU: Foreign Employment Unit (at the Department of Labour); SLBFE: Sri Lanka Bureau of Foreign Employment; OEAO: Overseas Employment Administration Office.

Notes: [1] There is no direct emigration clearance requirement but all workers require *Pusat AKAN* endorsement to obtain passports. [2] The Labour Code of the Philippines was enacted in 1984 but is has been periodically amended to take account of subsequent developments.

Source: Athukorala (1993a), p. 56.

recruitment took place largely on the basis of personal ties or was undertaken directly by employers. Soon, however, the commercialization of labour recruitment took hold, and businesses involved in international travel and tourism began to function also as recruitment agents. Governments reacted by setting up mechanisms to regulate the activities of those agents. In most cases, a government recruitment agency was set up to improve competition in the placement of workers abroad and to offer workers a reliable alternative to private recruitment agents. In practice, placements made by government recruitment agencies have usually accounted for only small proportions of workers employed abroad (see table 4.1). Hence, if the only statistics available were those on migrant workers placed by government agencies, they would be very poor indicators of the actual outflows of migrant workers. Fortunately, however, statistics are not derived exclusively from the placement activities of government agencies. Instead, as part of the regulatory mechanisms established to control the operations of private recruitment agencies, governments have set up procedures to check and approve the contracts of all prospective migrant workers before they leave the country. It is generally through this process of contract review that statistics on the number of citizens hired under contract to work abroad are compiled, though the situation varies somewhat from country to country. Indeed, one of the problems in assessing the statistics on contract migrant workers produced by labour administrations in the different labour-exporting countries is that information on the exact mode of generation of those statistics is often lacking. Thus, before proceeding to an assessment of the statistics available, it is important to review the modes of operation of the labour administration units in the major labour-exporting countries.

1. Labour-exporting countries of Asia

In Asia, Bangladesh, India, Indonesia, Pakistan, the Philippines, the Republic of Korea, Sri Lanka and Thailand have all been major sources of migrant workers, mostly to the oil-producing countries of western Asia. The experience of those countries in regard to the administration and control of labour migration is varied. In Bangladesh, for instance, the Bureau of Manpower, Employment and Training (BMET) was created in 1976 and began producing statistics on the outflow of contract migrant workers the same year (ILO, 1989; Athukorala, 1993a). Tabulations on the outflow of international migrant workers classified by region of destination, occupational group and district of origin are published in the *Monthly statistical bulletin* of the BMET (Athukorala, 1993a). Data also exist on the outflow of contract migrant workers by mode of recruitment: through the Government, a private recruitment agent, or directly by the employer (ILO, 1989). It is not clear at what point in the process statistics published are collected. Since Bangladesh requires that citizens leaving the country to work abroad be in possession of emigration clearance by BMET (proved by a stamp in their passports) and enforces such requirement through exit controls, statistics available may refer to the number of migrants who actually leave the country with a BMET clearance. Alternatively, they may reflect the number of contracts approved by BMET or the number of clearances issued. Although, in principle, these numbers should coincide, the experience of other countries suggests that the information is likely to be more complete if gathered at the time of approving contracts. It should be noted that, by law, citizens of Bangladesh possessing certain skills or belonging to certain occupational categories are not allowed to work abroad. In addition, women are not allowed to be employed abroad as domestic workers unless they are accompanied by their husbands (Abella, 1995).

In India, the 1983 Emigration Act established the Protector General of Emigrants (PGE) within the Ministry of Labour and seven field protectorates operating in different parts of the country. Their task is to set minimum standards for contracts governing the work of citizens abroad and to license recruitment agencies. Statistics on the number of contract international migrant workers are available since 1976 but it is not clear how they were obtained. As of 1983 they appeared to reflect the number of workers granted emigration clearance by PGE. However, certain categories of workers were exempt from obtaining emigration clearance to work abroad and these categories have been increasing over time. As of the end of 1990, they included persons holding professional degrees, persons planning to stay abroad for more than three years, seamen with accepted qualifications, persons subject to income tax payments, and persons holding graduate or higher degrees (Athukorala, 1993a). Workers belonging to the exempted categories can have their passports endorsed with an "emigration clearance not required" stamp by the Passport Office and may leave the country without PGE clearance. Consequently, statistics reflecting the number of workers subject to PGE clearance provide an underestimate of the number of persons leaving India to work abroad (Athukorala, 1993a). The statistics gathered also seem to be published irregularly, although they can be obtained from the Office of the PGE. They have also been compiled by the ILO (1989) and show the number of Indian contract migrant workers by country of destination.

In Pakistan, the Government established a Bureau of Emigration and Overseas Employment (BEOE) in 1971 to regulate recruitment activities by private agents and to recruit Pakistani workers under employment agreements with western Asian countries. The BEOE published the *Emigration statistics of Pakistan manpower* on a monthly basis until 1983 when publication was discontinued. The statistics available reflect the number of contracts approved by BEOE, classified by country of destination and occupation (Athukorala, 1993a). Prior to 1977, workers who obtained their visas directly from the country of employment were not required to go through the BEOE approval procedure. The requirement of BEOE clearance for all contract workers that was introduced that year resulted in a large increase in the number of BEOE approvals. Pakistan uses exit controls, checking that the passports of migrant workers are stamped by BEOE, to enforce the BEOE clearance requirement. In recent years, data on labour migration have been available through the Overseas Pakistani's Foundation, which has been granted access to the data collected by BEOE and by the Overseas Employment Corporation (created in 1976 as the recruiting arm of the Government). The ILO (1989) has published data of BEOE on the number of contracts approved by mode of recruitment and by both country of destination and occupation. The latter tabulation excludes, however, contracts obtained through the Overseas Employment Corporation.

The Government of Sri Lanka created the Foreign Employment Unit in the Department of Labour in 1976 to recruit Sri Lankan workers for employment abroad under contracts secured by the Government from employers in western Asian countries. In 1978 the Unit was upgraded to a Division and given the further task of controlling and monitoring the activities of private recruitment agencies. A further change was made as a result of the promulgation in

International migration statistics

1985 of the Foreign Employment Act, which established the Sri Lanka Bureau of Foreign Employment (SLBFE) to act as lead agency in overseas employment administration. The Act also empowered SLBFE to establish and maintain an information data bank to monitor the flow of Sri Lankans for employment outside Sri Lanka and their return after such employment. Statistics on labour migration are published by the Department of Labour in the *Sri Lanka labour gazette* and reflect SLBFE information on the verification of employment contracts. The data are classified by country of destination, by skill level, and by both simultaneously (ILO, 1989; Athukorala, 1993a). The SLBFE also publishes an *Annual statistical hand book on migration*. According to SLBFE, the information recorded on each worker whose contract is processed includes: age; sex; skill level; intended country of destination; intended duration of stay abroad; expected date of departure; expected occupation and sector of economic activity while abroad; expected type of employer; type of recruitment channel; type of exit visa; exit work permit and duration granted. The number of contracts approved by the SLBFE was low during its first years of operation, but has risen markedly since 1990. Such an increase is attributed to SLBFE's efforts to eradicate illegal recruitment practices, efforts that include direct inspection of private agents and publicity (Athukorala, 1993a). In Sri Lanka, clearance by SLBFE is not required for departure. Consequently, only workers who secure employment abroad through registered recruitment agencies are recorded in SLBFE statistics. Persons hired directly by employers abroad or placed by unregistered recruitment agencies almost certainly remain unrecorded (Athukorala, 1993a).

Of the labour-exporting countries of south-east Asia, the Philippines was the first to enter the international labour market. In 1974, the Government enacted a new Labour Code that set a framework for the regulation of the private recruitment of labour. The Bureau of Employment Services (BES) of the Department of Labour was charged with controlling private recruitment agents; the Overseas Employment Development Board (OEDB) was given the task of recruiting land-based workers for employment abroad, and the National Seaman's Board (NSB) was established to regulate shipping agencies engaging Filipino seamen. In an attempt to phase out private recruitment within four years of its enactment, the Labour Code prohibited the issuance of new licenses for recruitment agencies. But the result was the proliferation of illegal recruitment. The Labour Code was then amended in 1978 to permit increased participation of private recruiters. In 1982, the Philippine Overseas Employment Administration (POEA) was established as an integrated agency incorporating the Bureau of Employment Services, the Overseas Employment Development Board and the National Seaman's Board. The POEA was put in charge of issuing overseas employment certificates to workers whose contracts are approved. Only workers having certificates can obtain embarkation clearances from the Labour Assistance Center of POEA located at the Manila International Airport. Workers obtaining embarkation clearance must fill out an exit pass form that records the following information: name; date of departure; type of worker (construction, non-construction, seaman); address in Metro Manila or provincial address; place of birth; marital status; religion; highest educational attainment; vocational training completed; number of years working in the Philippines; name of last employer in the Philippines; position in last employment; number of years working abroad; name and address of last foreign employer; and immediate beneficiaries (name, date of birth, address and relationship to worker). In addition, with respect to the new overseas work contract, the following items are recorded: country of employment; contract period; position; monthly salary; percentage expected to be sent as remittances; name and address of foreign employer; and name and address of agency/contractor (Nigam, 1988).

The POEA publishes the *Overseas employment statistical compendium* annually, presenting summary statistics for the ten-year period preceding each issue. The tabulations included refer to the outflow of contract migrant workers processed by POEA classified by country of destination (ten major destinations only) and region of destination. A useful secondary source of information is the *Yearbook of labour statistics* published by the Bureau of Labour and Employment Statistics. It includes tables on the number of placements approved by POEA in the most recent year by region of destination, and the number of contract migrant workers over the five preceding years by year of departure and country of destination (Athukorala, 1993a). The ILO (1989) has compiled a set of retrospective tabulations, mostly containing annual data for the period 1975–89, which show the following: number of contract migrant workers processed by POEA or its predecessors by whether land-based or sea-based and, for the former, by whether newly hired or rehired and mode of placement (private or government); number of contract migrant workers by year of deployment (1984–89), whether land-based or sea-based, and mode of placement; number of processed land-based contract migrant workers by mode and year of placement; number of sea-based workers by occupational group and year of placement (1982–87); number of processed land-based contract migrant workers by year of processing and region of destination; number of processed land-based contract migrant workers by year of processing and occupation; and number of domestic helpers and entertainers deployed in 1987 by region and country of employment and whether they are newly hired or rehired.

As indicated in the tabulations listed above, the Philippines makes a distinction between processed and deployed contract migrant workers. This distinction is possible only since 1984, after the Labour Assistance Center of POEA was set up at the Manila International Airport. The Center issues embarkation clearances to workers processed by POEA who can prove it by showing overseas employment certificates. By exempting workers having embarkation clearance from the travel tax, the POEA provides an incentive for them to register at the Center. Because workers receiving embarkation clearance are ready to depart, they are described as deployed. That is, the statistics referring to processed workers represent the number of overseas employment certificates issued by POEA annually, whereas those referring to deployed land-based workers represent the number of embarkation clearances issued by the Labour Assistance Center at the airport. Ever since the two series have been produced, the two numbers have not quite matched: the number of deployed workers has been consistently lower than the number of processed workers, by at least 6 per cent during 1984–91 (Athukorala, 1993a). Part of the discrepancy may be due to the time-lag between obtaining an overseas employment certificate, which is valid for 120 days, and actual departure. Athukorala (1993a) suggests that the difference may also be attributable to data processing problems, since the data relative to rehired workers collected by the Labour Assistance Center had not yet been computerized by 1993, whereas those relative to other categories of workers were already being processed via computer. He suggests that problems in incorporating the full number of rehired workers in the total number of deployed workers may be responsible for the differences observed. In addition, some processed workers may leave from ports other than Manila International Airport. Moreover, there does appear to be agreement that, after undergoing the costly process of obtaining POEA approval, migrant workers are unlikely to stay in the Philippines.

In Indonesia, the Government began recognizing the activities of a small number of recruitment agencies only in 1978. They were then placed under the supervision of the Department of Transmigration, Manpower and Cooperatives, which would later become the Department of Manpower. Within that Department, the Centre for Overseas Employment (*Pusat AKAN*) was established to issue licenses to recruitment agents. Over time, the role of *Pusat AKAN* increased as it was assigned the duty of selecting migrants, checking their skills and health, and providing them with compulsory training and pre-departure orientation. In 1994, Indonesia announced an ambitious national programme for the export of Indonesian workers which included the replacement of *Pusat AKAN* with a new Directorate of Export of Indonesian Workers within the Ministry of Labour, the streamlining of administrative procedures, and the creation of a government recruiting agency, *PT Bijak*. The Government has thus entered the recruiting process directly for the first time, to curb the exploitative activity of some private recruitment agencies and to seek greater control over labour migration.

As part of its monitoring activities, *Pusat AKAN* gathers information on the number of migrant workers whose contracts are validated. The information is made available by the Department of Manpower but does not seem to be published on a regular basis. The ILO (1989) has compiled data on the number of contract migrant workers deployed annually by sex and country of employment (1979–88); number processed annually (1983–85) by sex and country of employment; and number of contract migrant workers overseas by sex and occupation group (1983–88). For those years in which data for both processed and deployed (actually overseas) contract migrant workers are available, the number deployed is generally considerably lower than the number processed (the only exception occurs among women in 1985). The difference seems to arise because, in Indonesia, the process involved in obtaining a contract to work abroad starts with the registration at local offices of the Department of Manpower of persons intending to find a job abroad, and only those who are successful in securing employment and proving that they have the necessary skills are eventually granted a work contract and a passport. The Director General of Immigration issues passports only if the application is endorsed by the *Pusat AKAN*. Data on the persons involved appear to be collected at both the time of initial registration and when the person with a prospective employer is undergoing pre-departure training. If the number of processed workers represents those registering initially and the number of actually deployed workers represents those undergoing pre-departure training, the difference may be explained by the fact that many of those seeking a job abroad do not follow through or are unable to find a job. The time-lag between initial registration and eventual departure may also play a role, though there is no information available to determine this.

In Thailand, the activities of private recruitment agents were regulated by the Employment and Job Seekers Act of 1968 until 1985 when the Overseas Employment Administration Office (OEAO) was established and a new Recruitment and Job-Seekers Protection Act was adopted (Athukorala, 1993a). The 1985 Act empowers the OEAO to maintain information on Thai migrant workers whose contracts are approved by the Office. Data relative to the number of Thai workers whose overseas employment has been processed by the OEAO are available since 1976. Starting in 1988, the number of workers reported also includes those who have found employment on their own and are enumerated at various ports of exit. The majority are workers whose contracts have been renewed (ILO, 1989). In Thailand, workers are allowed to leave the country only if they have emigration clearances stamped in their passports by the OEAO. The ILO (1989) has published tabulations on the number of workers whose contracts are processed by OEAO, with the addition of self-placed workers as of 1988, classified by: mode of recruitment (government, private recruitment agent, directly by employer, and self-placement); mode of recruitment and country of employment; country of employment and year of departure. According to OEAO, the information recorded on each worker whose contract is processed includes: age; sex; marital status; number of children ever born; educational attainment; current occupation and sector of economic activity; intended country of destination; intended length of stay abroad; expected departure date; expected occupation and sector of economic activity while abroad; expected type of employer (private/public); mode of recruitment; type of exit visa and reason for migration. However, most of the information collected is not processed.

Lastly, in the Republic of Korea, the Ministry of Labour compiles statistics on the number of Korean migrant workers departing annually, but there is no information on the procedures used. The ILO (1989) has published tabulations on the number of Korean migrant workers by year (1977–88), region of employment and whether employed by a foreign company; Korean migrant workers by country of employment in 1987 and 1988; and Korean

International migration statistics

migrant workers by occupation in 1988. The data appear to reflect annual flows. The Ministry of Labour itself publishes information on overseas workers by year and occupation as well as by year and region.

2. Labour-exporting countries in other regions

In general, the regulation of labour migration by labour-exporting countries outside of Asia has not been as extensive and data collection mechanisms focusing exclusively on migrant workers have not evolved. However, the possibilities of developing such mechanisms exist and are growing in countries that are beginning to experience labour outflows, especially in central and eastern Europe. The cases of a few countries will be used here to illustrate developments so far.

In northern Africa, Morocco has long been a source of migrant workers whose major destinations are in Europe. In the 1960s, when European countries were importing many migrant workers, Morocco was an important source of workers. More recently, Moroccans have been responding to employment opportunities in a wider range of countries. To facilitate the employment of Moroccan workers abroad, a Directorate of Employment of the Ministry of Labour was created to handle the requests of foreign employers. The Directorate routes requests to its Labour Service. After preliminary verification of the terms and conditions of employment offered, the Service distributes the requests received among the placement bureaux of the different provinces. A bureau receiving requests notifies workers who have registered previously and arranges interviews of qualified workers. Workers found acceptable are given skill tests. For those doing best, contracts are signed and sent to the Labour Service for validation and checking (contracts must meet certain conditions, especially when there is a labour agreement between Morocco and the country of employment). If the contract is validated and the worker's medical examination reveals no problems, the worker can proceed to obtain the other documents needed for departure (passports and visas). The period between the selection of a worker and the validation of a contract does not exceed ten days. As in Asian countries, the processing of work contracts is a potential source of information on contract migration. However, there is no concerted effort to derive statistical information on a regular basis from that information. Furthermore, in 1995 a law governing the recruitment of workers for deployment abroad was being debated and it was expected that private recruitment agencies would be legalized. If that were to happen, the number of contracts validated yearly by the Labour Service would cease being an acceptable indicator of migrant worker outflows unless the Labour Service is put in charge of checking contracts obtained through private recruiters.

In Eastern Europe, the State Migration Service of Belarus, as part of the State Labour Committee, registers citizens intending to work abroad and persons with work contracts obtained through some 40 authorized employment agencies. The process of registration involves gathering basic demographic information as well as nationality or ethnic group, educational attainment and place of previous residence. The data gathered are not published but are available on request. In Poland, the Voivodeship Central Labour Office in Warsaw issues approvals to work abroad to Polish citizens and maintains statistics on the numbers involved. Information on date of birth, sex, occupation, industry and country of destination is recorded. The data are computerized and transmitted to the Ministry of Labour, but are not published. To foster the migration of Polish workers, Poland has concluded agreements with Belgium, France, Germany, Lithuania, the Russian Federation, Switzerland and the Ukraine.

3. Scope and limitations of data derived from the control of contract labour migration by countries of origin

A major limitation of data derived from the control of contract labour migration by countries of origin is often their incompleteness, since they do not cover all workers who leave the country under a contract to work abroad. This is clearly the case when prospective migrants can obtain a contract with a foreign employer through a private recruitment agency or on their own and thereby avoid the clearance process involving the Government. Such procedure is facilitated when the prospective migrant already holds a passport or when passports can be easily obtained. It is also more likely in countries such as Sri Lanka where clearance by the Sri Lanka Bureau of Foreign Employment is not necessary for departure. Thus, a survey carried out among departing passengers at the Colombo international airport found that about 45 per cent of the persons departing to work abroad had not gone through the official clearance process (Sri Lanka Bureau of Foreign Employment, 1991).

Another possible source of incompleteness stems from the fact that certain migrants may be exempted from the clearance process. This is the case in India, where persons holding professional qualifications, persons holding first and post-graduate degrees, persons planning to stay abroad for more than three years, persons subject to income tax payments, and seamen with acceptable qualifications do not need clearance by the Protector General of Emigrants to leave the country as contract migrant workers. It must be noted, however, that persons in these categories often do not qualify as contract migrant workers anyway. That is, they may be hired without stringent contractual arrangements on the period of employment and on the specific job they can hold. Therefore, one should not assume that every Indian professional who emigrates is a contract migrant worker missed by the statistical system considered here.

Yet another group of migrants that the statistics derived from the control of contract migrant workers by countries of origin do not cover consists of those

International migration statistics

persons who leave the country with the intention of working abroad in an irregular situation. Thus, persons who leave a country on tourist visas but without a prearranged contract with a foreign employer and who subsequently find employment abroad without securing the required permits are not contract migrant workers and cannot be covered by a system set up to monitor the latter. This is the case for many migrants who work, including, for example, numerous Indonesians who cross the border between Malaysia and Indonesia illegally and work in Malaysia without the required permits. Clearly, they do not qualify for official clearance by *Pusat AKAN*. That is, the incompleteness of statistics based on the control of contract migrant workers *per se* cannot be attributed to the fact that irregular migrants are excluded.

The fact that many bona fide contract migrant workers avoid the clearance process is attributed to its lengthy, complicated and costly nature in many countries of origin. There is a need to simplify and expedite the administrative procedures involved and to streamline the process so as to make it both less time consuming and less costly. The development of better data processing tools would likely improve administrative efficiency and contribute to the improvement of the statistics. Having a computerized data bank with the records of all contract migrant workers processed would be particularly useful in solving the second major problem affecting the statistics available, namely, that they usually do not distinguish persons who leave the country for the first time and those who have gone to work abroad more than once. Indeed, since none of the labour-exporting countries that control contract migration has developed a mechanism to obtain continuous and sufficiently accurate statistics on return migration, there is as yet no way to assess the net effect that contract migration has on the country's labour force or on its population. Furthermore, by its very nature, contract migration implies a form of circulation between the country of employment and the country of origin. Contract migrant workers sometimes may be compelled to return to their country of origin before their contracts are renewed and thus may be counted several times as departing contract migrant workers during the course of their active migrant life. Data on the number of contracts processed over a given period cannot be interpreted to represent an equal number of persons when multiple counts are possible. Understanding whether the same persons continue to secure contracts and thus accumulate a lengthy period of work abroad or whether new migrants are continually being added to the pool is of crucial importance for social and economic planning. It is important, therefore, to ensure that the information needed to attain such an understanding is collected.

At present, the data obtained through the control of contract migrant workers in countries of origin have been mostly used to indicate trends over time. Yet one must be careful in interpreting the changes recorded, since some may result from regulatory and administrative modifications rather than actual changes in the underlying flows. The case of the Philippines is illustrative. Between 1982 and 1983 the number of land-based contract migrant workers processed increased markedly, passing from 250,000 to 380,000. However, whereas the 250,000 workers processed in 1982 were all classified as "new hires", among the 380,000 processed in 1983 only 237,000 were in that category (ILO, 1989). The rest, 143,000 workers, were classified as "rehires", a category for which data began to be collected only in 1983 as a result of changes in the clearance procedures initiated that year. That is, the increase observed was spurious since, in terms of comparable data, no major change had taken place (Athukorala, 1993a). Fortunately, the producers of statistics presented data according to both previous practice and the new categories, allowing the analyst to make inferences from comparable information. Such practice is to be commended.

As this example illustrates, the use and interpretation of statistics derived from the control of contract migrant workers by countries of origin is not devoid of problems, especially given that the data are known to have several limitations. Yet, with respect to labour migration within Asia, statistics on the outflow of contract workers provide one of the best sources of information available. It is therefore important to make the effort to improve their availability and use.

4. Recommendations for the improvement of statistics derived from the control of contract labour migration by countries of origin

- Agencies in charge of providing emigration clearance to contract migrant workers should produce a brochure describing the procedures involved in obtaining clearance and, most importantly, the point or points at which statistics are to be collected. Particularly in the case of countries gathering information on both processed and deployed workers, it is important to document at what point in the pre-departure process each set of data is gathered and from which types of migrant workers. Copies of the forms actually used to gather the relevant information should be included.

- A core set of information should be recorded for each person obtaining clearance to leave the country as a contract migrant worker. This should include:

Socio-demographic information:
  Name;
  Sex;
  Date of birth;
  Place of birth;
  Current residence, including whether:
    Urban;
    Rural;
  Marital status;

International migration statistics

    Educational attainment:
       Highest level of education attended;
       Technical or vocational training received;
    Foreign language proficiency;
    Number of dependents:
       Spouse;
       Number of children under 18 years of age;
    Country of residence of spouse;
    Country of residence of dependent children.

Administrative information:
    Date of application;
    Date clearance is issued;
    Mode of placement:
       Private recruitment agency;
       Government recruitment agency;
       Directly by foreign employer;
       Self-placement;
    Type of contract migrant worker:
       Land-based versus sea-based;
       Skilled versus unskilled;
    Amount paid to recruitment agent;
    Other official charges.

Information relative to the contract:
    Country of employment;
    Contract period (in months);
    Type of employer:
       Private enterprise;
       Public enterprise;
       Other public sector;
       Private individual;
    Position offered;
    Occupation;
    Sector of economic activity;
    Salary abroad (including allowances);
    Other benefits, if any:
       Travel expenses;
       Medical insurance;
       Free lodging;
       Free food;
    Amount of advances received, if any.

Migration history:
    Whether the person is going to work abroad for the first time;

Data collection systems concerning labour migration

If the person has worked abroad previously:
Date of first departure from the country to take employment abroad;
Country of employment during first work episode abroad;
Occupation during first work episode abroad;
Number of different overseas work contracts held so far (excluding the one being processed);
Period of most recent contract (beginning and ending dates);
Country of employment under most recent contract;
Occupation under most recent contract;
Date of most recent return to the country;
Whether the contract being processed is a renewal of the most recent contract (same employer).

The availability of the information listed above would make possible the classification of departing contract migrant workers according to whether they are leaving the country to work abroad for the first time or whether they already have prior migration experience. Such information on the type of migration (initial versus repeated) should be used in making any tabulation on the data gathered since it is crucial to understand the dynamics of labour migration.

- The following core tabulations should be produced:
    (a) Number of contract migrant workers processed in a year by type of migration (initial versus repeated), employer, sex, age group, completed education, and country of employment;
    (b) Number of contract migrant workers per year by type of migration (initial versus repeated), sex, expected occupation, and country of employment;
    (c) Number of contract migrant workers per year by type of migration (initial versus repeated), sex, expected sector of economic activity, and country of employment;
    (d) Number of contract migrant workers per year by type of migration (initial versus repeated), sex, educational attainment and country of employment;
    (e) Number of contract migrant workers per year by type of migration (initial versus repeated), sex, age group and expected occupation;
    (f) Number of contract migrant workers per year by type of migration (initial versus repeated), sex, education, and mode of recruitment;
    (g) Number of contract migrant workers per year who have been abroad at least once before, by sex and whether being rehired by the same employer or not;
    (h) Number of contract migrant workers per year who have been abroad at least once before classified by sex and by time elapsed since first departure;

International migration statistics

- (i) Number of contract migrant workers per year who have been abroad at least once before classified by sex and by time elapsed since most recent return to the country;
- (j) Number of contract migrant workers per year who have been abroad at least once before classified by sex and by number of overseas work contracts held before;
- (k) Number of contract migrant workers per year who have been abroad at least once before classified by sex, occupation the first time abroad, and expected occupation;
- (l) Number of contract migrant workers per year who have been abroad at least once before classified by sex, country of first employment abroad, and next country of employment;
- (m) Number of spouses and dependent children remaining behind in the origin country, classified by the sex of the migrant worker and type of migration (initial versus repeated) of contract migrant worker.

• All tabulations produced, whether in the list of recommended tabulations or not, should present data classified by sex of the contract migrant worker.

• An effort should be made to publish regularly the tabulations derived from the clearance of contract migrant workers, preferably through specialized publications devoted to international migration statistics. In addition, at minimum, tabulations (a) to (d), (h), (i) and (m) above should be included in more general government publications, such as statistical yearbooks or yearbooks of labour statistics. To the extent possible, tabulations (g) to (j) should also be included in widely available statistical sources.

• Agencies in charge of gathering the statistics should take whatever steps are necessary to ensure that, whenever changes of a legal, regulatory or administrative nature take place, their effect on the statistics produced is transparent. Such steps may include: adding appropriate explanatory notes to tables presenting time series data to indicate when a change took place and its consequences in terms of coverage or data reliability; and presenting simultaneously data conforming to the specifications in place before the change, and data incorporating the change, so that the differences introduced by the change itself can be determined precisely.

• Agencies in charge of processing statistics derived from the information collected during the work permit clearance process should attempt to computerize the data to facilitate not only the opportune extraction of information and preparation of cross-tabulations, but also the clearance process itself. Having electronic records on individuals facilitates following the migration history of each person and expediting the clearance process in cases of repeated migration. Such a database system would also permit the estimation of the number of migrant workers whose contracts abroad are valid at any particular point in time, thus providing an estimate of the stock of contract migrant workers abroad.

D. STATISTICS DERIVED FROM REGULARIZATION DRIVES

By its very nature, irregular international migration is difficult to capture statistically, especially by data collection systems whose objective is the quantification of authorized international migration. Perhaps the only exception is the statistics collected in relation to the regularization of irregular migrants. Although regularization drives vary considerably with respect to the sets of irregular migrants they target, the period allowed for registration, and the conditions established for regularization, they normally produce statistics that are useful indicators of the magnitude and characteristics of the irregular migrant stock at a particular point in time.

The use of regularization drives varies from country to country. In some countries, they have been used periodically as a means of trying to manage irregular migration. In others, they have been rare events, used only under special circumstances. Among European countries, recent regularization drives have been carried out by Austria (1974), Belgium (1974–75 and 1980), France (1981), Italy (1987 and 1990), the Netherlands (1975), Spain (1985–86 and 1991), and the United Kingdom (1974–77). There have also been important regularization programmes in the traditional countries of immigration: Australia (1973, 1976, 1982), Canada (1973) and the United States (1986–87). In Latin America, Argentina has had at least four regularizations – 1949, 1958, 1964–66 and 1974 – and Venezuela has had two, in 1974 and 1981 (Mármora, 1983; OECD, 1990). Lastly, in Asia only Malaysia seems to have carried out major regularizations in recent years. Before proceeding with a discussion of the scope, uses and limitations of the data derived from regularization programmes, it is useful to review the experience of countries that have conducted such programmes.

1. Europe

In France, as Garson and Moulier (1982) note, regularization has been a recurring phenomenon. It was the normal procedure for admitting foreign workers into the country during the periods of most intense migration, in 1920–26 and in 1960–73. Between 1948 and 1968, the percentage of foreign workers entering the country clandestinely whose status was later regularized rose from 20 to 82 per cent. In the 1970s, when the Government tried to exercise stricter control on entries, exceptional but successive regularizations of a varying nature were instituted (in 1973, 1974, 1976, 1979 and 1980). However, since the 1980 regularization programme was completed, there has been no further recourse to regularization on a sizeable scale.

International migration statistics

In 1981, the ministerial circulars of 6 July and 11 August established that foreign workers in an irregular situation who had entered France before 1 January 1981 and could present a work contract having a duration of at least a year or could prove that they could secure stable employment would have their status regularized if they applied before 31 December 1981. The 1981 regularization was the first allowing irregular migrants to apply directly to the competent authorities, independently of their employers. During the amnesty period, employers of irregular migrants were not subject to fines, but after 31 December, 1981, such employers would be subject to harsher penalties (Garson and Moulier, 1982; OECD, 1990). Because of problems in processing applications, the amnesty period was later extended to 15 January 1982 for most applicants and to 26 February 1982 for seasonal foreign workers seeking permission to work over the whole year. The 1981 regularization programme was accompanied by the issue of Law No. 81-973 of 29 October 1981 relating to the conditions of entry and residence of foreigners in France and was closely linked to the formulation of that law (OECD, 1990).

The circular of 11 August 1981 attempted to specify which irregular migrants were eligible for regularization. It stated that, among others, persons belonging to the following categories could apply: foreigners of any nationality in an irregular situation in respect to residence or employment who could provide official proof of identity; foreigners expelled for the new reasons provided for in the law of 10 January 1980; young foreigners who had failed to request a residence permit when they became 16 years of age and who were still living in France; foreigners who had been refused refugee status and who were living irregularly in France. However, these categories proved to be far from exhaustive and, since the list was not meant to be exhaustive or restrictive, persons in other kinds of irregular situations were also regularized. The unexpected cases most commonly found included: persons working for several employers on a part-time basis (such as domestic workers); persons employed illegally on a part-time basis; persons admitted as students who worked illegally; holders of valid temporary residence permits that forbid the exercise of an economic activity but who nevertheless worked; persons admitted as trainees who received a salary illegally during training; and irregular migrants who, because they had applied for regularization or expressed the intention to do so, had been dismissed by their employers. In addition, special provisions were made to allow the change of status of certain seasonal workers into "permanent workers", meaning that they could work the whole year. Essentially, seasonal workers whose status had been legal until 1 January 1981, who could prove that they had worked at least 21 months in France between 1 January 1977 and 31 December 1981, and who could present a current contract valid for at least four months were granted work permits allowing them to work the whole year (Garson and Moulier, 1982).

While the regularization process was ongoing, the authorities in charge were requested to publish statistics at regular intervals showing how it was proceeding. In addition, the Ministry of Labour undertook a study of the characteristics of a random sample of 9,500 regularized workers (Garson and Moulier, 1982). The total number applying for regularization was close to 140,000, 124,101 of whom were eventually regularized. The authorities did not strictly enforce the requirements for regularization, particularly with respect to the need to prove having stable employment. Thus, 20 per cent of those regularized did not present proof of stable or even occasional employment (OECD, 1990). In 1983, a follow-up survey of 650 immigrants in the Paris region who had been able to regularize their status in 1981 was carried out to assess their situation (OECD, 1990).

In Italy, Law No. 943/86 of 30 December 1986 established for the first time a comprehensive legal framework regarding the management of international migration. To set a clean slate for its application, it allowed for the legalization of foreigners who had been present in an irregular situation in Italy since before 27 January 1987 and who could prove that they were either employed or registered as unemployed. Registration took place between 27 January 1987 and 30 September 1988 and resulted in the regularization of 105,312 foreigners out of some 119,000 who applied (OECD, 1990 and 1991). When the 1986 law was revised in 1989, a second regularization programme was announced in December 1989 in connection with a new law on foreigners, known as the Martelli Act, which became Law 39/90 on 28 February 1990. The second regularization programme had less stringent eligibility criteria, requiring only that irregular migrants prove that they had been present in Italy since 31 December 1989. It was implemented during the first six months of 1990 and resulted in the regularization of 216,037 foreigners (OECD, 1991). Information on the number of foreigners regularized was gathered by the Ministry of the Interior which released some tabulations that were published in secondary sources (OECD, 1991). However, no statistical report devoted to the regularization results seems to have been published.

In Spain, the first Aliens Act came into effect on 1 July 1985 and, as in Italy, it called for a regularization programme of foreigners residing in Spain in an irregular situation. Eligibility depended on having been in Spain since before 24 July 1985, having a valid passport, and either sufficient means of support, an employment contract, or a license allowing self-employment. Applications for regularization were received between 24 July 1985 and 31 March 1986, and 43,815 persons were regularized. In 1991 the Government adopted a new policy aimed at imposing stricter controls on migration flows and adopting planning levels to manage migration intakes, but before implementing it, a second regularization programme was carried out. Foreign workers, whether self-employed or wage-earners, who had been working and living in Spain since before 24 July 1985 without proper authorization were eligible for legalization. Also eligible were foreigners living in Spain since before 17 May 1991 whose residence and work permits had expired and not been renewed; foreigners who had worked in Spain for at least nine months during the previous two years and who were living in Spain at the time of the application; and foreigners who had either a job offer or tangible plans to set up a business (OECD, 1992). Between

International migration statistics

10 June and 10 December 1991, 133,000 applications for regularization were filed. The Directorate-General for Migration gathered information on those regularized, but by 1992 it had still not released comprehensive statistics.

In the United Kingdom, a major distinction is made between foreigners who enter the country illegally and those who stay beyond the limits allowed by their visas. British authorities have long had the power to deport visa overstayers, but until the Immigration Act of 1971 could not deport illegal entrants. By way of transition after the Act was passed, an amnesty was granted in 1974 to citizens of Pakistan and the Commonwealth who had entered the country illegally before 1 January 1973 and who had stayed in the country continuously since then (North, 1979). By the end of 1977, 2,409 foreigners had applied for amnesty and 1,685 had been accepted. It has been argued that the low numbers resulted from the fact that early in the process some of those whose application was rejected were deported (North, 1979). Very few statistics were released on the regularization process, but those that were are published in the *Control of immigration statistics* prepared by the Home Office.

2. Traditional countries of immigration

All three of the main traditional countries of immigration – Australia, Canada and the United States – have undertaken regularizations at some point since 1970. In Australia, as immigration policies became more restrictive in the 1970s and the problems associated with economic recessions increased, concern grew about the number of migrants living and working in the country without official permission. At the time, the Minister for Immigration and Ethnic Affairs had the power to grant amnesties by administrative decision. Amnesties were granted in 1974 and again in 1976, but were considered unsuccessful because only 400 migrants applied in 1974 and 8,500 in 1976, at a time when migrants in an irregular situation were thought to number 30,000 to 60,000. The 1975 amnesty was first announced on 31 December 1975 and established that between 26 January and 31 April 1976 all persons residing illegally in Australia could have their status adjusted to become legal residents provided they were in good physical and mental health and had no criminal record in Australia or elsewhere. Although the amnesty period was extended somewhat, the statistics released during the process were few, consisting mainly of the number of persons applying for amnesty by the end of April (7,207). On the whole, the statistical information released about the 1976 amnesty seems to have been meagre.

In 1980, a more comprehensive approach to the problem of irregular migration was adopted. A regularization of status programme (ROSP) was announced by the Minister of Immigration and Ethnic Affairs on 19 June 1980, and in January 1981 changes to the Migration Act came into effect that severely limited the categories of persons who, once in Australia, were eligible to be considered for permanent residence (Storer, 1982). The Minister of Immigration and Ethnic Affairs thus lost the discretion to grant resident status to people who had entered Australia as tourists, visitors or other non-permanent status. The amended Act also implied that in any future amnesties, new legislation empowering the Minister of Immigration and Ethnic Affairs to grant them would have to be passed by the two Houses of Parliament. This change essentially ensured that the ROSP would be the last chance that irregular migrants would have to regularize their status.

Under the ROSP, foreigners, whether present legally or illegally, who had arrived in Australia prior to January 1980 and who wished to remain permanently in Australia could apply for permanent resident status before 31 December 1980. In addition, persons lawfully in Australia who had previously applied for permanent resident status and whose application had been denied or was still under consideration could re-apply or request by 31 December 1980 that their application be considered under the ROSP. Lastly, foreigners who had arrived after 1 January 1980 and who were residing illegally in Australia, but who were the spouses, parents or minor children of an Australian citizen or a legal permanent resident were also eligible for regularization. A total of 11,042 applications were presented under the ROSP, covering about 14,000 persons (Australia, 1982), but information on the characteristics of the migrants who applied or of those regularized was not available. However, data on persons filing in the Melbourne office (2,003) were used to analyse the age distribution of applicants, and their distribution by country of birth, marital status, type of visa used to enter Australia, and occupation (Storer, 1982).

In Canada, the Government made two decisions in 1967 regarding immigration that it would later reverse. The first was to allow foreigners with a non-immigrant status in Canada (tourists, students, short-term workers) to apply for immigrant status without leaving the country. Previously, those wishing to immigrate to Canada could apply only from outside the country. The second was to allow foreigners facing deportation to appeal their cases to the Immigration Appeal Board. Those changes resulted in an increasing number of persons applying for immigrant status within Canada and in a rise in the number of appeals filed by persons whose application for immigrant status was not successful. In 1972, the Government took steps to change those trends. The first was to revoke the section of the immigration regulations allowing non-immigrants to adjust their status to that of immigrants. The second was to expedite the processing of appeals to the Immigration Appeal Board by allowing immigration officers to make decisions on straightforward cases, most of which resulted in the granting of immigrant status to the aliens involved. The third was to adopt new legislation restricting the appeal rights of foreigners and instituting a sixty-day period in which all migrants in an irregular situation and non-immigrants who had been in the country since before 30 November 1972 could apply for immigrant status. The latter provision was the basis for the adjustment of status programme carried out in 1973 (North, 1979).

According to that programme, those eligible to be granted immigrant status were non-immigrants and foreigners who had entered Canada illegally, were present in the country on 30 November 1972, were still in Canada at the time of application, and did not have substantial criminal records. The period over which migrants could apply for regularization ran from 15 August to 15 October 1973. According to North (1979), statistical information on the results of the adjustment of status programme was slim. Some 39,000 persons were granted immigrant status, more than 3,000 of whom were already citizens or landed immigrants who simply had their status confirmed. Among the remaining 36,000 persons, 60 per cent were migrants in an irregular situation and their dependants, and the rest were non-immigrants and their dependants. Dependants were not necessarily present in Canada. Thus, by 29 November 1974 when, according to unpublished records of the Department of Employment and Immigration, the cases of 35,413 persons had been approved, only 26,088 persons had been "landed", that is, were present in Canada and had been granted immigrant status. The rest were either not present in Canada or the processing of their papers had not yet been completed. No information was available on the 14,510 persons who had applied but whose cases had not been approved as of the end of November 1974. Those who already were citizens or landed immigrants seem to have been included in that number. Most of the other information available, such as the proportion of irregular migrants, persons applying by country of origin or by place of residence within Canada, refers only to partial results of the regularization drive and was not published officially (North, 1979).

In the United States, the Immigration Reform and Control Act (IRCA) of 1986 established two regularizations programmes that would result in the eventual granting of permanent resident status to nearly 3 million migrants. The Act allowed two groups of irregular migrants to become first temporary and then permanent residents of the United States. The first group consisted of foreigners who had been present in the United States since before 1 January 1982 who were eligible for regularization under the regular programme, whereas the second consisted of foreigners who could prove that they had been employed in seasonal agricultural work for a minimum of 90 days between May 1985 and May 1986 (United States Immigration and Naturalization Service, 1992a). Applicants belonging to the second group regularized their status under the special agricultural worker (SAW) programme. Persons eligible under the regular programme could present their applications between 5 May 1987 and 4 May 1988, whereas the application period for SAW applicants began on 1 June 1987 and ended on 30 November 1988. The data on both the regular legalization programme and the SAW programme were reported in United States Immigration and Naturalization Service INS application forms, which are maintained in the Legalization applicant processing system (LAPS) database. Selected items of the information contained in each foreigner's application were entered in the LAPS data base (United States Immigration and Naturalization Service, 1988).

Between 1988 and 1992, the Immigration and Naturalization Service of the United States published the results of the legalization process in its annual

Statistical yearbook in which a table showing the number of applicants by type of regularization programme and country of citizenship, and another on the number of applicants by type of programme and selected state and city of current residence were included (United States Immigration and Naturalization Service, 1988 and 1992a). In addition, as successful applicants obtained permanent residence status, they were included in the immigration statistics under a separate category, thus allowing an analysis of their contribution to immigration levels. By incorporating the regularization results in its normal statistical publications, the United States ensured their adequate dissemination. Furthermore, to obtain a more detailed profile of the legalized population and its experience, the Immigration and Naturalization Service undertook a survey of a representative sample consisting of 6,193 legalized persons who were interviewed between February and June 1989 (United States Immigration and Naturalization Service, 1992b). In 1992, 4,012 of those persons were interviewed again by the Labour Department which was charged with assessing the labour market experience of legalized migrants (United States Bureau of International Labour Affairs, forthcoming).

3. Latin America

As noted above, Argentina has carried out at least four regularization drives since 1949, all under democratic Governments (Mármora, 1983). The first, in 1949, was directed mostly to overseas migrants who had arrived in Argentina after the Second World War, but it also covered the first contingents of migrants from neighbouring countries, who were in an irregular situation. Initially, the drive was to last 90 days but it was extended until March 1951. The second post-war amnesty was undertaken in 1958 and covered international migrants who had not satisfied the requirements to reside legally in the country. It lasted six months, during which irregular migrants were allowed to initiate the process of regularization, which then took months or even years to be completed. The third drive, directed only to migrants from neighbouring countries, started in 1964 and lasted until 1966. The fourth, undertaken in 1974 as a result of Decree No. 087 of 11 January, also targeted only irregular migrants from neighbouring countries and lasted six months (Mármora, 1983). The first three amnesties were promulgated on the basis of considerations related to the integration of international migrants, the existence of administrative obstacles to their regular admission, and considerations of national security in relation to migrants from neighbouring countries. In contrast, the 1974 amnesty was justified in terms of labour force concerns and the need to foster Latin American economic integration.

Data are available only regarding the legalizations carried out in 1958, 1964–66 and 1974. They usually show only the total number of migrants obtaining residence permits because of an amnesty. Thus, as a result of the 1958 amnesty, 31,526 migrants obtained residence permits over four years; the 1964 amnesty regularized 216,677 migrants from neighbouring countries over seven years; and the 1974 amnesty permitted the regularization of 147,383 persons over 6 months. Hence, between 1958 and 1980, among the 629,258 international migrants who were granted residence permits in Argentina, 395,586 or 62.9 per cent got them through the amnesties of 1958, 1964 and 1974 (Mármora, 1983).

In 1974, there was considerable bureaucratic opposition to the amnesty. Hence, various administrative and logistic problems developed that probably led to an undercoverage of the population eligible for regularization. Such problems included: a shortage of adequately trained personnel; a strike among amnesty workers during the second month of the amnesty period because of lack of salary payment; and the presence of few amnesty officials in rural areas and other remote areas, with most officials concentrated in the Buenos Aires Metropolitan Area. In order to qualify for legalization, a migrant had to prove that he or she had entered Argentina before 31 December 1973 either through documentary evidence (a passport or a migration entry form) or by presenting two witnesses who would swear that entry had taken place before the deadline. (Among a sample of 5,170 regularized migrants, only 18 per cent used witnesses.)

Data derived from information collected during the regularization process were not published formally. However, some tabulations are available through a mimeographed paper prepared by Gurrieri (1982), an official of the *Dirección Nacional de Migraciones*. They include: number of regularized migrants by citizenship; distribution of regularized migrants by citizenship and province; sex ratio of regularized migrants by citizenship; mean age of regularized migrants by citizenship; per cent illiterate among regularized migrants aged 5 years and over by sex and citizenship; distribution of regularized migrants by citizenship and port of entry; distribution of regularized migrants by period of entry into Argentina and citizenship; distribution of regularized migrants by citizenship, sex and economic activity; distribution of regularized migrants by citizenship and sector of economic activity; and distribution of regularized migrants by citizenship and occupation.

In Venezuela, a regularization programme was carried out in 1980–81, prompted in part by the fact that on 20 September 1978 the Andean Instrument on Labour Migration came into effect after having been ratified by Bolivia, Colombia, Ecuador, Peru and Venezuela. That treaty engaged State Parties to facilitate the regularization of the situation of irregular migrants from other State Parties, for migrants who had entered their respective territories before 20 September 1978. Venezuela's response was to issue, on 22 May 1980, a Regulation on the Admission and Stay of Foreigners whose main objective was to regularize the situation of workers originating in other State Parties (Michelena et al., 1984). In practice, however, the Regulation was used to allow the regularization of citizens of other countries in terms similar to those of Andean member States. The Regulation established that irregular migrants would be registered between 23 August and 23 December 1980. Those registering received a provisional identity document valid until 23 August 1981. They could then apply for a temporary residence permit (valid for a year) provided that they were citizens of Andean countries and had proper identification of citizenship, and that they could prove that they had exercised legal economic activities, on their own account or under employment contracts in Venezuela prior to 20 September 1978. Applications for temporary residence permits were received until 23 August 1981 (Michelena et al., 1984). Once a migrant obtained a temporary residence permit, which was renewable, and had lived in Venezuela for at least two years, he or she could apply for a permanent residence permit.

All foreigners, irrespective of citizenship, who complied with the formalities and requirements established by the 1980 Regulation were legalized. The registration of foreigners that eventually led to regularization encompassed 266,795 persons aged 10 years and over, among whom 92.3 per cent were Colombian and 54 per cent were men (Torrealba, 1985). Information gathered on those registering included: age; sex; literacy; educational attainment; number of children living in Venezuela; number of children who were Venezuelan citizens; marital status; citizenship of spouse; whether they had relatives in Venezuela; employment status; labour force participation; and occupation. Although being economically active and having an occupation was not a requirement to be registered, it was for regularization. Among those registered, 91 per cent of men and 41 per cent of women were economically active.

Certain tabulations of the data were made and released by the *Dirección Nacional de Identificación y Extranjería* of Venezuela (DIEX). Those available through secondary sources (Torrealba, 1985) include: distribution of registered migrants by age group and citizenship; number of registered migrants by sex and citizenship; number of registered migrants by sex and whether they had any children; number of registered migrants by sex, place of birth and place of residence of children; distribution of registered migrants by educational attainment and citizenship; number of registered migrants by state and region within Venezuela; distribution of registered migrants by sex and occupation; and number of registered migrants by most common occupation.

4. Asia

In Malaysia, the Government launched in January 1989 a regularization drive for Indonesian foreign workers employed illegally in agriculture. Workers coming forward were taken to the port of Malacca, then returned to Sumatra where they were issued travel passes allowing them to go back to Malaysia and obtain a work permit there. The process took a week and had a cost of $M300 per worker, a factor that reduced the effectiveness of the regularization drive. Almost no statistics regarding the drive are available, except that less than 180,000 persons applied for it (Awad, 1995).

International migration statistics

In October 1991, in conjunction with a change in labour migration policy, the Government of Malaysia launched another regularization programme (Awad, 1995). Initially, it required migrant workers in an irregular situation to register with the immigration authorities between 1 November and 31 December 1991. After a medical examination and the payment of fees, registered workers would obtain a temporary work permit valid for two years. The threat of stepped-up enforcement of the ban against hiring irregular migrants after the regularization period was over was used as a means of compelling eligible migrants to apply. In the event, the number registering was small and the registration period had to be extended to the end of June 1992. The Government announced that irregular migrants employed in plantations, construction and domestic services would be allowed to remain provided they registered before the extended deadline. By September 1992, the number of regularized workers reached 447,000, though other figures have been cited (Awad, 1995). In the case of Indonesian irregular workers, the registration involved two stages, the first with the Indonesian embassy and the second with the Malaysian labour authorities. It appears that by June 1992, 311,434 Indonesians had registered at the Indonesian Embassy, but that the requirement that all legalized workers had to be provided the same pay and conditions as Malaysian workers prevented many from proceeding to the second stage of the legalization process (Hugo, 1993a). Awad (1995) notes that by the 31 December 1993 only 190,000 of the foreign workers who had registered with Malaysian authorities had obtained machine-readable work permits valid for two years. Official statistics regarding the regularization drive seem not to have been published.

5. Scope and limitations of the data obtained through regularization programmes

The preceding description of country experiences reveals that, although the regularization programmes that have been implemented over the years by a variety of countries have had many features in common, there are sufficient variations among them to make the statistics that they may eventually produce differ considerably in terms of scope, meaning and limitations. To ensure, therefore, that any statistics emanating from the implementation of a regularization programme are properly used and interpreted, it is crucial that precise information be provided about both the conditions under which foreigners may obtain regularization and the actual implementation of the regularization process. In addition, sufficient attention must be given to a more complete gathering, processing and dissemination of statistical information. Such information is clearly needed while the regularization process is under way to guide managerial decision-making and help improve the logistics of implementation. But the need for quantitative information does not cease with the end of the regularization programme. The dissemination of statistics on the number of applicants and their characteristics; the number of those regularized and their characteristics; and the number of those whose applications were not approved and their characteristics is essential to assess the implementation of the programme, evaluate whether its goals were met, and guide the formulation of policy to prevent the most common types of irregular migration. Yet, as the review above reveals, very few countries accord priority to the elaboration of statistics that both help characterize the migrants involved and permit an objective evaluation of the effectiveness of a regularization programme.

According to the review of country practices, the target population of regularization programmes varies considerably from one country to another. Furthermore, some countries target not only migrants in an irregular situation but also foreigners whose situation is legal but who are given an opportunity to improve their status. Such was the case of France in 1981, where foreigners working legally as seasonal workers were granted work permits valid for the whole year; and of Canada in 1973 and Australia in 1980, where persons legally present in the country under temporary permits were allowed to adjust to permanent resident status as part of the regularization drive. In such circumstances, the total number of persons whose status is eventually regularized cannot be equated with the number of pre-existing irregular migrants. The distinction is straightforward when one has access to detailed information on the operation of a regularization programme but, given that in most cases only the total number of persons regularized is reported and insufficient attention is accorded to describing who exactly qualified for "regularization", the possibility of misinterpretation is high.

It should also be noted that only rarely do regularization programmes target all the irregular migrants present in a country at the time the programme is implemented. Since it is well known that the mere possibility of instituting a regularization programme can act as a magnet attracting new irregular migrants in the hope that they can regularize their status, the authorities in charge of instituting such programmes rarely allow the regularization of foreigners who have arrived recently. However, the longer the duration required for the presence of irregular migrants, the greater the number who will not be able to qualify for regularization. Hence, whatever the results of a regularization programme, it will not yield information on all irregular migrants present in the country at the time the regularization takes place. The case of the United States is illustrative: the migrants eligible to apply for regularization in 1987–88 had to prove that they had resided continuously in the country since before 1 January 1982. Even the most flexible interpretation of "continuous residence" could not transform recent migrants into eligible ones. The result was that, after the regularization programme had barely been completed in 1988, it was estimated that the number of irregular migrants still remaining in the United States was nearly 1.9 million persons, about half of whom had arrived after 1982 (Woodrow and Passel, 1990). The evidence available suggested that about one-third of the irregular migrants who qualified for regularization under the regular programme established by IRCA had not applied. However, with respect to the special agricultural workers (SAW) programme, there was evidence suggesting that the number of persons who eventually regularized their status was too high with respect to any reasonable estimate of the target population of that programme. Thus, the number of applications received was higher than the total number of agricultural workers in California in 1987. The Immigration and Naturalization Service Legalization Office suspected that as many as half of the applications under the SAW programme, which covered about 1.3 million persons, may have been fraudulent, but could not reject them because of a lack of disqualifying evidence (Hoefer, 1989). Thus, it is likely that the 3 million persons whose status was regularized as a result of IRCA included one component that underrepresented its target population and another that overrepresented a different target population.

This example indicates the difficulties involved in trying to assess whether the results of a regularization drive are consistent with its objectives or not. Usually the target population is ill-defined to begin with and, because of its clandestine nature, independent and reasonably reliable estimates of its magnitude are not available. The numbers cited are more often than not derived through procedures of dubious quality or from no procedures at all. Under such conditions, adequate evaluations of the completeness of coverage of regularization programmes are unlikely to be carried out, and both the misrepresentation and the misuse of the data based on those programmes is likely.

Better dissemination and analysis of the data from regularization programmes would go a long way towards avoiding or combating such problems. Data presentation should be accompanied by clear descriptions of the scope of the regularization programme, the target population or populations, changes made in that population as the programme was implemented, and problems encountered. Statistical results should include not only detailed information on the migrants whose status was eventually regularized but also on those whose applications were not successful. Characteristics of the regularized migrants should be explored in some detail, since they can reveal problems in coverage. The distribution by sex is particularly important. Thus, in the absence of strongly selective mechanisms, such as the need to be employed or to be employed in certain sectors of the economy, the proportion of women among migrants is likely to be high (at least 45 per cent). Lower proportions indicate that women in an irregular situation who were eligible may have either tended not to apply or been rejected more often than men. The distribution of applicants by region of the country or city of residence may also indicate areas not covered well by the regularization programme. Citizenship is also a key factor in assessing results: in most countries of destination irregular migrants tend to be highly concentrated among those originating in certain countries. The distribution by occupation and sector of economic activity is also likely to provide insights about how the regularization programme performed and about possible policy approaches to reduce unauthorized employment of foreigners. In sum, when countries that undertake regularization programmes fail to pursue an objective assessment of the results obtained and to allow for the analysis of the statistical information derived from the process of regularization, they are wasting a valuable opportunity to understand better the dimensions and characteristics of irregular migration.

6. Recommendations to improve the data derived through regularization programmes

- A strategy for the processing and timely release of statistical information regarding the implementation of regularization programmes should be integrated into the planning of any such programme. In cases where several months are allocated for the implementation of a regularization programme, statistical information on the number of applications received and their characteristics should be released at various points of the implementation phase to allow an intermediate assessment of the programme's performance and make any modifications deemed necessary.
- Upon completion of a regularization programme, a report showing the full results of the programme in terms of number of applications received, number of persons whose status was regularized, and number of applications that were not successful, should be prepared, published and disseminated. The report should contain a description of the conditions under which regularization was granted (with clear definitions of the population groups eligible); a description of how the programme was actually implemented, and of major problems encountered, if any; detailed tabulations of the results of the regularization programme; and, if possible, a description of the main features of the regularized population.
- If a report devoted solely to the results of a regularization programme cannot be prepared, an effort should nevertheless be made to disseminate the main results through regular statistical publications. Results published should be accompanied by a brief description of the regularization programme and of the conditions under which migrants in an irregular situation obtained regularization of their status.
- To the extent possible, the following information should be recorded about each migrant presenting an application for regularization:

Socio-demographic information:
  Name;
  Date of birth;
  Sex;
  Country of citizenship;
  Country of birth;
  Country of previous residence;
  Marital status;
  Educational attainment (level of education completed);

Whether the applicant has any dependents and country of their residence:
Spouse;
Number of children under 18 years of age.

Administrative information:
Date of application;
Type of category under which application is made, as appropriate:
Illegal entry;
Legal entry but illegal residence;
Legal residence but illegal employment;
Whether the decision is made to regularize the migrant or not;
If the migrant is regularized:
Type of permit granted to the migrant in case of regularization;
Date on which permit is granted;
Whether the migrant is economically active;
If the migrant presents a valid employment contract:
Type of employer hiring the migrant (private, public, mixed);
Location of employment;
Wage;
Current occupation;
Current sector of economic activity;
Number, type and country of residence of applicant's dependants who also qualify for regularization:
Spouse;
Number of dependent children.

Migration history:
Date of first arrival to live in the country where the migrant is seeking regularization (month and year);
Mode of entry: holding a valid entry permit or not; type of entry permit;
Port of entry;
First employment by the migrant in the country where his or her status is being regularized:
Period of employment: beginning and ending date;
Occupation in first employment;
Sector of economic activity.

According to the conditions under which the regularization is carried out, certain categories of migrants will need to be distinguished. Thus, if the regularization allows for the change of status of persons who are not irregular migrants, it is important to distinguish them from actual irregular migrants when presenting statistics on the regularization's results. Those in charge of implementing a regularization programme must decide which groups of regularized migrants it is important to distinguish and do so consistently in all the statistics released.

Data collection systems concerning labour migration

- The following core tabulations should be produced:

  (a) Number of persons covered by the applications classified by sex, age group and country of citizenship;

  (b) Number of persons covered by the applications classified by sex, age group and labour force participation;

  (c) Number of persons covered by the applications who are economically active by sex, age group and occupation;

  (d) Number of persons whose status was not regularized, classified by sex, age group and country of citizenship;

  (e) Number of persons whose status was not regularized, classified by sex, age group and labour force participation;

  (f) Number of persons whose status was regularized, classified by type of regularization, sex, age group and country of citizenship;

  (g) Number of persons whose status was regularized, classified by type of regularization, sex and educational attainment;

  (h) Number of persons whose status was regularized, classified by type of regularization, sex, age group and labour force participation;

  (i) Number of economically active persons whose status was regularized, classified by type of regularization, sex, age group and occupation;

  (j) Number of economically active persons whose status was regularized, classified by sex and whether they had an employment contract or not;

  (k) Number of persons whose status was regularized, classified by sex and place of residence at the time of regularization;

  (l) Number of spouses and dependent children regularized by virtue of being dependants of other regularized persons, classified by sex, country of citizenship and country of residence at the time of regularization;

  (m) Number of persons whose status was regularized, classified by sex, country of citizenship and year of arrival;

  (n) Number of persons whose status was regularized, classified by sex, country of citizenship and port of entry;

  (o) Number of persons whose status was regularized, classified by sex, country of citizenship and mode of entry (illegal or type of visa used);

  (p) Number of persons whose status was regularized, classified by sex and occupation in first job after entering the country;

International migration statistics

- (q) Number of persons whose status was regularized, classified by sex and time elapsed between entry and securing a first job;
- (r) Number of persons whose status was regularized, classified by sex and length of time in first employment.

- All tabulations produced, whether they be in the list of recommended tabulations or not, should present data classified by sex. The authorities in charge of implementing a regularization programme should ensure that, at the very minimum, tabulations (a), (f) to (j), and (m) are published and available for dissemination. Their inclusion in regular publications of the national statistical office or of the agency in charge of publishing statistics relative to international migration is strongly recommended.

DATA COLLECTION SYSTEMS PROVIDING INFORMATION ON ASYLUM-SEEKERS AND REFUGEES*

5

The international movement of people in search for asylum increased substantially during the 1980s and early 1990s, and that increase has been one of the major issues of concern in the international agenda during recent years. Although persons who can be identified as refugees have existed for centuries, the current regime for the protection of refugees was fashioned largely in response to the events following the end of the Second World War which culminated in the adoption by the United Nations of the Convention Relating to the Status of Refugees in 1951. The 1951 Convention and its 1967 Protocol are among the most widely ratified international instruments in existence and certainly the most widely ratified instruments relating to asylum. As of June 1995, 120 countries had ratified both instruments and a further eight had ratified at least one of them.

Jointly, the 1951 Convention and its 1967 Protocol provide an explicit definition of refugee. Thus, according to Article 1 A (2) of the Convention and Article 1, paragraph 2, of the 1967 Protocol, a refugee is a person who "owing to a well-founded fear of being persecuted for reasons of race, religion, nationality, membership of a particular social group or political opinion, is outside the country of his nationality and is unable or, owing to such fear, is unwilling to avail himself of the protection of that country; or who, not having a nationality and being outside the country of his former habitual residence, is unable or, owing to such fear, is unwilling to return to it."[1] By ratifying the 1951 Convention and its 1967 Protocol, countries incorporate this definition into their national legislation. In many countries, individual refugee-status determination procedures are used to evaluate the available evidence and establish if asylum claimants have a "well-founded" fear of persecution. Yet, while objective criteria are generally required to prove that a claim for refugee status is well-founded, the definition itself gives considerable weight to individual motives by acknowledging the "fear of being persecuted" as a reason for leaving one's country.

---

* An earlier version of this chapter was contributed by Bela Hovy, Statistician, Office of the United Nations High Commissioner for Refugees (UNHCR). The views and opinions expressed in it are those of the authors and do not necessarily reflect those of UNHCR.

Neither the Convention nor its Protocol guarantee the right to be granted asylum, but they establish that refugees cannot be forcibly returned to a country where their life or freedom would be threatened on the grounds cited in Article 1 A (2). The forcible return of refugees is known as *refoulement* and protection against it can therefore be considered the main obligation that States have in according protection to refugees.

In December 1950, just before the 1951 Convention was opened for ratification, the United Nations General Assembly adopted the Statute of the Office of the United Nations High Commissioner for Refugees (UNHCR),[2] thus creating the institution that would assume responsibility for protecting and assisting refugees worldwide during the rest of the century. The Statute of the Office contains a definition of refugee that is virtually identical to that contained in the 1951 Convention, but it also stipulates that the work of the High Commissioner "shall relate, as a rule, to groups and categories of refugees" (Ch. I, para. 2). The Statute further establishes that one of the tasks of the Office is to obtain "from Governments information concerning the number and conditions of refugees in their territories and the laws and regulations concerning them" (Ch. II, para. 8(f)).

It is worth noting that, as part of its mandate, UNHCR itself can grant protection to persons who qualify as refugees irrespective of whether the country in which they find themselves has signed the 1951 Convention or its 1967 Protocol or has accorded refugee status to the persons involved. Refugees whose status is granted by UNHCR are often referred to as "mandate refugees".

Although the definition of refugee as embodied in the 1951 Convention and its 1967 Protocol is recognized by a majority of the countries in the world, it is not without shortcomings. In fact, the original definition was subject to geographical and temporal limitations that severely restricted its potential usefulness, referring as it did only to events occurring before 1 January 1951 in Europe. Such limitations were lifted by the 1967 Protocol and are only operative today in a handful of countries. Yet the focus of the Convention and the Protocol on individual persecution rather than on that directed at groups of people and on a limited set of reasons for that persecution is increasingly perceived as a limitation.

In the 1960s, when problems of forced migration became important in the developing world, African countries formally recognized the need for an expanded definition of refugee by adopting in 1969 the Convention Governing the Specific Aspects of Refugees in Africa under the Organization of African Unity (OAU). The OAU Convention constitutes the second pillar in contemporary refugee protection. It incorporates the definition of refugee established by the 1951 Convention and expands it by adding that "the term 'refugee' shall also apply to every person who, owing to external aggression, occupation, foreign domination or events seriously disturbing public order in either part or the whole of his country of origin or nationality, is compelled to leave his place of habitual residence in order to seek refuge in another place outside his country of origin or nationality." (Article 1, para. 2). Under the OAU Convention, persons fleeing generalized violence in their home countries need no longer prove individual persecution in order to be granted asylum. As of 1993, the OAU Convention had 42 signatories (Rogers and Copeland, 1993).

In the early 1980s, countries in Central America experienced widespread violence that forced thousands of persons to flee their homes. As in Africa, the limitations of the 1951 Convention prompted the adoption of a wider refugee definition included in the Cartagena Declaration of 1984. The Declaration states that the definition or concept of a refugee to be recommended for use in the region is one which, in addition to containing the elements of the 1951 Convention and the 1967 Protocol, includes persons who have fled their country because their lives, safety or freedom have been threatened by generalized violence, foreign aggression, internal conflicts, massive violation of human rights or other circumstances which have seriously disturbed the public order (Rogers and Copeland, 1993). Unlike the 1969 OAU Convention, however, the 1984 Cartagena Declaration is not legally binding. Nevertheless, its principles have been adopted by most governments in the central American region.

Even at the level of international instruments there are, therefore, several definitions of the term refugee and, because not all countries are parties to the 1951 Convention or its 1967 Protocol, there is considerable variation in the way in which countries interpret such a term. In addition, among countries that have ratified the United Nations instruments relating to refugees, the criteria and procedures used in the determination of refugee status vary. Some countries have even established special admission categories for persons in need of protection who do not fully qualify for refugee status under the 1951 Convention (e.g. the "designated classed" of Canada or the "humanitarian status" granted by the Nordic countries). Nevertheless, there is probably more homogeneity in the definition of refugee used across countries than among the definitions of other types of international migrants. The point that bears stressing is that, as its Statute stipulates, UNHCR generally relies on governments to provide information on the number and characteristics of the refugees that they have admitted. Thus, although government practices may vary, their statistics are at the very minimum a good reflection of those practices and represent, even in cases where they are only rough approximations, a determination by the governments involved of which persons or groups of persons qualify for asylum.

With respect to UNHCR's activities, the extension of the definition of refugee by regional instruments has implied that, in certain regions, the UNHCR has extended its assistance and protection to persons fleeing armed conflict and generalized violence. As a consequence, a growing gap has developed between the functional responsibilities of UNHCR and the legal obligations of States. Thus, whereas UNHCR has assumed responsibility for groups of refugees, as stated in the Statute of the Office, or for persons who qualify as refugees only under regional instruments, most developed countries continue to adhere to the narrow interpretation of the definition of refugee contained in the 1951 Convention and its 1967 Protocol. Consequently, the statistics forwarded by governments to UNHCR often reflect considerably

International migration statistics

different approaches to the determination of refugee status. Developed countries tend to produce statistics derived from individual determination or from the admission of refugees for resettlement, whereas developing countries report overall numbers of persons recognized as refugees on a group basis who may not have been enumerated individually or at all.

This chapter will document both government and UNHCR practices in obtaining statistics on refugees and asylum-seekers. Other categories of forced migrants, such as internally displaced persons, will not be considered, since they have not crossed international borders. It must be noted, however, that UNHCR has provided assistance to internally displaced persons in Bosnia and Herzegovina, Iraq and in certain other countries. Such protection and assistance has been provided on an exceptional basis, at the specific request of the United Nations General Assembly, the Security Council or the Secretary-General of the United Nations. For operational purposes, UNHCR has developed a working definition of internally displaced persons as individuals who, had they managed to cross an international border, would have qualified as refugees of concern to UNHCR (UNHCR, 1994a).

A. DYNAMICS OF CHANGE OF THE REFUGEE POPULATION

Before proceeding with a discussion of the main sources of data relative to refugees, it is important to describe in general terms the components of change of the refugee population, since deficiencies in the measurement of any of those components will result in poor estimates of the stock of refugees in a country. Table 5.1 presents in schematic form the possible components of change of the refugee population in a country. As indicated in table 5.1, the number of refugees present in a country may increase because of new arrivals of refugees, because of the change of status of certain foreigners, or because of births to the refugee population already present in a country. Reductions of the refugee population can take place because of departures of different kinds, changes of status or deaths.

Table 5.1. Sources of change of the refugee population

Additions to the refugee population		Exits from the refugee population	
New arrivals	Admission of resettled refugees	Departures	Departures for resettlement
	Spontaneous arrivals		Spontaneous departures
	Admissions for family reunion		Organized voluntary repatriation
Changes of status	In-country applicants	Changes of status	Cessation of refugee status
			Naturalization
Natural increase	Births	Natural decrease	Deaths

Data collection systems providing information on asylum-seekers and refugees

1. Additions to the refugee population

In most circumstances, the components of change of greatest interest are those leading to an increase of the refugee population through new arrivals. Yet, the three categories of arrivals listed in table 5.1 have different relevance according to context. Until the early 1980s, the majority of refugees admitted by developed countries were those resettled from first countries of asylum. Generally, the status of those persons is determined while they are still outside of the country of resettlement and by the time they enter that country they have already been recognized as refugees or have been granted a similar status because of humanitarian considerations. Countries that differentiate between persons admitted as refugees under the 1951 Convention and its 1967 Protocol and other persons granted admission for humanitarian reasons use different terms to refer to each category. In this chapter, the first group will be denominated Convention refugees and the second, refugees for humanitarian reasons.

The major countries of resettlement in the developed world have been Australia, Canada and the United States, all of which establish an annual quota for the resettlement of refugees from countries of first asylum. Resettled refugees are either admitted directly as immigrants under special categories or are allowed to adjust their status to that of immigrant shortly after their arrival in the country of resettlement (in the United States, refugees may obtain a permanent residence permit one year after arrival). Consequently, resettled refugees are included in the normal immigration statistics of those countries, although the use of special categories allows their identification. The United States also gathers and publishes statistics on the actual arrival of resettled refugees in the country, and its refugee resettlement programme has the uncommon feature of allowing "in-country processing" of asylum applicants, thus granting refugee status to persons who have not yet left their own country.

In the European countries with market economies, refugee resettlement has occurred on a lower scale. Those countries resettle a few thousand refugees each year on the basis of a more or less formal refugee quota negotiated annually with UNHCR for the resettlement of especially needy cases. In addition, countries such as Austria, Belgium, France, Germany, Iceland, Ireland, Italy, Luxembourg, Spain and the United Kingdom provide resettlement places on an ad hoc basis. Statistics relative to the arrivals of resettled refugees in Europe are often not available or such arrivals are reported in conjunction with the numbers of persons seeking asylum. Denmark and the United Kingdom are among the few countries whose statistics report refugees admitted abroad as a separate category.

Over the years, UNHCR has published resettlement statistics. However, they reflect only those cases resettled through UNHCR mediation and are therefore not representative of the true level of resettlement taking place all over the world annually.

International migration statistics

Whereas relatively few countries admit refugees for resettlement, the number of countries receiving spontaneous arrivals of persons in need of protection is large. From both the legal and the statistical perspective, the consideration of spontaneous arrivals is simpler when a country recognizes refugee status on a group or prima facie basis. Then, all persons arriving in the country and belonging to that specific group can be considered refugees without the need of lengthy determination procedures. Developing countries are more likely to adopt the prima facie approach to refugee status determination, especially in regions where an expanded definition of refugee is common, as in Africa. In those cases, statistical accounting can focus on the recording of new arrivals which, in emergency situations or when the situation is very fluid, is not an easy task.

In most developed countries, persons arriving spontaneously and seeking asylum must undergo a refugee status determination procedure to establish the validity of their claims. Hence, they cannot be considered as additions to the refugee population immediately upon arrival. Only when their cases are adjudicated and the decision to grant them refugee status has been made can they be added to the stock of refugees. A further complication arises from the fact that, in a number of countries, asylum-seekers may not be granted refugee status under the 1951 Convention but may nevertheless be allowed to remain in the country for humanitarian reasons under a different status. The terms used to describe such status vary from country to country but, as in the case of resettled refugees, they can mostly be assimilated to the category of refugees for humanitarian reasons. In addition, as noted in Chapter 2, certain asylum-seekers whose claims are not granted and who are therefore not given any kind of formal status are nevertheless not deported immediately because it is recognized that they may be in danger if returned to their countries of origin. Persons benefiting from such stay-of-deportation decisions are not officially recognized as refugees and should not be considered as such. However, they represent a special category in the growing array of types of involuntary or forced migration. To the extent possible, their numbers should be reported separately in any statistical compilation dealing with asylum-seeker cases.

Returning to table 5.1, note that another source of additions to the refugee population is the change of status of other international migrants. In most circumstances, this category encompasses the cases of foreigners who are already present in a country, generally under another migrant status, and who present an application for asylum when the circumstances in their country of origin change. A significant number of asylum-seekers in developed countries fall into such category. Clearly, only if their applications for asylum are successful should they be added to the refugee stock and, for the purposes of transparent accounting, it is recommended that a distinction be made between them and persons who apply for asylum immediately upon arrival in the country.

The two other potential components of growth of the refugee population, family reunion and births, are generally very poorly documented, partly because it is not always certain that the persons involved will be considered as refugees. In the case of births, for instance, when refugees live in countries whose nationality laws are based on the principle of *jus soli*, children born in the country have a right to be citizens of that country irrespective of the citizenship of their parents. Consequently, children born to refugees living in such countries would not even qualify as international migrants, much less as refugees. In general, when refugees have been resettled in third countries or otherwise granted permission to stay permanently in the country of asylum, it is unlikely that their children born in those countries will continue to be considered as refugees.

The situation is different in cases where refugees are considered to be only temporarily present in the country of asylum or where refugee status is granted on a prima facie basis. In such circumstances, children born to refugees in the country of asylum are assimilated to the refugee population since their presence is also expected to be temporary and their need for assistance is likely to be similar to that of refugee children born abroad. Consequently, especially when statistics on refugee populations in camps are gathered periodically, the number of births occurring over a period is considered as an addition to the refugee stock.

With respect to family reunification, only countries that explicitly admit migrants for that purpose are likely to make a distinction between those who are admitted to join persons having refugee status and others. In some cases, family members are themselves granted refugee status and would therefore be included in the refugee stock. In cases where family members of refugees are not granted refugee status, their addition to the refugee stock would be debatable. Furthermore, the statistics available generally do not distinguish between principal applicants admitted as refugees and their accompanying family members, or between persons admitted as family members of refugees and those who are family members of other migrants. Consequently, unless family members are granted refugee status, they are unlikely to be included in the refugee stock.

As in the case of children born to refugees, family members joining refugees in countries where refugee status is granted on a prima facie basis would generally qualify as refugees in their own right and would be counted as new arrivals rather than as migrants for family reunification, thus becoming part of the refugee stock.

2. Exits from the refugee population

To estimate the size of the refugee population present in a country, it is imperative that the different components leading to its reduction be recorded with some accuracy. Yet, in most countries of asylum, refugees who leave the country are seldom counted, especially if they do so on their own (spontaneously). Generally, registration of refugee departures is limited to cases in which

International migration statistics

refugees receive special assistance to leave the country of asylum and to reintegrate themselves into the country of origin, that is, when they participate in organized voluntary repatriation programmes. Statistics on the beneficiaries of voluntary repatriation programmes therefore constitute an important, though incomplete, source of information on the departures of refugees, particularly for developing countries.

Information on departures is also obtained from camp statistics relative to the number of persons and families receiving assistance. However, those who depart spontaneously from refugee camps need not leave the country of asylum. Only by recording the number of persons who belong to refugee groups and actually cross the border can complete statistics on departures be obtained. That has been the case in Pakistan, where the number of Afghans crossing the border has been used as an indicator of the number of repatriated refugees.

With respect to departures for resettlement in third countries, their registration by the resettlement countries is more likely than that by the countries of first asylum. That has been the case of the thousands of Vietnamese who have been processed for resettlement in the United States by the orderly departure programme operating from Hanoi. In addition, departures for resettlement made possible through UNHCR mediation are usually well recorded and the statistics obtained have been published by UNHCR.

With respect to changes of status, the 1951 Convention establishes that refugee status can be revoked once the conditions in the home country have improved. Such cessation clause is seldom applied by countries of asylum, however, and the number of persons whose refugee status is withdrawn annually is negligible. More important is the possibility of changing from refugee to another migrant status. As already noted, the countries of immigration – Australia, Canada and the United States – either grant refugees permanent resident status upon arrival or allow refugees to adjust their status to that of immigrants at some point after arrival. It is an open issue whether persons who have thus adjusted their status and become permanent residents should continue to be considered as refugees.

According to the 1951 Convention, another reason for ceasing to be a refugee is to acquire a new nationality. Consequently, refugees who become naturalized citizens of the countries of asylum or resettlement should not continue to be counted as refugees. However, that is not the most common practice. Furthermore, since data on naturalization generally do not indicate whether the persons naturalizing were originally admitted as refugees or not, it is not possible to make the necessary downward adjustments to the refugee stock.

Lastly, while deaths of refugees are usually recorded in situations where the aim is to determine the size of the population requiring assistance, in countries of resettlement or in cases where refugees have ceased to require assistance, vital registration systems usually do not record the original migration status of persons dying and cannot, therefore, provide information on the number of deaths occurring to persons who can be considered to be refugees.

Data collection systems providing information on asylum-seekers and refugees

In conclusion, the measurement of the refugee stock as it evolves through time is unlikely to be accurate in most countries because of varying types of deficiencies in the availability and nature of the basic data needed to monitor the dynamics of change. In developing countries in which the determination of refugee status is made on a prima facie basis and statistics are gathered in relation to the provision of assistance, measures of the refugee population dependent on such aid are likely to reflect certain components of change better than others, including new arrivals, births, departures from camps, participation in voluntary repatriation programmes and deaths. In developed countries, data on the refugee stock are likely to be derived from general sources of migration statistics, such as population registers or registers of foreigners. When those sources are not available, stock estimates are unlikely to be sufficiently accurate since there are major deficiencies in the measurement of several of the components of change identified in table 5.1.

B. STATISTICS DERIVED FROM THE PROVISION OF ASSISTANCE

An important, though generally not comprehensive, source of information on refugee populations is constituted by registers of families or persons receiving assistance. In the context of the disbursement of aid, government agencies, international organizations and non-governmental organizations may keep some type of registers on the population covered by specific programmes. In developing countries in particular, the best documented refugee movements are those which are subject to registration for assistance purposes. Beneficiary statistics, as the statistics derived are normally called, are especially useful in contexts where statistics are generally lacking, as in many of the least developed countries of the world. However, the type and quality of beneficiary statistics varies considerably not only between countries but also within countries depending on the situation in which refugees find themselves. Thus, refugees who are confined to particular areas or are kept in closed camps are more likely to be enumerated with some accuracy than those who settle spontaneously among the local population.

Beneficiary statistics generally do not cover all the refugees living in a country. Refugees who do not request help are generally not included in those statistics. Furthermore, the statistics may relate only to heads of household, without listing all the members of each family. Average family sizes may be used to expand the number of heads of household to approximate numbers of persons receiving assistance. In addition, once refugees become self-reliant or otherwise cease receiving aid, they will generally be dropped from the statistics gathered even if they are still present in the country of asylum.

In some cases, even when assistance is provided, adequate registration may not be possible. That is the case in most emergency situations when large numbers of people cross borders over short periods. In such cases, only the most vulnerable are subject to individualized screening and food is distributed through refugee leaders without keeping records on the number of families involved. Once the emergency is over and refugees find themselves in a more stable situation, registration may be undertaken as a means of ensuring that the assistance programmes developed are adequately tailored to the needs of the people involved. Registration is especially likely in relation to food distribution, which is normally targeted to families and demands that the number of beneficiaries per household be known.

The quality of refugee registration depends also on the settlement pattern of the persons involved. When refugees are settled in well demarcated camps, it is generally possible not only to enumerate the population living in them but also the movements into and out of a camp or the births and deaths occurring in it. The data gathered are likely to be more accurate if the camps are "closed", meaning that the host government restricts the movement of the camp population. Refugees settled in "open" camps with unclear boundaries are less likely to be adequately enumerated and their numbers may not be kept up to date so easily. In south-eastern Asia, for instance, countries of first asylum have often kept Vietnamese refugees in closed camps where each shelter is numbered and movement outside the camp is limited. Statistics relative to those refugees have generally been fairly detailed and accurate. In contrast, in most of Africa, refugees have settled in open camps characterized by makeshift shelters and fluctuating boundaries from which refugees have been able to interact considerably with the local population. Under such circumstances, keeping accurate statistics is far from straightforward, especially when persons receiving assistance have an incentive to be registered and remain registered. Yet, for registration purposes, camps compare favourably to a dispersed pattern of settlement, where refugees intermingle with the local population. In cases where both refugees and the local population have the same ethnic origin, the collection of adequate beneficiary statistics is even more problematic since locals may pose as refugees in order to receive aid.

The type and level of assistance provided is another factor affecting the quality and coverage of beneficiary statistics. Registration of beneficiaries is usually more reliable when it is geared to the continuous provision of food to refugee families than when it involves a one-time provision of blankets to refugee groups.

Although beneficiary statistics are valuable indicators of the size of refugee populations, especially in contexts where no other data exist, they have several limitations. Information derived from the full registration of a refugee population may become outdated quickly because of departures which remain unrecorded or because of the new arrivals of refugees that are not immediately registered. Furthermore, registration must be carried out rapidly and under tight control to avoid an artificial inflation of refugee figures because of the inclusion of persons who are not refugees. Since registration is usually accompanied by the issue of ration cards, the cards themselves may remain in circulation long after the refugees have departed and may provide a weak basis for the derivation of statistics. To ensure that such problems are kept to a minimum, the registration of beneficiaries must be subject to periodic checks and verifications and, in some instances, registration must be repeated as necessary.

1. UNHCR registration guidelines

Registration of beneficiaries is not necessarily carried out by UNHCR, but in many cases the Office has assisted or been in charge of such registration. Aware of the need to improve its practices in that area, the UNHCR published in May 1994 its first registration guidelines, outlining a practical approach towards the registration of programme beneficiaries (UNHCR, 1994b). The guidelines are particularly useful for people who work with refugees, including field staff of UNHCR itself and of non-governmental organizations. The guide suggests that the planning of a registration drive be divided into at least four phases. The first includes the planning and organization of the drive in terms of staff needs, equipment, supplies, security arrangements, communications and transport. It also encompasses a campaign to inform refugees of the need for registration and of the benefits they will derive from it. In the second phase, the aim is to provide all those who claim to be of concern to UNHCR with a fixing token or a wristband, thus defining and freezing temporarily the size of the group for whom detailed information will be collected later. An alternative in spontaneously settled situations is the use of name lists by location which are collected and "closed" prior to more formal registration. This "fixing" phase is necessary to prevent registration from becoming a revolving door, open to distortion and abuse. This phase must be carried out rapidly (in one day) to avoid double or bogus registration. If properly implemented, the second phase will provide a preliminary count of the population involved.

During the third phase, limited information is collected on each person who can present the fixing token or the wristband, and temporary cards are issued for future identification and the distribution of benefits. Depending on the situation, temporary cards may be considered valid for up to six months. It is important that the fixing token be exchanged for the temporary card so that double counts are avoided. If the situation is pressing, the type of information collected would likely be limited to the name of the head of family, the number and distribution by sex of family members, the number of children under five years of age, and the number of the temporary card issued.

If the situation is stable, the third phase may consist of the completion of registration forms and the issuance of registration cards which double as ration cards. This phase ensures the collection of detailed information on individuals and families and provides a verifiable link between the identity of persons of concern and the simple forms of documentation needed for processing large numbers of people for the distribution of assistance. If this part of the third phase is carried immediately after the "fixing" stage of the second phase, there may be time pressures to complete it. If it can be carried out after issuing temporary cards, registration may take longer. It should be noted that it is the registration form that constitutes the core document of a UNHCR registration and that provides the basis for future reference, analysis, verification and the updating of information.

The fourth phase is devoted to verification. Some time after registration, when shelters have been given addresses, they can be linked to the family's registration information. The purpose of this phase is to verify that assistance is being provided to the population of concern and not to other groups. New registration cards can be issued annually and verification, including house to house calls, can become a regular part of monitoring.

The UNHCR registration form records the following information on each family: the country, site and location where they live currently; date of arrival; country, province and district of origin; country, province and district of previous residence if different from that of origin; ethnic origin; religion; number of male and female family members; number of children under five years of age; whether the head of family is a single parent; and whether the person involved is an unaccompanied minor. In addition, for each family member the following information is recorded: name, sex, year of birth, relationship to the head of the family, and whether the person is vulnerable.

The guidelines suggest that selected items of information gathered through registration forms be copied immediately onto control sheets and that all information in the registration forms be computerized for further analysis and use. The data copied onto control sheets can be used to produce preliminary statistics on the total number of beneficiary families, the number of adult men and women, the number of males and females aged 5 to 18 years, the number of children under age five years by sex, the total number of persons, the total number of vulnerable persons, and average family size. Field staff are instructed to obtain such data soon after registration is completed. After the computerization of the full information contained in registration forms, consolidated and updated statistics are to be obtained at the end of every year. It is recommended that the following tabulations be prepared: (a) the total beneficiary population by nationality or ethnic origin; (b) the total population by age and sex, using as a minimum age groups 0-5 years, 5-18 years, and 18 years and over; (c) the number of families by family size, total number of families and average family size; (d) the number of households headed by single men and by single women; (e) the number of vulnerable persons by type of vulnerability. Staff are instructed to prepare a brief registration report describing the main phases of the registration drive, including problems and lessons learned. The report should also contain the main results obtained.

It is too early to assess the success that the guidelines have had in improving data collection regarding beneficiaries. However, the results of some registration drives have begun to be available in some detail. That is the case of data relative to refugees from Burundi enumerated in the camps located in Rwanda during 27–31 December 1993 (UNHCR, 1994c). Furthermore, the UNHCR unit in charge of registration is monitoring closely the results obtained in that and other registration drives with a view to improving the procedures used.

It should be noted that persons receiving assistance from UNHCR are not necessarily recognized officially as refugees and that some may not be refugees at all. As already noted, the United Nations General Assembly, the Security Council and the Secretary-General have frequently asked UNHCR to act on behalf of groups of persons who are in need of protection or assistance but who do not qualify as refugees, even under regional instruments. Such groups have included local populations, war victims, internally displaced persons as well as former refugees who have returned to their country of origin (returnees). Therefore, statistics on the number of persons receiving UNHCR assistance cannot always be considered as indicative of the number of refugees present in a particular context. To facilitate interpretation, the UNHCR begun publishing in the early 1990s statistics that differentiate the various groups.

2. Recommendations regarding the collection and use of beneficiary statistics

- UNHCR should continue promoting the use of homogeneous registration procedures in developing countries. Its registration guidelines should be distributed widely (UNHCR, 1994b). In addition, as suggested in the guidelines themselves, efforts to evaluate experiences with a view to devising better means of implementation should be continued.

- In processing beneficiary statistics an effort should be made to produce more comprehensive tabulations. Thus, the tabulation of the beneficiary population by age and sex should be done in terms of five-year age groups, rather than in terms of the three age groups cited in the guidelines. The distribution by age and sex of dependants in households headed by single men or by single women should also be produced, classified by sex of the head of household. An age and sex distribution of heads of household by whether their partners are present or absent would also be useful. All tabulations made should present data classified by sex.

- An effort should be made to publish the results of registration drives with some detail and to disseminate the results obtained so as to raise awareness about the procedures being used, the results obtained and their utility.

C. UNHCR PRACTICES REGARDING THE GATHERING OF STATISTICS ON REFUGEES

In accordance with its Statute, the Office of UNHCR gathers information from governments concerning the number and conditions of refugees in their territories. Data collection is carried out annually by sending forms to all countries. For some types of populations of concern to UNHCR, information may be obtained not only from Governments but also from non-governmental organizations or from UNHCR records. Note that the information gathered is in terms of stocks at a particular time (end of the year) and that it relates not only to persons considered as refugees but also to other groups of people that are defined as "others of concern to UNHCR" which include internally displaced persons (IDPs), returnees and other groups. Information is also obtained on the number of persons repatriating voluntarily either on their own (spontaneously) or through organized programmes.

UNHCR has used the statistics it compiles to produce global estimates of the number of refugees and to report on the number of refugees present in different countries. Only recently, however, has the Office begun to publish on a regular basis a number of tabulations derived from the data gathered, showing in more detail the different components of the population of concern to UNHCR (UNHCR, 1994d and n.d.). The most recent statistical overview states that the populations covered by the data presented include refugees, returnees, internally displaced persons and others. The category of refugees includes Convention refugees, persons recognized as refugees under the 1969 OAU Convention, and persons recognized by UNHCR as "mandate" refugees. The returnees reported are persons who were of concern to UNHCR when outside their country and who remain so for a limited period after their return. The internally displaced persons included are only those who have become of concern to UNHCR as a result of a request from the Security Council, the General Assembly or the Secretary-General of the United Nations.

The category "others" includes persons who are in a refugee-like situation outside of their country but who have not been formally recognized as refugees. In Europe and Northern America, persons who have been granted protection on a group basis (sometimes referred to as being in a "temporarily protected status") or for humanitarian reasons are reported in this category. In addition, war victims of the former Yugoslavia assisted by UNHCR and groups of forced migrants, returnees and internally displaced persons in the former Commonwealth of Independent States (CIS) are included. Asylum-seekers in southeastern Asia whose claims have not been successful and who are assisted by UNHCR are also part of this category.

The report explains that the quality of the data presented varies considerably between countries, being based on detailed registration in some and on rough extrapolations based on health surveys or on "visual assessments" in others. In many countries, there are several partial sources of information on refugees, as is most commonly the case in countries where assistance is provided.

Data collection systems providing information on asylum-seekers and refugees

In those countries, separate registration systems exist for refugees in camps, in urban areas, or for those living among local populations. In addition, the organization responsible for registration varies between and within countries, being sometimes a governmental unit, a non-governmental organization, UNHCR or a combination of those.

In developed countries there are also a variety of sources of information on refugees and other groups in need of protection. The case of Switzerland illustrates the approach taken in estimating the number of persons of concern to UNHCR. At the end of 1993, the number of Convention refugees in the country was 27,300 and that of persons admitted for humanitarian reasons was 23,700. In addition, there were 24,900 persons admitted on a provisional basis, 30,000 asylum-seekers whose cases were pending, and 16,000 whose applications for asylum had not been granted but who were under stay-of-deportation for technical reasons. In total, therefore, the Government considered that at least 121,900 persons were relevant in terms of asylum. In addition, the Government estimated that between 70,000 and 75,000 citizens of the former Yugoslavia who had fled war in their country were living in Switzerland and could not return to their country (Switzerland, Office Fédéral des Réfugiés, 1994b). This example suggests that the task of recording with some accuracy the number of persons covered by temporary protection schemes, such as that used by Switzerland to allow the temporary presence of citizens of the former Yugoslavia in its territory, is not straightforward, partly because beneficiaries of the scheme need not register on an individual basis. Furthermore, the data available indicate that the number of Convention refugees constitutes only a small proportion of all persons relevant to the asylum system. Similar trends are noticeable in other European countries.

Germany provides another example of the difficulties faced in estimating the number of persons needing protection. Government figures put the "refugee" population in the country at 1,750,000 persons by the end of 1994. Although most of the data used in estimating such a figure are obtained from the central register of foreigners, certain components must be fully estimated. Thus, the central register of foreigners records: the number of persons officially granted asylum; the number of persons admitted as refugees (granted asylum while abroad); most of the "quota" refugees admitted under the framework of humanitarian assistance; the number of displaced foreigners; and the number of asylum-seekers whose applications are still pending. Components that must be estimated include: the number of persons admitted as dependants of foreigners granted asylum; the number of citizens of the former Yugoslavia who are allowed to stay under temporary protection; and the number of foreigners who have not filed an asylum application or whose application has been rejected but who cannot be returned to their country of origin. An estimated 1,110,000 persons belong to the last three categories implying that two-thirds of the population that Germany reports as in need of protection is estimated.

These examples show that much of the information available on refugees and persons in need of protection is tentative at best. UNHCR must rely on national sources for the generation of statistics, their interpretation and the preparation of suitable estimates. There is no guarantee that the approach used in a country matches that in other countries. Thus, asylum-seekers whose applications are still pending should not be included in the estimates of the refugee stock but both Germany and Switzerland seem to include them. Adjustments to ensure comparability of practices can only be made if, as in the cases of those countries, the process used to calculate the figures reported is spelled out. That is not the case for most countries in the world.

Consequently, the data published by UNHCR cannot be guaranteed to be comparable or accurate. Yet, by promoting the dissemination of more detailed information on the different groups of persons of concern to the Office, the UNHCR is performing a valuable service. Recent statistical overviews include several key tabulations. Those relative to stocks at the end of two consecutive years refer to: indicative number of persons of concern to UNHCR by assistance status, type and region; indicative number of refugees by country of asylum and assistance status; indicative number of returnee populations by country and region of return and assistance status; indicative number of other categories of concern to UNHCR by country, region and assistance status; and indicative number of internally displaced persons of concern to UNHCR by country, region and assistance status. In addition, regarding changes in the refugee population over a year, the following tables are included: major new arrivals of refugees by country of asylum and origin; resettlement departures by origin of the refugee; voluntary repatriation departures by country of departure; and number of asylum-seekers granted asylum by type of decision (UNHCR, n.d.). In addition, statistics reflecting UNHCR operational activities are gathered and reported with some regularity.

1. Recommendations on the statistics published by UNHCR

- UNHCR should continue to produce annually a statistical overview on the different groups of concern to it. The overview should be distributed among government officials working on refugee and asylum issues and key research institutions dealing with those issues.

- To the extent possible, UNHCR should include in the statistical overview a detailed analysis of the statistics reported by selected countries so as to illustrate the difficulties encountered in estimating the size of different groups of concern to it and to raise awareness about the different practices followed by various countries.

- UNHCR should modify its data collection forms to include the compilation of data on the populations of concern to it classified by sex. Its own data collection efforts should set an example by consistently producing the distribution by sex of persons registered.

Data collection systems providing information on asylum-seekers and refugees

- Countries having different sources of statistics on refugees, asylum-seekers and other categories of persons in need of protection should endeavour to prepare at regular intervals reports that describe the statistics available and analyse the trends they imply. Developed countries, in particular, are urged to improve the dissemination of their statistics and to ensure that UNHCR has access to all relevant statistical reports on refugees and persons of concern to the asylum system. In preparing those reports, special attention should be given to the presentation of all relevant data by sex.

D. STATISTICS ON ASYLUM-SEEKERS

As already noted, the terms of the 1951 Convention and its 1967 Protocol imply that the determination of refugee status should be made on an individual basis. In principle, all State parties to the Convention have established individual asylum eligibility procedures. In addition, UNHCR can process asylum claims under its Mandate. Most developed countries with market economies have complex procedures for asylum determination. Countries with economies in transition that have only recently acceded to the 1951 Convention and its 1967 Protocol are in the process of establishing such procedures. In south-eastern Asia, individual refugee status determination procedures for Indo-Chinese refugees were introduced in the late 1980s, principally by Hong Kong, Indonesia, Malaysia, the Philippines and Thailand.

Generally, status determination procedures include several stages. The first consists of the presentation of an application for asylum by the person or persons seeking asylum. In most countries, applications are filed in terms of cases and not persons, so that a case can cover several individuals: a principal applicant and members of his or her immediate family. Applications can be filed by foreigners upon their entry into a country or by aliens who are already residents of that country under a different status. In some countries, applications from certain foreigners are not receivable, that is, foreigners can be prevented from filing applications for asylum if they meet certain pre-established criteria. Among European countries, for instance, a foreigner is not eligible to apply for asylum if his or her country of citizenship is considered "safe", if the person has passed through another country where an application for asylum could have been filed, or if the person has already filed for asylum in another European country signatory of the Dublin Convention.

Once an application is filed, its merits may be considered within a certain time limit. If it is found unacceptable on legal or administrative grounds, it may be rejected at that stage. Otherwise it enters the adjudication procedure which generally consists of the formal consideration of the case by a court, a special board or panel that makes a decision on whether to grant asylum or not. If the decision is negative, it can usually be appealed and a judicial review takes place.

International migration statistics

A second negative decision normally implies that the asylum-seeker is not recognized as a refugee and must leave the country. However, as noted above, in a number of countries persons who are not formally granted refugee status are nevertheless allowed to remain in the country under stay-of-deportation orders because their lives may be in danger if they are returned to their country of origin. A positive decision at any stage of the process can take two forms: the granting of refugee status under the 1951 Convention or the granting of a similar status for humanitarian reasons. Statistics on asylum adjudication usually make a distinction between those two types of decision.

In recent years, countries confronted with large numbers of persons in need of protection who nevertheless did not qualify as refugees under the terms of the 1951 Convention and its 1967 Protocol have opted for another means of providing a temporary haven. Particular groups have been granted "temporary protected status", that is, they have been allowed to stay in the country for as long as the situation in their countries of origin remains dangerous. In 1990, the United States codified the principle of granting temporary protection to persons fleeing armed conflict in its Immigration Act. Salvadorians were one of the groups granted such protection and were required to register with the Immigration and Naturalization Service which was thus able to gather statistics on that group. In Europe, the conflict in the former Yugoslavia prompted a number of countries to grant temporary protection on a group basis to citizens of the former Yugoslavia, especially to Bosnians. In both cases, the persons granted such protection are expected to return to their countries once hostilities cease.

One of the by-products of the refugee status determination procedure is the compilation of statistics on various aspects of the process. The statistics most commonly available relate to the number of asylum applications filed. Although the statistics are complete in terms of covering the applications presented, as the discussion above suggests, they do not reflect the number of persons who are not allowed to file applications. Furthermore, the number of asylum applications may not equal the number of persons involved in countries where several persons can be covered by a single application.

Another common problem regarding asylum statistics is that their classification by country of citizenship of applicant may not be accurate, especially when asylum-seekers lack proper documentation or have an interest in hiding their country of origin. Clearly, differences in the practices of countries regarding the criteria for eligibility in filing an asylum application, the length of the adjudication process, and the possibility of appealing a first decision will be reflected in the statistics gathered. Of particular interest is the practice of checking whether an asylum-seeker has filed an application elsewhere. Before the Dublin Convention establishing the country in which an asylum application should be filed was adopted by most member States of the European Union, asylum-seekers could and did file applications in several countries and were thus counted several times at the regional level.

It is important to underscore that, even if complete and accurate statistics on the number of asylum applications filed were available, they would not be

Data collection systems providing information on asylum-seekers and refugees

adequate indicators of inflows of asylum-seekers since, as noted earlier, foreigners already residing in a country can and do apply for asylum. In the United Kingdom, for instance, 124,600 principal applicants submitted an asylum application during 1991-94, 90,400 or 73 per cent of whom were already present in the country. Consequently, in assessing general levels of migrant inflows, it is not valid to include all those persons filing asylum applications over a given period. Such a practice is even less acceptable in situations where the statistics on migrant inflows produced by other sources already include those asylum-seekers who are allowed to stay while their applications are being processed, as is the case of data derived from population registers and registers of foreigners in several European countries (see Chapter 3).

1. Recommendations on asylum statistics

Regarding asylum statistics, fairly sophisticated systems are already in place to gather and process the statistics obtained. The most pressing need concerns the production of comparable statistics by different countries and the dissemination of detailed tabulations on the results of the refugee status determination procedure. The recommendations presented here focus therefore on the types of tabulations needed to compare the performance of the asylum systems of different countries.

- It is recommended that the tabulations presented schematically in tables 5.2 to 5.5 be prepared by all countries gathering such information. A description of the terms used in those schematic tabulations is presented below:

Cases and persons: As explained above, it is common for a single application to cover several individuals. Hence, it is important to present for all categories of applications both the number of cases or applications involved and the number of persons they cover. Note that the number of cases is equivalent to the number of principal applicants.

Period: Usually refers to a year. Calendar years are recommended, but some countries may use fiscal years.

Applications pending at the beginning of the period: A backlog of applications develops when not all those submitted during a period are decided during that period. Information on the number of applications still pending at the beginning of the period for which data are being reported should be provided in terms of number of cases and number of persons involved.

Applications submitted during the period: All asylum applications should be reported, including those rejected during the initial or "pre-screening" phase of the refugee status determination procedure. Some countries make a distinction between the number of newly submitted applications and

International migration statistics

Table 5.2. Recommended tabulation on the results of the process to consider applications for asylum

Country of origin				Country A	Country B
1. Applications pending at beginning of period				Cases Persons	
2. Applications submitted during period	a.	Total		Cases Persons	
	b.	Of which, re-opened		Cases Persons	
3. Positive decisions during period	a.	Convention status granted		Cases Persons	
	b.	Humanitarian status granted		Cases Persons	
4. Negative decisions during period	a.	Total		Cases Persons	
	b.	Of which, stay-of-deportation		Cases Persons	
5. Cases otherwise closed				Cases Persons	
6. Applications pending at end of period				Cases Persons	
7. Convention recognition rate					
8. Total recognition rate					

Table 5.3. Recommended tabulation on the mode of reaching positive decision on asylum applications

Country of origin				Country A	Country B
Positive decisions during period	Convention status granted	First instance	Cases Persons		
		Appeal	Cases Persons		
	Humanitarian status granted	First instance	Cases Persons		
		Appeal	Cases Persons		

those re-opened, that is, those that were submitted during a previous period, closed without a decision and are being reconsidered. In all cases, both the number of cases and the number of persons involved should be reported.

Decisions granting Convention status: The number of cases in which the decision was to grant refugee status on the basis of the 1951 Convention and its 1967 Protocol should be reported, together with the number of persons affected by such decisions. All favourable decisions should be included, irrespective of whether they were reached at the first instance or on appeal.

Data collection systems providing information on asylum-seekers and refugees

Table 5.4. Recommended tabulation indicating number of asylum applications by status of person filing them, and decision taken by status of applicant

Country of origin				Country A	Country B
Applications submitted during period		Newly arrived	Cases Persons		
		From within country	Cases Persons		
Positive decisions during period	Convention status granted	Newly arrived	Cases Persons		
		From within country	Cases Persons		
	Humanitarian status granted	Newly arrived	Cases Persons		
		From within country	Cases Persons		
Negative decisions during period		Newly arrived	Cases Persons		
		From within country	Cases Persons		
Cases otherwise closed		Newly arrived	Cases Persons		
		From within country	Cases Persons		

Table 5.5. Recommended tabulation on the reasons for rejecting applications for asylum or for denying asylum

Country of origin			Country A	Country B
Applications rejected on formal grounds as manifestly unfounded	Safe country of origin	Cases Persons		
	Transit through safe third country	Cases Persons		
	Other grounds (specify)	Cases Persons		
	Total applications rejected through initial decisions	Cases Persons		
Applications rejected after full hearing	Cases granted stay-of-deportation	Cases Persons		
	Order to deport	Cases Persons		
	Total rejected after full hearing	Cases Persons		
Total number of applications rejected		Cases Persons		

Decisions to admit asylum-seekers on humanitarian grounds (humanitarian status granted): The number of cases in which the decision was not to grant the status of Convention refugee but rather to allow admission on humanitarian grounds should be reported, in conjunction with the number of persons covered by those decisions. All favourable decisions should be reported, whether they are reached at the first instance or on appeal.

Negative decisions: The number of cases which were decided negatively, that is, where the decision was not to grant refugee status of any kind, should be reported, distinguishing those where the persons concerned are allowed to stay temporarily under stay-of-deportation orders from the cases in which the persons involved are expected to leave the country. Both the number of cases and the number of persons involved under each category should be presented.

Cases otherwise closed: The number of cases that were closed without a decision should be reported together with the number of persons involved. Reasons for closing cases in this category should be indicated in a footnote. They usually include the impossibility of contacting the applicant to schedule an interview, or non-appearance of the applicant for an interview, the death or departure of the applicant. In some countries, this category also includes cases closed on formal grounds such as, "safe country of origin", "transit through a safe third country", etc. When that is the case, the separate reporting of the number of cases closed on formal grounds is recommended.

Applications pending at the end of the period: With respect to table 5.2, this number is equal to the number of applications pending at the beginning of the period (1), plus the number of applications submitted during the period (2), minus the number of positive (3) and negative decisions (4) and minus the number of cases otherwise closed (5).

Recognition rates: There are several possible measures of the extent to which asylum-seekers are being granted refugee status. The most narrow refers to the percentage granted Convention status, which is calculated as the ratio of the number of cases obtaining Convention status ((3.a) in table 5.2) over the total number of cases adjudicated (positive plus negative decisions: the sum of (3) and (4)). That percentage is commonly known as the "convention recognition rate" and refers to a particular period. Another possible measure is the percentage of positive decisions derived by including in the numerator the number of cases granted Convention status plus the number admitted on humanitarian grounds ((3.a) plus (3.b)) and dividing that number by the total number of positive and negative decisions ((3) plus (4)). This measure is called the total recognition rate. If all cases submitted over the course of a year are followed through to their

Data collection systems providing information on asylum-seekers and refugees

completion, the equivalent measures can be obtained on a cohort basis. Very few countries, however, produce data relative to cohorts by year of application.

First instance and appeal: It is recommended that the number of positive decisions taken be tabulated by type and by whether the decision was reached at the first instance or on appeal (see table 5.3). Systems allowing more than two instances for the consideration of asylum applications should present the results of each instance separately.

Status of applicant: Table 5.4 indicates the information that should be produced on the number of asylum applications filed and processed, classified by whether the applicant is newly arrived or has already been living in the country where the application is filed.

Grounds for rejection of applications: Table 5.5 indicates the data that should be produced on the number of asylum applications rejected according to reason for rejection. Also to be included is the number of applications that receive negative decisions after going through the full determination procedure by type of decision reached.

- Countries should endeavour to produce tabulations of the data as indicated in tables 5.2 to 5.5 classified by sex of the persons involved.

- In addition to the types of tabulations presented in tables 5.2 to 5.5, it is recommended that the distribution of principal applicants by sex and five-year age group be presented for the following sets: (a) applications submitted during a period; (b) cases granted Convention status; (c) cases granted asylum on humanitarian grounds; (d) all cases receiving negative decisions; and (e) cases receiving negative decisions but subject to stay-of-deportation. Similar tabulations are recommended regarding the total number of persons by sex and age group covered by the applications in each of the above categories.

- In countries admitting refugees for resettlement whose cases are processed abroad, it is recommended that those cases be excluded from the asylum tabulations discussed so far. A separate tabulation on the number of resettled refugees by sex, age group and country of origin should be prepared.

- In countries where migration for family reunification is permitted, immediate family members who do not accompany the principal asylum applicant during the period in which the application is considered but join him or her at a later stage should be excluded from asylum statistics. Family members who are admitted on the basis of their relationship with a person granted refugee status should be included in the statistics relative to migration inflows and treated in a manner similar to that accorded to other migrants for family reunification, though identification of the status of the sponsor would be useful.

International migration statistics

- To the extent possible, the number of applications processed over a year should be tabulated by type of decision made and year in which the application was filed so that cohort measures of recognition rates and processing times can be derived.

- In estimating the refugee stock, only those asylum-seekers who have been formally granted refugee status, either as Convention refugees or for humanitarian reasons, should be included.

Notes

[1] United Nations, Treaty Series, Vol. 189, No. 2545, p. 137; and Vol. 606, No. 8791, p. 267.

[2] United Nations General Assembly Resolution 428 (V) of 14 December 1950.

DESIGN OF SURVEYS TO INVESTIGATE THE DETERMINANTS AND CONSEQUENCES OF INTERNATIONAL MIGRATION

6

This chapter covers the use of specialized household surveys to collect data to study the determinants and consequences of international migration. Previous chapters have described the data collection systems producing information on international migration in general or on special types of international migrants. Although all the systems considered so far often gather some information that is relevant for the characterization of international migrants – in terms of sex, age, citizenship, education, date of arrival, country of previous residence, or occupation – the information gathered is too limited to allow the in-depth analysis of the likely causes of international migration or of its consequences for the persons involved. In addition, most of the data systems discussed earlier do not collect data on international migrants departing, and use restrictive definitions of international migrant, thus missing many migrants. Finally, none of those systems collects information on the situation of the migrants *prior to migration*, which will be seen below to be vital to understanding both the determinants and consequences of migration for international migrants. In particular, the most commonly available source of data on international migration, the population census, suffers from a narrow definition of international migrants (the foreign born); lacks information on out-migrants; collects very limited information, and nothing on the pre-migration situation of migrants; and usually identifies only the stock of lifetime migrants rather than recent migrants.

Specialized surveys constitute the best data collection system to gather the information needed to carry out a proper examination of the determinants and consequences of international migration. Although several types of surveys are reviewed, the focus is on household surveys. A household is usually defined as a group of persons who share the same living accommodation; who pool some, or all, of their income and wealth; and who consume certain types of goods and services together, such as food and shelter. Household surveys seek information from households as units of consumption, production, income sharing and decision-making. Most household surveys also include special schedules to collect information regarding particular members of the household or persons linked to a household in special ways. Surveys focusing on international

International migration statistics

migration can include special schedules or sections for members of the household who are international migrants or for persons who used to be members of the household but who have left the country in which the household is located to settle or work abroad. The design of surveys to quantify and assess the factors leading to the international migration of individuals and households, and to understand the effects that migration has on the persons involved, their households and the communities to which they belong is the main topic of this chapter.

Before addressing survey design, section A reviews selected existing survey approaches to the collection of data on international migrants, and their limitations. Section B presents the definition of international migrant recommended here for specialized surveys collecting data for the analysis of the causes or consequences of international migration, and on that basis discusses the identification of appropriate comparison groups for analysis. Section C provides guidelines for sample design for generalized surveys of international migration, and section D discusses certain more limited special approaches. Section E identifies and explains the need for information on many factors for the analysis of the determinants and consequences of international migration. Finally, section F introduces the set of model questionnaires for specialized surveys on international migration, which are presented in the annexes to this book.

A. USE AND LIMITATIONS OF EXISTING SAMPLE SURVEYS

1. General purpose surveys

General purpose household surveys are a potentially useful source of information on international migrants when they have large sample sizes and are conducted in countries where international migrants constitute a sizeable proportion of the population. The term "general purpose survey" is used here to indicate that the main focus of the survey is not the study of international migration. Most existing surveys focus on specific topics, such as labour force and employment, fertility and health, or income and expenditure. In the majority of countries, such surveys have sample sizes that are too small to yield statistically reliable data on international migrants. Thus, if we consider international migrants to be persons born outside the country in which they live, their share of the population is less than 6.5 per cent in three quarters of the independent countries of the world (United Nations, 1995a). Since the typical size of most nationally representative household surveys is in the range of 5,000 to 10,000 households,[1] assuming that there are five persons per household and that the proportion of foreign-born persons in the population is 3 per cent, the expected number of international migrants would range from 750 to 1,500, of whom perhaps 300 to 600 would be economically active adults. While numbers of that magnitude may provide some indication of the characteristics of the foreign born, the problems bias and high standard errors inherent in such small numbers are always present. These risks are magnified if, instead of considering all the foreign born, only those who had arrived within a specified period (such as five years) preceding the survey are to be the focus of analysis. The desirability of concentrating on *recent* migrants when analysing the causes or consequences of international migration implies that general purpose surveys are usually not useful because of the small numbers of recent migrants covered. In addition, general purpose surveys typically include few questions allowing the identification or characterization of international migrants, nor do they contain questions about the pre-migration experience of migrants or their adaptation. Although it is sometimes possible to add pertinent questions to general purpose surveys to discuss these limitations, this is recommended only in surveys with large sample sizes carried out in countries with high proportions of international migrants. Otherwise, the small numbers of migrants likely to be encountered do not justify the expense.

Examples of national surveys which may be large enough to capture sufficient numbers of international migrants for meaningful analysis include the monthly United States Current Population Survey (60,000 households), the annual National Population Survey (PMAU) of Brazil (65,000 households), the National Sample Survey of India, and the Labour Force Surveys of European Union countries (which have sample sizes of 60,000-100,000 for the larger countries and 10,000-50,000 for the smaller ones).[2] The Current Population Survey (CPS), which has been carried out every month since 1947, illustrates how general purpose surveys may be used to analyse some aspects of international migration. The CPS routinely gathers both basic demographic information and data on labour force participation and employment. The place of birth of each household member is recorded, as is the place of residence 12 months before interview in the survey carried out every March. Starting in January, 1994, country of citizenship has begun to be recorded. The CPS is a panel survey in which each household in the sample is interviewed over four consecutive months, then excluded for four months, and interviewed again for an additional four months before being dropped permanently from the sample. This scheme is meant to minimize interviewee fatigue while ensuring continuity and the comparability of results over time. There is a 75 per cent overlap of sampled households from one month to the next and a 50 per cent overlap from one year to the next. Consequently, the data relative to a particular household can be compared over a maximum interval of 11 months. That is, for the international migrants covered by half the CPS sample – 30,000 households – the data gathered have the potential for allowing an analysis of the short-term consequences of migration. Indeed, an analysis of the annual changes experienced by newly arrived cohorts of international migrants could provide insights about the short-term consequences of migration and the integration process. Changes in the status of migrants could be assessed in relation to the economic conditions prevalent in the United States during the relevant period or in relation to equivalent changes among non-migrants. This example illustrates the potential for using existing large-scale national surveys to study some limited consequences of international migration, but this potential has rarely been exploited.

The 1979 Population, Labour Force and Migration Survey of Pakistan (PLM) illustrates how the addition of a special set of questions to an on-going survey can allow a better characterization of international migration (Irfan et al., n.d.). Questions were added to two rounds of the national Labour Force, Income and Expenditure Survey. The head of household was asked to indicate whether any member of the household had ever migrated to live elsewhere since December 1971, when war with India erupted. Anyone moving abroad or returning from abroad within the 8 years preceding the interview was identified as an international migrant. The survey covered 10,242 household members, 0.15 per cent of whom were identified as return migrants and 0.48 per cent as international out-migrants. The information recorded on migrants was limited to age, sex, dependency status, year of departure or return, and labour force participation while abroad. This case suggests that, although there are significant cost advantages in latching onto an existing survey, the peculiarities of international migration demand special approaches because international migrants are rare elements in the population and are seldom represented satisfactorily in general purpose samples. In addition, the questions that can be added without disrupting the main function of an existing survey are usually too limited to allow more than a superficial characterization of international migrants.

Even when general purpose surveys include some questions on international migration, their use to study the consequences of migration for the migrants themselves is limited. In this regard, general purpose surveys have limitations similar to those of censuses. Thus, although it is common to use census or survey data to compare the status of international migrants with that of non-migrants in terms of occupation, income, unemployment levels, fertility, etc., and to interpret similarities between the two groups as indicative of the migrants' success, in reality such similarities reflect, at best, only the process of *integration*. To assess the *consequences* of migration for the migrants themselves, data are needed on their status at the time of migration so as to compare it with that at the time of interview (migrants could conceivably suffer a deterioration in their status even if they appear similar to non-migrants). An additional problem is that the status of the two groups can be compared only for the limited set of characteristics covered by general purpose surveys or censuses, and that both data sources fail to reflect the experience of migrants who have subsequently left or died. Studies focusing on return migration have shown that migrants who return to the country of origin tend to be those who are least successful in the country of destination.

To conclude, although large-scale general purpose surveys can provide some limited information relevant for the study of international migration, they have serious limitations in producing estimates of the stock or flow of international migrants into a country, since such estimates are generally subject to high variability. Yet in countries lacking other information on international migration, surveys have occasionally been used for that purpose. That is the case, for instance, of the surveys carried out in seven West African countries in 1993 under the coordination of CERPOD (1995).

2. Surveys of international migrants

Rather than households, certain international migration surveys focus on persons who cross or are about to cross international borders. A major problem in using data from border crossing at exit/entry points is the sheer volume of movements that take place, the vast majority for purposes other than to change residence. It is therefore difficult to find migrants among movers. In the case of the United States, for instance, there are about half a billion entries a year but less than a million persons are admitted as immigrants. The design of surveys of movers must confront the additional problem of the lack of an appropriate sampling frame. The surveys described below use innovative procedures to attempt to deal with these problems.

In Pakistan, the need for information on migration to the Middle East led to the implementation of an International Migration Project which included a survey of out-migrants at the major ports of departure (Gilani et al., 1981a). One of the aims of the survey was to identify families left behind; a second survey was conducted on these families to study the impact on them of temporary labour out-migration (Gilani et al., 1981c). Out-migrants were defined as workers who had departed for the Middle East within the two years preceding the survey. Since it was thought that most travelled by air, it was decided to undertake a survey of all passengers departing from the three international airports of Pakistan and to identify those leaving specifically to work in the Middle East. The survey was carried out during September-November 1979, and led to 12,516 male out-migrants being interviewed. Their age, occupation, place of residence in Pakistan, country of destination, and expected length of stay abroad were recorded. This information was then used to create a sampling frame to select households in Pakistan with migrant workers abroad for the second survey. The household survey gathered information on 1,710 households located in 250 villages and 50 cities and towns throughout Pakistan, 1,153 of which had migrant members (Gilani et al., 1981b). The procedures used to select households are unfortunately not described in the project documents, and the mean number of households per community was less than six, implying a high cost of data collection per household. A major problem in implementing the household survey was locating the addresses provided by departing migrants. Nearly 2,400 households had to be visited to complete 1,153 interviews in households with migrants, casting doubt on the representativity of the sample. Nevertheless, the approach followed has some novel features worth highlighting, especially the creation of a frame to select a sample of households on the basis of information provided by departing migrants. Such an approach may be useful in cases where most out-migration consists of individuals leaving their families behind and where the aim is to study the effects of migration on those families. The study also has the virtue of including a comparison group of non-migrant households.

Pakistan has also undertaken a survey of male migrants returning to Pakistan on incoming flights from the Middle East (Azam, 1994). The survey was carried out during April 1993 and obtained the following information on Pakistani men who had worked abroad: age; occupation; marital status; community of residence in Pakistan; country of employment; length of stay abroad; whether the migrant's work contract had expired or whether the migrant was returning home only for a short visit; whether the migrant had a written contract with an employer abroad; if so, whether it had been signed in Pakistan before departure and whether it had been processed by the Protector of Emigrants Office. Because in 1992 the Government of Pakistan stopped requiring that Pakistani citizens undergo immigration clearance upon re-entry into the country, the logistical problem of how to identify returning Pakistani citizens at the airport had to be addressed. Flight manifests were used to determine the total number of people on a flight as it arrived; women, children and foreigners were identified as they entered the arrival lounge and the remaining persons were screened to identify migrant workers eligible for interview. Interviewers were instructed to interview at least 20 per cent of the migrant workers on each flight, but managed to interview an average of 48.5 per cent. However, no attempt was made to ensure random selection. Out of a total of 36,155 eligible passengers, 17,524 were interviewed, 13,899 of whom were returning from working abroad. Among the latter, 5,170 were returning with the intention of staying in Pakistan. Although the survey has the virtue of being low cost, it is not based on a representative sample and its results cannot therefore be interpreted as indicating the experience of all return migrants. In addition, by covering only a given month, it cannot reflect differences from one time or season to another, which may be substantial.

Lastly, a survey on the northern border of Mexico, *Encuesta sobre migración en la frontera norte de México*, has been carried out since 1993 (Santibáñez-Romellón et al., 1994; Bustamante et al., 1994) and covers both inflows and outflows. The sampling universe is constituted by border crossings, that is, the survey aims at measuring actual flows. To obtain appropriate measures, space and time are divided into specific units each of which is assigned a probability of coverage according to its importance in terms of the flows that take place over that space and during that period. In terms of space, the 28 main border crossing points/areas were selected along the Mexico-United States border and the number of vehicles crossing at each was observed to determine relative weights for the observations to be sampled from each point. Sampling sites where migrants arrive or depart were then identified in each crossing area (e.g. highway points with immigration posts, bus terminals, train stations, and airports). The survey was planned so that each day two crossing areas were selected as locations for the survey, with two interviewers assigned to each site. Results are just beginning to emerge. Information on the dynamics of population movements from Mexico to the United States, including migrants crossing the northern border of Mexico is being collected. The results are likely to be useful for characterizing mobility across the Mexico-United States border, especially temporary and return migration. However, by covering only migrants, the survey lacks an adequate comparison group that would allow the study of the determinants of international migration.

3. Specialized surveys on international migration

A number of surveys focusing on international migration have been conducted over the past decade that illustrate both the potential usefulness of specialized surveys and the shortcomings inherent in the designs adopted by most of them. The Economic Commission for Europe, for instance, recently coordinated surveys in three countries of central and eastern Europe – Lithuania, Ukraine and Poland – aimed at the study of out-migration and short-term international travel originating in those countries. Although there is some variation across the three surveys, they are generally based on samples that are not representative of the population of origin (even of the few communities selected) and also suffer in data quality from using proxy respondents to obtain information on migrants absent from the household (Frejka, 1995; Mullan, 1995; Sipaviciene et al., 1995).

In Western Africa, CERPOD has coordinated a major survey programme entitled *Réseau d'enquêtes sur les migrations et urbanisation en Afrique de l'ouest* through which migration surveys have been carried out in Burkina Faso, Côte d'Ivoire, Guinea, Mali, Mauritania, Niger, Nigeria and Senegal in 1993 (CERPOD, 1995). All surveys are based on nationally representative samples and are aimed at both measuring migration flows as well as the characteristics of migrants. Full migration histories are recorded for the persons interviewed. The eight country surveys covered nearly 100,000 households but, because the sampling designs made no special effort to identify international migrants, the numbers of the latter are small. In addition, project documents do not explain clearly how samples were selected and problems of sample design may affect the data gathered (see, for instance, Senegal, n.d.). The CERPOD surveys do have the advantage, however, of covering both migrants and non-migrants, thus providing a basis for useful comparisons that may shed light on the determinants of migration. Furthermore, because the surveys simultaneously covered countries linked by major migration flows (such as Burkina Faso and Côte d'Ivoire; and Mali and Senegal), they may permit a more comprehensive analysis of the causes and consequences of international migration than any other data collection effort to date in Africa. However, the lack of detailed data on international migrants reduces the potential usefulness of the surveys for studying them.

Another project involving surveys in several countries is being carried out by the Netherlands Interdisciplinary Demographic Institute (NIDI) and Eurostat and is expected to be completed in 1997. The project aims at collecting the data needed to study the determinants of international migration to selected countries of the European Union. Surveys will be carried out in both countries of destination (covering only households with international migrants) and in countries of origin (covering households with and without out-migrants and their communities). The countries of origin where surveys will be carried out include Egypt, Ghana, Morocco, Senegal and Turkey; countries of destination are France, Germany, Italy, the Netherlands and Spain. Each country of origin has significant flows to at least two of the destination countries included in the study, and each country of destination has experienced large inflows from at least two of the countries of origin. Detailed information on international migrants is to be collected in single-round surveys in each country. To keep costs down, areas where international migrants are known to originate or settle are targeted *a priori*, without formal probability sampling. Sample sizes are to be around 2,000 households in each country of origin and 500-1,000 households per migrant group in each country of destination. The design of the project is consistent with the systems approach to the study of international migration (Zlotnik, 1992; Kritz and Zlotnik, 1992; Bilsborrow and Zlotnik, 1994), and has an overall survey design generally consistent with that recommended in this chapter (see section B). Its results will therefore be of particular interest both from a methodological and a substantive perspective.

The use of longitudinal surveys to study the consequences of international migration should also be mentioned. Australia has begun a Longitudinal Survey of Immigrants which involves interviewing international migrants both before and after they move to Australia. The survey began with annual cohorts of 3,000 immigrants. Principal applicants complete a detailed form prior to being accepted as immigrants. After arrival in Australia, they are interviewed four more times, after one month, one year, two years and five years. The data should be useful for analysing the integration of migrants and the consequences of migration for the migrants themselves if sample attrition is low.

In the United States, a similar survey is being proposed and tests of its feasibility are under way.[3] The survey will have as its universe all persons granted permanent resident status during a given year. A sample of 13,000 immigrants will be selected from a sample frame based on the administrative records of the Immigration and Naturalization Service, which are processed to grant permanent residence. Immigrants selected will be contacted by telephone soon after they obtain permanent residence to ascertain whether they are willing to participate in the survey and to obtain information to trace them later. In-depth interviews will be conducted soon after permanent residence is granted and then annually over a two-year period. Detailed information on the pre-migration and post-migration experience of the migrants will be collected. The data gathered are certain to be useful in assessing the short-term integration of legal immigrants in the United States and the consequences of international migration for the migrants themselves. However, as in the case of other longitudinal surveys covering only international migrants (including the Australian example above), the lack of information on non-migrants in the country of origin prevents an adequate assessment of the causes or consequences of international migration.

B. DESIGN OF SURVEYS FOR THE ANALYSIS OF THE DETERMINANTS AND CONSEQUENCES OF INTERNATIONAL MIGRATION

1. Defining international migrants

The proper design of surveys requires a clear definition of the population of interest. Therefore, a crucial step in designing international migration surveys is defining international migrants for purposes of the survey. As documented in other parts of this book, the characterization of international migrants varies considerably from one data source to another, and existing surveys are no exception. Indeed, given the flexibility that surveys offer in terms of the type and depth of information they can gather, there is ample room for considerable variability in the definitions of international migrant used in survey instruments. There is no single definition that will satisfy all needs and, consequently, the best a survey can do is to make explicit which group is the focus of attention, though data may still be collected for other international migrants and non-migrants as well.

As discussed in Chapter 2, there are three key criteria for the identification of international migrants: place of birth, citizenship and place of residence. Thus, international migrants can be considered persons whose country of birth is different from that in which the survey is being conducted; persons who do not have the citizenship of the country in which the survey is being conducted; or persons who have changed their place of residence from another country to that in which the survey is being conducted. In general, surveys use some version of the third formulation to identify international migrants of interest. For the purposes of analysing either the causes or the consequences of international migration, a change of residence from one country to another is clearly the critical event of interest and must be considered the main criterion for the identification of international migrants. However, leaving aside for the moment the problems inherent in the definition of "residence", it must be recognized that not all persons who change country of residence are equivalent from the analytical perspective. Thus, a person born in country A, who has always lived in country A and then moves to country Z cannot be considered similar to a person who is born in country Z, moves to country A and then returns to country Z. That is, return migrants must be distinguished from persons arriving in a country for the first time. Furthermore, distinguishing the inflows of persons who "belong" (insiders) to a country from those of persons who do not "belong" (outsiders) is crucial from the policy perspective. As stated in other parts of this book, the main marker of "belonging" is citizenship, an attribute of international migrants that should not be ignored.

Surveys gather information directly from the migrants themselves who have moved from one country to another or indirectly from (proxy) respondents who provide information on the persons who have moved and to whom they are related. In terms of retrospective information, "establishing residence" is normally taken to mean living in a place for at least a certain length of time. A period of six months or a year is usually adopted as the cut-off point. In the model questionnaires presented in the annexes to this book, six months has been used as the minimum period of stay to establish residence. Note that this definition tends to equate residence with presence and does not involve any legal considerations. Since the questions actually posed to respondents (see below) are phrased in terms of "having lived in another country for at least six months", there is little danger that the specific meaning of residence recommended here will be misconstrued in practice.

Having established what "change of residence" means for survey purposes, it is necessary to assess which changes of residence matter the most. To be most useful, the results of a survey should focus on current events so that they can provide timely information on the factors that shape them or on the consequences of such events. It is therefore advisable to concentrate on international migrants who have changed residence over a recent period preceding the survey. The choice of a cut-off point for that period is not obvious: The further the cut-off point from the date of the survey, the less likely that events encompassed are relevant for an analysis of the current situation. However, the closer the cut-off point to the date of the survey, the smaller the proportion of persons who would have changed residence during that period and hence the greater the difficulty of encountering a sufficient number of them. In addition, data quality considerations argue against adopting a cut-off point that is set too far in the past. Since respondents will be asked to provide detailed information regarding both the period immediately preceding the most recent change of country of residence and the period following that change, the further that event is in the past, the more likely the data will be affected by recall errors (Som, 1973; Bilsborrow et al., 1984, Ch. 4). Consequently, despite the problems associated with locating an adequate sample of recent international migrants, it is strongly recommended here that attention be focused on persons who have changed their country of residence within 5 or at most 10 years preceding the survey. The model questionnaires presented in the annexes assume a five-year cut-off point for the identification of international migrants subject to intensive interviews. Those migrants also constitute the main subjects for analysis based on the information gathered, whether to study the determinants or the consequences of international migration.[4]

To sum up, it is recommended that specialized migration surveys focus attention on international migrants defined as *persons who have lived for at least six months in a country other than that in which they are being interviewed and whose move into the country of interview occurred during the five years preceding interview.* This definition assumes that international migrants are being interviewed themselves in their country of current residence. When migrants cannot be interviewed because they have emigrated from the country in which the survey is being undertaken and information on them is being obtained from a proxy respondent, the definition has to be modified as follows: an international migrant is a person who used to live in the country in which the interview is being conducted and was a member of the household of the person being interviewed but who left at some point during the five years preceding the interview to live abroad for at least six months. These definitions provide the basis for the formulation of the questions needed to identify international migrants included in the model questionnaires presented in the annexes.

Once international migrants are identified, it is important for analytical purposes to distinguish return migrants from other international migrants. In previous chapters of this book return migrants have been identified as persons moving into their country of citizenship. Following that approach, if a survey is conducted in country A, a citizen of A who has lived in country B during at least six months and enters A during the five years preceding the interview with the intention of staying would be considered a return migrant irrespective of whether he or she had lived in country A before. Because, according to the nationality laws of most countries, few people can obtain the citizenship of a country without having lived in it, citizenship usually indicates previous presence in the country. Exceptions may arise, however, in the cases of countries that grant citizenship to descendants of previous emigrants or to persons with certain backgrounds. In such cases, the identification of "return migrants" may have to be based on both citizenship and place of birth, with a "return migrant" being a citizen born in the country of interview who has lived outside that country for at least six months and returns to live in it again during the five years preceding the interview. The use of citizenship as an organizing criterion is crucial because there are limits on the extent to which governments may regulate the international mobility of their own citizens. Therefore, the policy instruments that can be used to influence the international migration of citizens are generally different from those used in the case of foreigners. Consequently, if the analysis of factors influencing international migration flows is to have policy relevance, it is essential to make a distinction between those flows that are subject to full government regulation and those that are not.

In conclusion, specialized surveys on international migration should focus on international migrants characterized as persons who have changed their country of residence during the five years preceding the survey. If the survey is meant to cover inflows, it will encompass citizens as well as foreigners moving into the country of interview during the relevant five-year period. The former will be denominated return migrants (though this will also include persons with residence rights in country A who migrate to country B then return to country A). When the survey is aimed at obtaining information about migrants who are still abroad, it will focus on persons who left the country within the relevant five-year period, thus including both emigrating citizens and foreigners. Normally, emigrating citizens will be the object of study and emigrating foreigners may be disregarded.

To follow this approach, information on place of birth, citizenship, country of previous residence, and time of the most recent change of residence should be recorded for all persons interviewed. In addition, any change of citizenship and its timing should be recorded for each international migrant interviewed so as to ascertain whether the most recent change of residence took place before or after a change of citizenship.

2. Identification of appropriate comparison groups

A key decision that needs to be made at the outset in designing specialized surveys on international migration is whether the data collected are to be used for the analysis of the determinants or the consequences of international migration. This decision determines the most appropriate locus (country or countries) in which to carry out the survey and the group or groups of non-migrants that are to be used as the comparison or control group. There is a great deal of confusion in the literature regarding the data needed to investigate the determinants or consequences of international migration, with the result that the serious limitations of existing micro-level studies are not recognized. This section aims at elucidating the problems involved and makes explicit how the compromises typically made in the analysis have implications for the validity of inferences that can be drawn from particular types of surveys.

The discussion in this section assumes that international migrants have been precisely defined (for instance, following the guidelines in the previous section) and that a country can be characterized as being either a country of origin or a country of destination for the international migrants of interest. In addition, there is an implicit assumption that the country of origin of the migrant is the country of citizenship, although the framework presented below is relevant also for other conceptualizations of country of origin. In reality, every country has the dual role of being the country of origin for some international migration flows and the country of destination for others. The artificial dichotomy here is common in the analytical literature, and is used precisely to make evident the country perspective.

Perhaps the most straightforward approach for assessing the consequences of international migration for the migrants themselves involves a single survey in the country of destination which interviews international migrants to gather information on their status just before migration as well as at the time of interview. However, the need to minimize recall problems can make this approach usable only when migration is a relatively recent event.[5] Another approach to the collection of data to permit a comparison of the status of migrants over time is a longitudinal or panel survey, which reduces problems associated with recall but substantially increases the cost of data collection. Although it is possible to assess the consequences of international migration for the migrants themselves by examining changes in the migrants' situation over time using either of the two approaches above, such an assessment represents only a partial view of the whole picture and may even be misleading. Thus, suppose an index indicating the migrant's status in the country of origin just before migration has a value of 100 and that it rises to 150 five years after migration. The migrant is clearly better off. But suppose that for non-migrants remaining in the country of origin the status index changed from 70 to 140 over the same period. A comparison of the migrant's status five years after migration with that of non-migrants at the same time would still find the migrant better off, but in relative terms the migrant would have gained less from migration than non-migrants had gained in the country of origin. This example illustrates the importance of assessing change not only with respect to the migrant's own status but also in relation to appropriate reference groups. The remainder of this section discusses the key issue of selecting appropriate comparison groups according to the purpose of the survey, focusing first on the study of the determinants of international migration and then on its consequences.

Survey requirements to study the determinants of international migration

Table 6.1 presents in schematic form the various possible types of analyses relevant for the study of the determinants of international migration, together with what their requirements are in terms of data collection in the country of origin and the country of destination. The term "focal group" is used to denominate the population covered by the survey that makes possible the type of analysis indicated. An assessment of the quality of each type of analysis is provided on the basis of the adequacy of the focal groups involved and the likelihood of obtaining reliable information from those groups. Thus, whenever information on international migrants has to be obtained from proxy respondents because the migrants are not themselves present in the locus of the survey, the option is considered "barely acceptable". The adequacy of focal groups for a particular type of analysis is determined by whether they represent the population at risk of international migration. The greater the overlap between the combination of focal groups for a particular type of analysis and this population at risk, the more preferable the option.[6]

Nine possible types of analysis of the determinants of international migration are distinguished. The first three refer to the individual level and the next three to the household level. A further two deal with the determinants of return migration and the last one covers the determinants of potential migration. Cases are further differentiated according to whether they deal with a single country of origin, a specific pair of countries linked by migration (one country of origin

International migration statistics

Table 6.1. Focal groups for data collection at origin and destination to study the determinants of international migration

Type of analysis	Quality of option	Focal groups for data collection at origin	Focal groups for data collection at destination
1. Determinants of out-migration of individuals from country A	Barely acceptable	(a) Households in country A with members who have left the country (proxy respondent necessary) (b) Other households in A	None
2. Determinants of out-migration of individuals from country A to country Z	Acceptable	Non-migrants in country A	Migrants from country A in country Z
	Barely acceptable	(a) Households in A with members who have migrated to Z (proxy respondent necessary) (b) Other households in A	None
3. Determinants of out-migration of individuals from country A to main destinations (Z, Y, X, etc.)	Preferred	Non-migrants in country A	Migrants from country A in countries Z, Y, X, etc.
	Barely acceptable	(a) Households in country A with members who have migrated to Z, Y, X, etc. (proxy respondent necessary) (b) Other households in A	None
4. Determinants of out-migration of households from country A to country Z	Acceptable	Households remaining in country A	Migrant households from country A in country Z
5. Determinants of out-migration of households from country A	Preferred	Households remaining in country A	Migrant households from country A in countries Z, Y, X, etc.
6. Determinants of out-migration of individuals (and households) from countries A, B, C, etc. to Z, Y, X, etc.	Preferred	Non-migrant individuals and households in countries A, B, C, etc.	Individual and household migrants from countries A, B, C, etc. in Z, Y, X, etc.
7. Determinants of return migration of individuals from country Z to country A	Acceptable	Individuals who migrated from A to Z and returned to A	Migrants from country A remaining in country Z

Table 6.1. (continued)

Type of analysis	Quality of option	Focal groups for data collection at origin	Focal groups for data collection at destination
	Not acceptable	None	(a) Households in country Z with members that have returned to country A (proxy respondent necessary) (b) Migrant households from country A all of whose members are still in country Z
8. Determinants of return migration of households from country Z to country A	Acceptable	Households that migrated from A to Z and have returned to A	Migrant households from A remaining in Z
9. Determinants of potential out-migration of individuals (or households) from country A	Barely acceptable	(a) Households in A containing members intending to migrate (b) Other households in A	None

and one country of destination), or one country of origin and several countries of destination.

The most common type of analysis found in the literature (1) looks at the determinants of out-migration of individuals from country A based upon a survey in the country of origin A only. It allows for comparison of the individual characteristics and the household context of international out-migrants with those of non-migrants. Because the information on out-migrants must be obtained from proxy respondents (usually close relatives of the migrant remaining in the origin country and origin household), it cannot be very detailed or of high quality. Despite the apparent simplicity of this analytical approach, adequate data collection is still not as straightforward as usually assumed, since it should involve obtaining information about the out-migrants pertaining to the time of migration and about non-migrants for approximately that same time. Instead, information gathered on both has almost invariably been only on the time of interview. When the international migrants of interest are defined as those having left country A during the five years preceding interview, the relevant reference date for non-migrants should be 2.5 years preceding interview, that is, the mid-point of the period over which the change of residence of migrants would have taken place.

To study the determinants of out-migration of individuals from a particular country A to a particular country Z, the analyst has two options. In the first, considered acceptable, surveys are carried out in both the country of origin A and the country of destination Z, but the focal groups in each are different. The survey in the country of destination covers only migrants and indeed only migrants from country A, while that in the country of origin covers only non-migrants (that is, almost the whole population remaining in country A, which was at risk of international migration but did not migrate). Migrants are therefore interviewed directly in Z and not by proxy. The combination of non-migrants in A and migrants from A to Z in Z approximates well the total population at risk of international migration in A at the beginning of the observation period (say, five years before the survey). Those missing include persons who died during the period considered, those who migrated from A to countries other than Z, and those who migrated to Z but then migrated again to another country during the period. Each of these will normally be very small proportions of the migration flow from A to Z. Because the groups missing may differ from those covered in ways germane to the determinants of migration, this option is evaluated here as only acceptable.

The second option to study the determinants of individual out-migration from A to Z is to undertake a survey exclusively in the country of origin obtaining data on out-migrants from proxy respondents. The use of proxy respondents again makes this option barely acceptable. Note that the survey described here is similar to that in panel 1, the only difference being that here (in 2) only out-migrants to Z are of interest. In practice, it is not clear how one should treat households that contain out-migrants to countries other than Z. If any are encountered during the survey, they should probably be excluded from the analysis if the goal is really to focus on the determinants of those migrating to Z. But such a restriction makes little sense. (See discussion of the second option of panel 3.)

The third type of analysis involves the determinants of individual out-migration from a specific country A to several major countries of destination (3). The preferred approach involves undertaking surveys in the country of origin A to interview non-migrants and in each of the major countries of destination to gather information directly from the migrants originating in A. An alternative but barely acceptable approach is to carry out a survey of out-migrants and non-migrants (together with their households) only in the country of origin. In this approach information on out-migrants would have to be obtained from proxy respondents, but all out-migrants are considered since there is no need to focus only on those with a particular country of destination. The data gathered can be pooled to assess simultaneously the determinants of out-migration to various countries in comparison to the option of not migrating by using, for instance, multinomial logit analysis. It is likely that the coefficients of the determinants of the decision to migrate to a specific country Z versus not to migrate will be different from those of the decision to migrate to Z versus Y versus X versus to not migrate. Whether such differences are important or not is an empirical question whose relevance will depend on the degree to which Z is a more important destination for migrants from A than Y or X. This indicates the analytical advantage of this approach compared to panel 1, though the survey requirements are identical.

Design of surveys to investigate international migration

The next two panels are concerned with the international migration of households. The fourth type of analysis (panel 4) is concerned with the determinants of out-migration of households from a specific country A to a specific country Z. Because whole households are being considered as opposed to individuals, there is no possibility of using proxy respondents to report on those that have left a country (neighbours provide notoriously poor information). Consequently, the analysis envisaged requires that surveys be undertaken in both the country of origin A to interview households without out-migrants and country of destination Z to interview migrant households originating in A. It is important to stress that retrospective data on the situation of non-migrant households in country A must be obtained for the *mid-point of the period used to define international migration*, so that the situation of the migrants before migration can be compared with that of non-migrants at the (mean) time the migration decision was made. Information on households will generally be obtained from the head of household, supplemented by data from all other adult household members interviewed individually. Because this approach demands that only households originating in A be interviewed in Z, the problem of locating those particular households is greater. In the country of origin the households of interest are those that do not have any migrant members, whether the latter are in Z or in any other country. Consequently, if any household with out-migrant members is encountered in the sample, it should be excluded from the analysis. Note that the type of analysis possible in this case can provide an assessment of the effects of differences in individual and household factors on the propensity of households in A to migrate only to Z. Because only one country of destination is considered, nothing can be said about how differences in the factors at destination can influence out-migration from country A.

The fifth type of analysis focuses on the determinants of out-migration of households from a specific country A to several countries of destination. It therefore represents a generalization of (4), and requires that surveys be undertaken in the country of origin A covering households without out-migrants as well as in each of the (presumably major) countries of destination – Z, Y, X, etc. In each of the countries of destination, only households containing migrants from A would be included in the survey. The advantage of this approach over the previous one (4) is that it pools data from several countries of destination and thus permits an analysis of the factors determining the choice of destination by out-migrant households from A. Since the countries of destination may have different policies that affect the magnitude, timing and characteristics of flows of migrants from A, this type of analysis allows an assessment of the effects of policy differences on international migration from A, as well as, simultaneously, of cross-country differences in other factors including economic conditions. It is only when different countries of destination are included that such analysis is possible.

The sixth type of analysis represents the broadest approach to the study of the determinants of out-migration, since it considers both the out-migration of individuals and whole households from several countries of origin to several countries of destination. This requires that surveys be conducted in each of the countries of origin and each country of destination. Given the international migration linkages existing between countries today, it is often the case that a few countries of destination attract migrants from a common set of countries of origin (Zlotnik, 1992), and that the migrants from each country of origin gravitate to a small number of countries of destination. Therefore, implementation of this type of analysis is not as daunting as it would appear at first glance, as it would usually require undertaking surveys in a small number of countries, numbers that have proved manageable in projects such as the current NIDI and CERPOD projects (see section A.3). By gathering information on individuals and households without migrants in the countries of origin and on migrants from various countries of origin residing in the various countries of destination considered, this approach makes possible the analysis of the determinants of migration from several countries of origin to several countries of destination, thus making it possible to ascertain why out-migration differs from one country of origin to another as well as why some countries attract international migrants more than others. The results of such analyses could be very helpful in policy formulation, since they would encompass both the effects of differences in social and economic conditions in the countries of origin and destination, as well as those of policy differences in both countries of origin and destination. The surveys required should be carried out within a short period of time (preferably over one or two years) but need not be carried out simultaneously. The current multi-survey project being executed by NIDI provides a test case for undertaking these types of linked surveys.

The seventh type of analysis possible involves the determinants of return migration of individuals from a specific country Z to a specific country A (panel 7). There are two alternative approaches to gather data for this type of analysis. The most acceptable one requires a survey of individual migrants from country A to country Z returning to A and being interviewed in A plus a survey of migrants from A remaining in Z and interviewed in Z. Disregarding deaths and the possibility of re-migration to third countries, the two groups combined constitute the appropriate population at risk of returning to country A after migration to Z. An analysis of the determinants of return migration based upon the pooled data will provide useful information about the individual and household factors leading to return migration. However, surveys of return migrants should be undertaken only in countries where such migration is sizable; otherwise it will be very difficult and costly to locate a large enough and representative sample of return migrants in the country of origin. The barely acceptable alternative indicated is to gather information only in the country of destination, which would require using proxy respondents to obtain information about migrants who have returned to A. Because it is more likely for return migrants not to leave any household members in the country of destination when they return to their country of origin than it is for out-migrants not to leave family members in the country of origin when they initially leave, the need to use proxy respondents in the country of destination is likely to result in serious underrepresentation of return migrants. If only for that reason, the second approach to this type of analysis is not recommended.

The eighth type of analysis relates to the determinants of return migration of households from a specific country Z to a specific country of origin A. As in the case of individual migrants, such an analysis requires that surveys be carried out in both countries, comprising a survey in country Z of migrant households from A to Z remaining in Z and a survey in country A of households that had migrated from A to Z but returned to A. In both cases data can be obtained directly from the migrants themselves, though it may be very difficult to locate return migrants in the country of origin, especially if they are rare even with respect to the out-migrant population.

Both types of analysis involving the determinants of return migration (7 and 8) can be extended to include multiple countries of destination or several countries of origin. Thus, to study the causes of return migration from a set of various countries of destination to a single country of origin A, surveys should be executed in each country of destination focusing on migrants from country A while a survey in country A would cover return migrants from all of the relevant countries of destination. The data obtained would allow an analysis of how differences across countries of destination affect return (out-) migration to A. Similarly, a survey in a single country of destination Z could encompass all households with international migrants from various countries of origin and, combined with surveys of return migrants from Z carried out in each of those countries of origin, would provide the pooled data necessary to determine how differences across countries of origin influence the propensity of migrants to return from Z.

Lastly, to study the determinants of potential international migration from A, a survey in A can be carried out that covers all households and asks questions to distinguish those who intend to migrate internationally from those that do not. Although the reliability of the responses may be questionable because they are subjective, attitudinal, and therefore subject to change, studies based upon such data can provide useful results on the determinants of potential migration, and several have been carried out. They also have the advantage of requiring a survey only in a single country. This type of analysis is assessed as "barely acceptable" because of the subjective nature of the data it relies on.

Survey requirements to study the consequences of international migration

Paralleling the treatment of the analysis of the determinants of international migration, table 6.2 presents in schematic form the types of analysis relevant for the study of the consequences of international migration and their implications for data collection in the countries of origin and destination. As indicated in the above discussion on determinants, the preferred approaches are those in which the appropriate population at risk is covered, although the applicability of this concept is less straightforward in relation to the consequences of migration than with respect to the determinants. However, since

International migration statistics

Table 6.2. Focal groups for data collection at origin and destination to study the consequences of international migration

Type of analysis	Quality of option	Focal groups for data collection at origin	Focal groups for data collection at destination
1. Consequences of in-migration for individual migrants in country Z	Barely acceptable	None	(a) Migrants from countries A, B, C, etc. in country Z (b) Non-migrants in country Z
2. Consequences of in-migration for individuals from country A to country Z	Acceptable	Non-migrants in country A	Migrants from country A in country Z
	Barely acceptable	None	(a) Migrants from country A to country Z (b) Non-migrants in Z
	Barely acceptable	(a) Households in country A with members who have migrated to country Z (proxy respondent necessary) (b) Other households in country A	None
3. Consequences of in-migration for individual migrants in country Z from main countries of origin (A, B, C, etc.)	Preferred	Non-migrants in countries of origin A, B, C, etc.	Migrants from countries A, B, C, etc. in country Z
4. Consequences of in-migration for households from country A to country Z	Acceptable	Households in country A	Migrant households from country A in country Z
	Barely acceptable	None	(a) Migrant households from country A in country Z (b) Other households in country Z
5. Consequences of in-migration for households from countries A, B, C, etc. to country Z	Preferred	Non-migrant households in countries A, B, C, etc.	Migrant households from countries A, B, C, etc. in country Z
	Barely acceptable	None	(a) Migrant households from countries A, B, C, etc. in country Z (b) Other households in country Z

Design of surveys to investigate international migration

Table 6.2. (continued)

Type of analysis	Quality of option	Focal groups for data collection at origin	Focal groups for data collection at destination
6. Consequences of in-migration of individuals and households from countries A, B, C, etc. to countries Z, Y, X, etc.	Preferred	Households in countries A, B, C, etc.	Migrant individuals and households from countries A, B, C, etc. in countries Z, Y, X, etc.
7. Consequences of return migration for individuals returning to country A	Barely acceptable	None	(a) Individuals in households that migrated to country Z and who have returned to country A (proxy respondent necessary) (b) Other households that migrated from country A to country Z
	Acceptable	(a) Individuals who migrated from A to Z and returned to A (b) Non-migrants in country A	None
	Preferred	Individuals who migrated from country A to country Z and have returned country A	Individuals who migrated from country A to country Z
8. Consequences of return migration for households returning to country A	Acceptable	(a) Households that migrated from A to Z and have returned to A (b) Other households in country A	None
	Preferred	Households that migrated from country A to country Z and returned to A	Households that migrated from A to Z

international migrants are selected from a *pool of potential movers*, the best comparison group is always constituted by *non-migrants remaining in that pool*. Table 6.2 presents eight different types of possible analysis of the consequences of international migration, each of which is discussed below.

The first type of analysis (1), relating to the consequences of international migration for individual migrants in country Z, is also the most commonly undertaken, mainly because it requires only that a single survey be carried out in the country of destination Z and that the current status of migrants from whatever country of origin be compared with that of non-migrants. If migrants are doing as well as or better than non-migrants, the consequences of international migration are interpreted to be positive for the migrants concerned; they are considered negative if they are doing less well. Although it is important to control statistically for differences in the basic characteristics of migrants and non-migrants (i.e. age, sex, education, duration of residence in the country of destination, years of labour market experience, etc.), such appropriate controls have unfortunately generally not been used. In addition to such analytical problems, the main drawback of this approach is that it relies on an inappropriate comparison group because, in order to assess the consequences of international migration for the migrants themselves, their situation should be compared with that of non-migrants in the country of origin and not with non-migrants in the country of destination: the former had the potential of sharing the experience of migrants, not the latter. The comparison of migrants and non-migrants in the country of destination can, at best, shed light on the degree of integration of international migrants but not on the consequences of migration. Finally, another important methodological problem in the implementation of this type of analysis is that the survey must take care to ensure that a large enough sample of international migrants is obtained to be representative of that group, which will require specialized sampling techniques (see section C below). Otherwise, the rarity of international migrants in the population may render any type of analysis statistically unsound.

The second type of analysis is on the consequences of international migration for individuals originating in country A and residing in country Z. The most acceptable approach requires surveys in both countries, gathering information in Z on migrants from A and in A on non-migrants. Note that both migrants and non-migrants are interviewed directly, without recourse to proxy respondents. The survey in Z, however, has to contend with the difficulty of selecting a representative sample of migrants from country A, which are likely to be rare elements. The alternative, barely acceptable, option in panel 2 is similar to that described in panel 1 but with migrants from only a single country of origin considered. This will make the sampling problem even more severe.

The third type of analysis relates to studies of the consequences of migration for individual migrants in country Z whose countries of origin are A, B, C, etc. The preferred option requires a survey in country Z of migrants from the various countries of origin considered combined with surveys in each of those countries of origin focusing on non-migrants. The latter represent the appropriate comparison groups and, in principle, involve straightforward surveys that do not need to deal with the problem of rare elements. By comparing migrants in Z with non-migrants in their respective countries of origin, a broad assessment of the consequences of international migration for the migrants to Z can be made, and it can take into account the effects of both differences in the individual and household characteristics as well as of differences in the situations in countries of origin. An alternative, though barely acceptable option, is to carry out a single survey in the country of origin using proxy respondents to report on the current status of international migrants residing in country Z. The

Design of surveys to investigate international migration

data reported would then be compared with that of non-migrants covered by the same survey. Although such an approach has the advantages of involving a survey in only one country and uses the appropriate comparison group, it is in general not recommended because it is unlikely that proxy respondents can reliably provide the type of information needed to assess carefully the status of international migrants who are still living abroad. In addition, the selection of a sample that adequately covers households with out-migrant members living in a particular destination country Z is often likely to be an onerous task that is not justified by the weak results expected from this approach.

The fourth type of analysis involves studies of the consequences of migration for households that migrate internationally from a specific country of origin to a specific country of destination. The acceptable approach in this case requires a survey in Z of migrant households from A and a survey of the appropriate comparison group, non-migrant households remaining in A. This approach is similar to that discussed under type 2 above. A second but barely acceptable approach uses only a survey in the country of destination, and collects data from both migrant and non-migrant households to facilitate comparing the situations of the two at the time of observation. This approach is equivalent to that discussed under type 1 above, and allows the study of migrant integration but not the consequences of international migration.

The fifth type of analysis also centres on studies of the consequences of international migration for households but in this case considers several countries of origin simultaneously. The best approach for this type of studies involves surveys of the relevant non-migrant comparison groups in each of the countries of origin, plus a survey covering migrants from all the different countries of origin in the country of destination. A barely acceptable alternative approach involves a survey in the country of destination Z only, covering migrant households from the various countries of origin as well as non-migrant households. This approach provides a broad perspective on migrant integration but fails to address the consequences of international migration for the households involved.

The sixth type of analysis offers the most general study of the consequences of international migration, involving migrants from various countries of origin to several countries of destination, and comparing them with non-migrants in countries of origin. Just as its counterpart in approaches to the analysis of determinants – also type 6 in table 6.1 – this approach is especially useful to assess the consequences of international migration in countries that are linked by international migration flows (e.g. Kritz and Zlotnik, 1992). It requires that surveys of international migrants (individuals and households) living in various countries of destination be carried out in conjunction with surveys of non-migrants in the main countries of origin. The data gathered allow the examination of why the consequences of migration for international migrants differ according to both country of origin and country of destination, and to the specific origin-destination dyad. Thus, keeping the country of destination fixed but varying the country of origin allows for analysis of the consequences of

International migration statistics

migration according to country of origin; comparing data on international migrants from a single country of origin across several countries of destination allows an assessment of which country of destination provides the best experience for out-migrants from that particular country of origin; and considering several countries of origin and several of destination simultaneously allows the examination of which specific origin-destination flows have the best or worst consequences for the international migrants involved.

The seventh type of analysis involves the study of the consequences of return migration for individual migrants returning to country A. There are three possible approaches to that type of study which have very different, though rarely recognized, implications for the interpretation of the results obtained. The first one, which is considered barely acceptable here, is based on a survey undertaken in the country of destination Z, covering households that migrated from country A to country Z, some of which have members who have migrated back to A and for whom information is provided by proxy respondents. A second and better approach, which is commonly used, involves a survey undertaken only in the country of origin, where both individuals who migrated to another country and returned and comparable non-migrants are interviewed. The status of the two groups is compared to draw inferences about the benefits or lack thereof associated with international migration. However, the results of such comparisons do not really reflect the effects of return migration since the return migrants are being compared with persons who never migrated: thus any change in status reflects the joint effects of the original migration plus the return move. A better approach to investigate the effects of return migration *per se*, therefore, involves comparing the status of return migrants with that of other international migrants who have remained abroad, that is, with the rest of the population at risk of return migration. Such an approach requires that surveys be undertaken in both the country of destination Z of the migrants from A as well as in the country of origin A, the latter focusing only on return migrants from Z. This last requirement will require addressing the issue of selecting a representative sample of return migrants which, as a set of rare elements which is itself a subset of rare elements, is likely to be very difficult to locate.

The eighth and last type of analysis focuses on the consequences of return migration for households returning to country A. Since the use of proxy respondents is not possible in the country of origin because whole households have left, the two approaches presented in table 6.2 correspond to the last two of panel 7 and have the same advantages and limitations. Thus the option identified as acceptable cannot provide an assessment of the effects of return migration *per se* but only of the joint effects of emigration and return. The preferred approach, in contrast, isolates the effects of return migration by comparing migrant households from country A that remain in country Z with migrant households that have returned from Z to A.

As in the cases regarding the assessment of the consequences of international migration for the individual migrant and for the migrant household, the consequences of return migration may be studied by considering several countries of destination and a single country of origin, or several countries of origin and a single country of destination. The purpose of the former would be to assess which country of destination had the most positive impact on the status of return migrants by transmitting skills, allowing the accumulation of savings, etc. As for the latter, its purpose would be to study the differences in the consequences of return migration for migrants returning to different countries of origin. Carrying out surveys in multiple countries of origin and destination would allow both comparisons to be made.

Although the discussion above has assumed that the consequences of interest are those related to return migration *per se*, in some situations, such as the migration of contract workers, the main interest may be to assess the net overall effects of migration and return. In that case, use of the acceptable options within types 7 and 8 would be appropriate, provided measures are taken to obtain a representative sample of return migrants in the country of origin. An important issue to explore in that case, and in all cases in which migration separates members of the nuclear family (or of the household), is the consequences of migration for the family members remaining in the country of origin. The types of analyses presented in table 6.2 do not deal explicitly with this but, applying the same principles underlying table 6.2, the main comparison group for families or households with out-migrant workers is families or households without them in the country of origin, since taken jointly they constitute the population at risk of experiencing out-migration of family members as migrant workers. One key aspect of the consequences of international migration for the families remaining in the country of origin involves the receipt and use of remittances, a subject treated in detail in Chapter 7.

Implications of the selection of the preferred type of analysis for survey design

As the discussion in the previous sections makes clear, the preferred approach to the study of the determinants and consequences of international migration requires that surveys be carried out in both countries of origin and countries of destination, or at minimum in one such dyad. The question must therefore be addressed of whether the surveys involved can or should be undertaken in both the country of origin and the country of destination simultaneously. If perfect sampling frames allowing the identification of international migrants in the country of destination and of households with out-migrants in the country of origin were available, simultaneity would be desirable. However, while most countries have data on the presence of international migrants within their borders, few have reliable data on out-migration, in part because the migration of citizens is considered an international right. Because of this and because countries of destination are more likely to have the data needed to select a representative sample of international migrants, it is recommended that the survey be carried out first in the country of destination. From this survey detailed information on the place of origin should be obtained from the international migrants interviewed – at the level of the province,

International migration statistics

district and community. These data are then aggregated to get the total number of migrants in the destination country sample coming from each province and district in the country of origin. Then, given population estimates for those provinces and districts (e.g. from a census), ratios of the number of international migrants to the population can be calculated at the province level – and at the district level also if the number of international migrants in the sample in the destination country is large relative to the number of districts in the country of origin so as to provide reasonably reliable estimates of ratios for districts. (In general, this is likely only for those districts which account for most of the out-migration.) Then a national sample of selected provinces or districts may be derived using techniques such as those described in section C.6 below. Although the preferred options for the study of either the determinants or the consequences of international migration require selecting a sample only of non-migrants in the country of origin, to make the comparison with international migrants more meaningful it is important that those non-migrants be selected predominantly from the areas (provinces, districts, and perhaps cities or towns) where the relative propensity to out-migrate internationally to the country of destination is highest. Such a procedure ensures a more relevant comparison group of non-migrants in the country of origin.

An approach of this type has already been followed in a multi-country survey project undertaken in West Africa (Findley et al., 1988). First, areas in the destination country, France, thought to have the most migrants from francophone West Africa were selected by judgement (rather than probability sampling). The West African migrants interviewed in France were then asked to indicate their place of last residence in West Africa (down to the local area in their country of origin). That information was used, albeit again not in a probabilistic manner, to determine the main areas of exodus, which were then selected as the areas in the countries of origin for household surveys to be conducted.

There are also instances in which the reverse approach has been followed, that is, where the first survey is conducted in the country of origin to identify households with international out-migrants. The proxy respondent is then asked the place of residence of out-migrants, which is used to identify sites for the survey in the country of destination. Such an approach has the problem of missing households when the whole household migrates from the country of origin and also tends to overrepresent short-term migration.

Because preferred survey loci and comparison groups for studying the determinants of international migration are so similar to those for the study of the consequences (see tables 6.1 and 6.2), it is recommended that whenever a survey focusing on one of the two is planned it be designed also to collect data for the other topic as well. Substantial effort and expenditure will always be required to design and carry out surveys in two countries, one of origin and one of destination, so the data should be gathered so as to facilitate studying both the determinants and consequences of international migration, even if the intention of the survey design team is only to carry out analyses on one of the

Design of surveys to investigate international migration

two topics. Not only would this strategy be cost effective (the costly steps involved in mapping, sample selection and fieldwork would be carried out only once), it would also make the results more relevant for policy formulation. Studies of the determinants of migration clarify the factors affecting it and can therefore provide guidance regarding the policies to be changed with a view to altering international migration processes. But studies of the determinants provide no information whatsoever on whether this is a desirable thing to do. Studies of the consequences provide the latter information: if the consequences are found to be negative, then policy-makers would seek to decrease them, and *vice versa*. But studies of the consequences provide absolutely no information about what factors to change to alter the migration flows. Thus studies of both the determinants and consequences of international migration are desirable.

The minimum needed to study both the determinants and consequences of international migration is a survey in the country of origin covering households without out-migrants and a survey in the country of destination covering international migrants (individuals and households). The survey in the country of origin need not make any special effort to cover households with out-migrants since those migrants will be covered and interviewed directly in the country of destination. In the survey in the country of destination, the only population that need be covered is that of international migrants from the country of origin selected. However, in order also to permit an assessment of the integration of those migrants, coverage of a sample of non-migrants in the country of destination is also recommended. In all cases in which non-migrants are interviewed, in addition to recording information on their status at the time of the survey, retrospective information about their status at the mid-point of the period used to identify international migrants should also be recorded to permit the appropriate comparisons to be made. The relevant reference point is 2.5 years before the survey if international migrants are identified as those having changed country of residence within the 5 years preceding the survey.

3. Planning specialized surveys on international migration

Box 6.1 presents a list of the steps involved in designing, implementing and analysing specialized surveys aimed at gathering information for the analysis of the determinants and consequences of international migration, which requires surveys in both countries of origin and destination. The list is provided to ensure that all key steps are taken into account in planning the budget and the schedule of work to undertake surveys in at least two countries. Poor planning and failure to anticipate all the steps involved in carrying out a survey are often the source of serious budgetary and scheduling problems even when only a single survey is carried out. Carrying out linked surveys in more than one country is all the more complicated and therefore requires even more careful planning. Because unforeseen problems are likely to arise, the time allocated for the various steps should not be too tightly planned, particularly that assigned to fieldwork and data processing.

To the extent possible, the steps listed in box 6.1 are in chronological order, though several may be undertaken simultaneously. The initial steps in planning the survey, namely, the determination of survey objectives, the establishment of legal, contractual and budgetary parameters, and the development of an appropriate work schedule (steps 1 to 3) are crucial to a successful project.

BOX 6.1. STEPS INVOLVED IN CONDUCTING A SPECIALIZED SURVEY ON INTERNATIONAL MIGRATION

1. Determine survey objectives; establish definition of international migrants and of appropriate comparison groups; decide on countries of implementation (origin and destination).
2. Establish legal, contractual and budgetary parameters for the survey in each country; determine institutional responsibilities for implementation and budgetary accounting.
3. Plan work schedule identifying the role and responsibilities of main institutions and key personnel in the countries where surveys are to be undertaken.
4. Draft questionnaire(s) and manuals for interviewers and supervisors; translate them into the main languages needed to carry out the survey (this step can be carried out simultaneously in countries of origin and destination).
5. Determine who the main users of the survey data will be, solicit their suggestions regarding questionnaire content to ensure that, to the extent possible, their interests are incorporated.
6. Develop sampling frame for survey in the country of destination.
7. Carry out necessary cartographic work to select the sample in the country of destination (using, for instance, the most recent census maps and updating them in the field as necessary).
8. Design and select sample of migrants and non-migrants in the country of destination.
9. Develop documents to organize and monitor fieldwork.
10. Train first group of interviewers and supervisors to pretest questionnaires, and conduct pretests in the country of destination.
11. Evaluate results of pretests and revise questionnaires and manuals for interviewers and supervisors accordingly. Adjust translations of questionnaires and manuals; print final questionnaires and manuals for fieldwork.
12. Develop preliminary plans for the tabulation, analysis and dissemination of survey results.
13. Prepare editing and coding manuals; train editors and coders.

14. Prepare instructions and computer programs for data entry and cleaning; test and finalize those programs.
15. Recruit and train additional interviewers and supervisors.
16. Make logistic (housing, transportation etc.) arrangements for fieldwork in country of destination; assign fieldwork to teams comprising several interviewers and one supervisor each.
17. Implement survey in country of destination.
18. Code and edit responses to questionnaires; conduct data entry and cleaning; prepare data files for use in the analysis of results.
19. Prepare tabulations on international migrants interviewed in the country of destination to determine specific locations (province, district, community) of last residence in the country of origin. Use that information to select a sample of households without international migrants in the country of origin.
20. Repeat steps 6 to 18 in the country of origin.
21. Complete tabulation and analysis plans for the survey in the country of destination and for that in the country of origin; carry out the analysis planned.
22. Prepare database with the data gathered by the surveys implemented in the countries of origin and destination for dissemination and further analysis.
23. Prepare report on main findings that includes a clear and concise executive summary focusing on the implications of the results obtained.
24. Publish and disseminate findings through different publications (in the appropriate languages) so as to reach both the research and the policymaking community in participating countries.
25. Organize meetings or workshops to disseminate findings and seek feedback on the quality and relevance of the data gathered. Discuss the methodological issues involved in survey design and the analysis of results to seek ways of improving the approach adopted.

The drafting of questionnaires and manuals (step 4) should be carried out early for both countries of origin and destination. Pretests of the questionnaire to be used in the country of origin (steps 10 and 11) may also be conducted early, although the final printing of questionnaires may be postponed until the results (preliminary tabulations) of the survey in the country of destination are in and an assessment can be made regarding their implications for data collection in the country of origin. Steps 10 to 18 are standard in any survey, but all should be carefully planned and their sequence made clear from the beginning. Note that the preparation of tabulation plans, editing and coding manuals, as well as computer programs to clean and process the data gathered (steps 12 to 14) should be carried out as soon as possible after the questionnaires reach final form instead of waiting until the fieldwork is completed. Also note that data cleaning and processing should occur simultaneously with the fieldwork: as soon as the fieldwork in a given area is finished, the completed questionnaires should be sent to a central location for processing.

International migration statistics

The steps presented in box 6.1 assume that the survey will cover at least one country of origin and one of destination, and that the households without international migrants to be interviewed in the country of origin are to be selected from those areas within the country that are the most likely sources of international migrants to the country of destination considered; hence the relevance of step 19. Also important are steps 22 to 25 on the dissemination of both the data gathered and the findings derived from their analysis. Many data collection projects fail to exploit the full richness of the information collected or to disseminate adequately the analytical results. Further, in general no efforts are made to assess the methodological approach with a view to improving it.

Certain important aspects of planning a survey are not included explicitly in box 6.1. The first relates to the locus and mode of interview (e.g. telephone, mail survey, personal interview). Given the detailed information that will be sought from migrants and non-migrants alike, the personal interview is strongly recommended to obtain data of better quality and a higher response rate (and therefore lower non-response bias). In addition, the confidentiality of responses must be ensured, and interviewers are better able to convince certain types of international migrants (such as those in an irregular situation) that they should respond to the survey.

Concerning the choice of respondent, it is highly desirable to interview the migrant directly, because of the possibility of getting biased answers from anyone else serving as a proxy respondent. As noted above, the use of proxy respondents cannot be avoided when the survey is conducted in a country that the migrant of interest has left, but such a survey approach is not recommended anyway. Proxy respondents should be avoided because they often do not know certain things about the migrant, in particular details about potentially sensitive topics, such as earnings and savings accumulated, personal conflicts with employer, or motivations. In addition, even when they know the facts, they may deliberately distort them to give what they perceive to be more socially acceptable responses (Groves, 1989; Singleton et al., 1988). In the highlands of Ecuador, for instance, male heads of household tended to understate both the frequency of out-migration of their daughters and the extent to which they worked in the place of destination (Bilsborrow, 1993). Consequently, it should not be assumed that the head of household (usually a male) is the best proxy respondent for a migrant household member: the best respondent will often be instead another adult household member of the same sex as the migrant or another adult of the same generation as the migrant (for instance, a sibling).

The length of the questionnaire used and the duration of interview is another matter that needs to be settled early. Surveys undertaken in developing countries rarely encounter problems of resistance or non-response even when they last an hour or so, but there is a widespread presumption that interviews lasting longer will confront those problems and result in biased data. Surveys in developed countries and among upper income groups in large urban areas of developing countries sometimes encounter resistance even with shorter interviews. This issue must be assessed carefully during the pretesting of the questionnaires.

In designing questionnaires to gather retrospective information, the issue of whether to adopt a life history approach arises. The life history of an individual consists of the full record of dates on which salient events occurred, such as graduating from school, marriage, childbirth, entry into employment, job changes, changes of residence, etc. Events and their dates are sometimes recorded using a monthly calendar covering all years since the age of 12 or 15 years (Freedman et al., 1988). While the use of life history questionnaires has some advantages (especially in aiding the respondent to recall events and put them in the right chronological order), it also has some limitations, including the inability to obtain detailed information about specific events without the use of supplementary schedules and the fact that a wealth of information is gathered that is not used in the analysis. Given the objective of the surveys considered here, full life histories do not seem necessary.

Lastly, it must be noted that the definition of international migrant adopted for survey purposes makes no distinction between the different types of international migrants discussed in Chapter 2. Depending on the country of destination, some types of international migrants – as defined in Chapter 2 – will be more common than others among those who changed their country of residence within the five years preceding the survey. Questions to identify specific types of migrants may be included in the questionnaire. For example, it may be important to identify refugees and asylum-seekers; migrants admitted specifically for the exercise of an economic activity; or migrants admitted for family reunification. In countries where international migrants tend to stay for relatively short periods or where they do not live in private households but are rather housed in collective accommodation, special measures may need to be taken to ensure that they are not excluded from the sample selected. Given that the definition of international migrant adopted for survey purposes considers that a change of residence takes place only when a migrant stays in a country for over six months, short-term movers, such as border workers and seasonal workers, will not be covered. If those groups are of interest, different definitions and survey designs will be needed.

C. SAMPLE DESIGN

The quality of any survey depends on the quality of its sample. Sampling aspects are particularly complex in the case of surveys on international migration, mainly because international migrants constitute rare elements among the host population. Given that the preferred approaches to the analysis of either the determinants or the consequences of international migration require that surveys be conducted in both the country of origin and the country of destination, it will be assumed henceforth that the international migrants of interest are those originating in a particular country A who are still resident in Z. Extensions to more complex cases involving more than one country of origin or destination can be readily made based on the principles and procedures described below and will not be discussed explicitly.

This section describes in detail how to select the sample for specialized surveys on international migration. Whatever other limitations may be placed on the countries or areas covered by the survey owing to budgetary or logistical problems, it is crucial that the sample be a *probability sample* in the areas covered by the survey: Only probability samples allow statistically valid inferences to be made from the analyses based on the survey data. A probability sample is one in which every element in the sample (whether a migrant or non-migrant) has a known probability of selection. To ensure that the probabilistic nature of the sample is maintained, personal judgement must be assiduously avoided in the selection of the sample of persons to be interviewed. Thus during the fieldwork stage of the survey, measures should be taken to ensure that interviewers cannot exercise personal judgement in determining who to interview. Too many surveys have been marred by procedures that overtly or in a subtle fashion allow elements of judgement to enter into the selection of the sample, either at the stage of selecting areas to conduct the survey in or in the selection of persons to interview within those areas. Whenever probabilistic procedures are not adhered to, valid statistical inferences cannot be drawn about the populations covered by the survey and the validity of the survey findings cannot be properly assessed. Given the cost and effort involved in carrying out a survey, it is wasteful to compromise its results by disregarding the statistical principles underlying appropriate sampling procedures.

Devising an effective strategy for probability sampling is, however, particularly difficult in surveys focusing on international migrants, since the latter are very rare elements among the populations of most countries. Thus international migrants, as defined for survey purposes in section B.1 above, will usually constitute less than one per cent of the population. Consequently, specialized sampling techniques are required to locate such rare elements efficiently without wastefully dispersing field data collection efforts, which would result from a completely random sampling procedure. Such techniques are discussed in detail below. To make them understandable to the non-sampling expert, we first review basic sampling concepts relevant to the sampling of international migrants.

1. Domains of analysis and sampling frames

The first step in designing a sample is to define the *domains of analysis*. A domain is a well-defined set of elements about which one wants to draw inferences – such as the population living in a specific geographic region or city.

It may be part of a larger population but because the sample will be drawn only to cover a given domain or domains, inferences will only be valid regarding those domains. With respect to surveys on international migration, the domains of interest are the country of origin and the country of destination. However, because of budgetary restrictions, the domains actually used may be limited to small regions within those countries. The survey in the country of destination may, for instance, cover only the cities that attract most international migrants or only those that attract migrants from a particular country. The *population covered* in a survey thus depends on the domain or domains of analysis selected *a priori*, and inferences from analyses based on the data collected strictly refer to that population only. Thus, if the domain of analysis is a particular city in the country of destination, the findings regarding the consequences of international migration apply only migrants in that city and may not be meaningful for migrants in any area beyond it.

The *sampling frame* provides the basis for drawing a sample of *elements* belonging to the domains of interest. Elements are the ultimate units being analysed – in the present case, individual migrants and non-migrants or their households. The quality of the sampling frame is a major determinant of the extent to which the sample is representative of the population in the domain of interest. A sampling frame is a listing of elements in the domain of interest. A frame is perfect if every element appears on the list separately, once and only once, if no element is omitted, and if no inappropriate entries are on the list. With respect to international migration, a perfect sampling frame would be provided by a complete list of international migrants living in the country of destination at time t who had arrived in that country after t-5 (presuming a 5-year cut-off in the definition of migrant). To be usable, the list should include the current address of each of those migrants. In countries maintaining population registers, such a list is potentially available (see Chapter 3, sections B and C). The list might even include other information about recent international migrants, such as country of citizenship or country of previous residence, that may be relevant for sample selection. (Countries having registers of foreigners may also be able to use this as a sampling frame, although it would exclude all citizens returning after emigration abroad.) Even if the lists obtained from registers are not perfect (some migrants may have left without deregistering and irregular migrants are unlikely to be recorded at all), they provide a very useful basis for constructing a sampling frame, provided issues of privacy and confidentiality do not prevent the use of registration records altogether.[7]

Most countries, however, lack such data sources that can be used directly as a sampling frame. Population censuses, for example, usually do not process and store information on exact addresses. Furthermore, because they take place only once every decade, their information may not be current. If the survey is made soon after the census, however, census information can be used as a sampling frame. Thus, the 1990 census of France was used to identify a sample of international migrants for a specialized survey carried out in connection with the census (Tribalat and Simon, 1993; Tribalat, 1995). In some countries, census data have been incorporated into a geographical information system (GIS) that, without allowing the identification of the individuals enumerated, nevertheless provides information on the characteristics of the population of small geographic areas. Such information can be used to build a sampling frame when the ideal one does not exist. Indeed, the creation of a *population frame* requires that data on both population size and the number of international migrants be available for small geographic areas. To select the areas that will be included in the sample, the proportion of the population constituted by international migrants in each geographic area of the domains of interest is calculated and probabilities of selection are assigned as a function of those proportions.[8] Full details of the procedure are provided in sections 4 and 6 below. Note, however, that censuses may not have information on international migrants who have moved into the country during the five-year period of interest. If censuses identify international migrants in terms of place of birth (or current citizenship when place of birth is not recorded), the population frame they yield will be inadequate for the selection of recent migrants to the extent the geographic distribution of the latter differs from that of the foreign-born population, most of whom arrived much earlier. This is but one example of the type of frame problems that may affect the population frame.

The types of problems affecting frames include: the existence of missing elements, implying that some of the international migrants of interest are not covered by the data source being used; misclassification of elements, with some recent international migrants appearing as non-migrants and vice versa; the use of a definition of international migrant in the survey that is not identical to that used in the population frame (e.g. the survey focussing on migrants from a particular country and the frame only providing data on the foreign born, or only on those coming classified by region of origin); errors in recording or processing data on international migration in the population frame (since international migrants are so rare, small errors can cause significant distortions in the proportion of international migrants in small geographic areas); and the less recent the population frame, the more the number and geographical distribution of migrants it shows will differ from the true numbers at the time of the survey. Usually little can be done to alleviate frame problems such as those listed above since there is rarely any data available or other basis for "purifying" the sampling frame. One can only hope that the defects are small relative to the numbers of international migrants correctly identified by the population frame. For a detailed discussion of frame problems, see Kish (1965, pp. 53-59 and 384-433).

2. Fundamental need for probability samples

A *probability sample* is a sample in which every element (that is, every person or household) has a known, non-zero probability of being selected.

Probability samples are designed to permit statistical inferences about means, variances, regression coefficients and other statistical measures relative to the population in the domain of interest. All statistical inferences require that the sample be a probability sample. Inferences from non-probability samples cannot be considered to have statistical validity. Most of the few existing specialized surveys on international migration are not based on probability samples, a fact that vitiates any inferences made from them.

Probability samples do not allow personal or subjective judgement to play a role at any stage in the selection of the sample: not in the selection of the areas in which migrants are to be sought (called primary sampling units or PSUs), nor in the selection of persons or households to be interviewed in those areas. Thus, in a probability sample selection criteria are established *a priori* on the basis of survey goals and appropriate probabilistic procedures are used to select the areas to be included in the sample. The same is true for procedures to select households within those areas selected. The simplest probabilistic selection procedure is simple random sampling, whereby every element in a set has equal probability of being selected. When the number of elements is large, tables of random numbers can be used to effect the selection provided every element is assigned a unique number. If similar elements can be put into a list, the use of systematic sampling with a randomly selected starting point also results in a simple random sample.

When the elements to be selected are grouped, such as people living in different areas, and simple random sampling is used, the probability of selection of each subset is proportional to the number of elements it contains (this type of sampling is called "probability proportional to estimated size" or PPES). To illustrate PPES with systematic sampling, consider the following example. Suppose the domain of interest is divided into 20 areas with the following population sizes: 27, 42, 50, 100, 200, 48, 35, 24, 33, 21, 34, 37, 55, 40, 59, 80, 120, 410, 74, 32; suppose that four areas are to be selected with probabilities proportional to their population size. By cumulating the reported population sizes, the following list is obtained: 27, 69, 119, 219, 419, 467, 502, 526, 559, 580, 614, 651, 706, 746, 805, 885, 1,005, 1,415, 1,489, 1,521. The total population size is 1,521. To use systematic sampling, a sampling selection interval is calculated by dividing the total number of elements by the number of groups to be selected, namely, 1,521/4 = 380.25. Then, a starting point is selected at random between 1 and 380. Suppose it is 305. The key numbers to effect area selection are therefore, 305, 685 (305 + 380), 1,065 (685 + 380) and 1,445. These cumulated numbers correspond to the four areas which have population sizes of 200 (which accounts for all numbers between 219 and 419), 55, 410 and 74. These four areas are therefore the areas selected for the sample. This method can be used to select with equal probability any number of elements from a list and is most useful if a large number are to be selected since only a single random number needs to be determined as the starting point for the process.

It is important to note, however, that probability samples need not be based on such simple random sampling. Simple random sampling has the advantage of leading to self-weighting samples, because each element has the same probability of selection as any other. But when the purpose of a survey is to study rare elements, specialized sampling procedures are necessary to ensure that those elements are adequately represented (see section 6 below).

Deviations from probability sampling can occur under a variety of circumstances. A common one arises when budgetary constraints prevent a large number of areas being included in the survey. When only a few areas are to be sampled, it may be more advisable to use expert knowledge to select them than to select them on the basis of random probabilistic principles. The term "judgement sample" is used to describe the non-probabilistic selection of areas or elements to be surveyed. Judgement samples can be useful starting points for the selection of areas to be covered by pilot studies, but even in such cases the use of sloppy non-probability samples in the final selection of elements (households with international migrants) is not acceptable, nor is it necessary. The most common method of selecting non-probability samples of elements (households or individuals) is a quota sample, in which the types of elements to be sampled and the number of each to be selected are determined *a priori*, regardless of the actual relative prevalence of the different types of elements in an area. Thus, in a survey of international migrants in a city, interviewers could be instructed to each take an area of the city and seek out people (on the street, in dwellings or wherever), interviewing those who are international migrants until some fixed number or quota is achieved. Lack of information about the relative prevalence of international migrants across the areas studied means that there is no way to weight the observations (see section 7 below) to obtain a valid estimate for the city as a whole. In addition, the fact that the interviewer selects the persons to be interviewed inevitably leads to serious biases, even among the most experienced interviewers, since the persons selected tend to be the most accessible, those who wear attractive clothes or live in the nicer houses, who appear less busy or preoccupied, or who are of the same sex, age group, race, or social class as the interviewer. "Serious biases of subjective selection have been demonstrated time and again, whether choosing heads or tails, random samples of integers . . . plants from a field, or people on streets or in homes" (Kish, 1965, p. 29). Thus only in the case of a study limited to a small number of areas is judgement sampling somewhat justifiable, but even then only in the initial selection of areas. Quota samples should never be used in the selection of elements (persons or households).

3. Sample size

To estimate sample means and other statistics, the size of the sample is important. To begin with, the standard error of the sample mean is inversely related to sample size.[9] It does not depend on the fraction of the population in the sample, a common misconception. However, by using stratification (see next

Design of surveys to investigate international migration

section), a smaller sample can have more information content, implying that sample size is not the key factor in ensuring small variances. In addition, the quality of survey execution in the field is usually more important than sample size *per se* as a means of reducing total survey error. Non-sampling error, which comprises all sources of error other than sampling error, is usually both larger and more controllable (with careful field procedures) than sampling error.

Determining the desired sample size for a survey is seldom as easy in practice as it appears in textbook examples. As already noted, sampling error (or sampling variance) is inversely related to sample size, so that increasing the size of the sample reduces sampling error. In general, sample size should be determined by considering: the standard error of the key variable or parameter to be estimated from the survey; the size of error in that estimate that is considered within an acceptable range *a priori*; and the statistical power of the test of hypothesis used for the key variable or parameter. Textbooks focus on examples where the variable to be estimated is a sample mean, a sample proportion or a rate, such as mean income, the proportion of international migrants, or the rate of out-migration from an area. To determine the size of the sample required, *a priori* knowledge of the population variance of the key variable is needed. Moreover, in stratified samples (see below), such knowledge is required for every stratum. It is extremely rare that a recent survey in a given country would have a similar sample design and would have obtained data about the same key variable so as to provide the information needed.

Another critical factor in determining sample size is the identification of the key variable. In complex surveys, such as those needed for the study of the determinants and consequences of international migration, the measurement of a whole array of variables and relationships is of interest. Consequently, specifying in advance a single key variable or parameter to determine sample size is not only arbitrary but also extremely risky, since the variable selected may not be the most important for the population under study.[10]

In practice, budgetary considerations usually prove to be the main determinant of sample size. In view of the problems involved in selecting a sample size on the basis of statistical principles, as discussed above, some examples may indicate orders of magnitude. Bilsborrow et al. (1984, Chapter 4) provide a review of sample sizes and other characteristics of surveys of internal migration in low-income countries, finding sample sizes varying from less than 100 to over 5,000, with only the latter nationally representative. In a series of surveys of internal migration conducted in south-east Asia, ESCAP recommended the use of sample sizes of 6,000 to 8,000 households per country (Turner, 1979, pp. 19-20), though that size was later found to be inadequate and was raised to 15,000 households (United Nations ESCAP, 1980c, p. 9). Surveys of such dimensions are usually too costly for low-income countries and as a result only a few were carried out. To be conservative, surveys of international migration intended to be reasonably representative of a country or of a large region within a country should have minimum sample sizes for each domain of interest of 1,000 to 2,000 households. But there is so little experience in the design of such

International migration statistics

medium-sized surveys of international migrants that there are few examples to cite, and in none has sample size been based on the statistical criteria listed above. The ongoing multi-country survey project coordinated by NIDI (see section A.3 above) intends to use samples of 2,000 non-migrant households in each country of origin and 500 households containing international migrants for each of the flows covered in each country of destination. The latter will mean sample sizes of at least 1,000 households with international migrants in each country of destination. Samples two or three times as large are preferable whenever budgets allow, especially for countries with large, heterogeneous migrant populations, so as to permit analyses of differences across groups, such as for migrants originating in different countries.

Besides cost factors, the extent to which the population of interest is more homogeneous (requiring a smaller sample) or heterogeneous (requiring a larger sample) should always be taken into account in determining the desired sample size in different areas. To the extent possible, in order to compare international migrants with non-migrants in destination countries, for example, the aim should be to achieve a final sample in which close to half the households contain one or more international migrants. Large sample sizes are not necessary provided specialized sampling techniques are used to locate international migrants. Different sample sizes and sampling methods may also be desirable for different areas, such as urban and rural areas.

4. Stratification

Stratification is the division of the population into sub-groups or strata according to objective criteria or variables already measured for the population of interest. Once the population is divided into strata, the total variation in it can be divided into two parts: variation between strata and variation within strata. Because stratified sampling involves sampling separately from each stratum, sometimes using different (unequal) probabilities of selection or even entirely different sampling procedures, this procedure effectively eliminates the variation between strata from the computation of total variation in the sample selected, thus reducing total variance to the sampling variance within strata. Consequently, the gain from stratifying the population can be substantial, and will be substantial if stratification is carried out so that the elements within each stratum are as similar as possible to each another (that is, that the stratum has as little variance as possible), and that the strata differ as much as possible from each other (that is, that they have means for the stratification variables that differ as much as possible from each other). To be effective, stratification should be carried out on the basis of variables that are the main subject of study or that are closely associated with the variables being studied. Stratification can be performed on the basis of one or several variables. The latter, called multiple stratification, requires that the stratification variables used be related not only to the survey objectives but also be as different from each other as possible (uncorrelated). The number of variables used for stratification depends on the information available *a priori* about the population of interest.

How many strata should be formed? There is no general answer to this question, but certain principles can guide the decision. First, every stratum must have at least two elements to allow the calculation of within stratum variances. Second, (multiple) stratification on the basis of several independent variables that produce *k* strata is more efficient than stratification by a single variable also producing *k* strata. Thus, it is better to stratify according to place of residence (urban versus rural), socio-economic status (low, medium and high), and proportion of foreign-born (less than 0.1 per cent; 0.1 to 1.0 per cent; higher than 1.0 per cent) therefore producing 18 strata, than to create 18 categories on the basis of any one of the three variables alone.

In choosing the sampling probabilities for strata, an optimum sample design requires selecting a higher proportion of elements in strata where: the variance per element is greater; and the cost of data collection per element is less. Thus, proportions of observations should be selected in strata *j* such that

$$f_j = K s_j / \sqrt{C_j},$$

where K is a constant, C_j is the cost of data collection per element selected in j, and s_j is the standard deviation per element in j with respect to the stratification variable being used. Adequate information on either s_j or C_j is rarely available *a priori*, unless a survey with the same sample design has been conducted recently and gathered information on the stratification variables, thus allowing the estimation of s_j. In addition, information on costs (C_j) from that survey would have had to be collected and analysed, which is virtually never done.

In practice, urban areas tend to have both higher element variance with respect to the variables of interest and lower interviewer costs than rural areas (even allowing for the greater number of callbacks needed), both of which suggest that higher probabilities of selection be used in urban than in rural areas.[11] Desired sample size distributions, derived from survey objectives, may also affect the extent to which the probabilities of selection differ across strata. In all cases, the stratification variables should be correlated with the variables being studied. Thus, if the proportion of households having an international migrant differs markedly between urban and rural areas, or is correlated with population density or socio-economic status, each of those variables should be used in stratification. Different strata may, of course, be used in different domains.

Lastly, stratification allows the use of different sampling frames and different sampling procedures in the different strata. Thus, if adequate maps and sampling frames are available for urban but not for rural areas, different sampling procedures will need to be used.

5. Multi-stage and cluster sampling

The most efficient sampling designs usually involve more than one sampling stage. Up to this point it has been assumed, for simplicity that the sample is selected in two stages: the first involving the selection of first-stage areas, or primary sampling units (PSUs), and the second involving the selection of elements for interview within the PSUs. In practice, it is normally desirable to have more than two stages, thus making use of multi-stage sampling. In population surveys, the first stage in multi-stage sampling is usually the selection of PSUs in proportion to their estimated population size. In a single stage sampling design, areas within a country or region are selected and then all elements (e.g. households) within them are included in the survey. A survey on international migration should never use a single stage sampling design because the number of international migrants likely to be found in PSUs selected at random is so small that the effort would be wasteful.

Multi-stage sampling is particularly useful to ensure that a sample is representative of a whole country or a large region, since it allows a dispersed sample while at the same time keeping down the cost of field operations. In situations where no frame exists to select the final area elements of interest or the ultimate area units (UAUs) at the last stage of multi-stage sampling, a frame has to be created by a mapping operation. Because the cost of undertaking such an operation for a whole country is prohibitive, at the first stage an existing frame (derived from a census or other national data collection system) can be used to select a sample of relatively large area units (PSUs) from the domain of interest. Then mapping operations and the subsequent formation of next-stage units called segments or chunks within each mapped area can be carried out in the field only for those PSUs selected at the first stage.

Multi-stage sampling usually involves the use of cluster sampling, generally at the last stage of sample selection. In cluster sampling, sampling units are clusters of respondents, such as all households in the smallest or ultimate area unit or all clusters of a particular size (e.g. 20) closest to the northeast corner of the UAU, or all members of sample households. Clusters are used to reduce the cost of achieving a given sample size. Thus, the cost of locating 1,000 respondents in a large area is far greater if the 1,000 are widely distributed over the area than if only 50 places have to be visited containing clusters of average size 20.

Choosing the cluster size to use involves two important considerations. First, the larger the cluster, the lower the average cost per element of collecting data in the field, but the larger the average sampling error per element in the survey. There is thus a trade-off between cost and variance. The second consideration involves issues of practicality: the size of clusters used should relate to logistical aspects regarding the organization of the field work and the duration of interviews. Thus, the size of the cluster should take into account the desirable work load for a field team of interviewers and its duration of stay in each UAU. Suppose that the interview is expected to average one hour per household so that, on average, an interviewer is expected to complete three interviews per day (taking into account travel time within UAUs and the need for call-backs when the desired respondent is not at home). Suppose further that a field team consists of four interviewers and one supervisor. The team can therefore complete an average of 12 interviews per day, or 60 per five-day work week. Consequently, 12 might be considered a minimum desirable cluster size and 60 a maximum, assuming the team will have two days of rest a week. In urban areas, where inter-cluster transportation time is minimal, smaller clusters can be used without significantly increasing the duration or cost of fieldwork, but in rural areas, especially those of difficult access or with widely dispersed dwellings, larger clusters might be used to reduce intra-UAU travel time. Since urban areas usually have higher proportions of households with international migrants than rural areas, the use of fewer and larger clusters in rural areas is even more desirable in surveys of international migration than in surveys in general.

Turning now to the other determinants of desirable cluster size, it should be borne in mind that the use of clusters of elements increases the overall survey sampling error or variance. The sampling variance of an element is related positively to the heterogeneity of the population elements (persons) and negatively to the sample size. A basic statistic called the design effect (*deff*) is used to measure the loss in precision (increase in sampling variance) resulting from departures in the sample design actually used in a survey from simple random sampling. More precisely, *deff* is the ratio of the actual variance of the complex multi-stage cluster design typically used to the variance of a simple random sample with the same sample size (see Kish, 1965: pp. 88, 148-149, 161-163, 217-229):

$$deff = s_c^2/s_s^2 = 1 + \rho(\bar{b} - 1)$$

where s_c^2 and s_s^2 are the element variances of the complex and simple random sample designs, respectively, ρ (rho) is the intra-cluster correlation coefficient, and $\bar{b}$ the average number of respondents per UAU (which is the same as average cluster size, or the total sample size divided by the number of clusters). The more the *deff* ratio departs from (that is, is greater than) 1.0, the greater the "design effect", and the more all the sample statistics based on simple random sampling (including estimates of standard errors of regression coefficients in multivariate analyses) become inappropriate. That is, the standard errors are underestimates, so the statistical significance of regression coefficients is exaggerated. As ρ indicates the average degree of homogeneity within clusters, the more the variable of interest is distributed randomly within clusters – that is, the less homogeneous the cluster – the more ρ approaches 0 and the more *deff* approaches 1, implying that the actual sample design deviates little from simple random sampling. However, ρ is almost always above zero in human populations, reflecting the tendency of neighbouring elements (persons) to be similar. The maximum value of ρ, corresponding to complete uniformity or homogeneity within all clusters, is 1.0. The right side of the equation thus indicates that *deff* increases with cluster size and with homogeneity within clusters.

International migration statistics

Values of ρ are commonly found to range from 0 to 0.2. If clusters of size 21 are used and ρ is 0.05, $\textit{deff} = 2$, meaning that for a survey with a complex sample design to have the same precision as a simple random sample, it would have to have a sample size that is twice as large as that of the random sample. Since cluster sampling is less expensive, field costs may well still be lower with the larger sample size and a complex sample design than if simple random sampling is used. Note that if the average cluster size is raised to 31, $\textit{deff}$ rises only to 2.5, but if $\bar{b}$ remains at 21 and ρ rises to 0.1, $\textit{deff} = 3.0$. Thus changes in cluster size are less important than differences in ρ: a small change (positive or negative) in the value of ρ results in a large change in $\textit{deff}$ because it is multiplied by a relatively large $\bar{b}$, whereas variations in $\bar{b}$ have less effect on $\textit{deff}$ since they are multiplied by small values of ρ.

The value of ρ depends in complex ways on the particular type of sample design.[12] It also varies with the specific variables. For example, family income within urban or rural clusters is likely to have a high value of ρ because neighbouring dwellings tend to be economically similar, but ρ is likely to be smaller for variables such as fertility or age of head of household. In international migration surveys, a larger ρ is expected because international migrants tend to cluster geographically even more than the general population.

The definition of international migrant used also has implications for cluster size: the more stringent the definition of migrant (e.g. if limited to those arriving within the five years preceding the survey, or to migrants coming from or going to a single country), the rarer international migrants will be and the larger the cluster size should be to ensure that international migrants are encountered in the UAU. Fortunately, ρ will also tend to be lower, at least with respect to those factors that differ between international migrants and non-migrants. In a survey on internal migration in Ecuador in 1977-78, clusters of 20 households were found to be too small in urban areas to locate a sufficient number of rural-urban migrants arriving during the five years preceding the interview, whereas clusters of 60 households performed adequately in rural areas to capture out-migrants. In the case of international migrants, which constitute far lower proportions of the population, larger clusters will usually be desirable, of say 200 to 1,000 households, in both areas of in-migration in countries of destination and in areas of out-migration in countries of origin.

In conclusion, the interrelations between sample variance and cluster size are complex. The survey objective of achieving a desired number of households with and without international migrants and the survey budget are likely to be the major determinants of both average cluster size and total sample size. But the "cost" of using particular sizes in terms of design effects ($\textit{deff}$) must be borne in mind in planning the analyses that are to be based on the data gathered.

6. Finding "rare elements"

According to estimates of the number of international migrants present in each country of the world, in three-quarters of all countries the proportion of international migrants was at most 6.5 per cent in the early 1990s (United Nations, 1995a) and variations by region and level of development are considerable. Thus, for developed countries the upper quartile of the distribution of the proportion of international migrants was 16 per cent (meaning three-quarters of the developed countries had less than 16 per cent of their population being international migrants), whereas it was about 5 per cent for the developing countries. The median levels were 6 and 3 per cent, respectively, for developed and developing countries. Within the latter there was also wide variation, with the median being about 5 per cent in the Americas and less than 2 per cent in Africa and Asia. Since these estimates are based on the numbers of international migrants defined as persons living in a country other than the one in which they were born (the foreign born), the proportions would be far lower if only those international migrants who had changed country of residence during a five-year period were considered. The numbers above indicate that in almost all countries of the world and indeed in all large countries, international migrants constitute a small proportion of the population. Consequently, they are rare elements, difficult to locate. Similarly, in countries of origin, locating households with international out-migrants is at least as difficult. Indeed, households with international out-migrants are usually more difficult to locate in the country of origin because they are less clustered there than the migrants tend to be in countries of destination.[13]

The fundamental difficulty of locating international migrants in a survey of international migration is referred to in the sampling literature as the problem of locating "rare elements". Kish (1965) lists eight procedures that can be used to address this problem: use of multi-purpose samples; cumulation of rare cases from a series of continuing surveys; use of controlled selection; use of stratified sampling with disproportionate probabilities of selection (sampling fractions); use of two-phase sampling; use of large clusters; use of batch testing; and use of special lists prepared as part of multiplicity surveys. The use of multi-purpose samples helps spread the cost of locating migrants, but does not solve the problem of locating a large enough number of international migrants to make their analysis meaningful. The cumulation of international migrants from a series of surveys is impractical for the study of international migration because of the dynamism of international migration itself, which implies that the international migrants captured by one survey may have little in common with those captured by later surveys. The use of batch testing cannot be applied to human populations and is conceptually akin to the use of special lists as part of multiplicity surveys which is discussed in section D below. Consequently, the most viable strategies include the use of controlled selection techniques in conjunction with stratified sampling using disproportionate sampling fractions which can be strengthened by the use of two-phase sampling and large clusters. These are all discussed below.

Developing a sampling design to cover international migrants: The use of disproportionate sampling

Since most countries – particularly those hosting sizeable numbers of international migrants – have census data or data from population registers that can provide some basis for estimating both the number of international migrants and the total population in each area of the country, the following discussion assumes that a population frame exists which can be used to select a sample of international migrants. Although the international migrants identified in the population frame should ideally be the same as those that are to be the focus of the survey, differences in definition will often have to be accepted.

The usual source of data will be that of a population census, which will have information on the geographical distribution of the foreign born (as well as the rest of the population). If a question on time of arrival in the country was also asked in the census, the distribution of those arriving within five years of the census date might be available and should be used in the survey design. Information on country of previous residence, timing of the most recent change of residence and whether that change took place within a certain period prior to the census thus provides a better basis for selecting a sample than using data on all the foreign born. This is especially true if the focus is on recent migrants, as is presumed in this chapter.

Another issue to consider in constructing a population frame is whether the proportions used should refer to international migrants as a proportion of the total population in specific geographical areas or households with international migrants as a proportion of all households in those areas. Since the survey proposed has households as the ultimate sampling elements, the latter would be a better, but it may be difficult to obtain the desirable data. A practical alternative is to seek for each geographical area data on the number and proportion of households whose heads are international migrants.[14]

Once a population frame is available showing the relative proportions of international migrants (or of households whose heads are international migrants) in the different administrative areas of the country (or for the domains of interest), a three-stage sampling design can be implemented.[15] It is assumed that the administrative subdivisions of the hypothetical country under consideration include three levels: provinces, districts and census sectors. (Terminology will differ from one country to another.) The survey design has as ultimate area units (UAUs) the smallest geographical divisions, census sectors. Provided estimates of both the number and the proportion of international migrants are available at each administrative level, sample selection can proceed as follows. At the first stage, provinces constitute the primary sampling units (PSUs), so a sample of provinces is selected with probabilities of selection proportional to the estimated number of international migrants in each PSU (i.e. using PPES as described in section C.2 above). If the number of households whose heads are international migrants is available for each province, PSU selection should be made on the basis of those numbers instead.

In the second sampling stage, districts in the PSUs selected are classified into strata according to the proportion of international migrants in the population of each district. That is, the relevant proportions for the districts in the provinces (PSUs) selected are ordered from lowest to highest, appropriate intervals are defined (depending on the number of strata desired, and the extent to which the data fall into natural groupings), and districts whose proportions fall within each interval are classified in the same stratum. Note that districts are included in a stratum irrespective of whether they are urban or rural and irrespective of province.[16]

Once the strata are created, the key issue is how to select a sample of areas in the second stage from each stratum. In stratified sampling the optimal procedure is to select elements from each stratum in proportion to the estimated standard deviation of the stratum's elements with respect to the variable of interest. Using P, the proportion of international migrants, as the key variable of interest, the fraction of the districts to be selected from each stratum should be proportional to the estimated standard error of P for the stratum, namely, $\sigma = \sqrt{[P(1-P)]}$. Making sampling fractions proportional to σ implies that one is using disproportionate sampling, a highly efficient procedure to sample rare elements (see Kish, 1965, pp. 92-98, 142-144, 279-282). To complete the second sampling stage, therefore, districts in each stratum are selected in this manner.

With the data available at all levels as assumed, the third sampling stage is similar to the second. Again, it involves only those census sectors belonging to the districts already selected in the second sampling stage. Census sectors are again grouped into strata according to the proportion of the population constituted by international migrants. Then sectors within each stratum are selected in proportion to the standard deviation of the expected proportion of international migrants in their stratum, as described above.

While the major advantage of using multi-stage sampling is the resulting geographical concentration of field work (mapping, listing households, and interviewing), it can also reduce the work involved in preparing a sampling frame since tabulations on the proportions of population constituted by international migrants need to be prepared for the whole country only at the province level. After that, they are prepared at the district level only for those provinces already selected in the first stage; similarly, they are prepared for census sectors only for the districts selected at the second stage. However, there will be countries where the tabulations necessary for the third sampling stage are not available (either because of problems of confidentiality or because the information about international migrants is considered unreliable at such a small geographical level). In such situations, census sectors can be selected at the last stage simply by using probabilities proportional to the (estimated) population size of those sectors (PPES). In applying PPES in such cases, it is desirable to homogenize the sizes of census sectors by combining those with small sizes and splitting up larger ones so that each sampling unit in the list that constitutes the sampling frame for any given stratum contains UAUs of approximately equal size. From such a list census sectors may be selected randomly (or by systematic sampling), preserving the equal probability of selection of households across sectors within each stratum.

Returning to the use of disproportionate sampling, an example of its application may be useful. If four strata are created with mean expected proportions of households whose heads are international migrants of approximately[17] 0.2, 0.05, 0.01 and 0.001, then the standard deviations per stratum are, respectively, 0.40, 0.22, 0.10 and 0.03. Since the optimum sampling fractions for these strata must be directly proportional to the standard deviations, the probability of selecting an element from the first stratum must be approximately twice as high as that of selecting one from the second stratum, four times as high as that of selecting an element from the third stratum, and 13 times as high as that of selecting elements from the fourth stratum.

The actual probabilities (or intervals) to use in each stratum depend also on the overall population sampling fraction for each domain, n_d/N_d, where n_d is the total desired sample size in domain d and N_d is its estimated population size. Notice that although the sampling fractions may be very different across strata, as in the example above, the majority of elements ultimately selected may still be from the stratum with the lowest percentage of international migrants since that stratum will contain by far the largest number of census sectors. Therefore, although the method may assign a very low sampling fraction for that stratum, there should still be enough blocks selected to be representative of the stratum.

How different should the sampling fractions implied by disproportionate sampling be from those implied by the usual simpler, proportionate sampling across strata for it to be worthwhile to use disproportionate sampling? The question is important because proportionate sampling has the advantage of yielding a self-weighted sample that makes all the subsequent statistical analyses simpler since no weights need to be used (see section 7 below). Kish (1965, p. 94) suggests that the sampling fractions should differ by a factor of at least two, a view apparently accepted by Moser and Kalton (1972, p. 94). This means that the proportions of households with heads who are international migrants must differ by a factor of at least four between strata.

One possible variation of the sample design described above is the inclusion of "self-represented" areas, such as a city known to be the major cynosure of international migrants. The city can be included in the sample with certainty, meaning that it is treated as a separate domain where a different sample design may be used, while the rest of the country can be sampled using the three-stage design described above.

An important issue is whether those international migrants who are concentrated in the areas which will be selected with higher probabilities of selection using the sample design described in this section are somehow different in important ways from the international migrants living in areas selected with low probabilities of selection. While we are not aware of any evidence supporting (or contradicting) this widely held view, it does seem to have some *a priori* plausibility. Suppose that migrants who tend to concentrate in the same neighbourhoods are likely to be less successful than those who live dispersed among the non-migrant population. Even if this is the case, it presents no problem in the present context. In the type of national sample survey recommended here, even areas having low proportions of international migrants would still be included in the sample. Their characteristics and experience as migrants, when properly weighted, will be representative of that population of international migrants in the country. It is only when the domain of a survey is artificially restricted to areas with high concentrations of international migrants that the divergent experience of international migrants settled elsewhere would not be represented, and conclusions would be biased. This is therefore likely to be the case in surveys that select *a priori* only one city or a few regions where international migrants are thought to be concentrated, rather than taking a probability sample of areas to start with.

The selection of households for interview using two-phase sampling

Following the third stage of the sampling process described above, the census sectors or ultimate area units (UAUs) in which the survey is to be conducted have been selected. The last step is the sampling of the actual elements or households (or individuals) to interview, the goal being to identify reasonable numbers of households with international migrants compared to those without. Even in most of the UAUs belonging to strata with relatively high proportions of international migrants, the majority of the households will not have international migrants and the final sample will probably have a majority of UAUs with few or no households with migrants. It is thus still desirable at this last stage of household selection to use a procedure that ensures that most of the survey effort is not wasted in interviewing households without international migrants. The procedure recommended involves first making a list of all the households in the selected UAUs to determine which have international migrants and which do not, and then to oversample those with international migrants. This procedure is known as two-phase sampling.

Two-phase sampling, also called sequential sampling (an accurate description) or double sampling (a misleading term), involves the selection of a sub-sample of elements (households) from a larger sample (Kish, 1965, pp. 406 and 440-451). There are two main reasons[18] for using two-phase sampling: (a) to collect during the second phase more detailed information on a randomly selected sub-sample of the population covered in the first phase; or (b) to use the first phase as a screening device to identify respondents of special interest (given survey objectives) for the second phase. In (a), more detailed data may be collected from the sub-sample (by using additional questionnaire modules, for instance) and data from phase 1 may be used to provide overall means or other basic characteristics about the larger population, permitting an assessment of whether the phase 2 sample is representative of the whole population surveyed. While purpose (a) has some potential utility in international migration surveys (for example, for identifying migrants of particular interest for intensive interviews), the focus here is on (b) since the objective is to screen the entire sample in the UAU selected to seek out households with international migrants.

To implement the procedure, in phase 1 a field operation is used to identify and list all occupied households in the UAUs selected. Using a brief questionnaire, the answers to which are recorded on a single line per household on a sheet (the phase 1 listing questionnaire), the "lister" visits all households in the UAU in some sequential order to record the address, name of head of household, and whether the household contains one or more eligible international migrants (using the definition agreed upon for the survey – in the present case, noting only those who have come from abroad within the previous five years). Then, following a procedure determined in advance, some or all of the households containing international migrants and some of the households without international migrants are selected (sampled) for interview. In the second phase, interviewers administer the detailed questionnaire to the sample selected.[19] The selection procedure used in phase 2 can involve selecting either a fixed number or a large proportion of households with international migrants (depending on the final sample size desired) and similarly a fixed number or a small proportion of households without migrants. Use of two-phase sampling helps ensure that the number of households containing international migrants is not much smaller than the number without international migrants, a group that it is useful to collect data for in order to assess the integration of international migrants (see section B above). Note that if it is decided to exclude households without international migrants altogether, it is not necessary to use two-phase sampling. Instead, interviewers can be instructed instead to go from house to house in the selected UAUs to administer the questionnaire to all households containing international migrants.

To expedite phase 2, the rules for selecting households with and without international migrants in each UAU must be determined beforehand so that the selection of households can take place immediately after the household listing has been prepared at the end of phase 1, while the interviewing team is still in the UAU. Such a strategy minimizes travel time to the UAUs and is therefore particularly important in large countries or where the UAUs are widely dispersed. However, its successful implementation requires that the field supervisors be well trained to follow selection procedures established beforehand for household selection. Thus selection rules must be established *a priori*, covering all possible situations that may be encountered in the field (in terms of different populations, sizes of clusters, and numbers of migrant and non-migrant households), to prevent interviewers from making their own selection of households in the field, a practice that leads to inevitable biases.

The selection rules for phase 1 can take several forms, depending on survey objectives and on the information available regarding the proportion of households with international migrants in the population. Suppose that the aim is to obtain information from $M = 1,000$ households with international migrants and $N = 500$ households without, in a population where the estimated

Design of surveys to investigate international migration

proportion of households with international migrants is $P = 0.01$. Assume that the use of disproportionate sampling has raised by a factor of five the mean proportion of households with international migrants in the sample of UAUs selected, making it $P_u = 0.05$. If the average size of UAUs is 200 households, each UAU will be expected to contain on average 10 households with international migrants and consequently 100 UAUs would be selected in the country (or domain) to achieve the desired sample size of 1,000 households with international migrants. Suppose four strata have been used with mean proportions of households with international migrants equal to 0, 0.01, 0.05 and 0.2. The mean numbers of households with international migrants in the UAUs of each stratum are therefore 0, 2, 10 and 40. The numbers of UAUs selected in each of the four strata consistent with the above could be 40, 25, 15 and 20. Then the expected number of households with international migrants will be $40 \times 0 + 25 \times 2 + 15 \times 10 + 20 \times 40 = 1,000$. The selection rule in this case would be that every household with international migrants found during phase 1 should be interviewed during phase 2. It remains to be established how many households without international migrants should be selected in each UAU. Since there are 100 UAUs in the sample, 5 households without international migrants should be selected in each UAU. This number should be fixed *a priori*, before the fieldwork in phase 1 begins so that there is no subjectivity in selecting more or fewer households in the field. Systematic sampling can be used to select the sample of households without migrants from the lists made during phase 1, or a cluster could be selected randomly.

Note that, in the example above, if the average size of UAUs had been 500 instead of 200 households, the expected number of households with international migrants per UAU would have been 50 and, consequently, only 20 UAUs would have had to be selected at the third sampling stage. Though a smaller number of UAUs would reduce field costs and facilitate field logistics, it would also lead to larger sampling variance. Hence, to the extent that the size of UAUs can be controlled, opting for average sizes that do not concentrate the sample too much in a few areas is preferable since such concentration increases the design effect of the sample.

It is useful to provide another example to illustrate the value of two-phase sampling compared to other procedures. Suppose that the survey selects a random cluster of households within each UAU instead of relying on two-phase sampling. Suppose the clusters are of size 20 and that the average UAU size is 200 households. If a UAU has 198 households without international migrants and 2 households with migrants located in different clusters, the probability of finding even a single household with international migrants is only $2 \times 20/200$ or 0.2. That is, only one out of every five clusters selected (and only one of every 5 UAUs) would have a household with international migrants. This means that most of the time interviewers would be visiting households in the sample cluster, wasting their time, not finding any eligible households with international migrants for interview. In contrast, using two-phase sampling and an *a priori* rule stating that all households with international migrants are to be selected, the two households that qualify would be included in the sample. Furthermore, since the listing process documents the number of households with international migrants and those without in each UAU selected, it permits the calculation of appropriate weights (see section C.7 below).

To conclude, it is worth noting that a two-phase sampling procedure is also useful in designing samples in countries or regions where no data are available on the proportion of households with international migrants (e.g. the census does not contain a question to identify the foreign born). In such a situation, provinces will have to be selected in the first stage with probabilities of selection proportional to total population size (PPES), then districts are selected from those selected provinces the same way (PPES). Then all UAUs in the districts selected at the second stage may be screened through a phase 1 operation to list households and identify those with and without international migrants. Such lists are then processed in a central location and aggregated across UAUs to obtain the overall numbers of the two types of households to determine their respective sampling fractions. The census sectors are then stratified so disproportionate sampling can be used to select UAUs with probabilities of selection proportional to the known UAU sector variance. Once the UAUs are selected, the numbers of households with and without international migrants from each UAU is known. An advantage of this procedure is that the exact numbers of sample households with and without international migrants is known beforehand, which allows precise planning of the time and cost of phase 2 interviewing in the field. A significant disadvantage – and this is why it should be done only when no population frame is available for international migrants – is that it requires an extremely time consuming household listing operation in the districts selected, which are likely to be quite large.

In implementing any two-phase sampling procedure, it is very important to bear in mind that whenever it requires two separate field visits, phase 2 must be carried out as soon as possible after phase 1, particularly when the study of migration is involved. The longer the hiatus between the two phases, the more inaccurate the information gathered during phase 1 may become as individuals and households move into or out of the selected UAUs or die. In a 1975-76 survey of internal migration carried out by the National Statistical Office of Thailand, the migrants to re-interview, identified during phase 1, were sought for re-interviews only 6 to 7 months later; but by this time less than one-third of the households identified as having migrants contained exactly the same migrants as they had initially.

7. Use of weights in the analysis

Probability sampling is necessary in surveys of international migration so that statistically valid tests of hypotheses and inferences can be made regarding the characteristics of international migrants and the determinants and consequences of migration. In a probability sample, every element or observation – every migrant and non-migrant, or every household with an international migrant and every household without – has a known probability of having been selected or included in the sample. In the case of multi-stage sampling, the probability of selection is known at every stage and, consequently, the probability of selecting a particular element (individual or household) is the product of the probabilities of selection at each stage. For example, suppose the PSU or province in which a household is located has a probability of 0.1 of having been selected in stage one, and that the second stage unit (or UAU in this case, which may be a census sector) in which the household is located within the PSU selected has a probability of selection of 0.05. Then suppose further that the UAU contains 100 households of which 6 contain one or more international migrants, and that the *a priori* selection rule for UAUs in that stratum is that half of the households containing international migrants are to be selected. Then the household's probability of having been selected is (0.1) (0.05) (0.5) or 0.0025. This means that the values of any variable associated with that household need to be weighted (i.e. multiplied) by 1/0.0025 or 400 whenever all the survey observations are aggregated to represent the entire population in the domain. As this example indicates, the general procedure is to weight (multiply) the values pertaining to each element by the inverse of the probability of selection of that element.

Similarly, suppose that the survey also collects data for households without international migrants, and that in phase 1 of the last sampling stage the selection rule states that one out of every 32 households without migrants should be selected. Then, in the UAU described above, $(1/32)(100 - 6) = 2.94$ or about 3 households without international migrants would be selected, each with an overall probability of selection of (0.1) (0.05) (0.03125) or 0.00015625. The values of all observations for this non-migrant household should therefore be weighted by 1/(0.00015625) or 6,400, a number 16 times greater than that estimated for the household having international migrants and belonging to the same UAU.

In practice, to perform many statistical operations it is desirable to have the weights "normalized", meaning that each weight for each element is divided by the sum of all the weights for the observations in the final sample. The use of multi-stage stratified samples using clusters in the final stage complicates statistical analyses, but packages such as SUDAAN can handle complex sample designs. Moreover, in surveys of international migration, which inherently involve a serious problem of "rare elements", it is not advisable to use a simple sample design just so that the sample is self-weighting and statistical computations are easy. Simple sample designs imply very inefficient allocations of field work and must be avoided.

The procedures described in this section – using strict probability sampling methods, developing an appropriate sampling frame, grouping areas into strata according to their expected numbers and proportions of international migrants, using stratified multi-stage sampling with oversampling of areas with larger proportions of international migrants via disproportionate sampling, and employing two-phase sampling to identify households with international migrants in the ultimate area units selected – are appropriate for specialized surveys of international migration. They apply whether the goal is to interview only households with international migrants in a country of destination or households with international out-migrants in countries of origin, or either of these combined with households without international migrants in the same country. In most cases, the need to ensure that appropriate comparison groups are covered will involve undertaking a survey in both the country of destination and the country of origin. In developing a sample design for the country of origin, the information gathered through the specialized survey of international migration in the country of destination should be used to construct a population frame for the selection of PSUs in the country of origin.

D. OTHER DATA COLLECTION APPROACHES RELEVANT FOR INTERNATIONAL MIGRATION

1. Multiplicity surveys

Given the problem of identifying and locating international migrants, and the fact that, once located, an international migrant can often report the location of other international migrants, especially of those having the same country of origin as the migrant interviewed or those coming from the same community, "multiplicity surveys" are sometimes seen as a way to increase the size of the sample of international migrants at relatively low cost.

Sirken has defined multiplicity surveys as those in which "sample households report information about their own residents as well as about other persons who live elsewhere, such as relatives or neighbours, as specified by a multiplicity rule adopted in the survey" (Sirken, 1972, p. 257). They thus differ from conventional household surveys, where each individual has only one chance of being reported on through the dwelling where he or she resides. In a multiplicity survey, persons have different likelihoods of being reported on and often more than one chance of being reported upon. Thus, if a survey adopts a multiplicity rule saying that information about someone may be obtained from that person's sibling as well as from that person directly, then each person has $n + 1$ chances of being "observed", where n is the number of siblings of the person concerned that are part of the population sampled. Respondents thus do not have equal chances of being observed, a deviation from the usual probability sample. However, in principle, it is possible to adjust for the different probabilities of being reported on by using appropriate weights, provided the survey collects the information needed to identify the number of possible persons that could report on a person or an event. In the example just cited, recording the number of siblings living in the country of interview that everyone has would be sufficient.

Design of surveys to investigate international migration

An increase in the number of sources that can report an event evidently increases the total number of events reported as well as the opportunities to obtain information about an event or person for any given sample of households. Such a procedure also increases the chances of finding out about rare (and also about sensitive) events in a population. Sampling error can be reduced by the increased sample size obtained from using a multiplicity survey. Certain types of coverage bias may also be reduced by, for instance, obtaining information about whole households that leave an area from the remaining relatives or neighbours. The estimation of emigration based on the place of residence of siblings uses a similar approach (see Chapter 3.A.5).

Variations of multiplicity sampling, known as network or snowball sampling, have existed for many years (Goodman, 1961). All are used to locate or measure relatively rare elements or traits. Multiplicity surveys were originally developed to estimate components of population change, i.e. to measure demographic rates. In terms of the study of international migration, the class of persons allowed to report about an international migrant must be (a) carefully defined, so that there is no ambiguity which requires the interviewer to exercise judgement in the field; and (b) measurable. The need to characterize well the possible respondents severely limits the use of this technique to collect information from "neighbours", since most definitions of neighbour fail to result in either a fixed number that can be used universally or in a number that can be easily determined in the field for every household. This is unfortunate, since otherwise it would be possible to use at least basic information provided by neighbours concerning the emigration of whole households. The requirement that the number of informers should be measurable can best be met by focusing on the characteristics of persons who have specific relationships with the respondent, such as sons, daughters, mothers, fathers or siblings.

The experience of an exploratory test of the technique to assess the volume and character of movement into, out of and within a given area, may be instructive (Goldstein and Goldstein, 1979, p. 25). The study, carried out in 1978, focused on intra-state movements during 1976–78 reported by a sample of 201 migrant and non-migrant households in a city in Rhode Island, United States. Multiplicity rules were based on accepting information about events from parents, siblings, children and ex-spouses (a very imprecise procedure). Because of recall errors, only information about the migration of relatives in the year preceding the interview could be obtained, and even then only 62 per cent of the moves were reported. Out of these, only 70 per cent of the respondents reported the new address correctly, and only 61 per cent gave the same reason for the move as the migrant gave. The fact that this information was obtained only from immediate relatives in the smallest state in the United States suggests that multiplicity surveys have serious limitations in producing information about absent relatives because of the poor quality of the data obtained. It also provides further evidence that proxy respondents often give distorted answers.

It is still unclear whether multiplicity surveys are useful for sampling international migrants, and some experiments are currently under way in

Europe. Such procedures need to be used with far more care than has usually been the case, and cannot be considered generally or easily applicable methods.

2. Tracing migrants

Tracing is, in principle, an auspicious procedure for locating rare elements or persons such as international migrants. Even though it is not a sampling technique *per se*, it is discussed here because it can be considered an alternative procedure – albeit a survey procedure – for locating international migrants. Indeed, it has already been used a number of times for that purpose, primarily in studies of small numbers of international migrants. It has conceptual similarities with two-phase sampling but with the two phases taking place in entirely different geographic areas, in this case different countries. It is also similar to multiplicity surveys because information about how to reach certain persons is obtained from other persons.

There are two types of tracing that may be germane in the present context: (a) first interview households in the country of origin to identify the existence, name and last-known address of former household members who are international out-migrants, and then use the information to seek out and interview those migrants in the country of destination; and (b) first interview the international migrants in the country of destination to obtain the names and addresses of family members remaining in the country of origin, then interview the households of origin.

The purpose of both types of tracing is to obtain information first-hand rather than by proxy from both the international migrant and key household members. Note that tracing is useful only in cases where international migrants have left close relatives in the country of origin whom they are still in contact with, whether or not they are still considered household members. Among the studies that have used tracing, type (a) above is the most common. Not only does the use of tracing improve the quality and completeness of data on international out-migrants and their families in the country of origin, but it also makes possible certain consistency and data quality checks because it is likely that data are collected independently from the different family members in the two countries. Such checks are especially important regarding information on remittances, where the two parties involved (the migrant and family members remaining in the country of origin) may have vested interests in reporting figures that deviate from the true ones in opposite directions.

A survey of internal migration in Sierra Leone involved one of the largest attempts at tracing in a developing country (Byerlee and Tommy, 1976a; Byerlee and Fatoo, 1976b). The survey identified 1,900 rural households with one or more out-migrants to urban areas and then traced 825 migrants to various urban locations in the country. However, only 57 per cent of these were actually traced from households at the place of origin. The other 43 per cent were in-migrants from the same areas of origin reported by those who were successfully traced. The final result is that only 25 per cent of the out-migrants from rural areas were successfully traced, which is almost certain to be an unrepresentative sample.

Despite its attractions, tracing therefore has two major drawbacks. First, the proportion of persons successfully traced is generally too low to avoid serious biases. Taking less than 50 per cent of those eligible usually introduces serious biases in the representativity of the persons traced, and biases may also result when 70 to 80 per cent of those traced are successfully located. The fact that the direction of the bias can often be inferred may or may not help in interpreting the results. Migrants successfully traced will tend to be those who have left most recently, who have known addresses, who maintain close ties with their family members, and who are more economically successful (they send remittances and can afford to visit the country of origin). That is, those traced will usually be positively selected. In Sierra Leone, for instance, the migrants "traced" had a higher mean educational level than that of the larger sample of out-migrants reported by the rural households (five versus years of school completed).

The second major problem with tracing is its cost. A fully fledged tracing survey is likely to cost not only far more than a normal household survey in the country of origin but also more than the combined cost of separate, independent surveys in both the countries of origin and destination. Tracing international migrants from a country of origin to several locations distributed widely across the country of destination is not cheap, especially when the addresses provided may be inaccurate or when maps of the areas of destination may not be readily available or accurate. Similar arguments apply when tracing involves finding the migrants' households in the country of origin. The geographical dispersion of such households is likely to be greater than that of international migrants in the country of destination and therefore tracing back to the origin is at least equally costly. It is unfortunate that detailed information on the costs of tracing does not seem to be available for any survey. It would be useful to assess the additional cost involved in tracing.

In conclusion, although tracing is occasionally a useful procedure to enrich migration surveys, it cannot be recommended for general use: it is costly and, in most circumstances, it cannot produce a representative sample of the persons being traced. Consequently, it has greater value for exploratory purposes than as a tool to yield confirmatory information on the international migration process.

3. Use of qualitative survey methods to study international migrants

There are several types of procedures involving the collection of qualitative information on a selected group of persons. These include the use of intensive, in-depth interviews; ethnographic methods; focus groups (see Knodel et al., 1988; Wolff et al., 1991); and so-called "ethno-surveys" (see Massey et al., 1990). Studies based on such approaches are generally based on information obtained from a modest number of persons or a handful of communities that cannot be considered representative of anything larger than the group of surveyed individuals or communities themselves. A further fundamental shortcoming of most of these approaches is that the persons interviewed are not selected according to probabilistic principles and therefore statistically valid inferences cannot be made nor can statistical tests of hypotheses be carried out.

These qualitative methods have another important trait in common: they usually use open-ended questions, allowing the person interviewed to offer his or her version of events, different details and levels of detail about events and their reactions to them. They are thus not constrained by specific questions or precoded responses. Interviewers carrying out in-depth interviews must have the skills needed to keep the interview focused on the topics of interest, using pre-established questions or lines of inquiry to guide the interview so as to make sure that nothing important is completely omitted and that there is some comparability between the approaches used and the topics treated during the interviews of different individuals.

In carrying out specialized surveys on the determinants and consequences of international migration such as those described in previous sections of this chapter, intensive interviews with individual migrants and members of their families can be useful, either before a specialized survey is undertaken or just after the survey. The use of qualitative methods before the survey can provide valuable information about the nature of the international migration process in particular contexts or as viewed by particular types of persons or families, and can therefore be useful in developing questionnaires and in the formulation of hypotheses. After the main survey is completed, once migrants or households with international migrants have been interviewed using standardized questionnaires, some may be visited again for more intensive interviews to learn more about their experiences, their motives and the problems that they have encountered. Such re-interviews can be done for a probabilistically selected subsample of migrants, which would make possible the generalization of the findings of the intensive interviews but would also be expensive in terms of both personnel costs (especially well trained interviewers must be used) and data processing and analysis costs (a great amount of information is obtained in intensive interviews, much of which is not easy to analyse). Therefore, in most practical situations, the number of intensive interviews is usually small (10 or 20) and is not intended to be representative but rather the respondents would be selected by the judgement of the research team. In selecting specific migrants for intensive interview, an effort should be made to include different types of persons: young, middle-aged and older migrants; men and women; migrants from different major countries of origin, or households with out-migrants to different countries of destination; migrants living in different areas (cities, smaller towns, rural areas), etc. The dimensions for selection are evidently numerous. The information collected in the main survey could be used to characterize the main types of interest and to determine which are typical or atypical and therefore worthy of intensive interview.

One qualitative approach that may be used for the purposes above is that based on "focus groups". It consists of interviewing distinct groups of between 5 and 15 respondents, each group comprising a fairly homogeneous set of persons in terms of sex, age, socio-economic status or other relevant characteristic. The purpose is to learn about commonalities of experience or attitudes within each group by having similar people respond to a set of open-ended questions. The rationale for selecting homogeneous groups is that the more alike people are, the more they are likely to open up in a group interview situation, even stimulating each other to shed light on specific issues. Differences across the different groups in responses to the same general questions can then be revealing about different life experiences or attitudes.

The objective of intensive interviews carried out in conjunction with specialized surveys on international migration is to provide the depth of detail that can help better to understand the migration process, its determinants and consequences than may be possible through data from the usual structured interview lasting an hour or so in itself. In the best of circumstances, skilful interviewers can develop a much better rapport with the respondent during intensive interviews and thus obtain not only more nuanced but also new information, possibly quite revealing, about the person's migration experience. Of particular interest is the coverage of sensitive issues, such as the problems faced by international migrants (and irregular migrants) to enter or leave a country, bribes paid to officials, illegal activities engaged in (including illegal employment), unfair treatment by employers and family problems. Intensive interviews can thus complement and enrich the somewhat dry quantitative analysis based on large-scale surveys, and thus may provide additional insights that help in the interpretation of the quantitative results.

E. CONTENT OF QUESTIONNAIRES IN SURVEYS TO ANALYSE THE DETERMINANTS AND CONSEQUENCES OF INTERNATIONAL MIGRATION

In previous sections of this chapter, it has been argued that the best approach for the study of both the determinants and the consequences of international migration is to conduct linked surveys in countries of origin and countries of destination focusing on different groups (non-migrants in the country of origin and migrants in the country of destination). Taking that as the basic model for data collection, this section considers the types of information to seek from migrants and non-migrants, their households and their communities of destination and origin to make possible a thorough assessment of the factors

International migration statistics

leading to international migration and its consequences for the migrants involved.

Space restrictions do not allow a careful theoretical discussion or justification of the factors affecting migration at the micro level. Suffice it to say that there are a number of theoretical perspectives from the fields of microeconomics – e.g. human capital theory (cf. Sjaastad, 1962) and the Todaro model (1969) – sociology (e.g. Lee, 1966), geography, political science, and even psychology that can be drawn upon to justify collecting information on a wide range of factors hypothesized to play a role in international migration decisions. Many of the factors involved have been found to be associated with internal migration movements in one country or another. Much less is known about their effects on international migration, but it is clear that in order to understand and quantify specific determinants of international migration, it is important to examine simultaneously (or control for) the effects of the various factors on geographical mobility of individuals when the latter is not completely under State control. Indeed, a major distinguishing trait of international migration is that it is responsive to State policies regarding the admission and residence of foreigners. At the micro-level, individual migrants are normally well aware of the obstacles or barriers that the State erects to prevent the free movement of persons across its borders. Therefore, it is essential in studies of the determinants of international migration at the micro-level that information be collected from migrants and the non-migrant comparison group on contacts and experience abroad, perceptions about State policies, and legal aspects of their status that may be relevant for their international mobility, such as their citizenship or potential right to citizenship of another country.

In contrast to the determinants of international migration, there are no clear theoretical perspectives to guide the formulation of hypotheses pertaining to the consequences of international migration. Most approaches adapt or draw upon theories formulated to explain the determinants of migration. Consequently, there is considerable overlap in the types of factors that are considered relevant for the study of both the determinants and the consequences of international migration. Differences arise mostly in terms of whether the factors of interest are measured with respect to the period preceding the change of residence to another country (for the study of the determinants) or with respect to the current circumstances of the migrant, at the time of interview, after migration (for the study of the consequences). Because the surveys envisaged here generally have the dual purpose of collecting data to assess both the determinants and consequences, it will be necessary to record the status of migrants and their households at both those two points in time in terms of a variety of relevant factors.

Table 6.3 presents schematically a listing of factors thought to be relevant for the analysis of the determinants and consequences of international migration. Three major categories of factors are identified: those measured at the level of the individual migrant or non-migrant; those measured at the level of the person's household; and those relative to the community of residence. Within

Design of surveys to investigate international migration

Table 6.3. Factors relevant for the analysis of the determinants and consequences of international migration at the micro-level

	Some possible measures
Individual-level factors	
Demographic characteristics	Sex, ethnicity, country of birth; age and marital status at the time of migration and currently
Demographic events associated with migration	Actual or expected birth; actual or expected marriage/divorce; widowhood; orphanhood
Citizenship	Country of citizenship; right to other citizenship; dual or multiple citizenship; changes of citizenship; citizenship of close relatives; desire for naturalization (if applicable)
Migrant status in country of destination	Migration status; type of visa, residence permit, work permit; length of validity of permit(s); status upon first admission; changes in migration status; difficulties in obtaining visa or permit
Education	Level of education in completed years prior to migration; training or school attendance after migration; knowledge of languages before and after migration
Employment	Years of full time work experience, employment status, occupation and months worked in year prior to migration; current employment status, occupation and months worked in previous year; existence of employment contract and duration after migration
Earnings, income, benefits	Earnings per month (in money and in kind) in last job before migration or estimated income if self-employed before migration; whether had fringe benefits (health insurance, pension, paid vacation) in last job before migration; and same for current job
Labour migration	Whether transferred by employer; use of labour recruiter or other intermediary; cost of securing employment abroad; whether underwent employment clearance in country of origin; contacts with potential employers or recruiters in the country of destination before migration
Contacts with country of destination prior to migration	Close relatives or friends in country of destination prior to migration; previous visits to or stays in country of destination; reasons for those visits or stays
Aspirations, attitudes	Desire for further education, status, acceptance, material consumption and ownership of goods; marriage aspirations; conflicts with family members or with local norms; reasons for migrating
Community participation	Membership or participation in local community organizations prior to migration; participation in organizations with links to country of destination prior to migration
Household-level factors:	
Household size, composition	Number of members by sex and age (children or adult) in household prior to migration and currently

International migration statistics

Table 6.3. (*Continued*)

	Some possible measures
Household-level factors: (cont.)	
Household income	Total household income in money and in kind, in previous month/year and in year prior to migration (distinguishing labour income from other sources of income)
Household assets	Ownership in country of origin of land or dwelling; of producer durable goods or facilities; of consumer durable goods (type owned, estimated market value); of bank account and intangible assets. Whether goods are location-specific or are marketable or movable. Same for country of destination
Quality of housing and location in country of destination	Persons per room; whether has electricity, indoor plumbing, flush toilet, potable water, separate private kitchen; access to road, market, school
Current socio-economic characteristics of household members	Education of head of household, spouse, other adults; school attendance of children and other members; employment status of adult members, earnings and time worked
Ties to community or country of origin	Duration of residence of family in community or country of origin; presence of friends and relatives in community of origin
Ties to community of current residence	Presence of friends or relatives of household members in current community of residence prior to migration; assistance received from friends or relatives at the time of migration
Community-level factors:	
Population	Population size and density of community; composition of population by citizenship, ethnicity, religion, race
Migration flows at community level	Main countries or communities of origin of international in-migrants; major reasons for international in-migration; proportion of households with international in-migrants
Employment conditions	Overall average wage level; distribution of labour force by formal and informal sector employment; main occupations and wage levels; unemployment rate by sex, migration status; whether wages or unemployment rate are rising or falling; diversification of employment; whether recent establishment of factories, government development projects; existence of foreign employers; main employers of foreign workers
Poverty and distribution of wealth	Approximate percentage of income earned or land owned by top 5 per cent and bottom 50 per cent of inhabitants
Housing conditions	Proportion of dwellings with electricity, indoor plumbing/running water, flush toilet; degree of concentration of international migrant population; existence of ghettos; quality of housing in migrant neighbourhoods

Table 6.3. (*Continued*)

	Some possible measures
Community-level factors: (cont.)	
Communications, transportation	Modes of public transport; use of public transport by and usual commuter routes of international migrants; time required to get to provincial and to national capital; proportion of dwellings with telephones, motorized vehicle; newspaper circulation; existence of newspapers in languages of main migrant groups; number of television and radio stations available; proportion of dwellings with television and radio; access to (proportion of) radio/television programmes in language of international migrant groups; direct international transportation linkages (flights to main countries of origin); media from abroad; international trade and commercial linkages with main countries of origin
Community facilities and usage	Existence of primary and secondary school; existence of courses in language of international migrants; school enrolment rates by age group and migrant status; existence/number of hospitals, other health facilities per 1,000 population; doctors, other health personnel (per 1,000); use of health facilities by international migrants; existence of banks, post office, government office or police station; existence of cinema, theatre, recreational facility and whether language of international migrants is used; existence of community organizations, migrant associations, cooperatives; existence of welfare services; access by international migrants to welfare services
Environmental conditions	Existence of or degree of water or air pollution, toxic/nuclear wastes in community; whether community has drinking water, sewerage treatment facilities; garbage collection (per cent of solid waste collected); prevalence of health problems or contagious diseases, mortality levels
Topography, location, climate, natural disaster	Whether location on seacoast, lake, river; terrain; mean annual temperature, rainfall; whether recent drought, flood, hurricane or other natural disaster and proportion of population affected
Local governance, community tensions	Responsiveness of local authorities to community needs; degree of democratization; citizen empowerment; local respect for human rights; existence of targeted violence; indicators of social conflict and xenophobia
Community norms	Degree of openness to new ideas, to outsiders; traditional values fixed or in transition; norms regarding women's education, women's work outside the home, social and sexual equality; degree of homogeneity of society; existence of ethnic, linguistic or religious minorities; differences in norms among minorities

each category, several sub-categories are identified. In general, table 6.3 is constructed assuming that the information is obtained from the migrants themselves in the country of destination. As explained in previous sections, equivalent information needs to be obtained from non-migrants in the country of origin, making the relevant modifications because of the change of survey site and, more importantly, ensuring that appropriate retrospective information is also obtained.

The complexity of international migration and its diversity from one context to another means that the factors listed in table 6.3 can neither be exhaustive nor necessarily relevant in all circumstances. The list is thus intended to be suggestive of the factors that merit consideration but whose importance will vary from one situation to another. The discussion below, however, endeavours to highlight those factors most commonly considered relevant.

1. Individual-level factors

Most factors listed that refer to the individual level are expected to be relevant in most circumstances and, consequently, information on them should be recorded in any survey which gathers information for the study of the determinants or the consequences of international migration. The demographic characteristics of migrants at the time of migration are indicators of social status that influence the propensity to migrate. Sex, in particular, is a powerful control variable because the experiences of men and women that may relate to international migration often differ markedly according to acceptable sex role perceptions in the society of origin and that of destination (Hugo, 1993b; United Nations, 1995b). Demographic events that themselves can affect the propensity to migrate and the consequences of that migration for the person involved are listed separately so that they are not disregarded. The issue of whether international migration may be the cause of divorce or legal separation should also be borne in mind.

Information on citizenship and migrant status in the country of destination is crucial to assess the consequences of international migration, since migrants with restricted residence or work rights may not reap the same benefits from migration as those who are granted a wider range of rights. Distinguishing between migrants in an irregular situation and those whose presence is fully sanctioned by the State in which they reside is also fundamental. Investigating the problems faced by migrants in obtaining visas and other required permits and documents (for both travel and changes in nationality) sheds light on the effects of State efforts to control international migration. This has not been done adequately at the micro level.

With respect to socio-economic factors, education both affects migration and may be affected by international migration. Thus certain types of international migrants may be selected among the better educated, and some individuals move to improve their educational attainment (to attend a special training course or obtain a higher degree). Knowledge of languages is also likely to have some impact on the decision to migrate and, more importantly, on the selection of country of destination. Improved knowledge of the local language after migration has taken place indicates a more successful integration in the country of destination.

Economic variables are generally considered of key relevance in determining migration decisions, since most migrants seek to improve their standard of living by migration. People are usually less likely to migrate internationally if they are unemployed or poor and more likely to migrate if they have certain skills. Although the effect of differences in wages between the countries of origin and destination is considered a key determinant of international migration, empirical evidence to test its importance has been scant. According to human capital theory, people tend to migrate if predicted earnings[20] are greater in the place (or country) of destination than in the country of origin (provided the difference exceeds transportation, psychological and other costs). Examples confirming the relevance of such variables in influencing international migration are given by Adams (1993) and El-Saadani (1992), among others. Other approaches to the estimation of the determinants of migration use the actual wage prior to migration instead of the predicted wage. In most cases, migrants have some idea of their employment and earnings prospects prior to migration. Finding out more about their *a priori* expectations, their sources of information, and the extent to which the information was correct is important to assess whether migrants make well informed decisions and what their consequences are. Thus, migration will usually have great effects on the employment, occupation, wages and conditions of work of the migrant. To the extent that the migrant had accurate information before migrating, his or her aspirations are more likely to be realized.

In the specific case of labour migration, a crucial issue is the extent to which migrants are assisted in finding employment abroad by their current or prospective employers, labour recruiters, government agencies, and friends and relatives. Information on the existence of contracts, on the cost and benefits of moving abroad, and on the treatment the migrant received is essential in assessing the consequences of labour migration.

Social networkers are considered to play a crucial role in fostering international migration. They can both stimulate and facilitate changes of residence of persons linked to such networks. Among the many studies that have found support for the role of networks in promoting international migration are those by Hugo (1981), Taylor (1986), Fawcett and Arnold (1987y), and Massey (1990). Investigating the types of contacts that the migrant had with the country of destination prior to migration, both in terms of persons he or she knew there and previous visits to that country or even previous residence, is therefore essential.

An individual's own aspirations, attitudes and motivations are key determinants of migration, but are often ignored because they are difficult to measure objectively. Similarly, the realization of a migrant's aspirations might be used as an indication of success, but is generally not sufficiently explored in assessing the consequences of migration.

Participation in community organizations gives a feeling of belonging and provides more social contacts that may serve either to discourage someone from moving away or prompt migration when the organizations involved have linkages abroad. Furthermore, participation in local organizations in the country of destination can be an indicator of the level of engagement of the migrant with the host community and his or her commitment to stay in it.

2. Household-level factors

Household-level factors also include the demographic, economic and social characteristics of the household which may both affect the decision to migrate and be affected by migration. Demographic factors include household size and composition. Size prior to migration is relevant because large households have a lower propensity to migrate as a unit but at the same time are more likely to experience the out-migration of members. Such a relation may be stronger among lower income households for which migration is part of a survival strategy to diversify sources of income over space. After migration, household composition may reflect restrictions imposed by the receiving State on family reunification, and will evidently have important effects on the psychological consequences of international migration for both migrant household members and those remaining in the country of origin.

Household income can affect the likelihood of international migration in two opposite ways. Higher household income makes it easier to finance the often considerable costs involved in international migration, but to the extent higher income results mainly from higher earnings from employed household members, higher income also indicates a higher opportunity cost of international migration for those members and for the household as a whole. Household assets can also have positive or negative effects on international migration depending on their type (Oberai, 1984). Those that are easily marketable or "liquid" can be sold or realized to finance international migration[21] but assets that cannot be easily liquidated may have a negative effect on out-migration (DaVanzo, 1976). The latter include certain producer assets, such as specialized capital equipment or machinery used in industrial processes, and the value of good will built up over time by businesses and in certain professions, as measured by costumer loyalty. In terms of the consequences of international migration, changes in household income and assets associated with a change of residence are important indicators of the economic effects of migration on the household.

The type and quality of a migrant's dwelling prior to migration can be factors slightly influencing the decision to migrate, and after migration they indicate the status of the migrant's household. Similarly, the socio-economic characteristics and employment status of members of the migrant's household may be relevant. In particular, comparing the employment status (or other measure) of members of the household prior to migration and at the time of interview may indicate important effects of migration on household units. Certain household members may be "tied migrants", whose migration depends on the decisions of others. They may be particularly disadvantaged by household migration. In terms of the determinants of migration, the characteristics of household members prior to migration (including those of members who do not themselves migrate) may contribute to household decisions to migrate or not.

Ties to the community of origin can both determine in which circumstances international migration takes place and the orientation of migrants and their households while abroad (whether they remain attached to the community of origin or not). The strength of such ties is related to the number of years spent in the community of origin as well as to the breadth and depth of personal friendships and relationships with community dwellers. It is also of interest, particularly in relation to an assessment of the consequences of international migration, to explore the ties of migrants and their households to the communities of destination in terms of the presence of friends and relatives and the assistance received from such persons at the time of migration or subsequent to it. The anticipation or expectation of this assistance is widely considered to be a key factor in determining international migration. And the realization of the assistance is often instrumental in the migrant's initial successful integration.

3. Community-level factors and their utilization

Throughout the social sciences there is increasing recognition of the importance of context in affecting human behaviour. In the case of migration, this has long been recognized, but the specific desirability of collecting data at the community or contextual level to analyse the determinants or consequences of individual or household migration decisions can be traced back only to Wood (1981, 1982), Bilsborrow (1981) and Findley (1982). A discussion of the importance of taking community-level factors into account and of which factors to consider for the investigation of the determinants of internal migration in low-income countries is provided in Bilsborrow et al. (1984, Chapter XI). It is important to take those factors into account in international migration as well, along with State policy factors that may be measured at the community level. In practice, community factors are measured by using data obtained through specialized community-level questionnaires administered to community leaders, selected informants, or groups of residents.

Factors operating at the community level can be conceptualized as intermediate variables between those at the macro or national level and those at the individual or household levels. They thereby serve as a filter between national policies and the households of the community, influencing individual and household behaviour and themselves affected by higher level government policies. Table 6.3 presents a list of possible community-level factors relevant for the analysis of the determinants or consequences of international migration. From the point of view of the analysis of the determinants, factors characterizing the community of origin may be particularly important. Those characterizing the community of residence in the country of destination also may have some relevance in determining international migration (mainly the choice of destination) but are more relevant for assessing the consequences of migration.

As in the cases of individual and household level factors, demographic factors may be relevant at the community level as well. Communities with a larger population size and a higher density are likely to offer more opportunities than a smaller place and thus tend to be more attractive for international migrants. The composition of the community in terms of citizenship, ethnicity or religion is also likely to change because of migration, and in a community of origin may put pressure on minorities to leave. The community's migration history is also likely to influence current and future developments, whether the community acts as origin of or destination for international migrants, because it will be associated with direct ties and information flows. Investigating the internal migration flows that the community has experienced may also be relevant, since it is argued that international migrants may be substitutes for internal migrants in communities of destination or that they may drive out native residents in some communities. In addition, international migration may be the last step in a multi-stage process, following people's arrival in a large city with strong international ties after a series of internal migration movements.

Employment conditions in the community as a whole as well as the prevalence of poverty are factors that set the stage for the attraction of international migrants (or the retention of the local population in communities of origin). Recent (or planned) expansion of employment opportunities through investment by private sector employers or through government development projects in the community may have a significant impact on attracting international migrants (or in retaining the local population, when that expansion occurs in communities of origin).

Housing conditions in the community of destination are likely to be a minor factor in migration decisions, but may indicate broader aspects of quality of life, poverty and income distribution, which may promote or retard the integration of international migrants. Differences in housing conditions between international migrants (or particular groups thereof) and the general population of the community of destination may be related to the operation of networks, government housing policies vis-à-vis immigrants, or the location of employment opportunities, as well as the relative economic status of international migrants.

Given the importance of information and networks on international migration, both communications and transportation linkages between the

Design of surveys to investigate international migration

community of origin and the national capital or the world at large are most relevant. Thus the distance to the national capital, modes and frequency of public transport available, and time to get there are important, presuming that the capital is the centre for international contacts. Other potentially useful indicators of international influences in the community of origin are the availability of media programmes produced abroad for the local population, and the presence of persons who have lived abroad and brought in ideas about conditions in another country (return migrants, in particular). For the community of destination, the existence of transportation linkages with specific countries and of newsprint and media programmes in the languages of specific migrant groups is an indication of the cultural and social importance and degree of integration of those groups.

In the community of destination, the types of facilities and services in general, as well as their accessibility to international migrants, are commonly thought to play a role in attracting migrants. In the community of origin, the degree of access to such needed services can be a factor shaping the decision to migrate, though not necessarily internationally. Similarly, environmental conditions in communities of origin are increasingly being perceived as causes of migration, though most result in a change of residence within countries. In Mexico, for instance, a 1986 migration survey carried out in 16 cities showed that, for Mexico City, concerns about the deteriorating environment and the "agitated life style" were the two most commonly expressed reasons for intending to move away (CONAPO, 1987). The influence of environmental factors on decisions to move abroad has not been explored. Nor is there much information on how environmental factors in the community of destination shape the consequences of migration for the migrants involved. In a similar vein, the physical location of the community of origin and the likelihood that it may be affected by natural disasters are factors that probably influence decisions to migrate where they occur. As attributes of the community of destination, their role in influencing locational decisions of international migrants may have some relevance.

A more important factor shaping the decision to move from one country to another is the character of local governance, or the existence of tensions or outright conflicts in communities of origin. From the perspective of the community of destination, the consequences of migration will also be influenced by local governance issues and by those related to the existence of intolerance, discrimination or human rights violations affecting international migrants.

Lastly, community norms are part of the context in which people live and provide structure and familiarity to daily life. However, certain persons may consider the norms characterizing the community of origin as stultifying and may decide to migrate in order to avoid them. In some developing countries, norms regarding the roles and status of women may be a factor in prompting the out-migration of women who seek opportunities in a more egalitarian society. In such cases, the norms of the community of destination also play a role by providing the counterpart to the community of origin. Norms in the community of destination that foster prejudice and discrimination against minorities also evidently have an influence on the consequences of migration for migrants.

As noted earlier, current empirical approaches to the analysis of the determinants and consequences of migration at the micro level recognize that migration decisions are influenced not only by the characteristics and prospects of the individual migrant and his or her immediate family but also by factors associated with the community of origin and possible communities of destination. This view derives in part from the place-utility approach espoused by geographers and the earlier work of sociologists such as Stouffer (1940, 1960) and Lee (1966), and is concerned with the perceived utility of alternative places of residence. Since information on perceived utility is difficult to obtain, subjective and usually unreliable, it is rarely sought during data collection. Instead, information on the objective characteristics of places is collected. Thus differences in the characteristics of the community of origin and that of destination are important *a priori* contextual-level factors that influence the international migration decisions of individual migrants and their households. They should be taken into account explicitly in modelling migration functions to reduce the misspecification that characterizes models in which contextual-level factors are not included. Because contextual variables far more than individual variables reflect factors subject to policy intervention, models that include them (so called multi-level models) are potentially much more useful for deriving policy implications than the usual ones restricted to individual- and household-level factors. In multi-level models involving more than one country, policy factors differing across countries can be explicitly included (see also section B.2 above).

Figure 6.1 illustrates how factors at different levels may influence the international migration decisions of individuals and households. The figure shows the relevance of conditions in both the country of origin and that of destination. At the top left is the characterization of persons (migrants and non-migrants) in the country of origin. Their own characteristics influence who moves and who responds to the differences in conditions between origin and destination. Below are the contextual factors or conditions in the immediate community of residence or local reference area in the country of origin. At the bottom left, "national policies" indicates that the government of the country of origin may have policies to influence, directly or indirectly, the socio-economic situation and value systems of the local community, as well as policies which directly facilitate or restrict individual international migration decisions. The context of the community of origin acts as a filter through which factors from beyond the community, such as government policies, must pass in order to influence the decisions of households and individuals of that community. Similarly, the effects of factors in the country of destination are indicated on the right. In practice, the latter should refer to the initial community of destination of the migrant, which is most directly relevant to the study of the determinants of migration. To study the consequences of international migration, factors related to the current community of residence should be contrasted with those of the migrant's community of origin in order to assess change.

Design of surveys to investigate international migration

Figure 6.1. Illustration of multi-level model of determinants of international migration

Country of origin **Country of destination**

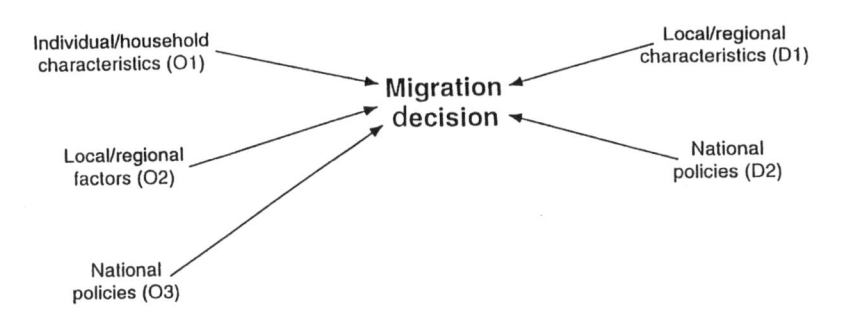

```
Individual/household                              Local/regional
characteristics (O1)                              characteristics (D1)
                        → Migration ←
                        ← decision →
Local/regional                                    National
factors (O2)                                      policies (D2)


National
policies (O3)
```

O1. e.g. age, sex, education; skill/work experience, occupation; current marital status; motivation; location-specific capital and other assets; household size and composition; income; attitudes/sex roles.

O2. e.g. employment conditions (overall wage levels, unemployment rate); wage levels of particular occupations; employment opportunities for women, children; availability of and quality of schools, health facilities, cultural and recreational facilities; transportation/communications links with national capital, other countries; ethnicity/religion; norms regarding women's roles; presence of close relatives, friends.

O3. e.g. level of economic development, wage/income level; policies relating to economic conditions in general; income/wealth distribution, poverty; tax/fiscal policy; exchange rate/foreign trade policies; expenditure policy, including share on social and economic services and infrastructure; policies to encourage people to work abroad, activities of foreign labour recruiters; restrictive policies on out-migration, or on allowing citizens to travel abroad as tourists, students.

D1. As in O2, viz. (relative) employment characteristics (overall wage and unemployment levels, levels for particular occupational groups); availability and quality of social and economic facilities; amenities; presence of friends, relatives, same ethnic or racial group; language; norms regarding women's employment.

D2. As in O3, viz. overall level of economic development, wage/income levels; economic polocies; tax/expenditure policies; foreign trade/aid flows; extent of business fixed investment; policies to recruit foreign workers; visa policies, border controls and other physical barriers to immigration and enforcement; quotas and other direct restrictions on immigration; political opposition to immigration, racism; official policies regarding family reunification; internal restrictions on illegal immigrants (employer sanctions, restrictions on their use of social services, etc.).

F. QUESTIONNAIRES FOR SURVEYS IN COUNTRIES OF DESTINATION AND ORIGIN

1. General questionnaire design and presentation issues

This section describes the content of questionnaires for specialized surveys of international migration. As explained in section B.2 above, it is highly desirable to obtain information for both the appropriate comparison group of non-migrants and for international migrants. Therefore, most issues of questionnaire design and content can be treated together both for international migrants and non-migrants and for countries of origin and destination. Hence, in the interests of saving space, a detailed discussion of questionnaire content for countries receiving international migrants (including the skip patterns necessary to accommodate non-migrants as well) will be presented first. Then, indications of how the questionnaires presented can be adapted for surveys in countries of origin of international migrants and for surveys of return migrants will be provided.

Prototype questionnaires are presented in the annexes. Because they are intended to serve only as models, the questions they include must be pretested in the field and modified as necessary for any actual application. Those conducting a survey will also want to include additional questions or exclude some questions, depending on the particular circumstances involved or on the objectives of the survey. In addition, prior to pretesting in the field, the questionnaires must be translated accurately into whatever languages are likely to be encountered (and translated independently back into the original, to ensure accurate translation).

The questionnaires are complete and self-contained, including skip patterns that make them appropriate both for households with international migrants and those without. Questions and skip instructions are grouped into sections or modules. Three full questionnaires are provided for countries of destination: a household questionnaire, an individual questionnaire, and a community-level questionnaire. The individual questionnaire comprises sections entitled migration and citizenship, pre-migration situation and activity, arrival in country, and current work. The first and fourth sections of the individual questionnaire should always be used to interview non-migrants as well as the household questionnaire. In addition, two optional modules are provided for individuals, one to be used to interview migrant workers and the other to interview women on fertility and family planning.

The definition of international migrant used has some effects on questionnaire design and especially on the time reference of information sought in both the household and individual questionnaires. In general, for reasons indicated in section B above, data will be sought from both migrants and appropriate non-migrants pertaining to both the time of the survey and the time before migration. If a five-year cut-off is used in defining international migrant, the mean time at which migration took place is 2.5 years before the survey. Retrospective data on the situation of non-migrant households (in the country of origin) should be sought for that reference date, as is done by the questionnaires presented in the annexes. If a ten-year cut-off were used, the mean time at migration would be about five years before the survey and the questionnaires would seek information from non-migrants for that reference data. The cut-off point used should not significantly affect questionnaire design, except that less detail should be sought if a cut-off further in the past is used.

The appropriate respondent for the household questionnaire is the person who knows the most about the household's economic situation and its sources of income, which will usually be the head of household, although the spouse or some other adult will sometimes be as knowledgeable. The appropriate respondents for the individual questionnaires are persons who may be involved in making migration decisions. That group is assumed to comprise every member of the household who is at least age 15 years at the time of the survey. While it takes more time to interview each such person separately compared to seeking information from a designated household respondent, such as the head of household, information of greater reliability and richer in detail can be collected when it is solicited directly from each person.[22]

Given space limitations, only selected questions are discussed below and the reasons for their inclusion are mentioned briefly. Some of the theoretical rationale for including the questions presented is discussed in section E above. Note that asterisks preceding question numbers in the prototype questionnaires included in the annexes are used to indicate those that the question is of secondary importance, of a subjective nature ("soft" or referring to attitudinal issues), more difficult to implement in the field, or less likely to produce reliable responses.

2. Questionnaire design for a survey in the country of destination of international migrants

Household questionnaire

A basic household questionnaire is provided in Annex 1 (pp. 363–402). As explained in section E above, it is crucial always to collect information on the current composition of households both with and without international migrants. Thus all households interviewed in the country of destination (or in the country of origin) must be asked to fill in the household roster and to provide other information on housing quality, household assets, unearned income, and location of dwelling. The respondent to the household questionnaire should be the head of household or the spouse of the head.

The household roster (questions H.1-H.10) provides for a complete listing of household members, based on the concept of *de jure* or legal residence, though the question on whether each person slept in the house during the past week makes possible a *de facto* classification and serves to check whether a person is in fact a *de jure* member who is temporarily away. The head of household should be listed first and each member's relationship to the head must be recorded. In addition, the following information is collected on each member: age, sex, level of educational attainment and current school attendance, current marital status, and work status. Consequently, at least this information is available for all adults household members, even if temporarily absent and therefore not available to respond to the individual questionnaire. The roster also includes a question on place of birth, to be coded by province or state for those born in the country and by country for those born abroad. Answers to that question provide an indicator of the net lifetime international migration of all current household members. If there are children in the household, data on their places and dates of birth provide some information on the international migration of the mother.

International migration statistics

Questions on household tenure, quality, and assets (H.11-H.18) and on household location (H.19-H.20) follow, the latter indicating the quality of location of the dwelling. Questions on household income from sources other than wage income and income from farm and business activities (both covered also in the individual questionnaire) are included in the household questionnaire (H.21) to provide for complete household income.

The household questionnaire should be administered also on the situation of the household prior to migration. Thus, in a survey in the country of destination, the migrant should be asked the composition of his or her household and its situation in the country of origin just prior to migration (see sections B.2 and E above). This is crucial to assess the extent to which the migrants have benefited from migration and also provides information on the situation of the migrant's household at the time migration took place. See also the discussion below on question 2.11 in the individual questionnaire.

Most questions in the household questionnaire do not usually encounter problems in field implementation. However, since the quality of data from responses to H.21 is sometimes suspect, the simpler questions H.17-H.18, which indicate socio-economic status, are also recommended.

Individual questionnaire

The individual questionnaire comprises four sections and two optional modules. Section 1 on migration and citizenship is fundamental since it identifies international migrants and thereby screens the sample population for non-migrants. The latter do not answer sections 2 and 3, and hence skip to section 4 of the questionnaire. The definition of international migrant used here is a person who has lived in another country for at least six months, has moved to the country of interview during the five years preceding interview and was at least age 15 years at the time of the move. The age cut-off at 15 years is intended to ensure that only those persons who might have actually participated in making migration decisions are interviewed.

Questions 1.1 and 1.2 identify the date and place of birth for all persons, aged 15 and over, who are the respondents to the individual questionnaire (as identified by the household questionnaire). Place of birth is one of the three aspects of international migration (along with citizenship and country of previous residence) that must be determined early in the survey, and is straightforward to collect. Question 1.3 identifies non-migrants, who skip a number of questions. Persons born in the reference country who moved to some other country (determined by questions 1.3 to 1.6) are native born returnees, while all persons who have lived in the reference country and come back (even if they were born in some other country) are return migrants. Evidently, the latter includes native born returnees as a special case. Anyone who has ever lived for over six months in any country besides the reference country and the country of birth is then routed by question 1.6 to a question on the international migration history of the respondent. Only moves from one country to another for more

Design of surveys to investigate international migration

than six months are to be recorded. Note that no information about activities in previous countries of residence is sought, to be consistent with the focus on the most recent move.

Questions 1.7-1.8 identify (recent) international migrants for purposes of the survey and question 1.9 records current citizenship. The sub-questions in 1.9 record whether the respondent has ever been a citizen of another country and the date of change of citizenship. Question 1.10 records the citizenship of immediate relatives and question 1.11 records their country of residence. Both are important in establishing the potential for further international migration (for family reunification purposes, for instance). Further questions on this topic for international migrants only are found in section 3.

Question 1.13 determines language knowledge and questions 1.14 to 1.17 explore the intentions of migrants and non-migrants for future migration. Seeking to determine whether the person has specific plans for departure – regarding both a time and a destination – has been found important for distinguishing those who are likely to move and those who are not, whatever their answers to 1.14.

Section 2 on pre-migration situation and activity seeks information on the situation of the migrant and the migrant's household prior to international migration. The first question, 2.1, confirms previous country of residence and establishes whether the migrant lived in an urban or rural area, information that is important in planning the survey in the country of origin. Question 2.2 identifies refugees and asylum-seekers who are routinely neglected in surveys of international migration but are increasingly important (see Chapter 5 above). Moreover, virtually all of the subsequent questions are relevant for those types of migrants as well, since refugees often exercise economic activities in the receiving country. Question 2.3 inquires why the respondent left the previous country of residence, listing conditions applying to that previous residence, thus distinguishing this question from that in section 3 on why the migrant chose the current country of destination. Failure to distinguish the two issues has created confusion in other surveys and led to excessive criticism about the value of data on reasons for migration. The two-part question seeks to identify both reasons spontaneously mentioned and the main reason.

Questions 2.4 and 2.5 ask about contact with the country of destination prior to migration, and questions 2.6 and 2.7 ask about sources of information about the country of destination and employment prospects in it: previous information and contacts play crucial roles in eliciting migration. Question 2.8 records marital status and changes therein in relation to migration. Question 2.10 inquires about who actually made the migration decision, a topic that should be explored before question 2.11 to minimize the contamination that might otherwise occur by posing that question in the context of compiling the roster pertaining to the household situation prior to migration. Note that question 2.11 calls for the full administration of the household questionnaire pertaining to the time immediately preceding migration. The respondent to that questionnaire will normally be the migrant himself or herself. In cases involving the migration of several adult members of a household who are still living together in the selected household, only the head of household (if also a migrant) need be asked to provide the information on the situation of the household prior to migration, thus avoiding unnecessary duplication. The next bloc of questions, 2.13-2.32, inquires about the economic activity of the migrant prior to migration, including job search activity. The information sought is essentially the same as that on current work, which is recorded for all migrant and non-migrant adults in section 4. It is also desirable to collect basic data on the earnings of all (other) members of the migrant's household just prior to the migrant's departure from the country of origin. In lieu of asking the migrant to provide the same level of detail as in questions 2.13-2.32 for each person, a few questions might be asked about the earnings of the head of household and income of any farm or household enterprise. These questions are 4.2, 4.4a, 4.6, 4.7, and 4.10, for employees, and 4.19 and the columns on estimated monthly income and (if appropriate) total land owned from the household questionnaire. Question 2.33 identifies if the person has had contact with a labour recruiter or contractor so as to identify the migrant workers to whom the optional module described at the end of this sub-section will be administered.

The need for documents, a fundamental aspect of international migration, is covered by questions 2.34-2.38 with respect to the country of previous residence or origin. Questions 2.34a-c explore whether the migrant was in possession of the documents needed to leave the country of origin. Questions 2.36-2.38 probe for further information about documents needed from other countries to leave the country of previous residence and difficulties in getting them. Question 2.38 seeks information about unauthorized payments (e.g. bribes to authorities or border personnel), though information about such topics will often not be forthcoming in an interview of this nature (see section D.3 above). Lastly, questions 2.39 and 2.40 are optional questions seeking the respondent's assessment of the relative status of his or her household in the previous country of residence and participation in community organizations. The former tests the "relative income hypothesis" for migration: are those who migrate from relatively well-off or relatively poor households?

Section 3 on arrival in country is the second major module addressed to international migrants. Whereas Section 2 covered the situation of migrants prior to migration, section 3 covers their arrival and adaptation to the country of destination, except for their current economic activity, which is covered in section 4. The first questions relate to the timing and experience of arrival. Question 3.2 asks why the migrant chose the country of interview as country of destination, and question 3.3 attempts to distinguish international migrants arriving with documents from those without. Questions 3.4-3.5 cover the problems confronted in gaining admission to the country of interview, and question 3.6 refers to documents possessed by the migrant, how they were obtained and whether any problems were encountered in acquiring them. Questions 3.7 and 3.8 ask about job transfers or about how the first job (apart from jobs arranged by labour contractors or recruiters, which are covered in the optional module discussed below) in the country of destination was obtained. It is important to distinguish the different ways of acquiring the first job to assess the extent to which migrants move because they know of such opportunities in advance or because such opportunities are expected from information obtained through relatives or friends (covered in question 3.9) or in the absence of any such contacts. Migrants without jobs on arrival are asked in question 3.11 about job search activity. Questions could also be asked regarding the migrant's first job in the country of destination, which would be useful to study the assimilation process over time, but this issue is not discussed here further.

Question 3.12 is the first of several questions on familial aspects of the migration, including marital status and whether other family members accompanied the migrant at the time of migration or followed later. Whether the migrant's family is with the migrant, provided he or she was married or wanted them to be with him or her, determines the consequences of migration for the migrant. Questions 3.13-3.15 ask about family members who had come to live with the migrant but who have since left. Those who had come only for short visits (less than six months) should not be mentioned here and only the most basic characteristics are obtained on those re-migrating (or dying). The data on age recorded should refer to the age at death or re-migration.

Question 3.17 covers the important topic of formal education and on-the-job training after arrival in the country of destination. Both reflect increases in human capital, which is a key positive consequence of migration in itself and is related to the migrant's overall economic success. Questions 3.17a and 3.19-3.20 cover the extent to which the migrant and his or her family use health and education facilities or receive other government benefits, the cost of which is a major policy issue in most of the major countries of destination of international migrants.

Question 3.21 inquires about visits back home, which are important for migrants away from their family (see question 1.11), but can also reflect lack of integration into the host society. Question 3.22-3.24 ask about changes in citizenship and intentions to change citizenship. The latter reflects long-term intentions to remain and integrate or not. Question 3.25 covers language ability and changes since arrival, a development that is closely tied to the migrant's success in the country of destination. Lastly, question 3.26 is an attitudinal question seeking to solicit the migrant's overall evaluation of his or her experience in the country of destination. It also suggests the existence of pull factors regarding relatives or friends remaining in the country of origin.

The last section of the individual questionnaire, section 4 on current work, seeks information from all migrant and non-migrant persons aged 15 years and over on their current economic activity. Most of the information is fairly standard and covers: labour force status; earnings, occupation, time worked in past year, and benefits; secondary work; age when first employed and total years of employment; whether the person has a written work contract; and income and assets from a family business or farm. For the latter, it is desirable to

International migration statistics

administer a series of questions if there is any hope of obtaining data of usable quality (see the enterprise questionnaire at end of section 4). For those respondents who are not currently "working", questions probe whether they are looking for work and why they are not working. Several questions are included on membership in a labour union and the ethnic composition of the labour force in the place of employment, the latter reflecting enclaves. Employment in such enclaves may not benefit migrants as much as other employment. The "soft" attitudinal questions 4.27-4.28 are optional, included to solicit attitudes towards women's work, from both women and men, to be able to study the relations between such attitudes and both women's participation in the labour force and their international migration. Question 4.29 determines if the migrant retains assets in another country, possibly the country of origin, which may provide income and facilitate a return move.

Optional module for migrant workers

This optional module covers a subset of international migrants which is particularly important to a number of countries of both origin and destination, namely, persons who migrate with the specific purpose of exercising an economic activity in the country of destination and who do so using some kind of intermediary to find a job abroad (this is a subset of migrant workers as defined in Chapter 2 and also includes persons migrating in an irregular situation to work abroad who find jobs through intermediaries). In certain contexts, such persons may work in a country other than their own for less than six months and, consequently, according to the definition of international migrant adopted for the survey, will not be covered by it. If persons working abroad for shorter periods are of interest, the survey takers may want to modify the instructions regarding coverage so that short-term migrant workers are interviewed, using mainly the module for migrant workers.

The perspective of the module presented here, as for other parts of the questionnaire, is that of the country of destination. The questions presented cover, first, the contacts the migrant had with recruiting agents and whether they influenced his or her migration decision (questions 1-5); whether any special training was received in the country of origin in advance of migrating (question 6); and the type of contract and its provisions as understood by the respondent (questions 7-8). The latter is vital for understanding the conditions under which people migrate and the consequences of that migration for their welfare and for policy. Question 9 deals with payments made to labour recruiters and question 10 covers sources of help prior to the trip, including cash advances, tickets for transport, and exit and entry documents. Questions 12-13 cover the extent to which the contract was fulfilled, and question 5.14 asks about the respondent's rights to and interest in bringing other family members into the country of employment. Question 15 deals with visits to the country of origin during the period of the contract. Question 16 obtains information on problems experienced in sending remittances back "home" and can serve as an introduction to the topic (covered in Chapter 7 below). Lastly, questions 17-20 ask about the worker's overall impressions regarding his or her experience as a migrant worker.

Optional module on fertility

A second optional module, on fertility, which also covers family planning and child mortality, is relevant for those interested in studying the interrelations between international migration and changes in fertility and the use of family planning. This module has fairly standard questions and is not discussed here further, other than to note that it obtains information on past fertility by using questions on children ever borne and surviving for each woman, as well as on and date of most recent live birth. It also asks about fertility and the use of family planning prior to and after international migration, perceived fecundity, and family size desires. The questions included have been used with considerable success in several hundred national fertility surveys in developing and developed countries over the past two decades. An alternative approach is to administer a complete birth history, recording the dates of all live births and the country of birth of each, thus obtaining data on the timing of births (and use of family planning) relative to international migration.

Community-level questionnaire

The administration of a community-level questionnaire is desirable both in communities of destination and in communities of origin, since the data thus gathered are useful in establishing contextual variables that are key for the analysis of migration decisions and the consequences of international migration (see section E above). The community questionnaire should be administered to community officials or key informants and covers a wide range of community characteristics, including population size and density, community facilities, housing quality, environmental conditions, education, and production and employment. Special questions pertaining to the study of international migration include the prevalence of foreigners in the community; the extent of international migration into and out of the community; transportation linkages to markets, to the national capital, and to other countries; the existence of foreign publications and frequency of foreign television programs; and the extent of commercial trade with other countries and of foreign business investment.

3. **Questionnaire design for a survey in the country of origin of international migrants: The comparison group**

As discussed in section B above, studies of either the determinants or the consequences of international migration require that a complementary survey be carried out in the country or countries of origin of the international migrants of interest. To study the determinants of international migration, data are needed from non-migrant households in the country of origin pertaining to the mean time of out-migration of the migrants involved. When a five-year cut-off point is used in the definition of international migrant, the relevant reference date for non-migrants is 2.5 years before the survey, assuming that the survey in the country of origin is carried out at about the same time as the survey in the country of destination. Consequently, all relevant information on non-migrants should be obtained not for the time of interview but for that earlier reference date, and information gathered through both household and individual questionnaires should refer to that date.

To study the consequences of international migration, however, the appropriate reference date for data collection in the country of origin is the time of interview, so as to make possible a comparison of the situation of international migrants in the country of destination with that of non-migrants in the country of origin at the same time (see upper entries in panels 2 and 4 in table 6.2). An even better analysis of the consequences of migration – valid even if the initial status of the two groups of migrants and non-migrants is different and not fully controlled for in the sampling design – can be carried out if data on both groups are collected for both time periods – the time of interview and the time of out-migration. Thus, in the questionnaire used in the country of destination, data on the situation of international migrants are collected for both the time of interview and for the time just prior to migration (using, for instance, section 2 of the model individual questionnaire). Availability of those data permits consideration of the change over time experienced by international migrants. In the country of origin, a parallel approach implies gathering information for the equivalent two reference dates: the time of the survey and the mean time of out-migration (2.5 years before the survey if the migration of interest is restricted to the five years preceding the survey), so as to be able to compare the changes experienced over time by non-migrants. Then, the changes over time of non-migrants can be compared with those experienced by international migrants. There is, therefore, a fundamental similarity of approach in studying the determinants and the consequences of international migration. The discussion below focuses on the appropriate questionnaire design in countries of origin that is consistent with such a comprehensive approach. Questionnaires should record information on households, working individuals within households, and their communities of residence.

In the country of origin, the survey procedure in the field begins with the household questionnaire (see Annex 2, pp. 403–409), first collecting data on the composition and condition of the household at the time of the survey. Thus, the same household questionnaire used for the country of destination should be administered. Then the same information should be recorded relative to the migration reference date, that is, for about 2.5 years prior to the date of interview. Given the short time interval involved, some data pertaining to the earlier time period could be collected quickly, such as those relative to the quality of the dwelling (questions H.11-H.16 and H.19-H.20). The two screening questions added to the questionnaire for the country of origin, H.10a-H.10b, determine when the short cut is possible. However, interviewers must be

Design of surveys to investigate international migration

carefully supervised to prevent them recording "yes" under H.10a and "no" to H.10b in order to save themselves time and effort. Furthermore, because changes are relevant and likely, in no case should questions on the composition of the household (household roster), assets and income be skipped in regard to the situation 2.5 years prior to interview. With regard to the household roster, for instance, even if all the members are the same, the educational level of children of school age will almost surely have changed, and the answers to questions H.6 and H.9 are also likely to have changed for someone in the household. Trying to get at this information by asking if there has been "any change" in the household composition or in each of the characteristics recorded is more cumbersome and certain to lead to incomplete information on changes.

The one change indicated in the household questionnaire for the country of origin is the transfer to it of two optional questions from the individual questionnaire so as to avoid collecting repetitive and secondary information more than once (questions H.22-H.23). Other similar changes could be considered, such as moving to the household questionnaire questions about relatives who are citizens of other countries or about relatives living in other countries (1.4-1.7). But such changes have their limitations because the relatives involved may vary depending on the respondent, even if the latter is always a household member. Lastly, in order to obtain comprehensive data on household income question H.21a on remittances should be added to the household schedule, even for households without international out-migrants and although it will mainly capture flows to and from internal migrants. If the situation of households in the country of origin that contain no international out-migrants is to be compared with that of households that do, which often receive remittances, the issue of remittance flows should be explored.

With respect to the individual questionnaire for the country of origin, the questions to be included are mostly a subset of those used in the individual questionnaire for the country of destination and therefore require no further explanation. The information in Section 1 of the individual questionnaire for the country of origin (part B of Annex 2) is sought only for the time of interview, assuming it has not changed much over the past 2.5 years. It would be awkward to ask the respondent to differentiate the present from the recent past for most of this information, which is unlikely to change rapidly anyway. Regarding specific questions, since it is possible for non-migrants to be citizens of another country, question 1.4 is needed, questions 1.5-1.10 and 1.17-1.18 are important because they make it possible to compare the responses from non-migrants with those of international migrants with a view to studying the determinants of international migration. Questions 1.10-1.16 relate to potential migration, and sections 2 and 4 (there is no section 3 for non-migrants) record work and income information relative to both the time of the survey and the mean time of migration.

With regard to the "mean time of migration", the discussion above assumes that surveys are being undertaken simultaneously in the countries of origin and destination. Following the discussion of sections C and E above, the desirable procedure is to link the two surveys, first carrying out the survey in the country of destination in order to determine from which part of the country of origin the migrants are coming. Then, having data on the number of migrants to country Z from country A and census data for A, areas in country A can be formed into strata based on the proportion of international out-migrants to Z, and areas in the country of origin can be sampled with probabilities proportional to those proportions (or disproportionately), in a manner similar to that used in the sample design for the country of destination. Such a linked survey procedure requires that the survey in the country of origin be carried out some time after that in the country of destination. If carried out one year later, for instance, an interval that is probably reasonable, then another 12 months must be added to the 2.5 years determining the migration reference date, so that the appropriate reference period for both the individual and household questionnaires used in the country of origin (and for the community questionnaire as well) is 3.5 rather than 2.5 years. Given the human tendency to forget as time elapses after the occurrence of an event (Som, 1973), it is desirable for this lag to be minimized. Thus the survey in the country of origin should be carried out as soon as possible after the survey in the country of destination.

4. Questionnaire modifications for a survey of out-migrants based on proxy respondents in the country of origin

Surveys based on proxy responses cannot obtain data of the same depth and quality as surveys in which the responses come directly from the person experiencing the event of interest (international migration in this case), henceforth called the reference person. Nevertheless, it is sometimes necessary to study the situation of international out-migrants and their households on the basis of a survey conducted exclusively in the country of origin, either because such surveys are less expensive than those involving two or more countries or because it is not possible to carry out a survey in the jurisdiction of the country of destination. Consequently, it is important to discuss how the individual questionnaire for countries of destination can be modified to form the basis for a survey carried out exclusively in the country of origin and using proxy respondents.

To identify international migrants who have left household members in the country of origin, the first question should be "Has anyone left this household to live or work abroad for at least 6 months in the past 5 years?" Then the age of the person at the time of departure and the date of departure should be recorded to ensure that each reference person for whom information is being sought qualifies as an international migrant according to the survey definition being used. From this point on, various questions from the individual questionnaire for countries of destination should be adapted, changing the pronouns and verbs as necessary. Thus, question 1.1 becomes "When was X born?", question 1.2 is "Where was X born?", and 1.4 asks when X first left the country (asking when X first left the household is also desirable). Question 1.9 records the current citizenship of X and questions 1.10 and 1.11 inquire about the citizenship and place of residence of the immediate relatives of X. Note that in all cases the reference is to relatives of X, not to the respondent, although the respondent will almost always be a close relative of X. While the focus in the data collection is on X, it is useful to modify question 1.12 to ask if the respondent or other members of the respondent's household intend to join X abroad or have initiated any steps to do so. Question 1.13 may ask both if X understands the language of his or her current country of residence as well as if the respondent and other members of respondent's household understand it. Question 1.14 becomes, "Does X intend to remain in that country?" but since it is an attitudinal question regarding the migrant, the response from a proxy is likely to have low reliability and should only be followed by question 1.14a.

Questions about the pre-migration situation of the migrant should follow, changing the pronoun in Section 2 from "you" to "X" and all country references from "here" to "there", or to X's current country of residence. The most relevant questions are 2.2, 2.3 (adding an asterisk), 2.4 and 2.5, 2.6, 2.8 through 2.8c, 2.9, 2.12, 2.12a, 2.12c, and 2.12e. In section 4, further details about the migrant's previous work should be limited to questions 4.4a, 4.5a and 4.5 (changing the verbs from the present tense to the past tense). Although problematic, questions 4.7, 4.10 and 4.11a are important, the respondent may well know the answers so they should be posed. Questions 4.19-4.20, 4.22-23, 4.26 and 4.29 on business activities before the migrant's departure should be retained. Lastly, question 2.33 is important to establish if the optional module on migrant workers should be administered to the proxy respondent and 2.34 is useful to inquire about documents.

Questions on the post-migration (current) situation of the migrant should be more limited because the respondent usually has no first-hand knowledge about it, whereas it is more likely that he or she had some first-hand information on the pre-migration situation of the migrant. Questions suggested for inclusion are 3.3-3.4 (without the details), 3.6, 3.7 through 3.7c, 3.8, 3.9-3.9c and 3.12-3.12a. The number and identity of accompanying family members are likely to be known by the respondent. Thus questions 3.12-3.14 are relevant. Question 3.15 inquires about the return of persons who accompanied the migrant. Questions 3.16-3.17 (but pertaining only to the migrant) provide sufficient information on education. Questions 3.21-3.21c refer to visits by the migrant to the respondent's country and the respondent is likely to know the answers. The migrant's acquisition of citizenship, question 3.23, is also likely to be known by the respondent. Questions on the migrant's current work and earnings abroad should normally be limited to those in section 4 cited in the paragraph above.

5. Questions for return migrant workers in the country of origin

The optional module on migrant workers may be modified to form the basis for an individual questionnaire to be applied to migrant workers once they have returned to the country of origin. The questionnaire could be used to interview the return migrant in his or her household of residence or at an entry point, though the latter may involve complex procedures of sample selection. Virtually all the questions included in the module may be posed to return migrant workers, with minimal and obvious modifications. First, the relevant migrant workers have to be identified by asking if they (or anyone in the household, if the questionnaire is being used as part of a household survey) have returned during the past five years from working for at least six months in another country. If they have, the module for migrant workers is used. Question 1 of that module becomes "Before you left this country to work abroad, were you ever contacted by a labour recruiter or contractor?" The questions that follow need to be modified to read "Were you interested in working in that country before you had that contact" and so on. At the end, additional questions should be asked on money and goods actually brought back, and changes in the household economy resulting from the whole process (see also Chapter 7 on remittances).

6. Questions of particular interest for policy analysis

Among the questions included in the model questionnaires that provide information potentially significant for policy analysis are those on citizenship and intentions to become a citizen, those on problems encountered in getting the documents to leave the country of current residence (if a non-migrant) or encountered in actually leaving the country of previous residence and entering the country of destination (if a migrant). Such information is useful to understand the effects of regulations and laws on the entry and departure of international migrants (and on the extent of evasion of those regulations). Questions on the existence of immediate family members who are citizens of other countries or living abroad, and questions on migration intentions are both useful for indicating future migration potential. Comparing the sources of information available to migrants and non-migrants, especially non-family sources, is also likely to be useful in shaping particular interventions. Documenting the activities of labour recruiters from the perspective of international migrant workers will certainly provide insights into the mobilization of those workers. Such information is useful both for countries of origin and of destination. The questions in section 3 on the use of services by migrants and their families in the country of destination collect information that is crucial for the assessment of the larger societal effects of international migration.

The effects of all the above and their consequences for the international migrants involved cannot be understood in a vacuum. It is therefore important to adopt a comprehensive approach to data collection that permits a thorough and scientifically sound analysis of the causes and consequences of international migration. To that end, gathering complementary information at the community level permits a better assessment of the likely effects of policy and thus contributes to providing a solid basis for the formulation of measures that enhance the effects of international migration and prevent its detrimental consequences.

Notes

[1] The Demographic and Health Surveys, for instance, typically have a sample size of 5,000 households and represent one of the major international survey undertakings carried out in recent years, covering some 35 developing countries.

[2] The small numbers problem is also evident in the European Union Labour Force Surveys, which find foreign employees to constitute only 2-6 per cent of the labour force. Independent sources suggest that these surveys miss at least 4-6 per cent of the foreign workers (Migration Research Unit, University College London, 1993).

[3] The pilot survey is being carried out by the Rand Corporation through a project financed by the National Institute of Child Health and Human Development of the United States National Institutes of Health.

[4] The NIDI survey of international migration to several European countries uses a 10-year cut-off for its definition of international migrants (see section A.3 above).

[5] In fact, there have been no studies assessing the incidence of recall problems in relation to a change of residence from one country to another, an event that is likely to be memorable for the person involved. It may be that recall problems in that case are less serious than is commonly assumed.

[6] The use of the concept "population at risk" is well-established in demography, for example, in computation of birth probabilities, parity progression ratios, and mortality rates in life tables.

[7] In the Netherlands, the system is decentralized such that each municipality makes its own decision regarding the provision of information from its register to researchers. This complicates, but does not prohibit, the process of gaining access to a national sample of foreigners from the population register.

[8] If data from a recent census are not available, the results of large sample surveys may be used in some countries to construct the necessary population frame. However, if international migrants constitute a very small proportion of the whole population, the data on international migrants generated by a nationally representative survey will likely have large variances (especially if disaggregated into several geographic regions) which may render them useless for the present purposes.

[9] In unrestricted simple random sampling (srs) the sample variance is:

$$s^2 = \Sigma(y_i - \bar{y}^2)/(n - 1),$$

where y_i is the ith observation for y, $\bar{y}$ is the sample mean, and n the sample size. The standard error is s, the square root of the sample variance. In simple random sampling the sample error is inversely proportional to the square root of n (ignoring the finite population correction factor, which is trivial in sample surveys).

[10] Since most surveys use multi-stage sampling with stratification, the standard error of estimate of the key variable (which is needed to determine the desired sample size) depends on the extent to which different weights are used across strata, the number of last stage sampling units (households), their average number of respondents, and the size of the design effect. Most of these parameters will not be known *a priori*.

[11] According to the experience of the World Fertility Survey programme, in most cases costs and variances with respect to fertility variables do not vary much between strata (WFS, 1975), but this is usually not the case for socio-economic variables and other factors relevant for the analysis of international migration (see, for instance, United Nations ESCAP, 1980c, pp. 10 and 13).

[12] Including the use of stratification, the extent to which the sampling probabilities per strata are equal or not, etc. For a full discussion, see Kish, 1965, Chapters 5 and 10.

International migration statistics

[13] This statement is based on roughly similar areas and populations in sending and receiving countries. The larger the receiving country relative to the sending country, the less likely in-migrants are geographically concentrated.

[14] Data on households are typically linked to the status of the head of the household, so information on the status of the head may be easier to obtain. The first line in the census or survey schedule usually refers to the head of household, so only the place of birth of the person identified on the first line need be processed to identify heads who are foreign born.

[15] Extension to four or more stages can be made, depending on the circumstances. A two-stage sampling design may be used in cases where a more appropriate sampling frame is available.

[16] For most countries, stratification by place of residence (urban versus rural) is not useful nor recommended in surveys of international migrants because a high correlation is expected between the proportions of international migrants and the urban nature of districts anyway. Only if the correlation between place of residence and proportion of international migrants is low, and if at the same time the character of international migration to urban and rural areas is different and itself a subject of interest would it be advantageous to stratify also according to the urban or rural nature of districts. For example, if migrants to Z from A mainly went to urban areas and tended to integrate quickly into the host society while migrants to Z from C went mainly to rural areas and did not integrate quickly, it might then be of interest to have separate strata for urban and rural areas to ensure representative selections from each independently.

[17] Each of the numbers is the mean of a *category*, with each category being the range for the stratum comprising all districts with observed proportions of international migrants within that range throughout the selected PSUs. For example, the values in the text could represent strata of 0.1 and over, 0.02 to 0.09, 0.00 to 0.02, and less than 0.005.

[18] Two-phase sampling also makes it possible to collect information from part of a surveyed population using a more expensive procedure than that used for the rest. For instance, all respondents may be asked to give subjective reports about their health status, but only those in a sub-sample undergo a medical examination.

[19] To investigate either the determinants or the consequences of international migration for the international migrants themselves, only households with international migrants need be interviewed in the country of destination, provided information is obtained on non-migrants in the country of origin from a separate survey in that country (see section B).

[20] Predicted earnings are estimated on the basis of age, educational attainment, and years of work experience.

[21] Countries with exchange controls, however, can make it difficult for people to convert assets in bank accounts or other liquid assets denominated in local currency into foreign currency to help facilitate migration. The existence of such controls should be explicitly taken into account in studying the causes of international migration.

[22] An alternative approach is being used by the multi-country survey of international migration being conducted by the Netherlands Interdisciplinary Demographic Institute (see section A.3 above). The NIDI approach is to identify the "main migration actor" (MMA), and only interview that person. When a group of people, including several persons over the age of 15 years, migrate as a family, the MMA approach can save interviewing time, though the depth and quality of data must be less for certain items. Whether one approach or the other is used depends on country circumstances and survey budgets, and the frequency among migrants of families that comprise more than two persons over age 15 years.

MEASUREMENT OF REMITTANCES 7

One of the major consequences of international migration is the generation of remittances, that is, of transfers in cash or kind from migrants to households resident in the country of origin. The main sources of official data on migrants' remittances are the annual balance of payments records of countries, which are compiled in the *Balance of payments yearbook* published by the International Monetary Fund (IMF). Global estimates of official remittance flows based on balance of payments statistics suggest that remittances increased from US$43.3 billion in 1980 to US$71.1 billion in 1990 (Russell, 1992; Russell and Teitelbaum, 1992). Although the data available on migrants' remittances have several deficiencies, they suggest that, for a number of countries, the level of remittances is very significant in proportion to the country's gross domestic product (GDP) and its merchandise exports (table 7.1). Given the importance of remittances, this chapter examines the problems involved in their measurement, describing first the concepts proposed in the most recent guidelines on balance of payments statistics and discussing next the way in which countries have actually measured the relevant items. The review suggests that there are many aspects of the transfers in cash and in kind between migrants and their families remaining in the country of origin that are not reflected adequately in balance of payments statistics. The need to use specialized surveys to gather more detailed information on such transfers therefore arises. The chapter concludes with a discussion of the types of questions that may be added to a specialized survey to obtain the necessary information (see also Chapter 6).

A. DEFINITION OF REMITTANCES IN THE SYSTEM OF NATIONAL ACCOUNTS AND IN THE BALANCE OF PAYMENTS

Box 7.1 presents the standard components of balance of payments statements. The balance of payments is a statistical statement designed to provide, for a specific period of time, a systematic record of an economy's

International migration statistics

Table 7.1. Migrant remittances in selected countries

Region/Country	Year	US$ millions				Remittances as % of	
		Workers' remittances	Migrant transfers	Labour income remitted	Total	GDP	Value of merchandise exports
Asia							
Bangladesh	1992		..		911.8	3.8	47.9
India	1990	2 352.0		32.0	2 384.0	1.6	13.3
Indonesia	1992	184.0[1]	..	..	184.0	0.14	0.5
Korea, Rep. of	1992	..	5.0	705.0	710.0	0.2	0.9
Pakistan	1992	1 566.0	..	..	1 566.0	3.7	21.5
Sri Lanka	1992	547.8	..	..	547.8	6.2	22.0
Thailand	1992	..	..	1 126.0	1 126.0	1.02	3.4
Africa							
Burkina Faso	1992	170.0	..	..	170.0	6.0	119.7
Lesotho	1992	..	..	455.4	455.4	84.9	..
Mali	1992	141.7	..	..	141.7	5.0	36.5
North Africa/ Middle East							
Algeria	1991	233.0	..	..	233.0	0.7	1.9
Egypt	1992	6 104.0	..	..	6 104.0	18.1	200.1
Jordan	1992	843.7	..	..	843.7	20.6	90.4
Morocco	1992	2 170.0	..		2 170.0	7.6	54.5
Senegal	1992	94.1	..	..	94.1	1.4	14.0
Sudan	1992	123.7	..	..	123.7	0.4[2]	30.0
Europe							
Cyprus	1992	..	22.4	81.0	103.4	1.6[3]	11.4[4]
Greece	1992	2 366.0	..	165.0	2 531.0	3.7	25.7
Portugal	1992	4 650.0	..	112.0	4 762.0	5.9	25.6
Spain	1992	2 218.0	77.0	241.0	2 536.0	0.4	3.9[5]
Turkey	1992	3 008.0	..	..	3 008.0	3.1	20.4
Latin America/ Caribbean							
Bolivia	1992	0.6	0.5	2.4	3.5	0.06	0.45
Colombia	1992	630.0	..	16.0	646.0	1.3	9.3
Dominican Republic	1992	346.6	..	..	346.6	4.5	61.2
Jamaica	1992	159.0	..	63.4	222.4	0.7	20.9
Mexico	1992	2 706.0	..	630.0	3 336.0	1.01	12.2

[1] World Bank estimates   [2] At current market prices, December 1991.   [3] At market prices, December 1992.   [4] Exports f.o.b. in trade returns.   [5] Merchandise exports f.o.b.   .. not available.
Sources: (i) IMF: *Balance of payments statistics year book 1994*, table 2. (ii) World Bank: *World tables 1994*, table 19. (iii) World Bank: *World development report 1994*, table 3; *World development report 1993*, table 3. (iv) Economist Intelligence Unit (EIU): *Country profile 1994-95*.

Measurement of remittances

transactions with the rest of the world. An economy is considered to be comprised of economic entities, described as "residents", which have closer associations with that specific economy than with any other. Economic entities that have closer associations with other economies are described as "non-residents". Consequently, the balance of payments reflects transactions between "residents" and "non-residents". Economic transactions include: transactions in goods, services, and income; transactions in financial assets and liabilities; and transfers in which real or financial resources are provided by one party to another without obtaining anything in exchange, that is, with no *quid pro quo*. The balance of payments classifies transactions as belonging to the current account or to the capital and financial account. The current account includes transactions in real resources (goods, services, income) and current transfers, while the capital and financial account shows the financing of real resource flows (generally through capital transfers or transactions of financial instruments).

Box 7.1. Balance of payments: Standard components

1. 1. *Current account*
2. A. *Goods and services*
3.   a. *Goods*
4.   1. General merchandise
5.   2. Goods for processing
6.   3. Repairs on goods
7.   4. Goods procured in ports by carrier
8.   5. Non-monetary gold
9.   5.1 Held as a store of value
10.   5.2 Other
11.   b. *Services*
12.   1. Transportation
13.   1.1 Sea transport
14.   1.1.1 Passenger
15.   1.1.2 Freight
16.   1.1.3 Other
17.   1.2 Air transport
18.   1.2.1 Passenger
19.   1.2.2 Freight
20.   1.2.3 Other
21.   1.3 Other transport
22.   1.3.1 Passenger
23.   1.3.2 Freight
24.   1.3.3 Other
25.   2. Travel
26.   2.1 Business
27.   2.2 Personal
28.   3. Communications services
29.   4. Construction services
30.   5. Insurance services
31.   6. Financial services
32.   7. Computer and information services
33.   8. Royalties and licence fees
34.   9. Other business services
35.   9.1 Merchanting and other trade-related services
36.   9.2 Operational leasing services
37.   9.3 Miscellaneous business, professional and technical services
38.   10. Personal, cultural and recreational services
39.   10.1 Audiovisual and related services
40.   10.2 Other personal, cultural and recreational services

International migration statistics

41.	11.	Government services, n.i.e.		73.		1.1.3 Other capital
42.	B.	Income		74.		1.2 In reporting economy
43.		1. **Compensation of employees**		75.		1.2.1 Equity capital
				76.		1.2.2 Reinvested earnings
44.		2. Investment income				
45.		2.1 Direct investment		77.		1.2.3 Other capital
46.		2.1.1 Income on equity		78.	2.	Portfolio investment
47.		2.1.2 Income on debt (interest)		79.		2.1 Assets
				80.		2.1.1 Equity securities
48.		2.2 Portfolio investment		81.		2.1.2 Debt securities
49.		2.2.1 Income on equity (dividends)		82.		2.2 Liabilities
				83.		2.2.1 Equity securities
50.		2.2.2 Income on debt (interest)		84.		2.2.2 Debt securities
				85.	3.	Other investment
51.		2.3 Other investment		86.		3.1 Assets
52.	C.	Current transfers		87.		3.1.1 Trade credits
53.		1. General government		88.		3.1.2 Loans
54.		2. Other sectors		89.		3.1.3 Currency and deposits
55.		2.1 **Workers' remittances**				
56.		2.2 Other transfers		90.		3.1.4 Other assets
57.	2.	*Capital and financial account*		91.		3.2 Liabilities
58.	A.	*Capital account*		92.		3.2.1 Trade credits
59.		1. Capital transfers		93.		3.2.2 Loans
60.		1.1 General government		94.		3.2.3 Currency and deposits
61.		1.1.1 Debt forgiveness				
62.		1.1.2 Other		95.		3.2.4 Other liabilities
63.		1.2 Other sectors		96.	4.	Reserve assets
64.		1.2.1 **Migrants' transfers**		97.		4.1 Monetary gold
				98.		4.2 Special drawing rights
65.		1.2.2 Debt forgiveness				
66.		1.2.3 Other		99.		4.3 Reserve position in the Fund
67.		2. Acquisition/disposal of non-product, non-financial assets		100.		4.4 Foreign exchange
				101.		4.4.1 Currency and deposits
68.	B.	*Financial account*				
69.		1. Direct investment		102.		4.4.2 Securities
70.		1.1 Abroad		103.		4.5 Other claims
71.		1.1.1 Equity capital				
72.		1.1.2 Reinvested earnings				

Source: IMF. 1993: *Balance of payments manual: Fifth edition* (Washington, DC), pp. 43–48.

Measurement of remittances

Given the nature of the transactions it reflects, an essential aspect of the balance of payments is the definition of "resident" and "non-resident". In the *Balance of payments manual: Fifth edition* (IMF, 1993) and the *Balance of payments compilation guide* (IMF, 1995), the definitions adopted of "resident" and "non-resident" coincide with those presented in the *System of national Accounts 1993* (United Nations, 1993b). Because those definitions are not simple and they have important implications for the measurement of remittances and other transactions involving international migrants, the full text characterizing "residents" and "non-residents" is reproduced in box 7.2. As the text notes, the concept of "centre of economic interest" is used to distinguish "residents" from "non-residents". Given that a household is defined as "a small group of persons who share the same living accommodation, who pool some, or all, of their income and wealth and who consume certain types of goods and services collectively, mainly housing and food" (United Nations, 1993b, para. 4.132), there is a strong presumption that the household's centre of economic interest coincides with that of each of its members and that it is determined by the place in which the household lives. Consequently, at the level of individuals, the definition of "resident" recommended for use in balance of payments statements links every person to a household and tends to equate the country in which the household has a dwelling with the centre of economic interest of each household member. Within such a framework, it is straightforward to make allowance for international migration when a household moves in its entirety from one country to another (such a move implies a change in the "centre of economic interest"). It is somewhat more problematic, however, to allow for the migration of only selected household members. The recommended treatment of such cases is to assume that the centre of economic interest of migrant members of a household remains the same as that of the household provided the length of absence of those members does not exceed a year. In those cases, migrant members continue to be considered residents of the country in which the household to which they belong is located. Only when the duration of absence is a year or longer do migrant members of households cease to be considered residents of the country in which the household lives. However, the recommendations suggest that duration of absence need not be the only criterion used to assign "centre of economic interest" to migrants. Thus, the fact that a migrant "sets up a new household or joins a household in the country of work" or that most of a migrant's consumption takes place in the country in which he or she lives or works would also lead to a "non-resident" status with respect to the country of origin. Taken as a whole, the recommendations on how to assign "resident" and "non-resident" status to mobile individuals for balance of payments purposes rely on criteria that are not easy to implement in practice and that often lack precision. Consequently, although the balance of payments recommendations make clear distinctions between different types of economic transactions involving international migrants, those recommendations are often not followed in practice because of the difficulties involved in distinguishing which international migrants change their centre of economic interest and which do not.

> Box 7.2. The concept of residence in the 1993 system of national accounts
>
> The sectors and sub-sectors of an economy are composed of two main types of institutional units which are resident in the economy: (a) households covering individuals who make up a household, and (b) legal and social entities, such as corporations and quasi-corporations (e.g. branches of foreign direct investors), non-profit institutions (NPIs), and the government of that economy. Residence is an important attribute of an institutional unit in respect of the rest of the world account, which records transactions between residents and non-residents. The residency status of producers determines the limits of domestic production and affects the measurement of gross domestic product (GDP) and many important flows in the system of national accounts. The concept and coverage of residence in the system are identical to those in the *Balance of payments manual: Fifth edition* (IMF, 1993).
>
> The concept of residence used for national accounts is not based on nationality or legal criteria (although it may be similar to concepts of residence which are used for exchange control, tax or other purposes in many countries). Moreover, the boundaries of a country which may be recognized for political purposes may not always be appropriate for economic purposes and it is necessary to introduce the concept of the "economic territory" of a country as the relevant geographical area to which the concept of residence is applied. An institutional unit is then said to be a resident unit when it has a centre of economic interest in the economic territory of the country in question.
>
> The economic territory of a country consists of the geographic territory administered by a government within which persons, goods, and capital circulate freely. In the case of maritime countries, it includes any islands belonging to that country which are subject to exactly the same fiscal and monetary authorities as the mainland, so that goods and persons may move freely to and from such islands without any kind of customs or immigration formalities. The economic territory of a country includes: (a) the airspace, territorial waters, and continental shelf lying in international waters over which the country enjoys exclusive rights or over which it has, or claims to have, jurisdiction in respect of the right to fish or to exploit fuels or minerals below the seabed; (b) territorial enclaves in the rest of the world (clearly demarcated areas of land which are located in other countries and which are used by the government which owns or rents them for diplomatic, military, scientific or other purposes – embassies, consulates, military bases, scientific stations, information or immigration offices, aid agencies, etc. – with the formal political agreement of the government of the country in which they are physically located); goods or persons may move freely between a country and its territorial enclaves abroad, but become subject to control by the government of the country in which they are located if they move out of the enclave; and (c) any free zones, or bonded warehouses or factories operated by offshore enterprises under customs control (these form part of the economic territory of the country in which they are physically located).
>
> The economic territory of an international organization consists of the territorial enclave, or enclaves, over which it has jurisdiction, these consist of clearly demarcated areas of land or structures which the

international organization owns or rents and which it uses for the purposes for which the organization was created by formal agreements with the country, or countries, in which the enclave or enclaves are physically located.

It follows that the economic territory of a country does not include the territorial enclaves used by foreign governments or international organizations which are physically located within the geographical boundaries of that country.

A member of a resident household who leaves the economic territory to return to that same household after a limited period of time (i.e. less than one year) continues to be a resident even if that individual makes frequent journeys outside the economic territory. The individual's centre of economic interest remains in the economy in which the household is resident. The following categories of such individuals are treated as residents:

(a) Travellers or visitors, that is, individuals who leave the economic territory for less than one year for recreation, business, health, education, religious or other purposes;
(b) Individuals who work some or all of the time in a different economic territory from that in which the household to which they belong is resident.

An institutional unit is said to have a centre of economic interest within a country when there exists some location – dwelling, place of production, or other premises – within the economic territory of the country on, or from, which it engages, and intends to continue to engage, in economic activities and trans actions on a significant scale, either indefinitely or over a finite but long period of time. The location need not be fixed so long as it remains within the economic territory.

In most cases, it is reasonable to assume that an institutional unit has a centre of economic interest in a country if it has already engaged in economic activities and transactions on a significant scale in the country for one year or more, or it intends to do so. The conduct of economic activities and transactions over a period of one year normally implies a centre of interest, but the choice of any specific period of time is somewhat arbitrary and it must be emphasized that one year is suggested only as a guideline and not as an inflexible rule.

The ownership of land and structures within the economic territory of a country is deemed to be sufficient in itself for the owner to have a centre of economic interest in that country. Land and buildings can obviously only be used for purposes of production in the country in which they are located and their owners, in their capacity as owners, are subject to the laws and regulations of that country. It may happen, however, that an owner is resident in another country and does not have any economic interest in the country in which he owns the land or buildings themselves. In that case, the owner is treated as if he transferred his ownership to a notional institutional unit which is actually resident in the country. The notional unit is itself treated as being entirely owned and controlled by the non-resident actual owner, in much the same way as a quasi-corporation is owned and controlled by its owner. In this way, the rents and rentals paid by the tenants of the land or buildings are deemed to be paid to a notional resident unit which in turn makes a transfer of property income to the actual non-resident owner.

The residence of households and individuals

A household has a centre of economic interest when it maintains a dwelling, or succession of dwellings, within the country which members of the household treat, and use, as their principal residence. All individuals who belong to the same household must be resident in the same country. If a member of an existing household were to be considered no longer resident in the country in which the household is resident, that individual would cease to be a member of that household.

(i) Workers who work for part of the year in another country, in some cases in response to the varying seasonal demand for labour, and then return to their households;
(ii) Border workers who regularly cross the frontier each day or somewhat less regularly (e.g. each week) to work in a neighbouring country;
(iii) The staff of international organizations who work in the enclave of those organizations;
(iv) The locally recruited staff of foreign embassies, consulates, military bases, etc.;
(v) The crews of ships, aircraft, or other mobile equipment operating partly, or wholly, outside the economic territory.

The circumstances in which an individual is likely to cease to be a resident are when that individual lives or works continuously for one year or more in a foreign country. If the individual rejoins his or her original household only very infrequently for short visits and sets up a new household or joins a household in the country of work, the individual can no longer be treated as a member of the original household. Most of the individual's consumption takes place in the country in which he or she lives or works, and the individual clearly has a centre of economic interest there.

Even if an individual continues to be legally employed and paid by an enterprise which is resident in his or her home country, that individual should be treated as resident in the host country if the individual works continuously in that country for one year or more. In these circumstances the person has to be treated as being employed either by a quasi-corporation which is owned by the enterprise and which is resident in the country in which the work takes place, or, alternatively, as being employed by a foreign agent. The latter case is intended to cover technical assistance personnel working in a foreign country on contracts or assignments of one year or more. Technical assistance personnel on long-term assignments should be treated as residents of the country in which they work and deemed to be employed by their host government on behalf of the government, or international organization, which is actually financing their work. A transfer of funds should then be imputed from the government or international organization which actually employs them to the host government to cover the cost of their salaries and allowances.

The situation of military personnel and civil servants, including diplomats, whom a government employs in its own enclaves abroad, is different. Those enclaves – military bases, embassies and the like – form part of the economic territory of the employing government and the personnel often live as well as work in the enclaves. Therefore, the employees whom a government transfers to work in such enclaves continue to have a centre of economic interest in their home country however long they work in the enclaves. They continue to be resident in their home country even if they live in dwellings outside the enclaves.

> Students should be treated as residents of their country of origin however long they study abroad, provided they continue to form part of a household in that country. In these circumstances, their centre of economic interest remains in the country of origin rather than the country in which they study. Medical patients abroad are also treated as residents of their country of origin even if their stay is one year or more, provided they continue to form part of a household in their country of origin.
>
> As to the treatment of individuals who have several international residences, where they may remain for short periods of time during a given year (for instance, three months in each of four countries), the centre of economic interest for such individuals often is "international", not a specific economy. Considerations should be given to such factors as tax status, citizenship (can be dual), etc., but the System does not recommend a specific treatment. The latter is left to the discretion of the economies concerned; the treatment should be coordinated, if possible, to foster international comparability.
>
> *Sources*: United Nations (1993b); IMF (1993).

According to the balance of payments recommendations, there are several international economic transactions that may involve international migrants. The first, included under the title *compensation of employees* (1.B.1 in box 7.1), comprises wages, salaries and other remuneration, in cash or in kind, earned by individuals in an economy other than the one in which they are resident for work performed (and paid by) a resident of that economy. Included are contributions paid by resident employers on behalf of non-resident employees to social security schemes or to private insurance schemes or pension funds – including imputed contributions to unfunded pension schemes – to secure benefits for employees. The non-resident employees of interest include seasonal or other short-term migrant workers staying in the country of employment for less than a year and border workers whose centre of economic interest is in their own economies. As the *Balance of payments compilation guide* (IMF, 1995) indicates, the credits part of the balance of payments includes two components in compensation of employees: (*a*) compensation earned by residents of the compiling economy working for enterprises abroad; and (*b*) compensation earned by local staff working for foreign embassies and similar institutions – including international organizations – and by local staff working for non-resident enterprises operating in the compiling economy. On the debit side, there are also two components: (*a*) compensation earned by non-residents working for resident enterprises in the compiling economy; and (*b*) compensation earned by local staff working for the compiling economy's foreign embassies and similar institutions located abroad and by local staff working for enterprises that operate abroad but are regarded as residents of the compiling economy. Note that this characterization of the components of the compensation of employees makes clear that it includes the earnings of both persons residing in economies that differ from the economies in which they work and who may therefore be considered international migrants under certain circumstances, and persons residing in their own economies. Consequently, even disregarding the problems involved in estimating the compensation of employees, this item is not necessarily a good indicator of the impact of short-term international migration (that lasting less than a year) on the compiling economy.

The instructions for the compilation of balance of payments statements further note that when residents of the compiling country work abroad for less than a year, their expenditures while abroad for food, clothes, accommodation etc. should be included in the debit part of the travel entry (1.A.b.2 in box 7.1) and any taxes paid to the government of the economy where they work or contributions to social insurance schemes of that economy should be included in the debit part of current transfers relative to the government or other sectors, as appropriate (see 1.C in box 7.1).

The second major item of the balance of payments statements that relates to international migrants is *workers' remittances*. According to the United Nations (1993b, para. 8.95): "Remittances are one type of current transfers between households. They consist of all current transfers in cash or kind from non-residents to resident households. Usually they are regular transfers between members of the same family resident in different countries, with the persons abroad being absent for a year or longer." However, it is recognized that "the distinction between those individuals whose earnings are to be classified as compensation of employees (persons who are not residents of the economy where they work) and migrants (persons who have become residents of the economy by virtue of being expected to live there for a year or more) is often hard to draw in practice" (United Nations, 1993b, para. 14.120).

Third and lastly, the balance of payments makes explicit allowance for the transfers of financial assets by migrants by including a specific item on *migrants' transfers* under the category of capital transfers. Capital transfers are those that transfer ownership of a fixed (capital) asset, are linked to the acquisition or disposal of a fixed asset, or involve forgiveness of a liability by a creditor. According to the *Balance of payments manual: Fifth edition* (IMF, 1993, p. 84), "in the strictest sense, migrants' transfers are not transactions between two parties but contra-entries to flows of goods and changes in financial items that arise from the migration (change of residence for at least a year) of individuals from one economy to another. The transfers to be recorded are thus equal to the net worth of the migrants." The *Manual* further specifies that "enterprises (including those that employ the land, structures, and movable capital goods that are not actually transferred) in which migrants retain ownership after departure become foreign claims of the migrants and, consequently, of the economies to which they have migrated. Migrants' claims on/liabilities to other residents of their former economies or claims on/liabilities to residents of a third economy also become foreign claims/liabilities of the economies to which they have migrated. Migrants' claims on/liabilities to the latter economies become claims between its residents. Changes in the net financial assets of the economies concerned and the offsets are recorded at the time of migration. In practice, it is recognized that few countries are in a position to record all assets, other than possessions and funds accompanying migrants upon entry to new economies, in the balance of payments." (IMF, 1993, p. 84).

The above descriptions of the different items in the balance of payments that include transactions involving international migrants or persons who have moved from one economy to another indicate the complexity of the concepts involved, not only with respect of the kinds of economic transactions covered but also with respect to the identification of different types of international movers. In that regard, although the latest editions of the *Balance of payments manual* and *Guide* of the IMF consistently make a distinction between persons who move from one economy to another for less than a year, who are not considered migrants for balance of payments purposes, and those who move for a year or longer and are therefore considered migrants, terms such as "foreign workers" or "nationals working abroad" are also used on occasion, especially in referring to actual sources of information about international migration or in relation to the international transactions reporting system (IMF, 1995, pp. 32, 141 and 143). Although an attempt is made to redefine "foreign worker" in terms of a duration of stay of at least a year (IMF, 1995, p. 141), the very use of the term suggests that actual balance of payments accounts are unlikely to abide strictly by the definitions of "resident" and "non-resident" underlying international recommendations and will more likely reflect reality by incorporating citizenship into the estimation of the relevant items in the balance of payments statements.

Given the complexity of the issues involved, it is not surprising to find that country practices vary considerably regarding the allocation of different types of transactions involving international migrants. Interestingly, the *Balance of payments compilation guide* (IMF, 1995) suggests that statistics on international migration be used to estimate some of the components of balance of payments statements that are not easily measured in terms of actual transactions. Yet, as chapters 3 and 4 of this book have shown, most sources of international migration statistics fail to make a distinction between international migrants who stay a year or more in the country of destination and those who stay less than a year. There is also very little information on the migration of household units or even of family units. Those statistical lacunae account, in part, for the varied and not necessarily consistent practices followed by different countries in assessing the magnitude of international transactions related to international migrants. Those practices are reviewed below, focusing particularly on the measurement of workers' remittances. Before proceeding, it is important to point out that the new guidelines for the production of balance of payments statements are too recent to have been implemented by countries. Consequently, the country practices examined below usually reflect the previous edition, the *Balance of payments manual: Fourth edition* (IMF, 1977), which included essentially the same categories of transactions relevant to international migration as

International migration statistics

those described above. Some terminology, however, was modified. Compensation of employees used to be called "labour income". In addition, there was a category labelled "other private transfers" under current transfers which included various types of transfers between residents and non-residents that are of relevance.

B. PROBLEMS INVOLVED IN MEASURING MIGRANTS' REMITTANCES AND OTHER TRANSACTIONS RELATIVE TO INTERNATIONAL MIGRATION

As already suggested, it is not easy to estimate the different items in the balance of payments statements that are relevant for the analysis of the impact of international mobility. Thus, the data on financial flows provided by commercial banks to the central bank of many countries usually cannot make the relevant distinction between transactions involving short-term migrants and persons who change country of abode for at least a year. Likewise, while transfers in kind by migrants may be recorded and included in total imports, migrants' transfers proper are difficult to measure with any accuracy and usually become part of "errors and omissions". Because of these data difficulties, countries have tended to report under a single item (usually under workers' remittances) the transfers made by all types of migrants, irrespective of their length of stay. Some countries have not even made a distinction between workers' remittances and other private transfers, tending to report both under a single item (usually as "other private transfers").

Table 7.2 presents data on gross inflows of the relevant sub-categories of current transfers for selected countries. The data serve to highlight some of the problems associated with differential reporting practices and illustrate the major differences in recording transfers between the old and the new classification systems. With regard to differential reporting, note that in the Philippines and Thailand the major emphasis is on compensation of employees (84 per cent and 67 per cent of gross inflows are recorded under this item, respectively), whereas other countries largely record transfers under workers' remittances (except for Bangladesh which records a higher percentage of receipts under other transfers than under workers' remittances). Interpreted at their face value, these data would suggest that the majority of persons moving from the Philippines and Thailand to work in other economies do so for periods of less than a year, whereas those originating in the other countries considered remain abroad for a year or longer. The existence of such marked differences between countries is not validated by available data on worker migration, a fact that suggests that the differences in balance of payments statistics arise from different practices rather than from a real difference in the phenomenon that they are supposed to reflect.

Given existing reporting and estimation problems related to the crucial items in the balance of payments statistics, those attempting to estimate the

Measurement of remittances

Table 7.2. Gross inflows of private unrequited transfers (including remittances) of selected countries, 1993 (in million US$)

Balance of payments components		Bangladesh	Dominican Republic	Mexico	Morocco	Pakistan	Philippines	Sudan (1992)	Thailand
Old classification (1977)	New classification (1993)								
Current account	**Current account**								
Goods, services and income	*Income*								
Labour income	Compensation of employees			647.0		406.0[1]	2 276.0		1 126.0
Unrequited transfers	*Current transfers*								
Workers' remittances	Workers' remittances	1 004.2	361.8	2 379.0	1 959.0	1 436.0	311.0	123.7	
Other private transfers	Other transfers	1 296.0		212.0	210.0	526.0	134.0		548.0
	Capital and financial account								
	Capital account								
Migrant transfers	Migrant transfers	NA	NA	NA	NA	NA	NA	NA	NA

[1] Pakistan includes these under "other goods, services and income" category. NA = not available.
Source: IMF (1993, 1994).

International migration statistics

global flow of remittances have usually added up the figures corresponding to the three relevant items – compensation of employees, workers' remittances and migrant transfers (Swamy, 1981; Russell and Teitelbaum, 1992). Such an approach has serious limitations and the estimates obtained should be interpreted with caution. It is often unclear how the data concerning compensation of employees are obtained and reported by the economies of origin. Estimates are likely to be derived from rough assessments of the stock of migrant workers abroad and assumptions concerning their average wages. Where this is the case, not only can the assumptions made regarding the size, composition or wage level of the migrant population be questioned, but there is the additional problem that the total compensation of employees cannot be considered as equivalent to the amount that is eventually remitted to the economy of origin to be usable in that economy. Moreover, to the extent that workers' remittances are reported separately and on the basis of actual reports of transfers through commercial banks, failure to distinguish which of those transfers are made by workers whose compensation has already been imputed and allocated to the compensation of employees item will lead to double counting and overestimate the gains by the economy of origin associated with international migration.

Another major problem is that data needed to estimate the relevant items of the balance of payments statement are not available for some countries. Recording and reporting practices differ considerably among countries (selected examples are presented in boxes 7.3 to 7.6). Thus, some countries include the value of in kind transfers and others do not. In India, for instance, reporting of remittances below 10,000 rupees has not been required (Russell, 1986).

This variety of practices has important implications for the calculation of key macro-economic indicators for labour-sending countries. The calculation of the gross national income (GNI) of a country, for instance, should in theory include only the production activities of residents. Consequently, it should incorporate the compensation of employees (i.e. the salaries and wages earned by residents from non-residents) but exclude workers' remittances (United Nations, 1993b, para. 2.181). Yet, countries do not necessarily follow these guidelines, partly because, as pointed out above, the basic data do not permit a clear distinction between compensation of employees and migrants' remittances. Thus, countries such as Bangladesh, Pakistan and the Philippines include workers' remittances in the calculation of GNI whereas India, Indonesia, Sri Lanka and Thailand do not.[1]

In addition to the methodological problems involved in distinguishing transactions that are part of compensation of employees from those that are workers' remittances, the measurement of the latter is fraught with difficulties because a significant proportion of the international transactions that can be considered remittances do not flow through official channels. In Sudan, for instance, only 24 per cent of a sample of international migrants reported using official channels to send remittances (Serageldin et al., 1981) and similar results

> ### Box 7.3. Pakistan: National reporting system
>
> Officially recorded data on remittances include only those foreign currency transfers which are made through regular banking channels and converted into domestic currency. Since 1984, an attempt has been made to include remittances in kind by incorporating contra entries for imports under personal baggage, the non-repatriation investment scheme and sales through duty free shops in Pakistan in the official remittances data. The share of official remittances in kind has ranged between 4 and 8 per cent of total recorded flows between 1985/86 and 1990/91 (Pakistan, State Bank, 1991).
>
> The inflow of remittances through informal channels is estimated at 30 per cent of officially recorded figures, although the choice between methods of remitting funds is likely to have been significantly influenced by the introduction of financial instruments denominated in foreign exchange and other measures designed to provide incentives to channel funds through the formal system. Nevertheless, the *Hundi* system is still popular because of its convenience: under this system funds get transferred immediately whereas the banking system can sometimes take up to two weeks.

> ### Box 7.4. Thailand
>
> Thailand records most of the transactions related to international migration as compensation of employees (wages or salaries of those who have been abroad less than one year). They amounted to 30.9 billion baht in 1993 (approximately US$1.13 billion). Transfers by migrants staying abroad at least one year are included among "other transfers" under current transfers. They amounted to 6.30 billion baht in 1993 (US$252 million). The actual amount of remittance inflows is therefore not known.
>
> With regard to the outflow of remittances (that is, money remitted by migrants in Thailand), migrants' transfers are recorded but are included in the category of "other transfers". Thus, there is no way of determining the outflow of remittances or net remittances. As migration inflows to Thailand grow, the need for better recording of inflows and outflows of remittances increases.

are common in other countries (see table 7.3). Informal channels are more likely to be used when the exchange rate of the country receiving remittances is overvalued, when there are taxes levied on remittances or when foreign exchange restrictions are in place.

There are several mechanisms to transfer earnings to the home country through informal channels. An important one is the *Hundi* system whereby the migrant transfers a sum in foreign currency to an agent in the country of destination under the agreement that the equivalent amount in the currency of

International migration statistics

> **Box 7.5. Republic of Korea: Recording of remittances**
>
> During the early 1980s when the economy was small and many Koreans were working abroad, particularly in the construction industry in the Middle East, remittances accounted for a significant proportion of GNP. Their significance has since declined. In 1993, the total inflow of remittances amounted to US$341 million. Remittances are defined as income transfers made by the Koreans working abroad to their relations in the Republic of Korea. These are recorded by commercial banks when the transfer is made and money is converted into local currency. Those transactions are reported to the central bank every week or month. Transfers of goods are recorded by customs officials and data tapes are made available to the central bank for consolidation of data on remittances.
>
> Remittance data are recorded by country of origin, but the breakdown is not published by the central bank. One problem is that the transactions of some commercial banks are not yet computerized and the central bank cannot process them in detail. Moreover, no information is obtained concerning transfers by period of stay of workers abroad.
>
> Resident Koreans are not allowed to keep a foreign currency account either in the Republic of Korea or abroad. However, non-resident Koreans (defined as persons working abroad for more than two years) have been allowed since 1993 to keep a foreign currency account in the Republic of Korea. Upon their return to the country, they become residents again and are obliged to bring back their money from abroad within 180 days. However, these rules have recently been relaxed and return migrants are permitted to keep an account abroad up to a maximum of US$20,000. Foreign currency deposits in the Republic of Korea held by the non-resident Koreans are shown as liabilities in the capital account of the balance of payments.

the country of origin of the migrant (determined at an exchange rate that is usually above the official one) is transferred by the agent's counterpart in that country to the migrant's family or nominee. This system or a variation of it is used in Bangladesh, India, Pakistan and the Philippines. Because the transactions it involves do not require actual transfers of money from one country to another, they are not reflected in normal balance of payments statements based on data produced by the banking system (Kazi, 1989; Alburo and Abella, 1992; Saith, 1989). Migrant workers often avoid banks because of the inefficiency and high cost of banking services. In countries where there is a wide gap between official and black market rates, the banks usually offer an unattractive rate of exchange. In Bangladesh, lack of banking facilities and unfamiliarity with banking procedures has also contributed to the widespread use of unofficial channels (Quibria and Thant, 1988). Private agents or "money couriers" have the added advantage of being able to deliver funds in remote places where banks do not operate. In the South Pacific, migrants wishing to remit funds to some of the more remote islands tend to use the services of one of the large, international retail merchants having branches in both the sending and receiving countries because they are a more efficient channel than the banks or post office (Brown, 1995).

Measurement of remittances

> **Box 7.6. Sri Lanka: Private transfers**
>
> Sri Lanka reports transfers made by migrants abroad under "private transfers" or "other transfers" in the balance of payments statement. The data on private transfers are reported periodically under the international transactions reporting system (ITRS) by all commercial banks operating in the country. These records are then classified into various subgroups depending on the purpose of the transaction and grouped according to the standard IMF classification.
>
> Private transfers include voluntary remittances for the maintenance of dependants; contributions to or by missionaries, educational or benevolent institutions; migrant transfers; transfers of assets; conversions of funds in non-resident foreign currency accounts (NRFC) and resident foreign currency accounts (RFC) into Sri Lanka rupees, and other private transfers. Prior to 1977, tight exchange restrictions prevailed and therefore, for each international transaction (both inward and outward), the applicant had to complete a form, as required under the Exchange Control Act, giving detailed information regarding the transaction. This information enabled the central bank to classify all transactions in a comprehensive manner, including the origin and type of transaction. However, with the gradual relaxation of exchange control regulations, form filling has been reduced and in the case of inward transfers has been completely eliminated. As a result, commercial banks are now entrusted with the task of classifying inward transfers for balance of payments purposes and are unable to allocate properly some transactions or to establish the country of origin of transactions. In the past, most bank drafts and other forms of transfers were denominated in the currency of the country of origin and that country could thus be identified. At present, most transfers are denominated in US dollars irrespective of the country of origin.
>
> Workers' remittances and compensation of employees are not distinguished in the balance of payments statements of Sri Lanka, nor are transfers in kind included in official statistics. The data on private transfers are classified by major geographical region, but not by the period of stay abroad of those making the transfer.

Table 7.3. Remittances sent through informal channels as a percentage of total remittances

Country	Source	Estimation period	Estimate[1]
Bangladesh	Mahmud (1989)	1981-86	20
India[2]	ESCAP (1986)	1983	40
Korea, Rep. of	Hyun (1989)	1980-85	8
Pakistan	ILO/ARTEP (1987)	1986	43
Philippines	Tan and Canlas (1989)	1982	60
Sri Lanka	Rodrigo and Jayatissa (1989)	1980-85	13
Thailand	Tingsabadh (1989)	1977-86	18

[1] Derived as $(TR - RB)/TR \times 100$, where TR = total estimated remittances, and RB = remittances through banking channels. For Pakistan and India the estimates are directly from the given source. For other countries, they were derived using data reported in the given sources. [2] Estimate represents remittance behaviour of migrant workers from Kerala only.
Source: Adapted from Athukorala (1993a), table 2.3.

International migration statistics

A more sophisticated way of avoiding exchange controls is a currency swap. While abroad, migrants operate on behalf of clients by buying goods for them or settling their invoices. In return, the client pays into the migrant's bank account in the country of origin an equivalent sum in that country's currency (at the black market rate). This practice has become common in the Maghreb countries, whose citizens are permitted to buy only restricted amounts of foreign currency (Stalker, 1994). Another informal channel is to hand-carry foreign exchange savings or send money through friends and relatives. Saith (1989) notes that in some Asian countries a traveller can carry up to US$10,000 in foreign currency without having to declare it. If at some stage the banking system is used for conversion of foreign currency into domestic currency, the funds are entered in the balance of payments account, but generally under the heading of travel (see box 7.1).

Sending or carrying remittances in the form of goods (remittances in kind) – either for personal use or for resale in the informal market – is also a common channel, especially when there are significant price differences between the countries of origin and destination of migrants. The goods involved range from inexpensive consumer items to highly priced durable goods and investment goods, which are either smuggled into the country or imported legally as personal effects (Saith, 1989). Kazi (1989) points out that this practice is widespread in Pakistan where remittances in kind amounted to an estimated 16 per cent of cash transfers among urban migrants and 11 per cent among those returning to rural areas. Remittances in kind appear to have become more significant since the introduction of liberal import policies allowing duty free imports under the "personal baggage/gift scheme" which includes such items as refrigerators and air conditioners. The practice of sending remittances in kind is also widespread among the remittance-dependent economies of the South Pacific (Brown, 1995). However, goods brought in under "personal baggage" rules or bought at duty free shops by return migrants are often not recorded either as remittances or as imports. There is evidence that hand-carried remittances and remittances in kind are significant, particularly among low-income migrants. According to survey-based evidence for Bangladesh (Mahmud, 1989), Pakistan (Kazi, 1989) and Sri Lanka (Rodrigo and Jayatissa, 1989), their combined share of total remittances could range between 10 and 15 per cent.

Most countries do not compile or publish data on remittances by country or region of origin. In India, the reserve bank publishes total private transfers by major currency area (sterling area, dollar area, OECD countries, rest of non-sterling area), but such data are of dubious quality. Most official transfers of remittances take place through American or European banks and the country of residence of the remitter is not recorded. Thus, remittances originating from western Asian countries, for example, are often shown as transfers from the sterling or dollar areas.

Balance of payments statistics, by their very nature, do not provide information about the distribution of remittances within a receiving country. Yet, the significance of flows at the regional or even city level can be large. Thus,

Measurement of remittances

the State of Kerala, where four per cent of India's population lives, received about half of all reported remittances sent to India from countries in western Asia until the early 1980s (Gulati, 1983).

A useful strategy to attract financial transfers from migrants abroad has been for countries of origin to allow non-resident citizens to open foreign currency accounts. From the balance of payments perspective, foreign currency deposits are part of the liabilities that the economy of origin has towards the rest of the world and are therefore not treated as realized workers' remittances. However, the amounts converted into local currency from foreign currency accounts are considered transfers from non-residents to residents and are included under remittances. Consequently, if the remittances that used to go through the usual banking channels are instead channelled to foreign currency accounts, trends in remittance data will give a misleading picture of the effectiveness of government policy in promoting the repatriation of migrants' income. Thus, in southern European countries during the 1970s the introduction of foreign currency accounts led to a reduction of remittances because they were redirected to the foreign currency accounts. But just as the decline in remittances was not indicative of changes in the tendency of migrants to repatriate income, the sharp rise in the holdings of foreign currency accounts was not an indication of success in attracting a greater share of that income. The recent Pakistani experience is similar. Total recorded remittances from overseas Pakistani workers during July 1991-March 1992 were 25 per cent lower than those for the corresponding period during the previous year (US$1,088 million versus US$1,448 million). According to the State Bank of Pakistan, this shortfall was mainly caused by the switch of remittances to foreign currency accounts in Pakistan held by non-resident Pakistanis, the total holdings of which increased by US$756 million during the period (Government of Pakistan, Ministry of Finance, 1992, p. 59).

Given this problem, a systematic analysis of the effectiveness of government policy in attracting remittances into banking channels would require data on both official remittances (as given in the balance of payments records) and on changes in foreign currency account balances by type and residence of owner. For most countries those balances are available from data on the operation of commercial banks as reported to the central bank. In the absence of direct estimates, the data on "time and saving deposits of non-residents denominated in foreign currency" as reported on the liability side of the consolidated balance sheet of commercial banks can be used as a proxy. These data are generally available from the annual reports of central banks.

C. FINANCIAL FLOWS AT THE MICRO-LEVEL: REMITTANCE DATA FROM HOUSEHOLD SURVEYS

As discussed above, the data on workers' remittances presented in the balance of payments statements have serious limitations, including inadequate coverage of actual flows, problems of establishing whether a migrant is a resident or not of the compiling economy, differences in recording and reporting practices across countries and even within countries over time, lack of sufficiently detailed information on financial flows through formal channels and the lack of reliable information on the use of informal channels and on remittances in kind. Since it is unlikely that major changes will occur soon regarding either the conceptualization or the measurement of workers' remittances and the compensation of employees, and since those economic transactions are not the only ones relevant for the study of the interlinkages between international migration and the functioning of the economy of origin of the migrants involved, it is important to devise other types of statistical instruments to obtain more detailed information on the relevant economic transactions. Specialized household surveys focusing on international migration can produce very useful information on the nature and flow of remittances.[2] Aside from its value for the in-depth analysis of the economic consequences of international migration, information from those surveys can be used to improve the estimates of remittances for balance of payments purposes. Thus, estimates of the proportion of remittances that go unrecorded can be used to adjust the time series on remittances derived from official sources.[3] For the adjustment to be appropriate, it is crucial that the data be obtained from representative surveys at the national level. Survey data are also necessary to study the factors affecting the use of remittances by the recipient households as well as the factors motivating migrants to send remittances. An understanding of such factors is valuable to explain and predict the levels of remittances over time and to assess their likely impact on the well-being of the migrants and their families.

However, assessing the impact of remittances by means of a survey raises several crucial issues. First, what is most relevant are the net remittances between households and their migrant members, meaning that both transfers from migrants to their families in the country of origin and those from families to the migrants abroad should be taken into account. Second, in interpreting the impact of remittances on households in the country of origin, it is important to bear in mind that the immediate use to which a specific amount of money is put is not necessarily the same as that which was made possible by the availability of remittances. Often the latter cannot even be identified by the recipient (Oberai and Singh, 1983; Standing, 1984). Thus, remittances may make it possible for children to remain longer in school than they would have otherwise, but the remittance transfers received need not necessarily be spent on school fees or materials. Third, there is the problem of defining "remittances", since the term is often used to encompass only monetary transfers but in fact encompasses both monetary and non-monetary transfers. Fourth, the period over which remittances are to be measured needs to be defined. Since the likelihood of sending remittances and their regularity will probably vary according to whether migrants leave on their own or are accompanied by immediate relatives and according to whether migrants remain abroad for short or longer periods, the choice of a short or long reference period can affect the estimates of gross and net flows obtained. In addition, the longer the period covered, the greater the need to devise appropriate ways to adjust the value of reported remittances for the effects of inflation and variations in exchange rates.

We present below the nucleus of a module on remittances for inclusion in specialized surveys on international migration. It is assumed that the identification of migrants from households and related issues (household composition, household income and assets etc.) are covered elsewhere in the survey questionnaire (see Chapter 6). The usefulness of the questions proposed here thus depends on the completeness of the complementary modules utilized. If the survey on remittances is to be carried out independently of a more comprehensive survey on international migration, then certain minimum questions concerning individual and household characteristics need to be added to the questions proposed below, as was done in two recent ILO/UNDP-sponsored studies in the South Pacific (Brown, 1995).

The modules presented below try to cover all the relevant aspects of the measurement of income transfers in cash and in kind between international migrants and households in the country of origin. They can be shortened or modified to suit particular needs. However, most of the detailed information sought is essential to estimate the magnitude of income transfers and therefore to assess the impact of such transfers on households and on the economy of origin in general.

The questions on remittances are divided into three modules. The first module covers transfers between households and international migrants abroad. The second deals with transfers related to return migration. The third concentrates on transfers made and received by international migrants in host countries. Since international migration surveys should be conducted in both countries of origin and destination, it is essential to design questions appropriate for each set of countries (see Chapter 6). Accordingly, the first module is addressed to households in countries of origin having absent members who are working or living abroad; the second is to be used in countries of origin if a household includes return migrants; and the third is to be used in countries of destination. The modules should be used in households having migrant members, and information on each and every international migrant should be gathered separately. However, a general question about the receipt of remittances should be addressed to all households, irrespective of whether they have migrant members or not. This last point is important because some persons may not have been identified as migrants in terms of the definition used for a particular survey but they may nevertheless be the source of remittances to the household. Thus, persons who have left the household and moved abroad over twenty years before the survey may not be identified as recent international migrants for survey purposes but may be a source of remittances. In addition, some income transfers may take place between international migrants and households to which those migrants never belonged.

The main items of interest to characterize the transfer of income and goods are: the amount transferred; its form; the uses to which such transfers have been put; and (*d*) the reciprocal obligations and expectations associated with such transfers. To obtain information on the transfer of income and goods to and from migrants who are not present in the household, the typical procedure has been to ask the head of household for information on income transfers. In many cases, however, the head of household may not be the best respondent, especially if the transfers are between husbands and wives and the head of household is someone else (Standing, 1984). It may be appropriate, therefore, to devise special procedures to select the best respondent in terms of relationship to the migrant or migrants involved.

1. Remittance questionnaire for households in countries of origin: Remittances to and from international migrants

Remittances sent to international migrants abroad

Question 1 is a two-part question concerning financial outflows often disregarded in the analyses of flows related to international migration. The financial flows of interest include cash and savings taken by the international migrant or sent to the country of destination around the time of the move through banks, post office transfers or transfers by other financial institutions. Interviewers must understand this broad definition and transmit it to the respondents. Q.1 (a) identifies the sources of the money taken by the international migrant at the time he or she left the household of origin and the country. All sources, including savings, gifts, loans and cash obtained from the sale of assets should be considered. The amounts obtained from each should be recorded. Q.1 (b) refers to the outflow of goods at the time of migration. It ensures that significant non-monetary transfers, such as those related to business activities, are recorded.

Question 2 further explores whether any money has ever been sent from the household of origin to the migrant while abroad and records who sent the money.

Question 3 is designed to identify the period during which the household has been sending money to the migrant. Q.3 (a) identifies the beginning of the process, Q.3 (b) determines whether there have been any recent transfers and screens for Q.3 (c) which establishes the amount transferred over the twelve months preceding interview. A period of 12 months is used to avoid seasonal variability dependent on the timing of the survey and to obtain the data needed to calculate net flows in relation to the remittances received from abroad. Q.3 (d) and Q.3 (e) gather information on the sender's intended use of the money sent to the migrant, with Q.3 (d) focusing on the main purpose of the transfer and Q.3 (e) probing for secondary purposes. It must be recognized, however, that the sender's purpose in sending money may not correspond to the actual use that the migrant makes of it. Furthermore, the response Q.3 (d) may be a rationalization of an actual outcome and not necessarily of the original intention of the sender. The codes suggested for Q.3 (d) have been used in several migration and

Measurement of remittances

remittances surveys but should be amended and refined after testing the questionnaire in a particular case. Interviewers should be encouraged to probe when posing Q.3 (e) and codification of responses should be carried out after the fieldwork is completed.

Question 4 is similar to Q.3 but it obtains information about non-monetary transfers. Once more, the first part of the question establishes the relevant timing of transfers of goods and focuses on those sent during the 12 months preceding interview. Although the types of goods of interest are listed under Q.4 (d), the list is not exhaustive and may need to be modified in each particular case. A longer list may be provided for interviewers to use in eliciting a better overall response to Q.4.

Question 5 explores whether any financial transfers have been made from the household to persons residing abroad who are not household members. It is a limitation of most migration surveys that they only consider financial transfers between household members. Yet, other transfers may take place, typically between relatives who have never been members of the same household. Q.5 focuses on such transfers, recording the relationship of the recipient to the head of household, the country where the recipient lives, the amount sent and the intended use. No attempt is made to explore the reciprocal obligations leading to such transfers or emanating from them. To explore that issue, additional questions would have to be added and tested as appropriate.

Module I-A: Transfers to international migrants from households in the country of origin having migrant members abroad

Serial number of migrant _____

Q.1 (a) When he/she [SPECIFY PERSON'S NAME] left this household, did he/she take any money from the following sources? (This should include cash and money transferred by banks, etc.)

	Yes	No	If yes, amount taken
From personal savings	1	2	_____
From savings of household head or other member(s) (specify _____)	1	2	_____
Gifts from friends or relatives	1	2	_____
Loans from friends or relatives	1	2	_____
Loan from money lender	1	2	_____
Loan from bank/government agency, etc.	1	2	_____
Pledge or sale of land, house or household assets	1	2	_____
Other (specify _____)	1	2	_____

International migration statistics

- (b) Besides all the above and personal belongings such as clothes, what else, if anything, did he/she take?

Goods	Quantity/value
_____	_____
_____	_____
_____	_____

Q.2 (a) After he/she [SPECIFY PERSON'S NAME] left, have you or any member of this household ever sent any money to him/her?

        Yes – 1   No – 2 [SKIP TO Q.6]

- (b) Who sent this money?

    Relationship to head of household: _____
    Relationship to migrant: _____

Q.3 (a) How long after he/she left was money first sent to [SPECIFY PERSON'S NAME]?

    Years _____   Months _____   Weeks _____

- (b) When was money **last** sent?

    Year _____   Month _____   [IF MORE THAN ONE YEAR SKIP TO Q.4]

- (c) In the past twelve months, how much money has been sent to him/her altogether?

    _____

- (d) Considering the money sent in the past twelve months, what was **your** (or the other sender's) main purpose in sending the money?

    01   Help pay for his/her daily needs (food, clothes etc.)
    02   Rent accommodation
    03   Purchase household goods, such as furniture, TV, refrigerator etc.
    04   Pay for school, university, training fees
    05   Pay his/her travel costs to return here to visit
    06   Purchase car/motorcycle/vehicle
    07   Purchase house, dwelling
    08   Marriage or other ceremony
    09   Purchase land
    10   Invest in business there
    11   Purchase goods to be sent back here
    12   Other, specify _____
    77   Don't know

- (e) Apart from that purpose, was there any other purpose for sending money? [USE CODES IN Q.3 (d)] _____

Q.4 (a) Have you or any member of this household ever sent any goods to [SPECIFY PERSON'S NAME]?

        Yes – 1   No – 2 [SKIP TO Q.5]

Measurement of remittances

(b) How long after he/she left were goods sent to [SPECIFY PERSON'S NAME]?

Years _____   Months _____   Weeks _____

(c) When were goods **last** sent?

Year _____   Month _____   [IF MORE THAN ONE YEAR SKIP TO Q.5]

(d) What goods have been sent in the **past** twelve months?

Goods	Quantity	Estimated value	Intended use[1]
1. Household furniture	–	–	–
2. Radio	–	–	–
3. Television	–	–	–
4. Refrigerator	–	–	–
5. Jewellery	–	–	–
6. Art objects/house decorations	–	–	–
7. Car/motorcycle/vehicle	–	–	–

Q.5 (a) In the past twelve months, have you or any other household member sent money to any other person living abroad?

Yes – 1   No – 2 [SKIP TO Q.5 (c)]   Don't know – 3 [SKIP TO Q.5(c)]

(b) Please indicate the relationship of the person(s) to household head, name of the country where he/she is living, the amount sent, and the main intended use of that money:

Person	Relationship	Country	Amount	Intended use
1.				
2.				
3.				

(c) In the past twelve months, have you or anyone else in this household sent goods to anybody else living abroad?

Yes – 1   No – 2   Don't know – 3

(d) If yes, what types of goods, to whom and the purpose for which they were sent?

Person	Relationship	Country	Quantity/Value	Intended purpose
1.				
2.				
3.				

---

[1] Codes for intended use:
01 Use them for the family
02 Use them as gifts
03 Sell them to others
04 Other (specify)

Remittances received from international migrants abroad

The questions in this sub-module should ideally be posed to the person with most knowledge of and contact with the international migrant or migrants concerned; this person is not necessarily the head of household.

Question 1 is the basic screening question to determine whether remittances have been sent to one or more members of the household. Q.1 (a) refers to money ever having been sent since the migrant left the household to live or work in another country. The transfers recorded should include those to members of the household who may have ceased being members as well as to persons remaining in the household. Those answering no to Q.1 (a) can skip the rest of Q.1 as well as Q.2 and Q.3. Q.1 (b) identifies the main recipient of the monetary transfers in terms of both relationship to the migrant and to the head of household. It is analytically important to identify the primary recipient of remittances, even if the recipient is not necessarily the person controlling the use of remittances. Q.1 (c) and Q.1 (d) seek to determine the beginning and the end of the period during which remittances have been sent, whereas Q.1 (e) obtains information on the regularity of remittances.

Question 2 records the channels used for the transfer of remittances, the frequency with which each channel is used, and the amount of money remitted through each channel during the 12 months preceding interview. By listing explicitly all possible channels, the reliability of the information obtained is improved.

Question 3 focuses on the use of remittances. Although the expenditure reallocation made possible by access to remittances is what matters, Q.3 (a) can only explore the actual use of remittances as perceived by the respondent. Q.3 (a) lists 14 possible uses which should be tested in each specific case. Q.3 (b) probes further by checking whether remittances have contributed indirectly to asset formation or increased production. It lists 13 types of expenditure, a list that may be expanded or reduced depending on local circumstances.

Question 4 focuses on non-monetary remittances. Q.4 (a) establishes whether any remittances in kind have been received and Q.4 (b) identifies the types of items received during the 12 months preceding interview and obtains information on how such items were sent or brought to the household and on their estimated market value. Q.4 (c) records whether the goods received were used mainly by the household or sold. Because responses to Q.4 may require considerable probing by the interviewer, they are susceptible to interviewer-induced bias and likely to suffer from widespread omission of items perceived as unimportant. Pilot surveys may be used to test for selective omissions and specific questions may be added to avoid them.

Question 5 records transfers from international migrants to local religious or social organizations. Q.5 (a) asks whether such transfers have ever taken place, and detailed information on the recipient organizations and the amount sent is recorded in Q.5 (b).

Measurement of remittances

Question 6 explores whether international migrants have paid insurance premiums, education fees or other fees on behalf of any member of the household during the 12 months preceding the interview. If that is the case, the type of fees paid and the amount involved are recorded.

Question 7 relates to transfers from persons living abroad who are either not identified as international migrants for survey purposes or who were never part of the household interviewed. It is important to collect this information to obtain a comprehensive picture of remittance flows.

Module I-B: Remittances from international migrants
(for households having a migrant member living abroad)

Serial number of migrant _____

Q.1 (a) Have you or any other member of this household ever received money from him/her [SPECIFY PERSON'S NAME]?

    Yes – 1   No – 2 [SKIP TO Q.4]

(b) Who received this money?

Relationship to head of household: _____
Relationship to migrants: _____
All household — 66
Various members – 77
Other, specify: _____

(c) How long after leaving here did he/she [SPECIFY PERSON'S NAME] first send money?

    Years _____ Months _____ Weeks _____

(d) When did he/she [SPECIFY PERSON'S NAME] last sent money?

    Year _____ Month _____

(e) Has he/she sent money regularly or only from time to time?

    Regularly – 1   From time to time – 2

Q.2 What methods has he/she used to send money to the household **in the past 12 months** and how much money has he/she sent or brought through these channels?

	Channel used Yes	Channel used No	Frequency in past 12 months	Total in past 12 months
Bank transfers (cheques, drafts, etc.)	1	2	_____	_____
Post office, money orders, etc.	1	2	_____	_____
Agent/courier	1	2	_____	_____
Brought personally (on home visits)	1	2	_____	_____
Through friends/relatives	1	2	_____	_____
Other, specify _____	1	2	_____	_____

International migration statistics

Q.3 (a) Considering the money received in the past 12 months, for what purpose has it been used? (Give up to three uses, in order of importance.)

_____   _____   _____

01 Daily needs (food, clothing, etc.)
02 Buy other household goods
03 Pay for schooling of household members
04 Pay off debt
05 Pay for wedding, funeral or other social function
06 Pay for visit abroad
07 Buy house
08 Improve house, repairs
09 Buy land
10 Rent land
11 Improve land
12 Buy farm inputs or implements
13 Invest in non-farm business
14 Save money, invest in securities, etc.
15 Other, specify: _____

(b) Did the money enable you or other household members to do any of the following?[1]

	Yes	No	Don't know
Buy food and clothing for family	1	2	3
Buy other household goods	1	2	3
Pay for schooling of household member	1	2	3
Pay off debts	1	2	3
Pay for wedding, funeral or other social function	1	2	3
Pay for visit abroad	1	2	3
Buy land	1	2	3
Rent more land	1	2	3
Improve land	1	2	3
Buy farm inputs/implements	1	2	3
Invest in non-farm business	1	2	3
Buy/improve house	1	2	3
Save money (bank or post office savings)	1	2	3
Other, specify: _____	1	2	3

Q.4 (a) **Apart from money**, have any goods been sent to you or brought to you or other household members in the last 12 months?

        Yes – 1   No – 2 [SKIP TO Q.5 (a)]

(b) What have been the main items received in the past 12 months and how were these sent or brought to you?

Type of goods	Method used in sending goods	Quantity	Estimated value
1. _____	_____	_____	_____
2. _____	_____	_____	_____
3. _____	_____	_____	_____

Measurement of remittances

    (c) What did you do with these goods?

		Yes	No	Don't know	Estimated value
01	Use them for the family	1	2	3	_____
02	Gifts to friends/other relatives	1	2	3	_____
03	Sell them to others	1	2	3	_____
04	Other, specify use and value: _____	1	2	3	_____

Q.5 (a) Has he/she also sent or brought money or goods for local organizations such as the church, sports clubs, community projects, relief work, etc., in the last 12 months?[2]

        Yes – 1   No – 2 [SKIP TO Q.7]   Don't know — 3 [SKIP TO Q.7]

    (b) About how much money or goods did he/she give to this organization?

        Organization [Name]   *Money*   *Estimated value of goods*

    1. _____   _____   _____

    2. _____   _____   _____

Q.6 (a) Has he/she paid on your behalf or on behalf of other household members any expenses here (e.g. insurance fees, etc.) during the last 12 months?[2]

        Yes – 1   No – 2 [SKIP TO Q.7]   Don't know — 3 [SKIP TO Q.7]

    (b) About how much was paid?

        Item   *Money paid*

    1. _____   _____

    2. _____   _____

    3. _____   _____

Q.7 (a) Have you or any other household member received any money or goods from any other person living abroad during the last 12 months?

        Yes – 1   No – 2

    (b) If yes, about how much money or goods were received and from whom?

Person	Relationship to household head	Money	Main use of money[1]	Value of goods	Main use of goods
1. ____	_____	____	____	____	____
2. ____	_____	____	____	____	____
3. ____	_____	____	____	____	____

---

[1] Use codes as in Q.3 (a). [2] Use codes as in Q.4 (c).

2. Remittance questionnaire for return international migrants in households in countries of origin

It is often claimed that return migrants stimulate the domestic economy, partly by virtue of their enhanced skills and experience and partly because they come back with accumulated savings or have sent back money beforehand. In order to test such claims, it is essential to have detailed information on the extent and use of income transfers associated with return migration. This section focuses on transfers that the migrant made from the country of destination prior to return, the transfers associated with the actual return, and any subsequent or continuing transfers. The questions suggested should be posed directly to the return migrants. It is assumed that relevant related information, such as length of stay abroad, years since return, name of the country where the migrant lived while abroad, whether any family members accompanied the migrant abroad etc., is recorded in other parts of the survey.

It is possible for the return migrant to have lived or worked abroad on more than one occasion. The questions on remittances in this module refer to the most recent period of absence from the home country to ensure better recall and because the most recent migration is likely to be more significant in explaining the current situation of the migrant.

Question 1 focuses on transfers made by the migrant before and after going abroad. Q.1 (a) and Q.1 (b) record the sources of funds and amounts taken abroad and the types of goods that the migrant took with him or her. Q.1 (c) explores whether the migrant received money or goods from the household of origin while abroad. Q.1 (d) focuses on monetary as well as non-monetary transfers sent by relatives, other household members or other persons in the country of origin to the migrant abroad. Asking specifically about transfers received from persons who are not members of the migrant's household is important because the migrant may have set up a separate household upon his or her return and that household may not be the source of the funds received while abroad. Note that Q.1 (d) records the sum total of transfers from the country of origin to the migrant. Because return may have occurred several years before interview or the length of stay abroad may have been lengthy, focusing on a specific period (such as the 12 months preceding return) would probably not elicit better information. However, the reference period that will produce the best results is an issue that cannot be resolved without having more information about the types of return migrants most likely to be present in a particular context. Questionnaire tests should be used to determine if a less encompassing reference period would produce more reliable results.

Question 2 is concerned with remittances made by the migrant to the household left behind while the migrant was living or working abroad. Note that the questions posed do not attempt to separate remittances sent through official or other channels from those brought back on home visits. Instead, they try to elicit reports on the overall total which, it is hoped, will be remembered better. As with respect to total transfers from the country of origin to the migrant while abroad, the possibility of using a specific reference period to report remittance must be explored in each context. The questions suggested here record information regarding the entire period that the migrant spent abroad.

Question 3 refers to the cash and savings brought back by the migrant upon return. It should be recognized that there is a certain ambiguity regarding financial transfers made just before return and those made at the time of return or immediately after. Interviewers must be trained to inform respondents that whatever is included in the response to Q.2 should not be included in Q.3, and vice versa. The version of Q.3 (a) proposed allows for an open-ended list, which may be long. To reduce it, specific assets or types of assets may be listed. Note that the value recorded should be the market value at the time of return.

Question 4 covers transfers received by the return migrant from the country of previous residence. Because the information sought includes both financial stocks and flows, they must be distinguished using appropriate codes. Q.4 (b) records the main sources of financial flows received since return and the amount received from each source. Q.4 (c) and (d) inquire about pension payments to which the return migrant may be entitled by virtue of having worked abroad.

Question 5 focuses on debt repayment so as to identify the extent to which international migrants remain liable to someone in the country of previous residence.

Question 6 relates to transfers from the return migrant to persons living in the country of previous residence. Q.6 (a) establishes whether such transfers have taken place since the return of the migrant, whereas Q.6 (b) focuses on transfers made during the 12 months preceding the interview. Q.6 (c) relates to goods sent during the 12 months preceding the interview to relatives or friends living or working abroad. Enough space must be left for the interviewer to record the main items sent.

Module II: Transfers related to return migrants

To be used in interviewing return migrants about their most recent period of absence from the country of origin.

Serial number of return migrant _____

Q.1 (a) Did you take any money from the following sources when you left this country for the last time? For each source, what was the amount taken? (Please include cash and funds transferred through banks, the post office, wire services, or any other means.)

International migration statistics

	Yes	No	If yes, amount taken
From personal savings	1	2	
From savings of household head or other household member(s), specify: _____	1	2	
Gifts from friends or relatives outside the household	1	2	
Loans from friends or relatives	1	2	
Loan from moneylender	1	2	
Loan from bank, government agency, etc.	1	2	
Pledge or sale of land, house or household assets	1	2	
Other, specify: _____	1	2	

(b) Besides all the above and personal belongings such as clothes, what other items did you take with you?

    Goods   *Quantity/Value*

    1. _____   _____

    2. _____   _____

    3. _____   _____

(c) While you were living or working abroad did you ever receive money or goods from any member of the household you had left or from other persons in this country?

    Yes – 1   No – 2 [SKIP TO Q.2]

(d) How much money did you receive during all the time you were abroad for the last time? What was the value of the goods that you received? What was the main use of the money and goods that you received?

	From household members	From other persons (non-household members)
Money	_____	_____
Main use of money[1]	_____	_____
Value of goods	_____	_____
Main use of goods[2]	_____	_____

Q.2 (a) Did you ever send or bring back money or goods to your household in this country while you were last living or working abroad?

    Yes – 1   No – 2 [SKIP TO Q.3]

(b) How much money did you send altogether to your household in this country during your last stay abroad, whether through banks, post offices, wire transfers, other channels or by bringing it back yourself when you came on home visits?

_____

---

[1] Use codes as in Q.2 (d).

[2] Codes for main use of goods

  01 Use them for the family   03 Sell them to others

  02 Gifts to friends/other relatives   04 Other, specify

Measurement of remittances

(c) During the time you were abroad what channels did you use for sending money back to this country? About what proportion was sent through each channel?

	Whether used		Proportion of money sent			
	Yes	No	0-25%	25-50%	50-75%	>75%
Banks	1	2	1	2	3	4
Post office	1	2	1	2	3	4
Agent/courier	1	2	1	2	3	4
Brought it personally	1	2	1	2	3	4
Sent through friends/relatives	1	2	1	2	3	4

Other (specify): _____

(d) What was this money mainly used for? Give up to three main uses in order of amount involved.

_____   _____   _____

01 Daily needs (food, clothing, etc.)
02 Buy other household goods
03 Pay for schooling of household members
04 Pay off debt
05 Pay for wedding, funeral or other social function
06 Pay for visit abroad
07 Buy house
08 Improve house, repairs
09 Buy land
10 Rent land
11 Improve land
12 Buy farm inputs or implements
13 Invest in non-farm business
14 Save money, invest in securities, etc.
15 Other, specify: _____

(e) In addition to money sent, did you send or bring back any goods on home visits?

Yes – 1   No – 2 [SKIP TO Q.3]

(f) What items of goods did you send or bring back before you returned?

Goods	Value	Main use[1]
1. _____	_____	_____
2. _____	_____	_____
3. _____	_____	_____

---

[1] Codes for main use of goods:

01 Use them for the family   03 Sell them to others
02 Gifts to friends/other relatives   04 Other, specify

International migration statistics

Q.3 (a) When you (last) returned here, what goods, if any, did you bring back with you?

        Goods   *Value*

    1. _____ _____
    2. _____ _____
    3. _____ _____

(b) Apart from money sent back before your return, how much money did you also bring back with you when you returned?

    _____ [IF NONE, SKIP TO Q.4]

(c) Since your return, what have been the main uses of these savings? (Give up to three uses in order of amount of money)

    _____   _____   _____

    01 Daily needs (food, clothing, etc.)
    02 Buy other household goods
    03 Pay for schooling of household members
    04 Pay off debt
    05 Pay for wedding, funeral or other social function
    06 Pay for visit abroad
    07 Buy house
    08 Improve house, repairs
    09 Buy land
    10 Rent land
    11 Improve land
    12 Buy farm inputs or implements
    13 Invest in non-farm business
    14 Save money, invest securities, etc.
    15 Other, specify: _____

Q.4 (a) Are you receiving, or have you received since your return, any money from the country where you were living or working before, such as income from a business or property that you still have there or from the sale of assets?

        Yes – 1   No – 2 [SKIP TO Q.4 (e)]

(b) How much money have you received from the following sources: *(i)* since your return? and *(ii)* during the last 12 months?

	Since return	During the last 12 months
Rent from house/property	_____	_____
Share of income/profits from business	_____	_____
Receipts from sale of assets or property	_____	_____
Income from bank deposits	_____	_____
Income from other financial instruments	_____	_____
Debt repayments	_____	_____
Other, specify: _____	_____	_____

(c) Do you receive a pension from work done while away from this country?

        Yes – 1   No – 2 [SKIP TO Q.5]

(d) How much do you receive monthly? _____

Measurement of remittances

Q.5 (a) Since returning, have you sent money or goods to someone living in your country of previous residence to pay off debts?

        Yes – 1   No – 2 [SKIP TO Q.6]

(b) About how much have you sent since returning? _____

(c) About how much have you sent in the past 12 months? _____

(d) And about how much more have you to send? _____

Q.6 (a) Since returning, have you sent money or goods to relations or friends living abroad for purposes other than paying debts?

        Yes – 1   No – 2

(b) If yes, how much and to whom have you sent money during the past 12 months? And what was the main use you expected the money to be put?

Person	Relationship to migrant	Money sent	Intended use[1]
1. _____	_____	_____	_____
2. _____	_____	_____	_____
3. _____	_____	_____	_____

(c) Besides money, have you sent any goods to relatives or friends living abroad during the last 12 months?

Goods	Sent to (relationship to migrant)	Value	Intended use[2]
1. _____	_____	_____	_____
2. _____	_____	_____	_____
3. _____	_____	_____	_____

3. Remittance questionnaire for households in migrant-receiving countries

Questions on remittances should also be posed to migrants still living abroad. This section focuses on migrants in the country of destination and the financial transfers they make to other countries. As in previous cases, it is assumed that the module presented here is part of a more detailed survey questionnaire which identifies international migrants and gathers relevant information on their employment status, income, household composition, length of stay in the country of destination, etc. Generally, data on remittances are more

---

[1] Code as in Q.3 (c).

[2] Codes for intended use of goods:
01 Use them for the family   03 Sell them to others
02 Gifts to friends/other relatives   04 Other, specify

accurate when the information can be obtained from the migrants themselves, especially in terms of the proportion of income remitted and the purpose for sending remittances. Information on the actual use of remittances can be gathered with greater accuracy from households receiving remittances in the country of origin.

Question 1 focuses on the transfer made by the migrant at the time of migration. It is analogous to similar questions used in previous modules.

Question 2 records monetary and non-monetary transfers from persons in the country of origin (generally relatives) to the migrant after the international move has taken place. Q.2 (a) focuses on transfers from relatives and friends living in countries other than that in which the migrant lives. It is important not to omit any such inflows. Q.2 (b) concerns detailed information on inflows during the 12 months preceding the interview, recording the sender's country and his or her relationship with the migrant. Q.2 (c) and Q.2 (d) record information on non-monetary transfers and their use. Of particular interest is the transfer of goods to be sold by the migrant.

Question 3 relates to remittances sent by migrants to relatives and others living abroad. As in Q.2, the relationship of the recipient of remittances to the migrant and the country of residence of the recipient are recorded. The monetary transfers of interest are those made within the 12 months preceding the interview. Information about the regularity of remittances and the financial obligations of migrants is also recorded. The latter is determined by establishing if the migrant's remittances account for at least 25 per cent of the recipient's income. This approach may need to be modified in particular situations and its performance needs to be tested because some respondents may respond in terms of the "dependent" status of the recipient and not in terms of the proportion of his or her income that the remittances sent represent.

Question 4 records information on the channels used in remitting money, a key issue in the estimation of remittances, as discussed earlier.

Question 5 focuses on non-monetary transfers from the migrant to persons living abroad. Detailed information concerning goods sent during the 12 months preceding the interview, including the methods used for sending goods, their value and their recipient is recorded.

Question 6 obtains information concerning transfers to social, religious or other organizations in the country of origin. Such transfers are often disregarded in surveys, resulting in downward biases in the estimation of transfers involving international migrants. Q.6 (a) asks about both monetary and non-monetary transfers made to religious and social organizations during the 12 months preceding the interview and Q.6 (b) obtains information about those organizations and on the intended use of such transfers.

Measurement of remittances

Module III: Remittances and international migrants abroad

(To be addressed to migrants in countries of destination)

Serial number of migrant _____

Q.1 (a) When you moved to live/work in this country, did you bring any money with you or transfer any funds ahead of the move?

        Yes – *1*   *No* – *2* [SKIP TO Q.1(e)]

  (b) How much money did you bring or transfer? _____ [IF NONE, SKIP TO Q.2]

  (c) What was the main source of that money?

      01 Personal savings
      02 Savings of head of household or other household member, specify _____
      03 Gifts from friends or relatives outside the household
      04 Loans from friends or relatives
      05 Loan from moneylender
      06 Loan from bank, government agency, other financial institution
      07 Pledge or sale of land, house, household assets
      08 Other, specify _____

  (d) What were the main uses of that money?
(Give up to three in order of money spent)

    _____   _____   _____

      01 Pay for daily needs (food, clothes, etc.)
      02 Renting accommodation
      03 Purchase household goods
      04 Purchase car/motorcycle/vehicle
      05 Purchase house, dwelling
      06 Pay for school, university, training fees
      07 Pay for travel costs of other members of household
      08 Marriage or other ceremony
      09 Purchase of land in country of destination
      10 Invest in business in country of destination
      11 Purchase goods to be sent back
      12 Other, specify _____
      77 Don't know

  (e) Besides all the above and personal belongings such as clothes, what else did you bring when you came?

    Goods   *Quantity/value*

    1. _____   _____
    2. _____   _____
    3. _____   _____

International migration statistics

Q.2 (a) Since arriving here, have you or any other member of your present household received any money or goods from relatives or others living in your home country or another country abroad?

        Yes – 1   No – 2 [SKIP TO Q.3]

(b) In the past 12 months, how much money or what goods have you received?

	Sender (Relationship)	Sender's country	Money		Goods	
			Amount	*What did you use the money for? [CODE AS FOR Q.1 (d)]	Description of goods	Value of goods
1.						
2.						
3.						

(c) Were any of the goods that you received during the last 12 months in turn sold to someone else?

        Yes – 1   No – 2 [SKIP TO Q.3]

(d) What goods were sold and where were these goods sold?

	Country	Goods	How did you sell the goods? 1. through a business 2. market stall 3. informally through home	Did you send any of the money from the sale back to your country of origin? (If yes, give amount)
1.				
2.				
3.				

Q.3 (a) Since arriving here, have you (or anyone else in this household) sent or given money to relatives or others living in your home country or another country abroad?

        Yes – 1   No – 2 [SKIP TO Q.5]

Measurement of remittances

(b) To whom and how much money did you send during the last 12 months?

	Relation-ship	Country	Money (Amount)	Do you send money to this person 1. regularly 2. from time to time	Does this person depend on you financially for more than 25% of his/her income?	What was the main purpose of sending money?[1]
1.						
2.						
3.						

[1] *Codes to be used*:
01 Daily needs (food, clothes, etc.)
02 Productive investment (farming)
03 Productive investment (non-farming), start a business
04 Purchase of land there/elsewhere
05 Land improvement
06 Marriage, other ceremony
07 Purchasing/paying for house/dwelling
08 Pay off his/her debt
09 Pay off own debt
10 Pay for his/her schooling/training
11 Pay taxes
12 Pay for migration/move of other family members
13 Saving
14 Other (specify)_____
77 Don't know

Q.4 (a) Did you use any of the following methods to send money during the last 12 months?

		Yes	No
1.	Bank transfer (cheques, drafts, etc.)	1	2
2.	Post office (money order, etc.)	1	2
3.	Agent/courier	1	2
4.	Carried personally	1	2
5.	Carried by relatives	1	2
6.	Carried by friends	1	2
7.	Other (specify) _____	1	2

(b) Which of the above methods do you use most often?
_____

Q.5 (a) During the last 12 months, did you or anyone else in this household send or give goods to anybody living in your home country or in another country?

        Yes – 1   No – 2 [SKIP TO Q.6]

International migration statistics

(b) What type of goods and to whom were they sent? Give examples: food products; handicrafts; clothing; stereo; TV; video; business goods; farm inputs, etc.

	Relation	Country	Goods	Value	Method of sending[1]	Intended use[2]
1.						
2.						
3.						

[1] *Code for method of sending:*
01 Post office
02 Shipped
03 Air freight
04 Carried personally
05 Carried by relatives
06 Carried by friends
07 Other, specify _____

[2] *Code for intended use:*
01 Family use/consumption
02 To give to relatives and friends
03 For sale
04 Other, specify _____

Q.6 (a) During the last 12 months, did anyone from this household send or give money or goods to any organizations in your home country or in any other country of previous residence?

        Yes – 1   No – 2

(b) If yes, what was the money or goods mainly used for?

Organization	Country	Money	Intended use[1]	Value of goods	Intended use[2]
1. _____	_____	_____	_____	_____	_____
2. _____	_____	_____	_____	_____	_____

---

[1] *Use codes in Q.3 (b).* [2] *Use codes for intended use in Q.5 (b).*

D. CONCLUDING REMARKS

Despite the need for data on workers' remittances to assess the impact of international migration on countries of origin, the data available are generally very deficient. Existing sources of information do not permit an adequate

Measurement of remittances

estimation of the main balance of payments items related to international migration. Consequently, crude estimates have to be used in place of moderately reliable information. Such a state of affairs can lead to serious overestimates or underestimates of the components of international transactions associated with the international flows of migrants' income. Although it is very likely that the data on remittances sent through official channels underestimate the true level of transfers by migrants to the households they leave behind, the adjustments that are sometimes made in estimating balance of payments items are arbitrary and more than counterbalance the possible underestimation inherent in official statistics. Consequently, it is not possible to rely on balance of payments information alone to assess the likely impact of remittances and other transfers on the economy of the country of origin or that of destination. Specialized surveys are an important tool to palliate existing data gaps.

There are strong reasons to doubt the quality of the available official data on remittances. In most commercial bank transaction records, there is no indication of the country of origin or the residence of the remitter, much less of the remitter's status as a migrant or as a "resident" of the economy of destination. This limitation has to be clearly stated in published data in order to avoid misleading interpretations. Until appropriate procedures are devised to overcome such shortcomings, meaningful data on both the components of the balance of payments and on the geographic origin of remittances can come only from specialized surveys on international migration. Such surveys permit an assessment of the net flow of remittances by allowing the measurement of the transfers not only from migrants to the households left in the country of origin but also of those from households to migrants abroad. Surveys are also a useful means of obtaining the data necessary to understand the impact of the use of remittances on the families left behind.

Very little research has been done to assess the importance of the availability and quality of institutional transfer mechanisms, such as banks and corporations, nor has there been much research into their role in facilitating remittance flows. Systematic survey-based research about remittance channels and the functioning of the remittance-related hidden economy is required to broaden our understanding of the impact of remittances on the economy of the country of origin. A clear understanding of the nature of the services offered by the private agents involved in the informal market would also be of value to financial institutions in the formal sector to aid them in redesigning their services to suit better the requirements of migrants and their families.

Notes

[1] Bangladesh uses the workers' remittances data directly from the balance of payments for this purpose. In the Philippines, the official remittances data are arbitrarily increased by 50 per cent (in order to allow for unrecorded remittances) before using them in the calculation of GNI. In Pakistan, official data on remittances are adjusted for income brought home by return migrants in the form of personal baggage (Athukorala, 1993b).

International migration statistics

[2] Standing (1984) provides a comprehensive treatment of remittances in internal migration surveys. The basic framework can be extended to cover remittances associated with international migration flows.

[3] The ILO has implemented a number of collaborative studies of remittances, especially in Asian labour-sending countries, which provide estimates of unrecorded remittance flows and which have been used to adjust the official time series data on remittances at the national level. Most of these efforts are reported in Amjad (1989). Mahmud (1989) bases his adjustments to the official remittance data of Bangladesh on the survey data generated by the Bangladesh Institute of Development Studies, which surveyed 368 return migrants, and on a survey of Rizwanul Islam (1980) undertaken for the World Bank which interviewed 277 recipients of remittances. Kazi (1989) has used the results of two micro-level studies to adjust the remittance estimates of Pakistan, one by Gilani et al. (1981a, 1981b and 1981c) and the other by ILO-ARTEP (1987). Burney (1989), in his macro-economic analysis of the impact of remittances on savings in Pakistan, adjusts official estimates of remittances using information on unrecorded transfers from the ILO-ARTEP (1987) study. For an example showing how such data can be combined for purposes of undertaking an alternative macro-economic analysis in the sub-Saharan African context, where official data are often even less reliable, see Brown (1992a and 1992b).

ANNEX 1. MODEL QUESTIONNAIRES FOR COUNTRY OF DESTINATION

A. HOUSEHOLD QUESTIONNAIRE

PLACE OF RESIDENCE: Country _____
  State _____
  District _____
  Name of city, town, village or rural area _____
  Classification as urban or rural _____
  Segment number (or census tract) _____

Date(s) of interview visits 1. _____ 2. _____ 3. _____ 4. _____ 5. _____

Result code for interview:
1 Completed satisfactorily
2 Incomplete
3 Desired respondent not available
4 Deferred
5 Refused
6 Vacant dwelling
7 Address not a dwelling
8 Unable to locate dwelling
9 Other, specify _____

ADMINISTER HOUSEHOLD SCHEDULE BELOW ONLY TO HEAD OF HOUSEHOLD OR SPOUSE. IF NOT AVAILABLE, MARK CODE 3 ABOVE AND ASCERTAIN WHEN EXPECTED TO BE AVAILABLE, AND RECORD HERE:

DATE: _____ HOUR: _____

INTERVIEWER: RECORD ANSWERS TO THE FOLLOWING (ASK IF NECESSARY)

What kind of dwelling is this? [CIRCLE CODE AS APPROPRIATE]
- 01 SINGLE DWELLING
- 02 MULTIPLE DWELLING WITH SEVERAL HOUSEHOLDS SHARING SAME SPACE OR FACILITY
- 03 APARTMENT, CONDOMINIUM BUILDING
- 04 RENTED ROOM IN HOUSE
- 08 OTHER, SPECIFY: _____

What is the roof made of?
- 01 TILE
- 02 CEMENT
- 03 METAL, TIN, ZINC
- 04 WOOD
- 05 MUD
- 06 THATCH, STRAW, LEAVES
- 08 OTHER, SPECIFY: _____

What is the floor made of?
- 01 CEMENT, BRICK
- 02 TILE, LINOLEUM, WOOD
- 03 STONES
- 04 STRAW, CANE
- 05 DIRT
- 08 OTHER, SPECIFY: _____

What are the exterior walls made of?
- 01 CEMENT, BRICK, CINDER BLOCK
- 02 DIRT, CLAY, MUD
- 03 WOOD
- 04 STRAW, CANE
- 08 OTHER, SPECIFY: _____

INDICATE BELOW WHO IS RESPONDENT FOR HOUSEHOLD QUESTIONNAIRE.
Name _____ ID code _____

Let me begin by asking about all the people who usually live in this household. [COMPLETE CURRENT COMPOSITION OF HOUSEHOLD TABLE BELOW, QUESTIONS H.1-H.10]

CURRENT COMPOSITION OF HOUSEHOLD

Please indicate the names of all the persons who normally live in this dwelling, beginning with the person mainly responsible for its economic functioning or economic decisions (referred to as the Head hereafter):

							For persons over age 6 years		For persons over age 15 years	
ID No.	H.1 Name	H.2 Relationship to head (CODE 1)	H.3 Sex (male = 1, female = 2)	H.4 Age (years completed)	H.5 Where was X born? (province/country)	H.6 How many days did X sleep here last week?	H.7 What is the highest level of education X completed? (CODE 2)	H.8 Is X currently attending school? (yes = 1, no = 2)	H.9 Did X work for pay, or in a family business or farm at any time in last 12 months? (yes = 1, no = 2)	H.10 What is the current marital status of X? (CODE 3)
1										
2										
3										
4										
5										
6										
7										

CODE 1
01 Head
02 Spouse
03 Child of head and spouse
04 Child of head only
05 Child of spouse only
06 Adopted child
07 Parent of head or spouse
08 Sibling of head or spouse
09 Child of sibling
10 Other relative
11 Domestic worker
12 Other non-relative

CODE 2
00 None
01 Primary incomplete
02 Primary complete
03 Secondary incomplete
04 Secondary complete
05 Technical school
06 University incomplete
07 University degree
08 Postgraduate or other professional degree

CODE 3
01 Single (never married)
02 Married
03 Consensual union
04 Separated
05 Divorced
06 Widow(er)

VERIFY: This includes all children and new babies who live here? And persons who are not relatives but live here? Also persons temporarily living/working away from the home? This also does not include temporary visitors?

International migration statistics

Now I would like to ask you a few questions about your dwelling.

H.11 Do you (or your spouse) own this dwelling? YES – 1 NO – 2 [SKIP TO H.12]

    * H.11a How much is your monthly mortgage payment? _____

    * H.11b (IF 0) About how much is the house worth if you wanted to sell it? _____ [SKIP TO H.13]

*H.12 Do you pay rent?

    01 YES, SPECIFY: How much do you pay in rent each month? $ _____
        [IF PAYMENT IS IN FOOD OR OTHER GOODS, INCLUDE ESTIMATE OF ITS VALUE]

    02 NO

H.13 How many separate rooms does your dwelling have, not counting bathrooms? _____

H.14 Does it have a separate kitchen or cooking area? YES – 1 NO – 2

H.15 What is your usual souce of drinking water? [CIRCLE APPROPRIATE CODE]

    01 PIPED, IN HOUSE   [SKIP TO H.16]
    02 PUMPED, IN HOUSE OR YARD   [SKIP TO H.16]
    03 RAINWATER, ROOF STORAGE   [SKIP TO H.16]
    04 PUMPED OR PIPED, PUBLIC FACILITY
    05 OPEN WELL
    06 SPRING, RIVER, LAKE
    07 PURCHASED
    08 OTHER, SPECIFY: _____

    * H.15a How long does it take you to go to this place where you get your water? MINUTES _____

H.16 What kind of toilet facilities do you have?

    01 FLUSH, INSIDE HOUSE   04 OPEN PIT
    02 FLUSH, OUTSIDE HOUSE   05 NONE (OPEN FIELDS, ETC.)
    03 LATRINE   06 OTHER, SPECIFY: _____

H.17 Do you have electricity in your dwelling? YES – 1 NO – 2 [SKIP TO H.18]

    H.17a Do you have the following items in your house? [CIRCLE THE CODES OF THOSE THAT THE HOUSEHOLD HAS]

        01 ELECTRIC FAN   04 REFRIGERATOR
        02 ELECTRIC IRON   05 COMPUTER
        03 TELEVISION

H.18 Does your household have these items? [CIRCLE THE CODE OF THOSE THAT THE HOUSEHOLD HAS]

    01 TABLE   06 BICYCLE
    02 CHAIR OR STOOL   07 CAR/JEEP/TRUCK
    03 RADIO   08 MOTORCYCLE
    04 CLOCK OR WATCH   09 TELEPHONE
    05 SEWING MACHINE

H.19 How close is this house to the nearest **paved** road? [IF FRONTS ON ROAD, RECORD 0] Kilometres from paved road _____

    *H.19a [IF NOT ON PAVED ROAD] How far is it from the nearest **unpaved** road? Kilometres from unpaved road _____

Annex 1

H.20 How far is this **house** from the nearest ... ? That is, how long does it take you to walk there? [IF IT DOES NOT EXIST IN THE COMMUNITY, OR CLOSE TO IT, AS FAR AS RESPONDENT KNOWS, WRITE X UNDER MINUTES]

Minutes

_____	Primary school
_____	Secondary school
_____	Health clinic, hospital
_____	Store for buying food
_____	Movie theater
_____	Bus stop or other public transportation
_____	Bank
_____	Telephone
_____	Pharmacy

H.21 Apart from the income your household receives from the work of household members and any family farms or business activities, which we will ask about later, have you or anyone else in the household received any income from any other sources in the **past 12 months**?

That is, did you or anyone else in your household receive any income from:	[CIRCLE RESPONSE]	What is the total amount received from [SOURCE] in the past 12 months? [IF NOT SURE, ASK]: How much did you receive per month (or in the last month)? [WRITE IN AMOUNT PER MONTH AND NOTE PER MONTH]
(a) renting out a building, house, or a room in a house to anyone (for them to live in or use for their business)?	YES – 1	
	NO – 2	
(b) renting out machinery, farm equipment or vehicles?	YES – 1	
	NO – 2	
(c) renting out farm animals?	YES – 1	
	NO – 2	
(d) interest or dividends, such as from a savings account in a bank, shares of stock owned in a company, etc.?	YES – 1	
	NO – 2	
(e) pension, retirement income?	YES – 1	
	NO – 2	
(f) unemployment/layoff benefits?	YES – 1	
	NO – 2	
(g) welfare benefits?	YES – 1	
	NO – 2	
(h) any other source? SPECIFY:	YES – 1	
	NO – 2	

International migration statistics

B. INDIVIDUAL QUESTIONNAIRE (FOR ALL ADULTS OVER AGE 15 YEARS)

NAME _____ MALE – 1   FEMALE – 2

ID NUMBER IN HOUSEHOLD LISTING _____

1. *MIGRATION AND CITIZENSHIP*

1.1 When were you born?   MONTH: _____   YEAR: _____   DON'T KNOW: _____

   *1.1a [IF RESPONDENT DOESN'T KNOW MONTH AND YEAR OF BIRTH] What is your age? _____

1.2 Where were you born?   HERE: _____
   (current village/town/city of residence)

   ELSEWHERE: COUNTRY   _____
                STATE   _____
                DISTRICT   _____
                VILLAGE/TOWN/CITY _____

   *1.2a At that time, was that place an urban or rural area?   URBAN – 1   RURAL – 2

[IF PRESENT COUNTRY OF RESIDENCE IS ALSO COUNTRY OF BIRTH, CONTINUE WITH 1.3. OTHERWISE SKIP TO 1.4]

1.3 Have you ever lived in another country for 6 months or more?
   YES – 1   [SKIP TO 1.6a AND COMPLETE MIGRATION HISTORY]   NO – 2
   [NON-MIGRANT – SKIP TO 1.9]

1.4 When did you (first) leave your country of birth? MONTH: _____ YEAR: _____

1.5 Where did you move to?
   THIS COUNTRY – 1   ANOTHER COUNTRY – 2   [1.5a What country? _____]

1.6 Have you ever lived in another country (besides your place of birth) for at least six months before coming to live in this country?
   YES – 1   NO – 2   [SKIP TO 1.7]

   1.6a How many other countries? _____   [COMPLETE MIGRATION HISTORY IN 1.6b]

   1.6b Please tell me all the countries in which you have lived for more than six months, starting with your country of birth, and indicate the date when you left each of them.

INTERNATIONAL MIGRATION HISTORY FOR MULTIPLE MOVERS

Country where you lived for at least 6 months (start with country of birth)	Date of departure	
	Month	Year
1.		
2.		
3.		
4.		

Annex 1

1.7 When did you come to live in this country (or most recently come to live, if you lived here earlier as well)?
MONTH: _____ YEAR: _____

1.8 What was your age when you (last) moved to live in this country? _____
YEARS

1.9 What is your country of citizenship? _____ [IF SAME AS COUNTRY OF BIRTH IN 1.2, SKIP TO 1.9b]

1.9a When did you become a citizen of that country? MONTH: _____
YEAR: [INDICATE IF AT BIRTH: _____]

1.9b Have you ever been a citizen of any other country?
YES – 1 [What country? _____] NO – 2 [SKIP TO 1.10]

1.9c Are you still a citizen of the country mentioned in 1.9b? YES – 1 NO – 2

1.10 We would like to know the country of citizenship of your immediate relatives, whether they are alive or not.

[INTERVIEWER: FOR FATHER OR MOTHER ASK]: What is or was the country of citizenship of your (father/mother)? [RECORD ANSWER IN APPROPRIATE CELL OF TABLE BELOW]

[REGARDING SPOUSE, INQUIRE]: Have you ever been married? [IF NO, RECORD "NA" IN APPROPRIATE CELL, OTHERWISE INQUIRE]: What is the citizenship of your current (or most recent) spouse? [RECORD ANSWER IN APPROPRIATE CELL]

[FOR EACH TYPE OF RELATIVE INQUIRE]: Do you have or have you ever had any (sons/daughters/brothers/sisters)? [IF THE ANSWER IS NO, WRITE "NA" UNDER NUMBER FOR THE RELEVANT TYPE OF RELATIVE. IF THE ANSWER IS YES, ASK]: Do or did they all have the same country of citizenship? [IF THE ANSWER IS YES, INQUIRE]: How many _____ do or did you have? What was their country of citizenship? [RECORD ANSWERS IN APPROPRIATE CELLS OF TABLE BELOW]. [IF THE ANSWER IS NO, INQUIRE]: What are or were their countries of citizenship? [RECORD ANSWERS IN APPROPRIATE CELLS]. How many _____ have or had the citizenship of _____ ? [RECORD NUMBERS IN APPROPRIATE CELLS].

	Country of citizenship	Sons		Daughters		Brothers		Sisters	
		Number	Country of citizenship	Number	Country of citizenship	Number	Country of citizenship	Number	Country of citizenship
Father			1.		1.		1.		1.
Mother			2.		2.		2.		2.
Spouse			3.		3.		3.		3.
			4.		4.		4.		4.

1.11 Do any of your immediate relatives we have just talked about currently live outside this country?
YES – 1 NO – 2 [SKIP TO 1.13]

1.11a We would like to know the country of current residence of your immediate relatives.
[FOR FATHER OR MOTHER ASK]: Is your (father/mother) alive? [IF NO, RECORD "NA" IN APPROPRIATE CELL OF THE TABLE BELOW, OTHERWISE ASK]: What is the country of residence of your (father/mother)? [RECORD ANSWER IN APPROPRIATE CELL]

International migration statistics

REGARDING SPOUSE, INQUIRE]: Are you currently married? [IF NO, RECORD "NA" IN APPROPRIATE CELL, OTHERWISE INQUIRE]: What is the country of residence of your current spouse? [RECORD ANSWER IN APPROPRIATE CELL]

[FOR EACH TYPE OF RELATIVE INQUIRE]: Do you have any (sons/daughters/brothers/sisters)? [IF THE ANSWER IS NO, WRITE "NA" UNDER NUMBER FOR THE RELEVANT TYPE OF RELATIVE. IF THE ANSWER IS YES, ASK]: Do they all have the same country of residence? [IF THE ANSWER IS YES, INQUIRE]: How many ____ do have? What is their current country of residence? [RECORD ANSWERS IN APPROPRIATE CELLS OF TABLE BELOW]. [IF THE ANSWER IS NO, INQUIRE]: What are their countries of residence? [RECORD ANSWERS IN APPROPRIATE CELLS]. How many ____ live in ____ ? [RECORD NUMBERS IN APPROPRIATE CELLS].

	Country of residence	Sons		Daughters		Brothers		Sisters	
		Number	Country of residence	Number	Country of residence	Number	Country of residence	Number	Country of residence
Father			1.		1.		1.		1.
Mother			2.		2.		2.		2.
Spouse			3.		3.		3.		3.
			4.		4.		4.		4.

1.12 Among your immediate relatives living in another country, do any of them wish to come to live in this country (or do you want them to come to live in this country)?

YES – 1   NO – 2   [SKIP TO 1.13]

1.12a Indicate which one(s)? [CIRCLE APPROPRIATE CODE AND INDICATE NUMBER IN EACH RELEVANT CATEGORY]

```
01  FATHER
02  MOTHER
03  SPOUSE
04  SONS, HOW MANY?        _____
05  DAUGHTERS, HOW MANY?   _____
06  BROTHERS, HOW MANY?    _____
07  SISTERS, HOW MANY?     _____
08  OTHER, SPECIFY WHO     _____
```

1.12b Have you taken any practical steps to bring these relatives to this country?

YES – 1   NO – 2   [SKIP TO 1.13]

1.12c What steps? Please explain: _____

1.13 What is your mother tongue? _____ [IF THE SAME AS MAIN LANGUAGE OF THE COUNTRY OF INTERVIEW, SKIP TO 1.13b]

1.13a Can you speak and understand the main language of this country? YES – 1 NO – 2

1.13b Do you speak and understand any other languages? YES – 1 NO – 2 [SKIP TO 1.14]

1.13c Which other language(s)? _____

1.14 Do you intend to remain in this country? YES – 1 NO – 2 [SKIP TO 1.15]

Annex 1

1.14a Why do you intend to remain? [CIRCLE CODE OF ALL REASONS MENTIONED]

01 HAVE A GOOD JOB AND SATISFACTORY INCOME
02 CLOSE RELATIVES AND FRIENDS ARE IN THIS COUNTRY
03 SCHOOLS ARE GOOD
04 GOOD HEALTH CARE
05 HAVE SUCCESSFUL BUSINESS HERE
06 HAVE GOOD HOUSE
07 HAVE NICE NEIGHBOURHOOD AND NEIGHBOURS
08 FREEDOM FROM POLITICAL PERSECUTION
09 FREEDOM FROM RELIGIOUS PERSECUTION
10 LOW LEVEL OF CRIME, GENERAL SECURITY
11 LOW COST OF LIVING
12 MANY SOCIAL ACTIVITIES AND THINGS TO DO
13 OTHER, SPECIFY: _____

1.14b Which is the **most important** reason for remaining in this country? _____
[SKIP TO 1.17a]

1.15 Do you have any specific plans to leave or do you just have a general feeling that you would like to leave?
SPECIFIC PLANS – 1   GENERAL FEELING – 2

1.15a Why are you thinking of leaving? [CIRCLE CODES OF ALL REASONS MENTIONED]

01 LACK OF CLOSE RELATIVES/FRIENDS IN THIS COUNTRY
02 UNEMPLOYED, CAN'T FIND WORK
03 POOR JOB, LOW PAY
04 POOR WORKING CONDITIONS
05 DON'T GET ALONG WITH BOSS OR CO-WORKERS
06 BUSINESS NOT DOING WELL
07 WORK CONTRACT OR WORK PERMIT IN THIS COUNTRY WILL EXPIRE
08 POOR SCHOOLS, LACK OF SCHOOLS
09 WILL COMPLETE TRAINING, STUDIES OR DEGREE IN THIS COUNTRY
10 DON'T LIKE COMMUNITY OF RESIDENCE, DIFFERENT VALUES
11 FAMILY PROBLEMS, DIFFERENT VALUES
12 TO GET MARRIED, SEEK SPOUSE
13 SEPARATION OR DIVORCE, WANT TO GET AWAY
14 HIGH COST OF LIVING
15 HIGH CRIME RATE
16 POOR PHYSICAL ENVIRONMENT, POLLUTION
17 DON'T LIKE CLIMATE
18 LANGUAGE PROBLEMS
19 VISA PROBLEMS, LACK OF DOCUMENTS
20 DISCRIMINATION
21 POLITICAL PERSECUTION, FEAR OF POLITICAL PERSECUTION
22 RELIGIOUS PERSECUTION, FEAR OF RELIGIOUS PERSECUTION
23 OTHER, SPECIFY: _____

1.15b Which is the **most important** reason? _____

1.16 Do you have a specific time when you plan to leave?   YES – 1   NO – 2
[SKIP TO 1.17]

1.16a When?   01 WITHIN A YEAR
              02 BETWEEN 1 AND 2 YEARS FROM NOW
              03 AFTER 2 YEARS
              04 NOT SURE

International migration statistics

1.17 Where do you think you will go? _____

    1.17a Have you ever actually tried to leave this country to move or migrate to another country?
        YES – 1   NO – 2 [SKIP TO 1.17c]

    1.17b Why didn't you migrate? [CIRCLE CODES OF ALL REASONS MENTIONED]
        01 CHANGED MIND
        02 COULDN'T GET EXIT PERMIT OR PASSPORT FROM THIS COUNTRY
        03 COULDN'T GET DOCUMENTS, VISAS OR PERMITS REQUIRED BY COUNTRY OF DESTINATION
        04 TOO EXPENSIVE
        05 TOO COMPLICATED, DON'T KNOW WHAT DOCUMENTS ARE NEEDED
        06 SPOUSE, FAMILY COULDN'T GET DOCUMENTS TO ACCOMPANY ME
        07 JOB FELL THROUGH
        08 SPOUSE, FAMILY OPPOSED
        09 JOB HERE IMPROVED
        10 OTHER PERSONAL REASON
        11 OTHER, SPECIFY: _____

    1.17c What documents are needed to leave this country? _____

INSTRUCTIONS FOR 1.18.

CHECK 1.3: IF NON-MIGRANT, CONTINUE WITH 1.18.
CHECK 1.8: IF IS MIGRANT BUT WAS NOT AT LEAST AGE 15 YEARS WHEN CAME TO THIS COUNTRY, CONTINUE WITH 1.18.
CHECK 1.7: IF CAME TO THIS COUNTRTY BEFORE (CURRENT YEAR MINUS 5), CONTINUE WITH 1.18.

THUS IF WAS BOTH (1) MIGRANT AND (2) CAME AFTER AGE 15 SINCE (CURRENT YEAR MINUS 5), SKIP TO SECTION 2.

1.18 What is your current level of education?
    01 NONE
    02 PRIMARY INCOMPLETE
    03 PRIMARY COMPLETE
    04 VOCATIONAL TECHNICAL TRAINING (POST-PRIMARY)
    05 SECONDARY INCOMPLETE
    06 SECONDARY COMPLETE
    07 VOCATIONAL TECHNICAL TRAINING (POST-SECONDARY)
    08 COLLEGE/UNIVERSITY INCOMPLETE
    09 COLLEGE/UNIVERSITY GRADUATE
    10 POSTGRADUATE DEGREE
    11 OTHER, SPECIFY: _____

    1.18a Has this changed in the past three years? YES – 1   NO – 2 [SKIP TO 1.19]

    1.18b During that time you completed _____ years at level _____.

1.19 What is your current marital status?
    01 NEVER MARRIED [SKIP TO 1.20]   04 SEPARATED [SKIP TO 1.19b]
    02 MARRIED [SKIP TO 1.19a]   05 DIVORCED [SKIP TO 1.19b]
    03 CONSENSUAL UNION [SKIP TO 1.19a] 06 WIDOW/WIDOWER [SKIP TO 1.19b]

Annex 1

    1.19a Did you get married in the last three years?
    YES – 1 [MONTH: _____ YEAR: _____]   NO – 2 [SKIP TO 1.20]
    1.19b Did you get separated or divorced or become a widow(er) during the last three years?
    YES – 1 [MONTH: _____ YEAR: _____]   NO – 2

1.20 Have you ever been contacted by a labour contractor or recruiter trying to persuade you to work in another country?
    YES – 1   NO – 2 [SKIP TO SECTION 4]
    1.21a To work in what country? _____
    1.21b Why didn't you leave? _____

[GO TO SECTION 4 – CURRENT WORK]

2. PRE-MIGRATION SITUATION AND ACTIVITY

    (FOR RECENT MIGRANTS WHO WERE AT LEAST AGE 15 UPON ARRIVAL IN THIS COUNTRY)

2.1 Where was your previous place of residence, that is, the place where you were living for at least 6 months before moving to live here?

                          COUNTRY: _____
                              STATE: _____
                            DISTRICT: _____
            VILLAGE/TOWN/CITY: _____
            OR NAME OF RURAL AREA

    2.1a Was this an urban or rural area?   URBAN – 1   RURAL – 2

2.2 Did you want to leave your previous place of residence or were you forced to leave by circumstances?
    FORCED TO LEAVE – 1   WANTED TO LEAVE – 2 [SKIP TO 2.3]
    2.2a Why did you have to leave? _____

2.3 Why did you leave your place of residence in (*previous country of residence, SEE 2.1*)? [CIRCLE ALL REASONS MENTIONED]
    2.3a [PROBE]: Any other reason?
        01 UNEMPLOYED AND SEEKING WORK
        02 TO SEEK WORK FOR THE FIRST TIME
        03 UNSATISFACTORY EARNINGS
        04 WORK CONDITIONS OR BENEFITS UNSATISFACTORY
        05 PERSONAL PROBLEM WITH EMPLOYER OR OTHERS AT WORK
        06 INADEQUATE EDUCATIONAL OPPORTUNITIES THERE, WANTED MORE EDUCATION FOR SELF
        07 INADEQUATE EDUCATIONAL OPPORTUNITIES THERE, WANTED MORE EDUCATION FOR CHILDREN
        08 INADEQUATE AMENITIES, SOCIAL ACTIVITIES THERE
        09 TO GET MARRIED, PROSPECTIVE SPOUSE BEING IN THIS COUNTRY
        10 DIVORCE, WANTED TO GET AWAY
        11 PERSONAL CONFLICTS OR FELT UNCOMFORTABLE WITH FAMILY/RELATIVES/FRIENDS/COMMUNITY THERE
        12 LACK OF CLOSE RELATIVES, FRIENDS IN AREA
        13 TO ACCOMPANY OR JOIN SPOUSE
        14 TO ACCOMPANY OR JOIN OTHER RELATIVE
        15 TO ACCOMPANY OR JOIN FRIEND
        16 POLITICAL PROBLEMS, FELT PERSECUTED OR AT RISK OF GOVERNMENT PERSECUTION
        17 OTHER, SPECIFY: _____

International migration statistics

    2.3b Which of these was **most** important? _____

2.4 Prior to migrating to this country, had you **ever** been to this country before? YES – 1 NO – 2 [SKIP TO 2.5]

    *2.4a When was the first time? MONTH _____ YEAR _____

    *2.4b About how many times altogether had you been in this country before? _____

2.5 Had you ever actually lived in this country (for at least six months) before moving here in (*year of in-migration* – SEE 1.7)?
    YES – 1   NO – 2

2.6 Before you came here, what were your main sources of information about this country? [DO **NOT** READ LIST: JUST CIRCLE EACH ONE MENTIONED]   PROBE: Any more?
    01 RELATIVES, FRIENDS ALREADY LIVING HERE
    02 RELATIVES, FRIENDS LIVING IN PREVIOUS COUNTRY OF RESIDENCE
    03 PRIVATE EMPLOYMENT AGENCIES, LABOUR RECRUITERS FROM THIS COUNTRY
    04 PRIVATE EMPLOYMENT AGENCIES, LABOUR RECRUITERS FROM PREVIOUS COUNTRY OF RESIDENCE
    05 GOVERNMENT EMPLOYMENT AGENCY FROM THIS COUNTRY
    06 GOVERNMENT EMPLOYMENT AGENCY FROM PREVIOUS COUNTRY OF RESIDENCE
    07 TELEVISION
    08 RADIO
    09 MOVIES
    10 WRITTEN MEDIA: NEWSPAPERS, MAGAZINES. SPECIFY EXACT SOURCE: _____
    11 OTHER, SPECIFY: _____

    2.6a Which of these do you consider to have been the most influential in affecting your decision to move to this country? _____

    *2.6b Please describe the kind of contact you had with this ["most influential"] source, including the first year of contact or information you remember, frequency of contact, how it affected your views about this country or other countries you may have been thinking about, etc. _____

2.7 Before you moved to live here, did you have any information specifically about employment/work opportunities in this country?
    YES – 1   NO – 2 [SKIP TO 2.8]

    2.7a What was the main source of this information? [CIRCLE THE CODES OF ALL SOURCES MENTIONED]
        01 RELATIVES/FRIENDS LIVING IN PREVIOUS COUNTRY OF RESIDENCE
        02 RELATIVES/FRIENDS LIVING IN THIS COUNTRY
        03 NEWSPAPER/RADIO/TV
        04 VISITED THIS COUNTRY EARLIER
        05 LABOUR RECRUITER, CONTRACTOR
        06 PRIVATE EMPLOYMENT AGENCIES IN PREVIOUS COUNTRY OF RESIDENCE
        07 GOVERNMENT EMPLOYMENT AGENCY IN PREVIOUS COUNTRY OF RESIDENCE
        08 EMPLOYER
        09 ORGANIZATION IN PREVIOUS COUNTRY THAT HELPS PEOPLE WHO WANT TO MOVE ABROAD
        10 ORGANIZATION IN THIS COUNTRY THAT HELPS PEOPLE WHO WANT TO MOVE HERE
        11 OTHER, SPECIFY: _____

Annex 1

2.8 What was your marital status when you left?
  01 NEVER MARRIED [SKIP TO 2.8c]   04 SEPARATED [SKIP TO 2.8b]
  02 MARRIED [SKIP TO 2.8a]   05 DIVORCED [SKIP TO 2.8b]
  03 CONSENSUAL UNION [SKIP TO 2.8a]   06 WIDOW/WIDOWER [SKIP TO 2.8b]

  2.8a Did you get married during the year (12 months) **prior to migrating**?
    YES – 1 [SKIP TO 2.9]   NO – 2 [SKIP TO 2.9]

  2.8b Did you get separated or divorced or become a widow(er) during the year (12 months) prior to migrating?
    YES – 1 [SKIP TO 2.9]   NO – 2 [SKIP TO 2.9]

  2.8c Did you move to this country to get married? YES – 1 [SKIP TO 2.9]   NO – 2

  2.8d Did you move to this country hoping to find someone to get married to later?
    YES – 1   NO – 2

2.9 What level of education had you completed before you left?
  01 NONE
  02 PRIMARY INCOMPLETE
  03 PRIMARY COMPLETE
  04 VOCATIONAL TECHNICAL TRAINING (POST-PRIMARY)
  05 SECONDARY INCOMPLETE
  06 SECONDARY COMPLETE
  07 VOCATIONAL TECHNICAL TRAINING (POST-SECONDARY)
  08 COLLEGE/UNIVERSITY INCOMPLETE
  09 COLLEGE/UNIVERSITY GRADUATE
  10 POSTGRADUATE DEGREE
  11 OTHER, SPECIFY: _____

2.10 Who primarily made the decision for you to move to this country? [CIRCLE CODES OF PERSONS MENTIONED]
  01 MYSELF   04 PARENT(S)
  02 SPOUSE   05 OTHER RELATIVE, SPECIFY _____
  03 CHILD(REN)   06 EMPLOYER
                          07 OTHER, SPECIFY _____

  2.10a Please explain how the decision was made for you to move to this country: _____

2.11 Who were you living with (who were the members of your household) in your previous country of residence before you moved to this country?

[COMPLETE HOUSEHOLD QUESTIONNAIRE, INCLUDING HOUSEHOLD ROSTER, ON SITUATION IN PREVIOUS PLACE OF RESIDENCE PRIOR TO MIGRATION]

2.12 During the year prior to leaving (*previous country of residence, SEE 2.1*), were you engaged in any kind of work, whether working for someone else or for yourself or in a family farm or business?
    YES – 1 [SKIP TO 2.13]   NO – 2

  2.12a Were you looking for work? YES – 1   NO – 2 [SKIP TO 2.12c]

  2.12b For how long had you been looking for work? WEEKS ____ MONTHS ____

  2.12c Had you **ever** worked in (*previous country of residence, SEE 2.1*) before coming to this country?
    YES – 1   NO – 2 [SKIP TO 2.33]

International migration statistics

    2.12d   During which (calendar) years did you work? _____

    2.12e   What was your main occupation? _____ [SKIP TO 2.33]

2.13-2.32   I would like to ask you some questions about your work during the year just before you left (*previous country of residence, SEE 2.1*).

Was your main work, during the 12 month period prior to departure, working for yourself, for someone else, or in some kind of family business, like a farm or store?

    01   For someone else   [REPEAT QUESTIONS 4.5-4.18, CHANGING VERB TO PAST TENSE.]

    02   For self   [REPEAT QUESTIONS 4.19-4.24, INCLUDING THE ENTERPRISE QUESTIONNAIRE, IF APPROPRIATE]

    03   In family business   [REPEAT QUESTIONS 4.19–4.24, INCLUDING THE ENTERPRISE QUESTIONNAIRE, IF APPROPRIATE]

2.33   Before you came to this country, had you ever had any contact with a recruitment agent, a labour recruiter or a contractor recruiting people to work in another country (a country different from *previous country of residence, SEE 2.1*)?

    YES – 1 **[POSSIBLE RESPONDENT FOR OPTIONAL MODULE ON MIGRANT WORKERS]**   NO – 2

2.34   When you left (*previous country of residence, SEE 2.1*), did you have any documents allowing you to travel abroad or specifically to leave (*previous country of residence, SEE 2.1*) or to come to this country?

    YES – 1   NO – 2 [SKIP TO 2.35]

    2.34a   What kind of documents did you have with you when you left your previous country of residence?

    [CIRCLE THE CODE OF ALL DOCUMENTS MENTIONED AND NOTE THE COUNTRY ISSUING THEM IN EACH CASE]

    01   PASSPORT, SPECIFY ISSUING COUNTRY _____
    02   EMPLOYMENT CLEARANCE FROM COUNTRY _____
    03   POLICE/SECURITY/MILITARY CLEARANCE ISSUED BY COUNTRY _____
    04   WORK PERMIT ISSUED BY COUNTRY _____
    05   RESIDENCE PERMIT ISSUED BY COUNTRY _____
    06   VISA ISSUED BY COUNTRY _____
    07   OTHER, SPECIFY TYPE AND COUNTRY OF ISSUE _____

    2.34b   Did you have any problems getting any of these documents?

        YES – 1   NO – 2 [SKIP TO 2.36]

    2.34c   Please explain: _____ [SKIP TO 2.36]

2.35   What kind of documents do you think you were supposed to have? _____
[USE CODES IN 2.34a]

    2.35a   Why didn't you have those documents?_____

2.36   Did you have to meet any requirements set by the government of (*previous country of residence, SEE 2.1*) to be able to leave that country?

    YES – 1   NO – 2 [SKIP TO 2.37]

    2.36a   What were those requirements? _____

    2.36b   Did you have any trouble meeting them?   YES – 1   NO – 2 [SKIP TO 2.37]

    2.36c   Please describe: _____

Annex 1

2.37 [IF CURRENT COUNTRY OF CITIZENSHIP IN 1.9 EQUALS PREVIOUS COUNTRY OF RESIDENCE IN 2.1, SKIP TO 2.38]

Did you have to meet any requirements of the government of (*country of citizenship, SEE 1.9*) to be able to leave (*previous country of residence, SEE 2.1*) for the purpose of coming to this country?

YES – 1   NO – 2   [SKIP TO 2.38]

2.37a   What were those requirements? _____

2.37b   Did you have any difficulties meeting them?   YES – 1   NO – 2   [SKIP TO 2.38]

2.37c   Please describe: _____

2.38 Did you have any (other) difficulties or did you have to make any special payments to anyone to leave (*previous country of residence*)?

YES – 1   NO – 2   [SKIP TO 2.39]

2.38a   What were these difficulties or payments? _____

2.38b   Please explain what you did or paid: _____

*2.39 With respect to your situation in (*previous country of residence, SEE 2.1*), compared to other people living in (*name of city, town, village from 2.1*), would you say you (and your family, if living with a family) was better off than most, worse off, or about average?

Better off   01 A lot better off than most
                     02 A little better off
About average   03 A little above average
                     04 Really average
                     05 A little below
Worse off   06 A little worse off
                     07 A lot worse off

*2.40 Were you or any members of your household in (*previous country of residence, SEE 2.1*) active in any organizations, say social, economic, religious, for sports, political or some other type?

YES – 1   NO – 2   [SKIP TO SECTION 3 – ARRIVAL IN COUNTRY]

*2.40a   Who was active? _____

*2.40b   What was the name of the organization to which (*person named in 2.40.a*) belonged? _____

*2.40c   Which type of organization was he or she active in? [CIRCLE APPROPRIATE CODE]

01 Social   04 Sports   07 Health
02 Economic   05 Political   08 Environmental
03 Religious   06 Educational 09 Other, specify _____

*2.40d   Did any of these organizations provide any information about migration to this country or any assistance to move to this country?   YES – 1   NO – 2 [SKIP TO SECTION 3 – ARRIVAL IN COUNTRY]

*2.40e   What information or assistance did it provide? _____

3. ARRIVAL IN COUNTRY

3.1   When did you come to live in this country?   MONTH _____   YEAR _____

3.2   Why did you come to this particular country?   [CIRCLE THE CODE FOR THE REASONS MENTIONED]

3.2a   [PROBE]: Any other reason?

01 HIGHER WAGES, HIGHER INCOME LEVELS HERE, HOPED TO GET BETTER JOB
02 OFFERED BETTER JOB HERE BEFORE I CAME
03 TRANSFERRED BY EMPLOYER

International migration statistics

        04 GOOD BUSINESS OPPORTUNITIES HERE, GOOD PLACE TO INVEST
        05 TO OBTAIN MORE EDUCATION FOR SELF
        06 TO OBTAIN BETTER OR MORE EDUCATION FOR CHILDREN
        07 HAD SPOUSE WAITING FOR ME HERE
        08 BETTER PROSPECTS FOR FINDING TYPE OF SPOUSE I WANTED
        09 BETTER AMENITIES HERE
        10 BETTER MEDICAL AND HEALTH SERVICES HERE
        11 LESS INSECURITY IN THIS COUNTRY
        12 FEWER ENVIRONMENTAL PROBLEMS
        13 THIS IS MY HOME COUNTRY
        14 HAVE FRIENDS AND RELATIVES HERE
        15 COULD OBTAIN ASYLUM IN THIS COUNTRY
        16 OTHER, SPECIFY: _____

3.2b Which of those reasons was **most** important? _____

3.3 Were you subject to border control when you moved to this country?
    YES – 1 [SKIP TO 3.4]   NO – 2

    3.3a Had you ever tried to enter before and had difficulties with border control?
        YES – 1   NO – 2 [SKIP TO 3.5]

    3.3b Please explain: _____ [SKIP TO 3.5]

3.4 Did you have difficulties with border control, customs clearance, health inspection, medical examinations and other types of checks when you moved to this country?
    YES – 1   NO – 2 [SKIP TO 3.4b]

    3.4a Please describe any difficulties that you had and what was done to resolve them:
        _____

    3.4b Did you have any other problems entering this country? YES – 1 NO – 2 [SKIP TO 3.6]

    3.4c Please describe: _____ [SKIP TO 3.6]

3.5 Why didn't you undergo border control? _____

    3.5a Did you have any problems entering this country?
        YES – 1   NO – 2 [SKIP TO 3.7]

    3.5b Please describe the problem, how it was resolved and how you got into the country:
        _____ [SKIP TO 3.7]

3.6 [CHECK 1.9: IF RESPONDENT WAS CITIZEN OF COUNTRY OF INTERVIEW AT TIME OF MIGRATION SKIP TO 3.7]

Did you have a visa when you last moved to live in this country (or when you came most recently to live here if you lived here earlier)?
    YES – 1   NO – 2 [SKIP TO 3.7]

    3.6a What kind of visa did you have?
        01 TOURIST VISA   05 WORK PERMIT
        02 BUSINESS VISA   06 TEMPORARY RESIDENCE PERMIT
        03 STUDENT VISA   07 REFUGEE VISA
        04 RESIDENT'S (IMMIGRANT) 08 OTHER, SPECIFY _____
              VISA

    3.6b Where did you get that visa?
        01 EMBASSY OR CONSULATE OF _____ IN _____
        02 THROUGH LABOUR RECRUITER OR CONTRACTOR
        03 THROUGH EMPLOYER
        04 THROUGH MARRIAGE (MY SPOUSE)
        05 OTHER RELATIVES GOT IT FOR ME, SPECIFY WHO: _____
        06 THROUGH OTHER INTERMEDIARY, SPECIFY WHO: _____

Annex 1

3.6c Did you have any problems getting it?   YES – 1   NO – 2   [SKIP TO 3.7]

3.6d Please describe these problems. [CIRCLE THE CODES OF ALL ITEMS MENTIONED SPONTANEOUSLY IN LEFT COLUMN. THEN PROBE FOR ANY ITEMS NOT MENTIONED AND CIRCLE ANY ADDITIONAL ITEMS MENTIONED WITH PROBING IN COLUMN TO THE RIGHT]

Spontaneous   Probing

01	01	LONG WAIT FOR APPOINTMENT
02	02	LENGTHY DELAYS WAITING IN LINES AT EMBASSY/CONSULATE OFFICE
03	03	LONG DELAYS IN WAITING FOR FOLLOW-UP APPOINTMENT OR FOR PAPERS TO CLEAR
04	04	COST OF VISA
05	05	OTHER PAYMENTS NECESSARY TO SPEED UP PROCESS
06	06	WAS NOT TREATED VERY WELL
07	07	TROUBLE FILLING OUT FORMS
08	08	TROUBLE MEETING QUALIFICATIONS, SPECIFY WHICH: _____
09	09	OTHER, SPECIFY: _____

*3.6e Please explain any problems encountered: _____

3.7 When you moved to this country, did you have a job waiting for you?
YES – 1   NO – 2 [SKIP TO 3.9]
THOUGHT THERE WOULD BE, BUT THERE WASN'T – 3   [SKIP TO 3.9]

3.7a Were you transferred here by an employer?   YES – 1   NO – 2   [SKIP TO 3.8]

3.7b Did you ask to be transferred here?   YES – 1   NO – 2   [SKIP TO 3.9]

3.7c What were the reasons for asking to be transferred?   [CIRCLE THE CODES OF ALL REASONS MENTIONED]

01 IMPROVE PAY
02 DISLIKED WORK I HAD BEFORE
03 PROMOTION
04 BROADEN EXPERIENCE
05 POOR WORKING CONDITIONS IN PREVIOUS JOB
06 WANTED TO MOVE BACK HOME
07 WANTED CHANGE OF ENVIRONMENT
08 FAMILY REASONS, FAMILY DIFFICULTIES
09 HAD RELATIVES ALREADY IN THE COUNTRY
10 OTHER, SPECIFY: _____

[SKIP TO 3.9]

3.8 Who helped you in getting a job? [CIRCLE THE CODE OF THOSE MENTIONED]
01 NO ONE
02 RELATIVE
03 FRIEND
04 EMPLOYER, BUSINESS CONTACT, OR ASSOCIATE
05 MIGRANT COMMUNITY OR ETHNIC ASSOCIATION, SPECIFY WHICH: _____
06 TRADE UNION
07 OTHER, SPECIFY: _____

3.9 Did you have any relatives or friends living in this country before you moved to live here?
YES – 1   NO – 2   [SKIP TO 3.9c]

3.9a Did any of your relatives or friends living in this country help you in any way when you first came here?
YES – 1   NO – 2   [SKIP TO 3.9c]

International migration statistics

3.9b What were the main types of assistance they gave you when you first moved to this country? [CIRCLE THE CODE OF THOSE MENTIONED]
   01 OBTAINED VISA
   02 PAID FOR TRANSPORTATION
   03 PROVIDED LODGING AND FOOD
   04 PROVIDED MONEY/LOAN
   05 PROVIDED INFORMATION ABOUT JOB POSSIBILITIES
   06 HELPED TO FIND EMPLOYMENT/WORK
   07 HELPED TO FIND HOUSE, APARTMENT OR OTHER LODGING
   08 PROVIDED FULL SUPPORT UNTIL I FOUND A JOB
   09 OTHER, SPECIFY: _____

3.9c Who paid for your transportation? [CIRCLE THE CODE OF THOSE MENTIONED]
   01 SELF
   02 RELATIVE
   03 FRIEND
   04 EMPLOYER, BUSINESS CONTACT, OR ASSOCIATE
   05 MIGRANT COMMUNITY OR ETHNIC ASSOCIATION
   06 TRADE UNION
   07 LABOUR RECRUITER OR CONTRACTOR
   08 OTHER, SPECIFY: _____

3.10 Apart from relatives in this country, after you arrived in this country, what was your **main** means of support? [CIRCLE ONE]
   01 THE JOB THAT I ALREADY HAD WAITING FOR ME IN THIS COUNTRY
   02 PERSONAL SAVINGS
   03 LOAN
   04 TRADE UNION IN THIS COUNTRY HELPED
   05 RELATIVES IN PREVIOUS COUNTRY OF RESIDENCE OR IN HOME COUNTRY
   06 MIGRANT COMMUNITY, ETHNIC OR MIGRANT ASSOCIATION IN THIS COUNTRY
   07 CASUAL JOBS IN THIS COUNTRY
   08 OTHER, SPECIFY: _____

3.11 [CHECK 3.7. IF PERSON ALREADY HAD A JOB WHEN HE/SHE MOVED TO THIS COUNTRY, SKIP TO 3.12] For how long were you in this country before you started looking for work?
   Less than a month – 00   MONTHS _____
   Has not started work – 88   [SKIP TO 3.12]

   3.11a What were the main methods that you used to seek work after you arrived? [CIRCLE ALL USED]
      01 FRIENDS, RELATIVES IN THIS COUNTRY
      02 FRIENDS, RELATIVES IN PREVIOUS COUNTRY OF RESIDENCE
      03 GOVERNMENT EMPLOYMENT AGENCY IN THIS COUNTRY
      04 PRIVATE EMPLOYMENT AGENCY IN THIS COUNTRY
      05 I ADVERTISED
      06 I READ NEWSPAPERS AND OTHER PRINTED MATERIALS LOOKING FOR JOB OPENINGS
      07 I ASKED OR VISITED POTENTIAL EMPLOYERS
      08 I TRIED TO SET UP BUSINESS
      09 OTHER, SPECIFY: _____

3.12 Since coming here, has your marital status changed?   YES – 1   NO – 2 [SKIP TO 3.13]

   3.12a Please explain each change that has occurred:
      First: From _____ to _____ in MONTH _____ YEAR _____
      Second: From _____ to _____ in MONTH _____ YEAR _____

Annex 1

3.13 Regarding your immediate relatives (father, mother, spouse, children, brothers and sisters), we want to know whether they have also moved to this country, either before, after or at the same time as you. Let me list first whether you had any immediate relatives alive at the time you moved to live in this country.

[INQUIRE ABOUT THE NUMBER OF RELATIVES OF EACH TYPE WHO WERE ALIVE WHEN THE RESPONDENT MIGRATED AND NOTE THE NUMBER IN THE FOLLOWING TABLE UNDER THE COLUMN LABELLED "Number alive when respondent moved to this country". IF A RESPONDENT DID NOT HAVE ANY RELATIVES OF A PARTICULAR TYPE AT THE TIME OF MIGRATION, RECORD "NA" IN THAT COLUMN]

    3.13a [FOR EACH TYPE OF IMMEDIATE RELATIVE INQUIRE]: Can you tell if your _____ has/have not moved to this country or if (he/she/they) died before moving to this country? [RECORD NUMBER OF THOSE WHO HAVE **NOT** MOVED UNDER COLUMN LABELLED "Number who have not moved to this country – those still alive" AND THOSE WHO HAVE DIED UNDER THE NEXT COLUMN. REPEAT "**NA**" IN CASES WHERE THE QUESTION IS NOT APPLICABLE BECAUSE THE RESPONDENT HAS NO RELATIVES OF THAT TYPE]

    3.13b [IF THE RESPONDENT HAS ANY IMMEDIATE RELATIVES WHO HAVE NOT MIGRATED TO THIS COUNTRY, ASK]:

    Why has or have these relatives of yours not migrated to join you? [CIRCLE APPROPRIATE CODES]

    01 NOT NECESSARY, NOT SEPARATED LONG
    02 TOO EXPENSIVE
    03 MY VISA DOES NOT ALLOW IT
    04 MY WORK CONTRACT OR TYPE OF EMPLOYMENT DOES NOT ALLOW IT
    05 GOVERNMENT IN THIS COUNTRY DOES NOT ALLOW IT
    06 GOVERNMENT IN THEIR COUNTRY OF RESIDENCE DOES NOT ALLOW IT
    07 FAMILY DOES NOT WANT TO COME
    08 CANNOT OBTAIN VISA FOR THEM
    09 CANNOT OBTAIN EXIT PERMIT

    3.13c [IF SOME RELATIVES ALIVE WHEN THE RESPONDENT MOVED TO THIS COUNTRY HAVE MIGRATED, INQUIRE ABOUT EACH TYPE]:

    Did your _____ move to this country together with you?

    [RECORD THE NUMBER WHO MOVED TOGETHER WITH THE RESPONDENT UNDER COLUMN LABELLED "Moved with respondent"]

3.14 [IF ALL RELATIVES MOVED TOGETHER WITH RESPONDENT, SKIP TO 3.15. IF ALL RELATIVES HAVE STAYED IN THE COUNTRY OF ORIGIN, SKIP TO 3.16. OTHERWISE INQUIRE ABOUT RELATIVES WHO MAY HAVE MOVED AT OTHER TIMES]:

Did your _____ move or migrate to this country before you did? When did (he/she/they) move here?

[RECORD NUMBER OF RELATIVES OF EACH TYPE THAT MOVED BEFORE RESPONDENT, MONTH AND DATE OF MOVE IN THE APPROPRIATE COLUMNS OF THE FOLLOWING TABLE. WRITE "**NA**" INSTEAD OF THE NUMBER IN ALL CASES IN WHICH THE QUESTION DOES NOT APPLY]

    3.14a [IF ALL RELATIVES ARE ACCOUNTED FOR, SKIP TO 3.15, OTHERWISE INQUIRE]:

    Did _____ follow you to this country later? When did (he/she/they) move here?

International migration statistics

[RECORD NUMBER OF RELATIVES OF EACH TYPE THAT MOVED AFTER RESPONDENT, MONTH AND DATE OF MOVE IN THE APPROPRIATE COLUMNS OF THE PRECEDING TABLE. WRITE "NA" INSTEAD OF THE NUMBER IN ALL CASES IN WHICH THE QUESTION DOES NOT APPLY]

*3.15 [INQUIRE ABOUT EACH TYPE OF RELATIVE WHO MOVED INTO THE COUNTRY OF INTERVIEW]:

Is your _____ still living in this country?

*3.15a Has/Have he/she/they died?

[RECORD NUMBER OF RELATIVES OF EACH TYPE THAT DIED SINCE MOVING TO THIS COUNTRY, TOGETHER WITH MONTH AND YEAR OF DEATH IN THE APPROPRIATE COLUMNS OF THE FOLLOWING TABLE. WRITE "0" IN CASES WHERE NO DEATH WAS RECORDED UNDER THE COLUMN LABELLED "Number"]

*3.15b Has/Have he/she/they moved to another country?

[RECORD NUMBER OF RELATIVES OF EACH TYPE THAT MOVED OUT OF THIS COUNTRY, MONTH AND DATE OF MOVE, AND CURRENT TOWN/VILLAGE/CITY AND COUNTRY OF RESIDENCE IN THE APPROPRIATE COLUMNS OF THE FOLLOWING TABLE. WRITE "NA" INSTEAD OF THE NUMBER IN ALL CASES IN WHICH THE QUESTION DOES NOT APPLY]

3.16 What is your **current** level of education?

```
01  NONE
02  PRIMARY INCOMPLETE
03  PRIMARY COMPLETE
04  VOCATIONAL TECHNICAL TRAINING (POST-PRIMARY)
05  SECONDARY INCOMPLETE
06  SECONDARY COMPLETE
07  VOCATIONAL TECHNICAL TRAINING (POST-SECONDARY)
08  COLLEGE/UNIVERSITY INCOMPLETE
09  COLLEGE/UNIVERSITY GRADUATE
10  POSTGRADUATE DEGREE
11  OTHER, SPECIFY: _____
```

3.17 Since you came to this country in (*year of arrival*, SEE *1.7*), have you (or any member of your family) ever attended school in this country?

YES – 1   NO – 2   [SKIP TO 3.18]

3.17a Please provide the following information for yourself and each person of your family who has attended school in this country after you moved to live here.

Name	ID no. if in current household	Dates attended	Level and grades attended in public schools	Level and grades attended in private schools

[INTERVIEWER: CHECK THAT 3.16 IS CONSISTENT WITH 2.9 PLUS 3.17a FOR RESPONDENT. CORRECT IF NECESSARY. IF RESPONDENT RECEIVED ANY MORE EDUCATION SINCE COMING TO THIS COUNTRY, CONTINUE WITH 3.17b. OTHERWISE, SKIP TO 3.18]

[TABLE TO BE USED TO RECORD ANSWERS TO QUESTIONS 3.13, 314 AND 3.15]

Relative	Number alive when respondent moved to this country	Number who did not move to this country		Moved before respondent to this country			Moved with respondent			Moved after respondent to this country			Has since left this country				Has since died in this country		
		Those still alive	Those who died since respondent moved	Number	Month	Year	Number	Month	Year	Number	Month	Year	Number	Month	Year	Country of residence	Number	Month	Year
Father																			
Mother																			
Spouse																			
Fiance(e)																			
Sons																			
Daughters																			
Brothers																			
Sisters																			
Other, specify:																			

International migration statistics

3.17b Did you receive any high school, college or other diplomas as a result of the schooling above?
YES – 1   NO – 2   [SKIP TO 3.18]

3.17c What kind of diploma did you receive?
01 HIGH SCHOOL DIPLOMA
02 VOCATIONAL DEGREE
03 COLLEGE DEGREE
04 GRADUATE DEGREE
05 OTHER DIPLOMA, SPECIFY _____

3.17d Has this degree/diploma/education helped you to....[READ EACH RESPONSE AND CIRCLE ANY WITH A POSITIVE ANSWER]
01 CHANGE YOUR PLACE OF WORK (EMPLOYER)
02 CHANGE YOUR OCCUPATION
03 IMPROVE YOUR SALARY/EARNINGS
04 TAKE ON HIGHER RESPONSIBILITIES IN YOUR PLACE OF WORK
05 CHANGE YOUR JOB SO AS TO USE THE NEW EDUCATION/ KNOWLEDGE YOU GAINED
06 NONE OF THE ABOVE
07 NOT APPLICABLE: HAS NOT WORKED SINCE STUDYING

*3.17e Please explain: _____

3.18 Since you moved to this country, have you received any on-the-job training?
YES – 1   NO – 2   [SKIP TO 3.19]

3.18a What kind of training was that, and how long did it last?
Please describe: _____ MONTHS: _____ YEARS _____

3.18b Did that help you improve your job or your earnings?
YES – 1   NO – 2   [SKIP TO 3.19]

3.18c In what way? _____

3.19 In the past 12 months, have you or any member of your family ever been ill or injured enough to have to go to a hospital?
YES – 1   NO – 2 [SKIP TO 3.20]

3.19a Please provide the following information about each such visit of any member of your household (include any members who were in the household one year ago but who have since left or died).

Name	ID no. if in household currently	Dates of treatment [EACH HOSPITALIZATION]	Public or private hospital?	Who paid for the treatment (USE CODES)?

CODES:
01 MYSELF OR MY FAMILY   05 RECEIVED FREE
02 EMPLOYER   06 OTHER, SPECIFY
03 INSURANCE   07 UNKNOWN
04 GOVERNMENT

Annex 1

3.20 Have you or any member of your family ever received any form of assistance from the government of this country, whether the local, state or national government, such as the following? [READ LIST AND CIRCLE CODE OF THOSE MENTIONED.]
  01 UNEMPLOYMENT COMPENSATION BENEFITS
  02 WELFARE BENEFITS
  03 FOOD OR LODGING (FREE OR SUBSIDIZED)
  04 RETIREMENT PENSION PAYMENTS OR SUPPORT
  05 HEALTH, MEDICAL BENEFITS
  06 OTHER, SPECIFY _____

  3.20a Please describe: _____

3.21 Have you, or anyone in this household, visited (*previous country of residence, SEE 2.1*) during the last 12 months?
  YES – 1   NO – 2 [SKIP TO 3.21c]

  *3.21a How many times during the last 12 months? ONCE – 1 TWICE – 2 THREE OR MORE – 3

  *3.21b Who made the visit(s)? [CIRCLE THE CODES OF ALL THOSE MENTIONED]
    01 MYSELF ALONE   03 MY SPOUSE
    02 MYSELF AND OTHER   04 MY CHILDREN
       CLOSE RELATIVES   05 OTHERS, SPECIFY _____
    [SKIP TO INSTRUCTIONS BEFORE 3.22]

  *3.21c When was the last time you or anyone in your household visited (*previous country of residence*)?
    MONTH _____ YEAR _____

CHECK 1.9: IF CITIZEN OF THIS COUNTRY AND NEVER BEEN CITIZEN OF ANOTHER, SKIP TO SECTION 4.

CHECK 1.9: IF CURRENTLY CITIZEN OF THIS COUNTRY BUT HAS CHANGED CITIZENSHIP, CONTINUE.

CHECK 1.9: IF NOT CITIZEN OF THIS COUNTRY, SKIP TO 3.24.

3.22 When you moved to live in this country in (*year of arrival, SEE 1.7*), were you already a citizen of this country?
  YES – 1 [SKIP TO 3.25] NO – 2

  3.22a When you moved here, had you intended to become a citizen?
    YES – 1 [SKIP TO 3.23] NO – 2

  3.22b What changed your mind? _____

3.23 When did you become a naturalized citizen? MONTH _____ YEAR _____

  3.23a What requirements did you have to satisfy to become a citizen? _____

  3.23b Did you have any problems satisfying those requirements?
    YES – 1   NO – 2 [SKIP TO 3.25]

  3.23c What kind of problems? [CIRCLE THE CODE OF ALL THOSE MENTIONED]
    01 PROVING LANGUAGE PROFICIENCY
    02 GETTING AN APPOINTMENT WITH THE RELEVANT AUTHORITIES
    03 FILLING THE NECESSARY FORMS, PROVIDING THE NECESSARY DOCUMENTS
    04 SATISFYING REQUIREMENTS RELATED TO LENGTH OF STAY IN COUNTRY

International migration statistics

      05 SATISFYING REQUIREMENTS RELATED TO ANCESTRY
      06 DELAYS IN PROCESSING THE APPLICATION
      07 COST OF NATURALIZATION PROCESS
      08 COST OF HIRING A LAWYER OR ANOTHER INTERMEDIARY TO FACILITATE PROCESS
      09 DIFFICULTIES IN PASSING A CITIZENSHIP EXAMINATION OR GOING THROUGH AN INTERVIEW
      10 PROBLEMS IN OBTAINING TYPE OF RESIDENCE PERMIT NEEDED FOR NATURALIZATION
      11 OTHER, SPECIFY: _____

3.23d Please explain further: _____ [SKIP TO 3.25]

3.24 Do you intend to become a citizen of this country (*name country*)? YES – 1 NO – 2 [SKIP TO 3.24b]

    3.24a Why? _____ [SKIP TO 3.24c]

    3.24b Why not? _____ [SKIP TO 3.25]

    3.24c Have you taken any practical steps to become a citizen? YES – 1 NO – 2 [SKIP TO 3.24e]

    3.24d What steps? _____ [SKIP TO 3.25]

    3.24e Why not? _____

3.25 Can you speak and understand the language of this country?
    01 YES, NATIVE TONGUE   [SKIP TO 3.26]
    02 YES, WELL   [SKIP TO 3.25c]
    03 YES, BUT NOT WELL
    04 NO

    *3.25a Do you feel this has been a handicap?
        YES – 1   SOMEWHAT – 2   NO – 3 [SKIP TO 3.25c]

    *3.25b Please explain in what way (or cite specific situations): _____

    3.25c Have you taken any course to improve your ability with the language of this country since coming here?
        YES – 1   NO – 2 [SKIP TO 3.25e]

    3.25d What course(s) did you take? _____ [SKIP TO 3.25f]

    *3.25e Why not? _____

    3.25f How well did you speak the main language of this country when you moved to live here?
        WELL – 1   SOMEWHAT – 2   NOT WELL – 3   NOT AT ALL – 4

3.26 What would you tell your friends or relatives in (*previous country of residence/place of origin, SEE 2.1*) regarding coming to this country?
    01 NOTHING
    02 ENCOURAGE THEM TO MOVE HERE
    03 DISCOURAGE THEM FROM MOVING HERE
    04 OTHER, SPECIFY: _____
    05 DON'T KNOW

4. *CURRENT WORK*

ADMINISTER QUESTIONNAIRE TO ALL HOUSEHOLD MEMBERS OVER AGE 15.

4.1 Are you currently engaged in some kind of work, whether working for someone else or for yourself or in a family farm or business?
    YES – 1 [SKIP TO 4.4]   NO – 2

Annex 1

4.1a Are you currently looking for work? YES – 1   NO – 2 [SKIP TO 4.1d]

4.1b For how long have you been looking for work?

MONTHS _____ WEEKS _____ DAYS _____

4.1c In what ways have you been looking for work? [CIRCLE THE CODE OF ALL THOSE MENTIONED]

01 ASKED FRIENDS/RELATIVES TO HELP
02 CHECKED WANTED ADS IN NEWSPAPER, OTHER PRINTED MEDIA
03 CONTACTED POSSIBLE EMPLOYERS DIRECTLY
04 CHECKED WITH EMPLOYMENT AGENCY—PRIVATE
05 CHECKED WITH EMPLOYMENT AGENCY—GOVERNMENT
06 CHECKED WITH LABOUR CONTRACTORS
07 OTHER, SPECIFY: _____
08 DONE NOTHING

[SKIP TO 4.2]

*4.1d Would you like to be working now, even if only in a part-time job?

YES – 1   MAYBE, DEPENDS – 2   NO – 3 [SKIP TO 4.2]

*4.1e Why are you not looking for work?

01 DO NOT HAVE RIGHT TO WORK
02 DO NOT HAVE WORK PERMIT
03 LOOKED FOR WORK, COULD NOT FIND ANY
04 NO JOBS AVAILABLE IN THIS AREA
05 NO JOBS AVAILABLE AT ADEQUATE PAY
06 NO JOBS AVAILABLE IN MY OCCUPATION
07 NO JOBS AVAILABLE IN MY LINE OF WORK
08 LACK NECESSARY EDUCATION, SKILLS
09 POOR HEALTH, DISABLED
10 EMPLOYERS THINK I AM TOO YOUNG OR TOO OLD
11 CANNOT ARRANGE CHILD CARE, NO ONE ELSE TO CARE FOR CHILDREN OR DO HOUSEWORK
12 IN SCHOOL, TRAINING
13 DO NOT KNOW
14 OTHER, SPECIFY: _____

4.2 Have you done any work, even part-time work, for at least two weeks in the past year?

YES – 1 [SKIP TO 4.4a]   NO – 2

4.3 Have you **ever** worked, that is, worked for someone else or for yourself or in a family farm or business whether at home or away from home, even if it was only for a few hours per week?

YES – 1   NO – 2 [SKIP TO 4.27]

4.4 I would like to ask you some things about your **most recent** job.

[INTERVIEWER: CHANGE VERB TENSE OF QUESTIONS BELOW IF NECESSARY AND CONTINUE]

4.4a What is (was) your main work: is it working for yourself, for someone else, or in some kind of family business, like a farm or store? [CIRCLE ONE]

01 FOR MYSELF   [SKIP TO 4.19]
02 IN FAMILY BUSINESS   [SKIP TO 4.19]
03 FOR SOMEONE ELSE

4.5 Please tell me about your work. What is the major activity of the place where you work?

_____

4.5a What is your work status? [PROBE AS NECESSARY]

01 LONG-TERM EMPLOYEE WITH A WRITTEN CONTRACT
02 LONG-TERM EMPLOYEE WITHOUT A WRITTEN CONTRACT
03 DAY LABOURER, CASUAL WORK

International migration statistics

        04   APPRENTICE, PAID
        05   APPRENTICE UNPAID, OTHER UNPAID WORKER
        06   TENANT (WORK ON FARM, PAY RENT)
        07   SHARECROPPER (WORK ON FARM, PAY PART OF PRODUCTION TO OWNER)
        08   OTHER, SPECIFY: _____

4.5b Where is this work mainly done?
        01   THIS AREA (VILLAGE, URBAN NEIGHBOURHOOD)
        02   ANOTHER PART OF CITY
        03   ANOTHER RURAL AREA
        04   A DIFFERENT CITY, URBAN AREA
        05   ABROAD, SPECIFY: _____

*4.5c How do you get to this job?
        01   WALK
        02   BICYCLE
        03   BUS, OTHER PUBLIC TRANSPORT
        04   PRIVATE CAR, MOTORCYCLE
        05   OTHER, SPECIFY: _____

*4.5d How long does it usually take you to get to work?
        MINUTES _____ HOURS _____

4.5e Is this job working for the government or an employer in the private sector?
        GOVERNMENT, PUBLIC SECTOR − 1   PRIVATE-SECTOR EMPLOYER − 2

4.6 What is your occupation? [IF NECESSARY, PROBE: What kind of work do you, yourself, do?] _____

4.7 How many weeks have you worked in the past 12 months? WEEKS _____

4.8 And how many days do you usually work per week? DAYS _____

4.9 How many hours per day do you work on average? HOURS _____

4.10 How much are you paid for this work? [NOTE THE AMOUNT AND CIRCLE THE TIME PERIOD OF RESPONSE. ALSO ASK IF RESPONDENT RECEIVES FREE FOOD, ETC., IF SO, INCLUDE ESTIMATE OF ITS VALUE IN THE TOTAL.]

        01   PER HOUR $ _____
        02   PER DAY $ _____
        03   PER WEEK $ _____
        04   PER MONTH $ _____
        05   PER YEAR $ _____

4.11 How long have you been doing this kind of work (in this kind of occupation), even if you were working someplace else? [WRITE "0" IF LESS THAN ONE YEAR] YEARS _____

    4.11a Do you have a written contract? YES − 1   NO − 2 [SKIP TO 4.12]

        Beginning date: MONTH _____   YEAR _____

        Ending date: MONTH _____   YEAR _____

        [WRITE "NONE" IF APPROPRIATE]

4.12 Some employers provide their employees with certain benefits, such as a retirement programme, health insurance, housing, etc. Do you receive any benefits like these from your current employer?
        YES − 1   NO − 2 [SKIP TO 4.13]

    4.12a What benefits do you receive? [CIRCLE CODE OF ALL THOSE RECEIVED; PROBE IF NECESSARY]
        01   HEALTH INSURANCE, MEDICAL CARE
        02   RETIREMENT PENSION

Annex 1

        03 UNEMPLOYMENT INSURANCE
        04 HOUSING
        05 SUBSIDIZED FOOD OR OTHER CONSUMER GOODS
        06 OTHER, SPECIFY: _____

4.13 On this job, are you a member of a labour union or similar employees' association?
        YES – 1   NO – 2

  *4.13a About what proportion of the workers in your place of employment are of the same country of origin as you? _____

  *4.13b How does this affect how you feel at work? _____

4.14 Do you currently do any **other** work, whether at home or away from home?
        YES – 1 [SKIP TO 4.16] NO – 2

4.15 In the past year did you have any other job besides the work that you have told me about?
        YES – 1   NO – 2 [SKIP TO 4.25]

4.16 What is this other work, is it working for yourself, for someone else, or in some kind of family business, like a farm or store?
        01 FOR MYSELF   [SKIP TO 4.19]
        02 IN FAMILY BUSINESS, FARM [SKIP TO 4.19]
        03 FOR SOMEONE ELSE

4.17 How many months did you work in this job in the past 12 months? MONTHS _____

4.18 And about how much did you earn per month for this work? $ _____ PER MONTH [SKIP TO 4.25]

4.19 In what kind of business do you work for yourself or for your family? [CIRCLE ALL THAT ARE APPROPRIATE. IF THE RESPONDENT OR HIS/HER HOUSEHOLD MEMBERS HAVE MORE THAN ONE BUSINESS, ANSWER QUESTIONS 4.20 AND 4.21 ABOUT EACH BUSINESS SEPARATELY]
        01 FARM, RAISE CROPS
        02 FARM, RAISE ANIMALS
        03 FISHING
        04 FORESTRY, SELL TIMBER
        05 COMMERCIAL, SELL SOMETHING
        06 MANUFACTURING, MAKE SOMETHING TO SELL
        07 SERVICES, PROVIDE SERVICE, REPAIR, LAUNDRY, ETC.
        08 OTHER, SPECIFY: _____

(4.20: see table overleaf.)

*4.21 When did you/your family acquire this business (or businesses)? YEAR _____ [RECORD A YEAR FOR EACH, AS APPROPRIATE]

4.22 What kind of main work do you yourself do in this business (or businesses)? _____

4.23 How many months did you work in this business (or businesses) in the past 12 months? MONTHS _____

4.24 And about how many hours per day did you work on average?
        HOURS PER DAY _____

4.25 Before the work that you did during the past 12 months, did you ever have any other work?
        YES – 1   NO – 2

4.26 How old were you when you **first** worked? _____ YEARS OLD

4.20 [CHECK 4.19: COMPLETE THE FOLLOWING ENTERPRISE QUESTIONNAIRE FOR EACH BUSINESS OWNED BY ANYONE IN THE HOUSEHOLD]

Business type (write code from 4.19)	Owner of business [USE CODES BELOW]	Value of gross sales last month (or usual month)	No. paid workers employed on average (full-time equivalent)	Total wage bill in average month	Total materials cost (of inputs) in average month	Total other costs per month (estimate)	Estimated net income of last (or average) month	Fixed assets (if any)			No. of cattle or other livestock
								Land (ha.)	Buildings (value in market, if sold)	Machinery & equipment (market value)	
1.											
2.											
3.											
4.											

CODE FOR OWNER OF BUSINESS:
01 RESPONDENT   03 OTHER MEMBER OF CURRENT HOUSEHOLD
02 SPOUSE   04 OTHER RELATIVE

Annex 1

*4.27 In some families, women work, while in others, they do not. Do you think a married woman should be able to work for pay away from home?
        01 YES   [SKIP TO 4.29]
        02 NO   [SKIP TO 4.29]
        03 IT DEPENDS
        04 DON'T KNOW

*4.28 Under what circumstances should a woman work away from home?
        01 WHEN FAMILY NEEDS MONEY
        02 WHEN HUSBAND IS SICK, AWAY, OR DEAD
        03 WHEN HUSBAND WANTS HER TO
        04 WHEN WOMAN IS NOT YET MARRIED
        05 WHEN WOMAN NEVER MARRIES
        06 OTHER, SPECIFY: _____
        07 DON'T KNOW

4.29 Do you yourself own any land, buildings, house, or business in any other country?
        YES – 1   NO – 2 [SKIP TO 4.30]

    4.29a What do you own and in what country? What would its approximate value be if sold?

	COUNTRY	VALUE
01 LAND	_____	_____
02 HOUSE	_____	_____
03 BUILDING	_____	_____
04 BUSINESS	_____	_____

    4.29b Who takes care of this asset (or assets)?

*4.30 In what country do you plan to retire? _____

C. OPTIONAL MODULE FOR MIGRANT WORKERS

THIS MODULE IS ONLY FOR MIGRANT WORKERS INTERVIEWED IN THE COUNTRY OF DESTINATION. MIGRANT WORKERS ARE IDENTIFIED HERE AS PERSONS LIVING IN A COUNTRY OTHER THAN THEIR OWN (THEY MUST **NOT** BE CITIZENS OF THE COUNTRY OF INTERVIEW) WHO HAVE HAD SOME CONTACT WITH A LABOUR RECRUITER WHILE LIVING IN A COUNTRY OTHER THAN THE COUNTRY OF INTERVIEW.

CHECK 1.9 TO ASCERTAIN THAT RESPONDENT IS NOT CURRENTLY A CITIZEN OF THE COUNTRY OF INTERVIEW AND CHECK 2.33 TO CHECK IF RESPONDENT HAS HAD CONTACT WITH A LABOUR RECRUITER.

FOR RETURN MIGRANT WORKERS LIVING IN THEIR OWN COUNTRY OF CITIZENSHIP, MODIFICATIONS TO THIS MODULE ARE NECESSARY (SEE CHAPTER VI.F).

1. You said earlier that when you were living in (*previous country of residence, SEE 2.1*) you had contact with a labour recruiter or contractor who contacted you about working in another country, correct?
        YES – 1   NO – 2   [END INTERVIEW]

2. Were you interested in coming to work in this country before you had this contact?
        YES –1   NO – 2

3. Was that contact regarding working in this country (*country of interview*) only or have such recruiters ever contacted you about working in other countries as well?
        01 YES, THIS COUNTRY ONLY
        02 NO, OTHER COUNTRIES AS WELL, SPECIFY WHICH: _____

    3a When did this contact occur (or the last such contact, if more than one)?
    MONTH _____ YEAR _____

4. Did this contact with the labour recruiter/contractor directly affect your decision to migrate here? YES – 1   NO – 2

International migration statistics

5. Did you migrate to take up a position/job offered by this (last) recruiter? YES – 1 [SKIP TO 5d] NO – 2

   5a Did you use the services of any other labour recruiter, whether private or affiliated to a government?
   YES – 1 [SKIP TO 5c]   NO – 2

   5b Why not? Please explain: _____ [END INTERVIEW]

   5c Did you get your first job in this country through a labour recruiter?
   YES – 1   NO – 2 [END INTERVIEW]

   5d Was this contact initiated by you or by the labour recruiter/contractor?
   MYSELF – 1   RECRUITER – 2

   5e Was that recruiter representing some company or government?
   YES – 1   NO – 2

   5f Was this a 01 Private labour recruiter from (*country of interview*) operating in (*previous country of residence*)?
   02 Private recruiter from (*previous country of residence*) recruiting for employer in (*country of interview*)?
   03 Agent of government of (*country of interview*) recruiting in (*previous country of residence*) for employer here?
   04 Other, specify: _____

   5g For which employer? _____

6. Did a labour recruiter or a government agency in (*previous country of residence, SEE 2.1*) offer any special training for persons wishing to work abroad?
   YES – 1   NO – 2

   6a Did you receive any special training to prepare you to work abroad while you lived in (*previous country of residence*)?
   YES – 1   NO – 2 [SKIP TO 7]

   6b Please describe the type of training you received: _____

   6c Who did the training? _____

   6d For what duration? DAYS _____ WEEKS _____ MONTHS _____

   6e Did you have to pay for it? YES – 1   NO – 2 [SKIP TO 7]

   6f How much did you pay? _____

7. Did the labour recruiter provide information about your work contract?
   YES – 1   NO – 2 [SKIP TO 10]

   7a Did the labour recruiter provide a written contract? YES – 1   NO – 2 [SKIP TO 7d]

   7b What language was it in? _____

   7c Could you read and understand it, or was it difficult?
   01 YES, I COULD UNDERSTAND COMPLETELY
   02 I COULD UNDERSTAND ONLY THE GENERAL POINTS, NOT THE DETAILS
   03 I COULD BARELY UNDERSTAND IT
   04 NO, I COULD NOT UNDERSTAND ANYTHING IN IT

   7d What were the terms of the contract?
   DURATION: FROM: MONTH _____ YEAR _____ ;
                  TO: MONTH _____ YEAR _____
   NAME OF PROSPECTIVE EMPLOYER: _____
   LOCATION OF WORK: COUNTRY _____ CITY _____

Annex 1

TYPE OF WORK SPECIFIED: _____
RATE OF PAY: _____ per _____
MODE OF PAYMENT OR WHERE TO BE DEPOSITED BY EMPLOYER:
_____

8. Were any other benefits of employment specified in the contract?
    YES – 1   NO – 2   [SKIP TO 9]

    8a Which benefits? [READ EACH RESPONSE AND CIRCLE THOSE INDICATED]
        01 FREE OR SUBSIDIZED HOUSING
        02 FREE OR SUBSIDIZED FOOD
        03 FREE OR SUBSIDIZED MEDICAL CARE OR HEALTH INSURANCE FOR YOURSELF
        04 PROVISION OF MEDICAL COVERAGE OR INSURANCE FOR IMMEDIATE FAMILY [IF APPLICABLE]
        05 PROVISION OF LIFE OR ACCIDENT INSURANCE
        06 RIGHT TO MATERNITY BENEFITS
        07 RIGHT TO DAYS OFF EVERY WEEK
        08 RIGHT TO UNEMPLOYMENT/TERMINATION BENEFITS
        09 RIGHT TO PAID SICK DAYS
        10 RIGHT TO PAID OVERTIME
        11 RIGHT TO VACATION DAYS WITH FULL PAY
        12 RIGHT TO ARBITRATION IN CASE OF A DISPUTE
        13 PAID RETURN TICKET OR TRANSPORTATION TO HOME COUNTRY
        14 OTHER, SPECIFY: _____

9. Did you have to pay anything or make other arrangements to get a work contract?
    01 YES, AMOUNT PAID: _____
    02 YES, OTHER ARRANGEMENT (describe): _____
    03 NO

10. Before you left (*previous country of residence, SEE 2.1*), did you receive any financial help from the labour recruiter, from the employer, or from your own government?
    01 FROM LABOUR RECRUITER
    02 FROM EMPLOYER
    03 FROM OWN COUNTRY'S GOVERNMENT
    04 FROM OTHER SOURCE, SPECIFY: _____

    10a Did they pay for your transportation to this country, in full or in part?
         YES – 1   NO – 2   [SKIP TO 10c]

    10b If yes, please explain: _____

    10c Did they provide you with a cash advance? YES – 1   NO – 2   [SKIP TO 11]

    *10d When? MONTH _____ YEAR _____

    10e How much was it? _____

    *10f What arrangements were made for you to pay it back? _____

    *10g How do you feel about this advance now? _____

11. Did they help you get the exit documents that you needed from your own country?
    YES – 1   NO – 2   [SKIP TO 11b]

    11a Please explain how they helped: _____

    11b Did they provide you with or help you get the documents that you needed to enter the country where you were to work?
         YES – 1   NO – 2   [SKIP TO 12]

    11c Please explain how they helped: _____

International migration statistics

12. Did you take up employment as you expected and according to the provisions of your work contract (if any)?
    YES – 1   [SKIP TO 13]   NO – 2

    12a In what way was the situation different from what you expected? [CIRCLE CODE OF STATEMENTS THAT APPLY AND ASK RESPONDENT TO EXPLAIN ANY STATEMENT SELECTED]
    01 THERE WAS NO JOB WITH THE EMPLOYER AFTER ALL
    02 I DID NOT RECEIVE THE RATE OF PAY EXPECTED
    03 THE WORK WAS DIFFERENT FROM WHAT I EXPECTED
    04 THE PAY WAS NOT TRANSFERRED TO ME OR TO MY ACCOUNT
    05 I DID NOT RECEIVE THE HOUSING (BENEFITS) ANTICIPATED
    06 I DID NOT RECEIVE THE FOOD (BENEFITS) ANTICIPATED
    07 I DID NOT RECEIVE THE HEALTH BENEFITS ANTICIPATED
    08 I DID NOT RECEIVE OTHER BENEFITS ANTICIPATED, SPECIFY: _____
    09 I COULD NOT BRING MY FAMILY, AS I HAD EXPECTED
    10 OTHER DIFFERENCE, SPECIFY: _____
       EXPLANATIONS: _____

13. Did you have the right to switch to another employer after you got here?
    YES – 1   NO – 2

    13a Did you want to change employer or take up some other work after you got here?
       YES – 1   NO – 2   [SKIP TO 14]

    13b Did you actually try to change employers?
       YES – 1   NO – 2   [SKIP TO 14]

    13c What happened? _____

14. Did you want members of your family to join you here?
    YES – 1   NO – 2   [SKIP TO 15]

    14a Did you try to get them in to join you?
       YES – 1   NO – 2   [SKIP TO 15]

    14b Were they able to join you?
       YES – 1   [SKIP TO 14d]   NO – 2

    14c Why not? _____ [SKIP TO 15]

    14d Were their health insurance needs covered by your health coverage with your employer?
       YES – 1   [SKIP TO 14f]   NO – 2

    14e How were their health insurance needs met? _____

    14f Did the employer provide any other benefits or assistance for your family members? [CIRCLE ALL THOSE MENTIONED]
       01 FREE OR SUBSIDIZED EDUCATION
       02 FREE TRANSPORTATION FROM HOME COUNTRY
       03 ASSISTANCE IN OBTAINING VISAS OR RESIDENCE PERMITS FOR IMMEDIATE RELATIVES
       04 FREE OR SUBSIDIZED HOUSING
       05 DEPENDENCY ALLOWANCE
       06 OTHER, SPECIFY: _____

15. Did you want to travel back to visit your family or your home country during the period of the contract?
    YES – 1   NO – 2

Annex 1

15a Are (or were) you allowed to do this during the period of the contract?
   YES – 1   NO – 2 [SKIP TO 16]

15b Have you actually visited your home country since you have been under contract?
   YES – 1   NO – 2

16. Did you want to send some of your earnings back to your family/home country?
   YES – 1   NO – 2 [SKIP TO 17]

16a Have you tried to send money home?
   YES – 1   NO – 2 [SKIP TO 17]

16b Have you had any problems sending money back?
   YES – 1   NO – 2 [SKIP TO 17]

16c What problems have you had?
   [READ EACH AND CIRCLE THE CODE OF THOSE MENTIONED]
   01 LIMITS ON AMOUNT THAT CAN BE SENT
   02 PROBLEMS IN CONVERTING CURRENCY
   03 BUREAUCRATIC OBSTACLES
   04 HIGH CHARGES OF CURRENCY CONVERSION
   05 HIGH CHARGES OF BANK TRANSFER
   06 LACK OF RELIABILITY OF THE BANKING SYSTEM
   07 NO ACCESS TO BANKS
   08 HAD NO ONE TO SEND IT WITH
   09 OTHER, SPECIFY: _____

16d Please explain any problems mentioned: _____

*17. Regarding the first job in this country that you secured through a labour recruiter, did you feel it offered job security for you? Or did you feel that you could be dismissed or laid-off at any moment?
   01 YES, IT OFFERED JOB SECURITY
   02 NO, IT DID NOT OFFER JOB SECURITY

*18. Regarding the employer in this country that first hired you through a labour recruiter, did you ever feel that the employer had taken advantage of or exploited you?
   01 YES, please explain: _____
   02 NO [SKIP TO 19]

   *18a Did you try to do anything about it? [CIRCLE CODE OF THOSE ACTIONS MENTIONED]
      01 SPEAK TO HIM/HER   04 QUIT JOB
      02 SEEK LEGAL HELP   05 SEEK OTHER EMPLOYMENT
      03 SEEK HELP FROM MY EMBASSY 06 OTHER, SPECIFY: _____

19. Overall, have you been satisfied with your work experience in this country resulting from being hired through a labour recruiter?
   YES – 1   NO – 2

   19a Please explain: _____

20. Would you do it again, or recommend that a friend take a job arranged by the same labour recruiter?   YES – 1   NO – 2

   20a Please explain: _____

D. *OPTIONAL MODULE ON FERTILITY*

   TO BE ASKED OF EACH WOMAN AGED 15 YEARS AND OVER.

1. Have you ever had a live birth?   YES – 1   NO – 2 [SKIP TO 10]

International migration statistics

2. How many children have you had who live with you now? _____
   2a How many sons? _____   2b How many daughters? _____
3. How many children have you borne alive who now live somewhere else? _____
   3a How many sons live elsewhere? _____
   3b How many daughters live elsewhere? _____
4. Have you ever given birth to a child who was born alive but who died later, even if he/she lived only a few minutes?
       YES – 1   NO – 2 [SKIP TO 5]
   4a How many children have you had who were born alive and died later? _____
   4b How many of your sons born alive died later? _____
   4c How many of your daughters born alive died later? _____
5. [INTERVIEWER: ADD TOTAL NUMBERS AND CONFIRM]: Altogether then, you have had a total of _____ live births, including _____ sons and _____ daughters? Is this correct? [IF NOT, PROBE AND CORRECT]
6. In what month and year did your **last** live birth occur?
   MONTH _____   YEAR _____
7. Where were you living when you had this last birth?   COUNTRY _____
                                                                                STATE _____
                                                                                DISTRICT _____
   7a Was this an urban or rural area?   URBAN – 1   RURAL – 2
8. In what country did this birth occur? COUNTRY: _____
   8a Where did the birth take place?
         01 OWN HOUSE
         02 GOVERNMENT HEALTH CENTRE, CLINIC OR HOSPITAL
         03 PRIVATE HOSPITAL, CLINIC, DISPENSARY, DOCTOR'S OFFICE
         04 OTHER, SPECIFY: _____
   8b Who attended the birth?
         01 DOCTOR   04 RELATIVE
         02 NURSE   05 OTHER, SPECIFY: _____
         03 MIDWIFE
9. Is this child still alive?   YES – 1   NO – 2
10. Are you currently pregnant?   YES – 1   NO – 2
11. Would you like to have any [**more**] children some day [*or any more after the current pregnancy, if currently pregnant*]?
    YES – 1   NO – 2 [SKIP TO 13]   CAN'T HAVE ANY MORE – 3 [SKIP TO 12a]
    11a How many more would you like to have? _____ -
    11b How soon would you like to have another child?
          01 WITHIN A YEAR
          02 BETWEEN ONE AND TWO YEARS FROM NOW
          03 AFTER TWO YEARS
          04 IT'S UP TO GOD, WHENEVER IT HAPPENS
          05 NOT SURE
12. Do you think you are capable of having more children?
    YES – 1 [SKIP TO 13]   NOT SURE – 2 [SKIP TO 13]   NO – 3
    12a Why do you think you can't have any more children?
          01 IS STERILIZED, HAD OPERATION
          02 HUSBAND STERILIZED

Annex 1

       03 IS MENOPAUSAL
       04 IS NOT FECUND ANY MORE
       05 NOT SURE

    [SKIP TO 14a]

13. Are you **currently** using any method of contraception or any procedure to delay or prevent pregnancies?
        YES – 1   NO – 2 [SKIP TO 14a]

14. What method are you using?   [CIRCLE THE APPROPRIATE CODE]
        01 PILL   06 INJECTION
        02 IUD   07 FEMALE STERILIZATION
        03 CONDOM   08 PARTNER VASECTOMY
        04 DIAPHRAGM   09 RHYTHM
        05 NORPLANT, INPLANT   10 WITHDRAWAL
                                             11 OTHER, SPECIFY: _____

    14a Are there any (other) methods you have used earlier at any time in your life?
            YES – 1   [USE CODES FROM 14]: _____ _____ _____
            NO – 2   [CHECK 1.3, IF NON-MIGRANT END INTERVIEW HERE;
                              IF MIGRANT AND HAS HAD A LIVE BIRTH (CHECK 1 THIS MODULE), SKIP TO 16;
                              IF MIGRANT AND HAS NOT HAD A LIVE BIRTH (CHECK 1 THIS MODULE), SKIP TO 19]

15. What method have you used for the longest time period?
    [USE CODE FROM 14] _____

        15a What was the **first** method you ever used? [USE CODE FROM 14] _____ -
        15b How old were you at that time? _____ YEARS

            [CHECK 1.3, IF NON-MIGRANT END INTERVIEW HERE;
            IF MIGRANT AND HAS HAD A LIVE BIRTH (CHECK 1 THIS MODULE), CONTINUE;
            IF MIGRANT AND HAS NOT HAD A LIVE BIRTH (CHECK 1 THIS MODULE), SKIP TO 19]

16. How many children born alive did you have in (*previous country of residence, SEE 2.1*), how many in any **other** countries (if you also lived in any other countries before the previous one), and how many have you had since coming to live in *this* country in (*year of arrival, SEE 1.7*)?

        IN EARLIER COUNTRIES, IF APPLICABLE   SONS _____
                                                                            DAUGHTERS _____
                                                                            TOTAL _____
        IN PREVIOUS COUNTRY OF RESIDENCE   SONS _____
                                                                            DAUGHTERS _____
                                                                            TOTAL _____
        IN THIS COUNTRY   SONS _____
                                                                             DAUGHTERS _____
                                                                            TOTAL _____

[CHECK 4: IF WOMAN HAS NEVER HAD A LIVE BIRTH THAT DIED LATER, SKIP TO QUESTION 19]

17. You said above that you have had _____ children born alive who died later. Did any of these children die in childhood, that is, before they reached their fifth birthday?
        YES – 1   NO – 2 [SKIP TO 19]

        17a For each of these children, in what country was he/she born and in what country did he/she die?

            Country of birth _____   Country of death _____
            Country of birth _____   Country of death _____

International migration statistics

        Country of birth _____   Country of death _____

[CHECK 16: IF WOMAN HAS **NOT** HAD BIRTHS IN PREVIOUS COUNTRY OF RESIDENCE, SKIP TO 19]

18. Think of the **last** child you gave birth to in (*previous country of residence, SEE 2.1*). In what kind of place did that birth take place?
    01 OWN HOUSE
    02 GOVERNMENT HEALTH CENTRE, CLINIC OR HOSPITAL
    03 PRIVATE HOSPITAL, CLINIC, DISPENSARY, DOCTOR'S OFFICE
    04 OTHER, SPECIFY: _____

    18a Who attended the birth?
        01 DOCTOR   03 MIDWIFE
        02 NURSE   04 RELATIVE
                                  05 OTHER, SPECIFY: _____

    18b Is this child still alive?   YES – 1   NO – 2

19. [IF WOMAN WAS **NOT** AT LEAST AGE 15 YEARS **WHEN SHE CAME** TO THIS COUNTRY, THIS CONCLUDES OPTIONAL MODULE]
Before you came to this country, had you ever used any methods of contraception or procedures to delay or prevent pregnancies?
    YES – 1   NO – 2 [SKIP TO 21]

    19a Which methods did you ever use before coming here?
        [USE CODES OF 14] _____ _____ _____ [IF USED MORE THAN ONE, CONTINUE. OTHERWISE, SKIP TO 20a]

    19b Which was the method that you used for the **longest** time while living in (*previous country of residence, SEE 2.1*)?
        [USE CODES OF 14] _____

20. What was the **first** method you ever used? [USE CODES OF 14] _____

    20a How old were you at that time? _____ YEARS

21. Since you came to this country, have you ever used any methods?
    YES – 1   NO – 2 [END OF OPTIONAL MODULE]

    21a After you came here in (*year of arrival, SEE 1.7*), in what year did you **first** use any method? _____

    21b What method was that? [USE CODES OF 14] _____

    21c Did you use any other methods?
        YES – 1   NO – 2 [END OF OPTIONAL MODULE]

    21d Which ones? [USE CODES OF 14] _____ _____ _____

    21e What method have you used for the longest time since you came to this country? _____

C. COMMUNITY-LEVEL QUESTIONNAIRE

Name of community _____ Date _____

Location (state, district, subdistrict) _____

Interviewer: _____ Administrative title/function (if any): _____

Urban/rural: _____

Names, titles, and official functions (if any) of respondents: _____

Written or published sources consulted (if any): _____

Annex 1

GEOGRAPHIC CHARACTERISTICS

Total area of community (sq. km.) _____ (DRAW SKETCH MAP, SHOWING BOUNDARIES WITH NEIGHBOURING COMMUNITIES)

Altitude, topography, bodies of water (note if on seacoast), quantity of rainfall during year and seasonality _____

Whether any major natural disaster in past 5 years (drought, flood, earthquake, etc.) and proportion of population in community affected _____

POPULATION

Total population _____ and total number of households _____

Distribution by age/sex in last census or other source, if available (note year to which data refer) _____

Distribution by ethnicity/race/religion (if appropriate) _____

MIGRATION

In general, over, say, the past five years, have there been more people coming to live in this community from other places, or are there more people from this community leaving it to live elsewhere?

Are there **any** residents of this community who were born in another country? [IF NOT, SKIP RELEVANT SECTIONS BELOW]

    How many individuals _____ (or families)? _____
    Main countries of origin _____
    Percentage of population of community from each major country of origin _____

Number of international migrants coming to community from **other countries** in past:

    12 months _____ , 5 years _____ , 10 years _____

    Main countries of origin _____
    Main years of arrival _____
    Mainly individual migrants or families? _____

What kind of work or economic activities do these migrants engage in here? _____

What are the attitudes in this community toward these migrants coming here? _____

Number of international migrants going from community to other countries in past:

    12 months _____ , 5 years _____ , 10 years _____

    Main countries of destination _____

    Main years of exit _____

    Mainly individual migrants or families? _____

Number of return migrants to this community in past:

    12 months _____ , 5 years _____ , 10 years _____

Attitudes in community towards return migrants: mainly favourable, not favourable? Please explain. _____

Do the return migrants bring money or goods back with them when they return? _____

What do return migrants do when they return to community? _____

Number of internal migrants to community from other parts of **this** country, in past:

    12 months _____ , 5 years _____ , 10 years _____

Number of out-migrants from this community to other parts of **this** country in past:

    12 months _____ , 5 years _____ , 10 years _____

International migration statistics

TRANSPORTATION

Does community have paved road (if not, distance and time required to walk to nearest)?
_____

Does community have bus transport **within** community _____

Does community have **other** main transport within community, (if so, describe)?
_____

Does community have public transport to nearby communities _____, if so, indicate its frequency _____

Travel conditions to reach nearest:	district capital	national capital	foreign capital
Distance from community			
Most common mode of transport			
Time of travel using above			
Condition of road			
Access limited in certain seasons?			

Existence of direct commercial transportation linkages with foreign countries: by air, water, or land

Distance/time to reach nearest foreign consulate

Distance/time to reach nearest government passport office

EDUCATION

Existence of educational facilities within community (circle as appropriate: if more than one, write in quantity just below each):

pre-school, primary school, secondary school, vocational school, university/college

Enrolment levels at each level by sex (compute enrolment ratios, if possible) _____

Males

Females

Indicate whether schools are public or private and cost of fees, uniforms, books, etc.
_____

(If primary school or secondary school is not in the community, estimate distance to nearest by walking or by most common means [indicate] used by children to get there, and include number of children attending elsewhere)

Proportion of adult men who can read and write _____

Proportion of adult women who can read and write _____

OTHER COMMUNITY FACILITIES

(If not IN the community, time to get to nearest by mode of transport most used by community residents)

	Mark with check if in community	Time to get to, if not
HEALTH CLINIC/HOSPITAL		
PRIVATE DOCTOR/CLINIC		
TRADITIONAL DOCTOR (OPTIONAL)		
PHARMACY		
POST OFFICE		
BANK/CREDIT UNION		
POLICE STATION		
STREET LIGHTS		
PUBLIC TELEPHONE		
MARKET FOR PURCHASING FOOD (FUNCTIONS AT LEAST WEEKLY)		
MOVIE THEATRE		
PARK OR ATHLETIC FIELD		
CHURCH/MOSQUE/TEMPLE		

Annex 1

Proportion of locally available (non-cable) television programmes originating abroad _____
Number of foreign newspapers, magazines available regularly _____

HOUSING/SANITATION/MODERNIZATION
Proportion of dwellings with dirt floor _____
Proportion of dwellings with piped water _____
Proportion of dwellings with electricity _____
Proportion of dwellings with flush toilet _____
Does community have garbage (solid waste) collection? _____ Frequency: _____
Does community have functioning water treatment facility for producing potable water?
_____
Does community have sewage facility for treating waste water? _____
Does community have regular shortages of water in certain seasons? _____
Is there air, water, solid waste, toxic waste pollution within the community? _____
   (If so) What are the main sources of wastes, and degree of human exposure? _____
Proportion of dwellings with radios _____
Proportion of dwellings with televisions _____
Proportion of televisions with cable/satellite connection _____
Proportion of dwellings with refrigerators _____
Proportion of dwellings with motorized vehicles _____
Proportion of women attended by doctor or nurse when they give birth _____
Proportion of children receiving DPT vaccination before they are two years old _____
Existence of serious contagious diseases and prevalence; outbreaks in past 5 years _____

ECONOMIC ASPECTS
Main economic (agricultural, non-agricultural) activities _____
Proportion of labour force in formal/informal sector activities _____
Extent of unemployment in community, whether rising or falling _____
Main employers _____
Are there any foreign-owned businesses? If so, number of local community residents employed by them and approximate proportion of local labour force _____
Is there significant seasonality of production/labour needs? What are the implications for migration?
_____
Distribution/proportion of working men/women in this community by main economic sectors
_____
For most common sectors for men/women, typical wage/salary levels _____
Whether any workers living in community belong to a labour union; if so, how many, and to what union(s)? _____
Existence of public development projects in past 5 years and effects on community employment, incomes, etc. _____
Expansion of private business establishments in past 5 years; effects on community employment, incomes, etc. _____
Existence, membership, and effects of producer/consumer cooperatives operating in community
_____

International migration statistics

(*OPTIONAL–ASK ONLY IF PRIMARILY RURAL COMMUNITY*)

Land distribution (number of families dependent on agriculture who have no land, number with less than 1 ha., 1 to less than 5 ha., etc.) _____

Largest 3 landholders; workers employed by each permanently (year-round) and seasonally _____

Quality of land (soil) _____

Main crops grown or animals raised _____

Trends or changes in crops/amimals raised in past 5 years _____

Use of technology (proportion of farms using fertilizer, irrigation, hybrid seeds, etc.) _____

Trends/changes in technology in past 5 years _____

Trends in prices of main crops or animals raised in past 5 years _____

ANNEX 2. MODEL QUESTIONNAIRES FOR COUNTRY OF ORIGIN

A. HOUSEHOLD QUESTIONNAIRE

[ADMINISTER THE SAME HOUSEHOLD QUESTIONNAIRE AS IN COUNTRY OF DESTINATION PERTAINING TO THE SITUATION AT THE TIME OF INTERVIEW, BUT ADD H.21a AND H.21b AS PRESENTED BELOW]:

H.21a Does anyone in this household receive money or goods (other than minor gifts) from any relative or person living in another country?

    YES – 1   NO – 2 [SKIP TO H.21b]

    [ADMINISTER MODULE I-B FROM CHAPTER VII]

H.21b Does anyone in this household send money or goods to any relative or other person in another country?

    YES – 1   NO – 2 [SKIP TO INSTRUCTIONS BELOW]

    [ADMINISTER MODULE I-A IN CHAPTER VII]

[NOW THE HOUSEHOLD QUESTIONNAIRE SHOULD BE ADMINISTERED AGAIN REGARDING THE COMPOSITION OF THE HOUSEHOLD, HOUSING QUALITY, HOUSEHOLD LOCATION, HOUSEHOLD INCOME FROM OTHER SOURCES, ETC., CORRESPONDING TO 30 MONTHS BEFORE INTERVIEW. FIRST COMPLETE THE HOUSEHOLD ROSTER, THEN ASK]:

H.10a Is this the same dwelling you were living in 30 months ago?

    YES – 1 [SKIP TO H.10b]   NO – 2

    [IF NO: ASK ALL QUESTIONS, INCLUDING THOSE ON THE MATERIALS OF THE ROOF, WALLS, ETC., THAT PRECEDE THE HOUSEHOLD ROSTER WITH REFERENCE TO 30 MONTHS AGO]

H.10b Have there been any changes at all in the house since that time? [PROBE]: Not in the materials of the house, in its supply of water or electricity, in the kitchen or toilet, or in the rent that you pay?

    YES, SOME CHANGES – 1   [ASK EVERY QUESTION ON THE HOUSEHOLD QUESTIONNAIRE WITH REFERENCE TO 30 MONTHS AGO]

    NO, NO CHANGES AT ALL – 2 [SKIP TO H.17]

[ADD QUESTIONS H.22 AND H.23 AT THE END OF HOUSEHOLD QUESTIONNAIRE IN ALL CASES]

*H.22 With respect to your situation at that time about 3 years ago, would you say that your family was better off than most, worse off, or about average?

Better off	01	A lot better off than most
	02	A little better off
About average	03	A little above average
	04	Really average
	05	A little below
Worse off	06	A little worse off
	07	A lot worse off
Don't know	09	

*H.23 Have you or any member of your household been active in any organizations, say social, economic, religious, for sports, political or some other type?

    YES – 1   NO – 2 [GO TO NEXT SECTION]

*H.23a Who has been active?_____

International migration statistics

*H.23b What is the name of the organization to which (*person named in H.23a*) belongs or belonged? _____

*H.23c Which type of organization was he or she active in? [CIRCLE APPROPRIATE CODE]
  01 Social   04 Sports   07 Health
  02 Economic   05 Political   08 Environmental
  03 Religious   06 Educational 09 Other, specify_____

*H.23d Does any of these organizations provide any information about migration to another country or any assistance to move abroad?   YES – 1   NO – 2

B. INDIVIDUAL QUESTIONNAIRE (FOR ALL ADULTS OVER AGE 15 YEARS)

NAME _____   MALE – 1   FEMALE – 2
ID NUMBER OF RESPONDENT IN HOUSEHOLD LISTING _____

1. *PLACE OF BIRTH, CITIZENSHIP AND CONTACT WITH OTHER COUNTRIES*

  1.1 When were you born? _____ MONTH: _____ YEAR: _____
      DON'T KNOW: _____
      *1.1a [IF MONTH AND YEAR OF BIRTH IS NOT KNOWN, ASK]: What is your age? _____
  1.2 Where were you born?   HERE: _____
                                    (current village/town/city of residence)
      ELSEWHERE: COUNTRY   _____
                    STATE   _____
                    DISTRICT   _____
                    VILLAGE/TOWN/CITY _____
      *1.2a At that time, was that place an urban or rural area?   URBAN – 1   RURAL – 2
[IF PRESENT COUNTRY OF RESIDENCE IS ALSO COUNTRY OF BIRTH, CONTINUE WITH 1.3. OTHERWISE SKIP TO 1.4]
  1.3 Have you ever lived in another country for 6 months or more?
          YES – 1   NO – 2 [NON-MIGRANT]
  1.4 What is your country of citizenship? _____ [IF SAME AS COUNTRY OF BIRTH IN 1.1, SKIP TO 1.4b]
      1.4a When did you become a citizen of that country? MONTH: _____
           YEAR: _____ [INDICATE IF AT BIRTH: _____]
      1.4b Have you ever been a citizen of any other country?
              YES – 1 [What country? _____]   NO – 2 [SKIP TO 1.5]
      1.4c Are you still a citizen of the country mentioned in 1.4.b?
              YES – 1   NO – 2
  1.5 We would like to know the country of citizenship of your immediate relatives, whether they are alive or not.
      [INTERVIEWER: FOR FATHER OR MOTHER ASK]: What is or was the country of citizenship of your (father/mother)? [RECORD ANSWER IN APPROPRIATE CELL OF TABLE BELOW]

Annex 2

[REGARDING SPOUSE, INQUIRE]: Have you ever been married? [IF NO, RECORD "NA" IN APPROPRIATE CELL, OTHERWISE INQUIRE]: What is the citizenship of your current (or most recent) spouse? [RECORD ANSWER IN APPROPRIATE CELL]

[FOR EACH TYPE OF RELATIVE INQUIRE]: Do you have or have you ever had any (sons/daughters/brothers/sisters)? [IF THE ANSWER IS NO, WRITE "NA" UNDER NUMBER FOR THE RELEVANT TYPE OF RELATIVE. IF THE ANSWER IS YES, ASK]: Do or did they all have the same country of citizenship? [IF THE ANSWER IS YES, INQUIRE]: How many _____ do or did you have? What was their country of citizenship? [RECORD ANSWERS IN APPROPRIATE CELLS OF TABLE BELOW]. [IF THE ANSWER IS NO, INQUIRE]: What are or were their countries of citizenship? [RECORD ANSWERS IN APPROPRIATE CELLS]. How many _____ have or had the citizenship of _____ ?
[RECORD NUMBERS IN APPROPRIATE CELLS].

	Country of citizenship	Sons		Daughters		Brothers		Sisters	
		Number	Country of citizenship	Number	Country of citizenship	Number	Country of citizenship	Number	Country of citizenship
Father		1.		1.		1.		1.	
Mother		2.		2.		2.		2.	
Spouse		3.		3.		3.		3.	
		4.		4.		4.		4.	

1.6 Do any of your immediate relatives we have just talked about currently live outside this country?

YES – 1   NO – 2   [SKIP TO 1.8]

1.6a We would like to know the country of current residence of your immediate relatives.

[FOR FATHER OR MOTHER ASK]: Is your (father/mother) alive? [IF NO, RECORD "NA" IN APPROPRIATE CELL OF THE TABLE BELOW, OTHERWISE ASK]: What is the country of residence of your (father/mother)? [RECORD ANSWER IN APPROPRIATE CELL]

[REGARDING SPOUSE, INQUIRE]: Are you currently married? [IF NO, RECORD "NA" IN APPROPRIATE CELL, OTHERWISE INQUIRE]: What is the country of residence of your current spouse? [RECORD ANSWER IN APPROPRIATE CELL]

[FOR EACH TYPE OF RELATIVE INQUIRE]: Do you have any (sons/daughters/brothers/sisters)? [IF THE ANSWER IS NO, WRITE "NA" UNDER NUMBER FOR THE RELEVANT TYPE OF RELATIVE. IF THE ANSWER IS YES, ASK]: Do they all have the same country of residence? [IF THE ANSWER IS YES, INQUIRE]: How many _____ do have? What is their current country of residence? [RECORD ANSWERS IN APPROPRIATE CELLS OF TABLE BELOW]. [IF THE ANSWER IS NO, INQUIRE]: What are their countries of residence? [RECORD ANSWERS IN APPROPRIATE CELLS]. How many _____ live in _____ ? [RECORD NUMBERS IN APPROPRIATE CELLS].

International migration statistics

	Country of residence	Sons		Daughters		Brothers		Sisters	
		Number	Country of residence	Number	Country of residence	Number	Country of residence	Number	Country of residence
Father		1.		1.		1.		1.	
Mother		2.		2.		2.		2.	
Spouse		3.		3.		3.		3.	
		4.		4.		4.		4.	

1.7 Among your immediate relatives living in another country, do any of them wish to come to live in this country (or do you want them to come to live in this country)?
   YES – 1   NO – 2   [SKIP TO 1.8]

   1.7a Indicate which one(s)? [CIRCLE APPROPRIATE CODE AND INDICATE NUMBER IN EACH RELEVANT CATEGORY]
   01 FATHER
   02 MOTHER
   03 SPOUSE
   04 SONS, HOW MANY?   _____
   05 DAUGHTERS, HOW MANY?   _____
   06 BROTHERS, HOW MANY?   _____
   07 SISTERS, HOW MANY?   _____
   08 OTHER, SPECIFY WHO   _____

   1.7b Have you taken any practical steps to bring these relatives to this country?
        YES – 1   NO – 2   [SKIP TO 1.13]

   1.7c What steps? Please explain: _____

1.8 Do you have any information or knowledge about life in any other countries?
   YES – 1   NO – 2   [SKIP TO 1.9]

   1.8a What are your main sources of this information about other countries? [CIRCLE THE CODES OF ALL SOURCES MENTIONED]
   01 RELATIVES/FRIENDS HERE
   02 RELATIVES/FRIENDS LIVING IN OTHER COUNTRIES
   03 PRIVATE RECRUITMENT AGENCIES OR LABOUR RECRUITERS FROM THIS COUNTRY
   04 PRIVATE RECRUITMENT AGENCIES OR LABOUR RECRUITERS FROM OTHER COUNTRIES
   05 GOVERNMENT EMPLOYMENT AGENCY FROM THIS COUNTRY
   06 GOVERNMENT EMPLOYMENT AGENCY FROM OTHER COUNTRIES
   07 TELEVISION
   08 RADIO
   09 MOVIES/FILMS
   10 WRITTEN MEDIA: NEWSPAPERS, MAGAZINES, SPECIFY EXACT SOURCES: _____
   11 OTHER, SPECIFY: _____

   *1.8b Which of these do you consider your most important source? _____

1.9 Have you ever travelled to any other countries?
   YES – 1   NO – 2   [SKIP TO 1.10]

   1.9a To which countries? _____

   1.9b [IF MORE THAN ONE]
        Which country have you visited most often? _____

Annex 2

1.9c When was the last time you visited that country?
MONTH _____ YEAR _____

1.9d What was the main purpose of that last visit? [CIRCLE CODE]
01 VACATION, TRAVEL, SHOPPING
02 VISIT FRIENDS, RELATIVES
03 BUSINESS, WORK, CONFERENCE, ETC.
04 LOOK FOR JOB, EXPLORE JOB MARKET
05 HEALTH
06 OTHER, SPECIFY: _____

1.10 What is your mother tongue? _____

1.10a Do you speak and understand any other languages?
YES – 1   NO – 2   [SKIP TO 1.11]

1.10b Which other language(s)? _____

1.11 Do you intend to remain in this country?
YES – 1   NO – 2   [SKIP TO 1.12]

1.11a Why do you intend to remain?
[CIRCLE CODES OF ALL REASONS MENTIONED]
01 HAVE A GOOD JOB AND SATISFACTORY INCOME
02 CLOSE RELATIVES AND FRIENDS ARE IN THIS COUNTRY
03 SCHOOLS ARE GOOD
04 GOOD HEALTH CARE
05 HAVE SUCCESSFUL BUSINESS HERE
06 HAVE GOOD HOUSE
07 HAVE NICE NEIGHBOURHOOD AND NEIGHBOURS
08 FREEDOM FROM POLITICAL PERSECUTION
09 FREEDOM FROM RELIGIOUS PERSECUTION
10 LOW LEVEL OF CRIME, GENERAL SECURITY
11 LOW COST OF LIVING
12 MANY SOCIAL ACTIVITIES AND THINGS TO DO
13 OTHER, SPECIFY: _____

1.11b Which is the **most important** reason for remaining in this country? _____
[SKIP TO 1.15]

1.12 Do you have any specific plans to leave or do you just have a general feeling that you would like to leave?
SPECIFIC PLANS – 1   GENERAL FEELING – 2

1.12a Why are you thinking of leaving? [CIRCLE ALL REASONS MENTIONED]
01 LACK OF CLOSE RELATIVES/FRIENDS HERE
02 UNEMPLOYED, CAN'T FIND WORK
03 POOR JOB, LOW PAY
04 POOR WORKING CONDITIONS
05 DON'T GET ALONG WITH BOSS OR CO-WORKERS
06 BUSINESS NOT DOING WELL
07 POOR SCHOOLS, LACK OF SCHOOLS
08 DON'T LIKE COMMUNITY OF RESIDENCE, DIFFERENT VALUES
09 FAMILY PROBLEMS, DIFFERENT VALUES
10 TO GET MARRIED, SEEK SPOUSE
11 SEPARATION OR DIVORCE, WANT TO GET AWAY
12 HIGH COST OF LIVING
13 HIGH CRIME RATE
14 POOR PHYSICAL ENVIRONMENT, POLLUTION
15 DON'T LIKE CLIMATE
16 LANGUAGE PROBLEMS
17 VISA PROBLEMS, LACK OF DOCUMENTS
18 POLITICAL PERSECUTION, FEAR OF POLITICAL PERSECUTION
19 RELIGIOUS PERSECUTION, FEAR OF RELIGIOUS PERSECUTION
20 DISCRIMINATION
21 OTHER, SPECIFY: _____

International migration statistics

       1.12b Which is the most important reason? _____

1.13 Do you have a specific **time** when you plan to leave?
       YES – 1   NO – 2 [SKIP TO 1.14]
       1.13a When?   01 WITHIN A YEAR
                             02 BETWEEN 1 AND 2 YEARS FROM NOW
                             03 AFTER 2 YEARS
                             04 NOT SURE

1.14 Where do you think you will go? _____

1.15 Have you ever actually tried to leave this country to move or migrate to another country?
       YES – 1   NO – 2 [SKIP TO 1.15b]
       1.15a Why didn't you migrate? [CIRCLE ALL REASONS MENTIONED]
              01 CHANGED MIND
              02 COULDN'T GET EXIT PERMIT OR PASSPORT FROM THIS COUNTRY
              03 COULDN'T GET DOCUMENTS, VISAS OR PERMITS REQUIRED BY
                     COUNTRY OF DESTINATION
              04 TOO EXPENSIVE
              05 TOO COMPLICATED, DON'T KNOW WHAT DOCUMENTS ARE
                     NEEDED
              06 SPOUSE, FAMILY COULDN'T GET DOCUMENTS TO ACCOMPANY
                     ME
              07 JOB FELL THROUGH
              08 SPOUSE, FAMILY OPPOSED
              09 JOB HERE IMPROVED
              10 OTHER PERSONAL REASON
              11 OTHER, SPECIFY: _____
       1.15b What documents are needed to leave this country? _____

1.16 Have you ever been contacted by a labour contractor or recruiter trying to persuade you to work in another country?
       YES – 1   NO – 2 [SKIP TO 1.17]
       1.16a To work in what country? _____
       1.16b Why didn't you leave? _____

1.17 What is your current level of education?
       01 NONE
       02 PRIMARY INCOMPLETE
       03 PRIMARY COMPLETE
       04 VOCATIONAL TECHNICAL TRAINING (POST-PRIMARY)
       05 SECONDARY INCOMPLETE
       06 SECONDARY COMPLETE
       07 VOCATIONAL TECHNICAL TRAINING (POST-SECONDARY)
       08 COLLEGE/UNIVERSITY INCOMPLETE
       09 COLLEGE/UNIVERSITY GRADUATE
       10 POSTGRADUATE DEGREE
       11 OTHER, SPECIFY: _____
       1.17a Has this changed in the past three years? YES – 1   NO – 2 [SKIP TO 1.18]
       1.17b During that time you completed _____ years at level _____

1.18 What is your current marital status?
       01 NEVER MARRIED   04 SEPARATED [SKIP TO 1.18b]
       02 MARRIED [SKIP TO 1.18a] 05 DIVORCED [SKIP TO 1.18b]
       03 CONSENSUAL UNION   06 WIDOW/WIDOWER
           [SKIP TO 1.18a]   [SKIP TO 1.18b]
       1.18.a Did you get married in the last three years?
       YES – 1 [MONTH: _____   YEAR: _____]   NO – 2
       1.18b Did you get separated or divorced or become a widow(er) during the last three years?
       YES – 1 [MONTH: _____   YEAR: _____]   NO – 2

Annex 2

2. *SITUATION AT TIME MIGRANTS LEFT*

2.1 During the year prior to 2.5 years ago, were you engaged in any kind of work, whether working for someone else or for yourself or in a family farm or business?

    YES – 1 [SKIP TO 2.2]   NO – 2

    2.1a Were you looking for work? YES – 1   NO – 2 [SKIP TO SECTION 4]

    2.1b For how long had you been looking for work?
        WEEKS _____ MONTHS _____

2.2-2.21 I would like to ask you some things about your work during that year, about 3 years ago.

Was your main work during that time working for yourself, for someone else, or in some kind of family business, like a farm or store?

01	For someone else	[REPEAT QUESTIONS 4.5-4.18, CHANGING VERB TO PAST TENSE.]
02	For self	[REPEAT QUESTIONS 4.19-4.24, INCLUDING THE ENTERPRISE QUESTIONNAIRE, IF APPROPRIATE.]
03	In family business	[REPEAT QUESTIONS 4.19-4.24, INCLUDING THE ENTERPRISE QUESTIONNAIRE, IF APPROPRIATE.]

3. *CURRENT WORK*

[ADMINISTER IDENTICAL SECTION AS IN THE QUESTIONNAIRE FOR THE COUNTRY OF DESTINATION TO ALL ADULTS OVER AGE 15 YEARS.]

BIBLIOGRAPHY

Abella, Manolo I. 1995. "Sex selectivity of migration regulations governing international migration in Southern and South-eastern Asia", in *International migration policies and the status of female migrants: Proceedings of the United Nations Expert Group Meeting on International Migration Policies and the Status of Female Migrants, San Miniato, Italy, 28-31 March 1990* (New York, United Nations), sales No. E.95.XIII.10, pp. 241-252.

Adams, Richard H. 1993. "The economic and demographic determinants of international migration in rural Egypt", in *Journal of Development Studies*, Vol. 30, No. 1, pp. 146-147.

Alburo, F. A.; D. Abella. 1992. *The impact of informal remittances of overseas contract workers' earnings on the Philippines economy* (New Delhi, ILO – Asian Regional Team for Employment Promotion, mimeograph).

Amjad, R. (ed.) 1989. *To the Gulf and back: Studies on the economic impact of Asian labour migration* (New Delhi, ILO – Asian Regional Team for Employment Promotion).

Arretx, Carmen. 1987. "Research on international migration and census data cooperation in Latin America", in *International Migration Review* (Staten Island, New York), Vol. 21, No. 4 (winter), pp. 1101-1103.

Asis, Maruja M. B. 1995. "The labour force experience of migrant women: Filipino and Korean women in transition", paper presented at the Expert Group Meeting on International Migration Policies and the Status of Female Migrants, San Miniato, Italy, 26-31 March.

Athukorala, Premachandra. 1993a. "Statistics on Asian labour migration: Review of sources, methods and problems" in *International labour migration statistics and information networking in Asia: Papers and proceedings of a regional seminar held in New Delhi, March 17-19* (Geneva, ILO – Asian Regional Team for Employment Promotion).

——. 1993b. "Improving the contribution of migrant remittances to development: The experience of Asian labour-exporting countries", in *International migration*, Vol. 31, No. 1, pp. 103-124.

Australia, Australian Bureau of Statistics. 1984. *1984 Year Book* (Canberra), No. 68.

Australia, Bureau of Immigration, Multicultural and Population Research 1995. *Australian Immigration Consolidated Statistics.* (Canberra, Australian Government Publishing Service), No. 18, 1993-94.

Australia, Department of Immigration and Ethnic Affairs. 1982. *Annual Review 1981* (Canberra).

International migration statistics

Awad, Ibrahim. 1995. *Labour immigration processes, policies and institutions in Malaysia* (Geneva, ILO), mimeograph.

Azam, Farooq-i. 1994. *A study of undocumented migrant workers from Pakistan* (Islamabad, ILO).

Bahrain. 1973. *Statistical Abstract 1972* (Bahrain, Oriental Printing Press).

——. 1976. *Statistical Abstract 1975* (Bahrain, Oriental Printing Press).

Bilsborrow, Richard E. 1981. *Surveys of internal migration in low-income areas: The need for and content of community level variables* (Geneva, ILO).

——. 1993. "Issues in the measurement of female migration in developing countries", in United Nations: *Internal migration of women in developing countries: Proceedings of the United Nations Expert Meeting on the Feminization of Internal Migration, Aguascalientes, Mexico, 22-25 October 1991* (New York, United Nations, Department for Economic and Social Information and Policy Analysis).

——; et al. 1984. *Migration surveys in low-income countries: Guidelines for survey and questionnaire design* (Beckenham (UK) and Sydney (Australia), Croom Helm).

——; United Nations Secretariat. 1993. "Internal female migration and development: An overview", in United Nations: *Internal migration of women in developing countries: Proceedings of the United Nations Expert Meeting on the Feminization of Internal Migration, Aguascalientes, Mexico, 22-25 October 1991* (New York, United Nations, Department for Economic and Social Information and Policy Analysis).

——; Zlotnik Hania. 1994. "The systems approach and the measurement of the determinants of international migration", in *Causes of international migration: Proceedings of a workshop, Luxembourg, 14-16 December 1994* (Luxembourg, Office for Official Publications of the European Communities, compiled by the Netherlands Interdisciplinary Demographic Institute on behalf of the European Commission), pp. 61-76.

Borjas, George J. 1990. *Friends or strangers: The impact of immigrants on the U.S. economy* (New York, Basic Books).

Botswana, Central Statistics Office. n.d. *1981 Population and housing census: Census administrative/technical report and national statistical tables* (Gaborone, Government Printer).

Bretz, Manfred. n.d. "Allemagne", in Poulain, Michel, et al. (eds.): *Projet d'harmonisation des statistiques de migration internationale au sein de la Communauté Européenne: Rapports nationaux* (Louvain-la-Neuve, Catholic University of Louvain), mimeograph.

Brown, R. P. C. 1995. "Migrants' remittances, savings and investment in the South Pacific", in *International Labour Review* (Geneva, ILO), Vol. 133, No. 3, pp. 347-368.

——. 1992a. "Migrants' remittances, capital flight and macroeconomic imbalance in Sudan's hidden economy", in *Journal of African Economies* (Oxford), Vol. 1, No. 1, pp. 86-108.

——. 1992b. *Public debt and private wealth: Debt, capital flight and the IMF in Sudan* (London, Macmillan).

Burney, N. 1989. "A macro-economic analysis of the impact of workers' remittances on Pakistan's economy", in Amjad R. (ed.): *To the Gulf and back: Studies on the economic impact of Asian labour migration* (New Delhi, ILO – Asian Regional Team for Employment Promotion).

Bibliography

Burundi, Département de la Population. 1982. *1979 Recensement général de la population: Résultats définitifs au niveau national* (Bujumbura, Ministry of the Interior), Vol. I.

Bustamente, Jorge A., et al. 1994. *Migration and immigrants: Research and policies, SOPEMI-Mexico*, Mexico's Report for the Continuous Reporting System on Migration (SOPEMI) of the Organisation for Economic Co-operation and Development (OECD) (Tijuana, Mexico, El Colegio de la Frontera Norte).

Byerlee, Derek; Tommy, J. L. 1976. *An integrated methodology for migration research: The Sierra Leone rural-urban migration survey* (East Lansing, Michigan State University; Sierra Leone, Nijala University College).

——; Fatoo, H. 1976. *Rural-urban migration in Sierra Leone: Determinants and policy implications*. University of Sierra Leone, Nijala University College, Department of Agricultural Economics, and East Lansing, Michigan State University, Department of Agricultural Economics, African Rural Economy Paper 13.

Canada, Statistics Canada. 1992. *Immigration and citizenship: The nation: 1991 Census of Canada* (Ottawa, Supply and Services Canada).

Carvallo-Hernández, Rahiza. 1993. *Informe sobre las fuentes de información estadística para el estudio de la migración internacional*, paper presented at the Conference on the Measurement of Migration in Latin America, Bogotá, Colombia, 21-23 October.

CELADE. 1977. "Investigación de la migración internacional en Latinoamérica (IMILA)", in *Boletín Demográfico* (Santiago, Chile), Vol. 10, No. 20 (July).

——. 1986. "Investigación de la migración internacional en Latinoamérica (IMILA)", in *Boletín Demográfico* (Santiago, Chile), Vol. 19, No. 37.

——. 1989. "Investigación de la migración internacional en Latinoamérica (IMILA)", in *Boletín Demográfico* (Santiago, Chile), Vol. 22, No. 43.

CENSIS. 1993. *Les mouvements migratoires en Italie: Rapport SOPEMI 1993* (Rome, Centro Studi Investimenti Sociali).

CERPOD (Centre d'Etudes et de Recherce sur la Population et le Développement). 1995. *Migrations et urbanisations en l'Afrique de l'ouest: Résultats preliminaires* (Bamako, Mali).

CONAPO. 1987. *Características principales de la migración en las grandes ciudades del país: Resultados preliminares de la encuesta nacional de migración en areas urbanas (ENMAU)* (Mexico City, El Consejo Nacional de Población).

Courgeau, Daniel. 1988. *Méthodes de mesure de la mobilité spatiale* (Paris, Institut National d'Études Démographiques).

DaVanzo, Julie. 1976. *Why families move: A model of the geographic mobility of married couples*, prepared under a grant from the Employment and Training Administration, Department of Labor (Santa Monica, The Rand Corporation).

Dinerman, Ina R. 1982. *Migrants and stay-at-homes: A comparative study of rural migration from Michoacán, Mexico* (La Jolla and San Diego, Center for U.S.-Mexican Studies, University of California), Monograph Series, No. 5.

Economic Commission for Europe. n.d. *Measuring international migration in Europe: The sources*, mimeograph.

El-Saadani, Somaya Mahmoud. 1992. *International migration functions for labor emigration from Egypt*, dissertation submitted to Cairo University in conformity with the requirements for the degree of Doctor of Philosophy.

International migration statistics

Employment and Immigration Canada. 1988. *Immigration Statistics 1986* (Ottawa, Minister of Supply and Services Canada).

Escribano-Morales, Fátima. n.d. "Espagne", in Poulain, Michel, et al. (eds.): *Projet d'harmonisation des statistiques de migration internationale au sein de la Communauté Européenne: Rapports nationaux* (Louvain-la-Neuve, Catholic University of Louvain), mimeograph.

Esser, Hartmut; Korte, Hermann. 1985. "Federal Republic of Germany", in Hammar, Tomas. (ed.): *European immigration policy: A comparative study* (Cambridge, Cambridge University Press).

Eurostat (Statistical Office of the European Communities). 1994a. *Special study on migration: Parts I and II*, Joint Eurostat/ECE Working Group on Migration Statistics, meeting held from 28 to 30 November in Luxembourg, DOC E1/MIG/5/94.

——. 1994b. *Migration statistics: Data collected by Eurostat*, Joint Eurostat/ECE Working Group on Migration Statistics, meeting held from 28 to 30 November in Luxembourg, DOC E1/MIG/3/94.

Fawcett, James T.; Arnold, Fred. 1987a. "Explaining diversity: Asian and Pacific immigration systems", in Fawcett, James T.; Cariño, B.V. (eds.): *Pacific bridges: The new immigration from Asia and the Pacific Islands* (New York, Center for Migration Studies).

——; ——. 1987b. "The role of surveys in the study of international migration: An appraisal", in *International Migration Review*, Vol. 21, No. 4, pp. 1523-1540.

Findley, Sally E. 1982. "Methods of linking community-level variables with migration survey data", in ESCAP, *National Migration Surveys, Survey Manuals X: Guidelines for Analysis* (New York, United Nations), pp. 276-311.

——; et al. 1988. "From seasonal migration to international migration: An analysis of the factors affecting the choices made by families of the Senegal river valley", in IUSSP, *African Population Conference, Dakar 1988* (Liège, International Union for the Scientific Study of Population (IUSSP), Vol. 2.

Finland, Tilastokeskus. 1994. *Statistical Yearbook of Finland 1994* (Helsinki, Statistics Finland).

Freedman, Deborah et al. 1988. "The life history calendar: A technique for collecting retrospective data", in *Sociological methodology*, Vol. 18, pp. 37-68.

Freedman, Ronald. 1974. *Community level data in fertility surveys* (London, World Fertility Survey), Occasional papers, No. 8.

Frejka, Tomas (moderator). 1995. *Panel session: Preliminary results of in-depth international migration surveys in Lithuania, Poland and Ukraine*, Panel at Demographic Processes and the Socio-economic Transformation in Central and Eastern European Countries, Population Activities Unit, United Nations Economic Commission for Europe, Geneva, 8-11 June.

García y Griego, Manuel 1987. "International migration data in Mexico". *International Migration Review*, Vol. 21, No. 4 (winter, pp. 1245-1257).

Garson, Jean-Pierre; Yves Moulier. 1982. *Clandestine migrants and their regularisation in France, 1981-82* (Geneva, ILO), International Migration for Employment, Working Paper, MIG/WP/6E.

Germany. 1982. *Statistisches Jahrbuch 1982* (Wiesbaden, Statistisches Bundesamt).

——. 1994. *Statistisches Jahrbuch 1994* (Wiesbaden, Statistiches Bundesamt).

Bibliography

Gilani, Ijaz et al. 1981a. *Labour migration from Pakistan to the Middle East and its impact on the domestic economy*: Part I (Islamabad, Pakistan Institute of Development Economics), Research Report Series No. 126.

——; ——. 1981b. *Labour migration from Pakistan to the Middle East and its impact on the domestic economy*: Part III (*sample design and field-work*) (Islamabad, Pakistan Institute of Development Economics), Research Report Series No. 128.

——; ——. 1981c. *Labour migration from Pakistan to the Middle East and its impact on the domestic economy*," Final Report, Research Project on Export of Manpower from Pakistan to the Middle East (Washington, The World Bank, June-July).

Gisser, Richard. 1992. "Switzerland, Liechtenstein and Austria", in Poulain, Michel: *Migration statistics for the EFTA countries*, Working Party on Demographic Statistics, meeting on 26, 27 and 28 February (Luxembourg, Eurostat), DOC E3/SD/12/92.

Giusti, Alejandro. 1993. *Argentina: Fuentes de datos sobre migración internacional, alcances y limitaciones de su uso*, paper presented at the Conference on the Measurement of Migration in Latin America, Bogotá, Colombia, 21-23 October.

Goldstein, Sidney; Goldstein, Alice. 1979. *Surveys of internal migration in developing countries: A methodological view*, background paper prepared for the International Statistical Institute/World Fertility Survey Expert Group Meeting on Methodology of Migration Measurement, London, 25-27 September.

Goodman, Leo A. 1961. "Snowball sampling", in *Annals of Mathematical Statistics*, Vol. 32, No. 1, pp. 148-170.

Government of Pakistan, Ministry of Finance, 1992. *Economic survey: 1991-92* (Islamabad, Government of Pakistan).

Groves, Robert M. 1989. *Survey errors and survey costs* (New York, John Wiley and Sons).

Gulati, Leela. 1983. *Impacts of male migrants to the Middle East on the family: Some evidence from Kerala*, paper presented at the Conference on Asian Labor Migration to the Middle East, Honolulu, East-West Population Institute, September.

Gurak, Douglas T.; Caces, Fe. 1992. "Migration networks and the shaping of migration systems", in Kritz, Mary M. et al. (eds.): *International migration systems: A global approach* (Oxford, Clarendon Press/Oxford University Press), pp. 150-176.

Gurrieri, Jorge. 1982. *Algunas características de los radicados por el Decreto No. 087/74*, Dirección Nacional de Migraciones, mimeograph.

Hill, Kenneth. 1981. "A proposal for the use of information on the residence of siblings to estimate emigration by age", in *Indirect procedures for estimating emigration*, International Union for the Scientific Study of Population (IUSSP), Paper No. 18, pp. 19-34.

Hoefer, Michael D. 1989. *Characteristics of aliens legalizing under IRCA*. Paper presented at the Annual Meeting of the Population Association of America, Baltimore, Maryland, 27-29 March, mimeograph.

Hoffman-Nowotny, Hans-Joachim. 1985. "Switzerland", in Hammar, Tomas (ed.): *European immigration policy: A comparative study* (Cambridge, Cambridge University Press).

Hugo, Graeme J. 1981. "Village-community ties, village norms, and ethnic and social networks: A review of evidence from the third world", in Gardner, R.W.; DeJong, G.F. (eds.): *Migration decision making* (New York, Pergamon), pp. 186-224.

International migration statistics

——. 1993a. "Indonesian labour migration to Malaysia: Trends and policy implications", in *Southeast Asian Journal of Social Science*, Vol. 21(1), pp. 36-70.

——. 1993b. "Migrant women in developing countries," in United Nations, *Internal migration of women in developing countries* (New York, United Nations), Chapter III.

——. 1994. "Introduction", in Wooden, M. et al. (eds.): *Australian immigration: A survey of the issues* (Canberra, Australian Government Publishing Service), pp. 4-28.

Hyun, Oh Seok; 1989. "The impact of overseas migration on national development: The case of the Republic of Korea", in Amjad (ed.), 1989.

Iceland, Statistical Bureau. 1994. *Statistical abstract of Iceland 1994* (Reykjavík, Statistical Bureau of Iceland).

ILO (International Labour Office). 1988. *Mediterranean information exchange system on international migration and employment (MIES)* (Geneva, MIES 1/88).

——. 1989. *Statistical Report 1989: International labour migration from Asian labour-sending countries* (Bangkok, ILO, Regional Office for Asia and the Pacific).

——. 1990. *International standard classification of occupations.*

——; ARTEP (Asian Regional Team for Employment Promotion). 1987. *Impact of out and return migration on domestic employment in Pakistan, Vol. II.* New Delhi: ILO–ARTEP.

IMF (International Monetary Fund). 1977. *Balance of payments manual: Fourth edition* (Washington, International Monetary Fund Publications Services).

——. 1993. *Balance of payments manual: Fifth edition* (Washington, DC, International Monetary Fund Publications Services).

——. 1994. *Balance of payments statistics year book 1994.*

——. 1995. *Balance of payments compilation guide* (Washington, DC, International Monetary Fund Publications Services).

Iraq. 1968. *Annual abstract of statistics 1968* (Baghdad, Al-Zahra Press).

——. 1970. *Annual abstract of statistics 1970* (Baghdad, Central Statistical Organization).

——. 1976. *Annual abstract of statistics 1976* (Baghdad, Central Statistical Organization).

Irfan, Mohammad et al. n.d. *Migration patterns in Pakistan: Preliminary results from the PLM survey, 1979* (Islamabad, Pakistan Institute of Development Economics), Studies in population, labour force and migration project report No. 6.

Islam, Rizwanul. 1980. *Export of manpower from Bangladesh to the Middle East countries: The impact of remittance money on household expenditure* (Dhaka, Bangladesh Institute of Development Studies), Research report, 94 pp.

Israel. 1992. *Immigration to Israel 1991* (Jerusalem, Central Bureau of Statistics).

Izquierdo-Escribano, Antonio. n.d. "Rapport synthéthique de les statistiques sur l'immigration en Espagne", in Poulain, Michel et al. (eds.): *Projet d'harmonisation des statistiques de migration internationale au sein de la Communauté Européenne: Rapports nationaux* (Louvain-la-Neuve, Catholic University of Louvain), mimeograph.

Japan, Immigration Bureau. n.d. *Immigration Control and Refugee Recognition Act and the Alien Registration Law* (Tokyo, Ministry of Justice).

Japan Immigration Association. 1994. *Basic plan for immigration control* (Tokyo, Japan Immigration Association).

Bibliography

Jaspers-Faijer, Dirk. 1993. *La estimación indirecta de la emigración internacional*, paper presented at the Conference on the Measurement of International Migration held in Bogotá, Colombia, 21 to 23 October.

Jones, H.M. 1968. *Report on the 1966 Swaziland population census* (Mbabane, Swaziland Government).

Jordan. 1989. *Statistical Yearbook 1989* (Amman, Department of Statistics).

——. 1992. *Statistical Yearbook 1992* (Amman, Department of Statistics).

Kazi, S. 1989. "Domestic impact of overseas migration: Pakistan", in Amjad, R. (ed.): *To the Gulf and back: Studies on the economic impact of Asian labour migration* (New Delhi, ILO – Asian Regional Team for Employment Promotion).

Kelly, John J. 1987. "Improving the comparability of international migration statistics: Contributions by the Conference of European Statisticians from 1971 to date", in *International Migration Review*, Vol. 21, No. 4 (winter), pp. 1017-1037.

Kish, Leslie. 1965. *Survey sampling* (New York, John Wiley and Sons).

Knodel, John E. et al. 1988. "Focus group research on fertility decline in Thailand: Methodology and findings" in Caldwell, John C. et al. (eds.): *Micro-approaches to demographic research* (London, Kegan Paul International), pp. 41-55.

Koszamanis, Byron. n.d. "Grèce", in Poulain, Michel et al. (eds.): *Projet d'harmonisation des statistiques de migration internationale au sein de la Communauté Européenne: Rapports nationaux* (Louvain-la-Neuve, Catholic University of Louvain), mimeograph.

Kritz, Mary M.; Zlotnik, Hania. 1992. "Global interactions: Migration systems, processes and policies", in Kritz, M. M. et al. (eds.): *International migration systems: A global approach* (Oxford, Clarendon Press), pp. 1-18.

Kuijsten, Anton, C. n.d. "Statistics on international migration flows in the EEC member countries", in Poulain, Michel et al. (eds.): *Projet d'harmonisation des statistiques de migration internationale au Sein de la Communauté Européenne: Annexe, rapports des experts internationaux* (Louvain-la-Neuve, Catholic University of Louvain), mimeograph.

Kuptsch, C.; Oishi, Nana. 1994. *Training abroad: German and Japanese schemes for workers from transition economies or developing countries* (Geneva, ILO).

Kuwait. 1974. *Statistical yearbook of Kuwait 1974* (Kuwait, Central Statistical Office).

——. 1978. *Public services statistics 1979* (Kuwait, Central Statistical Office).

——. 1979. *Annual statistical abstract 1979* (Kuwait, Central Statistical Office).

——. 1994. *Annual statistical abstract 1994* (Kuwait, Central Statistical Office).

Lange, Anita. n.d. "Danemark", in Poulain, Michel et al. (eds.): *Projet d'harmonisation des statistiques de migration internationale au sein de la Communauté Européenne: Rapports nationaux* (Louvain-la-Neuve, Catholic University of Louvain), mimeograph.

Langers, Jean; Ensch, Jean. n.d. "Luxembourg", in Poulain, Michel et al. (eds.): *Projet d'harmonisation des statistiques de migration internationale au sein de la Communauté Européenne: Rapports nationaux* (Louvain-la-Neuve, Catholic University of Louvain), mimeograph.

Lee, Everett S. 1966. "A theory of migration", in *Demography*, Vol.3(1), pp. 45-47.

Magescas, Jean-Bernard; Charbit, Yves. 1985. "Les étrangers en France", in *La population française de A à Z* (Paris, Cahiers Français), No. 219.

International migration statistics

Mahmud, W. 1989. "The impact of overseas labour migration on the Bangladesh economy", in Amjad, R. (ed.): *To the Gulf and back*, Studies on the economic impact of Asian labour migration (New Delhi, ILO – Asian Regional Team for Employment Promotion).

Mammey, Ulrich et al. 1989. *Country report: Federal Republic of Germany*, paper presented at the meeting of the Working Group on Immigrant Populations, Paris, France, 14-15 June.

Mármora, Lelio. 1983. *La amnistía migratoria de 1974 en Argentina* (Geneva, ILO), International Migration for Employment, Working Paper, MIG/WP/9S.

Massey, Douglas S. 1990. "Social structure, household strategies, and the cumulative causation of migration", in *Population Index* (Princeton, New Jersey), Vol. 56, No. 1, pp. 3-26.

——. et al. 1990. *Return to Aztlán: The social process of international migration from Western Mexico* (Berkeley and Los Angeles, University of California Press).

Mexico. n.d. *Anuario estadístico 1973-74* (Mexico City, Dirección General de Estadística).

——. 1981. *Anuario estadístico 1981* (Mexico City, Secretaría de Programación y Presupuesto).

Michelena, A. et al. 1984. *Immigración illegal y matrícula general de extranjeros* (Geneva, ILO), International Migration for Employment, Working Paper, MIG/WP/15S.

Migration Research Unit, University College London. 1993. *Comparison and evaluation of the labour force survey and regulation 311/76 data as sources on the foreign employed population in the EC*, December.

Mines, Richard. 1981. *Developing a community tradition of migration: A field study in rural Zacatecas, Mexico, and California settlement areas*, Monograph in U.S.-Mexican Studies 3, Program in United States-Mexican Studies, University of California – San Diego.

Moser, C.; Kalton, G. 1972. *Survey methods in social investigation* (New York, Basic Books), 2nd ed.

Mullan, Brendan. 1995. *Guidelines for preparation of country reports: International migration in the ECE region* (East Lansing, Michigan State University), unpublished, prepared for the Population Activities Unit, United Nations Economic Commission for Europe.

Nigam, S.B.L. 1988. *Data requirements and sources of information on international labour migration* (New Delhi, ILO – Asian Regional Team for Employment Promotion), Working Paper No. 11. ILO-UNDP Project.

North, David, S. 1979. *The Canadian experience with amnesty for aliens: What the United States can learn* (Geneva, ILO), World Employment Programme Research, Working Paper, WEP/2-26/WP.43.

Norway, Statistisk Sentralbyrå. 1994. *Statistical yearbook 1994* (Oslo, Statistics Norway).

Oberai, A.S. 1984. "Identification of migrants and collection of demographic and social information in migration surveys", in Bilsborrow, R.E. et al. (eds.): *Migration surveys in low-income countries: Guidelines for survey and questionnaire design*. International Labour Organization. (London and Sydney, Croom Helm), pp. 130-406.

——. 1993. *International labour migration statistics: Use of censuses and sample surveys* (Geneva, ILO), World Employment Programme Working Paper MIG WP.75.E.

Bibliography

———; Singh, H.K.M. 1983. *Causes and consequences of internal migration: A study in the Indian Punjab* (Delhi, Oxford University Press).

Oman. 1986. *Statistical year book* (Muscat, Development Council, Technical Secretariat).

———. 1992. *Statistical year book* (Muscat, Directorate General of National Statistics).

Ordoñez-Gez, Myriam et al. 1988. "Migración internacional", in *Colombia: Censo 1985* (Bogotá, Pontífica Universidad Javeriana), mimeograph.

OECD. 1986. *Système d'observation permanente des migrations (SOPEMI)* (Paris).

———. 1987. "Rapport du correspondant de la Suisse", in *Système d'observation permanente des migrations (SOPEMI)* (Berne), mimeograph.

———. 1990. *Système d'observation permanente des migrations (SOPEMI) 1989* (Paris).

———. 1991. *Système d'observation permanente des migrations (SOPEMI) 1990* (Paris).

———. 1992. *Trends in international migration: SOPEMI, 1992* (Paris).

———. 1994. *International movements of highly skilled labour*, Working Party on Migration, Paris, 31 May (Note by the Secretariat).

Peixoto, Joao. n.d. "Portugal", in Poulain, Michel et al. (eds.): *Projet d'harmonisation des statistiques de migration internationale au sein de la Communauté Européenne: Rapports nationaux* (Louvain-la-Neuve, Catholic University of Louvain), mimeograph.

Pellecer-Palacios, Sonia M. 1993. *Informe sobre la medición de la migración internacional en Guatemala*, paper presented at the Conference on the Measurement of Migration in Latin America, Bogotá, Colombia, 21-23 October.

Plender, Richard. 1987. *International migration law* (London and Dordrecht, Martinus Nijhoff Publishers).

Poulain, Michel. 1987. "The measurement of international migration in Belgium", in *International Migration Review* (Staten Island, New York), Vol. 21, No. 4 (winter), pp. 1107-1137.

———. 1992. *Migration statistics for the EFTA countries*, report presented to the Working Party on Demographic Statistics, meeting on 26, 27 and 28 February (Luxembourg, Eurostat), doc. E3/SD/12/92.

———; et al. n.d. *Projet d'harmonisation des statistiques de migration internationale au sein de la Communauté Européenne. Rapports nationaux* (Louvain-la-Neuve, Catholic University of Louvain), mimeograph.

Qatar. 1981. *Annual statistical abstract 1980* (Qatar, Central Statistical Organization).

Quibria, M.G.; Thant, M. 1988. "International labour migration, emigrant remittances, and ASEAN developing countries: Economic analysis and policy issues", in Dulta, M. (ed.): *Research in Asian economic studies* (Greenwich, Connecticut, JAI Press), pp. 287-311.

Rodrigo, C.; Jayatissa, R.A. 1989. "Maximising benefits from labour migration: Sri Lanka", in Amjad, R. (ed.): *To the Gulf and back: Studies on the economic impact of Asian labour migration* (New Delhi, ILO – Asian Regional Team for Employment Promotion), pp. 255-302.

Rogers, Rosemarie and Copland, Emily. 1993. *Forced migration: Policy issues in the post-Cold War period* (Medford, Massachusetts, Tufts University).

Russell, Sharon Stanton. 1986. "Remittances from international migration: A review in perspective", in *World Development*, Vol. 14, No. 6, pp. 677-696.

—. 1992. "Migrant remittances and development", in *International Migration Quarterly Review*, Vol. XXX, 3/4, Special issue: Migration and development, pp. 267-279.

—; Teitelbaum, Michael S. 1992. *International migration and international trade* (Washington, World Bank), World Bank Discussion Papers No. 160.

Saith, A. 1989. "Macroeconomic issues in international labour migration: A review", in Amjad, R. (ed.): *To the Gulf and back: Studies on the economic impact of Asian labour migration* (New Delhi, ILO – Asian Regional Team for Employment Promotion), pp. 28-54.

Salt, John. n.d. "United Kingdom", in Poulain, Michel et al. (eds.), *Projet d'harmonisation des statistiques de migration internationale au sein de la Communauté Européenne: Rapports nationaux* (Louvain-la-Neuve, Catholic University of Louvain), mimeograph.

Santibáñez-Romell, Jorge et al. 1994. *Encuesta sobre migración en la frontera norte de México: Síntesis ejecutiva* (Tijuana, Mexico, El Colegio de la Frontera Norte, Consejo Nacional de Población, and Secretaria del Trabajo y Previsión Social).

Saudi Arabia. 1965. *Statistical yearbook 1965* (Riyadh, Central Department of Statistics).

—. 1975. *Statistical yearbook 1975* (Riyadh, Central Department of Statistics).

—. 1978. *Statistical yearbook 1978* (Riyadh, Central Department of Statistics).

—. 1990. *Statistical yearbook 1990* (Riyadh, Central Department of Statistics).

—. 1993. *Statistical yearbook 1993* (Riyadh, Central Department of Statistics).

Senegal, Government of. n.d. *Reseau d'enquetes sur les migrations et urbanisation en Afrique de l'ouest (REMUAO)*. [Network of survey on migration and urbanization in Western Africa], CERPOD project (Dakar).

Serageldin, Ismail et al. 1981. *Manpower and international labor migration in the Middle East and North Africa* (Washington, World Bank), Research Project on International Labor Migration and Manpower in the Middle East and North Africa. Final Report, June.

Shryock, Henry S.; Siegel, Jacob S. 1975. *The methods and materials of demography* (Washington, United States Government Printing Office), Vol. 1.

Singleton, Jr., Royce et al. 1988. *Approaches to social research* (New York and Oxford, Oxford University Press).

Sipaviciene, Audra et al. 1995. "International migration in Lithuania: Causes and consequences", paper presented at the Second Training Workshop on International Migration Surveys in Central and Eastern Europe (United National Economic Commission for Europe and United Nations Population Fund), Warsaw, Poland, 5-7 June (preliminary report).

Sirken, Morris. 1972. "Stratified sample surveys with multiplicity", in *Journal of the American Statistical Association*, Vol. 67, No. 1, March, pp. 224-227.

Sjastad, Larry A. 1962. "The costs and returns of human migration", in *Journal of Political Economy*, Vol. 70, suppl. 5, pt. 2, October, pp. 80-93.

Sloan, J.; Kennedy, S. 1992. *Temporary movements of people to and from Australia* (Canberra, Australian Government Publishing Service).

Som, R.K. 1973. *Recall lapse in demographic enquiries* (New York, Asia Publishing House).

Somoza, Jorge L. 1977. "Una idea para estimar la población emigrante por sexo y edad en el censo de un país", in *Notas de población*, Vol. V, No. 15, pp. 89-106.

——. 1981a. "A proposal for estimating the emigrant population by sex and age from special census questions", in *Indirect procedures for estimating emigration*, International Union for the Scientific Study of Population (IUSSP) Papers, No. 18, pp. 3-18.

——. 1981b. "Indirect estimates of emigration: Application of two procedures using information on residence of children and siblings", in *Indirect procedures for estimating emigration*, International Union for the Scientific Study of Population (IUSSP) Papers, No. 18, pp. 35-60.

South Africa, Chamber of Mines. 1987. *Statistical tables 1987* (Johannesburg).

Spain, Instituto Nacional de Estadística. 1994. *Migraciones: Año 1993* (Madrid).

Sri Lanka, Department of Immigration and Emigration. 1993. *Sri Lanka migration control manual* (Colombo, Department of Government Printing).

Sri Lanka, Bureau of Foreign Employment. 1991. *Report of the airport survey of migrant workers* (Colombo), mimeograph.

Stalker, Peter. 1994. *The work of strangers: A survey of international labour migration* (Geneva, ILO).

Standing, Guy. 1984. "Income transfers and remittances", in Bilsborrow, Richard E. et al. *Migration surveys in low-income countries: Guidelines for survey and questionnaire design* (London and Sydney, Croom Helm), Ch. 8, pp. 264-316.

Storer, Desmond. 1982. *Out of the shadows: A review of the 1980 regularisation of status programme in Australia* (Geneva, ILO), International Migration for Employment, Working Paper, MIG/WP/7.

Stouffer, Samuel A. 1940. "Intervening opportunities: A theory relating mobility and distance", in *American Sociological Review*, Vol. 5, pp. 845-867.

——. 1960. "Intervening opportunities and competing migrants", in *Journal of Regional Science*, Vol. 2, No. 1, pp. 1-26.

Swamy, G. 1981. *International migrant workers' remittances: Issues and prospects* (Washington, World Bank), World Bank Staff Working Papers No. 481.

Sweden, Statistiska Centralbyrån. 1995. *Befolkningsstatistik 1994: Del 2. Inrikes och utrikes flyttningar* (Stockholm, Statistics Sweden).

Switzerland, Office Fédéral des Réfugiés. 1994. *Statistique en matière d'asile 1993* (Berne, Service d'Information et Service de la Statistique).

Switzerland, Office Fédéral de la Statistique. 1994. *Annuaire statistique de la Suisse 1995* (Berne, Verlag Neue Zürcher Zeitung).

Tan, Edita A.; Canlas Dante B. 1989. "Migrants' saving remittance and labour supply behaviour: The Philippines case", in Amjad (ed.) 1989.

Taylor, Jeffrey E. 1986. "Differential migration, networks, information and risk", pp. 147-171 in Stark, O. (ed.): *Research in human capital and development* (Greenwich, Connecticult, JAI Press) Vol. 4.

Tingsabadh, Charit. 1989. "Maximising development benefits from labour migration: Thailand", in Amjad, 1989.

Todaro, Michael. 1969. "A model of labor migration and urban unemployment in less developed countries", in *American Economic Review*, Vol. 59(1), pp. 138-148, March.

International migration statistics

Torrealba, Ricardo. 1985. *Migrant workers in an irregular situation and their regularisation in Venezuela* (Geneva, ILO), International Migration for Employment, Working Paper, MIG/WP/21.

———. 1987. "International migration data: Their problems and usefulness in Venezuela", in *International Migration Review*, Vol. 21, No. 4 (winter), pp. 1270-1276.

Tribalat, Michèle. n.d. "France", in Poulain, Michel et al. (eds.), *Projet d'harmonisation des statistiques de migration internationale au sein de la Communauté Européenne: Rapports nationaux* (Louvain-la-Neuve, Catholic University of Louvain), mimeograph.

———. 1989. "Rapport français", paper presented at the Meeting on the Working Group on International Migration of the European Association for Population Studies, Paris.

———. (ed.) 1991. *Cent d'ans d'immigration, étrangers d'hier, français d'aujourd'hui: Apport démographique, dynamique familiale et économique de l'immigration étrangère* (Paris, INED).

———. 1995. "Les immigrés et leurs enfants", in *Population and sociétés: Bulletin mensuel d'information de l'Institut National d'Études Démographiques*, April, No. 300, pp. 1-4.

———; Simon, Patrick. 1993. "Chronique de l'immigration", in *Population*, Vol. 1, pp. 125-182.

Turner, A. 1979. *Sample design for ESCAP multi-country survey of internal migration and urbanization* (Washington, DC, United States Bureau of the Census), mimeograph.

UNHCR. n.d. *Populations of concern to UNHCR: A statistical overview 1994* (Geneva, Office of the UNHCR).

———. 1994a. *UNHCR's operational experience with internally displaced persons* (Geneva, Office of the UNHCR).

———. 1994b. *Registration: A practical guide for field staff* (Geneva, Office of the UNHCR).

———. 1994c. *Résultats du recensement des réfugiés burundais (27-31 décembre 1993)* (Rwanda, Secrétariat Permanent du Comité de Crise and UNHCR).

———. 1994d. *Populations of concern to UNHCR: A statistical overview 1993* (Geneva, Office of the UNHCR).

United Arab Emirates. 1977. *Annual statistical abstract 1977* (Abu Dhabi, Central Statistical Department).

———. 1991. *Annual statistical abstract 1991* (Abu Dhabi, Central Statistical Department).

United Kingdom Office of Population Censuses and Surveys. 1995. *1993 International migration* (London, Her Majesty's Stationary Office), series MN, No. 20.

United Nations. 1949. *Problems of migration statistics* (United Nations publications, sales No. 1950.XIII.1), Population Studies No. 5.

———. 1953. *International migration statistics* (United Nations Publication, sales No. 50.XIII.1), Statistical Papers, series M, No. 20.

———. 1969. *Methodology and evaluation of population registers and similar systems* (United Nations Publication, sales No. E.69.XVII.15), Studies in Methods, series F, No. 15.

———. 1970. *Manual VI: Methods of measuring internal migration* (New York, United Nations), Population Studies No. 47.

Bibliography

———. 1978. *Demographic yearbook 1977* (United Nations Publication, sales No. E/F.78.XIII.1).

———. 1980a. *Recommendations on statistics of international migration* (United Nations Publication, sales No. E.79.XVII.18), Statistical Papers, Series M, No. 58.

———. 1980b. *Principles and recommendations for population and housing censuses* (United Nations Publication, sales No. E.80.XVII.8), Statistical Papers, series M, No. 67.

———. 1986. "The estimation of lifetime emigration from data on the residence of children: The case of Colombia", in *Population Bulletin of the United Nations* (New York), No. 18-1985, pp. 49-58.

———. 1987. *Demographic yearbook 1985* (United Nations Publication, sales No. E/F.86.XIII.1).

———. 1990. *Supplementary principles and recommendations for population and housing censuses* (United Nations Publication, sales No. E.90.XVII.9), Statistical Papers, series M, No. 67/Add.1.

———. 1991. *Demographic yearbook 1989* (United Nations Publication, sales No. E/F.90.XIII.1).

———. 1992. *World population monitoring 1991* (United Nations Publication, sales No. E.92.XIII.2).

———. 1993a. *International Migrant Stock*, database maintained by the Population Division, United Nations.

———. 1993b. *System of national accounts 1993* (United Nations Publication, sales No. E.94.XVII.4).

———. 1994. *Definition of total population: National practices and implications for population counts or estimates and projections*, paper presented to the Eighteenth Session of the ACC Subcommittee on Demographic Estimates and Projections, 28-30 June (ACC/SCDEP/1994/TP/3).

———. 1995a. *Trends in the international migrant stock*, database maintained by the Population Division, United Nations.

———. 1995b. *International migration policies and the status of female migrants* (United Nations Publication, sales No. E.95.XIII.10).

United Nations ESCAP (Economic and Social Commission for Asia and the Pacific) (Bangkok, Thailand). 1980a. *National migration surveys: I. Survey organization and monitoring*, comparative study on migration, urbanization and development in the ESCAP region, survey manuals (New York, United Nations).

———. 1980b. *National migration surveys: II. The core questionnaire* (New York, United Nations), comparative study on migration, urbanization and development in the ESCAP region, survey manuals.

———. 1980c. *National migration surveys: VI. Sample design manual* (New York, United Nations), comparative study on migration, urbanization and development in the ESCAP region, Survey manuals.

United Nations Statistical Division. 1994. *Definition of total population: National practices and implications for population counts or estimates and projections*, paper presented to the ACC Subcommittee on Demographic Estimates and Projections, Eighth Session, 28-30 June (ACC/SCDEP/1994/TP/3).

International migration statistics

——.; European Communities Statistical Office. 1995. *Revision of the United Nations recommendations on statistics of international migration* (New York), doc. MIG/EI/5A/95, mimeograph.

United States Bureau of International Labor Affairs (forthcoming). *Effects of the Immigration Reform and Contral Act: Characteristics and labour market behaviour of the legalized population five year following legalization* (Washington, DC, Department of Labor).

United States Commission for the Study of International Migration and Cooperative Economic Development. 1990. *Unauthorized migration: An economic development response* (Washington, United States Government Printing Office).

United States Immigration and Naturalization Service. 1988. *1987 Statistical yearbook of the Immigration and Naturalization Service* (Washington, DC, United States Government Printing Office).

——. 1990. *1989 Statistical yearbook of the Immigration and Naturalization Service* (Washington, DC, United States Government Printing Office).

——. 1992a. *1991 Statistical yearbook of the Immigration and Naturalization Service* (Washington, DC, United States Government Printing Office).

——. 1992b. *Immigration Reform and Control Act: Report on the legalized alien population* (Washington, DC, Immigration and Naturalization Service).

——. 1993. *1993 Statistical yearbook of the Immigration and Naturalization Service* (Washington, DC, Government Printing Office).

van den Brekel, J. C. 1977. *The population register: The example of the Netherlands system* (Chapel Hill, North Carolina, Laboratories for Population Statistics), Scientific Report No. 31.

van der Erf, Rob et al. n.d. "Sources on international migration and migrants: The Netherlands", in Poulain, Michel et al. (eds.), *Projet d'harmonisation des statistiques de migration internationale au sein de la Communauté Européenne: Rapports nationaux* (Louvain-la-Neuve, Catholic University of Louvain), mimeograph.

Vasquez, N.D. et al. 1995. *Tracer study on Filipino domestic helpers abroad* (Geneva, International Organization for Migration).

Verhoef, R. 1986. "The Netherlands population registers as a source of international migration statistics", in United Nations: *National data sources and programmes for implementing the United Nations recommendations on statistics of international migration* (United Nations publication, sales No. E.86.XVII.22), Studies in Methods, series F, No. 37.

Warren, Robert; Passel, Jeffrey S. 1987. "A count of the uncountable: Estimates of undocumented aliens counted in the 1980 United States census", in *Demography* (Washington, DC), Vol. 24, No. 3 (August), pp. 375-393.

WFS (World Fertility Survey). 1975. *Survey of organization manual* (The Hague, International Statistical Institute), basic documentation No. 2.

Wolff, Brent et al. 1991. *Focus groups and surveys as complementary research methods: Examples from a study of the consequences of family size in Thailand* (Ann Arbor, Population Studies Center, University of Michigan).

Wood, Charles H. 1981. "Structural changes and household strategies: A conceptual framework for the study of rural migration", in *Human Organization*, Vol. 40, No. 4 (winter), pp. 338-344.

——. 1982. "Equilibrium and historical-structural perspectives on migration", in *International Migration Review*, Vol. 16, No. 2, pp. 298-319.

Woodrow, Karen A.; Passel, Jeffrey S. 1990. "Post-IRCA undocumented immigration to the United States: An assessment based on the June 1988 CPS", in Bean, F. D. et al. (eds.): *Undocumented migration to the United States: IRCA and the experience of the 1980s* (Washington, DC, The Urban Institute), pp. 33-76.

Yemen. 1992. *Statistical year book 1992* (Sana'a, Central Statistical Organization).

Yemen Arab Republic. 1972. *Statistical year book 1972* (Sana'a, Statistics Department, Central Planning Organisation).

——. 1975. *Statistical year book 1974-75* (Sana'a, Statistics Department, Central Planning Organisation).

——. 1976. *Statistical year book 1976* (Sana'a, Statistics Department, Central Planning Organisation).

——. 1978. *Statistical year book 1977-78* (Sana'a, Statistics Department, Central Planning Organisation).

——. 1987. *Statistical year book 1986* (Sana'a, Statistics Department, Central Planning Organisation).

Zaba, Basia. 1986. "Measurement of emigration using indirect techniques", in *Manual for the collection and analysis of data on residence of relatives*, International Union for the Scientific Study of Population (IUSSP) (Liège, Ordina Editions).

——. 1987. "The indirect estimation of migration: A critical review", in *International migration review* (Staten Island, New York), Vol. 21, No. 80 (winter), pp. 1395-1445.

Zlotnik, Hania. 1987. "The concept of international migration as reflected in data collection systems", in *International migration review* (Staten Island, New York), Vol. 21, No. 4 (winter), pp. 925-946.

——. 1988. "The indirect estimation of emigration", in *African Population Conference*, Vol. 1 (Liège, Belgium, International Union for the Scientific Study of Population).

——. 1989. *Estimación de la emigración a partir de datos sobre la residencia de hijos sobrevivientes: El caso de Colombia*, Memorias de la Tercera Reunión Nacional sobre la Investigación Demográfica de México, Vol. I (Mexico, Universidad Nacional Autónoma de México (UNAM) and Sociedad Mexicana de Demografía (SOMEDE)), pp. 469-491.

——. 1992. "Empirical identification of international migration systems", in Kritz, Mary M. et al. (eds.): *International migration systems: A global approach* (Oxford, Clarendon Press/Oxford University Press), pp. 19-40.

Zolberg, Aristide R. 1981. "International migrations in political perspective", in Kritz, Mary M. et al. (eds.): *Global trends in migration: Theory and research on international population movements* (Staten Island, Center for Migration Studies), pp. 3-27.

INDEX

Note: The terms *migration, emigration* and *immigration* are largely omitted, due to their ubiquity.

Abella, D.   336
Abella, Manolo I.   154
"absentees"   64
Adams, Richard H.   411
additions, refugee   217-19
Afghanistan   147, 149, 220
Africa   180, 190
    border statistics   143-4, 145-6, 149
    census   55, 64-5, 71
    citizenship   17, 56, 62
    place of birth   59-61
    refugees and asylum-seekers   45, 214-15, 222, 225, 226
    remittances   322, 333, 334, 338
    residence permits   125
    surveys   241, 243, 262, 279, 290-1
    work permits   164, 166
Alburo, F.A.   336
Algeria   62, 118, 322
Americas   17, 45, 56-9, 71
    see also Canada; Central America and Caribbean; South America; United States
Amjad, R.   362n
Andorra   166
Angola   144
Antigua   144
Argentina   147, 197, 203-4
armed forces *see* military personnel

Arnold, Fred   299
Asia   48, 71, 180
    border statistics   143, 144-5, 147, 148-9
    citizenship   17, 61
    contract labour control   181-2, 184-90, 191-3
    place of birth   57-9
    population registers   29, 75-6
    refugees and asylum-seekers   220, 222, 229
    register of foreigners   102, 103, 107-8, 111
    regularization drives   197, 200, 205-6
    remittances   322-3, 334, 335, 336-9, 361-2
    residence permits   125-7
    surveys   239, 240-2, 244, 273, 279, 286
    temporary emigrants   65
    time criterion   23, 25, 26
    Western *see* Middle East
    work permits   166, 170-2, 173, 175, 176
    see also Soviet Union, former

assistance provision for refugees and asylum-seekers   221-5

asylum-seekers   34, 35, 39, 40, 41, 45, 49, 151, 213
    population registers   82-3, 91-2

427

statistics 229-36
see also refugees
Athukorala, Premachandra 183-9 *passim*, 193, 337n, 361n
Australia 46, 244
　border statistics 143, 148, 149
　refugees and asylum-seekers 217, 220
　regularization drives 197, 200-1, 207
　residence and permits 20, 120-1, 122-3
Austria 60, 197, 217
　population registers 76, 77, 82, 83-6, 91, 93-4, 95
　register of foreigners 102-3, 110
Awad, Ibrahim 172, 205, 206
Azam, Farooq-i 242

Bahrain 144, 170-1, 173
balance of payments and remittances 321-32
　components of 323-4
Baltic States 60, 134-5, 191, 243
Bangladesh
　contract labour control 181-2, 184
　remittances 322, 332-3, 334, 336-7, 338, 361, 362
Barbados 146
Belarus 25, 190-1
Belgium 109, 191, 197, 217
　population registers 75-6, 79, 80, 82, 83-6, 90, 91, 93, 95
　residence 88-90
　work permits 164-5, 173, 174
Belize 146
Bermuda 144
Bilsborrow, Richard E. 244, 246, 266, 273, 301
birthplace *see* place of birth
Bolivia 65, 67, 204, 322
borders
　frontier workers 33, 35, 43, 328

statistics 136-59
　problem of identification of migrants 138-41
　recommendations for improvement 156-9
　relevance 155-6
　UN recommendations 141-55
　surveys 241-3
Borjas, George J. 52
Bosnia and Herzegovina 216, 230
Botswana 62, 144
Brazil 147, 239
Brekel, J.C. van den 80
Bretz, Manfred 77, 91, 103, 110
British Virgin Islands 146
Brown, R.P.C. 336, 338, 341, 362n
Brunei 147
Bulgaria 75, 98
Burkina Faso 55, 243, 322
Burney, N. 362n
Burundi 55, 164, 225
business travellers 34, 35, 36, 38, 44
Bustamante, Jorge A. 242
Byerlee, Derek 290

Cameroon 55
Canada 16, 46, 125, 143
　place of birth 27, 57
　refugees and asylum-seekers 215, 217, 220, 226
　regularization drives 197, 200, 201-2, 207
　residence permits 120-1, 130
Cape Verde 144
Caribbean area *see* Central America
Cartagena Declaration 45, 169, 215
Carvallo-Hernández, Rahiza 169, 180
Cayman Islands 146, 149
censuses *see* population censuses
Central African Republic 60-1, 118

428

Index

Central America and Caribbean 27, 67, 75, 125
  border statistics 137, 144, 145, 146-7, 149-55
  refugees and asylum-seekers 215, 230
  remittances 322, 333
  surveys 242-3, 303
  work permits 168-9, 175
Central and Eastern Europe 48, 60, 159n, 243
  contract labour control 190-1
  exit permits 134-6
  population registers 75, 76, 97-9
  refugees and asylum-seekers 216, 226-7
  residence permits 120, 129
  time criterion 23, 25-6
  work permits 168, 174
  see also Soviet Union, former
CERPOD (Centre d'Etudes et de Recherche sur la Population et le Développement) 241, 243, 254
Ceuta 166
Charbit, Yves 62
children 66-7, 313, 315
  of refugees 218, 219
Chile 57, 147
China 71, 75
Christmas Island 148
CIS (Commonwealth of Independent States) 226
citizenship 5, 16-17, 30, 31
  and return migrants 33, 35, 36-7, 39-40
  censuses 56-9, 61-2, 70, 73
  questionnaire content 295, 298, 309, 318
  see also place of birth
classification of migrants *see* framework
cluster sampling 276-8
Colombia 67, 147, 159n, 169, 204, 322

Common Nordic Labour Market 82, 85, 87
Commonwealth, British 167, 200
Commonwealth of Independent States 226
communications and transport and questionnaire content 297, 302-3
community-level questionnaires 296-72, 301-5
  country of destination 398-400
  country of destination surveys 313
Comoros 144
comparison groups and surveys 248-63, 294
  analysis, preferred 261-3
  consequences 255-61
  country of origin 313-16
  determinants 249-55
concepts 8, 11, 15-50
  assessment considerations 29-32
  citizenship 16-17, 56-9, 61-2
  place of birth 26-8, 56-61
  purpose of stay 24-6
  residence 18-21
  time 21-4
  see also framework
consular and diplomatic personnel 33, 42, 53-4, 90, 151, 328
contract labour control 182-97
  recommendations for improvement 193-7
  scope and limitation of data 191-3
contract migrant workers 33, 35, 38, 43
Convention Governing Specific Aspects of Refugees in Africa 214-15, 226
Convention on Rights of All Migrant Workers and Members of Their Families 16, 30, 43, 46
Convention Relating to Status of Refugees 30, 45-6, 91, 213-14, 217, 218, 220, 229-30, 232, 234-5

Cook Islands   148
Copland, Emily   215
Costa Rica   144
Côte d'Ivoire   55, 125, 243
country of destination   3-4, 5-6
  households and remittances 355-60
  surveys   307-13
    community-level   313, 398-400
    comparison groups   251-62 *passim*
    fertility   313
    household   307-8
    individual   308-12, 368-98
    migrant workers   312-13
    model questionnaires   363-402
    planning   266
    questionnaire content   295, 304-5
    sample design   269, 279
    tracing migrants   290
country of origin
  households and remittances   342-55
    received from migrants   347-9
    sent to migrants   342-7
  surveys   313-18
    comparison groups   249-51, 252, 253, 256, 258-62, 313-16
    model questionnaires   403-9
    out-migrants *see* proxy respondents
    questionnaire content   295-305
    return migrants   317-18
    sample design   269, 279
    tracing migrants   290
Courgeau, Daniel   63
Cuba   75, 146
Cyprus   147, 149, 322
Czech Republic   98, 129
Czechoslovakia, former   60, 98, 135
data collection systems   10-11, 12
  all international migrants   51-160
  exit permits   134-6

see also population censuses; population registers; register of foreigners; residence permits; statistics *under* borders
  labour migration   161-212
    employers' reports   179-82
    see also control *under* contract labour; regularization drives; work permits
  refugees and asylum-seekers 213-36
    assistance provision   221-5
    dynamics of change   216-21
    recommendations for improvement   225, 228-9, 231-6
    see also UNHCR
DaVanzo, Julie   300
deff (design effect)   277-8
defining international migrants   245-8
demographic characteristics and questionnaire content   295, 298, 300, 302, 307, 308
  see also place of birth
Demographic Yearbooks (UN)   15, 19, 142-9, 151-3, 155
Denmark   109, 217
  population registers   75-6, 78-9, 82, 83, 84-7, 91, 93, 96
design of surveys   245-67
  defining international migrants 245-8
  and presentation   305-16
  specialized   263-7
  see also comparison groups; sample design
diplomats *see* consular and diplomatic
disproportionate sampling   280-3
documents, need for   310, 318
domains of analysis and sampling 268-70
  see also country of destination; country of origin

Index

Dominica 146
Dominican Republic 67, 147, 168-9, 322, 333
Dublin Convention 229-30
earnings/income
   questionnaire content 295, 296, 299, 300, 320
   see also remittances
Eastern Europe *see* Central and Eastern Europe
Economic Commission for Europe (ECE) 57, 120, 134, 243
Economic Community of West African States 125
economic migration/economic activity 34, 35, 36, 38, 44, 48-50
   censuses 69, 71
   see also migrant workers
ECOWAS (Economic Community of West African States) 125
Ecuador 147, 204, 266, 278
education
   level and questionnaire content 295, 311, 315
   see also students; trainees
Egypt 65, 146, 244, 322
El Salvador 169, 230
elements of sample design 269
employers' reports 179-82
employment
   questionnaire content 296, 299, 301, 302, 310-13
   see also migrant workers; work; work permits
Ensch, Jean 80
Equatorial Guinea 166
Erf, Rob van den 81, 87, 90, 91, 166
ESCAP 273, 319
Escribano-Morales, Fátima 78, 80, 104, 108, 166-7
Esser, Hartmut 106

established migrant workers 35, 38, 44, 111
Estonia 60, 135
Ethiopia 143, 144, 146
ethnicity 68
   see also return migrants
Europe
   border statistics 143
   contract labour control 197-8
   place of birth 28, 57-9
   refugees and asylum-seekers 227-8
   remittances 322, 339
   see also Central and Eastern Europe; European Union
European Union 5, 21, 191, 322
   border statistics 137-8, 143, 159n
   place of birth 28, 60
   population registers 75-88, 90-7, 100
   refugees and asylum-seekers 215, 217, 226, 228
   register of foreigners 102-11 *passim*
   regularization drives 197-200, 207
   residence 19-20, 88-90
      permits 115-19, 129, 130
   returning ethnics 40-1
   surveys 239, 244, 262, 319, 320
   time criterion 22-4
   work permits 162, 164-8, 173-6
exchange controls 320
exit permits 134-6
exits, refugee 219-21

Faeroe Islands 75
Falkland Islands 143, 144, 147
family
   reunification migrants 36, 39, 46-7, 69, 162, 218-19
   see also households
Fatoo, H. 290
Fawcett, James T. 299
fertility surveys 313, 319
Fiji 143, 145, 148
finance *see* earnings; remittances

431

Findley, Sally E.   262, 301
Finland   109
  population registers   75-6, 79, 82, 83-7, 93, 96-7
fixing token   223-4
foreigners   33-5, 37-50
  changes of status   48
  economic migrants   34, 35, 36, 38, 44
  family reunification migrants   36, 39, 46-7
  irregular migrants   34, 35-6, 39, 41, 49
  migrant workers   33-5, 37-8, 42-4, 48, 50
  returning ethnics   33, 35, 37, 40-1, 49
  settlers   33, 35, 37, 42, 49
  see also asylum-seekers; free movement; refugees; register of foreigners; special purpose admissions
framework for identification and classification   32-50
  citizens and return migrants   33, 35, 36-7, 39-40
  see also foreigners
France
  citizenship   62
  contract labour control   191
  place of birth   28
  population registers   82
  refugees and asylum-seekers   217
  register of foreigners   109
  regularization drives   197-9, 207
  residence permits   116-19, 129, 130
  surveys   244, 262, 269
  work permits   162
free movement, migrants with right of   33, 35, 37
  registers   81-6 *passim*, 111
Freedman, Deborah   267
Frejka, Tomas   243
French Guiana   144

frontiers *see* borders
Gabon   118
Gambia, The   144
Garcia y Griego, Manuel   151
Garson, Jean-Pierre   197-9
GATS (General Agreement on Trade in Services)   5
general purpose surveys   238-41
geographical conditions and questionnaire content   297, 303
geographical information system   270
German Democratic Republic   60
Germany   5, 159n
  place of birth   60
  population registers   29, 75-7, 80, 82, 83-6, 91, 93-4, 96
  refugees and asylum-seekers   217, 227, 228
  register of foreigners   29-30, 102, 103, 105-7, 110, 111
  returning ethnics   40
  surveys   244
  trainees   48
Ghana   146, 244
Gibraltar   166
Gilani, Ijaz   241, 362n
Gisser, Richard   77, 79, 87, 91, 102, 104, 108-9
Giusti, Alejandro   128
Goldstein, Sidney and Alice   289
Goodman, Leo A.   289
Greece   40, 82, 119, 159n, 165, 175, 322
Grenada   144
Groves, Robert M.   266
Guadeloupe   144
Guatemala   168-9, 175
Guinea   243
Guinea-Bissau   144
Gulati, Leela   339

Gurrieri, Jorge 204
Guyana 147
Haiti 67, 147, 169
highly skilled migrant workers 35, 38, 44, 48
Hill, Kenneth 66
Hoefer, Michael D. 208
Hoffman-Nowotny, Hans-Joachim 109
Honduras 144
Hong Kong 61, 147, 149, 229
households
  remittances 326, 327, 339-60
    in country of destination 355-60
    in country of origin 342-55
    residence concept 328-9
  surveys 6-7, 237-8, 298-300, 306-7, 320
    at borders 241-2
    comparison groups 249-62 *passim*
    country of destination 307-8, 363-7
    country of origin 403-4
    general purpose 238-41
    multiplicity 288-90
    questionnaire content 294, 295-6, 304-5
    sample design 269, 274, 276-7, 284-5
    selection in sample design 283-6
    specialized 243
housing and questionnaire content 296, 300-1, 302, 308
Hovy, Bela 213n
Hugo, Graeme J. 121, 206, 298, 299
humanitarian reasons and refugees 34, 35, 39, 45
Hungary 60, 120, 135, 168
Iceland 109, 217
  population registers 76, 80, 82, 83-6, 92, 93, 96-7

identification of migrants *see* framework
ILO (International Labour Office) 1, 8, 72, 341, 362
  on Asian labour-sending countries 184-9
  Interdepartmental Project on Migrant Workers 15, 17, 23
  on migrant workers 16, 30, 43
  Migration for Employment Convention 16, 30, 43, 49
IMF (International Monetary Fund) 321-2, 324-6, 329-31, 333
IMILA project 57-8, 71-2
improvement *see* recommendations
income *see* earnings
India 144, 239
  contract labour control 181-2, 184-5
  remittances 322, 334, 336-7, 338-9
individuals and surveys 6-7, 298-300, 306, 328-9
  comparison groups 249-52, 254, 256-60, 262, 269
  country of destination 308-12, 368-98
  country of origin 404-9
  questionnaire content 294, 295, 304-5
  specialized 244-5
Indonesia 147, 229
  contract labour control 184, 188-9
  regularization drives 205-6
  remittances 322, 334
intensive interviews 292-3
internal migration 63, 278, 290-1
International Conference of Migration Statisticians 1
International Labour Conference 1
International Labour Office *see* ILO
international migration statistics
  major findings and limitations 10-13
  need to improve 1-14

International migration statistics

see also concepts; data collection; remittances; surveys
International Monetary Fund *see* IMF
International Union for Scientific Study of Population   65-6
investors, immigrating   34, 38, 44
Iraq   144, 171, 180, 216
Ireland   60, 82, 109, 137, 217
   residence permits   119-20, 129
   work permits   165, 173
irregular migrants   34, 35-6, 39, 41, 49
Israel   5, 40, 75
   border statistics   147, 149
   residence permits   125-6, 130
Italy   109, 159n, 217, 244
   population registers   76, 77, 82, 83-6, 92, 93, 95
   regularization drives   197, 199
   residence permits   119, 129
IUSSP (International Union for Scientific Study of Population)   65-6
Izquierdo-Escribano, Antonio   104

Jamaica   322
Japan   5, 23, 48, 180
   border statistics   143, 147, 149
   population registers   29, 75-6
   register of foreigners   29-30, 102, 103, 107-8, 111
Jaspers-Faijer, Dirk   65, 67
Jayatissa, R.A.   338
Jones, H.M.   64
Jordan   144, 170, 173, 322

Kalton, G.   282
Kazi, S.   338, 362n
Kelly, John J.   87
Kennedy, S.   121
Kenya   60-1, 146, 149
key variable identification   273
Kish, Leslie   270, 277, 279, 281-3, 319n, 336

Knodel, John E.   292
Korea, Republic of   48, 75-6, 107
   border statistics   143, 147, 149
   contract labour control   181-2, 184, 189-90
   remittances   322, 336-7
Korte, Hermann   106
Koszamanis, Byron   119, 165
Kritz, Mary M.   7, 244, 259
Kuijsten, Anton C.   93, 95
Kuptsch, C.   48
Kuwait   127, 144, 180
   work permits   171, 173, 174, 175

labour *see* employment; migrant workers; work permits
Lange, Anita   79, 82, 91
Langers, Jean   80
language   68, 309
Latin America *see* Central America and Caribbean; South America
Latvia   60, 135, 243
Lebanon   170
Lee, Everett S.   294, 304
Lesotho   322
Liberia   146
Libyan Arab Jamahiriya   144
Liechtenstein: registers
   foreigners   102, 105, 109, 110
   population   76, 79, 80, 82, 83-6, 93-4, 95
life history questionnaires   267
Lithuania   60, 135, 191, 243
longitudinal surveys   244
Luxembourg   109, 217
   population registers   76, 79-80, 82, 83-6, 91, 93-4, 96

Macau   143, 144, 147, 149
Madagascar   144
Magescas, Jean-Bernard   62
Mahmud, W.   338, 362n

Index

"main migration actor" 320
Malaysia 172, 175, 197, 205-6, 229
Mali 243, 322
Mammey, Ulrich 106
Mármora, Lelio 197, 203, 204
Martinique 144
Massey, Douglas S. 292, 299
Mauritania 144, 243
Mauritius 145, 146
Mexico
 and USA 125, 242-3, 303
 border statistics 137, 147, 149-55
 remittances 322, 333
Michelena, A. 204, 205
Middle East (Western Asia) 40, 75, 180
 border statistics 144, 148
 contract labour control 181-2
 refugees and asylum-seekers 216
 remittances 322, 339
 residence permits 125-6, 127, 130
 surveys 241-2
 work permits 170-1, 173-5, 176
migrant workers 33-5, 37-8, 42-4, 48, 50, 111
 censuses 54, 55-6
 country of destination surveys 312-13
 questionnaires 295, 299, 391-8
 surveys 241-3
military personnel 33, 42, 53-4, 90, 328
MMA ("main migration actor") 320
Morocco 146, 190, 244, 322, 333
Moser, C. 282
Moulier, Yves 197-9
Mozambique 144
Mullan, Brendan 243
multi-stage sampling 276-8, 281, 319
multiplicity surveys 288-90
Myanmar 147, 149

national accounts 325, 329-30
national accounts and
 remittances 321-32
nationality, legal *see* citizenship
Nauru 148
Nepal 65
Netherlands 22, 109, 197
 population registers 19-20, 75-7, 78, 80, 81, 82, 83-8, 90-1, 93-4, 96
 residence 19-20
 surveys 244, 319, 320
 work permits 165-6, 174, 175
Netherlands Antilles 140-1
network sampling 289
New Caledonia 143, 145, 148
New Zealand 120-1, 143, 148, 149
Nicaragua 169
NIDI 254, 274, 319, 320
Nigam, S.B.L. 187
Niger 243
Nigeria 146, 243
Niue 143, 145, 148
nomads 54
non-migrants 35
 see also comparison groups
Norfolk Island 143, 145, 148
norms, community 297, 303-4
North America *see* Canada; United States
North, David S. 200, 201-2
Northern Ireland 60
Norway 109
 population registers 76, 79, 80, 82, 83-7, 91, 93, 96-7
OAU (Organization of African Unity) 45
 Convention on African refugees 214-15, 226
Oberai, A.S. 65, 300, 340
Oceania 71

435

border statistics   143, 145, 146, 149
place of birth   56-9
remittances   336, 338, 341
residence and permits   20, 120-1, 122-3
see also in particular Australia
OECD (Organization for Economic Cooperation and Development)   48
see also SOPEMI
Oishi, Nana   48
Oman   127, 130, 171, 180
open-ended questions   292
Ordoñez-Gómez, Myriam   65
Organization of African Unity see OAU
Organization for Economic Cooperation and Development see OECD
Pacific Ocean area see Oceania
Pakistan   200, 220
   contract labour control   181-2, 184, 185
   remittances   322, 333, 334, 335, 336-8, 339
   surveys   240, 241-2
   time criterion   25, 26
Panama   145, 147
Papua New Guinea   148, 149
Paraguay   65, 67
participation in community and questionnaire content   295, 299-300, 301
Passel, Jeffrey S.   55, 207
Peixoto, João   116
Pellecer-Palacios, Sonia M.   169
permits
   exit   134-6
   see also work permits and under residence
Peru   143, 144, 147, 204
Philippines   145, 166, 229

contract labour control   181-2, 184, 186-8, 192-3
   remittances   332-3, 334, 336-7, 361-2
place of birth   26-8, 56-61, 70, 71, 73, 307, 308
   see also citizenship; demographic characteristics
place-utility approach   304
Plender, Richard   82, 105, 159n
Poland   23, 25-6, 168, 174, 191, 243
population censuses   27-8, 52-75
   citizenship   56-9, 61-2, 70, 73
   information relevant   67-9
   measuring emigration   64-7
   place of birth   56-61, 70, 71, 73
   recommendations for improvement   73-5
   sampling   69-70, 269-70, 280
   tabulation   54, 57-9, 70-3
population frame   270, 280
population registers   75-102
   Central and Eastern Europe   97-9
   "establishing residence" meaning   88-90
   international migrants   92-4, 99-100
   recommendations for improvement   100-2
   special treatment groups   90-2
   structure and operation   76-81
   tabulation   84-6, 93, 94-7
   see also register of foreigners
Portugal   23-4, 82, 166, 322
   residence permits   115-16, 129
Poulain, Michel   78-80, 84-6, 88, 90, 93, 120, 164, 165
poverty and questionnaire content   296, 299
PPES (probability proportional to estimated size)   271, 281, 286
primary sampling units see PSUs
probability proportional to estimated size see PPES

Index

probability samples   268, 270-2, 286-8; *see also* sample design
project-tied migrant workers   33, 35, 37, 43
proxy respondents in surveys   246, 252, 266, 316-17
PSUs (primary sampling units)   276, 280-1, 287
Puerto Rico   27, 144
purpose of stay   24-6, 31

Qatar   144, 180-1
qualitative surveys   291-3
questionnaires *see* surveys and questionnaires
Quibria, M.G.   336

"rare elements" in sample design   279-83
receiving countries *see* country of destination
recommendations for improvement
  borders statistics   156-9
  citizenship data   61
  contract labour control   193-7
  data collection system for refugees and asylum-seekers   225, 228-9, 231-6
  employers' reports   181-2
  place of birth   28
  population censuses   73-5
  population registers   100-2
  register of foreigners   112-14
  regularization drives   209-12
  residence permits   131-4
  work permits   177-9
Recommendations on statistics of international migration (UN)   2-5, 54, 59, 71, 139-40, 156-7, 159
  border statistics   141-55
refugees   34, 35, 38-9, 45-6, 49, 69
  Conventions on
    in Africa   214-15, 226
    see also Convention Relating to Status of Refugees
  registers   106, 111
  see also asylum-seekers *and under* data collection systems
register of foreigners   29-30, 102-14
  data problems   110-11
  international migrants   105-10, 111
  recommendations for improvement   112-14
regularization drives   197-212
  recommendations for improvement   209-12
  scope and limitation of data   206-9
religion   68-9
remittances, measurement of   315, 321-62
  definition in national accounts and balance of payments   321-32
  problems   332-9
  see also under households
resettled refugees   38, 45
residence   18-21, 22, 63, 107
  censuses   55, 70
  "establishing", meaning of   88-90
  permits   115-28
    data limitations   128-31
    recommendations for improvement 131-4
  registers   82, 86, 106-7, 108
  see also visas
  remittances   326-9
  surveys   245-8
retirees, foreign   33, 35, 37, 42
return migrants   33, 35, 36-7, 39-40
  population registers   84
  remittances   350-5
  surveys   242, 247
    comparison groups   251, 254-5, 257, 260
    country of origin   317-18
returning ethnics   33, 35, 37, 40-1, 49, 111
Rodrigo, C.   338
Rogers, Rosemarie   215
Romania   98-9, 135-6

Russell, Sharon Stanton   321, 334
Russian Federation   99, 136, 191
Rwanda   55, 146, 164, 225
El-Saadani, Somaya Mahmoud   299
Saint Helena   145, 146, 149
Saint Kitts and Nevis   147
Saint Pierre and Miquelon   144
Saint Vincent   144
Saith, A.   336, 338
Salt, John   120, 167-8
Samoa   145, 148
sample design in surveys   267-88
  domains of analysis and sampling frames 268-70
  household selection   283-6
  multi-stage and cluster sampling 276-8, 281
  probability samples needed   270-2
  "rare elements"   279-83
  size   272-4
  weights used in analysis   286-8
  see also stratification
sampling
  frames   261, 268-70
  multiplicity   288-90
  population censuses   69-70, 269-70, 280
  see also sample design; surveys
Santibáñez-Romell, Jorge   242
São Tomé and Príncipe   144
Saudi Arabia   127, 130, 171, 173, 174, 175
seasonal migrant workers   33, 35, 37, 43, 54, 111
"self-represented areas"   282
sending countries see country of origin
Senegal   55, 243, 244, 322
Serageldin, Ismail   334
settlers   33, 35, 37, 42, 49, 111
sex roles   298
Seychelles   145, 146, 149

short-term migrants   33, 36, 42
Shryock, Henry S.   28, 60, 68
Siegel, Jacob S.   28, 60, 68
Sierra Leone   290-1
Simon, Patrick   269
Singapore   65, 143, 145, 148
Singh, H.M.K.   340
Singleton (Jr.)   266
Sipaviciene, Audra   243
Sirken, Morris   288
Sjastad, Larry A.   294
Sloan, J.   121
Slovakia   98
Slovenia   99
snowball sampling   289
social networkers   299
socio-economic characteristics and questionnaire content   295, 296, 298-9
Solomon Islands   148
Som, R.K.   246
Somalia   146
Somoza, Jorge L.   65, 66
SOPEMI (Système d'observation permanente des migrations)   109, 164, 166, 168, 197-200
South Africa   64, 65, 125, 180
South America   180, 322
  border statistics   143, 144, 145, 147, 149
  census   65, 67
  regularization drives   197, 203-5
  residence permits   127-8
  surveys   239, 266, 278, 279
  work permits   166, 168-9, 174-5
Soviet Union, former   25, 60, 99, 134-6, 191
  see also Central and Eastern Europe
Spain   159n, 217, 244, 322

Index

population registers 76-7, 78, 80, 82, 83-6, 92-4, 95
register of foreigners 102, 103-4, 108, 109, 111
regularization drives 197, 199-200
work permits 166-7, 174, 175, 176
special purpose admissions 33, 35, 37, 42, 48-9
special purposes migrants 33, 36, 42
special treatment groups 53-5, 90-2
specialized surveys 243-5, 263-7
Sri Lanka
  border statistics 143, 145, 148
  contract labour control 184, 185-6, 191
  remittances 322, 334, 337, 338
  residence permits 126-7
  time criterion 23, 26
Standing, Guy 340, 342, 362n
stay of deportation 34, 39, 45
stocks of migrants 51, 65-6, 70, 128-30
Storer, Desmond 200, 201
Stouffer, Samuel A. 304
stratification in sample design 272-3, 274-5, 281-2, 320
students 25, 33, 35, 37, 41, 42, 48-9, 102, 111, 329
Sudan 322, 333, 334
Suriname 75, 147
surveys and questionnaires 237-320
  community-level factors 301-5
  country of destination, model 363-402
  country of origin, model 403-9
  design and presentation *see* design of surveys
  household-level *see under* households
  individual-level *see under* individuals
  migrant workers 391-8
  multiplicity 288-90

policy analysis and 318-19
qualitative 291-3
specialized 243-5, 263-7
tracing migrants 290-1
use and limitations 238-45
see also comparison groups; sample design *and under* country of destination: country of origin *and* households
Swamy, G. 334
Swaziland 55, 146
Sweden 109
  population registers 75-6, 78, 80-1, 82, 83-7, 91, 93-4, 96-7
Switzerland
  labour migration data collection 191
  population registers 76-7, 84-6, 95
  refugees and asylum-seekers 227, 228
  register of foreigners 102, 104-5, 108-10, 111
  time criterion 23-4
Syrian Arab Republic 148
Système d'observation permanente des migrations *see* SOPEMI
tabulation
  border statistics 144-8, 150-3
  population censuses 54, 57-9, 70-3
  population registers 84-6, 93, 94-7
  refugees 232-5
  visa categories 122-3
Taiwan, China 61, 75
Tanzania, United Republic of 146
Taylor, Jeffrey E. 299
Teitelbaum, Michael S. 321, 334
temporary migrant workers 2, 33, 35, 38, 43-4, 111, 241, 320
temporary protected status 34, 35, 39, 45
temporary residence 108
Thailand 26, 229, 286
  border statistics 143, 145, 148

439

contract labour control 181-2, 184, 189
remittances 322, 332-3, 334, 335, 337
work permits 172, 173, 175, 176
three-stage sampling 280
time 21-4
  of arrival 62
  border statistics 140-1
  interview duration 266-7
Todaro, Michael 294
Togo 118
Torrealba, Ricardo 128, 170, 180, 205
tourists 2, 4, 33, 36, 41, 42, 150, 151
tracing migrants 290-1
trainees, foreign 25, 33, 35, 37, 42, 48
transfers *see* remittances
transients 54, 320
Tribalat, Michèle 116, 117, 119, 269
Trinidad and Tobago 145, 147
Tunisia 144
Turkey 143, 145, 148, 159n, 244, 322
Turner, A. 273
two-phase sampling 320
UAE *see* United Arab Emirates
UAUs (ultimate area units) 276-7, 278, 280, 281, 283-7
Uganda 146
Ukraine 191, 243
ultimate area units *see* UAUs
UN (United Nations)
  on Colombia 66, 67
  Convention on rights of migrant workers 16, 30, 43, 46
  on female migrants 49, 52
  on international migrant stock 1, 3, 17, 279
  on migration statistics 1-2, 8, 12, 137
  see also Recommendations . . .
  on national accounts 325, 329-30
  on population statistics 2, 15, 21, 53, 75
  censuses 53, 56, 61, 62, 63, 70
  on world population monitoring 46
  see also Demographic Yearbooks; UNHCR
unauthorized migrants *see* irregular migrants
UNHCR (Office of the UN High Commissioner for Refugees) 214, 215-16, 217, 220
  asylum-seekers 229
  registration guidelines 223-5
  statistics collection 226-9
  statistics recommendations 225, 228-9
Union of Soviet Socialist Republics *see* Soviet Union, former
United Arab Emirates 127, 171-2, 174, 180, 181
United Kingdom 22, 46, 61, 82, 109, 120
  border statistics 137-8
  refugees and asylum-seekers 217, 231
  regularization drives 197, 200
  work permits 167-8, 174, 176
United Nations *see* UN
United States 16, 22, 46, 48, 169
  border statistics 137, 143, 154
  census 27, 55, 72
  place of birth 27-8, 57, 60, 61
  refugees and asylum-seekers 217, 220, 226, 230
  regularization drives 197, 200, 202-3, 207-8
  residence permits 120, 121, 124-5, 130
  surveys 239, 241-5 *passim*, 279, 289, 319
Uruguay 65, 67, 147
USSR *see* Soviet Union, former

Index

Venezuela 67, 128, 180
  border statistics 147, 159n
  regularization drives 197, 204-5
  work permits 168, 169-70, 174, 175
Verhoef, R. 19
Vietnam 220, 222
visas 25, 82, 121-6
  see also permits under residence
Wallis and Futuna Islands 148
Warren, Robert 55
weights used in analysis 286-8
welfare statistics on refugees 221-5
Western Asia see Middle East
Western Sahara 144
Wolff, Brent 292
women 183
Wood, Charles H. 301
Woodrow, Karen A. 207
work permits 82, 105-6, 161-79
  recommendations for
    improvement 177-9
  scope and limitation of data 173-7
  see also employment; migrant
    workers
World Bank 322, 362
World Fertility Survey 319
Yemen, Democratic 127, 148, 170
Yugoslavia, former 60, 159n, 216, 226, 227, 230
Zaba, Basia 66, 67
Zaire 146, 164
Zambia 146
Zimbabwe 145, 146
Zlotnik, Hania 4, 7
  concepts 15, 17, 18, 22, 23, 24
  international migration data
    collection 65, 66, 159n
  surveys 244, 254, 259